ROUTLEDGE HANDBOOK
OF FOOD WASTE

This comprehensive Handbook represents a definitive state of the current art and science of food waste from multiple perspectives.

The issue of food waste has emerged in recent years as a major global problem. Recent research has enabled greater understanding and measurement of loss and waste throughout food supply chains, shedding light on contributing factors and practical solutions. This book includes perspectives and disciplines ranging from agriculture, food science, industrial ecology, history, economics, consumer behaviour, geography, theology, planning, sociology, and environmental policy among others. The *Routledge Handbook of Food Waste* addresses new and ongoing debates around systemic causes and solutions, including behaviour change, social innovation, new technologies, spirituality, redistribution, animal feed, and activism. The chapters describe and evaluate country case studies, waste management, treatment, prevention, and reduction approaches, and compares research methodologies for better understanding food wastage.

This book is essential reading for the growing number of food waste scholars, practitioners, and policy makers interested in researching, theorising, debating, and solving the multifaceted phenomenon of food waste.

Christian Reynolds is a Knowledge Exchange Research Fellow in the Department of Geography, University of Sheffield, a Technical Specialist in international food sustainability at WRAP, UK, and an adjunct Research Fellow at the Barbara Hardy Institute for Sustainable Environments and Technologies, University of South Australia. His research examines the economic and environmental impacts of food consumption; with focus upon food waste, and sustainable, healthy, and affordable diets.

Tammara Soma is an Assistant Professor in Planning at the School of Resource and Environmental Management at Simon Fraser University. She is the Research Director and also the Co-Founder of the Food Systems Lab, the first social innovation lab to address the issue of food waste and food insecurity in Canada.

Charlotte Spring is a postdoctoral researcher at the University of Calgary. Her PhD compared UK surplus food redistribution as charitable and activist practice. She has also undertaken considerable campaign work focusing critically on the relationships between food wastage and food insecurity.

Jordon Lazell is a Researcher at the Centre for Business in Society in the Faculty of Business and Law at Coventry University, UK. His research concerns sustainable consumption and production practices with a specific interest in food waste.

"In the global North, a post-war regime of sufficiency and surplus arguably rendered food waste politically and culturally visible. Academic researchers paid comparatively little attention to it. Over the last decade, the issue has gained significant momentum to become a recognised priority in the global policy arena. It engages a range of stakeholders including activists and campaigners, governments and legislators, citizens and consumers, and even food corporations. The task of understanding and responding to food waste requires attention from a range of academic perspectives. For example, there is a need for a credible definition of what food waste is as well as suitable techniques for measuring and modelling it. There is also a need to understand the social and spatial dynamics of waste generation; the dynamics of international food systems; the relationships between different elements of the food chain, and the interplay of society, economy, and environment. I could go on. The point is that the complexities of food waste can be quite overwhelming. This wide-ranging Handbook brings together leading authors who together possess a wealth of complementary experience and expertise. By distilling it and collecting it together in one place, this collection offers a much-needed and long-overdue overview and introduction to the various facets of the food waste crisis. Moreover, it offers the potential to develop solutions that are evidence-based, creative, and socially just. This will no doubt become the 'go-to' resource for interdisciplinary researchers and practitioners working on food waste."

David Evans, Professor of Material Culture and Food Security Lead at the Cabot Institute for Environment, University of Bristol, UK, author of *Food Waste* and *Waste Matters: New Perspective on Food and Society* (2013)

"Scholarly, original, comprehensive, *The Routledge Handbook on Food Waste* is timely, indeed long overdue – an invaluable compendium of cross-disciplinary essays and ideas systematically theorising and explaining key dimensions of today's global food waste crisis. Its critical and reflective analyses shine fresh light on the history of food loss and waste rooted in political economy and spirituality; its causes along the food supply chain and approaches to policy and practices around the world. It further considers different methodologies including how best to measure food waste as well as distinct cultural approaches to food waste prevention and reduction. Solutions are explored with debates in food waste studies about how best to respond. Whether or not you understand food waste as a symptom of a dysfunctional corporatised food system and/or structurally embedded within overproducing throwaway capitalism, as a researcher, policy maker, think tank analyst, activist, or campaigner this book will inform and stimulate your thinking and actions. An essential reference if you are concerned about feeding the world from a human rights perspective."

Graham Riches, Emeritus Professor of Social Work, University of British Columbia, Canada

"This book marks a major milestone in the global movement that has seen food waste surge from an ignored issue some years ago to a universally recognised environmental and development priority. It deftly brings together academics, practitioners, radical critics of the status quo, and very importantly gives voices from the global South their rightful place at the centre of debates about food security and sustainability."

Tristram Stuart, Founder of Toast Ale, Co-Founder of Feedback, author of *Waste: Uncovering the Global Food Scandal*

"This Handbook brings together writings from a stellar cast of leading writers and thinkers on wasted food. I expect it to be 'the' place to go, not only for an interdisciplinary overview of issues and strategies, but also for cutting-edge insights and critical perspectives. Readers will walk away with heightened awareness of the ways in which addressing waste of food effectively requires attention to systems, tradeoffs, unintended consequences, and the diverse manifestations of the issue in contexts across the world."

Roni Neff, Assistant Professor, Johns Hopkins
Center for a Livable Future, USA

"If you are interested in food waste, do not forget to read this book. It is an excellent, comprehensive, updated, and upgraded compendium of topics around food waste. The book I would have liked to read when I started working on food waste."

Chema Gil, Director, Center for Agro-Food Economics and
Development Parc Mediterrani de la Tecnologia, Spain

"This book contributes to our understanding of ways to reduce food loss and waste, which is important for creating a sustainable food system and at the same time tackling the challenges of climate change. It is a complex issue and many different players have a part to play. We need greater awareness and for more people to understand the issue so that we can develop robust solutions. As a Champion for the United Nations Sustainable Development Goal 12.3, I hope that it helps drive achievement of the goal of halving food loss and waste by 2030."

Liz Goodwin OBE, Senior Fellow and Director, Food Loss and Waste,
World Resources Institute

"*The Routledge Handbook of Food Waste* provides a no-stone-unturned analysis of food waste. Devour this volume to understand the topic from a practical, historical, political, religious, cultural, international, or most any perspective. Essential reading in the growing food waste canon."

Jonathan Bloom, author of *American Wasteland*

"What a fresh approach to food waste! This collection offers a diversity of perspectives from the global South and North and provides thoughtful insight into the morass of issues bound up in the industrial food system that creates so much food waste. It will certainly engage students and scholars alike."

Sarah Elton, Assistant Professor, Ryerson University, Canada

"This Handbook's impressively wide-ranging coverage is a first-rate introduction to the rapidly growing field of 'food waste studies'. It presents a variety of perspectives and analytic stances on food loss and food waste – juxtaposing campaigning impulses with technical discussions of measurement, moving from behaviour change approaches to political economy theorising. The editors demonstrate the considerable complexities involved, effectively demonstrating that there are no easy answers. They also remember to include upstream problems of post-harvest losses along with those of waste downstream, at household level. And commendably they work at including the 'global South' as well as the 'global North'. All in all, the book assembles an overview of many of the disparate approaches that now must be taken very seriously indeed by anyone sensitive to the fundamental value of food."

Anne Murcott, Honorary Professorial Research Associate, SOAS, University of London,
UK; Honorary Professor, University of Nottingham, UK; Professor Emerita,
London South Bank University, UK

ROUTLEDGE HANDBOOK OF FOOD WASTE

Edited by Christian Reynolds, Tammara Soma,
Charlotte Spring and Jordon Lazell

LONDON AND NEW YORK

from Routledge

First published 2020 by Routledge

2 Park Square, Milton Park, Abingdon, Oxon OX14 4RN

605 Third Avenue, New York, NY 10017

Routledge is an imprint of the Taylor & Francis Group, an informa business

First issued in paperback 2021

Publisher's Note

The publisher has gone to great lengths to ensure the quality of this reprint but points out that some imperfections in the original copies may be apparent.

British Library Cataloguing-in-Publication Data
A catalogue record for this book is available from the British Library

Library of Congress Cataloging-in-Publication Data
A catalog record has been requested for this book

ISBN: 978-1-138-61586-1 (hbk)
ISBN: 978-1-03-217573-7 (pbk)
DOI: 10.4324/9780429462795

Typeset in Bembo
by Swales & Willis, Exeter, Devon, UK

CONTENTS

Contents

FIGURES

TABLES

Tables

CONTRIBUTORS

Abdel Samie Felfel is an Associate at Value Chain Management International. He has 25 years' research experience in production and labour economics, food security, international trade policy, consumer behaviour, and the agribusiness industry. He worked on policy analysis and development in Canada. He has advised a few countries on developing national research strategies for economics diversification, food security, and trade policy. He holds a Doctorate in Agricultural Economics from the University of Guelph, Canada.

Abdul-Sattar Nizami is currently working as an Assistant Professor and Head of the Solid Waste Management Unit at the Center of Excellence in Environmental Studies (CEES) of King Abdulaziz University, Jeddah, Saudi Arabia.

Abigail Marie Favis obtained her MSc in Environmental Sanitation at the University of Ghent, Belgium and her undergraduate degree in Environmental Science from the Ateneo de Manila University. Currently she is a faculty member of the Department of Environmental Science, Ateneo de Manila University and is the Programme Manager for Campus Sustainability at the Ateneo Institute of Sustainability. Her research interests include sustainable consumption, waste management, and urban biodiversity and green spaces.

Adrianne Lickers Xavier is an Onondaga woman from the Six Nations of the Grand River First Nations Territory. She is currently in the Doctor of Social Sciences programme at Royal Roads University in Victoria, British Columbia, Canada, and is completing a Pre-Doctoral Fellowship in the Department of Global Development Studies at Queen's University. She holds a BA in Anthropology from McMaster University as well as an MA in Intercultural and International Communication from Royal Roads. Her doctoral thesis is an autoethnographic account examining the implementation of a food security initiative, 'Our Sustenance', at Six Nations. In addition to 'Our Sustenance', she has been involved with community initiatives addressing water, addictions, community health, and well-being. She has also pursued a lifelong education in her community's traditional ways of knowing and doing and, given her extensive training and experience in transcultural communication, she is regularly invited to share her knowledge and experience with Indigenous and non-Indigenous academic audiences across Canada and internationally. She has also published academically on the topic of Indigenous food security. Adrianne has taught courses on Traditional Ecological Knowledge as well as Women and Environmental Injustice.

Alex V. Barnard is an Assistant Professor of Sociology at New York University, USA. His book, *Freegans: Diving into the Wealth of Food Waste in America* (2016) examines social movements that use recovering and redistributing wasted food as a protest against capitalism. His current research project looks at the trajectories of people with severe mental illness between institutions of care and control in France and the United States.

Andrew F. Smith is the author or editor of 32 books. His most recent works include the three-volume *Food in America: The Past, Present and Future of Food, Farming and the Family Meal* (2017), *Savoring Gotham: A Food Lover's Companion to New York City* (2015), and *Fast Food: The Good, the Bad and the Hungry* (2016). He is the series editor for both the 'Edible Series' and the 'Food Controversies Series' in the United Kingdom. He has taught food history courses at the New School in Manhattan since 1996. His courses include 'Zero Food Waste' and he is the author of the forthcoming book *Why Waste Food? Feed People, Save the Planet, Make Money*.

Anne Sharp is an Associate Professor and has been a Senior Marketing Scientist with the Ehrenberg-Bass Institute, at the University of South Australia since its beginning. All Anne's work has the common theme of applying marketing science knowledge to sustainable marketing. Anne has a particular interest in interventions encouraging behaviour change for improved environmental outcomes. Her recent work includes the evaluation of bans on single-use plastics and plastic bags; householder waste and recycling behaviour; food waste; developing measures for repairing, reusing and waste avoidance; the sharing economy and transport; and the circular economy. Anne has published over 50 refereed academic papers and book chapters. Anne is a full member of the Australian Market and Social Research Society and teaches Market Research. She has a long track record of industry and government collaboration in her work.

Anton Nahman is a Principal Researcher at the Council for Scientific and Industrial Research. His main research interests include the economic valuation of environmental resources and impacts, the economics of environmental policy, the economics of pollution and waste, understanding consumer behaviour, operationalising and measuring the green economy, and the development of alternative indicators of well-being.

Atsushi Watabe is a Senior Researcher at the Institute for Global Environmental Strategies (IGES), Japan. He has worked for several programmes including the ODA programme on climate policies and the recovery of the communities affected by the Fukushima nuclear disaster. Since 2015, he has been on the Coordination Desk of the Sustainable Lifestyles and Education Programme of the UN 10-Year Framework of Programmes on SCP (also known as the One-Planet Network). Having majored in sociology on rural development with special attention to the narratives of the people living in the societies in transition, he is always interested in the ways the ordinary people organise their day-to-day living through interpreting various opportunities, threats, and resources.

Belinda Li, PEng is the Director of Innovation and Co-Founder of Food Systems Lab, a research and innovation hub at Simon Fraser University, Canada, for collaborative solutions in sustainable food systems. She uses a combination of participatory design and data-driven approaches to develop, test, and evaluate solutions to prevent food from being wasted. She led the development and implementation of Canada's first social innovation lab focused on food waste and research on the efficacy of household food waste interventions. As a consultant, she has worked throughout Canada and the United States on food waste measurement and solutions to reduce food waste for residential and commercial sectors. Publications she has contributed to include the Natural Resource Defense Council's 'Estimating Quantities and Types of Food Waste at the City Level', the National Zero Waste Council's 'How to Measure Food Waste: A Guide for Measuring Food Waste from Households in Canada', and the Commission of Environmental Co-operation's 'Characterization and Management of Food Loss and Waste in North America Foundational Report'.

Beth Vallen is an Associate Professor of Marketing at the Villanova School of Business, USA. Dr Vallen's research explores issues related to consumer health, focusing more specifically on choices made in the presence of various marketing and policy-related stimuli – such as nutrition labels, food menus, and food naming conventions. Her research has been published in journals including the *Journal of Consumer Research*, the *Journal of Consumer Psychology*, and *Appetite*.

Cansu Kandemir is a Research Associate at The University of Sheffield, UK. She is an Industrial Systems Engineer with eight years of experience in commercial and academic fields and is passionate about improvement of business systems/processes through modelling and simulation techniques.

Charlotte Spring is a postdoctoral researcher at the University of Calgary. Her PhD compared charitable and/or activist models of redistributing surplus food in the UK, through ethnographic engagement with a variety of organisations including FareShare and The Real Junk Food Project. After reading Poppendieck's *Sweet Charity* and observing resonances between UK discourses of surplus food redistribution as a 'win-win' solution to address food waste and food insecurity, and histories of foodbanking growth in North America, she undertook a Winston Churchill Memorial Trust Fellowship in the US and Canada to explore lessons for UK practice and campaigning. She brings practical as well as academic involvement in food waste recovery and campaign work focusing on intersections and root causes of food waste and food insecurity. Her current work explores intersections of housing and food injustice. She previously worked at the University of Sheffield as part of the Realising Just Cities programme, experimenting with digital coproduction as a way to enhance knowledge-sharing among urban food partnerships.

Chen Liu is a Senior Researcher at the Institute for Global Environmental Strategies (IGES), Japan. She earned a PhD in Biosphere Informatics from Kyoto University, worked as a researcher at the National Institute for Environmental Studies (NIES; 2001–2009) and an Associate Professor in Nagoya University Graduate School of Environmental Studies (2010–2014) in Japan before joining IGES. Her current research is mainly on 3R policies and municipal solid waste management, food waste, and good practice of sustainable consumption in Asian and Pacific countries.

Christian Reynolds is a Knowledge Exchange Research Fellow at the Department of Geography, University of Sheffield, UK, a Technical Specialist in international food sustainability at WRAP, and an adjunct Research Fellow at the Barbara Hardy Institute for Sustainable Environments and Technologies, University of South Australia. Christian's research examines the economic and environmental impacts of food consumption with a focus upon food waste, and sustainable, healthy, and affordable diets.

Christina O'Sullivan has an MSc in Food Policy from the Centre for Food Policy, City University, London. She has worked at the Cornell Food and Brand Lab and the Global Centre for Food Systems Innovation at Michigan State University. She manages Feedback's campaign on fish feed used by the Scottish farmed salmon industry and in 2018 produced a Supermarket Scorecard ranking UK supermarkets on their efforts to reduce food waste.

Claudia Fabiano joined the Environmental Protection Agency's Office of Resource Conservation and Recovery to work on Sustainable Management of Food in 2016 after 14 years in EPA's Office of Water. In addition to her role at EPA to reduce wasted food in the US, she is an active member of Washington DC's Food Recovery Working Group and her neighbourhood composting cooperative. She has a BS in Environmental Studies from The George Washington University, USA. She spends her free time chasing after her two daughters and coming up with creative solutions for how to cook what's left in the fridge.

Czarina Saloma is a Professor in the Department of Sociology and Anthropology of the Ateneo de Manila University, Philippines, and Alexander von Humboldt Foundation Fellow at the Faculty of Sociology of Universitaet Bielefeld, Germany. Her work examines questions about knowledge mobilisation in relation to the built environment, social development, and sustainable consumption and production. Her publications include *Possible Worlds in Impossible Spaces: Knowledge, Gender, and Information Technology in the Philippines* (2006); *Casa Boholana: Vintage Houses of Bohol* (with E. Akpedonu, 2011); *Many Journeys, Many Voices: Filipina Overseas Workers, 1960–2010* (with E. Manlapaz and Y. Buencamino, 2015); and *Food Consumption in the City: Practices and Patterns in Urban Asia and the Pacific* (edited with M. Sahakian and S. Erkman, 2016).

Daniel Hoornweg is an Associate Professor at Ontario Tech University and Senior Fellow at the Global Cities Institute, University of Toronto; a former member of the Urban Strategy Council of GDF Suez; Philips Livable Cities Think Tank; and an Adjunct Professor in Civil Engineering at the University of Toronto. Daniel was a lead urban specialist in the World Bank's central Urban Advisory Unit for almost 20 years prior to moving back to Ontario in 2012. Daniel was Solid Waste Manager for City of Guelph and Government of Bermuda and lead author on Canada's first municipal Green Plan and helped start the first local government round table on sustainable development (City of Guelph). He also started Canada's first retail store for environmentally friendly products (For Earth's Sake opened in Guelph in 1987).

David Boarder Giles is a Lecturer in Anthropology at Deakin University, Australia. He writes about cultural economies of waste, homelessness, and the politics of public space in global cities. He has done extensive ethnographic fieldwork in Seattle and several other cities in the United States and Australasia with dumpster divers, grassroots activists, homeless residents, and chapters of Food Not Bombs – a globalised movement of grassroots soup kitchens.

David Gray read Biochemistry at the University of Aberdeen, UK then gained a PhD in Plant Lipid Biochemistry (investigating the enzymes involved in the synthesis of poly-unsaturated fatty acids on sunflower seeds) from the University of Birmingham, UK. He was appointed to a Lectureship in Food Chemistry at the University of Nottingham, UK in 1993. Dr Gray has developed a biomaterials approach to sustainable ingredients and nutrition. He is exploring novel, bio-innovative approaches to incorporating functional lipids (such as galactolipids, phospholipids, essential fatty acids/omega-3 fatty acids, vitamin E, and carotenoids including pro-vitamin A) into foods as structuring agents, or to improve the health of the consumer. As part of this overarching theme, Dr Gray's team is recovering and characterising plant cell organelles such as oil bodies (oleosomes) from oilseeds, and chloroplasts from green leaf material. The recovery of intact, micron-sized oil bodies (the natural store of the seed-oil) offers a 'greener' way of processing oilseeds without the need for organic solvents. Underutilised plant biomass, such as post-harvest field residues, offers an abundant supply of chloroplasts, organelles enriched in a wide range of nutrients.

David Pearson is the Engage Program Leader in the Fight Food Waste Cooperative Research Centre. David's research expertise is in leading multidisciplinary collaborations addressing issues of concern in society. Most recently this has focused on encouraging consumers to make considered choices, such as dietary options to improve personal health and contribute to a more environmentally sustainable global food system. In addition, he has considerable leadership achievements in tertiary education as well as significant engagements with industry, government, and charity sectors. He is a Professor of Marketing in the School of Business and Law, and the Appleton Institute, at the Sydney campus of Central Queensland University.

Deepa Agarwal is a scientist researching in the food innovation portfolio at the New Zealand Institute of Plant and Food Research (PFR), Lincoln, NZ. She holds a degree in Biotechnology (Hons) from Amity University, India, Masters in Applied Biomolecular Technology and a PhD (Food Science) focused on food structures from the University of Nottingham. She has a keen interest in structuring food using alternative sources of ingredients such as cellulosic fibres, and utilisation of food waste streams to develop unique microstructures for food and the personal care industry. Currently, she is working on developing 3D printing technology and BioInks to create different food microstructures with various textures.

Dickella Gamaralalage Jagath Premakumara is a development planner, specialising in participatory environmental planning and low carbon cities. Currently he works as a programme manager for the IGES Centre Collaborating with UNEP on Environmental Technologies and focuses on developing integrated and holistic waste management strategies, policies, and institutions at national and local levels, application of participatory learning and action methods to promote the 3Rs (reduce, reuse, and recycling) and circular economy, integration of informal sector and women's participation in waste management, and linkages between waste and climate change as well as sustainable development goals.

Edson Talamini was awarded a Bachelor of Economics by the University of Passo Fundo, Brazil (2001); a Master's in Agribusiness by the Federal University of Rio Grande do Sul – UFRGS, Brazil (2003); and a PhD in Agribusiness by the Federal University of Rio Grande do Sul – UFRGS, Brazil (2008). He is an Associate Professor at the Department of Economics and International Relations – DERI/FCE/UFRGS and Professor of the Graduate Program in Agribusiness of the Interdisciplinary Center for Studies and Research in Agribusiness – CEPAN/UFRGS. He coordinates the Research Group on Bioeconomics applied to agribusiness.

Erica van Herpen is Associate Professor in the Marketing and Consumer Behaviour Group of Wageningen University, the Netherlands. Her research focuses on how consumers evaluate, use, and choose from (food) product assortments. Her research interests include influences of the general store context (store layout, social influence), on-shelf presentation of products (shelf organisation, product packaging, nutrition labelling), and consumers' use of food products at home and resulting food waste. In her research, she uses novel research tools such as virtual reality. In the EU project REFRESH, Erica leads the research on consumer understanding of food waste.

Ezra Ho is an independent researcher based in Singapore, and has authored articles on energy consumption, waste management, environmental education, and smart urbanism. He has a background in Environmental Studies, and completed his graduate degree at the University of Toronto. He is also affiliated with the Food Systems Lab, Canada's social innovation lab with a focus on food waste research.

Felicitas Schneider holds a diploma degree in Civil Engineering and Water Management and finished her PhD on the topic 'Generation and Prevention of Food Waste in Industrialised Countries'. Since 2001, her research has specialised on the topic of food loss and waste prevention. She was involved in the development of national strategies toward food waste prevention programmes, discussions related to the definition of food waste, designing applied methodology for measurement of food waste, and various implementation projects along the food supply chain. She chaired the International Waste Working Group task group on Prevention of Food waste for several years, co-founded the German-speaking Network on FLW prevention 'Essens-wert' and organised various FLW sessions and workshops at international conferences. Since June 2017, she works at the German Federal Research Institute for Rural Areas, Forestry and Fisheries, Thünen-Institute of Market Analysis, as coordinator of the Collaboration Initiative Food Losses and Food Wastes which was introduced by the Meeting of Agricultural Chief Scientists (MACS-G20) in 2015. She is member of the EIP-AGRI focus group 'Reducing food loss on the farm' and reviewer of scientific journals such as *Waste Management, Resources, Conservation & Recycling, Recycling, British Food Journal*, and *Sustainability*.

Gavin Stewart is Senior Lecturer in Evidence Synthesis at Newcastle University, UK. His research focuses on applying evidence-based methods to transdisciplinary problems relating to sustainable development and food security.

Geremy Farr-Wharton is affiliated with the Australian eHealth Research Centre, CSIRO. He has background experience in human computer interaction, innovation, entrepreneurship, and interaction design. His work has focused on leveraging enabling technologies to digital transform processes to meet the needs of a rapidly evolving digital economy. He has worked on very large and complex projects bringing together a nexus of environmental, economic, and social sustainability through exploring the very reaches of what technology can offer through out-of-the-box thinking.

Glenio Piran Dal' Magro is a PhD student in Agribusiness in the Postgraduate Programme in Agribusiness – CEPAN, Universidade Federal do Rio Grande do Sul – UFRGS, Brazil. Among the main research topics are: analysis of technical feasibility in rural properties, cooperativism, food supply chain, agri-food economy, rural organisations, food loss and waste, and food security.

Jan Mayer earned an MSc in Human Computer Interaction from the University of Munich, Germany, where he focused on solving real-world problems through user-centric (digital) applications. For his Master's thesis, he joined the QUT Urban Informatics Research Lab to explore the potential of digital food waste prevention strategies. His interest in sustainable food systems was sparked through a student job as an assistant chef at a small Italian restaurant. Building on his research at the QUT Urban Informatics Research Lab, Jan is exploring sustainable diets and their impact on people's health as well as environmental footprint. Currently, he is looking for an interdisciplinary PhD opportunity at the intersection of sustainable food systems and digital technology.

Jane Midgley is Reader in Urban Social and Economic Practice in the School of Architecture, Planning and Landscape at Newcastle University in the United Kingdom. Before this, Jane was a Research Fellow at the UK's leading think tank, the Institute for Public Policy Research, where she established and led its food policy research. Jane has an interdisciplinary social science background and explores the diverse practices of food provisioning and specifically those practices that are integral to the processes of making and managing surplus food and the diverse problems and possibilities offered by its redistribution by policymakers, the food industry, and voluntary and community sector actors.

Jaz Hee-jeong Choi is the Director of the Care-full Design Lab and Vice-Chancellor's Senior Research Fellow in School of Design, RMIT University, Melbourne, Australia. She founded FoodCHI (Food-Computer-Human-Interaction) as a SIGCHI Network and a field of research. As a transdisciplinary researcher, her approach to urban sustainability recognises 'play' and 'care' as the core of transformational encounters in cities as complex cyberphysical networks. She builds on this to explore, often through playful and co-creative engagements, how design – from interaction to experience, service, and strategic design – can be done care-fully in different cultural contexts. Currently, she is exploring care-full design for liveable and equitable urban futures across three inter-related domains: self-care and mutual aid, creative and impactful research methods, and co-creative urban transformation.

Jean C. Buzby is Chief of the Diet, Safety, and Health Economics Branch in the Economic Research Service's Food Economics Division. For over 25 years, Jean has worked either directly or indirectly for ERS, which is an Agency within the US Department of Agriculture. Prior to moving into management, her primary areas of work as an economist at ERS were food safety and food consumption research. Jean's food safety research included estimating the costs of foodborne illness, analysing the legal incentives for firms to produce safer food, and exploring international trade and food safety issues. Her food consumption research was primarily centred on using information gleaned from the Food Availability (Per Capita) Data System. She has also conducted research on food loss in the United States for well over a decade and continues to publish estimates of the amount and value of food loss at the retail and consumer levels in the United States, using data from ERS's Loss-Adjusted Food Availability Data Series. Jean received her PhD and MS in Agricultural Economics from the University of Kentucky, USA. She received a BS from the Pennsylvania State University, USA.

Jessica Aschemann-Witzel (Dr. habil. agr.) is Professor at the MAPP Centre – Research on Value Creation in the Food Sector at the Department of Management, Aarhus School of Business and Social Sciences, Aarhus University, Denmark. Her research focuses on marketing and consumer behaviour challenges along the supply chain of fast moving consumer goods in general, and specifically food, and especially issues around health and sustainability and opportunities for improvements to the benefit of society. Topics include healthy eating, health claims and food labelling, consumer-related food waste, organic food, sustainability claims, and protein food. She has been part of as well as managed projects on food waste research in Europe during the past years, among others the COSUS project on suboptimal food and consumer-related food waste, as well as WasteProm, which looks at the relation between food pricing and food waste.

Jon Cloke currently works as National Network Manager for the UK Low Carbon Energy for Development Network (LCEDN) and as Senior Research Associate at Loughborough University, UK. The LCEDN was set up as a network hosted by Loughborough University and the Durham Energy Institute to link the research expertise in the UK on energy and development and to improve research coordination and funding efficiency. Dr Cloke has worked closely with Professor Ed Brown on a variety of DfID-funded projects including Understanding Sustainable Energy Solutions (USES) and Transforming Energy Access (TEA) and he has been a Lecturer in Human Geography in the Geography Department at Loughborough from 2007 to date and worked as an NGO Consultant to different non-government organisations.

Jordon Lazell is a Researcher at the Centre for Business in Society in the Faculty of Business and Law at Coventry University, UK. Jordon's research concerns sustainable consumption practices with a specific interest in the wastage of food. His PhD thesis investigated the wider contextual factors that influence consumer food waste behaviours, employing a practice-based framework to understand how social, spatial, and temporal factors condition everyday performances. Jordon has also undertaken work on the circular economy, sustainable tourism, and the sharing economy. He has published in the *Journal of Consumer Behaviour*, the *Journal of Sustainable Tourism*, and *Social Business*.

Karen Luyckx holds a PhD in Geography from Leeds University, UK and has over 15 years of experience linking environmental campaigns with academic research. Karen's current work focuses on the microbiological safety and environmental aspects of using heat-treated surplus food in feed for omnivorous non-ruminant livestock. Karen has worked for six years in Bolivia where she witnessed the destruction of the Amazon caused by soya farming for animal feed.

Kate Parizeau, PhD, is an Associate Professor in the Department of Geography, Environment & Geomatics at the University of Guelph, Canada. Her research interests concern the social context of waste and its management. Dr Parizeau's research uses waste management practices as a lens through which to interrogate complex systems of social organisation and environmental change. Dr Parizeau co-leads the Guelph Food Waste Research Group, and recent research projects include explorations of food waste in Canadian settings, and informal recycling practices in diverse contexts.

Kirsi Silvennoinen, MSc, is a research scientist at the Natural Resources Institute (Luke), Finland. Her expertise includes projects on volume, quality, and reasons for food waste. Her studies have focused on the Finnish food chain, especially households and the hospitality sector, waste hierarchy, definitions, measurements and preventing methods, redistribution and impacts on the environment.

Laura C. Moreno is a PhD Candidate at the University of California at Berkeley's Energy and Resources Group, USA. Laura studies wasted food with a focus on household-level food waste and city-level measurement. Laura consulted for the Natural Resources Defense Council (NRDC) as a researcher for their city-level food waste assessment initiatives in New York City, Denver, and Nashville. Prior to graduate school, Laura was an environmental scientist at the US Environmental Protection Agency's Pacific Southwest Region. At the EPA, Laura worked primarily on wasted food and other organic wastes.

Lauren G. Block is the Lippert Professor of Marketing at the Zicklin School of Business, Baruch College, CUNY, USA. Dr Block's work is primarily in areas of food well-being, health persuasion, and perceptions of product efficacy. Her research includes how best to use marketing tools, such as food labelling and product packaging, to facilitate healthier food and lifestyle decisions. Current research also focuses on understanding the product-related and contextual influences that drive consumer judgements of the efficacy of pharmacological products. Her work in these areas has been published in outlets such as *Journal of Marketing*, *Journal of Marketing Research*, and the *Journal of Consumer Research*.

Lisa K. Johnson is a Senior Research Scholar at North Carolina State University, in the Department of Horticultural Science and the Center for Environmental Farming Systems. She has developed guidance for in-field measurement of losses, required in order to build industry capacity to utilise this supply, as well as prevent future losses. Through field data collection, she has demonstrated the need to reevaluate national loss estimates for vegetable crops. In addition, her qualitative research with growers has indicated that strategies used to reduce food waste in the downstream produce supply chain might not be well suited to the constraints of agricultural production. Dr Johnson engages commercial growers in the development of strategies that concurrently reduce agricultural losses, improve efficiency in resource use, and improve profitability through the marketing and use of blemished and surplus produce.

Lisanne van Geffen is a PhD at the Marketing and Consumer Behaviour Group of Wageningen University, the Netherlands. Her research focus lies on understanding the mechanisms behind avoidable food waste in households. She takes an inclusive perspective by focusing on individual, social, and societal factors driving food waste.

Marco Setti is an Associate Professor in the Department of Agro-Food Sciences and Technologies at the University of Bologna, Italy

Marie Mourad's PhD in Sociology focused on mobilisations and public policies against food waste, and new markets for surplus food in the United States and France. Her work has been published in international journals including the *Journal of Cleaner Production*. She currently works as an independent consultant and researcher for non-profits and governmental agencies in the US and France.

Marlyne Sahakian is Assistant Professor of Sociology at the University of Geneva, Switzerland, where she brings a sociological lens to consumption studies and sustainability. She gained a PhD in Development Studies from the Graduate Institute (2011), and co-founded SCORAI Europe in 2012 – a network for sustainable consumption research and action. Her research interest is in understanding everyday practices in relation to environmental promotion, social equity, and social change. She coordinates research projects on household energy and food consumption, and well-being, working with interdisciplinary teams. Her work outside of Switzerland is central to her research and teaching: she has focused primarily on the urban centre of South and Southeast Asia, whether tackling the changing food consumption practices and related food waste in Bangalore and Metro Manila, or considering the influence of built systems on air-conditioning usage and micro-climate diversity in Asian cities. She publishes in journals related to sociology, sustainability, and community development. Her books include *Keeping Cool in Southeast Asia: Energy Consumption and Urban Air-conditioning* (2014) and *Food Consumption in the City: Practices and Patterns in Urban Asia and the Pacific* (2016).

Mark Walker is a researcher and development engineer with expertise in anaerobic digestion and biogas; organic waste management; bio and renewable energy; integration of energy systems; and sustainable process engineering.

Martin Bowman holds an MSc in Globalisation and Development from SOAS University of London, UK. He has been a food waste activist for 10 years. Martin set up and coordinated a chapter of Food Not Bombs in London for five years, and helped set up Feedback's Gleaning Network, which mobilises volunteers to harvest food left unharvested in the field on farms for charitable redistribution, acting as UK Gleaning Coordinator for five years and delivering a TEDx talk on gleaning in 2016. In 2018, he moved to work on Feedback's Pig Idea campaign, campaigning to reform EU law to allow safely treated food surplus to be fed to omnivorous non-ruminant livestock. He co-authored Feedback's reports *Farmers Talk Food Waste* and *Feeding Surplus Food to Pigs Safely*. Martin has also worked for This Is Rubbish 2011 – helping to write their report on mandatory food waste audits *Counting What Matters*, acting as Campaign and Media Coordinator for their Stop the Rot campaign which targeted UK supermarket food waste policy, and leading their EU Food Waste campaign for ambitious food waste targets in the EU's revised Waste Framework Directive. Martin is currently Campaigns Manager for This Is Rubbish (www.thisisrubbish.org.uk/), and Policy and Campaigns Manager for Feedback (feedbackglobal.org).

Martin Gooch is co-founder and CEO of Value Chain Management International (VCMI), a global consulting company headquartered in Ontario, Canada. VCMI assists businesses in the agri-food and seafood industries to enhance their long-term profitability and environmental sustainability. Martin has two decades' experience in analysing businesses and value chains to identify where food and related waste occurs and why. He has authored or co-authored numerous publications on the topic. Martin and the VCMI team have participated in regional, national, and international initiatives that have resulted in reduced food and associated wastes along the value chain. Martin holds a PhD and Master's degree in agribusiness, a Bachelor of International Business, along with qualifications in agricultural production and farm management.

Matteo Vittuari is Associate Professor of Agricultural and Food Policy and Agricultural Policy Evaluation at the Department of Agricultural and Food Sciences (DISTAL) at the University of Bologna, Italy. His main fields of expertise include: food economics and policy; rural economics and policy; bioenergy system analysis; life cycle thinking; and behavioural economics. He has published over 80 scientific articles, reports, book chapters, and books. He coordinated the behavioural economics work package (Behavioural economic approaches and scenarios for food waste prevention, reduction and valorization) within the Horizon2020 REFRESH (Resource Efficient Food and Drink for the Entire Supply Chain) and the policy work package within the FP7 FUSIONS (Food Use for Social Innovation by Optimising Waste Prevention Strategies). He has participated in a number of other international and European projects (H2020, PRIMA, Interreg).

Matthew Grainger is a Research Associate at Newcastle University, UK. He has a background in ecology and conservation working for 15 years across three continents (Africa, Asia, and Europe). Currently he is focused on developing models to address the challenges of sustainable development, in particular on food waste in Europe.

Mattias Eriksson received a PhD in technology (2015) for his thesis titled 'Supermarket food waste: Prevention and management with the focus on reduced waste for reduced carbon footprint'. He currently works as a researcher at the Department of Energy and Technology at the Swedish University of Agricultural Science in Uppsala. In this position he teaches Life Cycle Assessment to undergraduate students, supervises thesis projects, and works as a Director of Studies for the research school Sustainable Biomass Systems. The focus of Eriksson's research has been on food waste in the retail sector and in the hospitality sector, and how a reduction of this waste could lead to a more sustainable food system.

Megha Shenoy is interested in the field of the environment and sustainable resource management. She currently teaches at the Valley School and is involved in the programmes at their science centre. She works with the editorial team of the academic publication *Journal of Industrial Ecology*. She is also an Adjunct Fellow at the Climate Change Mitigation and Development Programme at the Ashoka Trust for Research in Ecology and the Environment (Atree) and external consultant for the firm SOFIES. Megha was trained in industrial ecology during her postdoctoral fellowship at the Center for Industrial Ecology, Yale University, USA in 2009. Ever since, she has been involved in various projects that apply concepts and tools of industrial ecology to optimise resource (energy, water, and materials) flows and stocks in various systems. These projects range from examining waste management policies and practices of residential bulk generators in Bengaluru to enabling industrial symbiosis and collective recycling strategies in industrial areas and clusters across India. Megha completed her Integrated PhD (Masters in Biological Sciences and PhD in Ecology) at the Indian Institute of Science, Bengaluru.

Miranda Mirosa is Associate Professor in the Department of Food Science, University of Otago, Canada. Miranda is a Consumer Food Scientist with a background in agri-food marketing and consumer behaviour. She conducts consumer insights and strategic marketing communications-type work for the New Zealand (NZ) food and beverage industry. She is most passionate about her work on waste. Miranda has represented NZ on the committee of a multi-year APEC project 'Strengthening Public-Private Partnership to Reduce Food Losses'. She also was awarded a government 'Postharvest Loss and Food Waste Research Fellowship' to enhance business–research–government partnerships in NZ and China through commercially meaningful research. Miranda has recently served as the Specialist Advisor to Parliament's Environmental Select Committee's National Briefing on Food Waste.

Mirza Barjees Baig is a Professor of Agricultural Extension and Rural Society at the King Saud University, Saudi Arabia. He has published extensively and presented internationally about agriculture, natural resources, and the role of extension education.

Mohamed A. Gedi completed his PhD (Food Science) in the summer of 2017 and began working with an EU-funded project 'Enabling Food Innovation', based at the University of Nottingham's School of Biosciences as a Research Fellow in Food Waste Valorisation, UK. The project was funded up until 31st March 2019 to assist food and drink-producing SMEs around Nottingham and Derbyshire and was successfully completed.

Monica C. LaBarge is an Assistant Professor at the Smith School of Business, Queen's University, Canada. Dr LaBarge's research interests centre around public policy issues in marketing and how marketing can positively affect consumer well-being. Specifically, she has ongoing research projects in the areas of food well-being, health promotion, charitable giving, and non-profit marketing, as well as how vulnerable populations (such as older adults) cope with and overcome vulnerability in the marketplace. Her research in these areas has been published in the *Journal of Public Policy and Marketing*, *Non-Profit and Voluntary Sector Quarterly*, and *Media Psychology*.

Monika Verma has been a researcher at Wageningen University and Research since 2014, following four years spent as an interdisciplinary postdoctoral scholar at Purdue and Stanford universities. Her focus is on issues related to climate change, agriculture, and development in context of food, nutrition, consumption, poverty, and trade. Her research has used big simulation models as well as mathematical models and household data. She holds a doctorate in Agricultural Economics from Purdue University.

Rafaela F. Gutierrez PhD is a social scientist with expertise in waste policy. She has a keen interest in waste awareness, reduction, and literacy. Over the past decade she has studied up- and downstream plastic recycling processes, advocated and worked with low-income communities in Brazil focusing on how to improve socio-productive integration into formal recycling streams. She is currently a research fellow at Food System Lab, working on food waste awareness and reduction. She is also a member of the 'U of T Trash Team' developing strategies on how to increase waste literacy.

Ramy Salemdeeb is an Environmental Analyst at Zero Waste Scotland, UK, and the managing director of Zero Waste ME&A, a regional initiative that promotes sustainable waste management practices in the Middle East & North Africa (ME&A) in order to turn the region into one of ultimate resource efficiency.

Ran Yagasa is a researcher at IGES Centre Collaborating with UNEP on Environmental Technologies (CCET), a unit established within SCP Group, IGES, with the mandate of assisting countries to strengthen waste management systems and governance. Since 2015, he has been working as the Chief Coordinator for the centre's project in Cambodia for the development of national and city-level waste management strategies, while facilitating implementation of a pilot project in Phnom Penh for promoting environmental education in primary schools. He has also worked with the Government of Maldives as a member of the centre's country project team. Before joining IGES, he received an MA in Public Management and Policy Analysis from the International University of Japan (IUJ), and has previously worked in the private sector. His research interests are various topics under waste management governance and strategies including public participation, environmental education, selection of appropriate technologies, and donor coordination.

Randa Darwish is a Research Fellow at the University of Nottingham, UK. She has diverse experience in food processing and industry in both developing and developed countries.

Richard Worrall leads the SME engagement project for the Food Innovation Centre at the University of Nottingham, UK

Roger Ibbett is a Research Fellow at University of Nottingham, UK.

Sally Geislar is an interdisciplinary scholar drawing on theories and concepts from the social sciences to investigate the environmental sustainability and social equity of policy outcomes. Sally employs both quantitative and qualitative methods to investigate sustainable food and waste systems, decision-making and habitual behaviours, and questions of equity. Sally is a Postdoctoral Researcher at the Patel College of Global Sustainability. She earned a PhD in Urban Planning and Public Policy in the School of Social Ecology at the University of California, Irvine, USA, where she also earned an MA in Demographic and Social Analysis in the School of Social Sciences.

Sampsa Nisonen is a researcher currently employed by the Natural Resources Institute Finland. His areas of expertise are environmental modelling and food waste with focus on statistics and measurement methods. He is also working on his PhD on Bayesian decision support tools for cost-effective environmental improvements in the University of Helsinki, Finland.

Sandra Davison's background includes working as a clinical psychologist, lecturer, and course coordinator with the University of South Australia and the South Australian Institute of Business Technology, Adelaide. Clinically, much of Sandra's past work has been in health and rehabilitation areas, assisting people to adapt and change health and lifestyle behaviours. She has a strong interest in environment and pro-environmental behaviours and is currently a research scientist with the Ehrenberg-Bass Institute at the University of South Australia. Sandra's research focuses on developing a better understanding of lifestyle behaviours, and utilising psychological behaviour change theory to encourage more sustainable behaviours in the areas of food waste and transport.

Sarah Evans is a doctoral student in Marketing at the Smith School of Business, Queen's University, Canada. She earned a Master's in Health Psychology at the University of Alberta. Her research interests include the psychological and motivational factors that influence information processing of framed health messages, prosocial marketing, and, more specifically, cause-marketing. Her most current interests are in the co-production of online social platform regulations between media companies and consumers, and the role of political ideology in the marketplace.

Scott Lougheed is an Environmental Sociologist and was most recently a Postdoctoral Fellow in Geography and Planning at the University of Toronto, Canada, where he studied Ontario's ongoing transition to Extended Producer Responsibility for paper and plastic packaging. Scott received his PhD from the School of Environmental Studies at Queen's University, Kingston. His research interests include: environmental governance, particularly concerning waste and consumption; and the biopolitics of the food system. Scott is also interested in models of collective ownership and sharing as a means of community capacity-building, empowerment, and waste reduction.

Sean Geobey is Assistant Professor of Social Innovation and Social Entrepreneurship at the University of Waterloo, Canada. His teaching and research focus on participatory governance, social innovation, and sustainable finance. Sean has worked with the City of Kitchener, Filene Research Institute, Waterloo Institute for Social Innovation and Resilience (WISIR), the Atkinson Foundation, and the Canadian Index of Wellbeing. Dr Geobey led the research for the New Solutions for Youth Employment Lab and collaborated with the MaRS Solutions Lab on process design for this process. This lab was one of the first test sites for the WISIR Social Innovation Lab processes, and findings from this approach were incorporated into the *WISIR Social Innovation Lab Guide*.

Simone Piras is an agricultural and rural economist at the James Hutton Institute, UK. He has a background in development studies and a PhD in Agri-Food Economics and Statistics. From 2015 to 2018 he was a post-doc at the University of Bologna, Italy, where he worked on the EU projects H2020 REFRESH ('Resource Efficient Food and dRink for the Entire Supply cHain') and FP7 FUSIONS ('Food Use for Social Innovation by Optimising Waste Prevention Strategies'). Within REFRESH, he contributed to the creation of an agent-based model to simulate the generation of consumer food waste, and to its integration with a Bayesian network.

Simone Righi is Lecturer in Financial Computing at the University College London, UK, Department of Computer Science. He obtained a PhD from the University of Namur, Belgium, in 2012 and then worked for the Hungarian Academy of Sciences, University of Modena and Reggio Emilia, and University of Bologna, Italy. His research interests concern the evolution of cooperation in networks (theory and experiments); the study of companies' strategies in the digital economy; the analysis of microstructure, systemic properties, and behavioural bias of financial markets; and the economic consequences of social interactions on complex networks (theory and experiments).

Stephen Bede Scharper, a Fellow of Massey College, is Associate Professor at the School of the Environment and the Department for the Study of Religion at the University of Toronto, Canada. He is also cross-appointed in the Department of Anthropology at the University of Toronto Mississauga campus (UTM). Dr Scharper's research and teaching are in the areas of environmental ethics, worldviews and ecology, liberation theology, sustainability ethics, as well as nature and the city. His book, *For Earth's Sake: Toward a Compassionate Ecology* (2013), explores the notion of how we are being called to develop an affective relationship with the natural world in light of contemporary ecological challenges. His other books include *The Natural City: Re-envisioning Human Settlements* (co-editor, 2011), *The Green Bible*, co-written with his spouse, Hilary Cunningham (2008), and *Redeeming the Time: A Political Theology of the Environment* (1997).

Stephen D. Porter, PhD CFA, is a researcher, educator, and investor. Holding an MBA and CFA charter, he worked in the institutional investment management industry for nearly 20 years at some of the leading global firms. During that time, he engaged with asset owners such as sovereign wealth funds, public pension funds and charitable foundations to create custom solutions to meet their specific requirements. Subsequently, he taught on the same MSc in Carbon Management programme that he completed in 2013 while undertaking a PhD in Atmospheric & Environmental Science at the University of Edinburgh (completed in early 2019). He continues to supervise Master's students engaging in research. He joined the International Institute for Environment and Development (IIED)'s Climate Change Group as a Senior Researcher in 2019, focusing on public policy to promote investment in equitable climate resilient development, and is now affiliated with the University of Edinburgh. In addition to his work on food waste, Dr Porter has the following research interests: agri-food supply chain emissions; climate change resilience; investment management; carbon management; carbon accounting; sustainable development; communication; strategy development.

Suzan Oelofse is a Principal Researcher at the Council for Scientific and Industrial Research. Her research interests include the institutional and legal framework within which waste is managed in South Africa, waste information and data, reuse of industrial waste streams, and reducing the environmental impacts of waste. She is appointed as Extraordinary Professor in the Unit for Environmental Sciences and Management of the North-West University, South Africa and a Past-president of the Institute of Waste Management of Southern Africa.

Tammara Soma is an Assistant Professor at the School of Resource and Environmental Management at Simon Fraser University, Canada and is the Research Director and Co-Founder of the Food Systems Lab, the first social innovation lab to tackle the issue of food waste in Canada (foodsystemslab.ca). At Simon Fraser University she conducts research on issues pertaining to food waste, food system planning, community-based research, waste management, and the circular economy. Her dissertation investigated the factors that influence urban household food consumption and food wasting practices in Indonesia, and the ways in which food systems consideration can improve urban planning decision-making. She has published her work in the journals *Local Environment*, *Built Environment*, *Indonesia*, *Journal of Agriculture, Food Systems, and Community Development*, and in the books *Conversations in Food Studies* (2016), and *Learning, Food and Sustainability* (2016).

Tanhum Yoreh is an Assistant Professor at the School of Environment at the University of Toronto, Canada. His research focuses on the impact of religious values on environmental behaviour, faith-based environmentalism, faith-based environmental ethics, religious legal approaches to environmental protection, and religious approaches to environmental decision-making. He is particularly interested in the themes of wastefulness, consumption, and simplicity. He is the author of *Waste Not: A Jewish Environmental Ethic* (2019).

Tim Foster graduated, majoring in Plant Physiology, before undertaking a PhD in the 'Conformation and Properties of Xanthan Variants'. In 1992 he joined the Unilever R&D lab at Colworth House looking at the mobility of polymers in the plant cell wall. At Unilever he took fundamental knowledge into product design with numerous contributions to products reaching the supermarket shelves (e.g. Knorr Stockpot). In 2007 he joined the University of Nottingham as Reader in Food Structure and in 2014 was promoted to Professor. His current work focuses upon a further investigation of natural structuring agents and rehydration phenomena, and is centred on understanding the creation of required food microstructures from the most appropriate ingredient supply, utilising the most appropriate processes. This requires knowledge of both current and developing/emerging ingredient and process technologies. Current thoughts on minimising waste of manufactured foods, with a mindset on optimising processes, ingredient usage, and nutrient delivery and improving shelf life are key challenges faced. A biorefinery approach may benefit the utilisation of *all* of nature's renewable resources, including the use of waste vegetal material, and will benefit from taking a full supply chain view of resource provision in the future.

Timur Osadchiy's research interest is in using data-driven methods for improving the accuracy of automated dietary assessment. Timur works at the Open Lab at Newcastle University, UK. He works with a team of professionals from the fields of nutrition and medical statistics to develop a dietary monitoring and feedback system (Intake24.co.uk) addressing different populations, intervention targets, and contexts (disease, temporal, and spatial). His goal is to improve the accuracy and efficiency of automated dietary assessment by applying data mining and machine learning techniques. His ultimate target is to make scientifically proven methods of automated dietary assessment and intervention available to the general public all over the globe.

Tom Quested is the Lead Analyst at WRAP, specialising in food waste. He is the lead author of many key reports on food waste in the UK, including 'Household Food and Drink Waste in the UK 2012' and 'Household Food and Drink Waste – A People Focus'. He is also a co-author of both the World Resource Institute Food Waste and Loss Standard and the FUSIONS *Food Waste Quantification Manual*. He also developed the Milk Model, which simulates how decisions about purchasing, storage, and consumption influence waste levels. He advises governments and other organisations across the world on research, modelling, and measurement of food waste.

Ogueri Nwaiwu obtained his PhD (Biosciences) from the University of Nottingham, UK. He is a preventive control qualified individual (PCQI) for human food with a lot of experience from the industry and academia. He is currently with the research and teaching family at Nottingham where engagement with students across all levels (undergraduates and postgraduates) ensures the continuous probing of the frontiers of science. Part of his current role is the maintenance of a food safety plan which ensures that processed valorised new food ingredients meet the policies and specifications of different regulatory bodies. His interests include how different processing conditions affect the microbial quality, chemical structure, and functional properties of foods. The mechanism by which microorganisms survive in the environment and the excretions they produce which help them attach to food and processing equipment is also of interest.

Oona Pietiläinen, MSc Environmental Science and Policy (estimated 2019), is an early-career researcher from Luke, Natural Resources Institute Finland. Her multidisciplinary degree has provided her wide knowledge on sustainability issues. Her main fields of expertise are food waste in food services and sustainable food systems. She completed her Master's thesis on the reduction of plate waste created in primary school last year.

Peter Lyle has a background in human computer interaction, interaction design, participatory design, and urban informatics. He works in the Department of Computer Science at Aarhus University, Denmark. His current work contributes to an understanding of how diverse groups of people interact with constellations of technology, as 'artefact ecologies'. His other interests have been in the participatory design of a technology platform for precarious workers and other marginalised communities in Europe, and to study the opportunities for technology design to support urban food communities in Australia.

Vicki Mavrakis, BA, BSc, MEnvSt, PhD, undertook her PhD studies at Flinders University in South Australia looking at the generative mechanisms of food waste in South Australian household settings, using ethnographic techniques. She was involved in the initial bid for the Food Waste Cooperative Research Centre in 2014, and has co-lectured Consuming Passions: Anthropology of Food and Drink at the University of Adelaide. Publications she has contributed to include *Food Waste: The Blackwell Encyclopedia of Sociology* (2016); 'Food Waste' in *The SAGE Encyclopedia of Food Issues* (2015); 'Estimating Informal Household Food Waste in Developed Countries: The Case of Australia' (2014); 'Towards a Cookie Cutter Future' in *Have Fork Will Travel* (2014).

Vincenzo di Bari graduated (BSc hons and MSc) in Food Science and Technology from the Faculty of Agriculture of Foggia (Italy). He attained his PhD in 2015 from the School of Chemical Engineering of the University of Birmingham, UK. In October 2014 Vincenzo joined the EPSRC Centre for Innovative Manufacturing (CIM) in Food as a Research Fellow. Within this centre his research developed around the identification of suitable process-formulation approaches for the functionalisation of plant waxes (primarily 'rice bran wax') to manufacture oleogels as new biomaterials to reduce trans- and saturated fats in foods. In January 2019 Vincenzo joined the EPSRC project 'Formulation for 3D printing: Creating a plug and play platform for a disruptive UK industry' working on the identification of ingredients suitable for additive manufacturing technology (3D printing) for food applications.

Zainudin Umar is a Materials Scientist at PepsiCo International. He was previously a Researcher at Loughborough University, UK.

FOOD WASTE

An introduction to contemporary food waste studies

Charlotte Spring, Tammara Soma, Jordon Lazell, and Christian Reynolds

Food waste: our anthropocene legacy?

It is said that when looking back, our ancestors will recognise the legacy of the 'Anthropocene' age through the archaeological marker of rubbish. Such archaeology speaks of food waste as a particular continuity of humans' habitation on planet Earth. We have consistently left traces of food, from the earliest sites of human settlement to the trash heaps of today. This rubbish consists not only of ubiquitous plastics (Liboiron, 2016) or electronic waste (Lepawsky, 2015), it also consists of food, and lots of it, evidenced by the pristine-looking 40-year-old hot dog and 25-year-old lettuce found by 'garbologist' William Rathje during his *Garbage Project* excavation (Rathje, 1974). Our legacy will be marked by trails of uneaten food.

Global narratives of scale

The amount of food the world currently wastes is overwhelming. As Trentmann (2016, p. 622) posits, 'we appear to be drowning in waste', with perfectly edible food contributing a significant portion of what we discard. Studies continue to highlight the global scale of food waste, differentiating between 'avoidable' and 'unavoidable' – or edible and inedible (Nicholes et al., 2019). The preventability of vast quantities of thrown-away food has spurred ever-more concerted efforts in food waste practice and research. Well-rehearsed statistics mark out this trend, such as the Institute of Mechanical Engineers' estimate that '30–50% (or 1.2–2 billion tonnes) of all food produced never reaches a human stomach' (IMechE, 2013), and the common refrain that, if imagined as a country, food waste's climate-contributing emissions, at 4.4 GT CO_2E, would place it as the third greatest contributor to greenhouse gas emissions globally, behind China and the United States (FAO, 2015). This editorial aims to shed light on some explanations for the meteoric rise of food waste as a topic of public concern, as well as tracing some of the linguistic, philosophical, and representational means, beyond statistics, through which that concern has been expressed and understood.

Some commentators suspect that public alarm over food waste does not simply mirror the growing scale of the problem. Archaeologists have suggested that our ancestors tossed even more detritus on a daily basis than we do[1] – traces of foodscapes have long been central to understanding human–environment interactions. But some suggest that the tendency to

1

moralise and panic over waste as a 'crisis' prevents proper historiography and level-headedness in dealing with the problem (Rathje & Murphy, 2001; O'Brien, 2008). It also masks differences of understandings of where the roots of 'crisis' might lie: in profligate behaviour? Profit-prioritising business models? The policy environments that prevent or enable these? Registers of thought, language, and relationality?

This introductory chapter reviews some of these differences. Food waste is 'ontologically multiple' (Blake, 2019): it is political and bureaucratic, as shown in images of three frozen geese ceremonially pulverised by Russian officials in response to imports of 'banned' food from Ukraine (Lang, 2016). It is cultural, perhaps even evolutionary, as suggested in Stuart's (2009) account of potlatch ceremonies. It is microbial and mutable, as Lougheed (2017) shows in his study of food allergens, recalls, and biosecurity. It is visual, categorical, statistical, visceral, multi-scalar, spiritual, relational, biological, technological, historical, and re-thinkable, as the rest of this chapter aims to show.

A multi-dimensional concern

Chapters in this Handbook of Food Waste will help to demonstrate that the food waste problem affects all parts of the inhabited world. In the United States, as much as 40% of all food produced is wasted (Gunders, 2012), while 88 million tonnes are thrown away in Europe each year (Stenmark et al., 2016). Per-capita food waste in America has been calculated at more than 1,400 kcal per day (Hall et al., 2009) and the economic cost of food waste is estimated at more than $940 billion (FAO, 2015), a figure that continues to rise. These are, of course, estimations rather than approximations, with the true scale and costs of the impact of uneaten, discarded food difficult to quantify. The extent and problematisation of contemporary food waste is a marked consequence of the way that the current food system generates waste from food production through to retailing and consumption (Blake, 2019). Left unchecked, environmental impacts of the food system could increase by 50 to 90% by 2050 (Springmann et al., 2018; Willett et al., 2019), with food waste playing a substantial role in contributing to human-induced climate change. The wastage of food generates considerable environmental impacts not only through the use of energy, water, soil health, and labour of transforming uneaten or excessive food from farm to fork, but also in the deterioration of food itself, which generates methane gas once discarded. In Europe, estimates place food waste as responsible for 15% of the environmental impact of the entire food chain (Scherhaufer et al., 2018).

The 'global North' of Europe, North America, and industrialised Asia displays trends whereby the consumption end of the supply chain is considered most responsible for food waste. UK households, for example, generate 10.2 million tonnes of food waste annually (WRAP, 2018), whereas in many parts of the global South, the issue tends to be framed as food 'loss', as it is argued that wastage principally occurs during growing, harvesting, and processing stages (Parfitt, Barthel, & Macnaughton, 2010). While this particular and dominant framing is woven throughout the literature (Parfitt, Barthel, & Macnaughton, 2010; Gustavsson et al., 2011; IMechE, 2013; Schneider, 2013; Papargyropoulou et al., 2014), recent work from countries such as Indonesia challenges the reductionism of the 'food loss in the global South' and 'food waste in the global North' dichotomy. These analyses call upon food waste scholars to consider the changing demographic and rapidly urbanising landscapes of many countries in the global South (Soma, 2018), as well as the impact of 'supermarketisation' on people's consumption (Battersby, 2017).

Rising research interest in food and food systems more generally (Murcott, Belasco, & Jackson, 2013), particularly since the financial crisis of 2008, is mirrored in attention to food waste. Such attention has exposed food systems' instabilities, paradoxes, and injustices (Hossain et al., 2014, Trentmann, 2016), and extensive speculation and commodification (Clapp & Isakson, 2018). Amid turbulent struggles over the future direction of human cohabitation on a finite planet, food waste has emerged as an indictment of past patterns and decisions, posing the theoretical and practical challenges of new juxtapositions of scarcity and excess.

Growing public and policy attention

Public awareness of food waste has been bolstered by shocking footage of mountains of food waste in popular documentaries,[2] such as a viral scene from Craig Reucassel's *War on Waste* showing millions of bananas dumped not for their edibility, but for being too big, or too short. Such images have come to hint at a dynamics of neglect in how contemporary societies overconsume and exploit natural resources. The wastage of food symbolises for many the excesses of wealthy countries compared to the extent of food insecurity in others. For example, it is estimated that the 40 million tonnes of food that are wasted annually in the US could feed the world's 1 billion people who are food insecure (Stuart, 2009). Increasingly, this 'waste versus want' trope has highlighted not only inequities between countries in the global North and South. Research highlighting intersections of food waste and food insecurity demonstrates that such inequities exist *within* wealthy nations, cities, and neighbourhoods (e.g. Giles, 2016). The seeming paradox of food waste amid hunger was publicised in popular books such as Tristram Stuart's investigative book *Waste: Uncovering the Global Scandal* in 2009, and Jonathan Bloom's (2010) *American Wasteland*, both of which sparked global conversation and initiatives. While more detailed accounts of the environmental, social, political, and economic impacts of food waste can be found throughout this Handbook, suffice to suggest that the causes and impacts of food waste will help to determine whether life on Earth can continue within planetary boundaries.

As several chapters in this Handbook will demonstrate, the food waste crisis reflects multiple policy journeys, and arguably some failures, in how to mitigate and prevent the wastage of food. Turn-of-the-century changes in European waste policy represented an important redirection toward diverting food waste away from landfill and stimulating innovative solutions in action today (Evans, Campbell, & Murcott, 2013). Food waste has increasingly influenced mainstream political agendas at international and national levels, prompting legislation to actively reduce waste levels, as explored in Part III. Impacts of these regulatory efforts and interventions are hard to properly account and remain ambiguous. Mourad and Finn (2019), for example, suggest that, despite France's food waste law, efforts to *prevent* retailers from discarding food have shown little overall reduction. Strategies of surplus redistribution, date-marking and waste valorisation among others form multifaceted solution pathways, but the complexity and systematicity of food waste makes it clear that no single solution will address the root causes of its many manifestations (Gascon, 2018).

Governance bodies working across governments, industry, and civil society[3] have collaborated across sectors and multi-scalar levels of jurisdiction, responding to the clear need to tackle food waste holistically, often through public behaviour-change campaigns (e.g. 'Love Food Hate Waste') and voluntary business agreements such as the UK's Courtauld Commitment. Food waste reduction was included in the revised Sustainable Development Goals (SGDs), which set a clear global agenda for mitigation. SDG 12.3 aims to 'halve per capita food waste at retail and consumer levels and reduce food losses along production and supply chains, including post-harvest losses' by 2030 (UN, 2015). Certain chapters in this Handbook interrogate the assumptions, framings, and mechanisms of these mainstream approaches to food waste, asking what might they mask, exclude and, in the process of collaborating, who/which sectors might be ignored.

However, the purpose of this editorial is not to just detail the astounding facts and statistics surrounding the food waste problem. Nor do we subscribe to the need to give a thorough history on the topic. Andrew F. Smith's chapter in this Handbook covers this in detail, as does the opening chapter of Evans et al.'s 2013 book *Waste Matters: New Perspectives on Food and Society* (Evans, Campbell, & Murcott, 2013, see also Campbell, Evans, & Murcott, 2017). Rather, as the opening of this book indicates, it is important to explain the terrain over which food waste is situated after a relative intellectual invisibility in sustainability literatures up until the last 10 years (see Reynolds et al. (2019), and Chen et al. (2017) for bibliometric reviews). This editorial, therefore, hopes to go some way in opening up some intellectual doors to this Handbook as a resource that informs, facilitates, debates, and ponders food waste in the past, present, and future.

Addressing gaps in food waste studies: technology, innovation, and including diverse perspectives

Previewing possible futures and directions of debate in food waste studies, Part VI of this book considers the role of technologies and their potential disruptions of consumption patterns (Farr-Wharton, Osadchiy and Lyle, this volume). As technology such as smartphone 'apps' become more accessible, there may be new opportunities to share food and prevent waste through technology-mediated interactions (Davies & Legg, 2018). Online spaces have facilitated new relationships around food, such as 'Disco Soup' spaces and events that propose convivial solutions to minimise food waste through cooking and eating together (see Barnard and Mourad, this volume). New ideas and material innovations in packaging, labelling, and portion-sizing, it is hoped, might address some of the contextual, discursive, and environmental structurings of food wastage as the processual 'fallout' of everyday provisioning practices (Evans, 2014; see LaBarge et al., this volume). While the waste-mitigating potential of new technologies – and the political-economic contexts that mediate them – are up for debate, it is likely that they will play a key role.

Another issue we have aimed to tackle in the editing of this Handbook is that of over- or under-representation in food waste studies, discussed in further detail in following sections. Despite its 89 contributors and over 30 chapters, we make no claims that this Handbook is all-encompassing or all-inclusive, particularly because food waste is not attached to any single discipline but cuts across academic fields. We recognise, for example, the relative over-representation of global North perspectives. This regrettable marker of academia's uneven economic and socio-political structures of knowledge-production also reflects major inequalities embedded in food systems (Patel, 2007). It is not only global South scholars whose voices have been less apparent in dominant food waste discourses, but non-Eurocentric perspectives and ontologies more broadly. As Shilling (2013, p. 1) asks, 'who gets to define what is and what is not food and waste?'.

In recognising these gaps, we sought to include more diverse perspectives, scholars and case studies that may challenge certain well-received framings and interpretations of food and our relationship to it. The varied perspectives given in different chapters present just some of the possible approaches to food waste scholarship. This variability is partly rooted in the ways that food waste is woven into so many different aspects of everyday life, whether as a consumer, businessperson, and/or policymaker. In this Handbook, scholars, practitioners, and policymakers engage with food waste through the lens of religion and spirituality; supply chains; political economy; policy integration; behaviour change; waste measurement; social innovation; surplus food redistribution; infrastructure; inequality; activism; and a breadth of methodological approaches and innovations; among other broad themes. Today, those investigating the wastage of food continue to add to a rapidly expanding area of academic interest. The following section introduces a number of chapters analysing food waste activism and the visceral encounters with wasted foods that such activism frequently entails.

Encountering food waste: the response of scholar-activism

This volume includes authors whose current activism is rooted in scholarship, and others whose scholarship is rooted in activism, or at least visceral encounters with the ubiquitous stuff of food waste. Many food waste scholar-activists recall an experience of encountering food waste first hand, and often at scale, prompting questioning and an urge to somehow do something about it. Some years ago, beside a small supermarket in the UK, one editor noticed a bin overspilling with unopened, partly in-date packets of food: ice creams, whole chickens, bottles of beer, tomatoes, organic eggs, chocolate, and a preponderance of bread products and bananas – as would later come to be recognised as 'normal' for supermarket bins. Another recalls his part-time employment at a supermarket while in college and the shocking of the amount of unsold food that was generated at the end of each day, while another editor was taught from a young age through a traditional folktale, that to waste even one single grain of rice is unethical.

Our reactions and subsequent investigations led us, in different ways, to study causes and trajectories of wasted food. Discoveries of inexplicably wasted food might prompt horror or denial: close the bin, drive away. A combination of curiosity, greed, and consternation might prompt one to think how this very food could be put to good use: could I eat this? Share it? The materiality and symbolism of food, perhaps more so than other manifestations of waste, exerts a particularly strong call. The store bin's food was hastily bundled into the car (guiltily: the moral and structural line between gleaning and stealing has always been blurry and riddled with taboo[4]) and, once home, displayed and photographed. There is something about hoards of food, turned matter-out-of-place by their mediation within a furtively opened bin, that prompts urgings to tell others, seek explanations and solutions, expressed in Barnard and Mourad's recounting (this volume) of the 'Wave the banana at capitalism' speech. Emerging writing on 'dumpster-diving' (e.g. Edwards & Mercer, 2007) assured us that we were not alone.

The ontological perturbations induced by encountering food waste, and starting to learn how it is caused, can translate into political perturbations. Some Handbook authors have participated in social movements mobilising around food waste, convinced that individual efforts to 'waste less' will be futile in the absence of broader critical analysis and action to counter structurally entrenched causes (see Bowman in this volume). The past decade has seen an upswell of writings aiming to spur such critical attention. Curiosity and concern around food waste may have derived from reading Stuart's (2009) or Bloom's (2010) popularly written but thoroughly researched books, or the increasing number of academic papers and courses on food waste awaiting students of multiple disciplines. Equally, it may come from encounters with food waste while working in catering, or deep-rooted mores about the inadmissibility of wasting food from aphorisms around the childhood dinner table. Others' politicisations of food waste occur through involvement in broader social justice movements. Consider the origin story of Food Not Bombs (Barnard and Mourad, this volume): founder Keith McHenry, upon discovering an enormous wheel of cheese in a dumpster, announced: 'To heck with being vegan, let's be "freegan"!'. Noting that the politics of veganism rests in part on one's capacity to 'vote with the wallet' through market purchasing (Alkon & Guthman, 2017), Food Not Bombs aimed to highlight the destitution of many amid dominant logics of economic growth and military expansion. Yet despite burgeoning academic and popular writings, public awareness campaigns, and organisations making food waste visible, many of us relate to it in a personal way, often bringing a raft of moral conceptions to the table (O'Brien, 2008).

Embodying waste/guilt: a gendered perspective

The contradictions of a 'vastogenic' ('waste producing, waste dominated, and profiting from waste') economy premised on the manufacturing of scarcity (Cloke, 2013, p. 628 and this volume; Abbott, 2014) are swallowed and metabolised in political ecologies of bodies that complexify simple categorisations of how – and where – food waste is caused and manifested (Hayes-Conroy & Hayes-Conroy, 2013). The gendered and familial dynamics of domestic food waste have been documented (Cappellini & Parsons, 2013; Evans, 2014; Fraser & Parizeau, 2018). On the topic of food literacy and food waste reduction, Soma's Indonesian case study (2016) identified the critical role that women predominantly play (through food provisioning) in passing down traditional and intergenerational knowledge around food waste prevention, reduction, and attitudes. This knowledge is transferred through folktale storytelling, spiritual teachings, as well as gender-based domestic food work, which in a political economy perspective is categorised as 'unpaid' labour and often devalued (Soma, 2016). Further, a feminist perspective sheds light on how our bodies themselves become sites for the temporary resolution of capitalism's 'bulimic' contradiction of growth and bodily limitations (Guthman & DuPuis, 2006). Beyond metaphorical critiques, others have written highly personal and embodied accounts of experiences with bulimia, articulating experiential realities of dominant cultural dichotomies of gluttony and self-denial (Bullitt-Jonas, 1999), food's (over)use as a tool to manage self and social expectations (Squire, 2002), and racialised, classed guilt at 'wasting' food through culturally disordered eating (Stovall, 2017). Feminist accounts of obesity and fatness provide critical routes into understanding the relationships between minded bodies, foodscapes, and food economies whose excesses are both profitable and potentially life-threatening. Historical changes in cooking practices, gender roles, package/portion sizes, and food choice and availability, all nuance the enrolment of the 'rational individual' in the reckoning of what is, simply, enough.

Seeking root causes, recasting received wisdom

Social movements have coalesced around the problem of food waste, but differ in their framings, political diagnoses, and proposed actions to address it (Arcuri, 2019). Many such movements, for example, have attempted to situate food's wastage within a critique of the logics of neoliberal capitalism, where food's profitability exerts a greater influence on its journey than its capacity to nourish (Gascon, 2018). Ever-increasing excess becomes a business rationale rather than an effort to feed a growing number of humans equitably, as Cloke's chapter theorises through the concept of 'vastogenesis'. Far from being devoid of, or separate from, regimes of value, 'food/waste is both supportive of and necessary to the functionality of the system and therefore of direct value to it' (Cloke, this volume).

The values accorded to food and the ways in which it is perceived, narrated and treated, is a theme running through a number of chapters (Jane Midgley, for example, considers multiple values informing 'ideas and understandings of surplus food'). Several Handbook authors engage a Marxist analysis of food wastage, centred on the dominant logic of 'use values' over 'exchange values' and an unquestioned faith in the necessity (and assumption of the possibility) of economic growth in food markets. Such analyses trouble received ideas about who, or what, is responsible for food wastage. As Giles argues (this volume), 'the lion's share of public responses centre fickle consumers or technical inefficiencies. These narratives are a convenient exculpation for agribusiness and food retailers, ostensibly beholden to their customers' demands. In other words, they let capitalism off the hook' (see also Parizeau's chapter on household food waste, this volume). Such re-tellings unsettle explanations of food waste as 'accidents' – climatic, technical, or managerial – that interrupt the normal and desirable way of producing and distributing food. Rather, they shed light on normalised – but historically abnormal – conditions whereby food's commodification, rather than its provisioning as a commons (Morrow, 2019) appears natural. In this light, the bread tossed at the end of the supermarket day is seen in terms not only of depleted freshness that might deter fussy customers, but as a commodity whose cheap price, and industrialised sped-up mode of production allows for its overproduction.

Making space for newer items that can earn a greater premium for retailers than the old, daily remakes the visage of mass consumption, whose aesthetic standardisation stands 'diametrically opposed to the contingency of a natural world' (Giles, 2016, p. 84). Tackling the biopolitical structures that produce waste, Giles' chapter (this volume) analyses the wastage of edible food commodities as the necessary counterpart to the reckoning of exchange value through the constant flow (and uneven accumulation) of capital. Giles notes: 'where goods are produced in excess, and demand is produced through scarcity or rarefaction, the two strategies are in diametric opposition to one another'. These considerations of political economy perhaps help us understand why large food businesses can happily donate edible surpluses to charity, but will not simply allow passers-by or retail workers to take the food for free at the end of the day: why would people pay for food when they know 'it can be had for less, albeit not quite as fresh, in the alley?' (Giles, 2013, p. 46).

The variegated and visceral politics of food waste activism

Several Handbook chapters compare the variegated and shifting politics and practices of food waste activists (see especially chapters by Barnard & Mourad, and Bowman). Many involve encounters with the copious amounts of edible food that ends up in the waste stream; the lives of discarded foodstuffs do not always end in the dumpster. Food's use value – its capacity to nourish (and delight) bodies and commensal experiences – persists (Giles, 2016). Discarded foodstuffs trace an 'abject map of the conspicuous consumption of high-income earners' (ibid., p. 83), but can fuel practices of food sharing (Davies & Legg, 2018) and landscapes of 'social' eating where commodity values are no longer the dominant force (Blake, 2019). Giles' (2013) ethnographic delvings into Food Not Bombs' anarchist kitchens, open-air shared meals – and an array of dumpsters – take us into the topsy-turvy, shadowy worlds of value. Here, the 'abject labour' of those unwilling – or unable – to participate in the high-price urbanism of commodity capitalism, turns wasted foods into commensality and social solidarity through shared public meals.

Food Not Bombs thus transform wasted food materially but also discursively, naming contemporary waste as symptomatic of uneven structures and dynamics of resource distribution. Giles has studied how the globalised logics of waste production beget globalising, networked movements that not only critique those logics, but use the material stuff of waste to share food with people less able to participate in market economies in what he calls 'a kind of after-market shadow economy' (2016, p. 85). Yet there are conflicting visions of how the food waste problem should be understood and approached, with Lougheed and Spring's chapter (this volume) exploring conflicts around how different kinds of food waste can, and should, be divested and disposed of in the name of, at times contradictory, rationales of food safety and food insecurity.

UK campaign group This Is Rubbish have sought to counter what they see as neoliberal tendencies in dominant policy and industry responses to food waste. These tendencies include emphasising consumer-level, rather than pre-consumer, causes of wastage (Evans, 2011), and preferences for managing unsold excesses, rather than preventing their generation in the first place (Warshawsky, 2010), and for 'voluntary responsibility deals over mandatory regulation', which they attribute to a broader tendency for a politics of encouraging business efficiency with minimal government intervention (Stewart et al., 2013, p. 2). Over recent years, the group has lobbied for mandatory audits of industry waste generation and binding EU targets to halve farm-to-fork food waste by 2030, while supporting a parliamentary food waste bill (see Porter, this volume).

As well as creating discursive space for structural demands, sometimes through public stunts (a skipful of wasted food delivered to supermarket entrances, for example), groups such as This Is Rubbish have attempted to 'reconnect' consumers with food systems through public awareness-raising and educational efforts in schools but also outdoor events. Community-based surplus redistribution efforts may combine food waste reduction efforts premised on individuals' knowledge and skills (e.g. of expiry labels and food handling) with broader awareness-raising about food systems, to transmit understanding of causative factors and solutions. Spring, Adams, and Hardman (2019) explore the tensions between educational food waste activism that can shift the responsibility to young people rather than target systemic causes, yet whose attention to bodily, sensory dimensions of food access and handling can engender embodied and collective understandings of food and food systems that extend beyond a focus on waste alone (Hayes-Conroy & Hayes-Conroy, 2013). Many food waste movement actors themselves reflect on these tensions, and are aware of the potential contradictions of activism that seeks to contest, yet may inadvertently contain, food wastage and its causes (Heynen, 2010).

A concentration of this literature hails from North America, which has seen the growth of professionalised food charity as a response to the politically embarrassing contradictions of excess and poverty in wealthy nations. Riches (1997) critiqued charitable responses to 'first world hunger' as evidence of failing liberal welfare states, with Poppendieck (1998) noting the 'moral safety valve' food charity affords as a means to appease the discomfort of living in affluent-but-unequal societies. Fisher (2017) describes the globalising logics of industrial-scale surplus food charity in terms of 'Big Hunger', and research increasingly attends the growth of food banking in the global South (Warshawsky, 2018). Yet food charity has been framed as a 'win–win' solution in debates around interventions that often conflate food waste and food insecurity issues. Challenging such oversimplifications, this Handbook calls for a more inclusive approach to food waste studies and the need to explore alternative paradigms and solutions (see Yoreh & Scharper in this volume for a spiritual approach).

A more inclusive approach to food waste studies: alternative paradigms, alternative food waste conceptualisations, and alternative solutions

From the 'Tale of the Crying Rice' common in Java, Indonesia (Soma, 2016) to the Mohawk (Kanien'keh.:ka) telling of the Creation Story of the 'Sky Woman' (Horne-Miller,

2016) and the 'All My Relations' Indigenous teaching in Turtle Island (North America), a new wave of intersectional food waste scholars are recognising the need to include and (re)learn from paradigms, scholarships, cultures, and worldviews that might counter and challenge the industrial food system, while serving to reconnect identity, well-being, and relationships to food and land. This is especially relevant in a dominant global food system that numerous studies have defined as unjust and exploitative of labour (Weiler, Otero, & Wittman, 2016), destructive to biodiversity and natural resources (Willett et al., 2019), wasteful (Stuart, 2009), and a food system that has been commonly referred to as 'broken' (Holt-Giménez & Peabody, 2008).

Alternative worldviews on food systems (see Soma et al. in this volume) and alternative conceptualisations of relationships that are non-anthropocentric, non-human, or 'beyond human', are well established in post-humanist literature (Wolfe, 2010). Bennett (2010) notes the ecological importance of shifting the gaze from an anthropocentric focus on human experience to things-in-themselves. Food in this view becomes *actant*, with agency and vitality whose recognition may escape and challenge human mastery. In discussing waste matters, Bennett explores such vibrancy of matter, noting that 'our trash is not "away" in landfills, but generating lively streams of chemicals and volatile winds of methane' (2010, p. vii). This point is voiced in other registers within food waste literature; e.g. scholars and reports oft-repeat the point that food waste decomposing in landfills generates methane, a greenhouse gas with a warming impact 25 times more potent than carbon dioxide (FAO, 2015; CEC, 2017).

In large part, however, the dominant response to food waste has assumed the treatment of food waste as a resource, as a commodity, or as a problem for humans to master (Papar-gyropoulou et al., 2014). Bennett alerts us to a different approach to solving public problems that takes more seriously the agency of these matters (in the double sense), including edible matters such as food. She explains her advocacy for nondualistic distributed agency thus: 'my hunch is that the image of dead or thoroughly instrumentalized matter feeds human hubris and our earth-destroying fantasies of conquest and consumption' (2010, p. ix). Underlying our conceptions of power, Bennett implies, are ontologies of domination prem-ised on anthropocentric dualisms whose decentring might allow us to seek new possibilities for understanding action, community, and politics. Re-seen in this way, from the point of production, food deserves – and demands – to be elevated to a point where it is not merely a thing to be 'managed' but emphatically deserving of more respect and not to be wasted. Further, these points demand we seek ontological, systemic, and transformative – rather than symptom-managing – solutions. Lou's (2017) unveiling of everyday practices of reuse in Hong Kong is one example of ontological and ethnographic work that challenges the objectification and commodification of food matters.

Sensing wasted food materialities: a wellspring for politics … and art?

Other authors, especially those writing about waste from an Indigenous perspective (e.g. Liboiron, 2016), highlight the partialities of political economy for a comprehensive understanding of waste. While it has long been unfashionable in academic discourse to reinforce individual action as the locus of our analyses, 'assemblage' ontology troubles the very notion of the individual, arguing that our problems cannot simply be laid at the discursive door of 'government' or even 'capitalism'. How might recent efforts in social theorising to attend to sensoriality, affect, and emergence, help us make sense of the embodied, emotive, and multi-species experiences of many of those directly working in the generation, recapture, and transformation of wasted food (Korsmeyer & Sutton, 2011;

Waitt & Phillips, 2016)? Lougheed and Spring's chapter (this volume), for example, draws on assemblage thinking to consider the ethical, regulatory, and material infrastructures – or conduits – through which food is variously divested (Gregson, Metcalfe, & Crewe, 2007). How might food – and multiple conduits through which wasted food is rescued, repurposed, or land-filled – 'bite back' (Tenner, 1996) in unexpected and unintended ways?

What does it mean to give food agency, to be 'struck by its phenomenology' (Hawkins, 2006, p. 83)? Hawkins describes the heart-shaped potato picked out by *The Gleaners* documentary maker Agnes Varda not merely as effect of cinematic representation but as a 'sensuous, wondrous thing' (ibid., p. 84). The camera not so much renders the object as lively but allows us to witness 'objects becoming things and the ethical implications of this'. Hawkins notes of the close-up panning shot of potatoes on a table that we do not just 'see' them but 'touch' them and that 'through this imbrication of touch and vision … we experience Varda's sensuous enchantment with the thing' (ibid.). 'When we encounter waste as things,' she suggests, 'the affective energy that can accompany this … can be the impulse for new relations: a motivation for a different ethics, a sudden inspiration for a new use' (p. 85). What might be the ethical implications of engaging with various kinds of wasted food and the things we do with them? What happens if we let food itself speak as an actant? Perhaps Varda's art conveys an attunement to 'thing-power' that gives artists capacity to change hearts and minds (what is politics if not this?) that seems defunct in tired behaviour-change campaigns. Reno (2015, p. 568) notes the sleight-of-hand afforded by such weightings of blame: 'while economic incentives and moral shaming campaigns focus on consumer and retail practices, the possibility of compelling manufacturers to produce less waste is foreclosed'.

Austrian photographer Klaus Pichler is another such 'attuner'. His 'One Third' photo series,[5] inspired by UN reports on global food wastage (Gustavsson et al., 2011), re-presents decaying food – the stuff of waste – in ways that fascinate and affect differently from images of landfills of fruit. Their *affect* operates through their animation of *other beings* who lay claim to food when we do not eat it.[6] The photo collection as a whole manages to depict the global dimensions of food waste while invoking the most intimate, perhaps abject close encounters with food that Pichler allowed to rot in his apartment before photographing them. A beheaded, plucked chicken carcass sits bolt upright in its roasting dish, forearms splayed and chest skin splayed to reveal the green tinge of the putrefying flesh beneath. A mound of moulding beetroots 'bleed' down the side of their fluted white vase. A slab of beef teems with maggots and grubs. A pile of 'white' asparagus lay bare their yellowed, stringy innards like burned viscera. A bow-headed octopus gleams ghoulish and alien from its green bin-bag shroud. The smiles of potato 'smilies' are obscured by furring mould or squished into grimaces. Animated thus, the processual and dynamic nature of wastage is frozen in the photographic form, eerily inverting the fetishising aesthetics of food advertising (Keefe, 2014).

Animal relations and beyond-humans

There remains a lack of food waste literature that foregrounds the vitality of non-human matters, even in this Handbook. Another major gap in food waste literature is deeper consideration of animal welfare and categorisations of animals as 'waste', despite Alexander et al.'s (2013, p. 482) call for research to 'explore how food – particularly meat production – troubles post-humanist politics, in which the equivalence of life forms is often assumed' (for critical discussion on animal parts as waste see Coles & Hallett, 2012; Roe, 2013). This is particularly poignant in a food system where certain animals – the case of male dairy calves is a good example – are seen as of no use to the dairy industry and therefore considered 'waste product' (Gillespie, 2014). While not technically 'wasted' in the sense that the industrial system still sees some sort of use for those categorised as 'waste commodities', some of the male dairy calves live very short confined lives separated from the mother and are sold as veal, while others are killed at birth with their bodies composted or rendered (Gillespie, 2014). According to Ellendorff and Klein (2003), in the United States, 226 million day-old male chicks are culled every year almost immediately after hatching from layer breeders. Industry sees no reason to rear them due to slower growth rate and seemingly inferior meat in comparison to broiler chickens, raising significant ethical concerns (Krautwald-Junghanns et al., 2018). Culled chicks are generally processed industrially for animal feed so are not technically 'wasted' from the industrial food system perspective. However, instead of acknowledging wider ethical and environmental implications of industrial egg manufacturing and retailers/consumers' unrealistic expectations of chicken size, Ellendorff and Klein (2003, p. 7) suggest that killings 'could easily be avoided if only female chicks were born' or the unwanted gender could be identified at the stage of an embryo and then killed, assuaging public concerns around chick culling. While culled animals' categorisation as waste does not exclude them from being seen as a 'waste commodity' or 'resource' in other sectors – such as for rendering or animal feed – their vitality was never considered and they were not, as Bennett (2010) called for, treated with respect.

Relationships between animal agribusiness and waste trouble our very conceptualisations of what can be defined *as* food waste (Alexander, Gregson, & Gille, 2013). At a food waste symposium on a rural English farm, Henry Buller (2015) described the 'systemic waste of growing potentially human food to feed animals'. The idea of animal feed *as waste* challenges commonly held notions of 'efficiency' (Garnett & Little, 2015), while troubling narratives of the need to double food production by 2050 (Weis, 2015). Tomlinson (2013), indeed, argues that recognising food waste more broadly as part of this discourse offers alternative ways to feed the world than normative productivism.

Critical animal studies consider animal relations and how discourses around dirt, pests, vermin, and waste are reflected in stigmatic framings of both the unwanted non-human (in the case of Corman (2011), raccoons) and the unwanted human other (freegans/dumpster divers) within an urban context. Corman describes the cultural vilification of both freegans and raccoons, noting that urban 'civility' somehow becomes threatened by both the physical and symbolic disruption of trash when both freegans and raccoons reclaim what was once categorised as 'trash'. In re-valuing what others have deemed invaluable, freegans reclaim the discards of consumer culture and make the political choice to challenge excess consumption (Barnard, 2016). Despite stigma around garbage and dumpster diving, and the fact that many freegans eat from waste voluntarily and not due to lack of income (Edwards & Mercer, 2007), much food reclaimed from bins is not rotten, spoiled, or dirty but in many cases high-quality, though Clark's (2004) symbolic analysis of 'punk cuisine' highlights how the very categories of 'civility' may be rejected and inverted through activist food praxis.

Reconnecting the distance: alternative food systems

We argue that an alternative framing of value in edible matters can be found in various non-Eurocentric alternative paradigms, especially those focused on different forms of relationality and ethical responsibility. Alternative paradigms that delve deeper into intersections between human/non-human relations and non-Eurocentric forms of knowledge are evident in fields such as food studies and also economics (see the example of Buddhist Economics in Payutto

& Evans, 1994). For example, studies exploring Indigenous food sovereignty demonstrate the need to tackle the exploitation of land and resources due to colonisation (Rudolph & McLachlan, 2013; Grey & Patel, 2015; Kepkiewicz & Rotz, 2018) and the important role of traditional ecological knowledge (Coté, 2016) in the development of a more sustainable and just food system.

Addressing supposedly 'developed' nation-states, critical studies of equity and food justice, Alkon and Agyeman (2011) consider the importance of attending to class, race, and socioeconomic status in understanding determinants and measures of food security, hunger, and food accessibility. Food justice and non-Eurocentric approaches such as traditional ecological knowledge have not adequately informed debates and conversations in food waste literature (for some examinations of food waste through an equity lens see Spring (2016), Soma (2017), and Spring, Adams, and Hardman (2019) on the influence of class on food waste). One exception to this trend is the significant body of food insecurity research, already mentioned, which views the charitable redistribution of 'surplus' or donated foods as a symptom-alleviating- rather than system-challenging, response to food insecurity or 'hunger' (Henderson, 2004; Fisher, 2017). Thus far, paradigms with potential to challenge food system injustices by countering food's commodification while offering a decolonial approach to eaters and the food that they eat (see Todd (2014) on human–fish relationships), have not been made mainstream in current food waste studies literature. It is for this reason that we seek a more inclusive and intersectional approach to food waste studies that showcase scholarly work from the global South and from Indigenous scholars.

'All My Relations', an Indigenous worldview found in Canada (also referred to as Turtle Island) offers an interconnected framework of rights and responsibilities that is premised on the values of being in balanced relations with all creations (McGregor, 2009). When applied to food systems, it challenges the status quo and neoliberal paradox of the commodification that perpetuates wastage alongside hunger. It also seeks to counter the exploitative potentials of the distancing process, defined by Princen as, 'the separation of primary resource-extraction decisions from final consumption decisions' (2002, p. 157). The 'All My Relations' framework acknowledges that survival is possible through recognising our mutual relatedness, and responsibilities toward our kin (both human and beyond human). Histories of ever-greater distancing between food system elements and relations has disconnected these roles, responsibilities, and relations.

Despite widespread media and academic coverage showcasing the diversity of issues (health, environment, economic, animal welfare, etc.) around food production, consumption, choices, and wastage, simply being aware of an issue is not sufficient to mobilise action. As Carolan (2016) notes, 'we need to feel'. Elsewhere he writes that 'the experiential horizon of food consumers comes from the level of epistemic distance from the global nature of today's food systems' (2011, p. 32). This epistemic distance is reflected in a framework of severed relationships, which from an Indigenous ontological perspective (Manson, 2015), may also refer to our separation from our kin (note: plants, animals, the land, and food in general are considered 'kin'). Princen (2002) and Clapp (2014) have sought to explain how such spatial and mental distancing leads to overconsumption, exploitation, and waste. Thus, we pose the following question to the reader. In the context of wasting food, *what does it truly mean to waste one's kin?*

Building new foundations of relationality

Carolan (2017) documents examples of intentional efforts to distance eaters and producers, allowing issues such as farm labour exploitation or environmental injustices such as pollution for people living downstream of food processing plants to go unnoticed or unpunished.

These distancing processes are rooted in imperialist-turned-corporate regimes (Friedmann & McMichael, 1989), colonialism, and slavery (Mintz, 1986). Neoliberalism, through the liberalisation of global agricultural economies under structural adjustment policies, corporatisation, and regulations that promote unjust international trade (Bello & Baviera, 2009), have restructured landscapes, foodways, labour, and relationships, threatening the food sovereignty of various nations. Transnational corporations (TNCs) dominate global food supplies, from food production to food processing, distribution, and retail (Clapp & Fuchs, 2009). This process of intensified financialisation, as Clapp argues, has in turn 'abstracted food from its physical form into highly complex agricultural commodity derivatives' (2014, p. 797).

Viewed in this light, food waste solutions that do not challenge, disrupt, or address these systemic injustices could perpetuate further inequalities. It is rooted in the obfuscation and disregard of the interconnectedness of not only ecosystems, but also of land and human relations. Gille (2010) notes how cultural and social values have shifted to meet the demands of profits in waste regimes of disposability. Cheap food implies 'the decontextualisation of food in its broadest sense' (Carolan 2011, p. 2) and the externalisation of environmental, social, and political costs of food production, consumption, distribution, and waste management. In building a new foundation of relationality that honours vitality, challenges injustice, and considers the need to address the structural roots of globalised food waste, a number of chapters showcase diverse perspectives, theories, methodologies, and case studies from different regions. For example, Indigenous scholar Adrianne Lickers Xavier's (Onondaga from the Six Nations of the Grand River First Nations Territory) chapter in this volume, co-authored by Soma, Li, Geobey, and Gutierrez, asks 'how do we see food?'. This question will be useful to keep in mind when reading this book, considering whose lenses (individuals, academics, institutions, activists, corporations) have been privileged in approaches to food waste.

In addressing the 'wicked' problem of wasted food (see Soma et al. in this volume), it is thus important to recognise how problem framings and definitions influence interventions. In *Waste Matters* (Evans, Campbell, & Murcott, 2013), food and waste are firmly positioned as good for theorising. In thinking and acting, we hope that this book promotes interdisciplinary collaboration, cross-cultural learning, equitable policymaking, systems thinking, and alternative paradigms in approaching food waste. In doing so, it will become more possible to build a foundation of respect for the agency, vitality, and vibrancy of food and all of the relations embedded in its matter.

Joining the movement: a new wave of food waste studies and the international food loss and food waste studies group

We conclude this editorial with the genesis of how this book came to be, as to do so is our approach to challenge a linear framework by reconnecting the *present* to the *past*, in efforts to engage *future* food waste scholars. In early 2014 a whirlwind email thread discussing the expanding insights of the burgeoning field of food waste studies and deeply concerning statistics led to the beginnings of a global network of emerging food waste scholars. We responded to the alarming figures by helping to organise and aid the mobilisation of a new wave of global attention to the food waste problem, attention whose ambiguous implications and variegated politics are revealed by some chapter authors. First profiled and hosted as an online network and group by the Garbage Matters Project at Leiden University (Netherlands), The International Food Loss and Food Waste Studies Group (foodwastestudies.com) sought to create a space to nourish a new phase of food waste research. The group was born by autumn 2014, with a website and Google group platform enabling the exchange of research, knowledge, and debate within a growing community of academics and practitioners. As the Food Waste Studies network grew, the interdisciplinary nature of the field became increasingly apparent. The opening chapter of the seminal monograph *Waste Matters*,[7] noted that 'food waste is a hugely under-researched area of interest for social scientists' (Evans, Campbell, & Murcott, 2013, p. 5). Six years on, this Handbook includes contributions from 89 authors, among them scholars, practitioners, and policymakers. Clearly, food waste studies has come a long way, although much work remains to be done.

The Food Waste Studies group has encouraged discussion and debate both in-person and virtually, given the global nature of food waste studies. A significant milestone was the organisation of a special session at the 2015 Association of American Geographers conference in Chicago. The session, a 'Food Waste Tour of the Global North and Global South', was the first face-to-face meeting of many of the group members. Multiple paper presentations revealed food waste as an economic, ecological, and moral issue through a range of case studies from across the world. This was an attempt to unveil, compare, and conceptualise 'food waste' in its many aspects, interpretations, and politicisations. An Economic and Social Research Council Festival of Social Science event was held in 2015 on 'Innovation in Tackling Food Waste' as well as various seminars in Europe and North America. Further events followed, such as the organising of multiple food waste panels and a roundtable led by Food Waste Studies group members at the 2016 joint conference of the Association for the Study of Food and Society; the Agriculture, Food, and Human Values Society; and the Canadian Association for Food Studies in the City of Toronto, Canada.

Thus far, the group has provided a platform for advertising events far and wide, from 'Disco Soup' events to conferences, seminars, policy discussions, and film screenings. The group has provided a network of collaboration for research grants, book projects, and more. With the co-editors having been founding and/or active members since the group's inception, we see this book as a significant milestone in the group's journey and hope that as well as providing a valuable manual and point of reference for a variety of perspectives on food waste, it is also a call to arms to students, academics, and practitioners to further develop and act upon their interests in this critical field for addressing more sustainable and just food futures.

The community that has grown out of foodwastestudies.com, totalling more than 200 in number and spanning multiple countries, has shown us that an interdisciplinary response is needed to address the issue(s) of food waste in light of the urgency of climate change and the global inequities around food insecurity. For this community to operate effectively together we need a common starting point and language. For this reason, we have edited this book with two aims. First, we have edited this Handbook to appeal to a broad audience of food waste students, academics, policy makers, and practitioners. Second, we have edited the book to illustrate the breadth and scope of food waste literature, viewpoints, and research, and to provide an intellectual starting point from where others can launch themselves.

We recognise that food waste studies is rapidly evolving as a field of research. When the editors began their studies in the area, the number of academic papers related to food waste was under 100 – we (the editors) all had read sociological and cultural theorisations of waste by Douglas (2003 (1966)), Evans (2011), Hawkins (2006), Thompson (1979), and Rathje and Murphy (2001). Now every month we are alerted of new articles that expand the literature ever further, yet large gaps in knowledge – and voices – remain. This Handbook recognises the speed at which this field is growing, and provides a voice to emerging and established scholars to provide a snapshot of the swift proliferation of interest in this field. We encourage readers to join this community by visiting foodwastestudies.com.

Notes

1 Graphically depicted in Derf Backderf's (2015) lurid graphic novel of the societal ills of gluttony, *Trashed* (Abrams Comic Arts). Also Havlíček, F., & Kuča, M. (2017). Waste Management at the End of the Stone Age. *Journal of Landscape Ecology (Czech Republic)*, *10*(1), 45–57.
2 For example, *Wasted: The Story of Food Waste* produced by late celebrity chef Anthony Bourdain and *Just Eat It* by Grant Baldwin and Jenny Rustemeyer and public outcry following broadcasts such as Craig Reucassel's American Broadcasting Corporation's (ABC) 'War on Waste' (19 May 2017).
3 For example, the Waste & Resources Action Programme (WRAP) in the UK, World Resources Institute (WRI) and Natural Resource Defense Council (NRDC) in the USA, and World Wide Fund for Nature (WWF).
4 Exemplified with the case of Steven de Geynst, which has also been popularly dubbed the 'Muffin Man' case. On 22 March 2010, De Geynst was charged with robbery and sent for trial after taking two bags of muffins discarded at the back of a store in Rupelmonde, Belgium (O'Brien, 2012).
5 https://klauspichler.net/project/one-third/
6 Close attention to non-human forms of Serres' notion of parasitism offers new vantage points onto who – or what – decides what is waste (Burton & Tam, 2015).
7 This was originally published as a special issue in *The Sociological Review*.

References

Abbott, A. (2014). The problem of excess. *Sociological Theory*, *32*(1), 1–26.
Alexander, C., Gregson, N., & Gille, Z. (2013). Food Waste. In A. Murcott, W. Belasco & P. Jackson (Eds.), *The Handbook of Food Research* (pp. 471–485). London, New York: Bloomsbury Academic.
Alkon, A. H., & Agyeman, J. (Eds.). (2011). *Cultivating Food Justice: Race, Class, and Sustainability*. Cambridge, MA: MIT Press.
Alkon, A. H., & Guthman, J. (Eds.). (2017). *The New Food Activism: Opposition, Cooperation and Collective Action*. Oakland: University of California Press.
Arcuri, S. (2019). Food poverty, food waste and the consensus frame on charitable food redistribution in Italy. *Agriculture and Human Values*, *36*(2), 263–275.
Barnard, A. V. (2016). *Freegans: Diving into the Wealth of Food Waste in America*. Minneapolis: University of Minnesota Press.
Battersby, J. (2017). Food system transformation in the absence of food system planning: The case of supermarket and shopping mall retail expansion in Cape Town, South Africa. *Built Environment*, *43*(3), 417–430.
Bello, W. F., & Baviera, M. (2009). *The Food Wars*. London: Verso.
Bennett, J. (2010). *Vibrant Matter: A Political Ecology of Things*. Durham, NC: Duke University Press.
Biltekoff, C. (2016). The politics of food anti-politics. *Gastronomica*, *16*(4), 44–57.
Blake, M. K. (2019). More than just food: Food insecurity and resilient place making through community self-organising. *Sustainability*, *11*, 2942.
Bloom, J. (2010). *American Wasteland: How America Throws Away Nearly Half of Its Food (and What We Can Do About It)*. Cambridge, MA: Da Capo Lifelong Books.
Buller, H. (2015). Waste provocations: Introductory symposium remarks. *Food Geographies Working Group*. Retrieved from https://foodmatterssymposium.wordpress.com/2015/09/17/food-waste-symposium-introductory-remarks/
Bullitt-Jonas, M. (1999). *Holy Hunger: A Memoir of Desire*. New York: Vintage Books.
Burton, J., & Tam, D. (2015). Towards a parasitic ethics. *Theory, Culture & Society*, *33*(4), 103–125.
Campbell, H., Evans, D., & Murcott, A. (2017). Measurability, austerity and edibility: Introducing waste into food regime theory. *Journal of Rural Studies*, *51*, 168–177.
Cappellini, B., & Parsons, E. (2013). Practising thrift at dinnertime: Mealtime leftovers, sacrifice and family membership. *The Sociological Review*, *60*(S2), 121–134.
Carolan, M. (2011). *The Real Cost of Cheap Food*. New York, London: Earthscan, Routledge.
Carolan, M. (2016). Adventurous food futures: Knowing about alternatives is not enough, we need to feel them. *Agriculture and Human Values*, *33*(1), 141–152.
Carolan, M. S. (2017). *No One Eats Alone: Food as a Social Enterprise*. Washington D.C.: Island Press.
CEC. (2017). *Characterization and Management of Food Loss and Waste in North America*. Montreal, Canada: Commission for Environmental Cooperation, p. 48.

Chen, H., Jiang, W., Yang, Y., Yang, Y., & Man, X. (2017). State of the art on food waste research: A bibliometrics study from 1997 to 2014. *Journal of Cleaner Production, 140*, 840–846.

Clapp, J., & Fuchs, D. A. (Eds.). (2009). *Corporate Power in Global Agrifood Governance*. Cambridge, MA: MIT Press.

Clapp, J. (2014). Financialization, distance and global food politics. *Journal of Peasant Studies, 41*(5), 797–814.

Clapp, J., & Isakson, S. R. (2018). *Speculative Harvests*. Halifax: Fernwood.

Clark, D. (2004). The raw and the rotten: Punk Cuisine. *Ethnology, 43*(1), 19–31.

Cloke, J. (2013). Empires of waste and the food security meme. *Geography Compass, 7*(9), 622–636.

Coles, B., & Hallett, L., IV. (2012). Eating from the bin: Salmon heads, waste and the markets that make them. *The Sociological Review, 60*, 156–173.

Corman, L. (2011). Getting their hands dirty: Raccoons, freegans, and urban "trash". *Journal for Critical Animal Studies, 9*(3), 28–61.

Coté, C. (2016). "Indigenizing" food sovereignty. Revitalizing indigenous food practices and ecological knowledges in Canada and the United States. *Humanities, 5*(3), 57.

Davies, A. R., & Legg, R. (2018). Fare sharing: Interrogating the nexus of ICT, urban food sharing, and sustainability. *Food, Culture and Society, 21*(2), 233–254.

Douglas, M. (2003 (1966)). *Purity and Danger: An Analysis of Concepts of Pollution and Taboo*. New York: Routledge.

Edwards, F., & Mercer, D. (2007). Gleaning from Gluttony: An Australian youth subculture confronts the ethics of waste. *Australian Geographer, 38*(3), 279–296.

Ellendorff, F., & Klein, S. (2003). Current knowledge on sex determination and sex diagnosis: Potential solutions. *World Poultry Science, 59*(1), 7.

Evans, D. (2011). Blaming the consumer – Once again: The social and material contexts of everyday food waste practices in some English households. *Critical Public Health, 21*(4), 429–440.

Evans, D. (2014). *Food Waste: home Consumption, Material Culture and Everyday Life*. London: Bloomsbury.

Evans, D., Campbell, H., & Murcott, A. (2013). *Waste Matters: New Perspectives on Food and Society*. (Sociological Review Monograph). Oxford: John Wiley & Sons Ltd.

FAO. (2015). *Food Wastage Footprint & Climate Change*. Retrieved from www.fao.org/3/a-bb144e.pdf

Fisher, A. (2017). *Big Hunger: The Unholy Alliance between Corporate America and Anti-Hunger Groups*. Cambridge, MA: MIT Press.

Fraser, C., & Parizeau, K. (2018). Waste management as foodwork: A feminist food studies approach to household food waste. *Canadian Food Studies/La Revue Canadienne Des Études Sur l'alimentation, 5*(1), 39.

Friedmann, H., & McMichael, P. (1989). Agriculture and the state system: The rise and decline of national agricultures, 1870 to the present. *Sociologia Ruralis, 29*(2), 93–117.

Garnett, T., & Little, D. (2015). *Lean, Green, Mean, Obscene…? What is Efficiency? And Is It sustainable? Animal Production and Consumption Reconsidered*. Food Research and Climate Network. Retrieved from www.fcrn.org.uk/sites/default/files/fcrn_lmgo.pdf

Gascon, J. (2018). Food waste : A political ecology approach. *Journal of Political Ecology, 25*(1), 587–601.

Giles, D. B. (2013). *"A Mass Conspiracy To Feed People" Globalizing Cities, World-Class Waste, and the Biopolitics of Food Not Bombs*. PhD Thesis. University of Washington.

Giles, D. B. (2016). The work of waste-making: Biopolitical labour and the myth of the global city. In J. P. Marshall & L. Connor (Eds.), *Environmental Change and the World's Futures: Ecologies, Ontologies and Mythologies* (pp. 81–95). London: Routledge.

Gille, Z. (2010). Actor networks, modes of production, and waste regimes: Reassembling the macro-social. *Environment and Planning A, 42*(5), 1049–1064. https://doi.org/10.1068/a42122

Gillespie, K. (2014). Sexualized violence and the gendered commodification of the animal body in Pacific Northwest US dairy production. *Gender, Place & Culture, 21*(10), 1321–1337.

Gregson, N., Metcalfe, A., & Crewe, L. (2007). Moving things along: The conduits and practices of divestment in consumption. *Transactions of the Institute of British Geographers, 32*, 187–200.

Grey, S., & Patel, R. (2015). Food sovereignty as decolonization: Some contributions from Indigenous movements to food system and development politics. *Agriculture and Human Values, 32*(3), 431–444.

Gunders, D. (2012) 'Wasted: How America Is Losing up to 40 Percent of Its Food from Farm to Fork to Landfill'. NRDC Issue Paper [online] (August), 1–26. available from https://www.nrdc.org/sites/default/files/wasted-food-IP.pdf

Gustavsson, J., Cederberg, C., Sonesson, U., van Otterdijk, R., & Meybeck, A. (2011). *Global Food Losses and Food Waste- Extent, Causes and Prevention*. FAO. www.fao.org/fileadmin/user_upload/suistainability/pdf/Global_Food_Losses_and_Food_Waste.pdf

Guthman, J., & DuPuis, M. (2006). Embodying neoliberalism: Economy, culture, and the politics of fat. *Environment and Planning D: Society and Space*, *24*(3), 427–448.

Hall, K.D., Guo, J., Dore, M., and Chow, C.C. (2009) 'The Progressive Increase of Food Waste in America and Its Environmental Impact'. *PLoS ONE 4*(11), 9–14.

Hawkins, G. (2006). *The Ethics of Waste: How We Relate to Rubbish.* Lanham, Maryland: Rowman & Littlefield.

Hayes-Conroy, J., & Hayes-Conroy, A. (2013). Veggies and visceralities: A political ecology of food and feeling. *Emotion, Space and Society*, *6*(1), 81–90.

Henderson, G. (2004). "Free" food, the local production of worth, and the circuit of decommodification: A value theory of the surplus. *Environment and Planning D: Society and Space*, *22*(1), 485–512.

Heynen, N. (2010). Cooking up non-violent civil-disobedient direct action for the hungry: "Food not bombs" and the resurgence of radical democracy in the US. *Urban Studies*, *47*(6), 1225–1240.

Holt-Giménez, E., & Peabody, L. (2008). From food rebellions to food sovereignty: Urgent call to fix a broken food system. *Food First Backgrounder*, *14*(1), 1–6.

Horne-Miller, K. (2016). Distortion and healing: Finding balance and a "good mind" through the rearticulation of Sky Woman's journey. *Living on the land: Indigenous women's understanding of place.* In Kermoal, N., & Altamirano-Jiménez, I. (Eds.). *Living on the land: Indigenous women's understanding of place* (pp. 19–38). Edmonton: Athabasca University Press.

Hossain, N. et al. (2014). *"Them Belly Full (But We Hungry)": Food Rights Struggles in Bangladesh, India, Kenya and Mozambique.* Institute of Development Studies. Retrieved from http://foodriots.org/publication/view/them-belly-full-but-we-hungry-food-rights-struggles-in-bangladesh-india-kenya-and-mozambique

IMechE. (2013). *Global Food – Waste Not, Want Not.* Institute of Mechanical Engineers. Retrieved from www.imeche.org/docs/default-source/reports/Global_Food_Report.pdf?sfvrsn=0

Keefe, A. (July 16th, 2014) Visualizing waste: Klaus Pichler's gorgeous, rotting food. *National Geographic.* Retrieved from www.nationalgeographic.com/photography/proof/2014/07/16/visualizing-waste-klaus-pichlers-gorgeous-rotting-food/

Kepkiewicz, L., & Rotz, S. (2018). Toward anti-colonial food policy in Canada?(Im) possibilities within the settler state. *Canadian Food Studies/La Revue Canadienne Des Études Sur L'alimentation*, *5*(2), 13–24.

Korsmeyer, C., & Sutton, D. (2011). The sensory experience of food. *Food, Culture and Society*, *14*(4), 461–475.

Krautwald-Junghanns, M. E., Cramer, K., Fischer, B., Förster, A., Galli, R., Kremer, F., … Schnabel, C. (2018). Current approaches to avoid the culling of day-old male chicks in the layer industry, with special reference to spectroscopic methods. *Poultry Science*, *97*(3), 749–757.

Lang, G. (2016, March 29). Killing food: A theater of threat in Russia. Paper presentation at American Association of Geographers Annual Meeting.

Lepawsky, J. (2015). The changing geography of global trade in electronic discards: Time to rethink the e-waste problem. *The Geographical Journal*, *181*(2), 147–159.

Liboiron, M. (2016). Redefining pollution and action: The matter of plastics. *Journal of Material Culture*, *21*(1), 87–110.

Lou, L. I. T. (2017). The material culture of green living in Hong Kong. *Anthropology Now*, *9*(1), 70–79.

Lougheed, S. C. (2017). *Disposing of Risk: The Biopolitics of Recalled Food and the (Un)Making of Waste.* Canada: Queen's University.

Manson, J. (2015). *Relational Nations: Trading and Sharing Ethos for Indigenous Food Sovereignty on Vancouver Island* (Doctoral dissertation, University of British Columbia).

McGregor, D. (2009). Honouring our relations: An Anishnaabe perspective. *Speaking for Ourselves: Environmental Justice in Canada*, *27*, 27–41.

Mintz, S. W. (1986). *Sweetness and Power: The Place of Sugar in Modern History.* New York: Penguin.

Morrow, O. (2019). Sharing food and risk in Berlin's urban food commons. *Geoforum*, *99*(August 2018), 202–212.

Mourad, M. (2016). Recycling, recovering and preventing "food waste": Competing solutions for food systems sustainability in the United States and France. *Journal of Cleaner Production*, *126*, 461–477.

Mourad, M., & Finn, S. (2019, June). Opinion: France's Ban on Food Waste Three Years Later. *Food Tank.* Retrieved from https://foodtank.com/news/2019/06/opinion-frances-ban-on-food-waste-three-years-later/

Murcott, A., Belasco, W., & Jackson, P. (Eds.). (2013). *The Handbook of Food Research.* London; New York: Bloomsbury Academic.

Nicholes, M. J., Quested, T. E., Reynolds, C., Gillick, S., & Parry, A. D. (2019). Surely you don't eat parsnip skins? Categorising the edibility of food waste. *Resources, Conservation and Recycling, 147,* 179–188.

O'Brien, M. (2008). *A Crisis of Waste? Understanding the Rubbish Society.* New York, London: Routledge.

O'Brien, M. (2012). A 'lasting transformation' of capitalist surplus: From food stocks to feedstocks. *The Sociological Review, 60,* 192–211.

Papargyropoulou, E., Lozano, R., Steinberger, J. K., Wright, N., & Ujang, Z. (2014). The food waste hierarchy as a framework for the management of food surplus and food waste. *Journal of Cleaner Production, 76,* 106–115.

Parfitt, J., Barthel, M., & Macnaughton, S. (2010). Food waste within food supply chains: Quantification and potential for change to 2050. *Philosophical Transactions of the Royal Society B: Biological Sciences, 365*(1554), 3065–3081.

Patel, R. (2007). *Stuffed and Starved: the Hidden Battle for the World Food System.* London: Portobello.

Payutto, P., & Evans, B. (1994). *Buddhist Economics—A Middle Way for the Market Place.* Bangkok, Thailand: Buddhadhamma Foundation.

Poppendieck, J. (1998). *Sweet Charity? Emergency Food and the End of Entitlement.* New York: Viking.

Rathje, William L. (1974) The Garbage Project: A New Way of Looking at the Problems of Archaeology. *Archaeology, 27,* 236–241.

Princen, T. (2002). Distancing: Consumption and the severing of feedback. In Princen, T., Maniates, M. and Conca, K. (Eds.). *Confronting Consumption* (pp. 103–131). Cambridge, MA: MIT Press.

Rathje, W. L., & Murphy, C. (2001). *Rubbish!: The Archaeology of Garbage.* Tucson: University of Arizona Press.

Reno, J. (2015). Waste and Waste Management. *Annual Review of Anthropology, 44,* 557–572.

Reynolds, C., Goucher, L., Quested, T., Bromley, S., Gillick, S., Wells, V. K., Evans, D., Koh, L., Kanyama, A. C., Katzeff, C., & Svenfelt, Å. (2019). Consumption-stage food waste reduction interventions—What works and how to design better interventions. *Food Policy, 83,* 7–27.

Riches, G. (Ed.). (1997). *First World Hunger: Food Security and Welfare Politics.* Toronto: University of Toronto Press.

Roe, E. (2013). Global carcass balancing: Horsemeat and the agro-food network. *Radical Philosophy, 179* (May/June), 2–5.

Rudolph, K. R., & McLachlan, S. M. (2013). Seeking indigenous food sovereignty: Origins of and responses to the food crisis in northern Manitoba, Canada. *Local Environment, 18*(9), 1079–1098.

Scherhaufer, S., Moates, G., Hartikainen, H., Waldron, K., and Obersteiner, G. (2018) 'Environmental Impacts of Food Waste in Europe'. *Waste Management [online], 77,* 98–113. available from https://doi.org/10.1016/j.wasman.2018.04.038

Schneider, F. (2013, November). Review of food waste prevention on an international level. *Proceedings of the Institution of Civil Engineers-Waste and Resource Management, 166*(4), 187–203. (ICE Publishing).

Shilling, C. (2013). Series editor's introduction. In D. Evans, H. Campbell & A. Murcott (Eds.), *Waste Matters: New Perspectives on Food and Society. The Sociological Review* (pp. 1–4). Malden, MA: John Wiley & Sons.

Soma, T. (2016). The tale of the crying rice: The role of unpaid foodwork and learning in food waste prevention and reduction in Indonesian households. In J. Sumner (Ed.). *Learning, Food, and Sustainability: Sites for Resistance and Change* (pp. 19–34). New York: Palgrave Macmillan.

Soma, T. (2017). Gifting, ridding and the "everyday mundane": The role of class and privilege in food waste generation in Indonesia. *Local Environment, 22*(12), 1444–1460.

Soma, T. (2018). (Re) framing the food waste narrative: Infrastructures of urban food consumption and waste in Indonesia. *Indonesia,* (105), 173–190. https://www.jstor.org/stable/10.5728/indonesia.105.0173?seq=1#page_scan_tab_contents

Spring, C. (2016). *Learning Lessons from America's Surplus Food Redistribution Infrastructure.* Report of Winston Churchill Memorial Trust Fellowship. Retrieved from www.wcmt.org.uk/fellows/reports/learning-lessons-americas-surplus-food-redistribution-infrastructure

Spring, C., Adams, M., & Hardman, M. (2019). Sites of learning : Exploring political ecologies and visceral pedagogies of surplus food redistribution in the UK. *Policy Futures in Education, 17*(7), 844–861.

Springmann, M., Clark, M., Mason-D'Croz, D., Wiebe, K., Bodirsky, B.L., Lassaletta, L., de Vries, W., Vermeulen, S.J., Herrero, M., Carlson, K.M., Jonell, M., Troell, M., DeClerck, F., Gordon, L.J., Zurayk, R., Scarborough, P., Rayner, M., Loken, B., Fanzo, J., Godfray, H.C.J., Tilman, D., Rockström, J., and Willett, W. (2018) Options for Keeping the Food System within Environmental

Limits. *Nature [online]*, *562*(7728), 519–525. available from http://dx.doi.org/10.1038/s41586-018-0594-0

Squire, S. (2002). The personal and the political: Writing the theorist's body. *Australian Feminist Studies*, *17*(February 2015), 55–64.

Stenmark, A., Jensen, C., Quested, T., Moates, G., Buksti, M., Cseh, B., Juul, S., Parry, A., Politano, A., Relingshofer, B., Scherhaufer, S., Silvennoinen, K., Soethoudt, H., Zübert, C., and Östergren, K. (2016) Estimates of European Food Waste Levels [online] Stockholm: Fusions. Retrieved from https://www.eu-fusions.org/phocadownload/Publications/Estimates of European food waste levels.pdf

Stewart, B., Shepherd, C., Bellwood-Howard, I., & Bowman, M. (2013). *Counting What Matters. Report of the Industry Food Waste Audit Proposal*. This is Rubbish. Retrieved from www.thisisrubbish.org.uk/wp-content/uploads/2017/11/Counting-What-Matters.pdf

Stovall, M. (2017, September). Living on crumbs and air like my ancestors: Reflections on hunger, bulimia, and food waste in Black America. *Civil Eats*. Retrieved from https://civileats.com/2017/09/15/living-on-crumbs-and-air-like-my-ancestors/

Stuart, T. (2009). *Waste: Uncovering the Global Food Scandal*. London, New York: Penguin.

Tenner, E. (1996). *Why Things Bite Back: Technology and the Revenge of Unintended Consequences*. New York: Knopf.

Thompson, M. (1979). *Rubbish Theory: the Creation and Destruction of Value* (pp. 12–24). June edition, Encounter. www.unz.com/print/Encounter-1979jun-00012/

Todd, Z. (2014). Fish pluralities: Human-animal relations and sites of engagement in Paulatuuq, Arctic Canada. *Études/Inuit/Studies*, *38*(1–2), 217.

Tomlinson, I. (2013). Doubling food production to feed the 9 billion: A critical perspective on a key discourse of food security in the UK. *Journal of Rural Studies*, *29*, 81–90.

Trentmann, F. (2016). *Empire of Things: How We Became a World of Consumers, from the Fifteenth Century to the Twenty-First*. New York: Harper, pp. 862.

Waitt, G., & Phillips, C. (2016). Food waste and domestic refrigeration: A visceral and material approach. *Social & Cultural Geography*, *17*(3), 359–379.

Warshawsky, D. (2010). New power relations served here: The growth of food banking in Chicago. *Geoforum*, *41*(5), 763–775.

Warshawsky, D. N. (2018). The growth of food banking in cities of the global south (rep., pp. 1-10). Waterloo, ON: Hungry Cities Partnership. Hungry Cities Partnership Discussion Paper No. 13.

Weiler, A. M., Otero, G., & Wittman, H. (2016). Rock stars and bad apples: Moral economies of alternative food networks and precarious farm work regimes. *Antipode*, *48*(4), 1140–1162.

Weis, T. (2015). Meatification and the madness of the doubling narrative. *Canadian Food Studies / La Revue Canadienne Des Études Sur l'alimentation*, *2*(2), 296–303. https://doi.org/10.15353/cfs-rcea.v2i2.105

Willett, W., Rockström, J., Loken, B., Springmann, M., Lang, T., Vermeulen, S., … Jonell, M. (2019). Food in the anthropocene: The EAT–Lancet Commission on healthy diets from sustainable food systems. *The Lancet*, *393*(10170), 447–492.

Wolfe, C. (2010). *What is Posthumanism?* Vol 8. Minneapolis: University of Minnesota Press.

WRAP (2018). WRAP restates UK food waste figures to support united global action. http://www.wrap.org.uk/content/wrap-restates-uk-food-waste-figures-support-united-global-action

PART I

Understanding modern food waste regimes

Historical, economic, and spiritual dimensions

How did we get here? The four chapters in Part I offer several answers to this overarching question, aiming to understand the issue of contemporary food waste through a glimpse into the history, political economy, and regimes of consumption that have shaped and structured the pathways that have led us to the present. The chapters offer perspectives from anthropology, geography, history, and theology. Diverse approaches to understanding contemporary food waste issues are, and will continue to be, critical in the search for solutions. Together, these four chapters demonstrate transformations in how food has been valued, re-valued, framed, and re-framed throughout economic regimes, spiritual traditions, and historical timelines.

Part I's chapters begin a journey of understanding the shocking food waste statistics we have grown used to hearing. Some chapters demonstrate that there is nothing accidental about massive wastage. As anthropologist David Boarder Giles argues in 'After market: capital, surplus, and the social afterlives of food waste', much of the wastage that we see (or do not see) is deliberate. Giles questions the actual efficiency of market-based capitalist economies that invest in the cultivation, processing, manufacturing, transportation, and sales of food, only for it to be thrown away. Giles' chapter highlights multiple forms of biopolitical labour through which food becomes waste. However, surpluses culled by commerce – what he terms abject capital – form the basis of after-market, "shadow" economies of solidarity and food sharing with those marginalised from market life. Considering policies and corporate initiatives that also seek to make use of surpluses, Giles notes that these efforts nevertheless 'leave the linear capitalist value chain unchallenged'. Food's wastage as abject capital is not an accidental symptom, that systematic dis-use (desuetude) is what itself manufactures the scarcity upon which capitalist value-making is premised, upholding uneven processes of growth and marginalisation in contemporary market economies.

Complementing Giles, Jon Cloke's chapter, 'Interrogating waste: vastogenic regimes in the 21st century', describes systems that both generate and profit from waste. The regime approach to food waste follows from McMichael (2009) and Friedmann (2016)'s regime analyses (Gille (2012) applies this to food waste). Cloke coins the term 'vastogenesis', defined through the premise that waste generation is a critical component of mass consumption. Cloke analyses appetite-creation as one of the driving forces of vastogenesis, and outlines examples of how arbitrary marketing or classification standards (e.g. of apples), and best-before date legal requirements, serve to send food products to landfill despite their edibility and safety (for more on the issue of date labels, see Milne (2012)). Cloke's chapter also timelines the mechanisms and infrastructures that enabled the acceleration of food waste. These waste-accelerating mechanisms made massive transportation, storage, and consumption of food possible. The chapter also explains how diverse products are launched and are de-listed shortly after, as part of the 'appetite-creation' process that leads to wastage.

In Chapter 2, Andrew F. Smith of the New School outlines a historical trajectory of food waste (and its problematisation) in a chapter aptly titled 'The perfect storm'. From wartime propaganda materials encouraging citizens not to waste, to the growth of supermarket chains, food packaging, and the rise of food banks, Smith's overview helps to contextualise the ebb and flow of food waste in societal consciousness. The chapter describes stakeholders who have become involved in campaigning for food waste awareness and reduction, from not-for-profit organisations to mainstream authors, celebrity chefs, and individual champions. He argues that the current trajectory of food waste awareness (emerging rapidly after 2008's global price crisis) will continue to grow, as concerns around climate change and interest in economic opportunities from technological solutions become more widespread (see Barnard and Mourad, this volume, on how 'awareness-raising' solutions may fail to address systemic causes).

In 'Food waste, religion and spirituality: Jewish, Christian, and Muslim approaches', Tanhum Yoreh and Stephen Bede Scharper, scholars of theology, introduce the reader to ways in which Judaism, Christianity, and Islam approach the issue of food waste. The chapter engages with scripture and case studies from the three religions, showcasing the legal, ethical, and moral frameworks that admonish the respective faith communities to shun profligate wastefulness. The chapter also provides examples of how the three faith communities have mobilised to prevent and reduce waste. Yoreh and Scharper conclude that as faith communities have strong imperatives not to waste food, these communities may serve as worthwhile allies in the wider movement to prevent and reduce food waste.

Thus, the chapters in Part I introduce some of the complexity of the contemporary food waste problem, mirroring the complexity of dominant food systems. Here we are not speaking about leftovers or food scraps: the 'unavoidable' food waste (avocado pits, egg shells, clam shells) that is easily degradable and, in an ideal world – at an ideal scale – remnants that can be seamlessly incorporated as part of the natural environment back into a regenerative food production, or returned as nutrients back into the soil, the forest, the sand, river, and/or the sea. Contemporary issues around food waste reveal its global nature, with regimes that span multiple jurisdictions, involving both state and non-state actors, numerous types of packaging, cultures, and regulations. Food waste is also occurring at a scale (amount and cost) that defies individual interventions. Finally, due to the opaque nature of current international food trade, policies, and regulations, at an individual level, understanding the issues that lead to global wastage can be difficult. The chapters in Part I will hopefully assist readers and food waste scholars to better understand the historical, economic regimes, and spiritual trajectories of contemporary food waste.

References

Friedmann, Harriet (2016). Commentary: Food Regime Analysis and Agrarian Questions: Widening the Conversation. *The Journal of Peasant Studies*, 43(3), pp. 671–692.

Gille, Zsuzsa (2012). From Risk to Waste: Global Food Waste Regimes. *The Sociological Review*, 60, pp. 27–46.

McMichael, Philip (2009). A Food Regime Genealogy. *The Journal of Peasant Studies*, 36(1), pp. 139–169.

Milne, Richard (2012). Arbiters of Waste: Date Labels, The Consumer and Knowing Good, Safe Food. *The Sociological Review*, 60, pp. 84–101.

1

AFTER MARKET

Capital, surplus, and the social afterlives of food waste

David Boarder Giles

Introduction

Business as usual makes great waste. Much of it, edible. Somewhere, a perfectly ripe peach reposes in a supermarket dumpster because customers prefer one with a longer shelf-life. Day-old bread is pulled from bakery shelves to make room for fresh-baked loaves. An ugly potato lies in the fields. Extra pizzas are baked just to spruce up the buffet. Single-origin, fair-trade chocolate is poured in excess because the machines take time to shut down. A sealed, organic smoothie is abandoned by the distributor because its "best-by" (not even "use-by") date is too near its delivery schedule. And so on. At first glance, it seems incongruous that market economies—reputedly bastions of efficiency—should invest in the cultivation, refinement, manufacture, and transport of all that food, only to throw it away. Nonetheless, across the industrialised world they do. To what ends? What becomes of it?

Over the last decade, a wellspring of concern about food waste has emerged from the triumvirate of ecological, economic, and political anxieties that define our age. The lion's share of public responses centre fickle consumers or technical inefficiencies. But as Tristram Stuart suggests, these narratives are a convenient exculpation for agribusiness and food retailers, ostensibly beholden to their customers' demands (2009). In other words, they let capitalism off the hook.

In contrast, my ethnographic research in Seattle, Melbourne, and other American and Australasian cities has located the origins of these surpluses in the rhythms of commerce itself. I have traced the afterlives to which they are consigned both by dumpster-diving in the commercial waste stream and through participant-observation with chapters of Food Not Bombs (FNB), a global movement of anarchist soup kitchens who retrieve capitalist grocery surpluses, by dumpster and donation, prepare them safely, and distribute them in public spaces—usually to people who are homeless or hungry, and often in defiance of city feeding restrictions. (I will return to these below.) In this way, I have explored those waste-making regimes of late capitalism that render obsolete the former commodity that is yet edible.

While such surpluses abdicate their exchange value, this chapter agues, they nonetheless circulate elsewhere, establishing critical sites for the social reproduction—or transformation—of capitalism. From food banks in church basements to opportunistic after-market social enterprises, they remain structurally imbricated in the production of waste, value, and capital. As such, this chapter explores broad, polyvalent relationships among different economic sectors often ignored by recent work on food waste, from formal efforts such as the UK's "Love Food, Hate Waste" campaign to exposés like Jonathan Bloom's blog wastedfood.com, or the documentary film *Dive!*. Such popular interventions may save the spotty pear from the tip, but they rarely challenge the structure of the commodity chain that consigned it thereto. My goals here are twofold: first, to digest my research to-date on commercial food waste, waste-making labour, and after-market economies (e.g. Giles 2013, 2014, 2015, 2016); and second, to trace incipient trends in the commercial production, recapture, and recirculation of unspoiled food surpluses which may suggest something about the future of capitalism itself.

To that end, this chapter develops four related themes: (1) the role of edible commercial food waste and other useful-but-abandoned commodities, which I term "abject capital" (Giles 2014), in the production of capitalist value; (2) the waste-making labours that render commodities abject; (3) the non-market "shadow economies" constituted by food charities that simultaneously redistribute abject capital and segregate it from the market; (4) emergent practices of capitalist reclamation and recapitalisation, from profitable social enterprises that resell retail cast-offs, to energy generation through anaerobic digestion, by which supermarkets recoup the caloric surplus value trapped within their food surpluses. These reclamations, I argue, represent incipient possible futures for capital accumulation, allowing businesses to reclaim their waste and bolster their bottom line without fundamentally restructuring their commodity chains. In such ways, I argue, may the capitalism of the Anthropocene seek to throw away its cake and eat it too.

Abject capital

"I mean things that you find in dumpsters, you know?" gushes Karen. After dumpster-diving in Australia and the United States, she is gushing about her favourite discoveries. "A whole bag of plastic chopsticks that haven't been opened. And dolls. And clothes. And—what else—mango chutney."

"Anything you want," chimes in her partner, Terry. "Toilet paper," says Karen. "*Scented* toilet paper," adds Terry. "Yeah scented toilet paper," affirms Karen. "Anything and everything, if you keep it up. I mean just the other day, an entire dumpster full of oranges. *An entire dumpster.*"

Seven decades and several thousand miles removed from Steinbeck's classic *The Grapes of Wrath*, Karen and Terry are not consciously invoking his description of the Depression's forbidden fruits. But the resonance would not be lost on them: Steinbeck wrote of the bitter taste left by the fruits of agricultural and ecological labour, destroyed to maintain prices. Truckloads of oranges and other bounty, left to rot on the ground. "The people came for miles to take the fruit," he wrote, "but this could not be. How would they buy oranges at twenty cents a dozen if they could drive out and pick them up?" (Steinbeck 2006 [1939]: 348–349). Steinbeck's oranges were doused in kerosene and left in the Californian fields. Karen and Terry's oranges were merely secluded in a Melbourne dumpster. Either way, the effect is the same: unspoiled surpluses are taken off the market, and out of the hands of people who might use them. Underscoring this point, retailers often lock up their dumpsters to prevent its recovery (see Figure 1.1). One can gain access with the right tools, Karen teaches me, but that is another story. Terry's explanation for this is not unlike Steinbeck's: "They want it all hermetically sealed, the whole production process, from production to final disposal." Though he puts it rather conspiratorially, like Steinbeck he

Figure 1.1 "They want it all hermetically sealed … from production to final disposal": padlocked bins in Melbourne.

Source: Photo by David Boarder Giles.

captures something structural about such forcible desuetude. Its effect is to manufacture scarcity itself, the fundamental animus of market value. It produces demand, and hence value. The seclusion of good food in dumpsters and landfills is the denouement of a linear value chain—a one-way conveyer belt from manufacture to disposal that is the chief model of economic growth in a consumer economy.

This is no small matter. As Karen and Terry imply—and dozens of dumpster-divers I have met confirm—the scale of wasted surpluses abandoned in commercial dumpsters is consistent and consequential across market societies. Their findings are echoed by a growing literature on urban scavenging (e.g. Clark 2004; Ferrell 2005; Edwards and Mercer 2007; Vaughn 2011; Barnard 2016). "Chances are," wrote one anonymous dumpster-diver, "if they sell it in front, they throw it away out back" (CrimethInc 2004: 220). Although quantitative research regarding edible commercial food waste has been tellingly rare (distinguished from "food loss" through spoilage or other forms of unintended destruction), the most comprehensive, system-wide American research suggests that roughly five billion pounds of unspoiled food is discarded annually by retailers, distributors, and producers in the United States (Kantor et al. 1997). And in Seattle, food consistently claims the greatest share of the commercial waste stream,[1] most of it presumably edible (retailers and distributors not being in the business of storing food until it rots).

At first glance, the scale is baffling. While food waste narratives centred on consumer excess or inefficient technologies are easily legible within popular discourses of profligacy or progress, abject capital defies the hegemonic truism that free markets are rational and efficient. Why should for-profit enterprises invest in valuable stock, only to evacuate it from the shelves a little later, unsold?

In practice, there are many reasons. One cracked egg can doom eleven intact ones. A fast-approaching sell-by date renders milk obsolete if customers can reach past it for a newer carton. And so on. Tristram Stuart finds a telling case in the UK sushi chain K10, where the average product's retail price is two to three times its cost price; at the end of the day, it is cheaper to throw away two items than run out prematurely and lose a single sale (2009: 17). The latter example most acutely illustrates a structural logic common to each. They all entail a calculation, a pragmatic comparison between investment, markup, potential for sale, and the universe of other commodities that could take their place. In other words, a reckoning of *real* exchange value. Sometimes this calculation is made on paper by corporate policy-makers, sometimes in realtime by employees. Either way, if the opportunity cost of keeping a commodity on the shelf overshadows the cost of throwing it away, or if the price it will fetch at market is outweighed by newer stock, with few exceptions its exchange value is effectively null. Or more exactly, bequeathed to newer goods. And because a commodity qua commodity is defined by its exchange value, this renders it, in Barnard and Mourad's terms, an "ex-commodity" (this volume; see also Barnard 2016).

Such on-the-ground descriptions help us to locate abject capital *temporally*—a phase subsequent to the commodity's social life—and *spatially*—removed from spaces of market exchange. However, as Marx insisted, a commodity's value is determined simultaneously in microcosm and macrocosm, in relation to the sum total of capitalist social relations (2000 [1865]). Put another way, it is a "total social fact" (Mauss 2002 [1954]), bearing the holistic imprint of every relationship within a given society. In the same way, I have argued (Giles 2014) that the ex-commodity must be understood in both its ethnographic and structural contexts, as part of larger historically specific "regimes of value" (Appadurai 1986) or "waste regimes" (Gille 2010). The roots of abject capital, therefore, lie in the structural logic of capital accumulation.

Indeed, the history of capitalism has been defined by waste-making. Industrial capitalism, in particular, creates value by both mass-producing goods and producing demand itself. Both processes generate obsolescence or surplus, albeit differently. As Michael Thompson (1979) argued, where value is created through distinction and valorisation—for example, of innovation or style—there is inevitably a devalorised, wasted remainder. Meanwhile, critics of capitalism have long emphasised its overproduction. For Marx, this was the "fundamental contradiction of developed capitalism" (2000 [1941]: 399). In other words, capitalism's endless pursuit of growth and profitable return made it irrepressibly productive while at the same time compensating its workers—also its chief consumers—as meagrely as possible. The result was an overaccumulation of surpluses of all kinds, with no avenue for consumption. Moreover, where goods are produced in excess, and demand is produced through rarefaction, the two strategies are in diametric opposition. Where they intersect, waste emerges as a central paradox for capitalism. Abject capital represents a structural resolution of this paradox, and therefore an ever-present feature of capital accumulation. Its scale and significance vary with the particulars of a given regime of accumulation. Nonetheless, however many or few, these abject commercial surpluses necessarily constitute the material and discursive horizons of the market—a terminator between things' "commodity candidacy" (Appadurai 1986) and their post-commodity afterlives.

Capitalism's episodic crises have always navigated this tension between surfeit and scarcity. Each economic recovery and corresponding reorganisation has birthed new vectors of production and accumulation, often founded on new, profitable ways to dispose of surpluses (Liboiron 2013). And the faster surpluses are discarded, the more accelerated is capital's mean turnaround time between investment and return. From the mid-twentieth century's built-in product obsolescence and disposable consumerism (Packard 2011 [1960]) to the "vastogenic" or "waste-making" regimes of the global corporate food system (Cloke 2013), each phase of capitalism has practised distinct forms of "accumulation by disposal" (Giles 2016). Such industry-wide transformations are reflected, in turn, in individual diets and consumption practices. American per-capita food waste, for example, grew steadily by about 50 percent between 1974 and 2003 (Hall et al. 2009: 1–2). Guthman and Dupuis describe the vastogenic logic of the current neoliberal food system as a kind of "bulimic economy", constituted among the contradictions between excessive portions, empty calories, overeating, and expensive dieting, all with the effect of multiplying capital's opportunities to return a profit. As they put it, "neoliberalism's commodification of everything ensures that getting rid of food ... is as central to capitalist accumulation as is producing and eating it" (2006: 442).

It is in this context that we must understand the humble ex-commodity. Enclaved in a bin (or, in the case of derelict properties, boarded up against squatters), it generates value under economy-wide waste regimes that remediate capitalism's waste-making paradox.

Its disposal can never quite resolve the contradictions between nullified exchange value and persistent use value, however. Indeed, these contradictions are precisely what dumpster-divers exploit—and why the dumpsters are often locked. What this means is that disposal is not a momentary decision, but rather one continually reproduced through social and spatial practices that *dispose* objects—in both the sense of engendering their "disposition" (in the sense of both spatial and cultural orientation) and their "disposal" (Munro 2013). I will turn to some of those practices in the following section. Once abandoned, most commercial food surpluses must remain banished, segregated from the market, enclaved in a cultural "no man's land" (Navaro-Yashin 2003) where their existence is of little consequence to hegemonic price structures. The dumpster and places like it serve precisely this function. Therein the paradox is held in abeyance.

The work of waste-making

To maintain such a paradox takes a lot of work. Consider, for example, the tale of my twice-wasted melons and the zealous produce worker who threw them away. Throughout my research, one of my most important tasks was to gather produce for FNB each Sunday from Seattle's Pike Place Market. Rather than trash the food, some vendors donated it. But still, many a treasure was discarded in the bins; on occasion I would recover these too. One sunny Sunday morning, I found a crate full of cantaloupes, perfectly ripe, with barely a bruise. Eagerly, I set them aside and returned to forage deeper in the bin. But when I returned they were gone. Puzzled, I walked the market looking for them, and soon met a surly produce worker who, guessing my purpose, told me he had "taken care of them". In other words, he had thrown them away *again*. I explained that they were for a soup kitchen and he offered a nominal apology, but his tone remained harsh and he would not give back the melons.

Such waste enforcement is hardly exceptional. In my experience, employees' reactions upon finding me dumpster-diving varied from anger to condescension to anxiety about litigation (see also Vaughn 2011: 2). While not every employee is so enthusiastic about policing the garbage, and some even turn a blind eye or put the best food within reach, it is on their own initiative; even sympathetic employees often consider it their job to deter scavengers. April, a Seattle squatter and dumpster-diver told me, for example,

> There was a QFC on Capitol Hill up on 15th that always had a good dumpster but, boy, they were always really tight about kicking us out if they caught us. So it was always a matter of sneaking in and out of that dumpster. If you were in the dumpster when they came, you just had to sit in there and wait for them to dump the garbage on you and be all quiet and then sneak back out.

These employees are the tip of an iceberg. Whereas much political economy imagines that labour *adds* value to the commodity, theirs are some of the countless labours that rob things of their worth and commodity candidacy. I call this the "work of waste-making" (Giles 2015).

There is, after all, nothing inevitable about the end of a thing's shelf-life. To paraphrase Marx: could waste itself speak, it would say, "My 'uselessness' may be a thing that concerns men. It is no part of me as an object."[2] Just as Marx identified the "fetishism of commodities" as an expression of the sum of productive labours and capitalist social relations, so too is waste such a fetish, the production of value and waste being mutually entangled (cf. Barnard 2016). Yet, some labours are more directly implicated than others in the production of abject capital.

What is this work that so defies Marx's labour theory of value, displacing value rather than adding it? This is hardly the typical model of industrial labour, which combines materials and transforms products. Although one hears anecdotal reports of food waste doused in bleach or otherwise contaminated, what sets abject capital apart is that it is largely unchanged, unspoiled. To account for this devalorisation, therefore, we must widen our scope to encompass what Hardt and Negri call "biopolitical labour", work that "creates not only material goods, but also relationships and ultimately social life itself" (2004: 109). Capitalism has always relied on biopolitical labour in the production of workforces, consumers, and modes of production. However its significance is amplified in the ever-globalising economies of the twenty-first century.

The work of waste-making is, therefore, a constellation of biopolitical labours to produce distinct pathways of value that dispose commodities to an unnecessary or premature end, from the built-in obsolescence of electronics to the rapid turnover of grocery shelves. Some such labours, such as the zealous employees described earlier, represent an abject security detail, policing boundaries between abject and active capital. Others entail the repeated classifications and appraisals that enact market value (Tsing 2013). One can detect such labour, for example, in the split-second decisions of vendors at Pike Place, scanning the shelves for produce that will be overlooked by passers-by; rather than letting it languish on the shelves, they discard or donate it. These classifications simultaneously valorise some goods and devalorise others, entailing both practices of divestment and the management of absence that are central to the production of waste (Gille 2010).

Moreover, not all biopolitical labour is paid. As Hardt and Negri's interlocutor, Maurizio Lazzarato, puts it, "the postindustrial commodity is the result of a creative process that involves both the producer and the consumer" (2006: 142). Further to this devalorisation, therefore, the work of waste-making extends to the customer, who is embroiled in the discursive and affective labour of producing desire and sentiment toward goods (cf. Gibson-Graham 2006). A sentiment like disgust, for example, "helps create conditions of scarcity which build up demand and increase value" according to William Ian Miller (1997: 114). Precisely such disgust keeps most consumers away from the dumpster. The recovery of waste, therefore, represents a profound transgression according to capitalist norms (cf. Clark 2004; Vaughn 2011; Barnard 2016), a point to which I turn in the next section.

Shadow economies

On an average afternoon in Seattle—let's say, two o'clock on a Sunday—dozens of hungry Seat-tleites will assemble under a freeway overpass, waiting for lunch. Maybe even hundreds, depending on the day. They will crowd behind a chainlink fence in a parking lot at 6th Avenue and Columbia Street, Seattle's only officially sanctioned Outdoor Meal Site. Three times a day, seven days a week, one of the city's largest emergency meal providers, Operation Sack Lunch (OSL) and its partner organisations distribute well-balanced meals there to a cross-section of Seattle's homeless and food insecure denizens. Unlike many food banks and shelters, which require identification or evidence of residency, the Outdoor Meal Site aspires to an "anonym-ous, no barrier, non-denominational and all-inclusive environment" (OSL Nd.b). Ironically, however, to create such an "inclusive" space, the site must itself be excluded from public sight: although just two blocks from downtown, in the shadow of Interstate 5's massive cement pillars, it is largely hidden from tourists and businesses (see Figure 1.2). Everywhere else in the city, outdoor meals are forbidden (FNB's civil disobedience notwithstanding) largely as a result of Not-In-My-Back-Yard complaints and prejudice by local homeowners' groups and businesses (Giles 2013). Perhaps partly for that reason, without OSL's services, over half of their diners report that they simply would not eat (OSL Nd.b).

This is possible thanks to the excesses of the market. Along with the rest of the city's emergency meal providers, OSL represents one last chance for Seattle's commercial surpluses to avoid the trash. Once divested of their exchange value, as I described above, many retail-ers and distributors donate them rather than banish them to the dumpster. In this way, ex-commodities are diverted into a broad network of food-recovery organisations, from small grassroots endeavours like FNB to nonprofit agencies with multimillion dollar budgets like OSL—which recovered over a million pounds of food, and served over half a million meals in 2017 alone (OSL Nd.a). They comprise a city-wide web of gleaners and charities who comb farmers' markets, grocers, caterers, and other commercial food enterprises for their leftovers. This is not distinctive to Seattle. As Janet Poppendieck has argued, such networks have arisen across the United States and other industrialised countries to fill the gap left by neoliberal reforms (1998). Anthropologist Maggie Dickinson calls them an outsourced "third tier" of the safety net (2014: 118). While this emergency food sector also calls on philan-thropic and government funds, donated retail excesses and agricultural surpluses are crucial to its existence—the latter subsidised by the United States Department of Agriculture (Pop-pendieck 1998; Dickinson 2014). Collectively, therefore, they serve to absorb the abject capital and other wasted surpluses of the commercial food system. Indeed, the very first US "food bank" was so named in 1967 with a view to save unspoiled grocery surpluses as a bank does money (Poppendieck 1998). The emergency food sector, therefore, constitutes a network of after-market shadow economies.

What is most important to note about these shadow economies is that, while they put food surpluses back to work, they also divorce them spatially, temporally, and structurally from their former commodity candidacy in a manner analogous to the dumpster. Though the two pathways differ in important ways—charitable donations save the cost of waste dis-posal, for example, and earn the cultural capital of good corporate citizenship—both have

Figure 1.2 Excluded from public sight: Seattle's Outdoor Meal Site in the shadow of Interstate 5.
Source: Photo by David Boarder Giles.

the principal structural effect of keeping food off the market. In that sense, food charities, too, do the work of waste-making. What else are we to conclude if the retailer or whole-saler can as readily throw surpluses away or donate them (while employees feel obliged to keep them out of scavengers' hands)?

Their segregation from the space of the market is further secured by the norms of capitalist exchange that not only render dumpster-diving and other forms of scavenging transgressive, but also inflect a larger market-centric public sphere wherein the free dis-tribution of food surpluses is stigmatised, along with the receipt of charitable "handouts". In this fashion, the recipients are spatially and symbolically alienated from the market, and likely imagined by donors not to be potential customers anyway. This alienation is both presumed and exacerbated by the outdoor feeding prohibitions by which Seattle—and a growing number of other cities—banishes emergency food programmes from public view (cf. Giles 2013). In these ways, not only are marginalised people excluded from the public sphere, where the norms of capitalist exchange hold sway. So are the excesses of the capitalist food system.

This therefore represents a "shadow economy" not in the common sense of illicit or informal transactions beyond the reach of government surveillance, but rather in its defini-tive seclusion from public visibility, which capacitates pathways of circulation that coexist with the larger market economy without disrupting it. Or, as Vinay Gidwani might describe them, "an 'outside' that is fully 'inside'—that is to say, the creation of—the capitalist economy" (2015: 5). Although the surplus-to-requirements apple or pear is eventually eaten rather than left to decay in a dumpster, it is no less an ex-commodity. So excluded from the spaces of the market, it may remain, structurally, abject capital.

The recovery of the market

Given that these shadow economies work precisely because they are kept out of sight, it came as some surprise when I awoke one morning in 2011 to find my photograph splashed across the *Seattle Times'* front page (Long 2011). In a dumpster, no less. I had agreed to give the journalist a tour of Seattle's best dumpsters, assuming the story would be buried in the features. All the more surprising, then, that the Associated Press picked up the story. That month, it would be syndicated to nearly two dozen papers, across three countries (to my discomfort: while many Seattle dumpster-divers appreciated the public spotlight, others did not).

Wherefore the unexpected interest? In the shadow of the 2008 Global Financial Crisis, and the World Food Crisis of the same year, food waste had entered public consciousness. In the intervening years, that consciousness has only grown, driven by memories of those crises and the gnawing anxieties of economic and ecological precarity that succeeded them. Food waste has indeed become a concrete, actionable proxy for some of our direst fears about the twenty-first century.

In response, a flood of new enterprises, grassroots, governmental, and commercial alike, have spread across the industrialised nations, offering new salves for our collective profligacy. Prohibitions against grocery disposal. Tax incentives for its recovery. New business models. Technological fixes. The inevitable "app for that". Like many ostensibly progressive causes, however, behind their sincere concern, the majority—and arguably the most celebrated— reflect a conservative logic (in both political and material senses of the word "conserve"). Like the shadow economies above, they recapture wasted food without disrupting the structures of the market that wastes it. They innovate, developing new pathways of circulation—often allowing businesses to reduce their carbon footprint, earn tax credits, or circumvent the overhead costs of waste disposal—but leave the linear capitalist value chain unchallenged. (It is not irrelevant that globally this value chain benefits and is dominated by a handful of powerful agribusiness multinationals (Cloke 2013).) Socially and spatially at the margins of the marketplace, the lion's share of recent food waste activism lets the surplus remain structurally abject capital. For this reason, I term them "mechanisms of abject recapture" (Giles 2016). We can identify several forms.

One form engages, and potentially enlarges, precisely those shadow economies described above, such as OSL. Among the interventions most celebrated by food waste activists, for example, is the 2016 French legislation, passed unanimously, that bars supermarkets from abandoning edible food. Although the legislation only applies to supermarkets larger than 400 square metres, it may nonetheless conceivably impact a large quantity of France's would-be wasted produce. Further, it has inspired similar measures elsewhere, from Italy to California. However, while it is no longer destined for the dumpster, the afterlife promised to this waste is in some ways unchanged. It remains within the liminal space of charitable shadow economies.

More precisely, the law requires that supermarkets develop an ongoing contract to supply a food-recovery charity. Arguably, this merely formalises existing trends: as the emergency food systems described above demonstrate, even without legal compulsion businesses increasingly donate their waste. Moreover, a keen observer will note that French retailers can observe the letter of the law by donating a mere 1 percent of their surpluses. The law therefore illustrates the conservative, joint logics of waste-making and profit that anti-food waste measures are often obliged to preserve. Indeed, as the European Court of Auditors' (2016: 14) report on food waste points out, many such measures externalise the costs of waste-saving, passing it on to weaker competitors, charities, consumers, or the public purse.

Such legislation is articulated closely with new waves of grassroots food-recovery efforts. From the concerned undergraduates who founded the nationwide campus-based organisation, Food Recovery Network Food Recovery Network (Nd). to the earnest dumpster-divers who produce exposés like *Dive!* (Seifert 2009), these groups aim to channel further surpluses into a growing charitable shadow economy. As Barnard and Mourad argue (this volume), the typical emphasis of this activism on *reusing* the waste retreats from the more radical critiques of older waste redistribution projects—such as FNB, founded in the 1980s, or the Black Panthers' free breakfast programmes of the 1960s—which aimed explicitly to undermine the capitalist logics that produced waste and scarcity. Often inspired by this new grassroots enthusiasm, many recent technical fixes for food waste facilitate precisely this mode of abject recapture. Food waste apps like Ireland's FoodCloud—which connects retailers' surpluses with food charities in real-time—are often publicised with stories of the designer's earnest concern about food insecurity or waste (cf. Fox 2016); however, they also expand the infrastructure by which charitable shadow economies are articulated with the market, lending them both more instantaneous communication and more granular surveillance.

In contrast to these charitable shadow economies, another mode of abject recapture aims not to recirculate the surplus in some cultural no-man's land, but rather to recapitalise it within the same value chain—for example, by generating energy through anaerobic digestion. In the United Kingdom, for example, retailers such as Sainsbury's and Tesco have pledged to eliminate or significantly reduce their waste through a combination of charitable donations and energy generation (ambitious though such pledges have proven). As Martin O'Brien points out (2013), this strategy is attracting growing enthusiasm, particularly in the European Union, as it cuts the supermarkets' energy costs, allowing them to expropriate the maximum caloric surplus value from their product ("the works of the roots", as Steinbeck put it). But, crucially, this continues to keep the surpluses off the market in yet another post-commodity context analogous to the dumpster or the soup kitchen (Giles 2016). Paradoxically decommodified and recapitalised, it, too, remains abject capital with respect to the larger market.

In further contrast to these abject afterlives, another form of recapture—not quite abject, but bearing important parallels—has also grown in popularity: the secondary retail market. Unlike non-market endeavours such as FNB, restaurants like world-class Italian chef Massimo Bottura's Refettorio Ambrosiano, or Boston's more prosaic Daily Table, priced to compete with fast food outlets (and founded, not coincidentally, by a former president of the supermarket chain Trader Joe's), as well as niche marketing services such as US delivery service Imperfect Produce, cheaply procure unprofitable but unspoiled surpluses and find new markets for them. This represents an expansion of an older pattern of scale-sensitive relationships among various players in the food system—under which, for example, unsaleable products are returned to their distributor for credit, and then go on to be diverted into other markets. While this strategy *does* intervene in the structure of the market rather than enclave surpluses in non-market contexts, it remains redolent of other forms of abject recapture insofar as it removes the food socially and spatially from its immediate commodity context, never to return.

It remains unclear how these measures might actually transform the market. If the French law is any indication, the European Court of Auditors' (2016) report suggests that such forms of recapture are slow to impact the overall waste stream. And while food-recovery charities may be multiplying widely, this represents only an escalation of a decades-old trend that, far from challenging our bulimic neoliberal economy, in fact *heralded* neoliberal food systems, and dovetailed neatly within them (Poppendieck 1998). However, what these modes of recapture *do* suggest is that, in an era of growing economic and ecological anxiety, food waste has captured global capitalist imaginaries. And just as previous phases of post-crisis growth and reorganisation rested on the renegotiation of its waste-making paradox, if something called "capitalism" survives the twenty-first century, it will have wrestled with the quandary of food waste. We may, therefore, detect in these mechanisms of recapture the germ of certain future capitalist sensibilities. By all appearances, those sensibilities still cleave to a linear value chain that ends in an increasingly securitised or segregated set of after-market shadow economies. They envision new waste regimes to absorb abject capital, rather than transform the mode of production that relies upon its generation. While their practical effects further up the commodity chain cannot be predicted, their vision remains a conservative one.

Conclusion

These conclusions bear out Gregson et al.'s critique of the rhetoric of circular economies. "The concept is an endlessly cited ideal," they write, "yet, to effect a circular economy driven by producers through either industrial symbiosis or cradle-to-cradle manufacturing would require radical transformations to the economic order and property rights" (2015: 235). As they show, in the absence of such transformations, real-world instantiations of the concept often amount to recycling economies of the sort described above, dominated by technical fixes such as anaerobic digestion and post-consumer recommoditisation that relies on market logics that created the waste in the first place. This leaves intact the value chain so central to capitalism's waste-making paradox. This is "recovery done wrong" (ibid.: 227). The for-profit, privatised logic of capitalist accumulation as we now know it cannot yet generate the necessary efficiencies or public goods to establish a truly zero-waste economy of constant recapture and reuse—nor could such a circular system create the kind of privatised value necessary for capitalist accumulation and endless growth. Bluntly put, sustainable capitalism is still a pipe dream.

In the same vein, I have argued that industrialised market societies depend on waste-making in the form of abject capital. Premised as they are on scarcity, privatised profits, and linear value chains, they must externalise not simply costs, but also materials and use values in order to establish spheres of commodity exchange wherein the paradox of surplus production and market scarcity is resolved. This useful remainder is therefore spatially, temporally, and structurally enclaved from the spaces of public encounter and exchange that constitute the market. Excesses are consigned to exceptional spaces such as the dumpster and the soup kitchen. Because their abandonment remains integral to the structure of market exchange, they are "abject" both literally—thrown away—and because they fit Julia Kristeva's description of existential "abjection" as "the place where meaning collapses". As I have described above, a range of efforts to address food waste by recovering it for other purposes fail to challenge the logic by which such abject capital is removed from the market.

Fortunately, these are not our only options. The anxieties that give rise to them also inspire more radical imaginations that challenge capital's waste-making sensibilities. The French law that compels supermarkets to donate surplus groceries, for example, also bars them from spoiling the food they *do* discard (e.g. with bleach) and offers dumpster-divers some protection. Grassroots movements such as FNB continue to challenge capitalist norms dictating who eats where (see Barnard and Mourad, this volume). Cities from Detroit to Christchurch encourage microlocal food production and gleaning. And non-market projects such as Seattle's Beacon Food Forest exemplify modern-day commons wherein food is produced and shared collectively. As food systems are remade in conditions of ecological, economic, and political uncertainty, it remains to be seen whose imagination, and what kinds of value(s) will hold sway. One of the defining questions of our age therefore remains: how will we eat after market?

Notes

1   "Compostable organics", primarily food, constitute between 23 percent and 28 percent of everything local businesses throw away by volume depending on the season (Cascadia Consulting 2017).
2   In the first volume of *Capital*, Marx wrote: "Could commodities themselves speak, they would say: 'Our use-value may be a thing that interests men. It is no part of us as objects. What, however, does belong to us as objects is our value. Our natural intercourse as commodities proves it. In the eyes of each other, we are nothing but exchange values'" (2000 [1865]: 480).

References

Appadurai, Arjun. 1986. Commodities and the Politics of Value. In *The Social Life of Things: Commodities in Cultural Perspective*. Edited by Arjun Appadurai. New York: Cambridge University Press, pp. 3–63.
Barnard, Alex V. 2016. *Freegans: Diving into the Wealth of Food Waste in America*. Minneapolis: University of Minnesota Press.
Barnard, Alex V. and Marie Mourad. Forthcoming. *From Dumpster Dives to Disco Vibes: The Shifting Shape of Food Waste Activism*. In this volume.
Cascadia Consulting Group, Inc. in cooperation with Seattle Public Utilities Staff. 2017. *2016 Commercial Waste Stream Composition Study. September 2017*.
Clark, Dylan. 2004. The Raw and the Rotten: Punk Cuisine. In *Ethnology*, 43(1): pp. 19–31.
Cloke, Jon. 2013. Empires of Waste and the Food Security Meme. In *Geography Compass*, 7(9): pp. 622–636.
CrimethInc. Ex-Workers' Collective (collectively authored). 2004. *Recipes for Disaster: An Anarchist Cookbook*. Salem: CrimethInc. Ex-Workers' Collective.
Dickinson, Maggie. 2014. *Consuming Poverty: The Unexpected Politics of Food Aid in an Era of Austerity*. PhD Dissertation, Department of Anthropology, City University of New York.
Edwards, Ferne and David Mercer. 2007. Gleaning from Gluttony: An Australian Youth Subculture Confronts the Ethics of Waste. In *Australian Geographer*, 38(3): pp. 279–296.
European Court of Auditors. 2016. *Combating Food Waste: An Opportunity for the EU to Improve the Resource-efficiency of the Food Supply Chain*. Special Report No. 34. Luxembourg: Publications office of the European Union.
Ferrell, Jeff. 2005. *Empire of Scrounge: Inside the Urban Underground of Dumpster-diving, Trash Picking, and Street Scavenging*. New York: New York University Press.
Food Recovery Network. Nd. *Our Story*. foodrecoverynetwork.org/what-we-do, retrieved December 10, 2018.
Fox, Killian. 2016. *FoodCloud: New App Approves a Nourishing Idea for Wasted Food*. In *The Guardian*, Sunday, December 4.
Gibson-Graham, J. K. 2006. *A Postcapitalist Politics*. Minneapolis: University of Minnesota Press.

Gidwani, Vinay. 2015. The Work of Waste: Inside India's Infra-economy. In *Transactions of the British Institute of Geographers*, 40(5): pp. 575–595.

Giles, David Boarder. 2013. *"A Mass Conspiracy to Feed People": Globalizing Cities, World-Class Waste, and the Biopolitics of Food Not Bombs.* PhD Dissertation, Department of Anthropology, University of Washington.

———. 2014. The Anatomy of a Dumpster: Abject Capital and the Looking Glass of Value. In *Social Text* 118, 32(1): pp. 93–113.

———. 2015. The Work of Waste-Making: Biopolitical Labour and the Myth of the Global City. In *Environmental Change and the World's Futures: Ecologies, Ontologies, Mythologies.* Edited by Jonathan Paul Marshall and Linda H. Connor. London: Routledge, pp. 81–95.

———. 2016. Distributions of Wealth, Distributions of Waste: Abject Capital and Accumulation by Disposal. In *Anthropologies of Value: Cultures of Accumulation Across the Global North and South.* Edited by Luis Fernando Angosto-Ferrández, Geir Henning Presterudstuen. London: Pluto Press, pp. 198–218.

Gille, Zsuzsa. 2010. Actor Networks, Modes of Production, and Waste Regimes: Reassembling the Macro-Social. In *Environment and Planning A*, 42: pp. 1049–1064.

Gregson, Nicky, Mike Crang, Sara Fuller, and Helen Holmes. 2015. Interrogating the Circular Economy: The Moral Economy of Resource Recovery in the EU. In *Economy and Society*, 44 (2): pp. 218–243.

Guthman, Julie and Melanie DuPuis. 2006. Embodying Neoliberalism: Economy, Culture, and the Politics of Fat. In *Environment and Planning D: Society and Space*, 24: pp. 427–448.

Hall, Kevin D., Juen Guo, Michael Dore, Carson C. Chow. 2009. The Progressive Increase of Food Waste in America and Its Environmental Impact. In *PLoS ONE*, 4(11): pp. e7940. doi:10.1371/journal.pone.0007940.

Hardt, Michael and Antonio Negri. 2004. *Multitude: War and Democracy in the Age of Empire.* New York: Penguin Books.

Kantor, Linda Scott, Kathryn Lipton, Alden Manchester, and Victor Oliveira. 1997. Estimating and Addressing America's Food Losses. In *Food Review*, 20(1), Jan-Apr: pp. 2–13.

Kristeva, Julia. 1982. *Powers of Horror: An Essay on Abjection.* New York: Columbia University Press.

Lazzarato, Maurizio. 2006. Immaterial Labor. In *Radical Thought in Italy: A Potential Politics (Theory out of bounds).* Edited by Paolo Virno and Michael Hardt. Minneapolis: University of Minnesota Press, pp. 133–148.

Liboiron, Max. 2013. Modern Waste as Strategy. In *Lo Squaderno: Explorations in Space and Society.* Special edition on Garbage & Wastes. No 29.

Long, Katherine. 2011. *Dumpster-Diver's Thesis: Good Stuff Going to Waste.* In *Seattle Times*, November 3, 2011.

Marx, Karl. 2000 [1865]. Capital. In *Selected Writings.* Edited by David MacLellan. Oxford: Oxford University Press, pp. 452–525.

Marx, Karl. 2000 [1941]. Grundrisse. In *Selected Writings.* Edited by David MacLellan. Oxford: Oxford University Press, pp. 380–422.

Mauss, Marcel. 2002 [1954]. *The Gift: The Form and Reason for Exchange in Archaic Societies.* London: Routledge Classics.

Miller, William Ian. 1997. *The Anatomy of Disgust.* Cambridge, MA: Harvard University Press.

Munro, Roland. 2013. The Disposal of Place: Facing Modernity in the Kitchen-Diner. In *Waste Matters: New Perspectives on Food and Society.* Edited by David Evans, Hugh Campbell, and Anne Murcott. Malden, MA: Wiley-Blackwell, pp. 212–231.

Navaro-Yashin, Yael. 2003. 'Life is Dead Here': Sensing the Political in 'No Man's Land'. In *Anthropological Theory*, 3(1): pp. 107–125.

O'Brien, Martin. 2013. A 'Lasting Transformation' of Capitalist Surplus: From Food Stocks to Feedstocks. In *Waste Matters: New Perspectives on Food and Society.* Edited by David Evans, Hugh Campbell, and Anne Murcott. Malden, MA: Wiley-Blackwell, pp. 192–211.

Operation Sack Lunch. Nd.a *Home Page.* www.oslserves.org retrieved December 10, 2017.

Operation Sack Lunch. Nd.b *Outdoor Meal Site.* www.oslserves.org/outdoor-meal-site/retrieved December 10, 2017.

Packard, Vance. 2011 [1960]. *The Waste Makers.* Brooklyn: Ig Publishing.

Poppendieck, Janet. 1998. *Sweet Charity: Emergency Food and the End of Entitlement.* New York: Penguin.

Seifert, Jeremy. 2009. *Dive!: Living Off America's Waste.* (Self-released film).

Stuart, Tristram. 2009. *Waste: Uncovering the Global Food Scandal.* Penguin Books: London.

Steinbeck, John. 2006 [1939]. *The Grapes of Wrath.* New York: Penguin Books.

Thompson, Michael. 1979. *Rubbish Theory: The Creation and Destruction of Value.* Oxford: Oxford University Press.

Tsing, Anna. 2013. Sorting Out Commodities: How Capitalist Value is Made Through Gifts. In *HAU: Journal of Ethnographic Theory,* 13(1): pp. 21–43.

Vaughn, Rachel A. 2011. *Talking Trash: Oral Histories of Food Insecurity from the Margins of a Dumpster.* PhD Dissertation, Department of American Studies, University of Kansas.

2

THE PERFECT STORM

A history of food waste

Andrew F. Smith

Saving food and preventing waste are crucial matters that have confronted humankind for millennia. Failure to store or preserve food in times of plenty could result in hunger, famine, and death in times of want. Virtually every religion forbade wasting food, and saving food was a value built into the culture of communities around the world (see Chapter 3 in this book). Family culinary traditions, often passed down from mother to daughter, stressed the importance of wasting nothing and finding uses for every bit of edible food (see Broomfield 2007 for Victorian history and food preservation). Cookery manuscripts and later cookbooks offered adaptations of traditional uses to prevent waste, and recipes for leftovers. Notable examples of such a cookbook, identified by Evans et al. (2012), are Isabella Beeton's *Book of Household Management* (1861) and *Mrs Beeton's Cookery* Book (1899). Vegetable peel, bones, and less desirable animal products were used to make stocks and soups, or fed to livestock. Roots, leaves, feathers, bones, fish scales, and spoiled food were composted for use as fertilizer (Wilson 1991).

Beyond household culinary traditions of using peel and bones, food processors also contributed to food waste prevention. Some food processors considered by-products from processing as resources rather than waste (Bruttini 1923) and this perspective was exemplified by Chicago meatpacker Philip Armour. Armour hired chemists to exploit the inedible parts of cattle and hog carcasses. He noted that the goal of a slaughter facility, for instance, was to convert every part of the animal into a saleable product. This meant that the "waste" and leftovers from slaughter were transformed into gelatin, soap, glue, glycerin, grease, and fertilizer. Armour declared that waste was criminal and when asked which parts of the pig he used in his packing plants, he reputedly shot back, "Everything but the squeal" (Leech and Carroll 1938).

Reducing food waste continued as a concern among food processors throughout the twentieth century (Spooner 1918; Bruttini 1923; Benedict and Farr 1931). However, the issue received wider public attention mainly in periods of shortages and rationing, such as during the First and Second World Wars. Governments of nations affected by war launched propaganda campaigns, with newspaper articles, posters, and radio programs encouraging citizens not to waste food, which was desperately needed to support the war effort. War was declared on food waste (Harrison 1918) with messages equating the wasting of food to a lack of morality. Wasting food was declared a "sin," while preventing food waste was patriotic. Numerous slogans such as "Waste Not, Want Not," "Waste of Food Helps the Enemy Greatly," and "Save the Food of the Nation" were printed on flyers and posters, and pamphlets promised that "Food Will Win the War!" (Chambers and Mamburg 1918). When the wars were over, the anti-food waste campaigns ended.

Contributors to food waste

Throughout the twentieth century, food prices declined as mechanization increased crop yields, improved freight transportation, and fostered the rise of supermarkets. Simultaneous with the decrease in food prices was the increase in wages for many urban workers. The result of lower food costs and higher take-home pay was that families spent a smaller proportion of their income on food. In 1901, US urban households spent an estimated 42.5 percent of their take-home pay on food. By the twenty-first century, this had dropped to about 6.6 percent for food consumed at home (Bureau of Labor Statistics 2006; Sturm and An 2014). Similar patterns were seen in other affluent countries: By the twentieth-first century, UK households expended about 8.2 percent of their income on food, while French and South Korean households spent about 13.5 percent (Plumer 2015; Gray 2016).

Lower prices and higher wages encouraged waste throughout food systems. Farmers unable to profit by harvesting food, fed it to animals or ploughed it under (Howard and Wad 1931; Shover 1965; Rao 2015). Supermarket chains developed stringent standards for the produce they bought: fruits and vegetables had to be well-shaped, uniformly sized, and properly coloured, among other specifications; items that did not measure up to these standards were trashed. Supermarket managers found it easier to overstock items than to risk disappointing customers, but items that could not be sold when the items were at their peak ended up in the dump. Food manufacturers and retailers found it more efficient to discard surplus or outdated supplies than to try to salvage them (Stuart 2009). Restaurateurs supersized their offerings and plate waste surged with larger servings and larger plates used in restaurants and restaurant chains (Herzka and Booth 1981; Kosseva and Webb 2013). Consumers bought larger packages or two-for-one sales in supermarkets, and in some cases also discarded wholesome food due to aesthetic factors (Van Garde and Woodburn 1987).

By the 1950s, convenience became a major selling point for processed foods. "Instant" mixes, heat-and-eat frozen meals, and, later, microwaveable entrées could be served in a matter of minutes. Cafeterias, commissaries, buffets, snack bars, lunch counters, kiosks, coffee shops, canteens, and fast food chains flourished. By the early twenty-first century, consumers in some countries were spending almost half of their food budgets on meals prepared outside the home (Jamrisko 2015). Purchase of food prepared outside the home and convenience food for the home, contributed to the loss of traditional cooking skills once handed down through generations (Jaffe and Gertler 2006; Aschemann-Witzel 2018). There was little incentive for consumers to be concerned about leftovers in restaurants or food waste at home.

At home, kitchen refrigerators and pantries got bigger as the century progressed (Rees 2013). Ironically, overstocked refrigerators and brimful pantries contributed to waste as items were pushed to the back of a crowded fridge or pantry. In time, they soured or spoiled and ended up in the trash. Another invention, the in-sink garbage disposal solved the problem of unsightly, smelly, unsanitary kitchen garbage, but was just a convenient way of delivering scraps to the dump. As critics pointed out, they also wasted a lot of water, and fats, oils, and grease ground down garbage disposals occasionally clogged household drains and could cause "fatbergs," large masses of congealed cooking fat that blocked sewage systems (Hester 2018).

Another innovation is modern food packaging. Food packaging evolved as a way to prevent spoilage. Waxed paper, foil, cans, bottles, and jars preserved and conserved food, prolonging its useful life. Packaged food products enabled long-distance food supply chains as it was possible to ship food safely over long distances from processor to retailer to consumer. Constant innovation in plastic containers and wraps prolonged shelf life still further. Shoppers, however, could not see, smell, or touch the contents of the package, and only after opening it could spoilage be discovered. To help grocers and shoppers determine whether packaged products were still fresh and wholesome, processors began labeling packaged foods and beverages with a date indicating when the product had been packed, or when it was recommended that the food be consumed by, or when its shelf life would expire. Some processors began labeling milk products with a date in the 1930s. Marks & Spencer, a British department-store chain, began doing so in the 1950s. In the late 1960s, Kroger, an American supermarket chain, required sell by dates on cartons of milk and some other dairy products. These were intended to indicate when these products would begin to spoil or smell "off" (Newsome et al. 2014).

With "sell-by" or "best if used by" dates clearly marked, retailers and consumers could discard foods after the date had expired. But there was no consistency in the labeling: Food companies employed a variety of labeling systems and terminology, and by the 1970s there were more than 50 different versions of product dating, causing confusion among retailers and consumers (Salisbury 2016). Consumers who were (and remain) confused or obsessed with quality tend to discard perfectly edible food when the labeling shows it to be "outdated." A 2009 UK survey, for example, found that

> 53 per cent of British consumers did not eat fruit or vegetables that exceeded the 'best before' date, 56 per cent did not eat bread or cake; and 21 per cent never even 'take a risk' with food close to its date.
>
> *(Shields 2009)*

A 2011 report revealed that about 450,000 tonnes of food were thrown away because it had passed a "best before" date (Lyndhurst 2011). Had the food been stored properly, it would have been perfectly safe to eat up to and after this date. In addition, the report estimated that 380,000 tonnes of food were tossed out because it had passed a "use by" date – waste that could have been avoided had the food been cooked or frozen before that date (Lyndhurst 2011). Others have linked these behaviors to concerns around food safety, such as a 2017 study in Scotland showing that more than 50 percent of the country's population threw away perfectly edible food that was approaching or past its "best before" date, and the reason why 62 percent did so was the fear of "getting ill" (Luiza et al. 2017). Confusion around terminologies abound as a 2014 Belgian study found that 30 percent of those surveyed did not know the difference between "use by" and "best before" labels (Boxstael et al. 2014). This finding is further supported by a 2015 European Commission study, which found that fewer than half of those surveyed knew the meaning of "best before" labels (Shepherd 2016).

Concern with food safety contributes to increased waste and is often followed with the popular phrase, "When in doubt, throw it out," becoming the rule of the day beginning in the 1950s (Bracken 1960). Discarded food could be easily replaced, so rather than worry about off-flavors and potential food poisoning, it was easier for businesses and consumers to toss out discolored or bruised produce and packaged foods passed their prime. The following section explores the waste infrastructures enabling such ease of dumping food.

Early environmental concerns: landfills to climate change

Historically, refuse generated in populated areas was dumped outside town or city limits, often into nearby lakes, rivers, or swamps. Coastal cities shipped waste out to sea and dumped it in the ocean. As towns and cities grew and the composition of waste became more complex, new solutions were required and increasingly wastes were burned in bonfires or incinerators. The first so-called "sanitary landfill" was created in Fresno, California, in 1935 (Melosi 2002). After garbage was dumped by the truckload and compacted, it was covered each day with a layer of clean soil to reduce rodent activity and odours.

The environmental movement that emerged during the 1960s was concerned with conserving natural resources, controlling pollution, protecting endangered species, saving the rain forests, preventing desertification, and stopping exploitation of the oceans. Beginning in the 1970s, environmentalists in Europe, Japan, and North America began to focus on solid waste disposal, advocating recycling, reducing, and reusing rather than dumping it in landfill sites. Paper, metal, and glass were the first materials targeted for recycling. Progressive communities in North America began requiring residents and businesses to recycle, establishing collection and recycling programs for paper products, bottles, and cans (Strasser 2000).

Governmental agencies began to take action to limit the amount of material being dumped into landfills. For example, the European Union established the Landfill Directive in 1991, with the mission of reducing

> negative effects on the environment, in particular the pollution of surface water, groundwater, soil and on the global environment, including the greenhouse effect, as well as any resulting risk to human health, from the landfilling of waste, during the whole life-cycle of the landfill.
>
> *(European Commission 1999)*

Despite legislations to promote recycling, environmental hazards remain. In paper recycling programs, food particles, grease, and oil on paper recyclables, such as soiled pizza boxes or grease-stained paper products, could contaminate entire loads of recyclables, making them unusable or greatly reducing their value. In addition, food residue can create unsafe conditions for workers in recycling facilities. Estimates vary, but in the US alone an estimated 25 percent of paper recyclables are covered primarily with food waste (The Week 2019). Another serious environmental problem emerged with food waste sent to landfill. When food and other organic matter end up in landfills, they are compressed tightly underground and are deprived of oxygen. This results in the production of vast quantities of methane, which is 25 times more damaging to the earth's atmosphere than carbon dioxide (CO_2). The US Environmental Protection Agency (EPA) estimated that 63 million tons of food were sent to landfills each year, producing about 34 percent of American methane emissions (Scientific American 2019). Dumping food waste in landfills generates much more methane than do other mechanisms of handling such waste. In composting, food scraps are exposed to oxygen, and they produce CO_2; but decomposing food in a landfill is tightly compressed underground in an anaerobic state, resulting in the production of methane. Reducing food waste in landfills, therefore, was an early priority among environmentalists, but it was not until the early twenty-first century that the general public became aware of food waste's contributions to climate change.

Food waste's relationship to climate change has been on the international agenda since the late 1970s. In 1979 the World Climate Conference, organized by the World Meteorological Organization, called for nations to halt preventable environmental damage. In 1988, the United Nations established the Intergovernmental Panel on Climate Change. Most scientists believe that human actions – particularly the burning of fossil fuels and the release of greenhouse gases (GHGs) – including CO_2 and methane – have directly contributed to climate change (Smith 2017). Food systems are major contributors to GHGs throughout the world. Growing, processing, and transporting food make substantial contributions to these emissions, as does the food waste in landfills. In 2015, the Food and Agriculture Organization estimated that if food waste was a country, it would be the third largest emitter of GHGs in the world. Environmental efforts around the world have now jumped on the anti-food waste bandwagon in hopes of stemming global warming (FAO 2015).

Measuring the scale and impacts of food and organic waste

In 1973 William Rathje, an American archaeologist, began to examine garbage in the landfills in Tucson, Arizona. For several decades he and his collaborators tracked trends in what materials ended up in the trash (Harrison et al. 1975; Rathje 1984; Rathje and Murphy 2001). His research and subsequent studies revealed that food was the single largest component of solid waste. These studies did not include food scraps ground up in garbage disposals and washed into sewers, food-related packaging, or food scraps that ended up as compost or animal feed.

Others evaluated waste in a different way, by examining the availability of food in national systems. A 1980 study in the United Kingdom, for instance, reported that about 3,100 kilocalories of food were available to each person per day. As the average person required only 2,200 kilocalories, the authors concluded that a large portion of the remainder was wasted "in the home as well as in catering establishments and during the storage, distribution and processing of food" (Wenlock, Buss, and Derry 1980). In the same year, studies in the US found that about 35 percent of caloric value, including fat, liquid discards, disposal and compactor waste, and food fed to animals, was wasted (Gallo 1980). In 1997 the Economic Research Service of the US Department of Agriculture concluded that about 96 billion pounds of food, or 27 percent of the 356 billion pounds of edible food available for human consumption in the US, were lost to human use at these three marketing stages in 1995. Fresh fruits and vegetables, fluid milk, grain products, and sweeteners (mostly sugar and high-fructose corn syrup) accounted for two-thirds of these losses (Kantor et al. 1997). By the twenty-first century, the US produced 4,200 calories per person per day. As only about 2,200 calories are needed per day, almost one-half of the available food was lost somewhere in the food system (USDA, n.d.).

Developing solutions for food waste

There are many ways of dealing with waste, from reducing production to sending it to landfill. In 1979 Ad Lansink, a Dutch politician, developed a Waste Ladder with five rungs: disposal, recovery, recycling, reuse, and prevention. As food waste became an important topic within the environmental movement, several food waste reduction hierarchies were proposed, creating "Food Recovery Hierarchies," such as the one shown in Figure 2.1

Andrew F. Smith

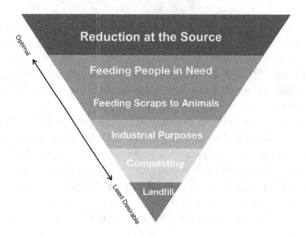

Figure 2.1 Food Recovery Hierarchy.
Source: Adapted from the US Environmental Protection Agency.

Traditionally, waste was the end result of a linear economy: food (and other goods) was produced, sold, and consumed, and the leftovers were discarded. During the 1980s, the concept of the "circular economy" was proposed (Pearce and Turner 1990). Circular economy advocates consider wasted food as a resource to be used, and not garbage to be thrown away.

Several approaches emerged to reuse or recycle food waste. Traditionally, excess food on farms was fed to animals (Bruttini 1923). Interest in conversion of waste to animal feed was renewed in the 1980s (Ledward et al. 1983). Another traditional solution was composting, which was easy to do in rural and suburban areas, but cities produce the vast majority of organic waste that ends up in landfill. During the late twentieth century, public and private projects emerged around the world to collect organic waste and convert it into compost for use on farms or in city parks (Karidis 2017).

New solutions emerged in the late twentieth century. Food waste and other organic material could be converted into biogas via anaerobic digestion – the process by which microorganisms break down organic material into methane. The science behind anaerobic digestion had been known for more than a century, but it garnered new interest during the oil crisis of the 1970s (Klinkner 2014). Beginning in the 1990s, Germany took the lead in constructing anaerobic digestion plants. Biogas production diverts organic waste from landfill and generates a renewable energy source that can be used to power vehicles, generate electricity, and supply fuel to homes and businesses. Anaerobic digestion facilities also produce nutrient-rich "digestate" which can be used as fertilizer. Despite these positives, low oil prices in the late 1990s made it unclear whether anaerobic digestion programs were financially viable.

Some countries made solid progress in reducing the amount of food waste sent to landfill. In 1991, Japan passed the Law for the Promotion of Effective Utilities of Resources and a decade later passed the Food Recycling Law. These encouraged businesses to create cyclical manufacturing processes that would reduce, reuse, and recycle any leftover waste. A revision of the laws in 2007 encouraged businesses to turn their waste into compost or animal feed (Marra 2014). South Korea required the separation of food from other waste in 1997, and implemented a "pay-as-you-throw" program in Seoul beginning in 2005. Its implementation was coupled with a major public relations campaign to gain support from consumers, and seven years later it was fully implemented in four million households. This system requires consumers to pay by weight for the food they throw away, the goal being to reduce food waste by creating a financial incentive to generate less garbage. The collected food waste is processed into animal feed or compost, or used to generate electricity. By 2015 household food waste had been reduced by 30 percent, and by 2019 South Korea recycled 95 per cent of its food waste (Hogan 2015). The following section explores the growth in efforts to ensure that food that might otherwise go to waste is fed to people.

Feed people

During the 1950s many prosperous countries established social welfare systems that provided minimum standards of living for all their citizens, with the goal of mitigating problems of malnutrition and hunger. The US did not develop such a system. In the 1960s, media exposés and government investigations brought the issue of hunger back to light (Poppendieck 1998). After massive media attention, public gatherings, government hearings, and high-profile reports, new federal programs were instituted, as were local plans to feed the hungry. However, during the 1980s President Ronald Reagan sharply cut funding to these programs to reduce the national debt. Local food pantries, soup kitchens, and food-rescue programs were launched or expanded by churches, unions, and civic organizations to take up the slack, providing food directly to those in need (Riches 2018).

Food banks – warehouses that receive food donations from processors, retailers, distributors, and individuals – were established throughout the US (Poppendieck 1998). Regional supermarket chains and wholesalers continue to donate tons of mislabeled or damaged packaged foods, overstock, test-market products, returned items, and short-dated foods. These are then sorted and distributed to affiliated food pantries, soup kitchens, and other hunger relief organizations, which are monitored by the supervising food bank to assure that the food is handled and distributed safely. This system "rescues" millions of tons of food that would otherwise end up in landfill – and, more important, it provides nourishment to millions of people who are hungry or food insecure. Riches (2018) provides a critical account of the ethics and efficacy of this system, however (see also Midgley's chapter, this volume).

The food bank model was also established in other countries. In 1985 the French comedian and actor Michel Gérard Joseph Coluche founded Les Restaurants du Cœur (Restaurants of the Heart) and in 1989 the Fondazione Banco Alimentare Onlus was founded in Italy to retrieve and distribute undamaged and non-expired food, that would otherwise have been destroyed, and distribute it to the needy. Food banks and food pantries, however, were not common outside the US until the economic crisis hit in the early twenty-first century. The geopolitical precursors of this crisis are outlined in the following section.

The storm hits

A major problem with industrialized food systems is that they are dependent on cheap oil to fuel farm equipment, power trucks and ships, make fertilizer, and operate food-processing facilities. When the Arab-Israeli War began in 1973, the oil-producing Arab nations embargoed oil, pushing up the prices of both fuel and food, but prices declined when the embargo ended in 1974 (Attarian 2002). Oil prices edged up again in 2002, when the US and other countries considered invading Iraq, a major oil producer in the Persian Gulf. When the invasion began in March of 2003, oil prices skyrocketed, causing a huge jump in global prices for food, particularly corn, wheat, and soy, which in turn bumped up the cost of grain-fed pork, beef, and chicken (FAO 2009).

To alleviate the fuel crisis, the US, Brazil, the European Union, Canada, China, and other nations subsidized production of ethanol (a renewable biofuel made largely from sugarcane, sorghum, corn, barley, and other grains) to promote energy independence (Shepherd 2008; FAO 2009). These programs diverted food crops from the market, pushing food prices even higher.

The global food system could likely have overcome rising oil prices and increased ethanol production had it not been for simultaneous adverse weather conditions. In Australia, two years of drought decimated the wheat crop (Wong 2008). Grain production in Ukraine and Russia, where much of the crop had previously been exported, was also curtailed (Kramer-aug 2010). India faced domestic food shortages. In June 2006, India stopped exporting sugar, wheat, and lentils in an effort to stabilize domestic food prices. India subsequently banned exports of rice except basmati (Bhupta 2008), and Vietnam, the world's third biggest rice exporter, cut its rice exports (Minh and Mukherji 2008).

As food prices soared globally, speculators jumped into commodities markets and began buying grain and other futures, pushing prices still higher (*Economist* 2007). In May 2007, the world price of wheat was $200 per ton; by early September it had risen to more than $400 – the highest price ever recorded (*Economist* 2007). Three months later, world cereal stocks based as a proportion of production were the lowest ever recorded. Russia imposed price controls on milk, eggs, bread, and other staples. Venezuela legislated price controls on food (Wroughton 2008). These policies further depleted food supplies worldwide as farmers stored or exported commodities rather than sell them at artificially low prices (Wroughton 2008).

Between 2005 and 2007, food prices jumped by 75 percent. From the spring to the fall of 2007 wheat prices doubled, as did the cost of milk, oilseeds, and other basics. In December 2007, *The Economist*'s food-price index was higher "than at any time since it was created in 1845" and the magazine proclaimed "the end of cheap food" (*Economist* 2007). In many parts of the world unstable oil and food prices made it difficult for farmers to make a living (Campbell 2008). In March 2008, the United Nations Secretary-General, Ban Ki-moon, reported that with the threat of hunger and malnutrition growing, millions of the world's most vulnerable people were at risk (Ki-moon 2008).

Yet another challenge was the financial meltdown initiated by a slowing US economy, worsened by the mortgage crisis that hit in December 2007 (Andrews 2007). As business and financial institutions succumbed, the result was the Great Recession, the largest global economic downturn since the Great Depression of the 1930s. Worldwide, both large corporations and small companies collapsed, and millions of workers lost their jobs. Despite rising unemployment, deflationary pressure on prices, and a strong US dollar, global food prices remained high (Araghi 2009).

Various commodity prices increased from 50 to 200 percent throughout 2007 to the end of 2008 (FAO 2009). Food insecurity, malnutrition, and hunger haunted millions of people throughout the world. An estimated 110 million people were thrown into poverty and 44 million were undernourished. Infant and child mortality also increased (Nellemann et al. 2009). During Ramadan in 2008, the government of Morocco fixed the price of bread so that people could afford it – if they could find any to buy (Streitfeld 2008). Consumer groups in Italy staged a one-day pasta strike (*Sydney Morning Herald* 2007). In Pakistan, paramilitary troops were deployed to guard trucks carrying wheat and flour. Malaysian leaders made it a crime to export flour and other products without a license. Food riots and other forms of unrest erupted in 30 countries, including Haiti, Egypt, Bangladesh, Somalia,

Burkina Faso, Guinea, Mauritania, Mexico, Morocco, Senegal, and Uzbekistan (Bush 2010; Lagi et al. 2011).

Projections varied, but some suggested that food prices would continue to increase by 5 percent per year for a decade (Chapman 2008). Reports by the United Nations Environment Programme and the World Bank projected that food prices could rise by 30 to 50 percent within decades, forcing those living in extreme poverty to spend up to 90 percent of their income on food (Nellemann et al. 2009). Even more worrisome were dire warnings about the negative effects of climate change on agriculture and food availability, while the world population was projected to reach 9.1 billion by 2050.

In the face of a looming food crisis, scientists, agriculture experts, and political leaders organized conferences, academics published articles and books, and foundations and governmental agencies issued reports addressing ever-rising food prices, growing world hunger, and threats to the environment. Some argued for sending more aid to developing countries and improving information systems to monitor and assess the impact of rising food prices (FAO 2009). Others proposed bringing new land into cultivation and expanding industrial agriculture – which many environmentalists strongly opposed.

As food prices rose, many countries also began to raise concerns about food waste. In the Netherlands, the Ministry of Agriculture, Nature and Food Quality began to focus on food waste in 2006 and, by 2010, was supporting many activities targeting food waste. In the UK, the Department for Environment, Food & Rural Affairs (Defra) concluded that waste could be reduced in agricultural operations (Defra 2006). Defra also funded the Waste & Resources Action Programme (WRAP), creating public–private partnerships intended to achieve a circular economy, which WRAP defined as

> an alternative to a traditional linear economy (make, use, dispose) in which we keep resources in use for as long as possible, extract the maximum value from them whilst in use, then recover and regenerate products and materials at the end of each service life.
>
> *(WRAP 2019)*

WRAP initially focussed on packaging and other materials that ended up in landfills, but food waste soon became part of its mandate.

WRAP reported in 2005 that it had "limited information about the amounts and types of food waste produced," so it launched a major research effort to quantify the nature, scale, origin, and causes of post-consumer food waste in the UK. The study was based on surveys of 2,000 households where families kept kitchen diaries – records of what they purchased, consumed, and discarded. In March 2007, WRAP published *Dealing with Food Waste in the UK*, a report concluding that there was "a genuine opportunity for the UK to take a lead in dealing with biowaste (i.e., food and organic garden waste) in Europe. It can learn from experience in other countries and manage biowaste more cost effectively and sustainably" (Hogg et al. 2007).

In May 2007, David Miliband, the UK Environment Secretary, announced the first new waste strategy for England since 2000. He proposed "pay-as-you-throw" rubbish taxes and encouraged local councils to collect food waste on a weekly basis. The waste was to be "converted into … gas in digesters, and can then be used to produce heat and electricity" (BBC News 2007a). That summer, Prime Minister Gordon Brown and his government tried to institute weekly food waste collections and to impose taxes on discarded food. The strategy brought opposition from many local councils, and in October Brown dropped plans for the taxes (BBC News 2007b; Channel 4 News 2008).

As food prices continued to rise, WRAP hired Trimedia, a public relations firm, to help develop a campaign encouraging consumers to reduce in-home food waste and keep food out of landfills. The campaign, called "Love Food, Hate Waste", was supported by leading chefs and food writers. The campaign was launched in November 2007 at London's Borough Market, a major wholesale and retail food market that operated in accord with campaign values and was accessible to journalists and film crews. Speakers included Joan Ruddock, Defra's Parliamentary Under Secretary of State. By June 2008 the campaign had amassed more than 550 pieces of coverage in print and electronic media (Black 2008).

On 8 May 2008, WRAP released a report called "The Food We Waste." It revealed that 6.7 million tons of food were thrown away each year in the UK, of which 4.1 million tons were avoidable. The report concluded that UK consumers spent £10.2 billion on wasted food each year, which worked out to £420 of annual avoidable waste for the average household. Even householders who claimed that they generated no food waste produced on average 2.9 kilograms of it per week (WRAP 2008). Since food prices were still climbing, it was a timely message. The press and online sources played up the "Shocking Food Waste Report," as one source headlined it (LetsRecycle 2008).

In November 2009, WRAP released two new reports: "Household Food and Drink Waste in the UK," and "Down the Drain." The first estimated that "8.3 million tonnes per year of food and drink waste is generated by households in the UK" (Quested and Johnson 2009). "Down the Drain" explored food and drink waste from UK households that was disposed of via sewer systems. The report estimated that "1.5 million tonnes of the food and drink disposed could have been avoided had it been better stored in the home or with better planning or preparation." It placed the cost of this to consumers at £2.7 billion, and also highlighted the environmental price: An estimated 4.6 million tons of CO_2 equivalent GHG emissions were released by UK households annually (Gray 2009).

The success of Trimedia's public relations campaign gave Gordon Brown the opportunity to revitalize his support for food waste reduction, and he found an excellent showcase for it at the G8 meeting of the world's major industrialized countries, held in Hokkaidō, Japan, in July 2008. At the meeting Brown announced a campaign to stamp out waste in the UK, declaring war on food waste as part of a global effort to curb spiraling food prices. Brown said that the solution to ever-rising food costs was to devise a "global plan" to reduce food waste, "which is costing the average household around £8 a week" (Lawson 2008).

Not everyone jumped on board with Brown's call to reduce global waste, but his comments set the stage for several significant events in 2009 in the UK. The first was Defra Minister Hilary Benn's announcement of a "War on Waste." Benn announced construction of new biogas facilities that would produce fuel from organic waste, and he argued for the end of "sell until," "sell by," "display until," and "best before" dates on packaged foods. These caused confusion, he said, and led to tremendous waste. The only useful label was the "use before" date, which was legally necessary for safety.

> When we buy food, it should be easy to know how long we should keep it for and how we should store it. Too many of us are putting things in the bin simply because we're not sure, we're confused by the label, or we're just playing safe.
>
> *(Smithers 2009)*

The second major event was the publication of *Waste: Uncovering the Global Food Scandal* (Stuart 2009). Written by Tristram Stuart, a writer, dumpster diver, vegan, and activist, the book contained jaw-dropping facts about food waste that came as a genuine shock to most readers. It was simultaneously released in the US and subsequently translated into French, German, Spanish, and Chinese.

To help reduce and recycle food waste, Stuart founded an environmental non-profit organization called Feedback, which, along with a coalition of other groups, staged a public "Feeding the 5000" meal in London's Trafalgar Square on 16 December 2009. Using only "recovered" food from supermarkets, bakeries, and other sources, the organizers fed thousands of Londoners while helping to raise a public outcry over the issue. The event garnered extensive media coverage, focusing the public's attention on reducing, reusing, and recycling food waste. The global war on food waste had commenced. The following section explores developments beyond the UK.

A globalizing social movement: The media and organizational deluge

The American filmmaker Jeremy Seifert released his documentary *Dive!* in October 2009. Its purpose was to publicize the staggering amount of food wasted in the US. Seifert filmed dumpster divers behind Los Angeles supermarkets, including Trader Joe's, salvaging thousands of dollars worth of edible food, some of which Seifert cooked to share with his wife and son. Seifert confronted supermarket executives, urging them to donate more food to local food banks. The film ends with a quotation from Noam Chomsky, the philosopher, social critic, and political activist: "Change doesn't trickle down from above, it grows from below." Managers of food banks thanked Seifert as they reported big jumps in donations from local supermarkets (Lenneman 2013).

Dive! was just the first in a series of films and television programs to address the issue. Olivier Lemaire's documentary, *Global Waste: The Scandal of Food Waste*, was released in August 2010. It starred Tristram Stuart, who traveled from Europe to Ecuador, India, the US, and Japan looking at the issue of food waste. The film targeted the culprits – food producers, industrialists, distributors, and consumers – and also noted innovations and solutions for decreasing waste (Lemaire 2011). At virtually the same time, BBC One released *The Great British Waste Menu*, a documentary that followed four chefs (Angela Hartnett, Richard Corrigan, Matt Tebbutt, and Simon Rimmer) as they sourced unwanted food from farms, supermarkets, and homes and then transformed the ingredients into "mouth-watering dishes" (Ratcliffe et al. 2010).

In Denmark, Selina Juul, a Russian émigrée, launched a Facebook group in 2008 that grew into a non-profit organization called Stop Spild Af Mad (Stop Wasting Food). Juul began publishing opinion-editorials and articles on food waste in Danish and international newspapers, many of them co-written with prominent politicians, and she collaborated with Danish chefs to publish *Stop spild af mad: en kogebog med mere* (Stop Wasting Food: A cookbook and more). Stop Spild Af Mad quickly became the country's largest consumer movement against food waste (Juul et al. 2011).

Ilse Aigner, the German Minister for Food, Agriculture, and Consumer Protection (BMELV), launched an anti-food waste campaign called "Better Appreciation of the Value of Food!" in 2010, but it generated little interest (GAIN Report 2013). This changed when Valentin Thurn released the documentary, *Taste the Waste: warum schmeissen wir unser Essen auf den Müll?* (Why do we throw our food in the trash?) in September 2011, followed the same year with the book, *Die Essensvernichter: warum die Hälfte aller Lebensmittel im Müll landet und wer dafür verantwortlich ist* (The Food Destroyers: Why half of our food ends up in the trash, and who is responsible) (Kreutzberger and Thurn 2011; Thurn et al. 2011). The book reported that European households threw away 100 billion euros worth of food every year, and that the amount of food wasted in Europe was "enough to feed all the hungry people in the world two times over." The film and book also revealed that food rotting in garbage dumps has a disastrous impact on the world's climate.

Thurn's work catalyzed a growing social movement against food waste in Germany. In March 2012, the University of Stuttgart reported that Germans wasted about 11 million tons of food each year, which worked out to 82 kg (176 lb) per person per year, about two-thirds of which came from private households (Kranert et al. 2012, p. 9). Ilse Aigner, the Minister for Food, Agriculture, and Consumer Protection (BMELV), announced a nationwide campaign to combat food waste. It informed Germans about how much food they throw away and why they do so, and enumerated steps citizens could take to reduce waste (GAIN Report 2013). The BMELV released an app called "Zu gut für die Tonne!" offering cooking suggestions and recipes to help homemakers shop, store, and utilize food with less waste (Too Good for the Bin 2012). The BMELV in cooperation with Slow Food Deutschland and Die Tafel (a non-profit that serves as the umbrella organization for the food surplus redistribution network), organized nationwide days of action called "Wir retten Lebensmittel!" (We save Food!).

Austrian activist David Gross launched Wastecooking, a collective that focussed on reducing food waste, in May 2012. Wastecooking opened Europe's first free supermarket in 2013. Two years later, Georg Misch filmed Gross as he journeyed through European countries gathering discarded food and preparing meals with it. His traveling kitchen was a converted garbage receptacle that he towed behind a biodiesel-fueled vehicle. This led to the series, *Wastecooking: Kochen statt Verschwenden* (Wastecooking: Make Food, Not Waste), which first aired in 2015. It featured chefs, scientists, and activists, and offered viewers simple ways to reduce food waste (Misch 2015).

Europe passed the Waste Framework Directive in 2008. It defined bio-waste as "biodegradable garden and park waste, food and kitchen waste from households, restaurants, caterers and retail premises, and comparable waste from food processing plants" and laid the basis for the EU to become a recycling society (European Commission 2008). The French Environment and Energy Management Agency launched an anti-food waste campaign aimed at consumers in November 2010 (ADEME 2010). The campaign included television and radio spots, print ads, and web banners. Consumer surveys were undertaken to improve understanding of why consumers wasted food. After due consideration, France committed to cut food waste in half by 2020.

In October 2014, the French chefs Cyril Lignac, Philippe Etchebest, Ghislaine Arabian, Yves Camdeborde, and Florent Ladeyn participated in a television program called "Gaspillage Alimentaire: Les Chefs Contre-attaquent" (Food Waste: The Chefs Fight Back) (LeclercMaisDrive 2014). It highlighted the importance of reducing food waste in France. Two months later, Arash Derambarsh, a city councilor of Courbevoie, France, started a "field experiment" that acquired unsold supermarket food destined for the trash and distributed it to the needy. The experiment was so successful that Derambarsh launched a change.org petition to demand that the French parliament pass a law requiring supermarkets to donate edible food to hunger programs. In just four months, the petition attracted more than 200,000 signatures along with celebrity endorsements. Within the year a law was passed prohibiting supermarkets from discarding edible excess food (Derambarsh 2016).

In Spain, La asociación de fabricantes y distribuidores (The Spanish manufacturing and distribution association) launched a campaign in 2012 to reduce waste along the whole food chain and optimize reuse of the excess food. Their tag line was "Food has no waste." The following year, the Spanish Ministry of Agriculture, Food and Environment (Magrama) launched the "More food, less waste" initiative that supported food waste studies, distributed guides to reduce loss and waste of food, and launched campaigns targeting consumers and the catering industry.

The European Commission declared the year 2014 the "European year of food waste." The following year, the EU adopted the Sustainable Development Goals, including a target of halving per capita food waste at the retail and consumer levels by 2030, and reducing food losses along the production and supply chains.

Jonathan Bloom, an American journalist, became interested in food waste while volunteering in a food pantry in Washington, DC in 2005. After five years of research into the problem, he published *American Wasteland: How America Throws Away Nearly Half of its Food (And What We Can Do about It)* (Bloom 2010). He created the "Wasted Food" website, a blog, and a Twitter feed, and began speaking throughout the US. The US EPA jumped on board the fast-expanding anti-waste movement, launching the Food Recovery Challenge in 2011. This supported universities, businesses, and community organizations in making their food management systems more sustainable. The National Resources Defense Council began publishing reports on related topics, including "Wasted: How America is losing up to 40 per cent of its food from farm to fork to landfill" (Gunders 2012) and "The Dating Game" (Leib et al. 2013). In 2013, Danielle Nierenberg and Ellen Gustafson co-founded Food Tank, a non-profit organization that continues to be a leader in promoting anti-food waste efforts.

In January 2012, The Food Network hosted a special, *The Big Waste*, that brought together four top chefs (Bobby Flay, Michael Symon, Anne Burrell, and Alex Guarnaschelli) to explore the potential of America's burgeoning food waste. The chefs collected discarded food from various sources and then prepared meals using only those ingredients. The program included discussions of waste in food preparation and distribution, a dumpster-diving session behind a supermarket, and a look at waste on the farm.

This was just the beginning of the anti-food waste blitz: Other documentaries and television series have kept the torch burning. Popular films include Grant Baldwin's *Just Eat It: A Food Waste Movie* (2015), Emily Broad Leib and Nathaniel Hansen's *Expired? Food Waste in America* (2016), and Anthony Bourdain's" (2017) showcasing celebrity chefs including Dan Barber, Mario Batali, Danny Bowien, and Massimo Bottura. In 2016, British chef and activist Hugh Fearnley-Whittingstall hosted a BBC series called *Hugh's War on Waste*, and Australian comedian Craig Reucassel presented a similar series on Australian television in 2017. In June 2018, the film *Food Fighter* was released in Australia to great acclaim. It followed Ronni Kahn, founder of the food-rescue organization OzHarvest, as she crusaded against food waste not just in Australia, but in other countries as well. Today, few weeks pass without the release of another television program, documentary, YouTube video, film, or other media program related to some aspect of food waste (Smith 2019).

Major conferences focussed on food waste are now regularly convened throughout the world. New projects, initiatives, and inventions intended to reduce the waste of food are launched by governmental agencies, non-profit organizations, and businesses. Academics release new studies and make recommendations on aspects of food waste. New facilities are funded or implemented to convert organic waste into compost or renewable energy, and innovators release new equipment or technology intended to reduce or "upcycle" food waste into a useable resource. There are frequent launches of new apps and platforms intended to reduce food waste, and governments continue to pass laws mandating new recycling programs or restricting certain types of waste. Food waste will likely continue to be on the agenda of farmers, businesses, governments, and consumers for the next decades.

As everyone wins – financially, morally, and environmentally – by reducing food waste, it will likely remain on the world's agenda for decades to come.

Note

This chapter has been compiled using sources from the "Food waste and food recovery bibliography." Currently in its 26th version, it is 614 pages long (and still growing). The bibliography catalogues all materials that have been found related to food waste and food recovery. These include books, academic journals, newspaper and magazine articles, web and blog posts, government reports as well as an eight-page list of Historical Material Pre-1955. For more information on how to access the bibliography, please contact Andrew F. Smith (www.andrewfsmith.com).

References

ADEME (2010) *Le Gaspillage Alimentaire Au Cœur De La Campagne Nationale Grand Public Sur La Réduction Des Déchets*, Agence de l'Environnement et de la Maîtrise de l'Énergie, Paris. www.docplayer.fr/33066156-Dossier-de-presse-le-gaspillage-alimentaire-au-coeur-de-la-campagne-nationale-grand-public-sur-la-reduction-des-dechets.html accessed 14 July 2019.

Andrews, E. (2007) 'Fed Shrugged as Subprime Crisis Spread', *New York Times*, 18 December. www.nytimes.com/2007/12/18/business/18subprime.html accessed 14 July 2019.

Araghi, F. (2009) 'Accumulation by Displacement: Global Enclosures, Food Crisis, and the Ecological Contradictions of Capitalism', *Political Economic Perspectives on the World Food Crisis*, vol 32, no 1, pp 113–114.

Aschemann-Witzel, J. (2018) 'Helping You to Waste Less? Consumer Acceptance of Food Marketing Offers Targeted to Food-related Lifestyle Segments of Consumers', *Journal of Food Products Marketing*, vol 24, no 5, pp 522–538.

Attarian, J. (2002) 'The Coming End of Cheap Oil', *The Social Contract*, vol 12, no 4, Summer www.thesocialcontract.com/artman2/publish/tsc1204/article_1095.shtml accessed 15 July 2019.

BBC News (2007a) 'Bin Charges 'to Boost Recycling', *BBC News*, 24 May. www.news.bbc.co.uk/2/hi/uk_politics/6685409.stm accessed 28 October 2018.

BBC News (2007b) 'Stop Wasting Food, Brown Urging', *BBC News*, 07 July. www.news.bbc.co.uk/1/hi/uk_politics/7492573.stm accessed 05 August 2019.

Benedict, F. G. and Farr A. G. (1931) '*The Energy and the Protein Content of Edible Food Waste and Mixed Meals in Sorority and Fraternity Houses*'. New Hampshire Agricultural Experiment Station, The University of New Hampshire Durham, New Hampshire www.library.unh.edu/find/digital/object/agbulletin%3A0224 accessed 14 July7 2019.

Bhupta, M. (2008) 'Price Vice', *India Today*, 03 April. www.indiatoday.in/magazine/economy/story/20080414-price-vice-735861-2008-04-03 accessed 14 July 2019.

Black, A. (2008) 'Campaigns: Public Sector - WRAP Tells Public to End Food Waste', *PR Week*, 05 December. www.prweek.com/article/867410/campaigns-public-sector—wrap-tells-public-end-food-waste accessed 14 July 2019.

Bloom, J. (2010) *American Wasteland: How America Throws Away Nearly Half of Its Food (and What We Can Do about It)*. Da Capo Press, Cambridge, MA.

Boxstael, S. et al. (2014) 'Understanding and Attitude regarding the Shelf Life Labels and Dates on Pre Packed Food Products by Belgian Consumers', *Food Control*, vol 37, March, pp 85–92 www.sciencedirect.com/science/article/pii/S0956713513004350 accessed 14 July 2019.

Bracken, P. (1960) *The Complete I Hate to Cook Book*. Fawcett Publications, Inc, Greenwich, Connecticut.

Broomfield, A. (2007) *Food and Cooking in Victorian England: A History*. Praeger, Westport, Connecticut.

Bruttini, A. (1923) *Uses of Waste Material; the Collection of Waste Materials and Their Uses for Human and Animal Food, in Fertilisers, and in Certain Industries, 1914-1922*. P. S. King, London.

Bureau of Labor Statistics (2006) '100 Years of U.S. Consumer Spending: Data for the Nation, New York City, and Boston', United States Department of Labor, BLS Report 991. www.bls.gov/opub/100-years-of-u-s-consumer-spending.pdf accessed 10 April 2019.

Bush, R. (2010) 'Food Riots: Poverty, Power and Protest', *Journal of Agrarian Change*, vol 10, no 1, pp. 119–129.

Campbell, A. (2008) *Paddock to Plate: Food, Farming and Victoria's Progress to Sustainability*. Australian Conservation Foundation, Melbourne.

Chambers, Charles Edward, and Mamburg, L.L.L. [artist]. 'Food Will Win the War: You Came Here Seeking Freedom, Now You Must Help to Preserve It: Wheat Is Needed for the Allies, Waste Nothing' [Washington, D.C.]: U.S. Food Administration, 1918. Poster. www.digital.library.unt.edu/ark:/67531/metadc360/.

Channel 4 News (2008) 'FactCheck: A 'binned' Tax?', *Channel 4 News*, 06 May. www.channel4.com/news/articles/politics/domestic_politics/factcheck%2Ba%2Bbinned%2Btax/2144557.html accessed 05 August 2019.

Chapman, J. (2008) 'As Supermarket Prices Spiral Brown Tells Families: "stop Wasting Food"', *Daily Mail*, 07 July. www.dailymail.co.uk/news/article-1032605/As-supermarket-prices-spiral-Brown-tells-families-Stop-wasting-food.html accessed 28 October 2018.

DEFRA (2006) *Saving Money by Reducing Waste: Waste Minimisation Manual: A Practical Guide for Farmers and Growers*. Department for Environment, Food and Rural Affairs, London. www.gov.uk/government/uploads/system/uploads/attachment_data/file/69393/pb11674-waste-minimisation-060508.pdf.

Derambarsh, A. (2016) 'I Helped Lead the Successful Campaign to Ban French Supermarkets from Wasting Food – It Must Now Work across Europe', *The Independent*, 19 February. www.independent.co.uk/voices/i-got-france-to-ban-supermarkets-from-wasting-food-and-now-im-fighting-for-it-to-happen-in-europe-a6884096.html accessed 14 July 2019.

Economist (2007) 'The End of Cheap Food', *The Economist*, 06 December. www.economist.com/node/10252015 accessed 28 October 2018.

European Commission (1999) 'Council Directive 1999/31/EC,' EUR-LEX', www.eur-lex.europa.eu/legal-content/EN/TXT/?uri=CELEX:31999L0031 accessed 28 October 2018.

European Commission (2008) 'Directive 2008/98/EC of the European Parliament and of the Council of 19 November 2008', p 4. www./extwprlegs1.fao.org/docs/pdf/eur83580.pdf accessed 14 July 2019.

Evans, D. et al. (2012) 'A Brief Pre-history of Food Waste and the Social Sciences', *The Sociological Review*, vol 60, pp 5–26.

FAO (2009) 'What Happened to World Food Prices and Why?', in *Food and Agriculture Organization of the United Nations*, Rome: Food and Agriculture Organization of the United Nations. March, pp 1–25. www.fao.org/3/i0854e/i0854e01.pdf accessed 14 July 2019.

FAO (2015) *Food Wastage Footprint & Climate Change*. UN FAO, Rome. www.fao.org/3/a-bb144e.pdf accessed 05 August 2019.

GAIN Report (2013) 'Anti Food Waste Movement Gets Government Support', Global Agricultural Information Network (GAIN Report GM13011), U.S. Department of Agriculture, 23 April www.gain.fas.usda.gov/Recent%20GAIN%20Publications/Anti%20Food%20Waste%20Movement%20Gets%20Government%20Support_Berlin_Germany_3-7-2013.pdf accessed 28 October 2018.

Gallo, A. E. (1980) 'Consumer Food Waste in the United States', *National Food Review*, Economic Research Service, Fall pp 13–16 www.openagricola.nal.usda.gov/Record/FNI81000609 accessed 28 October 2018.

Gray, A. (2016) 'Which Countries Spend the Most on Food? This Map Will Show You', *World Economic Forum*, 07 December. www.weforum.org/agenda/2016/12/this-map-shows-how-much-each-country-spends-on-food/ accessed 28 October 2018.

Gray, S. (2009) *Down the Drain: Quantification and Exploration of Food and Drink Waste Disposed of to the Sewer by Households in the UK*. Waste and Resources Action Programme, Banbury, Oxon November p1 www.wrap.org.uk/sites/files/wrap/Down%20the%20drain%20-%20report.pdf accessed 28 October 2018.

Gunders, D. (2012) *Wasted: How America Is Losing up to 40 Percent of Its Food from Farm to Fork to Landfill* (Research Report No. 12-06-B). National Resources Defense Council, August.

Harrison, M. W. (1918) 'War on Waste and Germany', *Housewives Magazine*, 11 August, 158.

Harrison, G. et al. (1975) 'Food Waste Behavior in an Urban Population', *Journal of Nutrition Education*, vol 7, January-March, pp 13–16 www.jneb.org/article/S0022-3182(75)80062-8/references accessed 16 July 2019.

Herzka, A. and Booth, R. G. (1981) *Food Industry Wastes, Disposal and Recovery*. Applied Science Publishers, London.

Hester, J. L. (2018) 'Meet the Fatbergs; Digging into the Science of Three Cities' Sewer-clogging Blobs', *Atlas Obscura*, 20 November. www.atlasobscura.com/articles/whats-inside-fatbergs accessed 15 July 2019.

Hogan, B. (2015) 'Technology Trumps Food Waste in South Korea', *LeanPath*, 29 May blog.leanpath. com/technology-trumps-food-waste-south-korea accessed 06 August 2019.

Hogg, D. et al. (2007) *Dealing with Food Waste in the UK*, Report prepared for WRAP by Eunomia Research and Consulting, Bristol, March www.wrapni.org.uk/sites/files/wrap/Dealing_with_Food_ Waste_-_Final_-_2_March_07.pdf accessed 28 October 2018.

Howard, A. and Wad, Y. D. (1931) *The Waste Products of Agriculture: Their Utilization as Humus*. Oxford University Press, Oxford.

Jaffe, J. and Gertler, M. (2006) 'Victual Vicissitudes: Consumer Deskilling and the (gendered) Transform-ation of Food Systems', *Agriculture and Human Values*, vol 23, no 2, pp 143–162.

Jamrisko, M. (2015) 'Americans' Spending on Dining Out Just Overtook Grocery Sales for the First Time Ever', *Bloomberg*, 14 April. www.bloomberg.com/news/articles/2015-04-14/americans-spend ing-on-dining-out-just-overtook-grocery-sales-for-the-first-time-ever/ accessed 10 April 2019.

Juul, S. et al. (2011) *Stop Spild Af Mad: En Kogebog Med Mere* [stop Waste of Food: A Cookbook and More] København Gyldendal.

Kantor, L. S. et al. (1997) 'Estimating and Addressing America's Food Losses', *Food Review*, vol 20, no 1, January-April, pp 2–12 www.gleaningusa.com/PDFs/USDA-Jan97a.pdf accessed 28 October 2018.

Karidis, A. (2017) 'How a Composting Program Flowered at a New York City Park', *Waste360*, 03 August. www.waste360.com/composting/how-composting-program-flowered-new-york-city-park accessed 05 August 2019.

Ki-moon, B. (2008) 'The New Face of Hunger', *United Nations Secretary-General*, 12 March.

Klinkner, B. A. (2014) 'anaerobic Digestion as a Renewable Energy Source and Waste Management Technology: What Must Be Done for This Technology to Realize Success in the United States', *U Mass. L. Rev.*, vol 9, p 68.

Kosseva, M. R. and Webb, C. eds (2013) *Food Industry Wastes: Assessment and Recuperation of Commodities*. Elsevier/Academic Press, Waltham, MA.

Krameraug, A. E. (2010) 'Russia, Crippled by Drought, Bans Grain Exports', *New York Times*.

Kranert, M. et al. (2012) 'Determination of Discarded Food and Proposals for a Minimization of Food Wastage in Germany', University Stuttgart, Institute for Sanitary Engineering, Water Quality and Solid Waste Management (ISWA), Stuttgart, February www.bmel.de/SharedDocs/Downloads/EN/Food/ Studie_Lebensmittelabfaelle_Kurzfassung.pdf?__blob=publicationFile accessed 28 October 2018.

Kreutzberger, S. and Thurn, V. (2011) *Die Essensvernichter: Warum Die Hälfte Aller Lebensmittel Im Müll Landet Und Wer Dafür Verantwortlich Ist. [The Food Killers Why Half of All Food Ends up in the Garbage and Who Is Responsible for It]*. Kiepenheuer & Witsch GmbH, Köln.

Lagi, M. et al. (2011) 'The Food Crises and Political Instability in North Africa and the Middle East', 15 August. www.papers.ssrn.com/abstract=1910031 accessed 08 August 2019.

Lawson, D. (2008) 'I'm Sorry, but Brown Is Talking Rubbish', *The Independent*, 07 July www.independ ent.co.uk/voices/commentators/dominic-lawson/dominic-lawson-im-sorry-but-brown-is-talking-rubbish-862009.html accessed 28 October 2018.

LeclercMaisDrive (2014) 'Gaspillage Alimentaire: Les Solutions', 12 October.

Ledward, D. et al. (1983) *Upgrading Waste for Feeds and Food: Proceedings of Previous Easter Schools in Agricul-tural Science*. Butterworths, Boston.

Leech, H. and Carroll, J. C. (1938) *Armour and His Times*. D. Appleton-Century Co., New York. p 44 (quote). This quote is also attributed to many others.

Leib, E. et al (2013) *The Dating Game: How Confusing Food Date Labels Lead to Food Waste in America*. The Natural Resources Defense Council and The Harvard Food Law and Policy Clinic September www. nrdc.org/sites/default/files/dating-game-report.pdf accessed 08 August 2019.

Lemaire, O. (2011) 'Global Waste: The Scandal of Food Waste' [Film] Website: www.imdb.com/title/ tt7443988/.

Lenneman, F. (2013) 'A Conversation with 'dive! ' director Jeremy Seifert, *Food & Nutrition*, 26 August www.foodandnutrition.org/September-October-2013/A-Conversation-With-Dive-Director-Jeremy-Seifert/ accessed 28 October 2018.

LetsRecycle (2008) 'Shocking Food Waste Report Published', *LetsRecycle*, 08 May. www.letsrecycle. com/news/latest-news/shocking-food-waste-report-published/.

Luiza, T. et al (2017) 'Impact of Consumers' Understanding of Date Labelling on Food Waste Behavior', *Operational Research*, 17 October. pp 1–18.

Lyndhurst, B. (2011) 'Helping Consumers Reduce Food Waste – A Retail Survey,' Banbury, Oxon Waste and Resources Action Programme (WRAP), May www.wrap.org.uk/sites/files/wrap/A_Retail_Survey.e5de3bec.9596.pdf accessed 14 July 2019.

Marra, F. (2014) 'Fighting Food Loss and Food Waste in Japan', *M. A. in Japanese Studies–Asian Studies,* Leiden University, 26 June. www.academia.edu/8853973/Fighting_Food_Loss_and_Food_Waste_in_Japan.

Melosi, M. V. (2002) 'The Fresno Sanitary Landfill in an American Cultural Context', *The Public Historian,* vol 24, no 3, Summer, pp 17–35 www.jstor.org/stable/10.1525/tph.2002.24.3.17?seq=1#page_scan_tab_contents accesses 08 August 2019.

Minh, H. B. and Mukherji, B. (2008) 'Vietnam and India Curb Rice Exports as Prices Double', Reuters 28 March.

Misch, G. (2015) 'Wastecooking - Make Food, Not Waste' www.idfa.nl/en/film/fe399608-2651-4490-9303-66d0e4f5fffa/wastecooking-make-food-not-waste accessed 14 July 2019.

Nellemann, C. et al (2009) *The Environmental Food Crisis: The Environment's Role in Averting Future Food Crises: A UNEP Rapid Response Assessment.* United Nations, Arendal, Norway www.gwp.org/globalassets/global/toolbox/references/the-environmental-crisis.-the-environments-role-in-averting-future-food-crises-unep-2009.pdf accessed 08 August 2019.

Newsome, R. et al (2014) 'Applications and Perceptions of Date Labeling of Food', *Comprehensive Reviews in Food* Science *and* Food Safety, vol 13, no 4, pp 745–769 www.onlinelibrary.wiley.com/doi/full/10.1111/1541-4337.12086 accessed 08 August 2019.

Pearce, D. W. and Turner, R. K. (1990) *Economics of Natural Resources and the Environment.* Johns Hopkins University Press, Baltimore.

Plumer, B. (2015) 'Map: Here's How Much Each Country Spends on Food', *VOX,* 19 August. www.vox.com/2014/7/6/5874499/map-heres-how-much-every-country-spends-on-food accessed 10 April 2019.

Poppendieck, J. (1998) *Sweet Charity?: Emergency Food and the End of Entitlement.* Viking, New York.

Quested, T. and Johnson, H. (2009) 'Household Food and Drink Waste in the UK', *WRAP,* November. www.wrap.org.uk/content/household-food-and-drink-waste-uk-2009 accessed 28 October 2018.

Rao, D. L. N. (2015) 'The Early History of Scientific Composting', *ResearchGate,* October. www.researchgate.net/publication/283052760_History_of_Composting accessed 16 July 2019.

Ratcliffe, P. et al (2010) 'The Great British Waste Menu', *BBC One* 25 August. www.bbc.co.uk/programmes/b00tkr88 accessed 14 July 2019.

Rathje, W. (1984) 'The Garbage Decade', *American Behavioral Scientist,* vol 28, no 1, September, pp 9–29.

Rathje, W. and Murphy, C. (2001) *Rubbish! the Archaeology of Garbage.* University of Arizona Press, Tucson.

Rees, J. (2013) *Refrigeration Nation: A History of Ice, Appliances, and Enterprise in America.* Johns Hopkins University Press, Baltimore.

Riches, G. (2018) *Food Bank Nations; Poverty, Corporate Charity and the Right to Food.* Routledge, New York.

Salisbury, S. (2016) 'Confused by 'sell-by' and 'use-by'' Food Labels? Changes are on the Way for Meat, Eggs, Dairy Products', *Palm Beach Post,* 15 December. www.protectingyourpocket.blog.palmbeachpost.com/2016/12/15/confused-by-sell-by-and-use-by-food-labels-changes-are-on-the-way-for-meat-eggs-dairy-products/accessed 28 October 2018.

Scientific American (2019) 'Waste Land: Does the Large Amount of Food Discarded in the U.S. Take a Toll on the Environment?', *Scientific American,* 02 May. www.scientificamerican.com/article/earth-talk-waste-land accessed 14 July 2019.

Shepherd, G. (2008) 'World Bank: Biofuels Caused Food Prices to Soar 75%', *Miami New Times,* 19 August. www.miaminewtimes.com/restaurants/world-bank-biofuels-caused-food-prices-to-soar-75-6583214 accessed 14 July 2019.

Shepherd, J. (2016) 'European Commission Date Labelling Study to Combat Food Waste,' *Just-Food,* 05 December. www.just-food.com/news/european-commission-date-labelling-study-to-combat-food-waste_id135166.aspx accessed 10 April 2019.

Shields, R. (2009) 'Kitchen Bin War: Tackling the Food Waste Mountain', *The Independent,* 06 June. www.independent.co.uk/environment/green-living/kitchen-bin-war-tackling-the-food-waste-mountain-1698753.html accessed 28 October 2018.

Shover, J. L. (1965) 'The Farmers' Holiday Association Strike, August 1932', *Agricultural History,* vol 39, no 4, October, pp 196–203.

Smith, A. (2017) *Food and the Environment.* ABC-CLIO, Santa Barbara, California.

Smith, A. (2019) 'Food Waste and Food Recovery Bibliography,' Version 26.

Smithers, R. (2009) 'Minister Calls for Food Date Labels to Be Made Clearer to Reduce Food Waste', *The Guardian*, 09 June. www.theguardian.com/environment/2009/jun/09/food-waste-sell-by-date accessed 28 October 2018.

Spooner, H. (1918) *Wealth from Waste: Elimination of Waste a World Problem*. G. Routledge & Sons, London.

Strasser, S. (2000) *Waste and Want: A Social History of Trash*. Macmillan, New York.

Streitfeld, D. (2008) 'A Global Need for Grain that Farms Can't Fill', *New York Times*, 09 March. www.nytimes.com/2008/03/09/business/worldbusiness/09crop.html accessed 14 July 2019.

Stuart, T. (2009) *Waste: Uncovering the Global Food Scandal*. W. W. Norton, New York.

Sturm, R. and An, R. (2014) 'Obesity and Economic Environments', *CA: A Cancer Journal for Clinicians*, vol 64, 22 May www.onlinelibrary.wiley.com/doi/10.3322/caac.21237/pdf accessed 10 April 2019.

Sydney Morning Herald (2007) 'Italians Stage Pasta Strike', 13 September. www.smh.com.au/world/italians-stage-pasta-strike-20070913-ywn.html accessed 14 July 2019.

Thurn, V. et al (2011) 'Taste the Waste: Warum Schmeissen Wir Unser Essen Auf Den Müll' [Taste the Waste: Why Do We Throw Our Food in the Trash] www.tastethewaste.com/info/film accessed 14 July 2019.

Too Good for the Bin (2012) www.zugutfuerdietonne.de/praktische-helfer/app/ accessed 14 July 2019.

USDA nd 'Nutrient Content of the U.S. Food Supply, 1909-2010', https://www.fns.usda.gov/resource/nutrient-content-us-food-supply-reports accessed 27 September 2019.

Van Garde, S. J. and Woodburn M. J. (1987) 'Food Discard Practices of Householders', *Journal of the American Dietetic Association*, vol 87, March, pp 322–329 www.ncbi.nlm.nih.gov/pubmed/3819252 accessed 08 August 2019.

The Week (2019) 'The Recycling Crisis', *The Week*, 30 March. www.theweek.com/articles/831864/recycling-crisis accessed 05 August 2019.

Wenlock, R. W. et al (1980) 'Household Food Wastage in Britain', *British Journal of Nutrition*, vol 43, no 1, pp 53–70.

Wilson, C. (1991) *Food and Drink in Britain: From the Stone Age to the 19th Century*. Academy Chicago Publishers, Chicago.

Wong, F. (2008) 'Australia Faces Worse, More Frequent Droughts-study', *Reuters*, 06 July. www.reuters.com/article/us-australia-drought/australia-faces-worse-more-frequent-droughts-study-idUSSYD6747620080706 accessed 14 July 2019.

WRAP (2008) *The Food We Waste*. Food Waste Report v2. Banbury, Oxon: Waste and Resources Action Programme, May; revised 05 July, p 209 www.ifr.ac.uk/waste/Reports/WRAP%20The%20Food%20We%20Waste.pdf accessed 28 October 2018.

WRAP (2019) *WRAP and the Circular Economy*, www.wrap.org.uk/about-us/about/wrap-and-circular-economy accessed 05 August 2019.

Wroughton, L. (2008) 'Price Controls on Food are Usually Futile, Economists Warn', *The New Times*, 07 April. www.nytimes.com/2008/04/07/business/../07iht-controls.4.11735373.html accessed 14 July 2019.

3

FOOD WASTE, RELIGION, AND SPIRITUALITY

Jewish, Christian, and Muslim approaches

Tanhum Yoreh and Stephen Bede Scharper

Introduction

To state the obvious, food is essential for all life. Faith traditions, particularly those with a lengthy history, have lived through times of drought, scarcity, and hunger. It is a great challenge to appreciate abundance, until it no longer is; appreciating food is easier when it is lacking. Theological explanations abound when there is scarcity. To address scarcity, legal, ethical, and spiritual discourses have been shaped over the course of millennia. Within these discourses, the importance of food is acknowledged, its presence celebrated, and its consumption regulated. As Anne Vallely (2016, p. 118) cogently frames it, "[food is] the builder of bodies and meaning, it is at the centre of all human cosmologies, ethics and social imaginings". All faiths have an inherent interest in sustainability. If the faithful do not survive, neither does the faith. Discourses of sustainability are most obviously connected to food and water. Without them, life is not possible. In this context it is easy to understand that food waste is considered abhorrent within faith traditions. When sustenance is actively considered a divinely granted blessing, wasting food and drink is not taken lightly.

While waste is a natural and enduring part of the cycle of life, wastefulness takes us into an ethical relationship with how we handle this feature of the life cycle. The Abrahamic traditions all have proscriptions against profligate wastefulness, stemming from their belief in the divine provenance of creation, and all express a concern for the just distribution of the fruits of the Earth. While they do so within the framework of their own traditions, they also possibly resonate with those outside these traditions.

The Abrahamic faiths reflect the desire to enter into relationships of food consumption and provisioning in ways that fall within the sacred covenant among the divine, the human, and the rest of creation. In this sense, they offer a spiritual grounding for responsible approaches to food provisioning, one rooted in a sense of both the common good and a common divine origin that unites all members of the biotic community.

In this chapter, we will address some of the ways in which Judaism, Christianity, and Islam approach issues of wastefulness, noting how in a time of climate chaos, massive ecological destruction, widespread hunger, and searing social and economic disparity, these issues take on new dimensions of urgency. The sections on Judaism and Islam will begin with a discussion of the literature on wastefulness, including primary texts, and continue with examples of how the legal and moral frameworks of food provisioning are put into practice in some communities. The section on Christianity will offer spiritual underpinnings of approaches to food wastefulness, with examples of how these are put into practice.

Judaism

Rabbi taught that a man shall not pour the water out of his cistern so long as others may require it.

(2nd century CE, Babylonian Talmud)

This is the way of the righteous and people of deeds who love peace and delight in the goodness of human beings and draw them near to the Torah; they do not waste even a grain of mustard in this world. Their instinct when encountering wastefulness and destruction is to try to prevent it with all their strength.

(The Book of Moral Education, *529, 13th century*)

"Do not waste anything" is the first and most general call of God, which comes to you, man, when you realize yourself as master of the earth.

(Rabbi Samson Raphael Hirsch, Horeb*, Hirsch, 1838[1968])*

Much has been written on *bal tashhit,* the Jewish prohibition against wastefulness (David, 2000; Nir, 2006; Schwartz, 2001; Shtasman, 1999; Vorhand, 2000; Wolff, 2009; Yoreh, 2019). The most comprehensive work to date which relates to the prohibition through an environmental scope has been written by Tanhum Yoreh (2019) which charts the intellectual history of the conceptualisation of *bal tashhit.* Yoreh argues that *bal tashhit* is more than a mere prohibition but encapsulates a powerful, yet simple environmental ethic: to harm the environment is to harm oneself. While his book focuses on the prohibition as a whole, many of the examples relate to food and drink.

Bal tashhit has its foundations in the book of Deuteronomy (20:19) in the Hebrew Bible. It began as an injunction against cutting down fruit trees during wartime, and later on was expanded by the sages of the Talmud to become a blanket proscription for all forms of wastefulness and destructiveness. Needless to say, especially based on the origins of the prohibition in cutting down fruit trees (Deuteronomy 20:19), *bal tashhit* includes in its scope all forms of wasting food and drink. Though there have been different schools of thought as to how to interpret the verse, one rationale for the prohibition is that human life is dependent on the food and to destroy it is commensurate to destroying oneself.

Some have cast doubt as to how relevant the prohibition is for combating contemporary environmental issues (Nir, 2006; Schwartz, 2001; Waskow, 2013). Nevertheless, Yoreh (2010) demonstrated that among Ultra-Orthodox communities, food is perhaps the most significant area in which *bal tashhit* is practised. In addition to falling under the prohibition against wastefulness, food and drink hold an elevated status, and causing them to be wasted is also considered to fall under the category of *bizui okhalin,* literally translated as contempt of foodstuff. When walking through Ultra-Orthodox neighbourhoods in Jerusalem, one often sees bread in various stages of decomposition on ledges and walls, because throwing the bread directly into the garbage is considered in these communities to be contemptuous of food.

In traditional Jewish thought, sustenance is considered to be divinely bestowed and one can only truly acquire food or beverage through the act of reciting a blessing over it. The recitation of the blessing is an acknowledgement of the dependence of humans on divine providence to ensure that life is continuously sustained; without food and drink there is no life, without providence there is no food or drink. Thus, not offering a blessing is akin to stealing what is given freely (Babylonian Talmud, *Berakhot* 35b). Wasting what has been received as a gift is a double affront: it is contemptuous of the food and of the divine.

Rabbi Zalman Schachter-Shalomi, one of the founders of the Jewish Renewal movement, coined the term eco-kosher. The Jewish dietary laws, known as *kashrut*, distinguish between what is permissible to eat (i.e. kosher) and what is not. Traditionally, these laws relate to the kind of animals a Jew is permitted to eat, the necessary guidelines that must be followed in the killing of permissible animals, and the separation of meat and dairy. Schachter-Shalomi was inclined to include contemporary notions of eating, consuming, and living in an ethical manner within a reconceptualised framework of *kashrut*. Within the eco-kosher system, food produced, consumed, or disposed of in a wasteful manner with a relatively high environmental impact would not be considered eco-kosher, even if from a traditional perspective it may be considered kosher (Waskow, 1992).

Faith in practice around wastefulness

One of the core themes for Hazon – The Jewish Lab for Sustainability, the umbrella Jewish environmental organisation in the United States and Canada – is food.[1] Hazon operates three programmes that specifically target food-related concerns – Teva (the Hebrew word for nature), Adamah (the Hebrew word for earth), and JOFEE (Jewish Outdoor Food/Farming and Environmental Education). Each of these programmes, with its own focus and target communities, highlights issues of food justice and sustainability through a Jewish lens. The film *Renewal* (Marty Ostrow & Terry Kay Rockefeller, 2007) provides a window into how faith-based environmentalism is put into practice by different faith communities, and offers a glimpse into the early days of the Teva programme. Teva's programming is geared toward children and youth and was designed with the aim of "helping students develop a more meaningful relationship with nature, and deepen their own connection to Jewish practices and traditions" (Hazon, n.d.). These include a commitment to *tikkun olam* (in this context, "repairing the world") and food sustainability. The short film depicts how the children weigh the collective leftovers on their plates at the end of each meal during their stay on the campgrounds. In the dining hall is a sign that reads *bal tashḥit*, reminding visitors to reduce their waste. After a few days on the programme, the children are empowered with knowledge and a sense of responsibility, and their food waste decreases substantially. The aim is for the children to take the values learned during the programme back to their daily lives at home in the city.

There has also been growing concern about food systems in Jewish communities. An increasing number of communities centralised around places of worship are taking action to reduce food waste. For instance, in 2010 the First Narayever Congregation, a traditional egalitarian community in Toronto, created a food policy for food served in the social hall at the synagogue.[2] The policy addresses food waste on multiple levels. In addition to opting for wholesome, non-processed foods, the policy calls for local, seasonal, fair-trade, and organic products. The synagogue does not serve any meat, and the animal products it does use must be produced with animal welfare in mind. The policy calls upon guests to minimise their food waste when filling their reusable plates, compost and recycle where possible, and donate surplus food to those in need. At its core, the Narayever's commitment to minimise waste and raise awareness about social, environmental, and health issues surrounding food is part of the synagogue's mission to engage in raising social awareness, and the Jewish value of *tikkun olam*.[3]

Christianity

When they had all had enough to eat, [Jesus] said to his disciples, "Gather the pieces that are left over. Let nothing be wasted."

(John 6:12)

Whenever food is thrown out it is as if it were stolen from the table of the poor, from the hungry!

(Pope Francis, 2013)

At a small Christian College in Toronto, Canada, the chaplain each week collects unused food from the college's food services and distributes it to hungry persons throughout the city.

In Alabama, USA, a Christian mother posts a regular blog focusing on food waste and her Christian faith for the Evangelical Environmental Network, providing statistics on food waste in the US, as well as tips on how not to waste food, including buying local, using smaller plates, and designating "weigh your own food waste" weeks on a regular basis.

In November 2018, members from 24 different congregations in Edinburgh and Glasgow participated in a Zero Waste workshop, organised by Eco-congregation Scotland. With workshops on "Love Food Hate Waste" and "Love Your Clothes", congregants learned about how food waste and the clothing industry significantly contribute to climate change, and reviewed some practical steps to reduce their environmental impact through waste reduction. They are now sharing these insights with their congregations across Scotland.

These are but a few examples of Christian communities who are linking food waste in pragmatic ways with a dual concern for the hungry and the planet.

Many Christians in North America recall their mother's prodding to "eat your peas" because there were people starving around the world, a familial linking of the food on comparatively affluent tables and the Christian demand to feed the hungry. This nexus is now being forged by established Christian groups around the world and expanded to include a deep concern over environmental destruction.

One such initiative is Food Waste Weekend, launched in the US in 2016 to help Christian and other faith communities shift their focus away from "feeding the hungry" to "ending hunger", partly through eliminating food waste. Linking up with AmpleHarvest.org, a non-profit which seeks to diminish food waste and hunger in the US, Food Waste Weekend provides sample sermons and "calls to action" for Christian clergy and their congregations, including tips on properly storing food to prevent spoiling and donating food from local gardens. As one of the sample sermons for the weekend reads:[4]

> Our faith teaches us that no one should be hungry and that we are supposed to help those who are. Jesus taught us that when we feed a hungry person, we are feeding him (Matthew 25:35–40). Our faith teaches us that we are stewards of God's good creation, responsible for caring for this remarkable gift. The book of Genesis – the very first book of the Bible – teaches that God put us in the Garden to work it, watch over it and protect it (Gen. 2:15). This weekend, these two concerns come together. We know that people in our country, and around the world, go hungry. That there are hungry families in our country, in our community, and quite possibly, even in our congregation. Around the world, over 800 million people suffer from hunger each day and 21,000 people die daily from hunger (one person every four seconds) – despite

the fact that it is well documented that there is more than enough food produced – healthy food, mind you – to feed everyone in the world. How is it that in a world so blessed with abundant food, so many can't count on this most basic blessing?

The text goes on to talk not only about perfectly fine but misshapen fruits and vegetables, or improperly refrigerated food, that ends up in the dumpster, but also the water, fuel, and electricity used to grow those items that is also wasted when such food items are tossed.

The sermon concludes: "We are blessed with food and should not be wasting that blessing. Ever. For the sake of hungry people. For the sake of our planet."

For many Christians, however, there is a sacramental prohibition against wastefulness that marks every celebration of the Eucharistic meal, a remembrance of Jesus' Last Supper with his disciples. For a number of Christian denominations, the bread and wine used at the altar during Communion celebrations are transformed into the "real presence" of Christ through the Christian ritual.

In certain communities, such as the Roman Catholic Church, the bread and wine are actually, it is believed, transformed into the body and blood of Christ through the Mass; hence, there is no wasting of the sacred bread and wine after Communion.[5] Celebrants carefully consume the last drops of consecrated wine and bread, and servers carefully clean the chalices and patens which hold the consecrated bread and wine. Traditionally, these utensils are cleaned in a special sink, with a direct conduit to the ground so that vestiges of the consecrated Eucharistic offering do not find their way into the sewage system.

In light of our contemporary awareness of both the sacredness of all creation, and the irresponsible wastefulness of its fruits, might there be an invitation to the Christian community to reflect on a spirituality of respectfully using God's precious gifts to us beyond the Eucharistic meal? Might there be room to reflect upon the wider sanctity of all life, and hence a deeper reverential care for its use?

Islam

It is He who produces both trellised and untrellised gardens, date palms, plants with different fruits, the olive, the pomegranate, alike and not alike. So when they bear fruit, eat some of it, paying what is due on the day of harvest, but do not be wasteful: God does not like wasteful people.

(The Qur'an 6:141)

The Prophet came upon Sa'd when he was performing ablution and asked, "What is the meaning of this extravagance, Sa'd?" He replied, "Is there extravagance in ablution?" He said, "Yes, even if you are beside a flowing river."

(Mishkat al-Masabih, 1340 CE)

Unlike the Hebrew Bible and New Testament, in which there is a dearth of explicit material relating to wastefulness, there is an abundance of such sources in the Qur'an. Depending on the translation to English, references to waste or associated terminology occur up to 50 times. It should, therefore, come as no surprise that the literature on Islam and Environment is replete with references to the Qur'anic verses and *hadīth* literature dealing with wastefulness (for example, see Dien, 2000; Kamali, 2012; Llewellyn, 2003; Ozdemir, 2003). What is gained in breadth, however, is somewhat lost in depth, as there are yet to appear studies that focus solely on Islamic conceptualisations of wastefulness.

The Arabic terminology associated with wastefulness is *isrāf* and *tabdhīr*. *Isrāf* means waste or excessiveness, while *tabdhīr* means extravagance. Muhammad Hashim Kamali (2012, p. 273) teases out some of the nuances of the terminology:

> Although Qur'ān and *hadīth* use these two Arabic words synonymously, a technical distinction has been drawn between them. *Isrāf* signifies extravagance and wasteful use of what is otherwise permissible. *Tabdhīr* on the other hand is spending on that which is unlawful in the first place.

Kamali continues this line of thought: "Thus one who exceeds the limits of moderation in what is lawful to him is a prodigal (*musrif*), such as one who consumes food to excess, or uses water wastefully even if for purposes of cleanliness and ablution." Tammara Soma (2016), in her ethnographic study on food waste in Indonesia, notes that many of her respondents used the Indonesian term *mubazir*, loosely translated as wasteful, as an Islamic value that influenced their approaches to preventing food waste.

Writing in reference to the *hadīth* mentioned above in which Sa'd is admonished for excessive use of water, Ibrahim Ozdemir (2003, p. 15) writes:

> If then ... it is ... "detestable" to use water from a river in excess while performing ablutions, and it was prohibited by the Prophet, how much stronger is the proscription on being wasteful and extravagant in those matters in which the above statements are not applicable?

Ozdemir is referring to the context of abundance in the *hadīth*. If excessiveness is prohibited in contexts of plenty, then it is *a fortiori* prohibited during contexts of scarcity. Othman Llewellyn is also a proponent of the *a fortiori* approach taken by Ozdemir. He writes:

> That the prohibition of extravagance applies in small matters as well as large, and in times of abundance as well as scarcity, was emphasized by the prophet Muhammad, upon him be peace and the blessing of God, when he forbade that a person waste water even in washing for prayer beside a flowing river.
>
> *(2003, p. 199)*

One of the great challenges with legal and ethical frameworks is the vagueness of definitions. Even though traditional Islam clearly frowns upon acts of wastefulness, what does it mean to be wasteful? Within the scope of Islamic environmentalism, Mawil Izzi Dien offers a useful definition: "wastage is deemed to be using anything improperly and without due consideration of its inherent value. The value of any object should be judged by the purpose for which it was created" (2000, p. 32). For many, food and water, the substances that sustain life, would be considered to have substantial inherent value.

Action

The focus on wastefulness in general and food waste specifically is central in Islamic environmental activism.

Ibrahim Abdul-Matin is a strong proponent of living as a Muslim in an environmentally responsible manner. In his book *Green Deen*, which means "green path", he spells out how to engage in a socially and environmentally conscious manner within an Islamic framework.

His book covers key aspects of life, and has a considerable section dedicated to food production and consumption. His chapters on food deal less with the issue of food waste and focus more on the environmental and social impact of food choices. He also brings up the issue of wasting water in the process of performing ablutions, asking readers what their *wudu* (ablution) number is; in other words, how much water they use while performing ablutions. This is meant to get adherents to be mindful of the water they use, a clear reference to the *ḥadīth* above.

The contrast between fasting and feasting is central to the month of Ramadan. Wastefulness during Iftar, the evening meal after a day of fasting during the month of Ramadan, has been a key issue for environmentally mindful Muslims. After sunset, Muslims will often gather in mosques, community centres, restaurants, or family homes to break the fast together. After a day of fasting, ingesting a big meal is physically challenging as the stomach shrinks during lengthy periods of inactivity. The availability of large quantities of food can lead people to put more on their plates than they can actually eat, resulting in large amounts of food being wasted. This is noticeable on both community and city scales. According to Jeanne Bedard writing for EcoMENA, a prominent environmental organisation operating in the Middle East, almost a quarter of all food prepared during Ramadan is wasted (Bedard, 2017). Surprisingly, more food is wasted during the month of Ramadan than during the rest of the year, despite the fact that one fewer meal is eaten during the day. Rehan Ahmad citing the Qur'anic teaching of not wasting through excess (6:141) argues that "the act of throwing away food during Ramadan is a complete contradiction to the philosophy behind fasting", encouraging a rethinking of how food is consumed during Iftar (Ahmad, 2018).

Initiatives to reduce wastefulness during Ramadan continue to move forward, as municipalities in Muslim majority countries, particularly in the Middle East, are working hard to ensure that waste management systems are in place so that, at the very least, less food is reaching landfills. Action is also being taken in Muslim communities around the globe. For instance, the environmental group Green Muslims based in Washington DC has issued guidelines on how to host a zero-waste Iftar (Strom, 2010). In the United Kingdom, the Islamic Foundation for Ecology and Environmental Sciences has taken to social media with a campaign called #plasticfreeiftar, aimed at eliminating the use of disposable dishes during Iftar (IFEES, n.d.). In the Greater Toronto Area, the Eco-Board of the Jaffari Community Centre has focused the majority of their efforts in mitigating food and associated waste during communal gatherings. Their campaign #BAM, "Bring A Mug", asks community members to bring a mug to mosque during the month of Ramadan, and is meant to eliminate the use of disposables and reduce overall waste.[6]

Conclusion

There is growing recognition of the role faith communities can play to achieve environmental goals. Faith communities and religious institutions have the necessary components to make an enormous positive impact. Faith groups have the moral imperative to act, they often have economic clout, and social and political capital (Veldman, Szasz, & Haluza-DeLay, 2014). This is not to say that barriers do not exist; rather, positive change is well within the scope of faith communities. The examples in this chapter are a clear indication that much is being done at the communal and organisational levels to mitigate food waste. This was not lost on the Environmental Protection Agency (EPA) in the United States, who in 2016 joined forces with faith communities across the USA to be part of the EPA's goal to reduce food waste by 50 per cent by the year 2030 (Godoy, 2016). Combating food waste is also an important area for bi-partisan cooperation. Regardless of political stances on climate change or environmentalism, minimising food waste is a cause that everyone can rally around.

It is important to note that while mitigating food waste is noble, and simultaneously feeding the hungry is doubly so, these efforts do not address the core causes of poverty and food waste. In fact, feeding the hungry with leftover, unwanted food has been critiqued as undignified, and ineffective at addressing the root causes of hunger. There are severe social stigmas associated with relying on food banks (Fisher, 2017). As we have demonstrated, there are significant efforts being undertaken in all three Abrahamic faiths to mitigate food waste through the distribution of leftovers to the hungry. Jewish, Christian, and Muslim sources, however, also relate to the importance of eliminating poverty over alleviating its symptoms. For instance, Maimonides, one of history's most prolific Jewish scholars (12th century, Egypt) wrote in his Laws of Charity (10:7) that the highest level of charitable giving is that which enables its recipient to no longer be reliant on charity; in other words, charity that ends poverty. A similar sentiment can be found in Islamic teachings about *sadaqah* (voluntary charitable giving). The highest form of charitable giving in Islam is *sadaqah jariyah* (recurring charity) (*Ṣaḥīḥ Muslim*, The Book of Bequests 3, 14-(1631), 9th century). *Sadaqah jariyah* provides its recipients with the tools to improve their life circumstances, such as funding educational facilities or putting children through school. In the Christian tradition, the notion of the social gospel, originating in the late 19th century, articulated the notion of "social" sin as well as personal sin, and advocated a Christian vocation to justice as well as charity. This understanding was also echoed in Catholic social teaching, beginning with Pope Leo XIII's *Rerum Novarum* (1891), continued in liberation theology of Latin America, and succinctly encapsulated in the "Justice in the World" statement (1971) of the world Synod of Bishops, which states that "action on behalf of justice ... appear[s] to us as a constitutive dimension of the preaching of the gospel".

The examples presented here are, of course, only rudimentary, and invite further reflection. On the one hand it is simple to find multiple examples from each faith tradition on food waste mitigation efforts. On the other hand, these efforts are not nearly as widespread or organised as they could be, and much work needs to be done to continue efforts to reduce wastage. What is abundantly clear, however, is that faith communities have a strong moral imperative to reduce food waste, and can offer hopeful avenues and models for mitigating waste and simultaneously addressing social justice issues.

Acknowledgement

Stephen Bede Scharper is grateful for the research assistance provided by Ms. Sharika Khan in the preparation of this chapter

Notes

1 Hazon Jewish Lab for Sustainability (https://hazon.org/)
2 Narayever Congregation (www.narayever.ca/food-kiddush).
3 *Tikkun Olam* (www.narayever.ca/mission-statement).
4 Sermon (http://foodwasteweekend.org/iamchristian).
5 During Roman Catholic Mass, for example, in the celebration of the Eucharist, Christ becomes actually present in a sacramental way in the consecrated bread and wine used at Communion. Through the celebration of the Eucharist led by the celebrant, the consecrated bread and wine are first consumed by the priest and then shared with the entire community.
6 Bring a Mug Campaign, Jaffari Eco-Board (www.jaffari.org/eco/)

Bibliography

Abdul-Matin, I. (2010). *Green Deen: What Islam Teaches About Protecting the Planet*. San Francisco, CA: Berrett-Koehler Publishers, Inc.

Ahmad, R. (July 12, 2018). Towards a Waste-Free Ramadan Iftar. Retrieved from www.ecomena.org/waste-free-ramadan-iftar/

Bedard, J. (June 4, 2017). Food Waste in Ramadan: An Infographic. www.ecomena.org/food-waste-ramadan-infographic/

Chavel, H. D. (Ed.). (1952). *Sefer HaḤinukh [The Book of Moral Education]*. Jerusalem, Israel: Mossad HaRav Kook. Original work 13th century.

David, S. T. (2000). *Sefer al Pakkim Qetanim: Hilkhot Bal Tashḥit [The Book of Small Flasks: The Laws of the Prohibition Against Wastefulness]*. Jaffa, Israel: S. M. Publishers.

Dien, M. I. (2000). *The Environmental Dimensions of Islam*. Cambridge, UK: The Lutterworth Press.

Epstein, I. (Ed.). (1961). *The Babylonian Talmud*. London, UK: Soncino Press.

Fisher, A. (2017). *Big Hunger: The Unholy Alliance Between Corporate America and Anti-Hunger Groups*. Cambridge, MA: MIT Press.

Food and Kiddush Guidelines. (n.d.). www.narayever.ca/food-kiddush

Francis. (June 5, 2013). General Audience. http://w2.vatican.va/content/francesco/en/audiences/2013/documents/papa-francesco_20130605_udienza-generale.html

Godoy, M. (January 18, 2016). Thou Shalt Not Toss Food: Enlisting Religious Groups to Fight Waste. www.npr.org/sections/thesalt/2016/01/18/463109192/thou-shalt-not-toss-food-enlisting-religious-groups-to-fight-waste

Haleem, M. A. S. A. (Trans.) (2004). *The Qur'an*. New York, NY: Oxford University Press.

Hazon, The Jewish Lab for Sustainability. (n.d.). https://hazon.org/

Hirsch, S. R. (1838 [1968]). *Horeb: A Philosophy of Jewish Laws and Observances – Volume Two* (2nd Edition). translated by I. Grunfeld. London: The Soncino Press.

Ibn Al Hajjaj, M. (2012) *Ṣaḥīḥ Muslim: The Authentic Hadiths of Muslim*. (M. M. Al-Šarif, Trans.). Beirut, Lebanon: Dar Al-Kotob Al-Ilmiyah. (Original work 9th century).

IFEES. (nd). Plastic Free Iftar. www.ifees.org.uk/plasticfreeiftar/

Jaffari Eco Board. (n.d.). www.jaffari.org/eco/

Kamali, M. H. (2012). Environmental Care in Islamic Teaching. *Islam and Civilisational Renewal 3*(2), 261–283.

Khatib Al-Tabrizi, M. (1960). *Mishkat Al-Masabih [A Niche for Lamps]*. Book 3. (J. Robson, Trans.). Lahore, Pakistan: Sh. Muhammad Ashraf Press. (Original work 14th century).

Llewellyn, O. A. (2003). The Basis for a Discipline of Islamic Environmental Law. In R. C. Foltz, F. M. Denny, & A. Baharuddin (Eds.), *Islam and Ecology: A Bestowed Trust* (pp. 185–247). Cambridge, MA: Harvard University Press.

Maimonides, M. (1979). *The Code of Maimonides. Book Seven. The Book of Agriculture*. (I. Klein, Trans.). New Haven, CT: Yale University Press. (Original work 12th century).

Mission Statement. (n.d.). www.narayever.ca/mission-statement

Nir, D. (2006). A Critical Examination of the Jewish Environmental Law of *Bal Tashchit*. *Georgetown International Environmental Law Review 18*(2), 335–353.

Ostrow, M. & Rockefeller, T. K. (Producers and Directors). (2007). *Renewal [Documentary]*. Cambridge, MA: Fine Cut Productions in association with the Center for Independent Documentary.

Ozdemir, I. (2003). Toward an Understanding of Environmental Ethics from a Qur'anic Perspective. In R. C. Foltz, F. M. Denny, & A. Baharuddin (Eds.), *Islam and Ecology: A Bestowed Trust* (pp. 3–37). Cambridge, MA: Harvard University Press.

Schwartz, E. (2001). *Bal Tashchit*: A Jewish Environmental Precept. In M. D. Yaffe (Ed.), *Judaism and Environmental Ethics: A Reader* (pp. 230–249). New York, NY: Lexington Books.

Shtasman, Y. E. (1999). *Sefer Etz HaSadeh: BeDinei Bal Tashḥit, Qetzitzat Ilanot UVizui Okhalin [The Book of the Tree of the Field: The Laws of the Prohibition Against Wastefulness, Cutting Down Fruit Trees, and the Contempt of Food]*. Jerusalem, Israel: The Foundation for the Advancement of Torah Study.

Soma, T. (2016). The Tale of the Crying Rice: The Role of Unpaid Foodwork and Learning in Food Waste Prevention and Reduction in Indonesian Households. In J. Sumner (Ed.), *Learning, Food, and Sustainability: Sites for Resistance and Change* (pp. 19–34). New York, NY: Palgrave Macmillan.

Strom, R. (2010). Green Iftars: A How-to Guide. http://greenmuslims.org/DCGM%20Green%20Iftar%20Guide.pdf

Teva. (n.d.). https://hazon.org/teva/

Vallely, A. (2016). Food and Religion. *Religious Studies and Theology 35*(2), 117–122.

The Holy Bible: New International Version Containing the Old Testament, and the New Testament. (1978). London, UK: Hodder and Stoughton.

Veldman, R. G., Szasz, A. & Haluza-DeLay, R. (2014). Social Science, Religions, and Climate Change. In R. G. Veldman, A. Szasz, & R. Haluza-DeLay (Eds.), *How the Wold's Religions Are Responding to Climate Change: Social Scientific Investigations* (pp. 3–19). New York, NY: Routledge.

Vorhand, M. Y. (2000). *Sefer Birkat HaShem: Leqet Dinei Issur Qetzitzat Ilanei Ma'akhal, Bal Tashḥit BiShe'ar Devarim, VeIssur Hefsed UVizui Okhalim [The Book of the Blessing of God: A Collection on the Prohibition Against Cutting Down Fruit Trees, the Prohibition Against Wastefulness, and the Prohibition Against Wasting and Degrading Food].* Jerusalem, Israel: private printing.

Waskow, A. (1992). What is Eco Kosher? *Jewish Quarterly 39*(4), 5–10.

Waskow, A. (2013). Jewish Environmental Ethics: Intertwining *Adam* with *Adamah.* In E. N. Dorff & J. K. Crane (Eds.), *The Oxford Handbook of Jewish Ethics and Morality* (pp. 401–418). New York, NY: Oxford University Press.

Wolff, A. (2009) *Bal Tashchit: The Jewish Prohibition Against Needless Destruction.* Ph.D. Dissertation, Leiden University.

Yoreh, T. (2010). Ultra-Orthodox Recycling Narratives: Implications for Planning and Policy. *Journal of Enterprising Communities: People and Places in the Global Economy 4*(4), 323–345.

Yoreh, T. (2019). *Waste Not: A Jewish Environmental Ethic.* Albany, NY: State University of New York Press.

4

INTERROGATING WASTE

Vastogenic regimes in the 21st century

Jon Cloke

Introduction

This chapter builds on two previous pieces (Cloke 2013, 2016) in which the author trialled the concept of vastogenesis, the premise that waste-generation should not be read as an unfortunate side-effect of consumer capitalism which is susceptible to a technological or organizational fix, but as a core, essential component of mass consumption. The operationalization of vastogenesis by various corporate actors increases the profitability of the consumer regime in which it is present, be it (for example) food, clothing or electronics. From the original idea the author loosely outlined the idea of vastogenic regimes ('waste producing, waste dominated and profiting from waste'; Cloke 2013: 628), based on previous work describing a 'Third Agro-Food Order' (Pistorius and van Wijk 1999: 51), a 'neoliberal food regime' (Pechlaner and Otero 2008, 2) and a 'corporate food regime' (McMichael 2009: 285).[1]

As globalizing capitalism in the 21st century has led to increased sectoral concentration across consumer goods in which groups of hegemons dominate globally in wholesale/retail goods, so vastogenesis has increased as a critical mechanism of profitability; in the case of food, vastogenic mechanisms connect global zones of mass food production to zones of mass consumption through reflexive production, distribution and transport systems. The core purpose of this chapter is to deconstruct the idea of waste-as-waste, proposing instead that the commodification of waste turns it into a proxy exchange value through (a) the value of the waste itself, but more importantly (b) as a mechanism for speeding up consumption and the throughflow of mass-consumed materials.

Using the UK as a case study, this chapter explores the conceptual territory of waste and how a growth in vastogenesis is intensified by sectoral concentration in and across globalizing capitalism. Contractual domination, sub-contracting and monopsonist practices (for example) by global food TNCs are all means by which waste and food production are locked into carefully controlled food production regimes which greatly enhance through-flow and profitability, as the ability to control commodity and food prices at the bottom of the food production chain is complemented by control over sale prices in zones of food consumption through food abundance.

The chapter will also examine the role of appetite creation as one of the driving forces of vastogenesis. Far from being mere suppliers of necessary foodstuffs and responders to demand, food wholesale/retail hegemons are actively involved in the creation of consumer demand through constant expansion of food ranges and through attempts to capture market share by appeals to the symbolism of sophistication, the exotic and modernity that sell a globalist, cosmopolitan diet in zones of mass food consumption.

The food waste paradox

Global food production and food waste are beset by paradox – although global agricultural production matched the doubling of the world's population between 1961 and 2007 and was 'sufficient to feed not only the current population but projected increases to 2050 (OECD 2009; Nature 2010[2])' (Cloke 2013: 625), by 2016 according to the UN Food and Agriculture Organization (FAO) roughly 10.7% of the world's population was still suffering from 'chronic undernourishment'.[2] Additionally, one-third of that increase in agricultural production was wasted, even though material estimates of current global food waste would feed the undernourished four times over.[3] How to explain over-production, waste and mass consumption alongside undernourishment and early death, a world in which 41 million children under the age of five were overweight or obese in 2016[4] and in which simultaneously a third of child deaths every year are caused by malnutrition?[5]

Current official interpretations of food security and food waste leave systemic, regime-induced factors out of the picture, failing completely to depict the internal mechanisms through which such regimes enhance profitability through waste. Rather than looking at the complex systems of power and control that produce these social paradoxes, where the particular issue of waste is concerned they concentrate on narrow technical and scalar issues, reifying waste as an unfortunate systemic side-effect. Institutions such as the FAO continue to address the contradictions of massive over-production, massive waste and coexisting undernourishment and obesity through the optics of enhanced technical efficiency, increased productivity, increased use of genetically modified organisms (GMOs) and a range of security strategies aimed at individual households, local and national governments.[6] What is lacking from such analyses is any understanding of corporate food regimes (McMichael 2009) and their systemicity.

Despite the invisibilization of corporate systemicity and its related biopolitics[7] in official writing on food production, food security and food waste, there is an extensive literature of academic takes on food security and food production problematizing these global food regimes. From the suggestion of a third agro-food order (Pistorius and van Wijk 1999) to Nally's 'historically new modality of biopower' (2011: 44), various authors have moved the totality of food production issues toward what is suggested here is a form of 'new materialism' (Coole and Frost 2010) about which 'primarily textual accounts are insufficient for an adequate understanding of the complex and dynamic interplay of meaning and matter' (Lemke 2015: 3).

Explaining the food waste paradox therefore is not just a question of systemic analysis but of interrogating the signifier 'waste' (in this case food waste[8]), what is signified by it and the hegemonic regimes that produce it. Having introduced the idea of vastogenic systems – put simply, biopolitical systems produced of and for waste (Cloke 2013, 2016) – the author now seeks to push the interrogation further by deconstructing waste-as-*doxa* – Bourdieu's (1977) concept of something so generally accepted that it 'goes without saying because it comes without saying'.[9] Waste needs to be explicated as a form of biopolitical power, as a social relationship rendering it both co-constitutive of and interdependent with value – food (indeed all consumer products) in this view is more than just a vehicle for waste – the potential for waste in food products and the waste involved in producing them is part of their value.

The practice of knowledge about waste, therefore, dovetails with Foucault's practices of knowledge produced through relationships of power (Peters 2007: 166), but the relationships of power here are not specifically those of the sovereign state, but those of a state/corporate/consumer hybrid. The state/corporate biopolitics concerned are in addition not focused on the 'population' but on 'consumer/consumption', which acts to re-focus Foucault's 'specific knowledges and techniques' (Foucault 1989: 106). The biopower of vastogenic systems and how waste is interpreted through them is 'intimately linked to the constitution and transformation of human bodies and human life', defining a 'set of mechanisms through which the basic biological features of the human species became the object of a political strategy' (Foucault 2007: 1, cited in Lemke 2015: 7). To put it another way, in this take the key biopolitical mechanisms through which biopower is expressed in 21st-century capitalism are not those of the state – the state has been suborned by a complex mixture of multi-scalar organizations, relationships and mechanisms under corporate regimes which control the fundamental biological mechanisms underpinning human existence – food, water, air (through pollution/non-pollution) and health.

Getting to know waste

As the systemicity of food waste has changed over time and what is perceived as food waste has greatly increased, so definitions of waste have also changed to try to incorporate the ways in which the official *doxa*, waste, is enacted. Despite the changes in definition over time, one constant can be detected, an all-absorbing focus on the 'discarding' of materials, from 'Wholesome edible material intended for human consumption, arising at any point in the food supply chain (FSC) that is instead discarded, lost, degraded or consumed by pests' (FAO 1981) to 'Food waste is part of food loss and refers to discarding or alternative (non-food) use of food that is safe and nutritious for human consumption along the entire food supply chain, from primary production to end household consumer level' (FAO 2014).[10]

Focusing on the materiality of waste as 'any substance or object the holder discards, intends to discard or is required to discard'[11] first makes the mistake of treating waste 'as abstraction rather than as always existing in a concrete materiality and in concrete social relationships'(Gille 2010: 1053), and second, it detaches waste from value. As Gille points out, in fact 'without waste there is no value' (2013: 28); not only that, but as the changes in official definitions illustrate, try as we might to reify the concept of waste, definitions keep changing, not just because the physical content is changing, but because changes in type, volume and location are created in the first place by the changing reality of waste as a social relationship.

The themes of vastogenic social relationships and value add another dimension to an older literature on consumer citizenship (see, for instance, Gabriel and Lang 1995), where waste is a constitutive part of the value of consumption and therefore a mediating mechanism for the establishment of value. Returning to the biopolitics of waste, the social relationships that determine waste, value and consumption are increasingly critical components of the 'government of things' which 'takes into account the interrelatedness and entanglements of men and things, the natural and the artificial, the physical and the moral' (Lemke 2015: 3); vastogenesis is central to the interrelatedness of people and things and therefore the governmentality of corporatized global capitalism.

Reconsidering a new 'epistemological, ontological and political status of materiality' (Lemke 2015: 3–4) in global food production regimes brings the observer to the inescapable conclusion that the distinction between 'edible' and 'waste' food is a false binary – what matters in vastogenic systems is accelerated throughflow of material, and the only difference between food and waste is the different processes the systemic material goes through in order to create co-constitutive forms of value for the system – food system material is 'active, forceful and plural rather than passive, inactive and unitary' (Lemke 2015). That active role is directly related to the profitability of the system, '[p]rofitability is contingent upon unit sales: the imperative is throughput' (Sage 2013: 4). The food/waste dyad is an 'active object' through which the profit-focused biopower of corporate food regimes is mediated.

Systemic practices of food/waste: the UK

The reflections in the previous section invite us to consider the shape and extent of the *dispositive*,[12] the apparatus of the food/waste vastogenic system and what is included among the mechanisms through which biopower is exercised. Accepting food production regimes as mechanisms for vastogenic biopolitics liberates the observer from the narrow, highly restrictive diktat of 'waste-as-waste' and invites a far more extensive examination of the apparatus of 'waste-as-value'. Examining some (but by no means all) of the key elements in the development of how food production regimes have developed in the UK as a case study, allows us to look at the lived reality of vastogenic territory and to interrogate how food/waste is practically expressed and what its components are.

The governmentality of waste in the UK

At the time of writing, there are four overriding pieces of legislation guiding the regulation of food products in the UK: (1) the Food Safety Act 1990, the framework for food legislation which creates offences relating to safety, quality and labelling; (2) the General Food Law Regulation (EC) No. 178/2002 on principles and requirements of food law across Europe; (3) the Food Safety and Hygiene (England) Regulations 2013, which deal with enforcement and penalties for infringement, and (4) the European Communities Act 1972, which brought European food laws into UK legislation. These micro-manage every aspect of any business, non-profit or profit, and 'any undertaking or activity carried on by a public or local authority ... in relation to any food or contact material' in an exhaustive list of food-based activities, including:

> selling, possessing for sale and offering, exposing or advertising for sale; consigning, delivering or serving by way of sale; preparing for sale or presenting, labelling or wrapping for the purpose of sale; storing or transporting for the purpose of sale; importing and exporting.[13]

Underneath these food safety macro-structures are thousands more covering the nature of the food product, ingredients, nutritional information, medicinal/nutritional claims, production and sale dates, storage conditions, product business and address details, origin, instructions for use, presentation, batch identifiers, sectioning (which information must be in the same place), standard specifications, additives and allergens. Irrespective of the function of these regulations in determining the quality of the food, breaches of these regulations transsubstantiates[14] food, through inspection or through self-selection by vendors or consumers.

Under these prescriptive, discursive legal structures that act to delineate the food/waste interface are thousands more regulations governing food quality standards, developed over decades. The Commission Implementing Regulation (EU) No. 543/2011, for instance, contains marketing standards for apples inside the EU which set out the minimum requirements for apples sold within the EU, but this is just the start – the regulation sets out in minute detail the colouration of an apple necessary to be sold in particular classes of apples (see Table 4.1).

The regulation goes on to specify weights, numbers per box and also provides a substantial table of apple varieties which are classified according to the types above and which therefore have the appropriate colouration standards applied depending on the variety.

These laws and regulations are discursive mechanisms that strictly shape the 'sociomaterial assemblages, or collectives' of the food/waste hybrid. Adherence to these diktats[15] decides not just whether individual products or categories in the throughflow of material are sold in a shop or rejected for sale and end up in a landfill. What these laws, regulations and standards also accomplish is not only the acceleration of flows, but the determination of how each flow is 'transformed, not just in terms of its function and value, but also as material, as it traverses networks and flows' (Gille 2010: 1049–1050).

The final discursive mechanism negotiated by the food/waste hybrid before arrival (or not) in the household are the array of 'use by' and 'best before' dates which structure both retailer and consumer deployment of food products. In the UK, 'use by' and 'best before' dates are a legal requirement under Regulation (EU) No. 1169/2011 and the Food Information Regulations 2014 (FIR) and, although they are precautionary indicators having no basis in the food quality of the product, are persuasive signals that influence food consumers to choose whether to consume the product or not. The EU calculates that some 10% of food products that end up in landfill unnecessarily each year is created by date marking,[16] irrespective of the edibility, safety and nutritional value of the product.

The sociotechnical waste *dispositif*

The vast array of actors, actants[17] and sociotechnical agencements[18] involved in global food production regimes are intimately intermingled with and expressive of the built environment, as much as in the technical innovations and innovative social practices of material flows. Neither is correlation and causation between the social, technical and physical

Table 4.1 Extra Class from Regulation (EU) No. 543/2011

Extra Class from Regulation (EU) No. 543/2011

Apples in this class must be of superior quality. They must be characteristic of the variety and with the stalk which must be intact. Apples must express the following minimum surface colour characteristic of the variety:

1   3/4 of total surface red coloured in case of colour group A,
2   1/2 of total surface mixed red coloured in case of colour group B,
3   1/3 of total surface slightly red coloured, blushed or striped in case of colour group C.

necessarily easy to determine: 'Causal relations do not pre-exist but rather are intra-actively produced. What is a "cause" and what is an "effect" are intra-actively demarcated through the specific production of marks on bodies' (Barad 2007: 236). In the case of the food/waste *dispositif* in the UK, there has been a concomitant development of transport infrastructure, urban development, population growth, legal, social and technical advances that accompanied the development of food production systems since 1945, at different junctures and in different rhythms.

The large food retail outlets that accelerate material throughflows for global food production regimes would have been impossible (for instance) without a range of technical and infrastructural developments from the shopping trolley to the acceleration of the car economy and the accompanying road networks, without the growth in post-war employment and accompanying increases in household income, and without the consecutive 'baby booms' in population growth which determined patterns of house-building, house ownership and urban and suburban spread.

The retail outlet foundations for the current set of sociotechnical food/waste production relationships in the UK began immediately after the end of the Second World War, but by 1947 there were still only ten 'self-service' shops in the UK, Tesco and Sainsbury's among them; at that point, possibilities for large food waste outlets were limited by social constructs inside the UK such as food rationing (which ended in 1954), car ownership (which limited the quantity of products that could be physically transported), road networks and public transport systems (limiting the possibilities for transporting food), household employment and income (limiting consumer ability to purchase). Outside the UK, fast transport systems (e.g. container shipping, air lines) were virtually non-existent, the networks of collection and storage had yet to be built and, as importantly, the dense network of supranational trade relationships, inter- and intra-governmental agreements, inter- and intra-corporate commercial relationships, collateral and vertical obligations and interconnected contractor/producer relationships did not exist at all.

The end of rationing allowed the rapid development of a more complex consumption-focused infrastructure in the UK, widespread changes in income and employment and the transfer of technical innovations, commercial organization and business practices that constantly crossed the Atlantic from the US rapidly transformed food production and retail in the UK. By 1961, three commercial outlets alone (Premier, Victor Value and Fine Fare) owned 330 supermarkets (from only 50 in total in 1950) and by 1969 there were around 3,400 supermarkets in the UK with a concomitant growth in the range of products available.[19] Following this initial expansionary boom, however, the numbers of firms involved began to contract rapidly; from a market share by independent firms of over 30% in 1970, by August 2018 the largest four retailers (Tesco, Sainsbury's, Asda and Morrisons) controlled 68.5%[20] of the national market, despite recent fierce competition from price-cutting rivals; these large retailers occupy a dominant position over a complex meshwork of over 7,000 suppliers.[21]

A diagram of the development of the food production *dispositif* in the UK during the course of over 70 years since the Second World War by comparison with estimated food waste figures allows an entirely new interpretation of the different technical innovations, social changes and functionality of various aspects of material throughflow, which can be sorted between food/waste processing and accelerating mechanisms, as the illustration in Table 4.2 shows.

It should be noted that the imbricated meshwork of sociotechnical food/waste mechanisms greatly accelerated food waste following the substantial take-up of consumer transport

Table 4.2 The development of food/waste processing and accelerating mechanisms in the UK

Year	UK household food waste	Food/waste processing mechanisms	Food/waste accelerating apparatus
1939	1–3% (Cathcart and Murray 1939)		
1950			Shopping trolley introduced by Sainsbury's
1951			Estimated 85% of UK population have no car
1952		First automatic coffee pot	
1956			37% of UK households have a TV
Mid-1960s			Vacuum-sealed food domestically available
1970			Majority of UK population owns a fridge
1970–1973			Sell by dates introduced by Marks and Spencer
1972		First coffee percolator	
1975			97% of UK households have a TV
1976	6.0% (Osner 1982)		Majority of UK households have one car
Mid-1970s			Commercial uses of freeze-drying developed; 1/3 of UK population owns a freezer
1980s		Microwaves becoming widespread in the UK	Use of sorbic acid as a food preservative
Mid-1980s			½ UK population owns a freezer
1990			Pascalization (HPP) of commercial products
2000			Widespread use of chemical preservatives
2008	25% (WRAP 2008; WRAP 2009; Pantzar, Shove, Southerton and Strandbakken 1999)		

and storage goods from the late 1950s to the mid-1970s. In 1951, 85% of households have no car, making the transport of large amounts of food difficult; they have few possibilities for storing it because fridge ownership only becomes a majority in the late 1960s. The drive to create appetites through advertising on TV and persuade consumers to purchase and waste more food begins in the 1950s but only hits full flow in 1975 when 97% of UK households have a TV, at a time when the ability to store more frozen food is still hindered by only a third of UK households having a freezer, which increases to half by the 1980s. The take-off phase for mass food consumerism doubled food waste from 1939 to 1976, but the biggest increase in food/waste took place when car, TV, fridge, freezer and road networks, plus the spread of supermarket networks, combined to produce a veritable explosion in throughput of food/waste materials.

The development of the food/waste *dispositif* in the UK, then, is comprised of a wide range of sociotechnical changes, ranging from the end of food rationing in 1954 through the development of an extensive road network, rapidly increasing car and white good ownership, increases in household income linking into the spread and development of food/waste accelerating conduits and nodes of distribution (retail supermarkets and their associated sourcing, contract, purchase, transport, storage and distribution networks) and the development of a sophisticated advertising industry dedicated to providing a powerful 'pull' mechanism for food/waste consumption through the creation and intensification of appetites for increased consumption. By the mid-1970s most of these sociotechnical components for accelerated food/waste consumption were in place, and whereas what is estimated as food waste merely doubled between 1939 and 1976 due to the limitations created by a *dispositif-in-development*, once the major components of the food/waste mechanism were interconnected, food/waste material throughflows more than quadrupled.

Creating vastogenic behaviours and appetites for waste

Material throughflow in vastogenic systems does not become 'materially, socially, and spatially' food/waste (Gille 2010: 1050) purely through the creation of physical systems and infrastructure supporting its sourcing, production, collection, distribution and sale – neither is the creation of the food/waste hybrid produced solely by the mechanisms of governmentality and regulation constructed to control the flows. In the scenario described above in the UK, as in every other country dominated by mass consumption, the speed and intensity of food/waste throughflows depends on creating new forms of behaviour, inside and outside the food/waste production system.

Creating the consumer involves entraining different behavioural modification processes to normalize new forms of behaviour. In the specific example of the food/waste hybrid, persuading the consumer to greatly accelerate household throughflow of material in the UK was preceded and then accompanied by creating appetites for the mechanisms that acted to accelerate flows – ownership of cars, fridges, freezers, TVs and microwaves had to penetrate the majority of the population as the roads and the food/waste distribution networks were being built and completed. At that point, media and communications began to dominate as the critical conduits for behavioural change; printed matter, cinemas and TV before the ICT revolution and then a far broader spectrum of e-mechanisms, all deploying an underlying universal theme of emphasizing inferiority and discontent that can be satisfied only by increased consumption.

Inside the global food production regimes, the behaviours of human agents have evolved to increase material throughflow. As pointed out elsewhere (Cloke 2016), actually physical spoilage and loss of the food/waste hybrid declines dramatically from the point where it leaves the realm of producers or external storage and moves through the internal realm of the food production regime. Once entered into the retail section, however, a range of behaviours on the part of production regime workers and consumers alike act to speed up throughflow again. Globally, supermarkets are controlled by regulators and mechanisms that see continuing waste in individual stores as an indication of an enhanced customer experience and 'non-trivial waste figures' (Mena, Adenso-Diaz and Yurt 2011: 657) as indicators of stores that are efficiently managed. But these behaviours are not restricted to store managers or system regulators or to transubstantiation of materials; they come from different

Table 4.3 Appetite creation: alternative spreads

Alternative spreads	Launched	Delisted
Tesco Avocado Spread	May 2016	Nov. 2017
Tesco Coconut Spread	May 2016	June 2017
Asda Avocado Spread	June 2016	June 2017
Waitrose Rapeseed and Coconut Oil Spread	June 2016	June 2017
Flora Freedom Avocado Oil & Lime	May 2017	Oct. 2017
Flora Freedom Coconut and Almond	May 2017	Oct. 2017
Flora Freedom Walnut	May 2017	Oct. 2017
Vitalite Coconut	Feb. 2017	Oct. 2017

Source: *The Grocer*

sources and are generated by more complex motives than mere replacement of older stock with newer.

One of the most important of these behavioural control systems is appetite creation, systematized demand that actively involves every human agent in the system and deploys a range of actants and agencements in a continuous search for market share. As one small example, Table 4.3 above depicts a range of 'alternative spreads'[22] launched by some of the major UK retailers over the period May 2016 to November 2017 to detect one possible market for vegan/vegetarian products. Each of these products involved substantial human activity and use of capital, material and financial resources through market research, product and packaging creation, advertising, placement and contracting with sources through some part of the 7–8,000 retail sources that supply UK food retailers – yet none of these stayed on the shelves for longer than 18 months.

Figuratively and literally, as a result of compulsive behaviours shaped by the demand for material flows, food/waste hybrid material such as these alternative spreads is continuously accumulated and mobilized in one sphere of the food production regime, transformed into a consumer-focused actant in another sphere and transported to the retail/consumer interface as part of a continuous process of product creation involving thousands of new consumer products a year in the UK alone – some 1,351 new grocery products are launched annually in the UK and the failure rate is estimated at 76%, with an annual cost of £30.4 million.[23] The quantities of energy, water, raw materials and human effort utilized in transubstantiating the food/waste hybrid from source raw components outside the system to land-filled end-product once it has successfully transited through the vastogenic regime to the consumer are actually mobilized by learned, consumption-driven behaviours inside and outside the production regime, a regime that responds to a variety of commercial stimuli as well as product failure. In 2015, Tesco decided to simultaneously cut a third of its product lines as a result of competition from cost-cutting retailers Aldi and Lidl,[24] for instance, whereas in 2006 Heinz spontaneously jettisoned 20% of the lines it had acquired as a result of a merger with HP Foods,[25] as being surplus to the strategic direction of the new corporate entity.

This constant demand for and motion of material requires sources conditioned to providing the raw physical materials on terms that are openly in favour of the retail system; the complex of contractual systems that suppliers are subjected to has developed over decades into an incredibly detailed behavioural modification system. A brief list of these socio-systemic conditioners of supplier behaviours includes:

- payment terms discouraging smaller growers which include unilateral contract changes by purchasers;
- retailer product quality standards deterring smallholders from supplying produce to the market;
- exclusive dealing arrangements restricting the number of contracts a supplier can make;
- exclusive purchasing agreements restricting the retailer to buy from contracted suppliers only;
- discounts demanded by the retailer for differing quantity needs;
- damage/waste payments demanded by retailers from suppliers for produce damaged in transport/storage;
- high contractual penalties for partial or total non-delivery of orders by suppliers;
- slotting allowances and pay-to-stay fees to retailers (also known as 'listing fees') for new products;
- product take-back clauses in supplier contracts allowing retailers to return product to suppliers once a residual shelf-life has been reached;
- category management to suit the sales strategies of retailers;
- marketing 'contributions' paid by supplier to retailers toward the cost of marketing promotions;
- often poor demand forecasting and replenishment systems and a lack of FSC transparency;
- other payments – for store re-fitting, etc. demanded by the retailer.

(Based on Parfitt, Barthel and Macnaughton 2010)

Conclusion: There is no 'food waste'

In the official and much of the academic literature, waste in general, and the concept of food waste in particular, revolves around a core of socially constructed characteristics; waste is material that is 'discarded', not useful or desirable; waste stands apart from 'value production and realization' (Gille 2010: 1055); and waste derives from the 'assumption that the economy is constituted by the production and exchange of intended things' (Gille 2010: 1054). Re-envisioning the idea of waste through a new materialist biopolitics highlights that it is none of those things. Far from being discarded, food/waste plays a vital supporting role as a lubricant-actant, generating a massive over-supply of material flows through a flexible and adaptable socio-legal structure. Far from being apart from value, in the complex socio-cultural environment inside global food production regimes, food/waste is both supportive of and necessary to the functionality of the system and therefore of direct value to it. Last, as the overview of the vastogenic *dispositif* clearly illustrates, what is discursively dismissed as waste is very much an 'intended thing'.

The orthodox tendency in literature on food waste and food security, moreover, has the effect of detaching a simulacrum of waste from the materialist biopolitics of which it is the core component, allowing a discourse that removes it from the practical and political dimension it shapes and which places it in a moral dimension that conceals its systemic realities and prevents proper discussion of vastogenic regimes. Food waste is inevitably written as a moral problem (Stuart 2009) that creates food crises (Nellman et al. 2009), causes pollution (Griffin, Sobal and Lyson 2009) and has harmful economic effects to consumers (Ventour 2008) – but this is reverse-engineering some of the symptoms of vastogenic regimes to conceal the totality of what food/waste is, a critical component of mass food consumption.

Critically reviewing the idea not just of food waste, but of all waste in vastogenic systems, is vital to understanding how corporate regimes are dependent on vastogenesis to create and increase value in a mass consumer society. The recent spate of reportage on plastic waste in oceans, for instance, plus the attempts of governments, supranational organizations and even corporations to 'address' the problem is almost purely phenomenological and utterly absent the systemic analysis and biopolitical understanding which are required to act in a realistic fashion to counter the moral dilemmas waste is said to represent. Every vastogenic phenomenon created by mass consumption, from mobile phones and e-waste, through plastic and food waste to carbon emissions, has at its heart the production of what is dismissed as waste through ignoring the dependency of global consumption regimes on it – there can, however, be no effective action to address the physical phenomenon of waste without addressing its systemic causation.

Notes

1 'Food regime analysis …. identifies stable periods of capital accumulation associated with particular configurations of geopolitical power, conditioned by forms of agricultural production and consumption relations within and across national spaces' (McMichael 2009) but see Friedmann (2016) for an overview of the continuing debate on this topic.
2 '2018 World hunger and poverty facts and statistics', accessed 15/10/18 at www.worldhunger.org/world-hunger-and-poverty-facts-and-statistics/
3 Thalif Deen, 'Food waste enough to feed world's hungry four times over', Inter Press Service, Wednesday, August 8, 2018, accessed 15/10/18 at www.ipsnews.net/2018/05/food-waste-enough-feed-worlds-hungry-four-times/
4 'Obesity and overweight', WHO, accessed 15/10/18 at www.who.int/news-room/fact-sheets/detail/obesity-and-overweight
5 'Fast facts about malnutrition', GAIN, accessed 15/10/18 at www.gainhealth.org/knowledge-centre/fast-facts-malnutrition/
6 See the new edition of *Food Wars: The Global Battle for Mouths, Minds and Markets* by Tim Lang and Michael Heasmann (Routledge, 2015) for more in-depth exploration of some of these issues.
7 There is substantial, continuing debate about the origins, meaning and over-use of the term biopolitics (see Lemke 2011), but for the purposes of this chapter, biopolitics is deployed in the sense of exploring growing corporate mechanisms of power and control over 'the biological or biosociological processes characteristic of human masses' (Foucault 2003).
8 It should be noted here that although this text refers to food waste, the analysis here is relevant to all forms of waste: plastic, e-waste, fabrics, etc.
9 'This is what I mean by doxa – that there are many things people accept without knowing', Pierre Bourdieu in 'DOXA and common life, Pierre Bourdieu and Terry Eagleton, *New Left Review* I/191, January–February 1992.
10 'Technical platform on the measurement and reduction of food loss and waste', FAO, accessed 16/10/18 at www.fao.org/platform-food-loss-waste/food-waste/definition/en/
11 EU Council Directive Waste 75/442/EEC [91/156/EEC].
12 'A thoroughly heterogeneous ensemble consisting of discourses, institutions, architectural forms, regulatory decisions, laws, administrative measures, scientific statements, philosophical, moral and philanthropic propositions … the system of relations that can be established between these elements' (Foucault 1980).
13 Food Safety Act 1990, c. 16 Part I Section 1, accessed 23/10/18 at www.legislation.gov.uk/ukpga/1990/16/section/1

14 Taken from the Catholic concept through which the sacrament (wine and wafer) of the Eucharist during the Mass is converted literally into the body and blood of Jesus Christ, at the moment of consumption; in this instance, blessing or condemnation by the secular Mass of food regulations and standards transubstantiate food into 'edible' or 'inedible' irrespective of the actual quality and healthfulness of the food.

15 'An order or decree imposed by someone in power without popular consent' (Oxford Dictionaries).

16 'Date marking and food waste', European Commission, accessed 24/10/18 athttps://ec.europa.eu/food/safety/food_waste/eu_actions/date_marking_en

17 'Non-human, nonindividual entities' (Latour 1996: 369).

18

> The word agencement has the advantage of being close to the notion of agency: an agencement acts, that is, it transforms a situation by producing differences. The modifier "socio-technical" underscores the fact that the entities which are included in the agencement and participate in the actions undertaken are both humans and non-humans.
>
> *(Callon 2008: 38)*

19 'The rise of the supermarket in Britain', Exeter Business School, accessed 24/10/18 at http://business-school.exeter.ac.uk/research/consumer_landscapes/shopping/rise.html

20 'Market share of grocery stores in Great Britain from August 2012 to August 2018', Statista, accessed 24/10/18 at www.statista.com/statistics/300656/grocery-market-share-in-great-britain-year-on-year-comparison/

21 C-Tech (2004) 'United Kingdom food and drink processing mass balance: a Biff award Programme on sustainable resource use'.

22 'Eight alternative spreads that have disappeared from shelves', *The Grocer,* accessed 19/10/18 at www.thegrocer.co.uk/reports/the-dairymen/eight-alternative-spreads-that-have-disappeared-from-shelves/571462.article

23 'Failed product launches cost UK grocery sector £30.4 million', *New Food Magazine,* 10 November 2017, accessed 30/10/18 at www.newfoodmagazine.com/news/46262/failed-product-launches/

24 'Tesco's decision to cut a third of its total 90,000 products', *Marketing Week,* accessed 30/10/18 at www.marketingweek.com/2015/05/13/how-brands-can-bounce-back-from-supermarket-de-listings/

25 'Heinz says it is cutting back on 20% of its lines, including some of those it inherited when it bought HP Foods in 2006', *Campaign,* accessed 30/10/18 at www.campaignlive.co.uk/article/delisting-frenzy-brand-owners-retailers-drastically-cut-number-variants-pack-sizes/967431

References

Barad, K. (2007). *Meeting the Universe Halfway: Quantum Physics and the Entanglement of Matter and Meaning.* Durham/London: Duke University Press.

Bourdieu, P. (1977). *Outline of a Theory of Practice.* R. Nice (Transl.) Vol. 16 Cambridge, UK: Cambridge University Press, 167–169.

Callon, M. (2008). Economic markets and the rise of interactive agencements: from prosthetic agencies to habilitated agencies. *Living in a material world: Economic sociology meets science and technology studies* 1, pp. 29–56.

Cathcart, E. and A. Murray (1939). A note on the percentage loss of calories as waste on ordinary mixed diets. *Journal of Hygiene* 39, pp. 45–50.

Cloke, J. (2013). Empires of Waste and the Food Security Meme. *Geography Compass* 7(9), pp. 622–636.

Cloke, J. (2016). Chapter 11: Food Security and Food Waste. In: P. Jackson et al. (ed) *Eating, Drinking: Surviving, Springer Briefs in Global Understanding.* pp. 99–105, Springer, SpringerBriefs eBook availablt at https://www.springer.com/gp/book/9783319424675

Coole, D. and S. Frost (2010). Introducing the new materialisms. In: D. Coole and S. Frost (eds) New Materialisms: Ontology, Agency, and Politics. Durham/London: Duke University Press, 1–43.

FAO. (1981). *Food loss prevention in perishable crops.* FAO Agricultural Service Bulletin, no. 43, FAO Statistics Division.

Foucault, M. (1980). The Confession of the Flesh (1977) Interview. In: Colin Gordon (ed) *Power/Knowledge Selected Interviews and Other Writings*. London: Longman, 194–228.

Foucault, M. (1989). *Resume des cours 1980–1982*. Paris: conferencs, essais et lecons du Collège de France. Paris, Julliard.

Foucault, M. (2003). *"Society must be defended": lectures at the Collège de France 1975–1976*. D. Macey (trans.) New York: Picador.

Foucault, M. (2007). *Security, Territory, Population: Lectures at the Collège de France, 1977–78*. New York: Palgrave.

Friedmann, H. (2016). Commentary: Food regime analysis and agrarian questions: widening the conversation. *The Journal of Peasant Studies* 43(3), pp. 671–692.

Gabriel, Y. and Lang, T. (1995). The unmanageable consumer. Thousand Oaks, CA: Sage.

Gille, Z. (2010). Actor networks, modes of production, and waste regimes: reassembling the macro-social. *Environment and Planning A* 42, pp. 1049–1064.

Gille, Z. (2013). From risk to waste: global food waste regimes. *The Sociological Review* 60(S2), pp. 27–46.

Griffin, M., Sobal, J. and Lyson, TA. (2009). An analysis of a community food waste stream. *Agriculture and Human Values* 26, pp. 67–81.

Latour, B. (1996). *On actor-network theory: A few clarifications*, Soziale Welt, 47. Jahrg., H. 4, pp. 369–381. Accessed 24/ 10/18 at http://transnationalhistory.net/interconnected/wp-content/uploads/2015/05/Latour-Actor-Network-Clarifications.pdf.

Lemke, T. (2011). *Biopolitics: an advanced introduction*. E.F Trump (trans.). New York & London: New York University Press.

Lemke, T. (2015). New Materialisms: Foucault and the 'Government of Things'. *Theory, Culture & Society* 32(4), pp. 3–25.

McMichael, P. (2009). A food regime genealogy. *Journal of Peasant Studies* 36(1), pp. 139–169.

Mena, C., Adenso-Diaz, B. and Yurt, O. (2011). The causes of food waste in the supplier–retailer interface: Evidences from the UK and Spain, Resources. *Conservation and Recycling* 55(4), pp. 648–658.

Nally, D. (2011) The Biopolitics of Food Provisioning. *Transactions of the Institute of British Geographers* 36, pp. 37–53.

Nature (2010). How to feed a hungry world. Nature 466(7306), pp. 29.

Nellman, C., MacDevette, M., Manders, T., Eickhout, B., Svihus, B., and Prins, AG. (2009). *The environmental food crisis – the environment's role in averting future food crises*. Norway: United Nations Environment Programme (UNEP); 2009. Accessed 1/ 11/18 at www.gwp.org/globalassets/global/toolbox/references/the-environmental-crisis.-the-environments-role-in-averting-future-food-crises-unep-2009.pdf

OECD. (2009). The bioeconomy to 2030: designing a policy agenda. OECD International Futures Project. Accessed 15/ 10/18from: www.oecd.org/futures/bioeconomy/2030.

Osner, R. (1982). Food Wastage. Nutrition and Food Science, 13–16. July/August.

Pantzar, M., Shove, E., Southerton, D., and Strandbakken, P. (1999). Configuring domestic technologies: the normalisation of freezers in Finland, Norway and the UK. Consumption, Everyday Life and Sustainability Summer School. Accessed 12/ 10/18 at www.lancaster.ac.uk/fass/projects/esf/papers.htm.

Parfitt, J., Barthel, M., and Macnaughton, S. (2010). Food waste within food supply chains: quantification and potential for change to 2050. *Philosophical Transactions of the Royal Society of London B: Biological Sciences* 365(1554), pp. 3065–3081.

Pechlaner, G. and Otero G. (2008). The third food regime: neoliberal globalism and agricultural biotechnology in North America. *Sociologia Ruralis* 48(4), pp. 1–21.

Peters, M. (2007). Foucault. biopolitics and the birth of neoliberalism, *Critical Studies in Education* 48(2), pp. 165–178.

Pistorius, R. and van Wijk, J. (1999). *The exploitation of plant genetic information: Political strategies in crop development*. Oxon: CABI Publishing.

Sage, C. (2013). The interconnected challenges for food security from a food regimes perspective: energy, climate and malconsumption. *Journal of Rural Studies* 29, pp. 71–80.

Stuart, T. (2009). Waste: uncovering the global food scandal. London: Penguin Books.

Ventour, L. (2008). *The food we waste: food waste report V.2*, *WRAP*, Banbury, UK. Accessed 24/ 10/18 at http://wrap.s3.amazonaws.com/the-food-we-waste-executive-summary.pdf

WRAP. (2009). *Household food and drink waste in the UK*. Banbury, UK. Accessed 24/10/18 at www.wrap.org.uk/sites/files/wrap/Household_food_and_drink_waste_in_the_UK_-_report.pdf

PART II

Food waste (and loss) along the food supply chain and institutions

Part II 'follows' food waste (and loss) along the supply chain; from farm to fork. Attention to each stage reveals causes and solutions for food waste throughout. Each chapter provides information on measurement, reviews literature, and discusses future developments and current best practice regarding prevention and diversion of food waste.

In 'Produce loss and waste in agricultural production', Lisa K. Johnson explores farm-level issues of food loss and waste. She highlights that agricultural losses are often missing from discussions of food waste, and that although definitions of food 'loss' and 'waste' are varied, many losses are driven by constraints outside the farmers' control, and are linked to factors (and waste) in other parts of the food system. She also shares her groundbreaking fieldwork assessing harvests and losses for eight vegetable crops in North Carolina. (For those further interested in postharvest loss, we encourage reading the posthumously published paper by Baker et al. (2019) as well as Lisa's earlier work.)

In 'Food loss and waste in processing and distribution', Martin Gooch and Abdel Samie Felfel follow food through wholesale and logistics phases of the supply chain, providing quantification and a business case for reducing food loss and waste, starting from the common reference point of internationally recognised food loss and waste measurement and reporting standards. They highlight different approaches, tools, and techniques to reduce and prevent food waste, including the memorable 'Plan → Do → Check → Act' and 'TIM WOOD'.

Although the proportion of food waste generated within the retail sector itself is relatively low (~10% of mass), retail has a significant influence on other stakeholders along the food supply chain. Felicitas Schneider and Mattias Eriksson explore this topic in 'Food waste (and loss) at the retail level'. They review previous global literature on retail food waste, list quantification studies, and highlight influencing factors and prevention measures for retail food waste.

In 'Household food waste', Kate Parizeau covers the area of the food system where the largest amounts of food waste are currently generated, providing a comprehensive discussion of generative mechanisms and drivers of household food waste (such as socio-demographic and behavioural factors as well as emotions, values, and identity). After summarising these complex issues, Kate leads the reader into an exploration of disposal paths and interventions for households.

Finally, in 'Food waste in the service sector: key concepts, measurement methods and best practices', Kirsi Silvennoinen, Sampsa Nisonen, and Oona Pietiläinen provide a review of the most elusive (until recently) parts of the supply chain to waste food: the service sector. They provide definitions of key concepts and give amounts and types of food waste in different kinds of outlets, e.g. school canteens, and compare studies from different countries. They then give the best practice of food waste management, and guidance on food surplus management.

Reference

Baker, N., Popay, S., Bennett, J., and Kneafsey, M. (2019). Net yield efficiency: Comparing salad and vegetable waste between community supported agriculture and supermarkets in the UK. *Journal of Agriculture, Food Systems, and Community Development, 8*(4), 1–14.

5

PRODUCE LOSS AND WASTE IN AGRICULTURAL PRODUCTION

Lisa K. Johnson

Agricultural losses often missing from discussions of food waste

In order for the fruit and vegetable supply to meet US dietary recommendations for the current population, the supply of fruit would need to double, and the supply of vegetables on hand should be increased by 70% (Krebs-Smith et al., 2010). The United Nations recommends that food supply chains need to be restructured in order to handle changes in climate, demographics, fuel costs, water scarcity, loss of biodiversity, and food insecurity (Nellemann et al., 2009). Further, in order to improve food security, Godfray and colleagues (2010) call for "radical" changes to the way food is produced, similar to "those that occurred during the 18th- and 19th-century Industrial and Agricultural Revolutions and the 20th-century Green Revolution." There is some consensus surrounding the idea that reducing food loss and waste could improve sustainability while increasing food availability (Beddington et al., 2012; Kader, 2003, 2005; Nellemann et al., 2009). Certainly, utilizing more of what is produced on farms would have the effect of immediately increasing the food supply, without increasing some of the resources used in their production.

Importantly, the portion of production that remains on-farm is not included in the widely recognized 40% of US food that is not consumed (Gunders, 2012). The figure simply calculates the kilocalorie difference between the total US per capita food supply and average consumption (Gunders, 2012; Hall et al., 2009). The omission of the farm-level loss discussion in the US is further evidenced by reports and datasets that provide information or recommendations to reduce food loss and waste, yet are unable to report estimates of farm-level loss due to a lack of data (Buzby and Hyman, 2012; Gunders, 2012; Hodges et al., 2011; Kantor et al., 1997). Data describing fruit and vegetables that are edible but unmarketable is not recorded by the United States Department of Agriculture (USDA), nor is it typically recorded by growers (Buzby et al., 2014; Evans-Cowley and Arroyo-Rodriguez, 2013). For example, the US Department of Agriculture's Economic Research Service collects the most comprehensive data available on the US food supply, yet their "Loss-Adjusted Food Availability" dataset omits supply that may still be available on the farm (Buzby et al., 2014). The USDA's National Agricultural Statistics Service does report on a portion of farm supply that is unutilized, by reporting grower survey data on planted area that was not harvested in each year's vegetables annual summary (USDA-NASS, 2017). However, this data leaves out fields that have been harvested once or several times, but are still producing a viable crop that is subsequently destroyed.

Differentiating "food loss" and "food waste"

Definitions of food "loss" and "waste" are varied, and differ across organizations important to global agriculture, including the Food and Agriculture Organization of the United Nations (FAO), and the USDA. The World Resources Institute defines food "loss" as "the unintended result of agricultural processes or technical limitations in storage, infrastructure, packaging, and/or marketing," whereas "waste" occurs in the storage, processing, and distribution stages of the supply chain (Lipinski et al., 2016). The most straightforward definitions divide the supply chain at one point, though each stage can be subdivided to include both "loss" and "waste."

"Postharvest losses" have historically been described as quantitative or qualitative reductions in crop volume that occur between harvest and consumption, setting definitional boundaries from farm gate to consumption (Kader, 2005; Kays, 1997). More recently, definitions of on-farm food loss have expanded to include the loss of mature produce crops that are ripe for harvest and intended for human consumption. These are crops that may be left unharvested due to constraints outside the control of the grower, such as weather and market demand. In addition, it includes produce crops that may have been graded out in sorting and packing, provided those activities are occurring on-farm. In this chapter, the term "food loss" will be used to describe unutilized food that would be fit for human consumption, but remains in the field or on the farm, never reaching downstream stages of the food supply chain. "Food waste" will be used to describe food intended for human consumption, lost during distribution, retail, restaurant, or consumer stages.

Growers aim to prevent a wide variety of losses

A fruit or vegetable is ready for harvest when it meets expectations for consumption (FAO, 1989), which will vary based on the type of produce described. These expectations result in fruit and vegetables being selected at harvest on the basis of appearance and maturity, which can include color, size, shape, texture, aroma, or soluble solids content (FAO, 1989).

Losses in agricultural production that occur at the time of harvest may have the greatest potential for recovery and utility of the food. However, losses can and do occur at each stage within production and can include loss of yield potential, reductions in yield, reductions in quality, or a loss of resources and inputs used to produce the crop (Figure 5.1). All can translate to loss of profits or sales for growers, which leads growers to focus according to their available resources.

Growers often plant improved cultivars, optimize fertility and irrigation strategies, maintain strict pest and disease control schedules, reduce food safety hazards, form cooperatives, seek contracts, or any combination of these strategies and others, all in an effort to minimize losses. When food that was produced for humans is not consumed, the resources used in its production, such as water, cropland, fertilizer and labor, are also lost (Hall et al., 2009; Kummu et al., 2012; Lundqvist et al., 2008). In addition, market price, shifting market location, imports, oversupply, or a reduction in demand could influence profit margins or sales negatively, leading to losses. Further, losses of the entire crop do occur, often due to weather-related incidents, recalls for food safety, or unavailable labor.

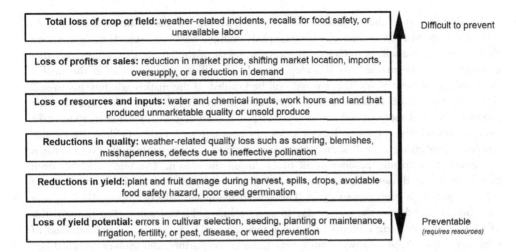

Figure 5.1 Some of the ways in which losses occur in the production of fruit and vegetable crops, ranked according to the difficulty of prevention.

Losses in production are driven by constraints outside the growers' control

Critically important to understanding the volumes of fruit and vegetable crops lost on-farm is the decision-making leading to the harvest of specialty crops, which is heavily influenced by the requirements of produce buyers. Even though losses can be found in agricultural production, that does not mean growers are responsible for, or have the capacity to change, these losses. Losses of mature produce crops fall broadly into two categories: products that do not meet buyer specifications for quality, and production exceeding demand, or surplus. The drivers that influence losses can often be found in other portions of the supply chain, such as retail and foodservice distribution. Growers make decisions about what to harvest based on market activity, price, and buyer requirements, suggesting that the system rather than individual growers needs improvement, in order to realize reductions in on-farm losses.

Several reports have determined that the grade standards are one of the causes of food losses, and recommended the development of new markets for edible products not meeting current standards (BSR, 2013; Gunders, 2012; Milepost, 2012). Quality standards have an important role to play in current industry operations. Standards allow for some harmonization throughout the industry, are a marketing tool that provides a common language, assist producers and handlers in labeling, comprise the basis for reporting, help settle disputes, and reward top quality (Abbott, 1999; Beierlein et al., 2003; Kader, 2002). As fresh produce is often sold unbranded, its quality must equal the produce that filled the shelf the previous week, even if that product came from another grower, or even another region or country. US standards are developed and implemented by the USDA Agricultural Marketing Service, and inspectors work to enforce standards at shipping points and terminal markets (Kader, 2002). Buyers can also shift their specifications based on current market supply, thereby asking growers to provide even stricter standards (Milepost Consulting, 2012). Despite the importance of standards, they tend to define quality according to aesthetic appearance, such as shape and size, rather than flavor or nutritional value (Abbott, 1999; Kader, 2003).

In addition, when the conditions for producing a crop are good, surpluses can and do arise. Growers without insurance sometimes plant multiple fields on multiple dates to ensure their crop available will be sufficient to meet the needs of the buyers they supply, whether contracted or uncontracted. As the crop matures, it will at some point meet the market demand, and at some point, the demand will be fulfilled. If the market window has passed, or the produce in a field does not meet the specified standards, the entire field full of edible produce can be abandoned and left to rot (Milepost Consulting, 2012). Growers must make decisions on whether or not to harvest a field, or continue to harvest a field, under variable conditions, balancing several factors. They may not have a relationship with a buyer that is interested in purchasing produce at all times during the season. The price available from buyers fluctuates throughout the season, and may or may not be sufficient to cover the inputs required for each harvest cycle. The appearance quality of the crop in the field may have been reduced over the season, due to aging plants or harvest traffic. The financial risk of packing and shipping a crop that has this reduced quality increases, as the likelihood of rejection is greater, and growers often bear these costs. Further, the grower must balance the need to move the harvest crew to a field which is producing a higher quality crop, perhaps for the first or second picking, and cannot afford to keep the crew in a field nearing the end of its useful life.

The amount of fresh produce lost in agricultural production is not yet well understood

Only a few studies that estimate fruit and vegetable crops lost at the production level in the US are included in Schneider's (2013) and Van der Werf and Gilliland's (2017) reviews of food waste research. Both reviews list studies that do provide data on losses in agricultural production, but they use a calculation approach to determine estimates that are based on indirect data. Including a few other studies with the reviews' shortlists, a wide range of definitions, data collection, sampling strategies, reporting styles, and results can be found.

Fresh fruit and vegetable crops are lost at higher rates than other foods, such as meat, dairy, and grain crops, according to the Swedish Institute for Food and Biotechnology's report for FAO (Gustavsson et al., 2011). An estimated 20% of the marketed fruit and vegetable crops is lost at the farm level in North America (Gustavsson et al., 2011). However, this figure is not based on inquiry or field-level measurement, but instead cites other literature, which is also not based on field measurement (Cappellini and Ceponis, 1984; Golumbic, 1964; Harvey, 1978; Kader, 2005; LeClerg, 1964; Parfitt et al., 2010). These estimates might no longer apply to modern vegetable production, as techniques, varieties, and efficiency have all improved.

The primary benefit of field measurement is that it provides assumption-free, sample-derived estimates of the total amount of not just marketable but usable produce lost, rather than a broad rate of loss that does not distinguish what is included. Because estimates of food loss and waste at the national level can vary widely based on data sources and assumptions, systematic research is necessary to determine baselines for reduction (Bräutigam et al., 2014). Studies comparing interview estimates with field-based data in the UK and Scandinavia have confirmed that growers underestimate losses from the farm in interviews or surveys (Hartikainen et al., 2018; WRAP, 2017). Therefore, methods to determine remaining volumes quantitatively, including field measurement, may be preferable to qualitative methods (Chaboud and Daviron, 2017; Muriana, 2017; Reutter et al., 2017), and are available for production styles similar to the US (Johnson et al., 2018a).

Research in food loss in agricultural production in developed countries and the US has used qualitative methods such as interviews and surveys to describe growers' self-reported rates of edible produce lost at the primary production level. Almost all of the interview-based studies have emphasized the imprecision or inaccuracy that may be present in their estimates, one describing a "reluctance to disclose" data (Milepost Consulting, 2012), along with wide variability and no way to confirm the estimates (Berkenkamp and Nennich, 2015; Hartikainen et al., 2018; Neff et al., 2018; Rogers, 2013; WRAP, 2011). The variability in reporting and data collection methods makes the figures reported by these studies difficult to synthesize.

Qualitative inquiry on small Minnesota farms primarily using alternative production practices by Berkenkamp and Nennich (2015) utilized survey and interview data to describe the opportunities and challenges of harvesting and marketing cosmetically imperfect produce. A range of crops studied resulted in estimates of up to 20% of the crops being cosmetically imperfect, and therefore considered unmarketable (Berkenkamp and Nennich, 2015). Neff and colleagues (2018) reported that small, diversified farms in Vermont leave just 5% of edible vegetables unharvested in the field, and, using that figure, calculated a statewide estimate of food loss. A preliminary study commissioned by the Natural Resources Defense Council used a small set of grower interviews to determine estimates and causes of fruit and vegetable losses (Milepost Consulting, 2012). Sixteen growers estimated losses in the field and during packing for four tree fruit and two vegetable crops in California at 0–30%. The report called for further research including extensive cross-commodity data collection across many regions (Milepost Consulting, 2012).

A few recent studies have generated estimates of food loss in agricultural production through sampling and scaling field-generated data, rather than qualitative data.

In European countries, field measurement has resulted in carrot, onion (Hartikainen et al., 2018), lettuce (Strid et al., 2014; Waste & Resources Action Programme (WRAP), 2017), and potato (Schneider et al., 2019) estimates, which determined that 26% of the marketed carrot crop, 15% of the marketed onion crop, 16.8% to 19% of the marketed lettuce crop, and 1–9% of the marketed (mechanically harvested) potato crop was left unharvested in the field in primary production. In Australia, field measurement of tomatoes indicated 28.7% of the marketed yield was left unharvested in the field (McKenzie et al., 2017). Often a difference between those specialty crops with a relatively lower rate of loss in the field can be attributed to mechanical harvest, which has been optimized to collect nearly the entire crop, and may in turn be connected to the processing industry. Interestingly, a Scottish study investigating the relationship between farm size and loss rate concluded that the portion of the crop that is not utilized increases with farm size (Beausang et al., 2017).

In their report, "No Food Left Behind," the World Wildlife Fund detailed studies performing field-based research that generated estimates in four important US crops (WWF, 2018). Field losses included 2.5% in mechanically harvested potatoes (Idaho), 41% of tomatoes (Florida), 40% of peaches (New Jersey), and 56% in romaine lettuce (Arizona).

In a 2017 North Carolina study (Johnson et al., 2018b), data was collected from sixty-eight fields on nine farms that market fresh produce into the wholesale supply chain. The overall average rate of produce crops evaluated remaining in the field that could be utilized was 42% of the three-year average marketed yield in North Carolina. The grand mean of produce remaining in the field that was either edible or marketable (excluding watermelon) was 5,114.59 kg/ha.

The overall average of just the *marketable* crops left unharvested totaled 16% of the three-year average marketed yield in North Carolina, which aligns with current national estimates, underscoring the possibility that growers may consider only the *marketable* crops left behind as a loss when self-reporting. Marketable cabbage and summer squash left unharvested totaled just 1% of the marketed yield, which could serve to confirm very low estimates provided by growers in US interview studies, depending, again, on what growers consider edible produce in their reported figures. When produce of correct maturity and condition conducive to long shelf-life (considered *edible*) are included, a more accurate picture of the produce that could be recovered and utilized available in the field is presented, which increases the rate of losses in all crops (Figure 5.2).

A 2016 case study reporting on losses in thirteen fields on a 121-hectare farm in North Carolina found an average rate of field losses at 57%, again including vegetable crops that remained unharvested, yet were suitable for harvest and use (Johnson et al., 2018a). An average of 8,840 kg of fresh produce remained in the field per hectare. The marketable quality remaining in each field differed, even among fields of the same crop. However, the average over all fields indicated that over half of the remaining crop was of a quality suitable for recovery and use (Figure 5.3).

The estimates derived from these field-based studies are higher than previously estimated, suggesting more field-based measurement is needed in order to generate more reliable estimates. This idea has been promoted by FAO (Parfitt et al., 2010), suggested again during

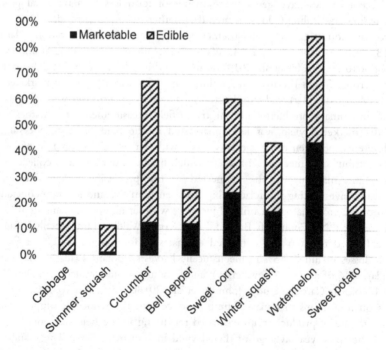

Figure 5.2 The portion of the three-year average North Carolina marketed yield that remains in the field for eight vegetable crops. Percentages included are marketable produce that meets traditional buyer specifications for quality, and produce that is edible but may not meet specifications.

Source: Johnson et al. (2018b).

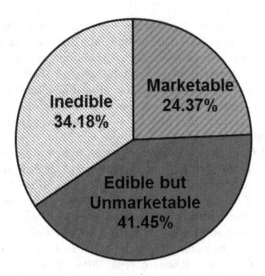

Figure 5.3 Vegetable crops remaining in the field after the primary harvest was completed in thirteen fields on a North Carolina farm displayed a range of quality, including marketable, edible but unmarketable, and inedible. The average quality over all fields is shown.

Source: Johnson et al. (2018a).

the renewal of interest in food loss and waste (Gunders et al., 2017; Kader, 2005; ReFED, 2016), and has been requested in proposed US policy (HR 4184, 2015).

Strategies that can reduce agricultural food loss may not incentivize growers

Focusing on prevention of losses, food recovery, and recycling, the options often suggested for the agricultural level include development of emerging markets for produce of low appearance quality, improvement of processing opportunities for growers, and facilitating donation through improving infrastructure and tax policy (Rethink Food Waste through Economics and Data (ReFED), 2016). Most of the suggested strategies focus on recovery and recycling, however, rather than prevention. Measurement is considered the best strategy for those portions of the supply chain from distribution through consumption, and it can work for agricultural production as well. Each farm operation is unique, and when provided with detail on what is lost in the field and why, strategies can target the reduction of losses within the constraints of the operation. Yield can be increased by preventing or recovering food losses in agricultural production, but will that increase in yield translate to profit or loss?

In an economic analysis from the World Resources Institute, an average benefit-cost ratio for investing in food waste reduction strategies was determined to be 14:1. This exciting financial incentive was described for businesses specializing in food manufacturing, retail, hospitality, and foodservice (Hanson and Mitchell, 2017). However, the same benefit-cost ratio for agricultural production was found to be just 1.3:1, revealing one reason growers may not have the capacity to develop new strategies for food loss in their operations.

If the produce lost in agricultural production were recovered, yields could be increased by at least the FAO estimate of 20% (Gustavsson et al., 2011). In that event, essentially an increase in supply, the price of fresh produce may be lowered to levels that do not support input costs, a cause for concern among vegetable growers (Berkenkamp and Nennich, 2015). Emerging businesses and programs are now promoting the sale of blemished or mis-shapen produce through retail, restaurant distribution, and direct-to-consumer. Often these programs offer a reduced price for produce of this quality, which continues to dis-incentivize growers and distributors.

An economic analysis of six southeastern vegetable crops has described some scenarios that may lead to profit for growers that aim to utilize more of their production, including the full range of appearance quality. The study showed that no single strategy resulted in a potential profit in all of the crops studied (Table 5.1). If the entirety of the crop remaining in the field after harvest were recovered, the scenario most likely to generate a profit for the grower was to sell the marketable portion of the remainder through a regular wholesale marketing channel, and sell the edible portion in bulk to an alternative market for approxi-mately 50% of the wholesale price (Dunning et al., 2019). Realizing that each crop, field, region, and season presents unique challenges on farms is important in understanding that in some years one scenario might work well, but in others, it might not.

Suggested strategies for reducing food loss that promote food donation are cost-effective, provide high relative net economic value, and can divert high relative volumes of food, according to a recent economic analysis (Rethink Food Waste through Economics and Data (ReFED), 2016). Donation can be a challenge for producers, as reliable infrastructure is not available nationwide, and there are few incentives to donate. The US EPA and other groups also suggest the donation of excess produce to feed hungry people as a strategy for food loss reduction (EPA, 2015; Gunders et al., 2017; Rethink Food Waste through Economics and Data (ReFED), 2016). Gleaning fresh produce from the field, which recovers food that would be lost, increases fresh food in the emergency food supply. However, gleaning can be inefficient due to its nature as an activity undertaken by charitable groups using a non-

Table 5.1 Estimates of per acre profitability of harvesting and selling recovered volume for selected North Carolina vegetable crops

Harvest scenarios	Returns ($/acre)					
	Bell pepper	Cabbage	Cucumber	Summer squash	Sweet corn	Sweet potato
Scenario 1: Packed in bins at 50% of wholesale price	466	(557)*	823	(137)	(178)	88
Scenario 2: Field packed, sold in bins at $0.07/lb	(97)	(338)	38	(277)	(155)	106
Scenario 3: Packed in cartons for marketable and bins for edible; wholesale price for marketable and 50% of this for edible	1,059	(538)	1,135	(116)	5	515
Scenario 4: Packed in cartons for marketable and bins for edible; wholesale price for marketable and $0.07/lb for edible	580	(580)	211	(289)	(111)	364

Note: * Figures in brackets denote losses.
Source: Dunning et al. (2019)

agricultural volunteer workforce, and further research is required to determine how to optimize its output (Sonmez et al., 2015). A few states now support programs that compensate growers for harvest and packing costs, which makes donation much more likely.

An estimated 21% of water, 19% of fertilizer, and 18% of cropland is devoted to producing food that is not consumed in the US (Rethink Food Waste through Economics and Data (ReFED), 2016). Innovative solutions that reduce losses at the agricultural level are needed. As the utility of crops is maximized, land and chemical resources on farms are used more efficiently, improving environmental sustainability. Although, food lost in the field has not yet generated the environmental cost of food that has reached the consumption stage of the supply chain, as it has not yet been harvested, sorted, packed, cooled, and transported. A plant that is still bearing when tilled back into the soil may provide some nutrient cycling. Therefore, fruit and vegetable crops lost on-farm are likely not generating the same environmental damage as those discarded after a full trip through the supply chain.

Growers must strive for economic resiliency, and therefore might not be able to balance that with environmental or social goals in their operations. When strategies that reduce losses through donation are not financially supported for growers, there might be only a small group that participates in donation. Targeting environmental sustainability itself presents intangible benefits for growers. However, the potential to manage a smaller area, or use chemical resources more efficiently because more of the crop produced has been sold, presents cost savings for the grower, with the same desired result.

Quantification of losses in agriculture leads to new knowledge about food production

Understanding that growers continuously work to avoid losses in addition to maximizing yield is important to consider when discussing the volumes of food lost in agricultural production. In addition, it is critical to realize that constraints outside growers' control could be influencing the amount of losses seen in agriculture.

The need for more accurate estimates is necessary in order to determine the true environmental, economic, and societal costs of food loss and waste. Setting national or global targets for reduction is challenging without accurate baseline measurements, currently missing for food loss in agricultural production. However, as consumer-level food waste is assumed to represent the highest value contributor to food loss and waste in the supply chain, and because it may be easier to quantify than agricultural losses, the emphasis for prevention, recovery, and recycling efforts has remained on consumer-related food waste (Griffin et al., 2009; Gustavsson et al., 2011).

Globally, researchers agree more study is needed to quantify the amount of edible crops that is lost at the production level and what factors contribute to these losses. Field-based measurement is needed to understand the opportunities available for further utilizing crops either for profit, or to supplement the emergency food system (Gunders, 2012; Gunders et al., 2017; Harvey, 1978; Kantor et al., 1997; Lundqvist et al., 2008; Neff et al., 2015).

Emphasizing further research on food loss in the US and globally, and providing resources that assist growers in reducing their losses, will lead to new knowledge about whether the current system is sufficiently working to meet the needs of the population now and in the future. Working toward the prevention and recovery of on-farm food losses might hold the potential to improve public health through an increased supply of nutritious food (Neff et al., 2015), lessen the environmental burden of farming through more efficient use of resources (Beddington et al., 2012), and improve the economic resiliency of farms by ensuring growers are incentivized (Dunning et al., 2019).

References

Abbott, J. (1999) 'Quality measurement of fruits and vegetables', *Postharvest Biology and Technology*, vol 15, pp 207–225.

Beausang, C., Hall, C. and Toma, L. (2017) 'Food waste and losses in primary production: Qualitative insights from horticulture', *Resources, Conservation and Recycling*, vol 126, pp 177–185.

Beddington, J., Asaduzzaman, M., Clark, M., Fernandez, A., Guillou, M., Jahn, M., et al. (2012) Achieving food security in the face of climate change: Final report from the commission on sustainable agriculture and climate change, CGIAR Research Program on Climate Change, Agriculture and Food Security (CCAFS), Copenhagen, Denmark, www.cccafs.cgiar.org/commission.

Beierlein, J., Schneeberger, K. and Osburn, D. (2003) *Principles of agribusiness management*. Third Edition. Waveland Press, Inc., Prospect Heights, IL.

Berkenkamp, J. and Nennich, T. (2015) 'Beyond beauty: The opportunities and challenges of cosmetically imperfect produce, Report 1: Survey results from Minnesota produce growers', www.ngfn.org/resources/ngfn-database/Beyond_Beauty_Grower_Survey_Results_052615.pdf.

Bräutigam, K-R., Jörissen, J. and Priefer, C. (2014) 'The extent of food waste generation across EU-27: Different calculation methods and the reliability of their results', *Waste Management & Research*, vol 32, no 8, pp 683–694.

Business for Social Responsibility (BSR) (2013) 'Losses in the field: An opportunity ripe for harvesting', www.bsr.org/reports/BSR_Upstream_Food_Loss.pdf.

Buzby, J. and Hyman, J. (2012) 'Total and per capita value of food loss in the United States', *Food Policy*, vol 37, pp 561–570.

Buzby, J., Wells, H. and Hyman, J. (2014) 'The estimated amount, value, and calories of postharvest food losses at the retail and consumer levels in the United States', *USDA-ERS*, www.ers.usda.gov/media/1282296/eib121.pdf.

Cappellini, R. and Ceponis, M. (1984). 'Postharvest losses in fresh fruits and vegetables', in H. Moline (ed) *Postharvest pathology of fruits and vegetables: Postharvest losses in perishable crops*, University of California Bulletin no 1914, Berkeley, California, USA, pp 24–30.

Chaboud, G. and Daviron, B. (2017) 'Food losses and waste: Navigating the inconsistencies', *Global Food Security*, vol 12, pp 1–7.

Dunning, R.D., Johnson, L.K. and Boys, K.A. (2019) 'Putting Dollars to Waste: Estimating the Value of On-Farm Food Loss.', Choices. Quarter 1. Available online: http://www.choicesmagazine.org/choices-magazine/theme-articles/food-waste-reduction-strategies/putting-dollars-to-waste-estimating-the-value-of-on-farm-food-loss.

EPA (2015) 'Sustainable management of food', *Food recovery hierarchy*, www2.epa.gov/sustainable-management-food/food-recovery-hierarchy.

Evans-Cowley, J. and Arroyo-Rodriguez, A. (2013) 'Integrating food waste diversion into food systems planning: A case study of the mississippi gulf coast', *Journal of Agriculture, Food Systems, and Community Development*, vol 3, no 3, pp 167–185.

Food and Agriculture Organization of the United Nations (FAO) (1989) *Prevention of post-harvest food losses: Fruits, vegetables and root crops*. FAO, Rome, Italy.

Godfray, H., Beddington, J., Crute, I., Haddad, L., Lawrence, D., Muir, J., Pretty, J., Robinson, S., Thomas, S. and Toulmin, C. (2010) 'Food security: The challenge of feeding 9 billion people', *Science*, vol 327, pp 812–818.

Golumbic, C. (1964) 'Maintaining quality of farm crops', in A. Stefferud (ed) *Yearbook of Agriculture*, Washington, DC: USDA, pp. 291–302.

Griffin, M., Sobal, J. and Lyson, T. (2009) 'An analysis of a community waste stream', *Agriculture and Human Values*, vol 26, pp 67–81.

Gunders, D. (2012) 'Wasted: How America is losing up to 40 percent of its food from farm to fork to landfill', Natural Resources Defense Council Issue Paper: 12-06B, www.nrdc.org/food/files/wasted-food-ip.pdf.

Gunders, D. et al. (2017) 'Wasted: How America is losing up to 40 percent of its food from farm to fork to landfill', Natural Resources Defense Council Issue Paper: R10-05A.

Gustavsson, J., Cederberg, C. and Sonesson, U. (2011) '*Global food losses and food waste*, Food and Agriculture Organization of the United Nations, Sweden, www.fao.org/fileadmin/user_upload/ags/publications/GFL_web.pdf.

Hall, K., Guo, J., Dore, M. and Chow, C. (2009) 'The progressive increase of food waste in America and its environmental impact', *PLOS ONE*, Nov 25, vol 4, no 11: e7940. doi: 10.1371/journal.pone.0007940.

Hanson, C. and Mitchell, P. (2017) 'The business case for reducing food loss and waste', *Champions*, vol 12, no 3, https://ec.europa.eu/food/sites/food/files/safety/docs/fw_lib_business-case_en.pdf

Hartikainen, H., Mogensen, L., Svanes, E. and Franke, U. (2018) 'Food waste quantification in primary production – The Nordic countries as a case study', *Waste Management*, vol 71, pp 502–511.

Harvey, J. (1978) 'Reduction of losses in fresh market fruits and vegetables', *Annual Review Phytopathology*, vol 16, pp 321–341.

Hodges, R., Buzby, J. and Bennett, B. (2011) 'Postharvest losses and waste in developed and less developed countries: Opportunities to improve resource use', *Journal of Agricultural Science*, vol 149, pp 37–45.

HR 4184 (2015) 'Food recovery act of 2015', *Introduced by Chellie Pingree to the House*, www.congress.gov/bill/114th-congress/house-bill/4184/text.

Johnson, L., Dunning, R., Bloom, J., Gunter, C., Boyette, M. and Creamer, N. (2018a) 'Estimating on-farm food loss at the field level: A methodology and applied case study on a North Carolina farm', *Resources, Conservation & Recycling*, vol 137, pp 243–250.

Johnson, L., Dunning, R., Bloom, J., Gunter, C., Boyette, M. and Creamer, N. (2018b) 'Field measurement in vegetable crops indicates need for reevaluation of on-farm food loss estimates in North America', *Agricultural Systems*, vol 167, pp 136–142.

Kader, A. (2002) *Postharvest technology of horticultural crops*, Third edition. University of California, Agricultural and Natural Resources Publication 3311, Oakland, California, USA.

Kader, A. (2003) 'A perspective on postharvest agriculture (1978–2003)', *HortScience*, vol 38, no 5, pp 1004–1008.

Kader, A. (2005) 'Increasing food availability by reducing postharvest losses of fresh produce', *ActaHorticulturae*, vol 682, pp 2169–2175.

Kantor, L., Lipton, K., Manchester, A. and Oliveira, V. (1997) 'Estimating and addressing America's food losses', *USDA-ERS Food Review*, webarchives.cdlib.org/sw1tx36512/www.ers.usda.gov/publications/foodreview/jan1997/jan97a.pdf.

Kays, S. (1997) *Postharvest physiology of perishable plant products*, Exon Press. Athens, GA.

Krebs-Smith, S., Reedy, J. and Bosire, C. (2010) 'Healthfulness of the U.S. food supply', *American Journal of Preventative Medicine*, vol 38, no 5, pp 472–477.

Kummu, M., de Moel, H., Porkka, M., Siebert, S., Varis, O. and Ward, P. (2012) 'Lost food, wasted resources: Global food supply chain losses and their impacts on freshwater, cropland, and fertiliser use', *Science of the Total Environment*, vol 438, pp 477–489.

LeClerg, E. (1964) 'Crop losses due to plant diseases in the United States', *Phytopathology*, vol 54, pp 1309–1313

Lipinski, B. et al. (2016) 'Food loss and waste accounting and reporting standard, 'food loss and waste protocol', *World Resources Institute*, www.wri.org/sites/default/files/REP_FLW_Standard.pdf.

Lundqvist, J., de Fraiture, C. and Molden, D. (2008) *Saving water: From field to fork-curbing losses and wastage in the food chain*, SIWI Policy Brief, Stockholm International Water Institute, Stockholm, Sweden.

McKenzie, T., Singh-Peterson, L. and Underhill, S. (2017) 'Quantifying postharvest loss and the implication of market-based decisions: A case study of two commercial domestic tomato supply chains in Queensland, Australia', *Horticulturae*, vol 3, no 3, Article 44.

Milepost Consulting (2012) 'Left-out: An investigation of the causes and quantities of crop shrink', commissioned by the Natural Resources Defense Council, www.nrdc.org/sites/default/files/hea_12121201a.pdf.

Muriana, C. (2017) 'A focus on the state of the art of food waste/losses issue and suggestions for future researches', *Waste Management*, vol 68, pp 557–570.

Neff, R., Dean, E., Spiker, M. and Snow, T. (2018) 'Salvageable food losses from Vermont farms', *Journal of Agriculture, Food Systems, and Community Development*, vol 8, no 2, pp 39–72.

Neff, R., Kanter, R. and Vendevijvere, S. (2015) 'Reducing food loss and waste while improving the public's health', *Health Affairs*, vol 34, no 11, Nov, pp 1821–1829. doi: 10.1377/hlthaff.2015.0647.

Nellemann, C., MacDevette, M., Manders, T., Eickhout, B., Svihus, B., Prins, A. and Kaltenborn, B. (eds). (2009) *The environmental food crisis – The environment's role in averting future food crises*, A UNEP rapid response assessment. United Nations Environment Programme, GRID-Arendal, www.grida.no.

Parfitt, J., Barthel, M., and Macnaughton, S. (2010) 'Food waste within supply chains: Quantification and potential for change to 2050', *Philosophical Transactions of the Royal Society*, vol 365, pp 3065–3081.

Rethink Food Waste through Economics and Data (ReFED) (2016) 'A roadmap to reduce US food waste by 20 percent', www.refed.com/downloads/ReFED_Report_2016.pdf.

Reutter, B., Lant, P., Reynolds, C. and Lane, J. (2017) 'Food waste consequences: Environmentally extended input-output as a framework for analysis', *Journal of Cleaner Production*, vol 153, pp 506–514.

Rogers, G. (2013) 'Identifying new products, uses and markets for Australian vegetables: A desktop study', http://ausveg.com.au/infoveg/infoveg-search/multipurpose-vegetables-factsheet-for-vg12046/.

Schneider, F., Part, F., Göbel, C., Langen, N., Gerhards, C., Kraus, G. and Ritter, G. (2019) 'A methodological approach for the on-site quantification of food losses in primary production: Austrian and German case studies using the example of potato harvest', *Waste Management*, vol 86, pp 106–113.

Schneider, F. (2013) 'Review of food waste prevention on an international level', *Waste and Resource Management*, vol 166, no WR4, pp 187–203

Sonmez, E., Lee, D., Gomez, M. and Fan, X. (2015) 'Improving food bank gleaning operations: An application in New York state', *American Journal of Agricultural Economics*, vol 98, no 2, pp 549–563.

Strid, I., Eriksson, M., Andersson, S. and Olsson, M. (2014) *Losses of iceberg lettuce during primary production and whole sale in Sweden* (in Swedish), report 146, Swedish Board of Agriculture, Jönköping, Sweden.

USDA-NASS (2017) 'Vegetables annual summary', http://usda.mannlib.cornell.edu/MannUsda/view DocumentInfo.do;jsessionid=2EA4BC5594C40D7A93C885EEC9495710?documentID=1183.

Van der Werf, P. and Gilliland, J. (2017) 'A systematic review of food losses and food waste generation in developed countries', *Waste and Resource Management*, vol 170, no WR2, pp 66–77.

Waste & Resources Action Programme (WRAP) (2011) 'Fruit and vegetable resource maps: Mapping fruit and vegetable waste through the retail and wholesale supply chain', www.wrapni.org.uk/sites/files/wrap/Resource_Map_Fruit_and_Veg_final_6_june_2011.fc479c40.10854.pdf.

Waste & Resources Action Programme (WRAP) (2017) 'Food waste in primary production: A preliminary study on strawberries and lettuces', www.wrap.org.uk/sites/files/wrap/Food_waste_in_primary_production_report.pdf.

World Wildlife Fund (WWF) (2018) 'No food left behind', https://c402277.ssl.cf1.rackcdn.com/publica tions/1170/files/original/WWF_No_Food_Left_Behind_111018.pdf?1542040595.

6

FOOD LOSS AND WASTE IN PROCESSING AND DISTRIBUTION

Martin Gooch and Abdel Samie Felfel

Introduction

Food losses and waste (also referred to as FLW or food wastage) include the edible portions of foods produced that are intended for human consumption, but that are not consumed (FAO, 2011; FLWP, 2016; CEC, 2019). As illustrated in Figure 6.1, food losses generally refer to unintended spills or spoilage or technical problems that reduce production before it reaches the retail or foodservice distribution system and consumers. Food waste is generally associated with behavior such as negligence or suboptimal processes, along with conscious decisions by businesses to discard food during distribution and by consumers in the household or when dining out at foodservice establishments (Lipinski et al., 2013; Gooch et al., 2010; CEC, 2019).

Not all FLW can be avoided. Unavoidable FLW includes generally inedible materials, such as bones, egg shells, tea bags, fruit and vegetable peels, etc. Possibly avoidable FLW is food or drink disposed of due to its cooking or preparation method, or consumer preferences, e.g. potato skins or bread crusts. Avoidable FLW is considered edible prior to disposal, and was either over prepared, not used on time, or disposed of for other reasons (WRAP, 2009; Bagherzadeh et al., 2014).

An international review by Schneider (2013) identified that research undertaken to quantify FLW occurring in "logistics, wholesale and redistribution," (p. 187) and methodologies for reducing FLW at any point along the food supply chain are underrepresented topics compared to the amount of research conducted into FLW that occurs in households. This

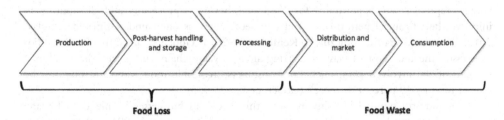

Figure 6.1 Commonly accepted distinction between food loss and food waste.

lack of data pertaining to supply chain FLW has led to households incorrectly being viewed as the place where the majority of FLW occurs in industrialized nations such as Canada (Gooch et al., 2019).

FLW can be qualitative or quantitative. Qualitative losses arise due to deterioration of taste, texture, or nutrients. Quantitative losses are due to reduced volume or weight (Buzby et al., 2014). Throughout this chapter, the term food loss and waste (FLW) is used to describe loss and waste occurring throughout the foods and beverages value (supply) chain.

While typically food loss is highest in developing countries and food waste is highest in developed countries (Gooch et al., 2013; FAO, 2016), the breadth of this distinction can differ enormously by food type. It also differs according to how individual food value chains operate (Simons et al., 2003; Hines et al., 2006; Food Chain Centre, 2007; Barclay, 2012; Tanner, 2012; Gooch et al., 2014, 2019).

FLW during processing and distribution

Within the primary and further processing[1] sectors, three forms of FLW occur: (1) *planned* (unavoidable) FLW – such as animal bones and hide; (2) *unplanned* (potentially avoidable) FLW – such as production and operational management related FLW due to ineffective equipment operation reducing yields below expectations; and, (3) *post-processing* (avoidable) FLW – such as finished products that due to inaccurate forecasts or cancelled orders reach their expiry date[2] before being sold (Barclay, 2012; FLWP, 2016; Gooch et al., 2019; Provision Coalition, 2019). In distribution, it is rare for planned (unavoidable) FLW to occur. Products reaching their expiry dates, inaccurate forecasts, cancelled orders, cool chain malfunction, and incorrect handling are among the most common causes of avoidable FLW in foods and beverages during distribution (IGD, 2009; Tanner, 2012; Gooch et al., 2017a, 2017c, 2019).

Because it is preventable, both types of avoidable FLW described above represent the greatest opportunity to reduce FLW. This can be achieved by improving the processes involved in production and manufacturing, then distributing foods and beverages to customers. However, all FLW can be reduced to a degree (Gooch et al., 2019). Reducing avoidable FLW would result in a reduction in unavoidable FLW created during its production. An example is bread: less avoidable waste in foodservice, retail stores and in the home (due to better forecasting, handling and storage) would result in less production waste further up the chain. This would be because less grain would be milled in the production of the flour, and in turn less flour used in the manufacturing of the bread.

The business case for reducing FLW

The extent to which reducing FLW, by controlling the factors that cause it and associated wastes, represents an opportunity for food and beverage processors and distributors to improve their financial performance and competitiveness, is often underestimated (Barclay, 2012; Whitehead, Parfitt, Bojczuk & Keith James, 2013; Gooch et al., 2014, 2017c). "For businesses, the total cost of waste occurring along a value chain can exceed the combined margins of the involved companies. For consumers, avoidable food waste can increase the cost of food by 10 percent or more" (Gooch et al., 2014: 5).

In an industry typified by slim margins, this results in businesses having to sell many items simply to break even on each item lost or wasted (Gooch et al., 2014). Why the true value of FLW and associated impacts are often underestimated (typically significantly) includes disjointed financial reporting systems and employee incentive systems that pit employees operating within a business against each other (Hines et al., 2006; Food Chain Centre, 2007; Barclay, 2012; Gooch et al., 2019). The improvement opportunities that arise from this situation include cost reduction, resource efficiency and competitive positioning.

Volume of FLW occurring in processing and distribution

Based on primary Canadian industry data, Gooch et al. (2019) identified that, in terms of metric tonnes, primary and further processing account for a considerably greater proportion of total food supply chain FLW than previously estimated: 34 percent and 13 percent, respectively. Distribution accounted for 4 percent of total FLW by volume. This combined FLW (51 percent of total FLW estimated to occur along the food supply chain) is over three times the volume of FLW estimated to occur in Canadian households (14 percent). Gooch et al. (2019) found that the occurrence of potentially avoidable and avoidable FLW during processing was highest in the production of products derived from field crops (bread, beer, etc.), followed by products derived from horticultural crops (bagged salads, fruit juices, etc.). Other research, including Simons et al. (2003), Hines et al. (2006), Food Chain Centre (2007), IGD (2009), CEC (2017), and Provision Coalition (2019) shows that the potential for high levels of FLW to occur during the processing of foods and beverages is a global phenomenon.

Reduction of food loss and waste is becoming an integral part of efforts to reduce costs along food supply chains to improve the efficiency of the chain by using resources more effectively (Provision Food Chain Centre, 2007; Gooch et al., 2010; Barclay, 2012; Schneider, 2013; Zokaei, 2014; WRAP, 2015; Provision Coalition, 2019). Food losses and waste represent unsold products and therefore reduced revenues and higher costs for businesses in the food supply chain. Additionally, when consumers purchase too much (or are served too much food), food wastage represents unnecessary expenditures.

Why reducing FLW represents such a significant opportunity for businesses, from fishers and farmers through to retailers and foodservice, is that it never occurs in isolation. Whenever FLW occurs, so do myriad associated wastes – energy, water, labour, packaging, transport and equipment wear – plus transaction costs, due to, for example, poor collaboration between different businesses and reconciling financial accounts (Simons et al., 2003; Barclay, 2012; Zokaei, 2014; Provision Coalition, 2019). These associated wastes can massively exceed the face value of the food or beverage item itself. The FAO (2013) estimates the value of food product wastage alone at US$936 billion per year, while the costs of managing waste from an environmental and social costs perspective is estimated at about US$1,200 billion. Gooch et al. (2019) estimated the annual value of solely avoidable FLW in Canada at CA$50 billion.

With quality (including appearance and taste) impacting consumers' purchasing decisions, addressing the root causes of FLW can also increase revenue by driving sales and increasing consumers' willingness to pay above commodity prices for products to which they apportion recognized value (Gooch and LaPlain, 2010; Tanner, 2012; Mazhar, 2015). The root causes of FLW do not just create avoidable costs, they also reduce businesses' revenue (Simons et al., 2003; Hines et al., 2006; IGD, 2009; Gooch and LaPlain, 2010; Gooch et al., 2014); for example, fresh produce that is bruised through inappropriate handling practices or cool chain irregularities, and manufactured products that have reached their best before date lead to food and beverages being discounted to encourage their purchase by consumers (INCPEN, 2013). The amount that consumers purchase whenever a product's quality is negatively impacted during production, processing and distribution, and the frequency of those purchases, is also reduced compared to what would otherwise occur (Gooch et al., 2011; Barclay, 2012; Mazhar, 2015). This leads to avoidable losses upstream, due to unexpected and potentially severe fluctuations in supply and demand (Food Chain Centre, 2007; Gooch et al., 2014, 2019; WRAP, 2015).

Reducing FLW in processing and distribution

Value Chain Management International's (VCMI) work with the international food industry has concluded that FLW is a symptom of ineffective processes (Gooch and LaPlain, 2010; Barclay, 2012; Tanner, 2012; Gooch et al., 2014, 2019). VCMI has proven that (1) the further FLW reduction efforts extend along the value chain, the more opportunities businesses and their business partners have to address FLW; and (2) the greater the resultant benefits from an FLW reduction initiative, the more difficult it can be for competitors to remain competitive. Taking a value chain approach also provides greater opportunity to implement improvements that can be sustained over the long term and continually improved upon.

Our work to assist businesses to capture commercial opportunities by having reduced FLW has included the development of innovative tools and techniques. These have produced significant benefits for businesses and involved stakeholders; in turn, highlighting the sustainable benefits that can be achieved by addressing FLW from a whole of chain perspective. The effectiveness of techniques developed by VCMI has been assisted by an internationally recognized measurement protocol that was introduced in 2016. This was the Food Loss and Waste Accounting and Reporting Standard (FLWARS), an important and admirable first step in addressing FLW (FLWP, 2016).

As its name suggests, however, the FLWARS is focused on measuring and reporting FLW; its primary purpose is not to enable businesses to improve performance by reducing FLW. Hence the need for pragmatic tools and techniques that can be applied widely by food and beverage processors and distributors in developed and developing countries. Mitigating the environmental and social issues that result from FLW also rests on quantifying, analyzing and managing the root causes of FLW (Roussant et al., 2009; CEC, 2017; Provision Coalition, 2019; Nikkel et al., 2019).

The importance of adopting a value chain approach to FLW

Much of the food industry operates from a produce, batch-and-queue[3] standpoint (Simons et al., 2003; LaPlain, 2007; Zokaei, 2014). In an effort to minimize per unit fixed production costs, respond to inaccurate forecasts and dysfunctional replenishment[4] systems, and maximize return on capital employed, businesses operate at (or close to) maximum capacity. This invariably leads to excess production, avoidable FLW, widespread inefficiencies, and unnecessary costs (Nikkel et al., 2019; Provision Coalition, 2019). It also ties up enormous amounts of capital. A focus on quantity versus quality results in defects, creating further costs and missed revenue-generating opportunities.

The alternative approach is the process-improvement methodology known as "lean six sigma" (LSS). The basis of lean is matching capacity to customer and consumer demand, and reducing cycle time (Simons et al., 2003; Barclay, 2012; Zokaei, 2014). The basis of six sigma is minimizing variations in quality and supply, resulting in greater predictability and consistency than otherwise possible (LaPlain, 2007; Ali and Ahmed, 2016).

A key reason why the food industry operates in non-LSS fashion and finds it difficult to adopt LSS approaches is that the internal reporting and coordination mechanisms that determine how a business is managed are arranged vertically, while the activities that determine business performance and profitability occur horizontally. This mismatch produces a reiterating internal culture characterized by competition, adversity and distrust between individuals and functions (Hines et al., 2006; Food Chain Centre, 2007; Barclay, 2012; Gooch et al., 2014, 2019). This leads to individuals apportioning blame at those operating at different levels and within different departments. Seeking to continually improve performance by developing then implementing increasingly sophisticated solutions is simply not on the cards (Barclay, 2012; Gooch et al., 2019). Hence this results in fragmented financial reporting systems, ineffective processes, waste and missed revenue-generating opportunities (Tanner, 2012; Provision Coalition, 2019).

Extend this scenario across multiple businesses and the true impact of businesses being vertically structured in relation to product flow comes into view (Simons et al., 2003; Food Chain Centre, 2007; Barclay, 2012; Gooch et al., 2019). Enormous waste and unnecessarily high cost structures result from individuals, functional departments and entire businesses lacking the incentive to ensure operations are correctly managed in relation to customer and consumer demand (Hines et al., 2006; Gooch et al., 2019; Provision Coalition, 2019). This is particularly true in agriculture and food, an industry that is characterized by slim margins, adversarial relationships, distrust and short-term opportunistic behavior (Barclay, 2012; Gooch, 2012; Gooch et al., 2014).

Enabling businesses to balance vertical and horizontal considerations in their own operations, and in how they interact with customers and suppliers, is the primary purpose of easily implementable tools and techniques described in the next section. Balanced operations enabled businesses to proactively engage with other members of the value chain(s) in which they operate.

The term "value chain management" (VCM) describes a process where businesses situated along the value chain purposely work together to attain shared sustainable competitive advantage. In developing closer strategic and operational relationships, businesses acquire the ability to profit by continually improving their efficiency and effectiveness in ways that are not otherwise possible (Collins and Dunne, 2002; Barclay, 2012; Gooch, 2012; Tanner, 2012). VCM regards efficiencies as outcomes of having improved the effectiveness of processes employed to create and capture value.

How to reduce FLW in processing and distribution

Improving performance to reduce FLW for commercial, social and environmental reasons relies "more on individuals' determination to learn and the ability to communicate effectively than on statistical prowess" (Gooch et al., 2013: 22). When businesses have informal and inconsistent processes or built-in inefficiencies, they would benefit from embracing process-improvement approaches that have the potential for saving time, money and/or resources (Miller and Vollman, 1985; Lokrantz et al., 2018). As previously mentioned, they also negatively impact (1) commercial relationships – including customer loyalty, and (2) businesses' ability to create and capture revenue.

Plan → Do → Check → Act

The PDCA (Plan–Do–Check–Act) cycle (Figure 6.2), also known as a Deming cycle or Shewhart cycle, can be applied to develop and implement measures to counteract food waste (Strotmann et al., 2017). The tools' design and the descriptions of how to apply them to achieve sustainable improvements in performance, leading to reduced FLW and wider benefits that extend across the business, reflect over 40 years' experience assisting businesses operating in multiple industries and jurisdictions to profit from reducing waste.

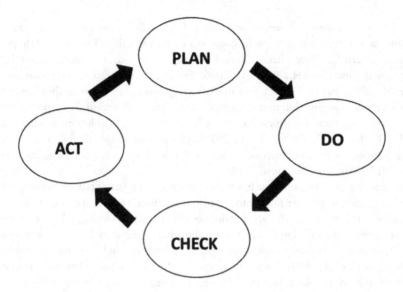

Figure 6.2 Plan → Do → Check → Act cycle.

The PDCA methodology provides a disciplined process for testing small, carefully designed changes, the impact of which is evaluated before changes are extended across the company or more ambitious efforts are undertaken (Gooch and LaPlain, 2010; Gooch et al., 2017d: 3). The four activities that together form the methodology are:

- *Plan*: Determine improvement opportunities, and establish objectives and processes that you believe will enable targeted improvements in performance to be achieved;
- *Do*: Implement the plans established during the planning phase on a small scale;
- *Check*: Verify the robustness and suitability of changes by having analyzed data gathered during the pilot; and
- *Act*: Monitor the rollout process by measuring performance and supervising the implementation of new processes.

Applying the four activities sequentially in a robust manner will enable most food processor or distribution businesses – regardless of their size, location, analytical capabilities, and products produced/handled – to measurably improve their performance. The tools and techniques that together form the PDCA methodology enable them to address basic process problems and achieve measurable results in a relatively short time span, without the need for capital investment. Improvements are achieved by accurately targeting "hot spots" and then monitoring progress, these efforts translating into higher margins and profits, and ultimately creating a culture of continual improvement.

Tools and techniques

The ten-step process that VCMI has developed for enabling businesses to translate the PDCA methodology in commercial gains are listed in Table 6.1. The steps are listed in the order in which they typically occur, particularly by those new to the concept of LSS.

Table 6.1 Ten-step process to enable businesses to translate PDCA

Step	Title	Purpose
1	Project charter	Ensure team agreement on the problem(s) seeking to be resolved, and the project can be documented in terms of desired outcomes, timelines and scope.
2	Map the current process	Understand how current processes associated with the problem operate, to identify waste or non-value-added process steps and potential causes of the problem.
3	Cause and effect diagram	Identify potential root causes of the problem identified, which will guide development of pragmatic solutions.
4	Ideas board	Capturing then categorizing ideas for solving the problem and achieving improvement objectives.
5	Ideas sorter	Sort ideas according to their ability to deliver meaningful results, and to be quickly and easily implemented.
6	Action log	Establish responsibility and accountability by shortlisting actions to be undertaken, timelines and team members.
7	Future state process	Know how future processes will operate when ideas are implemented and waste has been reduced or eliminated.
8	Pre-mortem	Minimize the number of potential risks associated with the new processes, and their impact, should any occur.
9	Pulling it together	Documentation for communicating and training staff on the improved processes, monitoring/reporting progress.
10	Process data and performance	Enable continual improvement by having ability to monitor performance and manage determining factors.

Source: Gooch et al. (2017d)

Together, they form a roadmap for change and the basis of a continual improvement program. As users' familiarity with the tools and their implementation grows, some tools and techniques – such as those used to measure process performance – may be applied at multiple phases of an improvement program. This enables businesses to evaluate performance and quantify the impact of piloted improvements at the earliest possible opportunity, then benchmark their progress over time.

Investing time in the comprehensive and accurate completion of the first five steps in particular is critical to achieving sustainable change (Strotmann et al., 2017). The most effective means of implementing impactful sustainable change is by establishing a collaborative effort from the outset, by forming a team of people from across multiple business functions, and from different businesses situated along the value chain (Food Chain Centre, 2007; Gooch and LaPlain, 2010; Tanner, 2012, 2012; Gooch et al., 2017c).

The remainder of this chapter provides a high-level illustration of how the PDCA cycle has been implemented to enable businesses to achieve significant reductions in FLW and wider commercial benefits, by having addressed the root causes of FLW and associated wastes/inefficiencies. The flexibility of the tools and techniques is shown by this cycle having successfully been used to measurably reduce FLW at the farm, primary and further processing, distribution, and retail levels along the food supply chain. The primary source of the material is taken from work completed for a Canadian mainline distributor (Gooch et al., 2017c).

Project charter

The purpose of the project charter is to ensure that individuals from different departments across the business(es) agree on the problem that they are seeking to resolve, and that the problem can be documented in terms of desired improvements (how much), by when these improvements will be achieved, and the project's scope. Table 6.2 contains the project charter from an initiative completed with a mainline distributor. While, for commercial in-confidence reasons, specific amounts have been omitted, the metrics included in the examples are those applied during the project.

Table 6.2 Project charter, mainline distributor

Current undesirable effects (UDEs)
- Inconsistent quality
- Increased costs per case; costs incurred include:

  - the produce item
  - handling returns/rejections
  - labour
  - disposal/donation
  - replacement process, including additional transportation

- Strained, unconstructive internal relationships and apportioning of blame among employees
- Dissatisfaction among external customers, impacting customer loyalty/future sales
- Disconnects between procurement, inventory management, warehouse management and delivery routing systems

Problem statement
Too much reactive noise masking root causes of shrink[5] in processed leafy green stock keeping units (SKUs). The current situation leads to dissatisfaction and potentially unconstructive relationships developing with internal and external customers.

Objective
Measurably reduce level of shrink caused by processed leafy green SKUs reaching their "best if used by"[6] (BIUB) date.
Produce insights, skills and processes that can be replicated to reduce shrink in other categories of foods and goods distributed.

Scope
Top five processed leafy green SKUs experiencing shrink due to reaching BIUB date

Process output measure *(for chosen SKUs)*	**Potential savings**
- Donations to food banks: %, # - Credits: %, #, $ - BIUB incidents and cartons: %, # - BIUB shrink: %, #, $ - BIUB shrink as % of sales/revenue	- Reduce frequency of BIUB incidents by 50 percent - Reduce total number of cases going to shrink due to BIUB incidents by 50 percent

Source: Gooch et al. (2017c)

It is not uncommon for a food processor's problem statement to be along the lines of

> Overall and premium product yields can vary by x percent and x percent, respectively, on any given day, resulting in target margins regularly not being met. Financial performance is exacerbated by 8 hours' overtime a week typically being required to meet schedule.

Process-improvement initiatives that result in significant reductions in FLW and associated wastes might not state that their purpose is to reduce loss or waste. This is because the focus of PDCA initiatives is on improving processes per se – which results in improved performance and reduced waste.

Process map

Process mapping is an important FLW reduction tool (LaPlain, 2007; Gooch et al., 2013, 2017a, 2017b). It details how the processes associated with the problem statement actually work currently, the purpose being to identify waste or non-value-added process steps and potential causes of problems experienced. If any of those steps is not sufficiently focused on maximizing businesses' value proposition from the perspective of their customers and consumers, the cumulative impact on the profitability of an individual business, and the entire value chain in which it operates, can be significant.

In the case of the mainline distributor, the mapping process identified all steps involved in: (1) order taking and the building of a purchase order issued to vendors; (2) transportation and delivery of ordered products to the distribution center; (3) warehouse management including order receipt, quality assurance checks, inventory management, order pick/pack/preparation, and loading of trucks; (4) transport routing, dispatch and arrival at destination. Layered onto the process map is any of seven types of inefficiency that are known to potentially result in FLW or associated wastes.

Tim Wood

The acronym TIM WOOD is used to identify any processes where inefficiencies are found to occur, or believed to occur. As can be seen in the Table 6.3, each letter refers to a particular inefficiency that the LSS approach targets to improve the predictability and consistency with which processes are performed, resulting in less FLW and wider benefits across the business and the overall chain.

The term given to overall inefficiencies created by TIM WOOD is the "hidden factory"[7] that increases businesses' overhead costs (Miller and Vollman, 1985). FLW is an observable symptom of opportunities created by the hidden factory that exists in all businesses. In some businesses, the hidden factory can be enormous – equating to 20+ percent of their income. Costs saved and inefficiencies eliminated by having addressed the root causes of FLW go straight to the bottom line. Addressing the hidden factory also allows businesses to increase revenue and sales by having improved quality, availability and other aspects of operational performance (Miller and Vollman, 1985; IGD, 2009; Gooch et al., 2017b).

The process map produced with staff drawn from different departments located across the mainline distributor identified the two areas of activity where considerable chance existed for inefficient processes to arise, resulting in losses and associated wastes. The first of these is the quarantining of deliveries received at the warehouse. Quarantining is a manual process,

Table 6.3 TIM WOOD described

Letter	Inefficiency
T	Unnecessary **T**ransportation
I	Unnecessary **I**nventory – required to buffer against defects, variation in demand or supply, etc.
M	Unnecessary **M**otion or **M**ovement by people
W	Unnecessary **W**aiting or delays
O[1]	**O**ver Producing – making or producing more than is required which leads to Inventory
O[2]	**O**ver Processing – doing more than required to meet customer requirements
D	**D**efects of any kind

Source: Gooch et al. (2017b)

as is the disposal and the subsequent claiming of credit from vendors when products are rejected.

The second and more serious cause of inefficiency and losses was identified as the sale of part cartons.[8] Part sold cartons were monitored, picked, packed and staged differently to full cartons. This led to the sale of part versus full cartons being identified as a common creator of avoidable losses and inefficiencies. That "these same inefficiencies occur in the absence of shrink, underlines why businesses should view shrink as a symptom, not a finite issue" (Gooch et al., 2017c: 9). Other factors identified by the process mapping included sales representatives' ability to (1) override surcharges that should be applied to the sale of part cartons, and (2) grant all customers the same option of splitting cartons.

These and other hotspots of losses and inefficiencies identified by the process mapping shared a common theme: the lack of, or not adhering to, standard operating procedures and control points.

Once processes have been mapped in sufficient detail, there are two options on how to proceed. The first option is to identify the root causes of loss and waste hotspots identified during the mapping process by conducting a cause and effect analysis.[9] The second option is to measure process performance before conducting the root causes analysis. The chosen approach will likely depend on: (1) whether root causes are obvious, (2) the complexity of the processes being examined, (3) individuals' familiarity with the PDCA methodology, and (4) available resources. The benefit of measuring before commencing the cause and effect analysis is that conclusions will be based on quantitative data and facts relating to the quality of goods and process performance in relation to customer satisfaction, not qualitative assumptions and emotions.

Measure

The effectiveness of process measurement rests squarely on the execution of a well-designed data collection plan and the attitudes of those involved (LaPlain, 2007; Gooch et al., 2013; FLWP, 2016; CEC, 2019). The measurement plan should be designed to both enable users to determine current process performance, and allow any improvements made to the process to be measured and confirmed.

The measurement plan must include what information is required. This will determine the type of data that you need to collect. Information commonly sought includes (1) cycle time (how long); or (2) percentage of production within specification, on time, or saleable.

The measurement plan is not to be developed without having: (1) observed how the process is performed, and (2) determined what data and information is currently available. If process data and information already exist, but do not provide the required insights, the current reporting systems with which operators are familiar can be modified rather than implementing wholly new systems.

If exploring the potential impact of multiple factors on process performance – for example: the impact of transportation arrangements on warehouse management and the occurrence of rejects by end customers; the impact of growing methods, storage practices and variety on potatoes' suitability for manufacturing into French fries; or the impact of orchard management practices, harvesting methods and forced air cooling on the shelf life and eating quality of peaches – the design of experiment philosophy and regression analysis should be incorporated into the measurement process. Instructions on how to apply these measurement and analytical processes to produce statistical data are widely available. Examples include Gooch et al. (2013, 2017d), FLWP (2016), CEC (2019).

In the case of the mainline distributor, it was determined that sufficient data already existed to determine where hotspots of inefficiencies lay within their operations, and the incidence with which specific outcomes related to FLW (such as products passing their BIUB date and therefore not being saleable, or being damaged) occurred as a percentage of overall shrink and turnover/sales. This data had existed prior to the project being undertaken, though it had not been analyzed to identify patterns and trends pertaining to issues identified during the process mapping exercise.

Cause and effect (fishbone) diagram

Almost invariably, some root causes of FLW and associated inefficiencies or missed opportunities will have been identified during the mapping process. Others will have been identified during the measurement phases.

The purpose of the cause and effect analysis is to identify potential root causes of the problem; or identify if further analysis is required before root causes can be identified with certainty. The analysis conducted with the mainline distributor to identify causal relationships that, if addressed, would produce measurable improvements in the distributor's performance is presented in Figure 6.3. The problem summary contained in the "head" of the fish stems from the process mapping exercise having identified that losses and other inefficiencies often stemmed from current processes not being enforced.

The root cause analysis identified the extent to which unnecessary complexity that had resulted from the current situation impacted business performance, and the extent to which the current situation forced managers to repeatedly address issues that are merely symptoms of underlying problems. The introduction of clear, objective, cross-functional accountability systems would address the current UDEs created by the dynamics that existed between and within functional departments.

Examples of root causes identified in processors that led to significant reductions in FLW and associated wastes include the extent to which assumptions and tribal knowledge had driven commercial decisions. A French fry manufacturer had assumed that large potatoes were the ideal source of long French fries. The analysis identified that large potatoes were in fact a good source of hash browns, which were of considerably lower value than French fries. Large potatoes were also a significant cause of avoidable FLW and associated wastes. Further analysis identified that (1) the specifications provided to vendors was incorrect, and (2) the production of

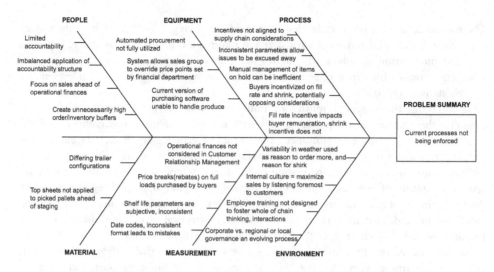

Figure 6.3 Cause and effect (fishbone) diagram.

medium potatoes possessing attributes required by the processor offered cost benefits to both them and producers. The production of medium-sized potatoes is readily achievable by implementing on-farm practices that are specifically designed with that task in mind.

Whole of chain framework

As mentioned previously, the ability to reduce FLW and capture wider opportunities within a complex processing facility or at multiple levels of the value chain requires the collection and reporting of standardized data and information. The framework presented in Table 6.4 provides a means for researchers to view the food supply chain as one interconnected system. This aids the analysis and benchmarking of FLW from a whole of chain perspective and, in so doing, the development of sustainable solutions for reducing FLW and capturing wider opportunities (Gooch et al., 2019).

The recommended measure is metric tonnes: a measure that can be accurately correlated to the array of different metrics presently used to monitor food and beverage production, distribution, sales, FLW, and waste prevention practices. For example: kilograms, pounds, litres, quarts, gallons, dozens of eggs, and bushels can all be translated directly into metric tonnes; albeit the precise formula for doing so differs by crop or product. This allows the effectiveness of all FLW reduction initiatives to be accurately monitored and directly benchmarked.

By having translated approaches and protocols contained in the FLWARS into a structured process, and standardized the overall reporting metric to tonnes, the framework provides a practical tool for monitoring and reporting FLW. While processed foods typically contain multiple commodities, the categorization system for foods and beverages produced by Gooch et al. (2019) enables direct correlations to be established between consumer foods and beverages and the terrestrial and marine products from which they are derived. The natural resources required to produce, for example, a meat pie can be estimated by calculating the comparative amounts of specific meat, bakery and dairy inputs used in their

Table 6.4 Whole of chain analytical framework

Point in chain	On-farm loss	Primary processing			Further processing			Distribution	Retail	Foodservice	Redistribution
		Planned loss	Unplanned loss	Post-process loss	Planned loss	Unplanned loss	Post-process loss				
Type of loss	Harvest loss	Planned loss	Unplanned loss	Post-process loss	Planned loss	Unplanned loss	Post-process loss	Waste during distribution	Store waste	Preparation, serving, plate waste	
Percent of volume (metric tonnes) that is lost at each stage of the value chain											
Most impactful root causes	Root causes of this loss at this point in chain	Root causes of each type of loss at this point in chain			Root causes of each type of loss at this point in chain			Root causes	Root causes	Root causes	Root causes of this loss at this point in chain
Root cause #1 Root cause #2 Root cause #3											
Destinations Rescue/gleaning Animal feed Biomaterial/ processing Compost/anaerobic Controlled combustion Land application Landfill Sewer											

Source: Gooch et al. (2019)

manufacture. The standardized measure of metric tonnes enables businesses and researchers to monitor inputs, processes and outputs from a whole of chain perspective.

Developing and sorting ideas

With the location of FLW hotspots and the root causes of these and associated wastes identified, the FLW reduction process transitions to beginning to develop solutions for eliminating problems and achieving improvement objectives identified in the project charter. In a group setting, this is achieved by inviting each participant involved in the initiative to review the process map, performance data, and the cause and effect diagram. Ideas for reducing FLW by improving the process are discussed and analyzed.

Next, sort the ideas. The idea sorting process has two overarching objectives. The first is to arrive at a set of ideas that will deliver meaningful results and can be implemented quickly and easily. The second is to avoid ideas that will be difficult to implement or will deliver minimal improvement. This is achieved by engaging people from across the business(es) to categorize ideas into the four groups listed in Table 6.5.

The mainstream distributor's FLW reduction team – comprising individuals from procurement, warehouse operations, transport, marketing, finance, and account management – identified ten ideas that they believed would translate into reduced FLW and wider benefits across the business. The categories into which they were grouped are presented in Table 6.6.

The top-right quadrant contains six ideas that the distributor's team proposed to measurably reduce shrink, each of which requires a low level of effort to implement and enforce. They include means to reduce the incidence of carton splitting and other inefficiencies that stemmed from sales representatives (SRs) having the ability to (1) override the surcharges that should be applied to the sale of part cartons; and (2) once an option is granted to one customer, offer it to all customers. Addressing the disconnects that existed between sales and operational considerations represented enormous financial and strategic opportunities.

The revision of training and incentive systems, particularly for SRs, was considered too ambitious an undertaking as a first step. Therefore, they were categorized as "do later," even though they are expected to have a significant impact on performance. The remaining two ideas (review buying geography and introduce supply chain related monitoring of SRs' performance) were deemed of insufficient benefit and requiring too much effort to warrant their implementation.

Big reward/low effort ideas proposed and implemented by the French fry manufacturer included (1) redesigning the potato payment structure to incentivize farmers to produce the

Table 6.5 Ideas sorter categories

Category description	Anticipated timing of their implementation
Big rewards/big effort	Do later
Big rewards/low effort	Do now
Low rewards/big effort	Park
Some reward/low effort	Do when can

Source: Gooch et al. (2017d)

Table 6.6 Mainline distributor: ideas to reduce FLW and improve performance

Big reward/big effort	*Big reward/low effort*	
Do later	**Do now**	
7. Educate SRs on supply chain considerations …	1	Restrict the splitting of cartons
8. Review and revise SRs' incentive programs to ensure supply chain requirements enacted …	2	Correct wrapping of skids on dock … .
	3	Choose six items for auto-ordering trial …
	4	No filling of inbound trucks with unrequired items …
	5	Validate accuracy of shelf life parameters …
	6	Bring in leafy greens three times a week, *instead of the current twice a week* …
Low reward/big effort	**Some reward/low effort**	
Park	**Do when we can**	
9. Review buying geography and pick-up options …		
10. SR performance tracked to assess relationships between order placing, forecasting and shrink …		

Source: Gooch et al. (2017b)

type of potato required to most effectively and efficiently process potatoes into French fries; (2) streamlining changeovers occurring on the packing line; (3) establishing and enforcing standardized protocols for all the manufacturing and bagging equipment; and (4) working with farmers to establish common standardized processes for growing potatoes.

The growing of smaller potatoes resulted in environmental benefits, such as reduced fertilizer usage and less usage of irrigation water – potentially resulting in less run-off. Harvesting potatoes sooner also offered farmers new cropping and market opportunities. Having established common standardized on-farm processes led to the formation of a learning network that saw producers benchmarking themselves against each other. This benefited them by further reducing production costs and increasing their margins, by continually improving their operations in line with the needs of both the processor and other customers.

Action log

The purpose of the action log is, as it suggests, to translate ideas into action. The process involves writing a concise statement of the actions required to implement each idea. The person who will be responsible for the action's completion (the owner), along with supporting actors, is then identified, and an intended completion date agreed. Update meetings are regularly held to report on progress and identify any challenges that require remedial action to address.

Table 6.7 shows a redacted version of the action log used to monitor the implementation of the ideas listed in Table 6.6. Each item is described concisely, based on findings that emerged from the development of the process map, data analysis, and cause and effect diagram. Listed alongside each action item was an owner (the person responsible for its completion), the date by when the activity is expected to be completed, and its current status.

Table 6.7 Mainline distributor action log

Idea #	Action	Owner	By when	Status
1	Restrict the splitting of cartons	xx (operations) xx (warehouse) xx (marketing)	xx	xx
2	Correct wrapping of skids on dock	xx (warehouse)	xx	xx
3	Choose six vendors/items for auto-ordering trial	xx (warehouse) xx (purchasing)	xx	xx
4	No filling of inbound trucks with unrequired items	xx and xx (marketing)	xx	xx
5	Validate accuracy of shelf life parameters	xx (purchasing) xx (marketing) xx (warehouse)	xx	xx
6	Bring in leafy greens three times a week	xx and xx (marketing)	xx	xx
7a	Educate SRs on supply chain considerations	TBD		
7b	Review and revise sales force incentive programs to ensure supply chain requirements enacted	TBD		
8	Distribute articles on supply chain incentives, demand amplification	Xx (VCMI)	xx	xx
9	Review buying geography and pick-up options	xx (purchasing) xx (marketing) xx (warehouse)	xx	xx
10	SR performance tracked to assess relationships between order placing, forecasting and shrink	Parked	N/A	N/A

Source: Gooch et al. (2017b)

Future state process

Translating ideas into action may require processes to be re-engineered. This step in the FLW reduction initiative produces a roadmap to assist the implementation of effective and sustainable solutions, by allowing people to see what the process flow will look like once all the ideas are implemented and TIM WOOD (as defined above) has been reduced or eliminated.

Pulling it together to ensure continual improvement

The final step in the PDCA methodology for reducing FLW, and which closes the circle to begin the PDCA cycle over again, is the creation of a standardized operating procedure and instructional document that describes how to perform and measure the process. It is structured to provide a clear, unambiguous and auditable document that can be communicated to staff. Having established a means to measure process performance, evaluate the performance of those conducting the process, and determine appropriate remedial actions to drive continual improvement. It ensures that the benefits of having improved processes are realized and sustained – resulting in long-term reductions in FLW and wider benefits across the business(es). An example of a process instruction document forms Table 6.8.

Table 6.8 Example of a process instruction document

Instruction title:
Supplier scorecard parameters
Revision and date:
#1, May 2019
Prepared by:
Christine Smith
Approved by:
Susan Falconer
Purpose of this instruction

- To ensure supplier performance remains within agreed to and documented parameters, such that we do not experience unacceptably low yields or short our customers.

Reference documents

- The company quality manual – refer to sections on product specifications and vendor performance.

Process definitions

- Delivery in full, on time, to quality (DFOTQ)

Roles and responsibilities

- Purchasing determine required volumes by SKU, delivery dates, pricing.
- Quality assurance reports when acceptable quality parameters or service levels have breached the green zone.
- Management conducts a monthly review of vendor performance to determine whether any remedial action is required and advise purchasing on operational decisions.

Process flow chart

- Potato process map

Process instructions
1) Safety issues

- Use the designated PPE and mobile (wheeled) steps when taking test samples from load.
- All four of the step wheels must be locked prior to using the steps.
- Ensure that there is no doubt about the condition of the wheeled steps that must not be used until checked by the supervisor.
- No employee shall use the steps without a supervisor being present.
- PPE includes safety shoes and hard hat for both the person using the steps and second person in attendance.

2) Conducting the process

1. Conduct random sampling, testing and documentation process as described in company quality manual.
2. If initial sample falls outside of green zone and within yellow zone, repeat test. If test produces similar result, notify manufacturing supervisor and purchasing supervisor of results.
3. If initial sample falls outside of green zone and within red zone, repeat test. If test produces similar result, notify manufacturing supervisor and manager and purchasing supervisor and manager that load has been rejected. Notify plant manager of decision.

Conclusions

Researching FLW in wholesale and logistics, and producing methodologies for reducing FLW, are topics that have received comparatively little attention internationally. Influencing the factors that result in the creation of FLW and associated wastes provides businesses with potentially enormous opportunities to improve financial performance, by having reduced costs, mitigated risks, increased revenues and achieved more effective use of resources. Influencing the factors that result in the creation of FLW produces wider commercial benefits, including competitive positioning. Significant environmental and social benefits result from organizations having addressed FLW and associated wastes.

This chapter described practical management tools and techniques that incorporate internationally recognized FLW measurement and reporting standards. Developed from decades of international experience in multiple industries, including food, the materials provide a robust, readily implementable means for managers to measure, monitor and mitigate FLW and associated wastes by addressing their root cause. The whole of chain analysis framework enables businesses, researchers, NGOs and governments to embrace a vigorous, more academic whole of chain approach to benchmarking the impact of initiatives designed to reduce FLW.

Notes

1 Often referred to as manufacturing.
2 Policies, rules and regulations pertaining to the setting and enforcement of "expiry," "best before" and "display by" dates differ by country, product and individual business.
3 Producing more than one piece of an item and then moving those items forward to the next operation before they are all actually needed there.
4 Replenishment is the movement of inventory from upstream – or reserve – product storage locations to downstream – or primary – storage, picking and shipment locations.
5 Shrinkage is a term that often is used to describe losses occurring in wholesale and retail. Shrink is the shortened version of shrinkage and is defined here as food and beverage products that are available for sale but not sold, for whatever reason. Shrink includes both the edible and inedible portions of food (Buzby et al., 2015).
6 "Best if used by" is the term that the distributor uses to determine the latest date that a product could be shipped, thereby ensuring that it reaches its destination with a shelf life that is acceptable to customers.
7 Hidden factory is the term used to describe activities performed within an organization that increase overhead costs, but do not create customer recognized value or are not required to create customer recognized value.
8 Carton is the term given to a cardboard box that contains a number of separately packed items; for example, bags of premixed salads.
9 Cause and effect analysis is a structured method used to identify possible reasons for why FLW is occurring within a single facility or along an entire supply chain (IGD, 2009).

References

Ali, F., Ahmed, A. 2016. A review on the statistical concepts of six sigma; AIP Conference Proceedings, V. 1775, Issue 1. 030053-1 to 030053-7. 1–7 Accessible at: https://aip.scitation.org/doi/pdf/10.1063/1.4965173?class=pdf
Bagherzadeh, M., Inamura, M., Jeong, H. 2014. *Food waste along the food chain; oecd food, agriculture and fisheries papers, no. 71*, OECD Publishing. Accessible at: www.oecd-ilibrary.org/docserver/5jxrcmftzj36-en.pdf?expires=1552401205&id=id&accname=guest&checksum=D2F72DF69BD928C55A45FCEF1A485B65

Barclay, J. 2012. *Purpose for Profit & Profit for Purpose: Adapting to Market Demands by Partnering with Produ-cers.* Value Chain Innovation Forum: Creating a More Profitable and Competitive Canadian Agri-Food Sector, Delta Meadowvale, Mississauga Ontario, April 3-4, 2012. Gooch, M., Brandle, J. Eds Accessible at: https://vcm-international.com/wp-content/uploads/2013/04/VCIF-Final-Report-English-Feb-27-2013.pdf

Buzby, J.C., Bentley, J.T., Padera, B., Ammon, C., Campuzano, J. 2015. Estimated fresh produce shrink and food loss in U.S. supermarkets Agriculture, 5 (2015), pp. 626–648.

Buzby, J.C., Wells, H.F., Hyman, J. 2014. *The Estimated Amount, Value and Calories of post-harvest food losses at the retail and consumer levels in the United States.* EIB No. 121, Feb, 2014. Economic Research Service, USDA.

CEC. 2019. *Why and How to Measure Food Loss and Waste: A Practical Guide.* Commission for Environ-mental Cooperation, Montreal, Canada. Accessible at: www3.cec.org/islandora/en/item/11814-why-and-how-measure-food-loss-and-waste-practical-guide-en.pdf

CEC. 2017. *Characterization and management of organic waste in north america—foundational report.* Commission for Environmental Cooperation, Montreal, Canada. Accessible at: www3.cec.org/islandora/en/item/11771-characterization-and-management-organic-waste-in-north-america-foundational-en.pdf

Collins, R., Dunne, T. 2002. *Learning from others*; CD ROM; Agriculture, Forestry and Fisheries Australia.

FAO. 2011. *Global food losses and food waste - Extent, causes and prevention.* Rome, Italy.

FAO. 2013. *Food wastage footprint: impacts on natural resources,* Technical Report, Rome, Italy.

FAO (Food and Agriculture Organization). 2016. *Food Loss And Food Waste.* Food and Agriculture Organization of the United Nations, Rome, Italy. Accessible at: www.fao.org/food-loss-and-food-waste/en/

FLWP. 2016. *Food Loss and Waste Accounting and Reporting Standard.* Food Loss and Waste Protocol. World Resources Institute, Washington DC. Accessible at: www.wri.org/sites/default/files/REP_FLW_Standard.pdf

Food Chain Centre. 2007. *Best practice for your business: completion report*; Food Chain Centre; Institute of Grocery Distribution, England.

Gooch, M. 2012. *Evaluating the Effectiveness of Applying an Adult Learning Approach to Value Chain Manage-ment Education.* PhD Dissertation; University of Queensland; Australia. Accessible at: https://espace.library.uq.edu.au/view/UQ:283726

Gooch, M., Bucknell, D., LaPlain, D., Dent, B., Whitehead, P., Felfel, A., Nikkel, L., Maguire, M. 2019. *The Avoidable Crisis of Food Waste: Technical Report.* Value Chain Management International and Second Harvest, Ontario, Canada. Accessible from: https://secondharvest.ca/wp-content/uploads/2019/01/Avoidable-Crisis-of-Food-Waste-Technical-Report-January-17-2019.pdf

Gooch, M., Bucknell, D., Whitehead, P. 2017a. *Quantifying packaging's potential to prevent food waste.* Value Chain Management International, Oakville, Ontario.

Gooch, M., Felfel, A., Glasbey, C. 2014. *"$27 billion" revisited: the cost of Canada's annual food waste.* Value Chain Management International, Oakville, Canada. Accessible at: https://vcm-international.com/wp-content/uploads/2014/12/Food-Waste-in-Canada-27-Billion-Revisited-Dec-10-2014.pdf

Gooch, M., Felfel, A., Marenick, N. 2010. *Food waste in Canada.* Value Chain Management Centre. George Morris Centre, Guelph, Canada. Accessible at: https://vcm-international.com/wp-content/uploads/2014/01/Food-Waste-in-Canada-November-2010.pdf

Gooch, M., LaPlain, D. 2010. *Platinum peach playbook ; value chain management centre.* George Morris Centre. Guelph, Canada. Unpublished.

Gooch, M., LaPlain, D., Felfel, A., Marenick, M. 2011. *Collaborating to increase the value of Ontario peaches.* Value Chain Management Centre, George Morris Centre, Guelph, Canada. Accessible at: https://vcm-international.com/wp-content/uploads/2013/04/Collaborating-to-Increase-The-Value-of-Ontario-Peaches-May-2011.pdf

Gooch, M., LaPlain, D., Glasbey, C. 2017b. *Profiting from improving table potato quality and pack-out.* Value Chain Management International, Oakville, Ontario. Accessible at: https://vcm-international.com/wp-content/uploads/2017/06/EarthFresh-Food-Waste-Case-Study-June-2017.pdf

Gooch, M., LaPlain, D., Glasbey, C. 2017c. *Profiting from balancing customer wants with process profi-ciency.* Value Chain Management International, Ontario, Canada. Accessible at: https://vcm-international.com/wp-content/uploads/2017/12/OPMA-FW-Project-Distributor-Case-Study-December-2017.pdf

Gooch, M., LaPlain, D., Glasbey, C., Whitehead, P. 2017d. *Reducing Food Waste in Fresh Produce*. Value Chain Management International, Ontario, Canada, Accessible at: www.theopma.ca/education-training/food-waste-reduction/

Gooch, M., Marenick, N., LaPlain, D., Dent, B. 2013. *Cut waste, grow profit: reducing food waste by addressing the disconnect between the attitude and behaviour of producers and managers of businesses situated along the value chain*. Value Chain Management International, Oakville, Canada. Accessible at: https://vcm-international.com/wp-content/uploads/2013/06/Cut-Waste-GROW-PROFIT-Food-and-Associated-Wastes-May-30-2013.pdf

Hines, P., Francis, M., Baley, K. 2006. Quality-based pricing: a catalyst for collaboration and sustainable change in the agrifood industry. *International Journal of Logistics Management*, 17(2), pp. 240–259.

IGD. 2009. *Sell more, waste less*. Institute of Grocery Distribution, London, England.

INCPEN. 2013. *Checking out food waste*. INCPEN: The Industry Council for research on Packaging and the Environment. Reading, England. Accessible at: www.incpen.org/checking-out-food-waste-2/

LaPlain, D. 2007. *Continual process improvement*; Value Chain Management: Adding Value to Agriculture, George Morris Centre, Guelph, Ontario, DVD.

Lipinski, B., Hanson, D., Lomax, J., Kitinoja, L., Waite, R., Searchinger, T. 2013. *Reducing food loss and waste*, Working paper, Installment 2 of Creating a Sustainable Food Future. World Resources Institute, Washington DC.

Lokrantz, A., Gustavsson, E., Jirstrand, M. 2018. Root Cause Analysis of Failures and Quality Deviations in Manufacturing Using Machine Learning. 51st CIRP Conference on Manufacturing Systems; Science Direct; Elsevier. Accessible at: https://reader.elsevier.com/reader/sd/pii/S2212827118303895?token=882456B0B5EB066A90152260877157B39C8CD2618E4FED5CF28FCB2A5AE9593F0BA6ACA38CC07B5887273D1186C40B05.

Mazhar, M.S. 2015. *Bruising in avocado (Persea Americana M.) CV 'hass' supply chains: from the ripener to the consumer*. PhD Dissertation. University of Queensland. Gatton, Australia. Accessible at: https://espace.library.uq.edu.au/view/UQ:364746

Miller, J.G., Vollman, T.E. 1985. *The hidden factory*; Harvard Business Review; September, 1985. Accessible at: https://hbr.org/1985/09/the-hidden-factory

Nikkel, L., Maguire, M., Gooch, M., Bucknell, D., LaPlain, D., Dent, B., Whitehead, P., Felfel, A. 2019. *The avoidable crisis of food waste: roadmap*; Second Harvest and Value Chain Management International, Ontario, Canada. Accessible at: https://secondharvest.ca/wp-content/uploads/2019/01/Avoidable-Crisis-of-Food-Waste-The-Roadmap-by-Second-Harvest-and-VCMI.pdf

Provision Coalition. 2019. *Food loss and waste library*. Provision Coalition: Making Food Sustainably; Guelph, Ontario, Canada. Accessible at: https://provisioncoalition.com/Resources/FoodWaste/foodlosswastelibrary

Roussant, N., Dujet, C., Méhu, J. 2009. Choosing a sustainable demolition waste management strategy using multicriteria decision analysis. *Waste Management*, 29(1), January 2009, pp. 12–20.

Schneider, F. 2013. Review of Food Waste Prevention on an International Level. *Proceedings of the Institution of Civil Engineers; Waste and Resources Management*, 166, pp. 187–203. Accessible at: www.wau.boku.ac.at/fileadmin/data/H03000/H81000/H81300/upload-files/Forschung/Lebensmittel/warm166-187_offprint.pdf.

Simons, D.W., Taylor, D., Francis, M. 2003. *Cutting costs – adding value to red meat*. Food Chain Centre in Partnership with the Red Meat Industry Forum, London, England.

Strotmann, C., Göbel, C., Friedrich, S., Kreyenschmidt, J., Ritter, G., Teitscheid, P. 2017. A participatory approach to minimizing food waste in the food industry—a manual for managers. *Sustainability*, 9(66), pp. 1–21. https://www.mdpi.com/2071-1050/9/1/66.

Tanner, D. 2012. *Managing the Value Chain to Deliver on Consumer Perceptions of Value*. 2012 Value Chain Innovation Forum: Creating a More Profitable and Competitive Canadian Agri-Food Sector, Delta Meadowvale, Mississauga Ontario, April 3-4, 2012. Gooch, M., Brandle, J. Eds Accessible at: https://vcm-international.com/wp-content/uploads/2013/04/VCIF-Final-Report-English-Feb-27-2013.pdf

Whitehead, P., Parfitt, J., Bojczuk, K., James, K. 2013. *Estimates of waste in the food and drink value chain*. Waste & Resouces Action Program. Banbury. Accessible at: www.wrap.org.uk/sites/files/wrap/Estimates%20of%20waste%20in%20the%20food%20and%20drink%20supply%20chain_0.pdf

WRAP. 2009. *household food and drink waste in the UK*. Waste & Resources Action Program Final Report, Banbury, www.wrap.org.uk

WRAP. 2015. *Whole Chain Resource Efficiency*. Waste & Resources Action Program, Banbury. Accessible from: www.wrap.org.uk/content/whole-chain-resource-efficiency

Zokaei, K. 2014. *Sustainability, Lean and Enterprise Excellence, Profiting from Reductions in Waste*. Presentation to Food and Drink Federation on Managing Sustainability Opportunities & Risks in the Food & Drink Industry; SA Partners. Accessible at: www.slideshare.net/keivanz/food-waste-43074628

7

FOOD WASTE (AND LOSS) AT THE RETAIL LEVEL

Felicitas Schneider and Mattias Eriksson

Introduction

Within Sustainable Development Goal 12.3 of the United Nations (UN), the retail sector is named explicitly as a target level to fulfil the 50% food waste reduction goal by 2030 (UN, 2015). In recent years, more information has emerged about food losses and waste in retail, but in most cases the dataset is restricted to one company (e.g. Lebersorger and Schneider, 2014a), a few product groups (e.g. WRAP, 2011; Eriksson et al., 2012, 2016; Lebersorger and Schneider, 2014a; Buzby et al., 2015) or a restricted number of outlets (e.g. Eriksson et al., 2012; Buzby et al., 2015; Cicatiello et al., 2016; Mattsson et al., 2018). In addition, the available literature world-wide is limited to mostly industrialised countries and to retail chains or supermarkets, while data from wholesalers, street markets and small grocery stores are lacking. While the scope of available data and the options for extrapolation are limited, the available data show that the proportion of waste in the retail sector is smaller than in many other stages of the food supply chain (FSC). The retail level is generally estimated to produce less than 10% waste in relation to delivered mass (Eriksson, 2015), whereas other stages in the FSC exceed this value. Nikkel et al. (2019) reported that retail food waste contributed 12% to entire food waste along the Canadian FSC and according to Stenmarck et al. (2016) retail is believed to produce about 5% of the total food waste in EU.

Nevertheless, taking the retail sector into account is essential in prevention of food waste, for several reasons. For example, the retail stage is located near the end of the FSC and thus food offered on retail shelves comprises all resources used and environmental impacts generated upstream in food production, processing, packaging, etc. Furthermore, supermarkets represent a relatively manageable number of sites where good-quality surplus food, mostly still fit for human consumption, could be collected and utilised for other nutrition purposes (Eriksson et al., 2015; Eriksson and Spångberg, 2017; Porat et al., 2018). According to Gruber et al. (2016), four additional factors explain the high relevance of the retail sector within the food waste issue.

First, retail plays an important gatekeeper function within the FSC (as do wholesalers). In countries with highly concentrated markets dominated by few companies, retail has high purchasing power and influence over the food items produced and offered, the amounts and the quality (Parfitt et al., 2010; Gruber et al., 2016; Feedback, 2017; Eriksson et al., 2017). Sweden is a good example of such a country, since the market share of the five largest food retail companies amounted to 94.7% in 2002, which was the highest in Europe (average 69.2%) (Vander Stichele et al., 2006). These five companies also own or control large parts of the distribution chain and, via private brands, some of the production. This reflects the typical situation in industrialised countries, where food retail involves national or international supermarket chains with many outlets. However, within emerging and developing countries the situation may be similar or completely different. Some, such as Indonesia, are facing an increasing growth of modern supermarkets in comparison to traditional wet markets such as "pasar" (Soma, 2018). Other countries, such as South Africa, are in transition, depending both on small kiosks known as "spazas stores" and informal street vendors, and on (inter)national supermarket chains, which are rapidly increasing in importance, especially in high-income urban areas (Battersby, 2017). In Brazil, public marketplaces such as the so-called CEASAs (Centrais de Abastecimento), which are mostly managed by public authorities, are important food supply sources for both retailers and consumers (Menezes et al., 2015). In all cases, as Gruber et al. (2016) point out, retail controls the point of sale and can stimulate specific purchasing habits by households. Second, the outlet is the real distribution point of food items and the corresponding food waste is generated there. Third, due to the high absolute concentration of surplus products which are not sold due to high turnover, retail outlets are easier to target in food waste prevention measures than, for example, households. Fourth, the cooperation paths of various stakeholders (e.g. suppliers, consumers, authorities) converge at the retail outlet (Gruber et al., 2016).

Most retail companies record non-sold products as a cost within their data warehousing. As non-sold products represent a loss of sales/turnover, information about food waste is hidden within cost accounting, but normally not determined in detail. Thus, the term used for non-sold products in cost accounting tools is "loss", expressed in terms of financial loss. This means that the available economic data must be converted into mass if waste topics or environmental issues are to be addressed. Corresponding uncertainties result from that conversion. Moreover, many studies on retail food waste use terms such as "loss", "shrinkage" or "shrink" (cf. Buzby et al., 2015) or similar terms, rather than "waste". A precise definition of the food streams included or excluded is not always given in the literature.

Irrespective of the term or definition used for food waste in supermarkets, data from different supermarket departments provide different perspectives on the problem. Figure 7.1 exemplifies this by showing the share of waste generated in different product categories. As can be seen, fresh fruit and vegetables are the dominant category from a mass perspective, but are less dominant if the focus is shifted to economic value or environmental impact (here represented by the carbon footprint). The opposite trend can be seen for animal products, which have a higher value in terms of both economic and environmental impact and represent a more significant share of retail food waste when it is quantified in monetary units or environmental impact units.

Following increasing concerns among consumers about topics such as fair trade, healthy food, regional supply and responsible food production, in recent years retailers have started to broach the issue of food waste, reporting their responsibilities, strategies and measures within corporate social responsibility (CSR), sustainability reports and member mailshots (cf. Tesco, 2014; Spar AG, 2014; Spar Holding AG, 2017). Retailers are now also more interested in supporting food waste reduction initiatives and in cooperating with other stakeholders on this issue.

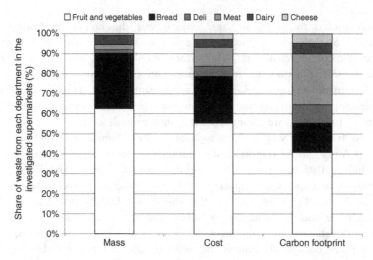

Figure 7.1 Depending on the units used, different supermarket products contribute different shares of food waste. Meat is a good example of products where a small mass of waste represents a much larger share of the environmental impact and cost.

Source: Based on data presented in Scholz et al. (2015), Eriksson (2015) and Brancoli et al. (2017), with the dairy department used to normalise the data.

Generation and composition of food waste in retail

One of the first retail companies to publish internal data on food waste generated within operations was Tesco, in 2013. The data showed that less than 1% of the offered food was wasted, which corresponded to 46,000 tonnes per year for Tesco's UK activities (Parfitt et al., 2010). This was an important signal to other international companies to begin playing a more active role in reducing food waste. Table 7.1 provides a brief overview of international results on food waste in the retail sector.

As mentioned, total assessments of the national food retail sector or of individual retailers are still scarce, mostly due to data confidentiality. As food waste generated by retail is not restricted to the company itself, more information on the influence of retail on other levels of the FSC (pre-store, in-store and post-store) is provided in the following sub-sections.

Pre-store food waste induced by retail

Due to the strong influence of retail on quality issues, especially related to fresh produce, individual marketing standards have a strong influence on losses at global supplier level. Although 26 of the former specific marketing standards for fruit and vegetables in the European Union were replaced by general marketing standards in 2009, imperfect or "wonky" products are still generally not sold at the retail level by international or national chains. Products not meeting specifications set by the purchasing department of retail chains are rejected on-site, as return transport is too costly. If they are returned to the supplier, they are mostly used for animal feed, biogas production or soil amendment. There are also take-back agreements and rejection policies that allow retailers to waste food at the expense of the supplier. These procedures make the waste problem less visible to retailers, as there is no internal recording, and suppliers are often not in a position to challenge the system (Parfitt et al., 2010; Eriksson et al., 2012, 2017; Feedback, 2017; Ghosh and Eriksson, 2019). In

Table 7.1 Summary of published studies quantifying relative food waste in supermarkets. FFV = fresh fruit and vegetables, FSC = food supply chain. The relative waste refers to the percentage waste in relation to the specified reference base

Reference	Country	Data collection method	Reference base	Product group	Relative waste (%)
Fehr et al. (2002)	Brazil	Quantification at retailer	Delivered mass	FFV	8.8
Tofanelli et al. (2007)	Brazil	Interviews	Delivered mass	FFV:	3.2
Tofanelli et al. (2009)	Brazil	Interviews		in supermarkets	1.9
				in grocery stores	4.2
				in street markets	21.5
Buzby et al. (2009)	USA	Supplier records	Supplier shipment data	Fruit	8.4–10.7
				Vegetables	8.4–10.3
Göbel et al. (2012)	Germany	Analysis of national statistics	Delivered mass	Retail sector	1
Buzby & Hyman (2012)	USA	Analysis of national statistics	Food supply value	FFV	9
				Dairy products	9
Eriksson et al. (2012)	Sweden	Store records	Delivered mass	FFV	4.3
Beretta et al. (2013)	Switzer-land	Estimate from store records	Volumes of sales	FFV	8–9
Katajajuuri et al. (2014)	Finland	Interviews	Not specified	Retail sector	1–2
Stensgård & Hanssen (2016)	Norway	Store records	Sales value	Fruit	4.5
				Vegetables	4.3
				Milk products	0.8
				Cheese	0.9
Lebersorger and Schneider (2014a)	Austria	Store records	Sales in cost price	FFV	4.3
				Bread & pastries	2.8
				wasted by retail	9.7
				Bread & pastries returned to bakery	1.3
				Dairy products	
Lebersorger and Schneider (2014b)	Austria	Store records	Sales in cost price	Total	1.82
				FFV	5.05
				Dairy products	1.67
				Bread & pastries	2.91
Eriksson et al. (2014)	Sweden	Store records	Sold mass	Organic perishable animal products	0.70
				Conventional perishable animal products	0.56
Mattsson & Williams (2015)	Sweden	Store records	Sold mass	FFV (only in-store waste)	1.9
Eriksson (2015)	Sweden	Store records	Sold mass	FFV	4.7
				Dairy	0.34

(*Continued*)

Table 7.1 (Cont).

Reference	Country	Data collection method	Reference base	Product group	Relative waste (%)
				Cheese	0.55
				Deli	1.5
				Meat	1.3
Ju et al. (2017)	Japan	National statistics	Initial total net food supply to FSC	Retail sector	2.2
			Input into retail sector	Retail sector	2.3
Eriksson et al. (2017)	Sweden	Supplier records	Returned volume	Premium bread	32
Porat et al. (2018)	Israel	Interviews	FFV marketing volume	Bananas, tomatoes, cucumbers	15–17
				Oranges, peppers, grapes	7–11
				Potatoes, apples	4–5

2009, a case study in Austria showed that bread and pastries are generally governed by take-back agreements between supplier and retail (Schneider and Scherhaufer, 2009). The supplier is only paid for the amounts sold, while non-sold products must be redistributed and handled at the supplier's expense, a system which has considerably impaired the economic performance of bakeries. Discounters do not participate in such agreements and take responsibility for the whole order (Schneider and Scherhaufer, 2009). In addition to marketing standards, contracts for agreed amounts of delivered produce lead to systematic overproduction in agriculture in order to overcome the risk of inability to deliver due to poor harvest, which would incur penalties (Feedback, 2017).

In-store food waste

As mentioned, non-sold food is usually recorded internally as a financial loss within the book-keeping tools of major food retailers. In order to determine the food waste prevention potential, these financial data must be converted into mass data and then divided into damage/breakages (e.g. products damaged/broken by staff or customers and no longer useable), stolen products, products used for own purposes (e.g. cleaning agents used for cleaning the outlet) and products removed from the shelf for other reasons. The last group is the primary target for food waste prevention measures, although such measures could also seek to reduce the share of damaged/broken products. However, part of this amount of waste may already have been donated to social organisations or used for animal feed, which does not account for food waste but is an economic loss for the retailer. Thus, calculation and interpretation of data from cost accounting tools often needs some manual processing for the accurate assessment that is required to achieve reliable datasets and enable appropriate prevention measures to be formulated. Both Eriksson et al. (2012) and Cicatiello et al.

(2017) quantified the share of food that is wasted without being recorded – the unrecorded in-store waste. In contrast, Lebersorger and Schneider (2014a) did not find evidence for such variations in the book-keeping tool in comparison to test sorting in some outlets.

One of the first studies on food loss and waste along the entire FSC was published by the Economic Research Service of the US Department of Agriculture in 1995. The authors, Kantor et al. (1997), estimated that approximately 2 mass-% of available food in the USA was lost within the retail sector. Available data from the literature show that fruit and vegetables, dairy products, bread and fresh meat products are the most wasted products at retail level (e.g. Kantor et al., 1997; Schneider and Wassermann, 2005; Eriksson et al., 2012, 2014, 2017; Lebersorger and Schneider, 2014a, 2014b; Cicatiello et al., 2016; Brancoli et al., 2017).

Among the product groups with high levels of waste there are single products contributing high shares of waste. For Swedish retail this is described in detail by Eriksson (2015) where tomatoes, bananas and lettuce were the most wasted products in the FFV section while pork chops, minced beef and pork legs were the most wasted in the meat section and skimmed and semi-skimmed milk and flavoured yoghurt were the most wasted in the dairy section.

Post-store food waste induced by retail

As mentioned, retailers strongly influence the shopping and consumption habits of consumers. In particular, special offers on multipacks and so-called BOGOF (buy one, get one free) offers are reported to lead to household-level surpluses of food, which is wasted once the "sell-by" or "use-by" date is reached. According to Parfitt et al. (2010), UK consumers attribute half their food impulse buying at retail outlets to in-store promotions. Mondejar-Jimenez et al. (2016) claim that the layout of goods in supermarkets also has a strong influence on the shopping behaviour of consumers and, as a consequence, on household food wasting behaviour. Moreover, a study in South Korea found evidence that travel time and buying frequency can influence food over-purchasing, with the individual effects differing depending on the format of the retail outlet visited (Lee, 2018). In surveys, consumers themselves blame retailers for not offering useful pack sizes or for selling poor-quality perishable food (e.g. for bread and FFV) (cf. Brook Lyndhurst Ltd., 2007; Schmidt et al., 2018).

Reasons and influencing factors for food waste in retail

There are multiple reasons for food losses at retail level, some of which are described in detail by Kantor et al. (1997), Schneider and Wassermann (2005), Mena et al. (2010), Lebersorger and Schneider (2014a), Canali et al. (2014), Buzby et al. (2015) and Lewis et al. (2017). Common reasons for food being discarded in supermarkets are: expired shelf-life (past the best-before or use-by date), visual defects/damage to the food item itself or the packaging, which make food unsellable (at least at full price), and overstocking due to difficulties in accurate sales prediction. Some of these issues are addressed below.

Because food can be wasted for a large variety of reasons, the food waste issue is difficult to solve with a single solution. As pointed out by Lindbom et al. (2014), it is important to identify not just the reason for food being discarded, but also the underlying root cause of the problem. However, such identification is problematic, since there are so many potential root causes: for example, expired shelf-life, shortened shelf-life due to high piles at display, too large inflow of products, unexpected lack of demand, or a combination of all these.

Since it is very difficult to identify a single root cause, it may be more useful to assess risk factors, since these can potentially better capture the multiplier effect when several risk factors are present and include factors not necessarily leading to food waste, but increasing the risk of waste. Possible risk factors can be low demand, short shelf-life, unsuitable packaging or storage conditions and inappropriate handling by staff and customers.

Among others, Mercier et al. (2017) show that a poor cold chain due to long transport distances, improper or overloaded display cabinets in retail outlets and permanent rotation of stock between display and cooling facility within outlets leads to significant reductions in the shelf-life of perishables, even in developed countries such as Canada. This may have an impact at the retailer level or ultimately in the household, but is difficult to identify.

From an economic perspective, retailers try to order just the right amount of all products, meaning that there are no empty shelves (to avoid opportunity costs) and no unsellable surplus (to avoid loss of purchase costs). Unfortunately, there are several influencing factors that can introduce variation in demand and make prediction difficult. These include the weather, public holidays and school holidays, and also greater product variety (Lindbom et al., 2014), since having more different types of products decreases turnover for each and makes forecasting more difficult. On the other hand, providing a large variety of products also means freedom for customers, which supermarkets might use as a competitive advantage to differentiate them from their competitors. Since a larger variety might thus be expected to increase profits, retailers may be unwilling to reduce their product range, with waste simply being part of the price they have to pay for the larger range of products sold. In practice, Lebersorger and Schneider (2014b) show that food discounters with a smaller assortment of products generate less in-store food waste.

Promotions have a similar effect on food waste, since they temporarily shift the turnover of products and make forecasting more difficult. According to Eriksson (2015), some promotions prompt the customer to buy the promoted product, but to reject similar products (so-called substitute goods) as a consequence. Since forecasting of sales is more difficult when there are many aspects to consider, temporary shifts in sales can be difficult for retailers to predict accurately. This leads to a larger than necessary stock of non-promoted products and, since the store must not run out of the promoted product, a surplus of the promoted product. The result of the promotion is increased waste of the promoted product and also increased waste of similar products. Added to the cost of the waste is the lack of profit that arises when the store sells products at a lower margin than usual. Thus promotions can seem like a waste of effort, but they are unlikely to disappear since they are there to attract customers and thereby increase overall profits. Promotions can thus be viewed as a marketing cost, and waste as simply part of that cost.

The literature is somewhat inconclusive regarding the effect of supermarket outlet size and the corresponding food waste generated within the outlet. Based on a review of a large range of results in the literature, Alexander and Smaje (2008) concluded that larger retailers have more losses as only perfect fruit and vegetables are offered to consumers. In contrast, Parfitt et al. (2010) concluded that future demand is more difficult to predict for small grocery outlets, as slight changes in consumer behaviour have more impact on stock and therefore generate a greater proportion of waste than in large supermarkets. Based on a detailed statistical analysis of 612 outlets of an Austrian supermarket chain, Lebersorger and Schneider (2014a) found that food loss rates decline with increasing sales area, increasing number of purchases per year and increasing sales of the retail outlet. They also found that these factors only explain 33% or less of the variation in food loss rates within the outlets of the same retailing company, depending on food category. This indicates that food loss rates depend on other influencing factors such as individual work routines, planning approaches or staff experience (Eriksson et al., 2014; Leber-sorger and Schneider, 2014a). A closer assessment of 83% of Austrian food retailers indicated that food retail discounters achieve a lower level of food waste than other supermarkets, which may be due to restricted assortment (Lebersorger and Schneider, 2014b).

Unexpected external events may cause irregular food waste at retail, e.g. if customers decide to stop buying a certain product. This decision might be caused by food scandals, such as presence of toxin-producing *Escherichia coli*, and it makes no difference whether the suspicion is proven or not. Several thousand cases of *E. coli* illness were reported in Germany in early summer 2011 and for some weeks it was not possible to identify the source. However, consumers were cautioned by the authorities about the safety of cucumbers and other vegetables and the market for these items collapsed after the first notice of suspicion, not only in Germany but also in surrounding countries. Beside the economic loss due to price deterioration, thousands of tons of good-quality fresh produce were wasted at produc-tion and retail levels (Gaul, 2011). In less dramatic cases, such as discussions about unhealthy food, affected products are also likely to end up as food waste if the supplier cannot stop production fast enough or find an alternative market. According to Taylor (2006), there are a number of actions in the supermarket that can lead to a "bullwhip effect", where the amp-litude of the customer reaction increases from retail to wholesale, from wholesale to industry and from industry to primary production, and everyone along the chain increases/decreases production and increases/decreases stock in order to compensate for the customer reaction. Increased communication along the logistics chain, so that primary producers get their sig-nals directly from the end customers, could be one way to deal with this problem. Another way to decrease the risk of a bullwhip effect could be to reduce the activities that increase variation. According to Taylor (2006), these activities include promotions, large numbers of products and/or actors in the logistics chain, and ordering and producing in large batches with large stocks. Therefore, the same risk factors for food waste can be problematic both within supermarkets and in other parts of the FSC.

Literature from emerging and developing countries mentions other reasons for losses in the food retail sector. Improper storage (e.g. lack of cold chain during transport and retail), poor transport conditions (such as poor roads, lack of protecting packaging, huge distances), poor quality of produce coming from smallholders, and challenging environment (such as temperature, humidity, rainfall) are some of the problems, in addition to those reported for industrialised countries (Tofanelli et al., 2007, 2009). Lack of sufficient transport capacity and lack of regular access to new stock due to the rural location of retailers can also result in even non-perishable products having already reached their expiry date before the products reach the retailers. This situation has been reported, for example, in South Africa and leads to losses for the shop owners (Pereira et al., 2014).

Prevention measures

The varying food loss rates indicated by Table 7.1 and the weak influence of the outlet characteristics described above suggest that there is great potential for further food waste pre-vention in retail in practice. In recent years, many different prevention policies have been developed and implemented at retail level. These policies can be categorised as:

- targeting internal staff only, or including external stakeholders too;
- brought into force by law (obligatory measures) or developed as voluntary agreements;

- focusing on prevention of surpluses before generation, or finding alternative purposes for already generated surpluses.

Most types of waste and loss are unintentional, but since several risk factors are inevitably a natural part of any activity, waste must also be accepted as natural. A common reason for accepting the presence of risk factors is that they are too expensive or too difficult to prevent. There can also be a conflict of interest between waste reduction and increased profit, with waste reduction likely to be a lower priority. On the other hand, there are also many measures that could easily be economically justified and therefore should be implemented in order to reduce food waste (Eriksson & Strid, 2013). The problem is knowing which problems have low required management intensity (Garrone et al., 2014), meaning that they are cheap and/or easy to solve.

Possible measures include in-house measures, training of staff, restrictions on BOGOF offers and multipacks, reduced product range toward the end of opening hours, use of damaged/ripe products for in-house catering or ready-to-eat products, selling imperfect products, selling surplus products at a cheaper price, food donation and fair trading rules. A retail company in the UK tested a change in promotion strategy from BOGOF to "buy one, get one free later", where consumers were able to convert a coupon within two weeks and did not have to purchase double amounts of perishable food at once (Gooch et al., 2010).

A well-known nationwide voluntary agreement on prevention of food waste is the Courtauld Commitment, which was introduced in the UK in 2005. The latest version, called Courtauld Commitment 2025, sets clear targets for the whole FSC, e.g. a 20% per person reduction in food and drink waste associated with food production and consumption (WRAP, 2018). The signatories from retail comprise 95% of the UK grocery retail sector by value of sales and have promised to report their food waste separately from other waste streams on an annual basis (WRAP, 2018). Another voluntary agreement, set up by The Consumer Goods Forum in 2015, aims to "first prevent food waste, then maximise its recovery towards the goal of halving food waste within our own retail and manufacturing operations by 2025, versus a 2016 baseline" (Consumer Goods Forum, 2016). About 400 retailers and manufacturers around the globe are affected by this agreement. Implemented actions include advanced forecasting, pricing down food items near expiry date and partnerships with social organisations or restaurants using surpluses from retailers (Consumer Goods Forum, 2016).

Reducing the price of products near their expiry date in the course of routine monitoring of shelves is a widespread prevention measure targeted at consumers who value reduced costs for slightly imperfect products. In order to increase demand for those price-reduced products and to automate recognition of expiry date, a mobile app called Chowberry has been developed in Nigeria. It informs supermarket owners about products expiring soon and informs deprived clients and social organisations about the price reduction. In 2018, the app already succeeded in tests covering 20 shops and 300 clients in Lagos and Abuja (http://chowberry.com/). Other research indicates that issues such as the introduction of dynamic shelf-life for perishable products, in combination with price reduction, could be a more effective strategy for retailers than single measures (Buisman et al., 2017).

Donation of edible surplus food from retail to social organisations is gaining increasing attention. This measure has been applied globally through voluntary agreements since the 1960s, and on an obligatory basis since 2014. A particular characteristic of surplus food donation is that it must make a threefold contribution to sustainability, by resolving ecological, economic and social issues for all stakeholders. Long-time experience of voluntary agreements on donation of food surpluses shows that almost the total amount of food items offered by retail is suitable for redistribution to people in need (Alexander and Smaje, 2008; Schneider, 2013). Nevertheless, case studies show that the potential for food donation has not yet been exploited to the full, although some products are donated in amounts that exceed demand (Schneider, 2013; Capodistrias, 2017). Following years of voluntary activities, legislation governing surplus food donations from retail to social organisations was implemented in Wallonia in 2014 (Wallex, 2014) and in France in 2016 (*Journal Officiel de la République Française*, 2016). Similar legislation has been recommended in other countries, such as Norway, in order to exploit a greater share of the existing food waste reduction potential (Capodistrias, 2017).

Another statutory activity is mentioned by Lee (2018), who suggests introducing a regulatory framework for food retailers' marketing procedures, especially for developing countries, in order to avoid the development of disadvantageous lifestyles from the outset, including over-buying of food which leads to household food waste.

Food waste reduction measures that promote alternative uses for surpluses already generated are also addressed within the literature as valorisation measures. These aim to create value from the surplus/waste occurring and thereby reduce the negative effect of the waste. Donation of surpluses to charity can be considered a valorisation measure, since it handles the surplus food rather than reducing the production of food. Using surplus bread from bakeries for the production of beer is another example.

The order of different waste prevention and valorisation options for supermarkets is shown in Figure 7.2. The concept of waste prevention differs depending on the perspective.

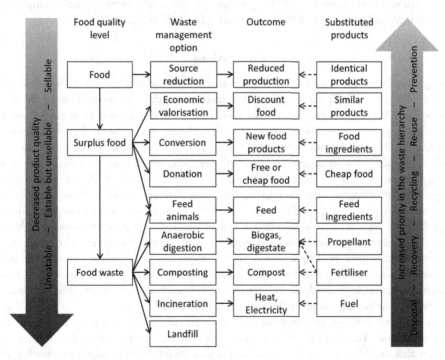

Figure 7.2 Waste management framework showing the priority of different destinations for retail food waste.

Source: Eriksson (2015).

From an environmental perspective, waste is prevented as long as the food is never produced or used for its intended purpose, i.e. eaten by humans. From an economic perspective, it would be a waste to sell the food at a reduced price, since that is a loss of money.
With this logic, the measure of cutting the price by 50% on the day before the best-before
date may prevent food from being wasted, but still wastes some of the value of the product.
However, since a price reduction also means that half the value is saved, this type of measure can be categorised as prevention through economic valorisation (Figure 7.2), as the food
is sold through normal channels with a price reduction in order to save some of the economic value and possibly the whole environmental value.

In Figure 7.2, there are also a few important trends that follow the order of priority
in the EU waste hierarchy. First, the less prioritised measures are all general and do
not require food waste with high levels of product quality, biosecurity, separation or
storage conditions. Therefore, these options are cheap and general, but have an outcome with much lower economic value than the original food products. In order to
prevent food from being wasted (i.e. using it for human consumption), there are high
hygiene requirements that need to be met, which makes separation and proper storage
important. These options, therefore, need more effort from the supermarket, but in
return provide a more valuable outcome. The problem is that the outcome of most
waste management options is profitable for society (SEPA, 2011, 2012), but not necessarily for the supermarket.

Prevention measures suggested to have an impact on retail located in emerging and
developing countries include optimisation of infrastructure (e.g. roads, cold chain), prioritising regional suppliers in order to cut long shipping distances and avoid damage during transport, and increased product quality from the start (Tofanelli et al., 2007, 2009).

Conclusions

Although the proportion of food waste generated within the retail sector itself is relatively
low (~10% of mass), retail has a significant influence on other stakeholders along the FSC.
This available power and retail networks should be used to enhance cooperation among
stakeholders and to provide/create a trading and purchasing environment that promotes prevention of food loss and waste. Retailers can actively influence the behaviour of stakeholders
and also of their own management and staff members, which enables a broad range of
potential measures to be implemented. In recent years, retailers have shown a remarkable
change in acknowledging and shouldering their responsibility for food waste in the retail
sector, which is promising, but their responses could sometimes be implemented in a more
straightforward approach. As at all other levels of the FSC, there is no single food waste
prevention measure that could solve the problem within retail. However, there is a raft of
measures which could be implemented within food retail companies or together with
cooperation partners along the FSC. Some issues can be addressed on a voluntary basis,
through agreements by individuals and market conditions. For other topics, obligatory measures may be needed, e.g. unfair trading practices that reflect the market power of retail and
lead to food waste along the upstream FSC are currently under consideration within the
European Union. There are several pros and cons that have to be balanced in formulating
measures that consider the regional characteristics of member states, while also sharing the
risk of natural uncertainties in product yield and quality, especially in agricultural produce
and between suppliers and retailers.

Acknowledgement

The authors would like to thank all colleagues involved in the research studies mentioned within this chapter for their valuable work.

References

Alexander C., Smaje C. (2008) Surplus retail food redistribution: An analysis of a third sector model. *Resources, Conservation and Recycling*, 52, 1290–1298.

Battersby J. (2017) Food system transformation in the absence of food system planning: The case of supermarket and shopping mall retail expansion in Cape Town, South Africa. *Built Environment*, 43, 3, 417–430. doi: 10.2148/benv.43.3.417.

Beretta, Claudio, Stoessel, Franziska, Baier, Urs, Hellweg, Stefanie. (2013) Quantifying food losses and the potential for reduction in Switzerland. *Waste Management*, 33, 764–773. http://dx.doi.org/10.1016/j.wasman.2012.11.007

Brancoli, P., Rousta, K., Bolton, K. (2017) Life cycle assessment of supermarket food waste. *Resources, Conservation and Recycling*, 118, 39–46.

Brook Lyndhurst Ltd. (2007) WRAP Food Behaviour Consumer Research - Findings from the qualitative phase. Draft Final Report, May 2007.

Buisman M.E., Haijema R., Bloemhof-Ruwaard J.M. (2017) Discounting and dynamic shelf life to reduce fresh food waste at retailers. *International Journal of Production Economics*, in press, 1–11. doi: 10.1016/j.ijpe.2017.07.016.

Buzby, J.C., Farah Wells, H., Axtman, B., Mickey, J., (2009). Supermarket loss estimates for fresh fruits, vegetables, meat, poultry, and seafood and their use in the ERS loss-adjusted food availability data. *Economic Information Bulletin Number*, 44, United States Department of Agriculture, Economic Research Service, Washington, USA.

Buzby J.C., Hyman J. (2012) Total and per capita value of food loss in the United States. *Food Policy*, 37, 561–570, http://dx.doi.org/10.1016/j.foodpol.2012.06.002.

Buzby J.C., Bentley J.T., Padera B., Ammon C., Campuzano J. (2015) Estimated fresh produce shrink and food loss in U.S. supermarkets. *Agriculture*, 5, 626–648. doi: 10.3390/agriculture5030626.

Canali M., Östergren K., Amani P., Aramyan L., Sijtsema S., Korhonen O., Silvennoinen K., Moates G., O'Connor C. (2014) Drivers of current food waste generation, threats of future increase and opportunities for reduction. FUSIONS final report, Bologna, ISBN 978-94-6257-354-3.

Capodistrias P.V. (2017) Norwegian Supermarkets and Food Waste – Prevention and Redistribution Strategies. *Oslo*, available at www.refreshcoe.eu/wp-content/uploads/2017/06/supermarkets-and-food-waste-FIVH.pdf (last accessed April 8th, 2019).

Cicatiello C., Franco S., Pancino B., Blasi E. (2016) The value of food waste: An exploratory study on retailing. *Journal of Retailing and Consumer Services*, 30, 96–104. doi: 10.1016/j.jretconser.2016.01.004.

Cicatiello C., Franco S., Pancino B., Blasi E., Falasconi L. (2017) The dark side of retail food waste: Evidences from in-store data. *Resources, Conservation and Recycling*, 125, 273–281.

Consumer Goods Forum (2016) Food Waste - Committments and Achievements of CGF members. www.theconsumergoodsforum.com/files/Publications/2016_CGF_Food_Waste_Booklet.pdf (last accessed April 8th, 2019).

Eriksson M. (2015) Prevention and Management of Supermarket Food Waste: With Focus on Reducing Greenhouse Gas Emissions, Doctoral thesis 119, Acta Universitatis agriculturae Sueciae, Swedish university of Agricultural Science, Uppsala.

Eriksson, M., Ghosh, R., Mattsson, L., Ismatov, A. (2017) Take back policy in the perspective of food waste generation in the supplier-retailer interface. *Resources, Conservation and Recycling*, 122, 83–93.

Eriksson, M., Spångberg, J. (2017) Carbon footprint and energy use of food waste management options for fresh fruit and vegetables from supermarkets. *Waste Management*, 60, 786.799.

Eriksson M., Strid I., Hansson P-A. (2012) Food losses in six Swedish retail stores: Wastage of fruit and vegetables in relation to quantities delivered. *Resources, Conservation and Recycling*, 68, 14–20.

Eriksson, M., Strid, I., (2013), *Svinnreducerande åtgärder i butik - Effekter på kvantitet, ekonomi och klimatpåverkan [Waste reducing measures in supermarkets – Effects on quantity, economy and greenhouse gas emissions]*, Report 6594, Swedish Environmental Protection Agency, Stockholm.

Eriksson M., Strid I., Hansson P-A. (2014) Waste of organic and conventional meat and dairy products: A case study from Swedish retail. *Resources, Conservation and Recycling*, 83, 44–52.

Eriksson, M., Strid, I., Hansson, P-A. (2015) Carbon footprint of food waste management options in the waste hierarchy – a Swedish case study. *Journal of Cleaner Production*, 93, 115–125.

Eriksson, M., Strid, I., Hansson, P.-A. (2016) Food waste reduction in supermarkets – net costs and benefits of reduced storage temperature. *Recourses, Conservation and Recycling*, 107, 73–81.

Feedback (2017) Causes of Food Waste in International Supply Chains. www.refreshcoe.eu/wp-content/uploads/2017/07/Causes-of-food-waste-in-international-supply-chains_Feedback.pdf (last accessed April 8th, 2019).

Gaul B. (2011) Schlimmste Krise seit Tschernobyl (Worst crisis since Chernobyl). Kurier, Print version from 08.06.2011, p. 16.

Garrone P., Melacini M., Perego A. (2014) Opening the black box of food waste reduction. *Food Policy*, 46, 129–139, http://dx.doi.org/10.1016/j.foodpol.2014.03.014.

Ghosh, R., Eriksson, M. (2019) Food waste due to retail power in supply chains: Evidence from Sweden. *Global Food Security*, 20, 1–8.

Göbel, C., Teitscheid, P., Ritter, G., Blumenthal, A., Friedrich, S., Frick, T., Grotstollen, L., Möllenbeck, C., Rottstegge, L., Pfeiffer, C., Baumkötter, D., Wetter, C., Uekötter, B., Burdick, B., Langen, N., Lettenmeier, M. & Rohn, H. (2012). *Reducing Food Waste - Identification of causes and courses of action in North Rhine-Westphalia*. Abridged version, University of Applied Sciences Münster, Institute for Sustainable Nutrition and Food Production – iSuN, Münster, Germany.

Gooch M., Felfel A., Marenick N. (2010) *Food Waste in Canada - Opportunities to increase the competitiveness of Canada's agri-food sector, while simultaneously improving the environment*. Georg Morris Centre, Value Chain Management Centre.

Gruber V., Holweg C., Teller C. (2016) What a waste! Exploring the human reality of food waste from the store manager's perspective. *Journal of Public Policy & Marketing, Ahead of Print*, doi: 10.1509/jppm.14.095.

Journal Officiel de la République Française (2016) LOI no 2016-138 du 11février 2016 relative à la lutte contre le gaspillage alimentaire (1). Paris, 12.02.2016.

Ju M., Osako M., Harashina S. (2017) Food loss rate in food supply chain using material flow analysis. *Waste Management*, 61, 443–454. doi: 10.1016/j.wasman.2017.01.021.

Kantor L.S., Lipton K., Manchester A., Oliveira V. (1997) Estimation and addressing America's food losses. *Food Review*, 20, 1, 2–12.

Katajajuuri J.M., Silvennoinen K., Hartikainen H., Heikkilä L., Reinikainen A. (2014) Food waste in the Finnish food chain. *Journal of Cleaner Production*, 73, 322-329, http://dx.doi.org/10.1016/j.jclepro.2013.12.057.

Lebersorger S., Schneider F. (2014a) Food loss rates at the food retail, influencing factors and reasons as a basis for waste prevention measures. *Waste Management*, 34, 1911–191. doi: 10.1016/j.wasman.2014.06.013.

Lebersorger S., Schneider F. (2014b) Aufkommen an Lebensmittelverderb im österreichischen Lebens-mittelhandel. Endbericht im Auftrag der ECR Arbeitsgruppe Abfallvermeidung. Wien, www.ecr.digital/wp_contents/uploads/2016/09/Aufkommen_an_Lebensmittelverderb_im_Oesterr_Lebensmittel handel.pdf (last accessed April 8th, 2019).

Lee K.C.L. (2018) Grocery shopping, food waste, and the retail landscape of cities: The case of Seoul. *Journal of Cleaner Production*, 172, 325–334. doi: 10.1016/j.jclepro.2017.10.085.

Lewis H., Downes J., Verghese K., Young G. (2017) Food waste opportunities within the food wholesale and retail sectors. Sydney, Prepared for the NSW Environment Protection Authority by the Institute for Sustainable Futures at the University of Technology Sydney.

Lindbom, I., Gustavsson, J., Sundström, B. (2014) Minskat svinn i livsmedelskedjan – ett helhetsgrepp, Report SR 866, SIK, Gothenburg.

Mattsson, L., Williams, H., (2015), Waste reduction potential of fresh fruit and vegetables at retail stores: A case study of three supermarkets in Sweden. 2nd International Conference on Global Food Security, October 11-14, 2015, Ithaca, USA.

Mattsson, L., Williams, H., Berghel, J. (2018) Waste of fresh fruit and vegetables at retailers in Sweden – Measuring and calculation of mass, economic cost and climate impact. *Resources, Conservation and Recycling*, 130, 118–126.

Mena, C., Adenso-Diaz, B., Yurt, O. (2010) The cause of food waste in the supplier-retailer interface: Evidences from the UK and Spain. *Resources, Conservation and Recycling*, 55, 648–658.

Menezes F., Porto S., Grisa C. (2015) Food Supply and Public Procurement in Brazil - A Historical Review. *Food and Social Policies Series 1, Centre of Excellence against Hunger*, available at https://documents.wfp.org/stellent/groups/public/documents/research/wfp286644.pdf (last accessed April 8th, 2019).

Mercier S., Villeneuve S., Mondor M., Uysal I. (2017) Time–temperature management along the food cold chain: A review of recent developments. *Comprehensive Reviews in Food Science and Food Safety*, 16, doi: 10.1111/1541-4337.12269.

Mondejar-Jimenez J.A., Ferrari G., Secondi L., Principato L. (2016) From the table to waste: An exploratory study on behaviour towards food waste of Spanish and Italian youths. *Journal of Cleaner Production*, 138, 8–18. doi: 10.1016/j.jclepro.2016.06.018.

Nikkel L., Maguire M., Gooch M., Bucknell D., LaPlain D., Dent B., Whitehead P., Felfel A. (2019) The Avoidable Crisis of Food Waste: Roadmap. *Second Harvest and Value Chain Management International*, Ontario, Canada. https://secondharvest.ca/wp-content/uploads/2019/01/Avoidable-Crisis-of-Food-Waste-The-Roadmap-by-Second-Harvest-and-VCMI.pdf (last accessed April 8th, 2019).

Parfitt J., Barthel M., Macnaughton S. (2010) Food waste within food supply chains: quantification and potential for change to 2050. Phil. Trans. R. Soc. B 365, 3065–3081. doi: 10.1098/rstb.2010.0126.

Pereira L.M., Cuneo C.N., Twine W.C. (2014) Food and cash: understanding the role of the retail sector in rural food security in South Africa. *Food Security*, 6, 339–357. doi: 10.1007/s12571-014-0349-1.

Porat R., Lichter A., Terry L.A., Harker R., Buzby J. (2018) Postharvest losses of fruit and vegetables during retail and in consumers' homes: Quantifications, causes, and means of prevention. *Postharvest. Biology and Technology*, 139, 135–149.

Schmidt T., Schneider F., Claupein E. (2018) Lebensmittelabfälle in privaten Haushalten in Deutschland – Analyse der Ergebnisse einer repräsentativen Erhebung 2016/2017 von GfK SE (Food waste in private households in Germany – Analysis of results from a representative survey 2016/2017 done by GfK SE). Thünen Working paper 92, Braunschweig.

Schneider F. (2013) The evolution of food donation with respect to waste prevention. *Waste Management*, 33, 755–763. doi: 10.1016/j.wasman.2012.10.025.

Schneider F., Scherhaufer S. (2009) Aufkommen und Verwertung ehemaliger Lebensmittel - am Beispiel von Brot und Gebäck (Generation and utilisation of former food – the example of bread and pastry). Report on behalf of the Austrian Ministry of Business, Family and Youth, Vienna.

Schneider F., Wassermann G. (2005) The second life of food losses. In Edmonton Waste Management (ed.): Waste – The Social Context, 11-14 May 2005, Edmonton, Alberta; Canada; Proceedings (CD); 588–594.

SEPA. (2011). *Nyttan med att minska livsmedelssvinnet i hela kedjan.* Report 6454, Swedish Environmental Protection Agency, Stockholm.

SEPA. (2012). *Nyttan med att minska livsmedelssvinnet.* Report 6527, Swedish Environmental Protection Agency, Stockholm.

Scholz K., Eriksson M., Strid I. (2015) Carbon footprint of supermarket food waste. *Resources, Conservation and Recycling*, 94, 56–65. doi: 10.1016/j.resconrec.2014.11.016.

Soma T. (2018) (Re) framing the Food Waste Narrative: Infrastructures of Urban Food Consumption and Waste in Indonesia. *Indonesia*, 105, 173–190.

Spar AG (2014) Nachhaltigkeitsbericht 2013. Spar AG, Salzburg, available at www.spar.at/content/dam/sparatwebsite/nachhaltigkeit/nachhaltigkeitsbericht/NH-Bericht2013-SPAR.pdf (last accessed April - 8th, 2019).

Spar Holding AG (2017) Nachhaltigkeitsbericht 2016. Salzburg, available at www.spar.at/content/dam/sparatwebsite/nachhaltigkeit/nachhaltigkeitsbericht/Nachhaltigkeitsbericht_2016_Gesamt.pdf (last accessed April 8th, 2019).

Stenmarck, Å., Jensen, C., Quested, T., Moates, G. (2016) Estimates of European food waste levels, ISBN 978-91-88319-01-2, Fusions, Stockholm.

Stensgård A.E., Hanssen O.J. (2016) Food Waste in Norway 2010-2015 - Final Report from the ForMat Project. ISBN No.:978-82-7520-750-8.

Taylor, D. (2006). *Demand management in agri-food supply chains: An analysis of the characteristics and problems and a framework for improvement*, The International Journal of Logistics Management 17, 163–186.

Tesco (2014) Tesco and society: Using our scale for good. 2013/14 half year update, UK. Available at www.tescoplc.com/media/1184/tesco_and_society_review_2014.pdf (last accessed April 8th, 2019).

Tofanelli M.B.D., Fernandes M.S., Carrijo N.S., Martins Filho O.B. (2009) Survey on fresh vegetables' losses in the retail market of Mineiros, Goiás State, Brazil (Levantamento de perdas em hortaliças frescas na rede varejista de Mineiros). *Horticultura Brasileira*, 27, 1, 116–120.

Tofanelli M.B.D., Fernandes M.S., Martins Filho O.B., Carrijo N.S. (2007) Fresh fruit losses at retail markets in Mineiros, State of Goiás, Brazil (Perdas de frutas frescas no comércio varejista de Mineiros-GO: Um estudo de caso). *Revista Brasileira de Fruticultura*, 29, 3, December 2007, doi: 10.1590/S0100-29452007000300020.

UN (2015) Resolution adopted by the General Assembly on 25 September 2015-70/1.Transforming our world: the 2030 Agenda for Sustainable Development. www.un.org/ga/search/view_doc.asp?symbol=A/RES/70/1&Lang=E (last accessed September 25th, 2018).

Vander Stichele M., van der Wal S., Oldenziel J. (2006) Who reaps the fruit? Critical issues in the fresh fruit. Amsterdam: SOMO, Centre for Research on Multinational Corporations.

Wallex (2014) Décret modifiant le décret du 11 mars 1999 relatif au permis d'environnement en vue de favoriser la distribution des invendus alimentaires consommables aux associations d'aide alimentaire. *Namur*, 13, 03.

WRAP (2011) Fruit and Vegetable Resource Maps. Final report, Bunbury.

WRAP (2018) Courtauld Commitment 2025 food waste baseline for 2015. Final report, Banbury, prepared by Bill Harris, available at www.wrap.org.uk/content/courtauld-2025-baseline-and-restated-household-food-waste-figures (last accessed April 8th, 2019).

8

HOUSEHOLD FOOD WASTE

Kate Parizeau

Introduction

Patterns of household food waste vary across contexts: in affluent countries, post-consumer waste accounts for the greatest proportion of food waste across the value chain (Parfitt et al., 2010). For example, it has been estimated that households are responsible for between 42% (Monier et al., 2010) and 53% (Stenmarck et al., 2016) of all food waste in Europe, and 47% of food waste in Canada (Gooch et al., 2014). In low-income countries, more wastage occurs post-harvest due to a lack of infrastructure and technology, including processing capacity, refrigeration, and transportation systems. Waste in this segment of the value chain is termed food loss. While the trend seems to be that more food waste occurs at the consumer level as the proportion of a population's income spent on food decreases, insufficient data and research attention to emerging economies/BRIC countries limits our understanding of the dynamics of food waste versus food loss on an international scale (Parfitt et al., 2010; Xue et al., 2017).

This chapter will discuss the methodological difficulties in defining and measuring household food waste, summarize the findings of household food waste research from different contexts, and consider the diverse drivers of household food waste (including individuals' behaviours, attitudes, and self-perceptions; as well as broader societal-level factors including infrastructure, policy contexts, systems of social organization, and cultural norms).

An overview of household food waste generation and management

Estimates of the amount of food wasted in households vary based on the estimation method and the place of the research. Xue et al. (2017) note that only 20% of published studies on food waste across the value chain involved direct observations of food waste, while the rest relied on indirect measurements or estimates calculated from secondary data. However, direct observational methods included diaries and self-report of waste generation rates; both of these methods are prevalent in household food waste research. While it can be difficult and costly to conduct observational studies or composition audits of household waste, recent research suggests that self-reports of food waste amounts are problematic and unreliable. This method assumes that people can accurately remember how much food they have wasted, accurately estimate the weight or volume of that waste, and also faithfully report the amount of food they have wasted despite social desirability bias (whereby respondents may provide responses that they believe will be viewed favourably; Xue et al., 2017). Delley and Brunner (2017) compared house-holders' self-reported food waste generation rates to national waste compositional analyses in Switzerland, finding a tenfold discrepancy (8.9 kg of self-reported avoidable food waste, versus 89.4 kg of mostly avoidable food waste extrapolated from national data). While food waste diaries do require that householders pay more conscientious attention to their self-reporting via measurement guidelines, Quested et al. (2011) suggest that diar-ies also lead to underreporting of approximately 40% when compared to waste stream analyses. Comparing across all three methodologies in Italy, Giordano et al. (2018) found that household questionnaires underreported the amount of food waste recorded in diar-ies by 53%, and that diaries underestimated the amount of food waste observed in audits by 23%. Surveys and questionnaires can provide useful information on householders' food waste-related beliefs, opinions, and motivations. However, this source of data is not a reliable means for reporting amounts or types of food waste generated.

A lack of measurement consistency and variable data quality have been noted as major bar-riers in the comparability of food waste research (Xue et al., 2017); cross-cultural differences in what constitutes membership in a household may also limit the comparability of food waste research (Soma, 2017a). In general, the highest rates of household food waste generation seem to be in North America, followed by Europe and other Western nations, with lower average rates of household food waste generated in the global South (see Table 8.1). It is important to note that there is a relative paucity of research on household food waste (and particularly household-level audits) in the global South.

While food waste generation patterns vary substantially from place to place, trends do emerge across contexts. For example, fresh produce is one of the most wasted categories of food in households in diverse locales (e.g. UK – Langley et al., 2010; UK – Quested et al., 2011; Iran – Monavari et al., 2012; Finland – Silvennoinen et al., 2014; China – Song et al. 2015; Denmark – Edjabou et al., 2016; Germany – Richter and Bokelmann, 2018; Israel – Elimelech et al., 2018). There are public health implications to this finding: householders might buy fruit and vegetables with the intention of meeting their nutritional needs and dietary recommenda-tions, but these may be aspirational food purchases that regularly lead to food waste.

Different types of food wasted in households have diverse environmental impacts. Conrad et al. (2018) suggest that produce-intensive "higher quality diets" are associated with greater amounts of wasted water and pesticides, largely because of the high rates of fruit and vegetable waste in the US. From a different perspective, Venkat (2011) highlights that while animal products make up 30% of food waste, they account for 57% of wasted greenhouse gas emissions because of the emission-intensive nature of animal food systems (see also Song et al. 2015). While some of the environmental impacts of household food waste may be mediated through diversion and recovery activities such as anaerobic diges-tion, composting, or incineration, prevention of food waste is a much better way to mediate global warming impacts compared to end-of-pipe treatment options (Bernstad Saraiva Schott and Andersson, 2015). Although many householders think it is important to reduce their food waste, many do not understand the environmental aspects of this issue (Hoek et al., 2017; Mccarthy and Liu, n.d)., or else wrongly perceive that the packaging associated with wasted food has greater environmental impact than the wasted food itself (Jungbluth et al., 2000; Tobler et al. 2011; Principato et al., 2015).

Household treatment of food waste varies across contexts. Some communities have access to municipal organic collection streams, and some places have strong cultures of at-home

Table 8.1 Examples of household food waste generation rates in different locales

Locale	Annual food waste per capita	% that is avoidable or possibly avoidable[1]	Source
US	124 kg total	–	Buzby and Hyman, 2012
US	77 kg total	–	Commission for Environmental Cooperation, 2017
Canada	85 kg total	–	Commission for Environmental Cooperation, 2017
Europe	76 kg total	–	Monier et al., 2010
Europe	92 kg total	–	Stenmarck et al., 2016
Denmark	48 kg avoidable	56%	Edjabou et al., 2016
Norway	79 kg total/46 kg avoidable	59%	Hanssen et al., 2016
Finland	23 kg avoidable		Koivupuro et al., 2012; Silvennoinen et al., 2014
Sweden	–	35%	Bernstad Saraiva Schott and Andersson, 2015
UK	70 kg avoidable	81%	Ventour, 2008
Hungary	68 kg total/33 kg avoidable	49%	Szabó-Bódi et al., 2018
Austria	33 kg total/19 kg avoidable	56%	Lebersorger and Schneider, 2011
Israel	95 kg total/50 kg avoidable	54%	Elimelech et al., 2018
China	16 kg total	–	Song et al., 2015
South Africa	8–12 kg total	–	Oelofse et al., 2018

composting. Even in locations where householders have access to source-separated collection of organics, many still use alternative disposal practices, including home composting, feeding animals, and using the sewage system or the garbage stream to dispose of food waste (Ventour, 2008; Langley et al., 2010; Seng et al., 2011; Reynolds et al., 2014; Parizeau et al., 2015; Szabó-Bódi et al., 2018). In the global South, informal household treatment of food waste may include composting, feeding animals, and giving food to friends or low-income people (e.g. Parizeau et al., 2006; Seng et al., 2011; Leray et al., 2016; Soma, 2017a).

It is clear that there is variety in the amounts and types of food wasted in households, and also in the treatment and disposal of these wastes. The following section turns to a discussion of research assessing the reasons for household food waste.

Assessing diverse drivers of household food waste

Socio-demographic factors

The impacts of household socio-demographics on food waste generation are not clear in the literature. One pattern that does emerge is that while big households waste more food in total, they waste less per capita than smaller or single-person households (Quested et al., 2013;

Parizeau et al., 2015; Do Carmo Stangherlin and de Barcellos, 2018; Schanes et al., 2018). Otherwise, the data are less clear. For example, some studies have found that older people waste less food, but it is not clear if this is a generational effect (Quested et al., 2013; Melbye et al., 2017), or rather the result of retired people having more time and better cooking skills to address household food waste (Qi and Roe, 2016; Visschers et al., 2016). Some suggest that youth have a poorer understanding of the impacts of food waste, and so are less likely to take action on this issue (Neff et al., 2015; Nikolaus et al., 2018), while other studies have found no food waste generation differences according to age (Ventour, 2008).

The relationship between income and food waste generation is also difficult to decipher. In the global North, it has been observed that more food is wasted by higher income households (Szabó-Bódi et al., 2018) and by households that spend more money on food (Parizeau et al., 2015). Some attitudinal surveys suggest that affluent people are less likely to try to reduce food waste (Principato et al., 2015), or that they may even see value in wasting food as a way of avoiding food-borne illness, saving time, or ensuring the freshness of meals (Qi and Roe, 2016). Other studies find no income effect on food wasting and related attitudes (Koivupuro et al., 2012; Melbye et al., 2017 – this study did not include very low-income respondents, however). In the global South, different patterns emerge. Some studies suggest higher relative amounts of food waste in low-income households, possibly due to a heavy reliance on produce and traditional packaging in their meals, greater reliance on restaurants among higher income homes, or lack of planning in low-income households that are already stretched thin (Sujauddin et al., 2008; Qu et al., 2009; Monavari et al., 2012; Porpino et al., 2015; Thi Thuy Trang et al., 2017).

Overall, there is little compelling evidence to clearly explain how socio-demographic factors influence food wasting at the household level. In their systematic review of the household food waste literature, Schanes et al. (2018, p. 985) summarize the contradictory findings among studies assessing demographic variables as follows: "[I]t is hardly possible to single out any socio-demographic factor(s) as explanatory variable(s) for food waste generation." In part, demographic trends are not clear because so many other factors intervene (at both personal and systemic levels). These trends may also be an artefact of the limited methods used to assess food waste at the household level.

Behavioural factors

The generation of food waste is not a behaviour in itself, but results from the interaction of multiple behaviours relating to planning, shopping, storage, preparation and consumption of food. … Indeed, by the time food is thrown away, the opportunity to prevent that food from becoming waste has often passed.

(Quested et al., 2011, p. 463)

Much of the research on household food waste focuses on the internal dynamics of the home, including the behaviours and routines residents use to manage food and waste, and the values and identities of the people within the household. Although most of the available English-language research on this topic focuses on households in Europe (and particularly the UK and Italy: Do Carmo Stangherlin and de Barcellos, 2018; Schanes et al., 2018), there are some trends that emerge across locales with respect to the factors influencing food waste generation.

It has been observed that the origins of food waste generation are seeded throughout food planning and preparation processes. Households that do not plan their food consumption tend to generate more organic waste (Parizeau et al., 2015) or food waste (Quested et al., 2013). Planning behaviours that can mediate food waste include using shopping lists, meal planning, and checking inventories of food in the household (Farr-Wharton et al., 2014; Jörissen et al., 2015). Shoppers who purchase according to their plans report wasting less food (Ponis et al., 2017). In contrast, food stock-piling behaviours have been associated with increased food waste (Graham-Rowe et al., 2014; Porpino et al., 2016). The exception to this pattern is people who make bulk purchases as a means of saving money, who report wasting less food (Koivupuro et al., 2012; Williams et al., 2012; Jörissen et al., 2015; see Porpino et al. (2015) for contrasting evidence from Brazil, however).

Stefan et al. (2013) suggest that planning and shopping activities are an indicator of consumers' perceived behavioural control over their waste generation: "This implies that in order to change consumers' food waste behaviour, efforts should be directed towards providing consumers with skills and tools to deal with their food-related activities" (p. 375). However, shoppers often do not have control over the food options available at retail, or the ways these foods are packaged and presented to them (Evans, 2011; Quested et al., 2013). Some may overbuy food due to price discounts, promotions on bulk purchases, or because the only package size available is larger than they require (Koivupuro et al., 2012; Jörissen et al., 2015). The choices that householders make in purchasing food are therefore constrained, and may lead to unintentional food waste.

Improper storage of food can also contribute to food waste. In order to extend the edibility of perishable foods, they must be kept in optimal temperatures and stored in appropriate locations. Failure to store food properly can be a cause of food waste, as is storing food in a way that allows it to be forgotten until it spoils (Farr-Wharton et al., 2014; Jörissen et al., 2015; Porpino et al., 2016; Waitt and Phillips, 2016; Romani et al., 2018). Some studies have assessed how the prolonged storage of food until it rots may be a procrastination strategy that alleviates the guilt associated with disposing of edible food (Blichfeldt et al., 2015); in this vein, Evans (2012b) describes storage solutions such as fridges, freezers, containers, and food wraps as "coffins of decay that play an active part in carrying discarded food towards the waste stream" (2012b, p. 1132). In such instances, it is not poor storage that leads to food waste, but wilful forgetfulness.

There is some indication that those with stronger cooking skills are predisposed to avoid food waste (Graham-Rowe et al., 2014; Melbye et al., 2017). Other ways that cooking practices may contribute to food waste include the generation of excess trim waste (Roodhuyzen et al., 2017), burning or otherwise over-preparing food, and improper portioning, or the preparation of too much food (Graham-Rowe et al., 2014; Silvennoinen et al., 2014; Romani et al., 2018). Cooking too much food is particularly a problem when householders are resistant to eating leftovers, which can lead to waste (Ventour, 2008; Monier et al., 2010; Quested et al., 2013; Silvennoinen et al., 2014; Stancu et al., 2016). Cappellini (2009) highlights the general reluctance to eat leftovers within households: those who do eat leftovers are seen as performing an act of sacrifice on behalf of the household. Andrews et al. (2018) suggest that leftovers may have positive ("tasty foods") or negative associations ("dangerous foods," "looks like spoiling," "used or second hand"). Leftovers, therefore, are an example of a type of edible food carrying social meanings that facilitate or impede their consumption.

Another major source of food waste generation associated with preparation and consumption is reliance on date labels, which are often misunderstood as indicators of food safety (Abeliotis et al., 2014; Qi and Roe, 2016). Many consumers use date labels to help them decide whether food is still edible, or whether it should be disposed of (Farr-Wharton et al., 2014; Neff et al., 2015; Parizeau et al., 2015). The reliance on date labels as indicators of edibility changes depending on the type of food product (Van Boxstael et al., 2014), the type of label (e.g. "use by" vs. "sell by"; Wilson et al., 2017), and across regional contexts (Toma et al., 2017). Labels are often combined with other strategies in determining whether people want to eat food beyond its labelled date (Williams et al., 2012; Watson and Meah, 2013; Waitt and Phillips, 2016). Nonetheless, date labels are not a meaningful proxy for food safety (Van Boxstael et al., 2014; Qi and Roe, 2016), and their widespread use as an indicator of when food should be discarded suggests a need for improved household food literacy. Date labels are an example of a factor influencing behaviours via emotional registers (Watson and Meah, 2013). It is therefore important to consider the affective and identity-based aspects of food waste generation as well.

Emotions, values, and identity

At an individual level, it has been suggested that wasting behaviours are the result of complex emotional and value-based relationships to waste. Many studies have catalogued the guilt that householders experience about wasting food (Ganglbauer et al., 2013; Quested et al., 2013; Graham-Rowe et al., 2014; Parizeau et al., 2015; Qi and Roe, 2016; Hoek et al., 2017). Other emotions related to food waste include anxiety, disgust, and shame (Evans, 2012a; Watson and Meah, 2013; Blichfeldt et al., 2015; Waitt and Phillips, 2016; Fraser and Parizeau, 2018). However, positive affect has also been observed in practices related to wasting food (such as when householders provide excess food or dispose of spoiled food in order to be a "good provider" (Evans, 2012a; Graham-Rowe et al., 2014; Porpino et al., 2015, 2016; Visschers et al., 2016); or expressions of pride related to preventing waste (Waitt and Phillips, 2016; Fraser and Parizeau, 2018)).

It is not clear how different emotional states impact food wasting behaviours. Russell et al. (2017) suggest that negative emotions lead to an increased intention to reduce food waste, but paradoxically also lead to increased self-reported wasting behaviours. In contrast, Blichfeldt et al. (2015) suggest that feelings of guilt and wrongdoing lead to reduced food wasting. The source of consumer guilt about food waste has also been investigated at the household level. While there are likely multiple associations that lead to feelings of guilt, there is some indication that for most people food waste is associated with moral norms and imperatives to "not waste," rather than an environmentally motivated sense of guilt (Quested et al., 2013; Qi and Roe, 2016). Indeed, when asked about their motivations for reducing food waste, respondents in diverse locales tended to prioritize economic (Quested et al., 2013; Watson and Meah, 2013; Neff et al., 2015; Stancu et al., 2016) and ethical/social rationales, including allusions to hunger (Ganglbauer et al., 2013; Parizeau et al., 2015) over environmental concerns. However, it has also been observed that environmentally conscious people expressed more negative attitudes toward wasting food (Melbye et al., 2017), and also wasted less food (Williams et al., 2012). It is important to note that motivations to reduce food waste can be quite diverse across and within households, including a desire to improve household management or eat healthier (Quested et al., 2013). It is therefore difficult to reduce the emotional and cognitive associations with food waste to a singular concept.

In order to capture some of the complexity of factors influencing food waste behaviour at the individual scale, some scholars have suggested clusters of characteristics that help to describe food waste generation patterns. For example, Gaiani et al. (2018) describe typologies that characterize perspectives and lifestyles related to food waste patterns. They detail seven profiles, including the "conscious-fussy type" who wastes food that no longer appeals to them, the "frugal consumer" who claims to waste very little and also avoids fresh produce, and the highly wasteful "confused-about-labelling" type. Richter (2017) uses survey data to contrast "guilty food wasters," who are well informed and conscientious consumers who feel guilty about food waste, with "unwitting food wasters," who are generally less informed and less concerned about food waste, and "careless food wasters," who are reluctant to plan their food purchases, tend not to use leftovers, misunderstand best before dates, and are unaware of the environmental impacts of food waste. Andrews et al. (2018) describe how householders characterize themselves with respect to leftover reuse, identifying three themes: the "responsible ones" who avoid risk, say they do not prepare more food than is needed, and reuse leftover food when possible; "virtuous ones" who enact moral pathways for uneaten leftovers via feeding animals or composting; and "blameless ones" who see others in the household as more responsible for wasted leftovers than themselves. Parizeau et al. (2015) found that householders who expressed higher levels of food and waste awareness generated less organic waste at the kerbside, whereas busy family and convenience lifestyles were associated with higher rates of organic waste. Similarly, others have identified convenience lifestyles as a key factor in household food waste generation (Graham-Rowe et al., 2014; Aschemann-Witzel et al., 2015; Mallinson et al., 2016; Hebrok and Boks, 2017). The factors affecting household food waste behaviours are therefore complex and interrelated, and these factors also vary according to context.

The household in context: food waste as a systemic phenomenon

In addition to research that investigates the internal dynamics of food wasting within households, there are studies that investigate factors outside of the home that may influence household food waste patterns. For example, some researchers consider how decisions made at other points in the food value chain impact household food waste. Lee (2018) describes how retailers in Seoul, South Korea make marketing decisions that influence household food consumption patterns (such as promotions and packaging formats that encourage over-purchasing), and how retailers can more broadly shape food shopping choices. Decisions to reduce the price of foods may also influence consumer choices at retail (Aschemann-Witzel et al., 2017). Similarly, Aschemann-Witzel (2018) suggests that Uruguayan retailers may be able to help consumers to waste less food (e.g. through pricing policies, the conversion of suboptimal foods into convenience/ready-to-eat options at retail, and the provision of information about food storage and handling), and that consumers are interested in seeing more of these types of interventions. Decisions made at the manufacturing stage can also influence household food waste patterns. Williams et al. (2012) estimate that 20–25% of the food waste recorded in household diaries was related to package design, including the size and configuration of the packaging, as well as the best before dates printed on the packaging. It has been suggested that the imposition of aesthetic standards by which foods are accepted and rejected at the production level are based on retailers' assumptions about consumer preferences (Aschemann-Witzel et al., 2015).

Researchers have observed the influence of waste management infrastructure on food waste-related behaviours at different scales. While these factors may interface with households directly, their design and implementation are largely beyond the control of individual residents. For example, increased access to refrigeration might reduce food waste generation among low-income households in China (Song et al., 2015), and the presence of appropriate and convenient in-home sorting equipment can facilitate source separation of organics where municipalities offer collection services (Metcalfe et al., 2013; Bernstad, 2014). In the US, Geislar (2017) found that the provision of both supportive infrastructure (in the form of carts) and the communication of norms supporting source separation increased self-reported participation in a municipal organics collection programme. Refsgaard and Magnussen (2009) compared two Norwegian municipalities, one of which provided source-separated collection of organics. They found that the technical provision of a collection system combined with institutional context (e.g. information provision, supportive norms, system planning) encouraged waste separation behaviours, and influenced local attitudes about food waste diversion. At a larger scale, Soma (2017b) argues that the phenomena of urbanization and long-distance modern supply chains contribute to the growth of food waste in rapidly urbanizing areas, such as Bogor, Indonesia, by enabling the distancing of food production from sites of food waste, and also distancing food waste away from the privileged urbanites who create it.

It has also been observed that the regulatory context may influence food waste generation. In an international macro-level analysis of food waste generation rates, Chalak et al. (2016) conclude that well-defined regulations and policy approaches (such as acts, plans, and strategies regulating food waste management activities) more effectively mitigate household food waste than fiscal measures. They note that the consideration of context-specific behaviours, attitudes, and cultural factors would complement their findings, and allow for place-based regulatory design that addresses local dynamics. In Australia, Benyam et al. (2018) similarly find that the inclusion of local community perspectives is integral to the successful design and implementation of food waste prevention and diversion policies.

Broader social and cultural phenomena also influence household-level food waste behaviours. For example, Soma (2017a) documents how unequal power dynamics between affluent householders and their domestic helpers in Bogor, Indonesia can influence patterns of household wasting and diversion:

> Upper-income consumption patterns are reliant upon the domestic helper or a lower-class group (orang belakang) absorbing the unwanted foods and in some cases, "ridding" to the lower income helps to assuage the anxieties around wasting food. By demonstrating the food gifting practice of the upper-class, which leads to excessive wasting, and the utilisation of the low-income group as conduits for food disposal, this paper has shown that the existence of a large amount of food waste within a household while others have to consume rice that has gone bad is based on structural and systemic inequality.
>
> (p. 1457)

Leray et al. (2016) observed similar household dynamics with respect to domestic helpers in Bangalore, India. In the global North, the off-loading of surplus food to low-income or food-insecure individuals has also been identified as a strategy for mitigating food waste and assuaging waste-related guilt; however, these patterns usually take place at manufacturing and retail points of the food value chain, rather than within households (Henderson, 2004; Riches, 2018).

Other systemic factors that influence household food waste generation include cultural norms around food risk and best before dates (Alexander et al., 2013; Milne, 2013; Watson and Meah, 2013; Waitt and Phillips, 2016); gendered norms that place responsibilities on women to provide abundant food, and to bear primary responsibility for management of waste arising in the household (Graham-Rowe et al., 2014; Porpino et al., 2016; Fraser and Parizeau, 2018); and the influence of macroeconomic phenomena such as recessions on household spending and consumption patterns (Abeliotis et al., 2014). It is therefore apparent that household food wasting behaviours do not exist in a vacuum. The waste-related decisions and strategies implemented at the household level are influenced by infrastructure; regulation, policy, and planning; social systems and hierarchies; and cultural factors (see also Bulkeley and Askins, 2009; Evans, 2011). As an example of this interplay, Leray et al.'s (2016) small-scale study of middle-class households in Bangalore, India highlights how the very low rates of avoidable food waste observed (2%) may be the result of a combination of infrastructure, social systems, and cultural norms:

> [H]alf of the respondents draw on a "buy today, eat today" mentality, enhanced by a normative understanding of food freshness, supported by elements such as food retailing infrastructure diversity, domestic helpers, and influenced by contextual factors such as erratic power supply. All these elements contribute to shape provisioning and storage practices, which in turn leads to minimal food wastage.
>
> *(p. 53)*

In their systematic review of the literature, Roodhuyzen et al. (2017) emphasize the importance of accounting for diverse factors influencing household food waste behaviours: "Not taking into account the breadth and diversity of factors potentially involved not only hampers scientific advancement, but may also reduce the effectiveness of reduction strategies in practice" (p. 46). In order to better accommodate a breadth of personal and structural factors into their conceptualizations of household food waste behaviours, researchers in this field are increasingly turning to theories of planned behaviour (Ghani et al., 2013; Graham-Rowe et al., 2015; Visschers et al., 2016; Russell et al., 2017) and social practice theory (Quested et al., 2013; Evans, 2014; Revilla and Salet, 2018), both of which allow for the consideration of multiple factors at multiple scales.

Interventions

Although the research demonstrates the complexity of the factors influencing household food waste at multiple scales, many of the interventions to reduce food waste that have been tested continue to focus on the household as the main unit of analysis. For example, informational campaigns are premised on the notion that householders may be capable of, and motivated to, change their food wasting behaviours if provided with more information. However, the evidence on this approach is mixed: some studies suggest that raising awareness empowers householders to change their behaviours (Gillan et al., 2004) or can shift norms (Nomura et al., 2011), whereas others have found no change in food waste generation rates as a result of informational campaigns (Bernstad, 2014). It may be that awareness-raising is a necessary but insufficient condition for influencing household attitudes and local cultures of food waste. Overall, there is relatively little research that assesses the impact of different interventions on the generation of household food waste.

In their overview of interventions most commonly proposed in the food waste literature, Hebrok and Boks (2017) identify three categories: in-home technologies to help with food management and sharing, packaging and storage solutions, and informational campaigns to raise householder awareness of food waste. They suggest that such interventions might not effectively address the practice-based ways in which food waste is an outcome of the routines and demands of everyday life. It is clear that household food waste is a complex and "wicked" problem: this phenomenon has many causes, and its solution will require diverse interventions, including the development of policy and regulatory measures to prevent avoidable food waste and divert unavoidable waste to locally appropriate treatment systems, transitioning the modern agri-food system to a waste reduction model that does not encourage surplus food at the household level, shifting cultures of abundance and convenience toward mores that value food and the reduction of waste, addressing social systems that normalize unequal access to high-quality foods and inequitably distribute food waste, and facilitating household routines and practices that allow for the effective management of food and its waste in the home.

Future research efforts can support the prevention and reduction of household food waste in the following ways: assessing baselines of household food waste generation through composition audits in diverse locales, documenting the self-reported and ethnographically observed factors that influence household wasting behaviours and related beliefs among diverse groups of people, analysing the diverse structural and cultural factors that enable and encourage widespread food wastage at the household level in different contexts, and rigorously investigating the effectiveness of waste reduction interventions undertaken at local, regional, and societal scales.

Note

1 Avoidable food waste is defined as "food and drink thrown away that was, at some point prior to disposal, edible" (WRAP, 2009, p. 4).

Bibliography

Abeliotis, K., Lasaridi, K., and Chroni, C. (2014). Attitudes and Behaviour of Greek Households Regarding Food Waste Prevention. *Waste Management and Research*, 32(3), 237–240. doi: 10.1177/0734242X14521681

Alexander, C., Gregson, N. and Gille, Z. (2013). Food waste. In Murcott A, Belasco W and Jackson P (eds.) *The Handbook of Food Research*. London, UK: Bloomsbury, pp. 471–483.

Andrews, L., Kerr, G., Pearson, D., and Mirmosa, M. (2018). The attributes of leftovers and higher-order personal values. *British Food Journal*, 120(9), 1965–1979. doi: 10.1108/BFJ-08-2017-0442

Aschemann-Witzel, J., de Hooge, I., Amani, P., Bech-Larsen, T., and Oostindjer, M. (2015). Consumer-related food waste: causes and potential for action. *Sustainability*, doi: 10.3390/su7066457

Aschemann-Witzel, J., Haagen Jensen, J., Hyldetoft Jensen, M., and Kulikovskaja, V. (2017). Consumer behaviour towards price-reduced suboptimal foods in the supermarket and the relation to food waste in households. *Appetite*, 116, 246–258. doi: 10.1016/j.appet.2017.05.013

Aschemann-Witzel, J., Giménez, A., and Ares, G. (2018). Convenience or price orientation? Consumer characteristics influencing food waste behaviour in the context of an emerging country and the impact on future sustainability of the global food sector. *Global Environmental Change*, 49, 85–94. doi: 10.1016/j.gloenvcha.2018.02.002

Benyam, A., Kinnear, S., and Rolfe, J. (2018). Integrating Community Perspectives into Domestic Food Waste Prevention and Diversion Policies. *Resources, Conservation and Recycling*, 134(Complete), 174–183. doi: 10.1016/j.resconrec.2018.03.019

Bernstad, A. (2014). Household food waste separation behavior and the importance of convenience. *Waste Management*, doi: 10.1016/j.wasman.2014.03.013

Bernstad Saraiva Schott, A. and Andersson, T. (2015). Food waste minimization from a life-cycle perspective. *Journal of Environmental Management*, 147, 219–226. doi: 10.1016/j.jenvman.2014.07.048

Blichfeldt, B. S., Mikkelsen, M., and Gram, M. (2015). When it Stops Being Food. *Food, Culture and Society*, 18(1), 89–105. doi: 10.2752/175174415X14101814953963

Bulkeley, H., and Askins, K. (2009). Waste interfaces: biodegradable waste, municipal policy and everyday practice. *The Geographical Journal*, 175(4), 251–260.

Buzby, J. and Hyman, J. (2012). Total and per capita value of food loss in the United States. *Journal of Food Policy*, 37, 561–570. doi: 10.1016/j.foodpol.2012.06.002

Cappellini, B. (2009). The sacrifice of re-use: the travels of leftovers and family relations. *Journal of Consumer Behaviour*, 8, 365–375. doi: 10.1002/cb.299

Chalak, A., Abou-daher, C., Chaaban, J., and Abiad, M. G. (2016). The global economic and regulatory determinants of household food waste generation: A cross-country analysis. *Waste Management*, 48, 418–422. doi: 10.1016/j.wasman.2015.11.040

Commission for Environmental Cooperation. (2017). Characterization and Management of Organic Waste in North America: Foundational Report. Retrieved from www3.cec.org/islandora/en/item/11771-characterization-and-management-organic-waste-in-north-america-foundational-en.pdf

Conrad, Z., Niles, M.T., Neher, D.A., Roy, E.D., Tichenor, N.E., and Jahns, L. (2018). Relationship between food waste, diet quality, and environmental sustainability. *PLoS ONE*, 13(4), e0195405.

Delley, M., and Brunner, T. A. (2017). Food waste within Swiss households: A segmentation of the population and suggestions for preventive measures. *Resources, Conservation and Recycling*, 122, 172–184. doi: 10.1016/j.resconrec.2017.02.008

Do Carmo Stangherlin, I. and de Barcellos, M. D. (2018). Drivers and Barriers to Food Waste Reduction. *British Food Journal*, doi: 10.1108/BFJ-12-2017-0726

Edjabou, M.E., Petersen, C., Scheutz, C., and Fruergaard, T. (2016). Food waste from Danish households: Generation and composition. *Waste Management*, doi: http://doi.org/10.1016/j.wasman.2016.03.032

Elimelech, E., Ayalon, O., and Ert, E. (2018). What Gets Measured Gets Managed: A New Method of Measuring Household Food Waste. *Waste Management*, 76(Complete), 68–81. doi: 10.1016/j.wasman.2018.03.031

Evans, D. (2011). Blaming the consumer–once again: the social and material contexts of everyday food waste practices in some English households. *Critical Public Health*, 21(4), 429–440. doi: 10.1080/09581596.2011.608797

Evans, D. (2012a). Beyond the throwaway society: Ordinary domestic practice and a sociological approach to household food waste. *Sociology*, 46(1), 41–56. doi: 10.1177/0038038511416150

Evans, D. (2012b). Binning, gifting and recovery: the conduits of disposal in household food consumption. *Environment and Planning D: Society and Space*, 30, 1123–1137. doi: 10.1068/d22210

Evans, D. (2014). *Food Waste: Home Consumption, Material Culture and Everyday Life*. London: Bloomsbury Academic.

Farr-Wharton, G., Foth, M., and Choi, J. H. (2014). Identifying Factors that Promote Consumer Behaviours Causing Expired Domestic Food Waste. *Journal of Consumer Behaviour*, 13(6), 393–402. doi: 10.1002/cb.1488

Fraser, C. and Parizeau, K. (2018). Waste management as foodwork: A feminist food studies approach to household food waste. *Canadian Food Studies*, 5(1), 39–62. http://canadianfoodstudies.uwaterloo.ca/index.php/cfs/article/view/186/224

Gaiani, S., Caldeira, S., Adorno, V., Segrè, A., and Vittuari, M. (2018). Food wasters: Profiling consumers' attitude to waste food in Italy. *Waste Management*, 72(Complete), 17–24. doi: 10.1016/j.wasman.2017.11.012

Ganglbauer, E., Fitzpatrick, G., and Comber, R. (2013). Negotiating Food Waste: Using a Practice Lens to Inform Design. *ACM Transactions on Computer-Human Interaction*, 20(2), 11–25. doi: 10.1145/2463579.2463582

Geislar, S. (2017). The new norms of food waste at the curb: Evidence-based policy tools to address benefits and barriers. *Waste Management*, 68, 571–580. doi: 10.1016/j.wasman.2017.07.010

Ghani, W. A., Rusli, I. F., Biak, D. R. A., and Idris, A. (2013). An application of the theory of planned behaviour to study the influencing factors of participation in source separation of food waste. *Waste Management*, 33(5), 1276–1281. doi: 10.1016/j.wasman.2012.09.019

Gillan, D. A., Leland, L. S., Davies, A. M., and Walsh, K. (2004). Reducing curbside waste volumes by promoting household composting. *Journal of Environmental Systems*, 30(4), 317–332.

Giordano, C., Piras, S., Boschini, M., and Falasconi, L. (2018). Are questionnaires a reliable method to measure food waste? A pilot study on Italian households. *British Food Journal*, 120(12), 2885–2897. doi: 10.1108/BFJ-02-2018-0081

Gooch, M., Felfel, A., and Glasbey, C. (2014). '$27 billion' revisited: The cost of Canada's annual food waste. *Value Chain Management Centre*. https://vcm-international.com/wp-content/uploads/2014/12/Food-Waste-in-Canada-27-Billion-Revisited-Dec-10-2014.pdf

Graham-Rowe, E., Jessop, D. C., and Sparks, P. (2014). Identifying Motivations and Barriers to Minimising Household Food Waste. *Resources, Conservation and Recycling*, 84, 15–23. doi: 10.1016/J.RESCONREC.2013.12.005

Graham-Rowe, E., Jessop, D.C., and Sparks, P. (2015). Predicting Household Food Waste Reduction Using An Extended Theory of Planned Behaviour. *Resources, Conservation and Recycling*, 101, 194–202.

Hanssen, O.J., Syversen, F., and Stø, E. (2016). Edible food waste from Norwegian households - Detailed food waste composition analysis among households in two different regions in Norway. *Resources, Conservation and Recycling*, 109, 146–154. doi: 10.1016/j.resconrec.2016.03.010

Hebrok, M., and Boks, C. (2017). Household food waste: Drivers and potential intervention points for design: An extensive review. *Journal of Cleaner Production*, 151, 380–392. doi: 10.1016/j.jclepro.2017.03.069

Henderson, G. (2004). 'Free' food, the local production of worth, and the circuit of decommodification: A value theory of the surplus. *Environment and Planning D: Society and Space*, 22(4), 485–512.

Hoek, A. C., Pearson, D., James, S. W., Lawrence, M. A., and Friel, S. (2017). Shrinking the food-print: A qualitative study into consumer perceptions, experiences and attitudes towards healthy and environmentally friendly food behaviours. *Appetite*, 108, 117–131. doi: 10.1016/j.appet.2016.09.030

Jörissen, J., Priefer, C., and Bräutigam, K.-R. (2015). Food Waste Generation at Household Level: Results of a Survey among Employees of Two European Research Centers in Italy and Germany. *Sustainability*, 7(12), 2695–2715. doi: 10.3390/su7032695

Jungbluth, N., Tietje, O., and Scholz, R.W. (2000). "Food purchases: Impacts from the consumers' point of view investigated with a modular LCA". *The International Journal of Life Cycle Assessment*, 5, 134–142. doi: 10.1007/BF02978609

Koivupuro, H., Hartikainen, H., Silvennoinen, K., Katajajuuri, J., Heikintalo, N., Reinikainen, A., and Jalkanen, L. (2012). Influence of socio-demographical, behavioural and attitudinal factors on the amount of avoidable food waste generated in Finnish households. *International Journal of Consumer Studies*, 36(2), 183–191. doi: 10.1111/j.1470-6431.2011.01080.x

Langley, J., Yoxall, A., Heppell, G., Rodriguez, E. M., Bradbury, S., Lewis, R., … Rowson, J. (2010). Food for thought?–A UK pilot study testing a methodology for compositional domestic food waste analysis. *Waste Management and Research*, 28(3), 220–227. doi: 10.1177/0734242x08095348

Lebersorger, S. and Schneider, F. (2011). Discussion on the methodology for determining food waste in household waste composition studies. *Waste Management*, 31(9-10), 1924–1933. doi: 10.1016/J.WASMAN.2011.05.023

Lee, K. C. L. (2018). Grocery shopping, food waste, and the retail landscape of cities: The case of seoul. *Journal of Cleaner Production*, 172(Complete), 325–334. doi: 10.1016/j.jclepro.2017.10.085

Leray, L., Sahakian, M., and Erkman, S. (2016). Understanding Household Food Metabolism: Relating Micro-Level Material Flow Analysis to Consumption Practices. *Journal of Cleaner Production*, 125(Complete), 44–55. doi: 10.1016/j.jclepro.2016.03.055

Mallinson, L. J., Russell, J. M., and Barker, M. E. (2016). Attitudes and Behaviour Towards Convenience Food and Food Waste in The United Kingdom. *Appetite*, 103, 17–28. doi: 10.1016/J.APPET.2016.03.017

Mccarthy, B., and Liu, H.-B. (n.d.). "Waste not, want not": Exploring green consumers' attitudes towards wasting edible food and actions to tackle food waste. doi: 10.1108/BFJ-03-2017-0163

Melbye, E., Onozaka, Y., and Hansen, H. (2017). Throwing It All Away: Exploring Affluent Consumers' Attitudes Toward Wasting Edible Food. *Journal of Food Products Marketing*, 23(4), 416–429. doi: 10.1080/10454446.2015.1048017

Metcalfe, A., Riley, M., Barr, S., Tudor, T., Robinson, G., and Guilbert, S. (2013). Food waste bins: bridging infrastructures and practices. *The Sociological Review*, 60(S2), 135–155. doi: 10.1111/1467-954X.12042

Milne, R. (2013). Arbiters of waste: Date labels, the consumer and knowing good, safe food. *Sociological Review*, 60(2), 84–101. doi: 10.1111/1467-954X.12039

Monavari, S. M., Omrani, G. A., Karbassi, A., and Raof, F. F. (2012). The effects of socioeconomic parameters on household solid-waste generation and composition in developing countries (a case study: Ahvaz, Iran). *Environmental Monitoring and Assessment*, 184(4), 1841–1846. doi: 10.1007/s10661-011-2082-y

Monier, V., Mudgal, S., Escalon, V., et al. (2010). Preparatory study on food waste across EU 27: European Commission. Retrieved from http://ec.europa.eu/environment/archives/eussd/pdf/bio_foodwaste_report.pdf

Neff, R. A., Spiker, M. L., and Truant, P. L. (2015). Wasted Food: U.S. Consumers' Reported Awareness, Attitudes, and Behaviors. *PLoS ONE*, doi: 10.1371/journal.pone.0127881

Nikolaus, C. J., Nickols-Richardson, S. M., and Ellison, B. (2018). Wasted Food: A Qualitative Study of U.S. Young Adults' Perceptions, Beliefs and Behaviors. *Appetite*, 130, 70–78.

Nomura, H., John, P. C., and Cotterill, S. (2011). The Use of Feedback to Enhance Environmental Outcomes: A Randomised Controlled Trial of A Food Waste Scheme. *Local Environment*, 16(7), 637–653. doi: 10.2139/ssrn.1760859

Oelofse, S., Muswema, A., and Ramukhwatho, F. (2018). Household Food Waste Disposal in South Africa: A Case Study of Johannesburg and Ekurhuleni. *South African Journal of Science*, 114(5/6), 1–6.

Parfitt, J., Barthel, M., and Macnaughton, S. (2010). Food Waste Within Food Supply Chains: Quantification and Potential for Change to 2050. Philosophical Transactions of The Royal Society of London. *Series B, Biological Sciences*, 365(1554), 3065–3081. doi: 10.1098/rstb.2010.0126

Parizeau, K., Maclaren, V., and Chanthy, Lay (2006). Waste Characterization as An Element of Waste Management Planning: Lessons Learned From A Study in Siem Reap. *Cambodia. Resources, Conservation and Recycling*, 49(2), 110–128.

Parizeau, K., von Massow, M., and Martin, R. (2015). Household-Level Dynamics of Food Waste Production and Related Beliefs, Attitudes, and Behaviours in A Municipality in Southwestern Ontario. *Waste Management*, 35, 207–217. doi: 10.1016/j.wasman.2014.09.019

Ponis, S. T., Papanikolaou, P.-A., Katimertzoglou, P., Ntalla, A. C., and Xenos, K. I. (2017). Household food waste in Greece: A questionnaire survey. *Journal of Cleaner Production*, 149, 1268–1277. doi: 10.1016/J.JCLEPRO.2017.02.165

Porpino, G., Parente, J., and Wansink, B. (2015). Food Waste Paradox: Antecedents of Food Disposal in Low Income Households. *International Journal of Consumer Studies*, 39(6), 619–629. doi: 10.1111/ijcs.12207

Porpino, G., Wansink, B., and Parente, J. (2016). Wasted Positive Intentions: The Role of Affection and Abundance on Household Food Waste. *Journal of Food Products Marketing*, 22(7), 733–751. doi: 10.1080/10454446.2015.1121433

Principato, L., Secondi, L., and Pratesi, C. (2015). Reducing Food Waste: An Investigation on The Behaviour of Italian Youths. *British Food Journal*, 117(2), 731–748. doi: 10.1108/BFJ-10-2013-0314

Qi, D., and Roe, B. (2016). Household food waste: Multivariate regression and principal components analyses of awareness and attitudes among U.S. consumers. *PLoS ONE*, 11(7), E0159250. doi: 10.1371/journal.pone.0159250

Qu, X., Li, Z., Xie, X, Sui, Y., Yang, L., and Chen, Y. (2009). Survey of composition and generation rate of household wastes in Beijing, China. *Waste Management*, 29(10), 2618–2624. doi: 10.1016/J.WASMAN.2009.05.014

Quested, T. E., Marsh, E., Stunell, D., and Parry, A. D. (2013). Spaghetti soup: The complex world of food waste behaviours. *Resources, Conservation and Recycling*, 79, 43–51. doi: 10.1016/j.resconrec.2013.04.011

Quested, T. E., Parry, A. D., Easteal, S., and Swannell, R. (2011). Food and drink waste from households in the UK. *Nutrition Bulletin*, 36, 460–467. doi: 10.1111/j.1467-3010.2011.01924.x

Refsgaard, K., and Magnussen, K. (2009). Household behaviour and attitudes with respect to recycling food waste–experiences from focus groups. *Journal of Environmental Management*, 90(2), 760–771. doi: 10.1016/j.jenvman.2008.01.018

Revilla, B.P. and Salet, W. (2018). The social meaning and function of household food rituals in preventing food waste. *Journal of Cleaner Production*, 198, 320–332. doi: 10.1016/j.jclepro.2018.06.038

Reynolds, C. J., Mavrakis, V., Davison, S., Høj, S. B., Vlaholias, E., Sharp, A., and Dawson, D. (2014). Estimating informal household food waste in developed countries: The case of Australia. *Waste Management and Research*, 32(12), 1254–1258. doi: 10.1177/0734242x14549797

Riches, G. (2018). *Food Bank Nations: Poverty, Corporate Charity and the Right to Food*. New York: Routledge

Richter, B. (2017). Knowledge and perception of food waste among German consumers. *Journal of Cleaner Production*, 166(10), 641–648. doi: 10.1016/j.jclepro.2017.08.009

Richter, B., and Bokelmann, W. (2018). The significance of avoiding household food waste – A means-end-chain approach. *Waste Management*, 74(Complete), 34–42. doi: 10.1016/j.wasman.2017.12.012

Romani, S., Grappi, S., Bagozzi, R. P., and Barone, A. M. (2018). Domestic food practices: A study of food management behaviors and the role of food preparation planning in reducing waste. *Appetite*, 121, 215–227. doi: 10.1016/j.appet.2017.11.093

Roodhuyzen, D. M. A., Luning, P. A., Fogliano, V., and Steenbekkers, L. P. A. (2017). Putting together the puzzle of consumer food waste: Towards an integral perspective. *Trends in Food Science and Technology*, 68, 37–50. doi: 10.1016/j.tifs.2017.07.009

Russell, S. V., Young, C. W., Unsworth, K. L., and Robinson, C. (2017). Bringing habits and emotions into food waste behaviour. *Resources, Conservation and Recycling*, 125, 107–114. doi: 10.1016/j. resconrec.2017.06.007

Schanes, K., Dobernig, K., and Gözet, B. (2018). Food Waste Matters - A Systematic Review of Household Food Waste Practices and their Policy Implications. *Journal of Cleaner Production*, 182, 978–991. doi: 10.1016/j.jclepro.2018.02.030

Seng, B., Kaneko, H., Hirayama, K., and Katayama-Hirayama, K. (2011). Municipal solid waste management in Phnom Penh, capital city of Cambodia. *Waste Management & Research*, 29(5), 949–960.

Silvennoinen, K., Katajajuuri, J.-M., Hartikainen, H., Heikkilä, L., and Reinikainen, A. (2014). Food waste volume and composition in Finnish households. *British Food Journal*, 116(6), 1058–1068. doi: 10.1108/BFJ-12-2012-0311

Soma, T. (2017a). Gifting, ridding and the "everyday mundane": the role of class and privilege in food waste generation in Indonesia. *Local Environment*, 22(12), 1444–1460. doi: 10.1080/13549839.2017.1357689

Soma, T. (2017b). Wasted infrastructures: Urbanization, distancing and food waste in Bogor, Indonesia. *Built Environment*, 43(3), 431–446. doi: 10.2148/benv.43.3.431

Song, G., Li, M., Semakula, H. M., and Zhang, S. (2015). Food consumption and waste and the embedded carbon, water and ecological footprints of households in China. *Science of the Total Environment*, 529(Complete), 191-197. doi:10.1016/j.scitotenv.2015.05.068

Stancu, V., Haugaard, P., and Lähteenmäki, L. (2016). Determinants of Consumer Food Waste Behaviour: Two Routes to Food Waste. *Appetite*, 96, 7–17. doi: 10.1016/J.APPET.2015.08.025

Stefan, V., van Herpen, E., Tudoran, A. A., and Lahteenmaki, L. (2013). Avoiding food waste by Romanian consumers: The importance of planning and shopping routines. *Food Quality and Preference*, 28(1), 375–381. doi: 10.1016/j.foodqual.2012.11.001

Stenmarck, Å., Jensen, C., Quested, T., and Moates, G. (2016). FUSIONS: Estimates of European food waste levels. www.eu-fusions.org/phocadownload/Publications/Estimates%20of%20European% 20food%20waste%20levels.pdf

Sujauddin, M., Huda, S. M. S., and Hoque, A. T. M. (2008). Household Solid Waste Characteristics and Management in Chittagong, Bangladesh. *Waste management*, 28(9), 1688–1695.

Szabó-Bódi, B., Kasza, G., and Szakos, D. (2018). Assessment of Household Food Waste in Hungary. *British Food Journal*, 120(3), 625–638. doi: 10.1108/BFJ-04-2017-0255

Tobler, C., Visschers, V.H.M., and Siegrist, M. (2011). Eating green. Consumers' willingness to adopt ecological food consumption behaviors. *Appetite*, 57(3), 674–682. doi: 10.1016/j. appet.2011.08.010

Toma, L., Montserrat Costa Font, B., Bethan Thompson, B., and Res Int, O. J. (2017). Impact of consumers' understanding of date labelling on food waste behaviour. *Operational Research*, doi: 10.1007/s12351-017-0352-3

Thi Thuy Trang, P., Quoc Dong, H., Quang Toan, D., Thi Xuan Hanh, N., and Thi Thu, N. (2017). The Effects of Socio-economic Factors on Household Solid Waste Generation and Composition: A Case Study in Thu Dau Mot, Vietnam. *Energy Procedia*, 107, 253–258. doi: 10.1016/j.egypro.2016.12.144

Van Boxstael, S., Devlieghere, F., Berkvens, D., Vermeulen, A., and Uyttendaele, M. (2014). Understanding and attitude regarding the shelf life labels and dates on pre-packed food products by Belgian consumers. *Food Control*, 37, 85–92. doi: 10.1016/j.foodcont.2013.08.043

Venkat, K. (2011). The climate change and economic impacts of food waste in the United States. *International Journal on Food System Dynamics*, 2(4), 431–446.

Ventour, L. (2008). The food we waste. WRAP: Banbury/Oxon. Retrieved from www.lefigaro.fr/assets/pdf/Etude%20gaspillage%20alimentaire%20UK2008.pdf

Visschers, V. H. M., Wickli, N., and Siegrist, M. (2016). Sorting out Food Waste Behaviour: A Survey on The Motivators and Barriers of Self-Reported Amounts of Food Waste in Households. *Journal of Environmental Psychology*, 45, 66–78. doi: 10.1016/J.JENVP.2015.11.007

Waitt, G., and Phillips, C. (2016). Food waste and domestic refrigeration: a visceral and material approach. *Social and Cultural Geography*, 17(3), 359–379. doi: 10.1080/14649365.2015.1075580

Watson, M. and Meah, A. (2013). Food, waste and safety: Negotiating conflicting social anxieties into the practices of domestic provisioning. *The Sociological Review*, 60(2), 102–120. doi: 10.1111/1467-954X.12040

Williams, H., Wikström, F., Otterbring, T., Löfgren, M., and Gustafsson, A. (2012). Reasons for household food waste with special attention to packaging. *Journal of Cleaner Production*, 24, 141–148. doi: 10.1016/j.jclepro.2011.11.044

Wilson, N. L. W., Rickard, B. J., Saputo, R., and Ho, S. T. (2017). Food waste: The role of date labels, package size, and product category. *Food Quality and Preference*, 55, 35–44. doi: 10.1016/j. foodqual.2016.08.004

WRAP. (2009). Household Food and Drink Waste in the UK. Retrieved from www.wrap.org.uk/sites/ files/wrap/Household_food_and_drink_waste_in_the_UK_-_report.pdf

Xue, L., Liu, G., Parfitt, J., Liu, X.,Van Herpen, E., Stenmarck, Å., O'Connor, C., Östergren, K., and Cheng, S. (2017). Missing food, missing data? A critical review of global food losses and food waste data. *Environmental Science & Technology*, 51(12), 6618–6633. doi: 10.1021/acs.est.7b00401

9

FOOD WASTE IN THE SERVICE SECTOR

Key concepts, measurement methods and best practices

Kirsi Silvennoinen, Sampsa Nisonen and Oona Pietiläinen

Introduction

Background on food waste in the food service sector

While food waste (FW) occurs at all stages of the food supply chain, in high-income countries the largest contributors are consumers (Parfitt et al., 2010; Gustavsson et al., 2011). Consumer FW is produced in households and in the food service sector, and is estimated to be 95 to 115 kg/year per capita in Europe and North America (Gustavsson et al., 2011). In EU countries, food services are the third largest sector producing FW which accounts for 12% of all EU FW (Stenmarck et al., 2016). The food service sector is a part of hospitality services which also includes lodging and meetings (Myung et al., 2012). Food service providers can be private enterprises such as restaurants, hotels and bars (European Agency for Safety and Health at Work, 2008) or municipal catering services providing food for institutions such as hospitals and schools. It is important to note that these definitions can vary in different countries. The food service sector employs a considerable number of people with the catering industry steadily growing in Europe, particularly in the Nordic countries (HOTREC, 2018). Reduction of FW has become a high priority for many enterprises in this sector according to surveys in the US and the UK (British Hospitality Association, 2015; National Restaurant Association, 2018).

FW occurring at the end of the food supply chain is especially harmful to the environment because of the resources used and emissions produced in previous stages of the supply chain to grow, transport and retail foodstuffs (Priefer et al., 2016). There are significant economic costs here also; food is lost after being transported, processed and prepared with many working hours' energy expended in vain. Also, the percentage of food ending up as waste is relatively high when compared to other stages of the chain. For example, in the Finnish food service sector, 20% of all the prepared food is wasted (Silvennoinen et al., 2015).

In education institutions, the food service sector has seen a drive to mitigate FW and ensure it is properly handled (Priefer et al., 2016). Research suggests that when people are informed of the importance of FW reduction, they become aware of and better equipped to handle the problem. To be the most effective, educating consumers about FW should start at an early age (Priefer et al., 2016). A study of Italian university students showed they were more likely to reduce leftovers if they were aware of problems related to FW (Principato et al., 2015).

A growing number of studies and research articles have investigated FW from food service in the education sector, with significant literature on schools. The amount of FW generated in schools has primarily been measured in Europe (WRAP, 2011; Martins et al., 2014; Falasconi et al., 2015; Silvennoinen et al., 2015; Eriksson et al., 2017) and in the US (Cohen et al., 2014; Smith and Cunningham-Sabo, 2014; Wilkie et al., 2015) where plate waste and inefficient nutrient intake of children have been the main concerns. FW quantifications have also been conducted within hospitals, day-care centres, student and workplace canteens as well as in homes for the elderly (Sonnino and McWilliam, 2011; Dias-Ferreira et al., 2015; Silvennoinen et al., 2015; Painter et al., 2016; Eriksson et al., 2017). Studies covering hotels, restaurants and cafés are few, for instance Wang et al. (2017) measured restaurant plate waste in China, Pirani and Arafat (2016) audited FW in hotels in the United Arab Emirates, Tatàno et al. (2017) and Kallbekken and Sælen (2013) looked at FW in restaurants, and Betz et al. (2015) studied the magnitude of FW in the Swiss food service industry.

Results from these studies are difficult to generalise because of the nature of the measurement periods (typically conducted over short periods) and the limited number of individual food service providers included in such studies. According to Stenmarck et al. (2016) there is only enough data of a good quality in the EU to roughly estimate the amount of FW in the food service sector. This makes it hard to ascertain whether food reduction targets for halving FW (UN, 2015) will be met. Various studies have also concentrated on finding reasons for FW generation and ways to reduce FW in the food service sector. FW measurements, workshops, surveys, interviews and mixing methods have been commonly used in these studies (e.g. Betz et al., 2015; Heikkilä et al., 2016; Lazell, 2016; Mirosa et al., 2016; Pirani and Arafat, 2016). FW reduction practices have been empirically tested mainly with plate waste, for instance using written messages, decreasing plate size and using a trayless system (Kallbekken and Sælen, 2013; Thiagarajah and Getty, 2013; Whitehair et al., 2013).

As well as knowledge derived from literature about FW and food services in Europe and globally, we also draw upon our experience of conducting research projects during 2010–2018 in Finland. These studies include several projects (FOODSPILL 2010–2012, WASTESTIMATOR 2015–2017, CIRCWASTE 2017–2020) concerning FW in food services and other parts of the food supply chain (Katajajuuri et al., 2014; Silvennoinen et al., 2015; Heikkilä et al., 2016; Silvennoinen et al., 2019a; Hietala et al., 2018; Nisonen and Silvennoinen, 2018; Silvennoinen et al., 2019b). These involved administering direct FW measurements in different subsectors as well as undertaking interviews, workshops and surveys to develop reduction methods and best practices. We also draw on data on the EU FUSIONS project in the sections below.

Key concepts

In current food service literature there have been several ways to approach and analyse the question of FW, leading to variance in how its key concepts can be explained. To ensure rigour we introduce the key concepts and terms used in this chapter below (Table 9.1).

To begin, we define *food waste* (FW) as the sum of originally edible and inedible food products produced in the food service sector that ends up as waste arising from several different sources. *Kitchen waste* is generated in the kitchen and storage as a result of spoiling or mistakes in food preparation. *Serving waste* is food that results from over production and is

Table 9.1 Definition of key concepts

Food waste and food waste categories	Food service sector and restaurant types	Metrics of food waste
Food waste Sum of originally edible and inedible food products and food produced in the food service sector that ends up as waste.	**Food service sector** The horeca sector (the food service industry) with the addition of municipal hospitality services, e.g. hospitals, schools and day-care centres as well as their private counterparts.	**Food waste percentage** The percentage of prepared food that ends up as waste. Metric of efficiency.
Kitchen waste FW generated in kitchen and storage as the result of spoiling or mistakes in food preparation.	**Buffet restaurants** Includes schools, workplace and student restaurants; buffets produce serving food waste.	**Food waste per customer** Metric of efficiency with sense of scale. Complemented by eaten food per customer.
Serving waste Food left over from a buffet.	**Cooked to order and fast food restaurants** Food is served in prepared portions. No serving waste is produced.	**Eaten food per customer** Complements food waste per customer.
Customer plate waste Scraps of food taken on plates by customers, but never eaten. **Originally inedible parts of food and food products** E.g. coffee grounds or peelings.		

not used, e.g. left over from a buffet. Finally, *customer plate waste* are the scraps of food taken on plates by customers, but not eaten. FW is generated very differently in each category and so the measures taken to reduce FW must be different as well. *Originally inedible food and food products*, such as coffee grounds or peelings, are part of FW but should be separated from originally edible parts.

The food service sector has several subsectors. Our definition of the food service sector includes the catering industry with the addition of municipal hospitality services such as hospitals, schools, elderly care homes and day-care centres as well as their private counterparts. Within the sector, it is important to separate *buffet restaurants* from the rest as they produce serving waste, unlike *cooked to order and fast food restaurants*, where food is served in prepared portions.

Additionally we define important FW metrics that should be used when comparing the FW situation. A simple comparison of the weight of FW from different outlets or in different countries is not satisfactory as the scale of the operation may influence the amount of food wasted much more than the efficiency of the operation. Thus we define *food waste percentage* as the percentage of prepared food that ends up as waste. This metric accurately describes the efficiency of the operation of the outlet. *Food waste per customer* is also a useful metric of efficiency as it incorporates a sense of scale. Paired with *eaten food per customer* the same estimation of efficiency as with food waste percentage can be calculated. Both food waste percentage and food waste per customer can be calculated separately for each food waste category. A summary of the key concepts is presented in Table 9.1.

The current situation: food waste amount, origin, composition and consequences

There are a fair number of weighing studies of restaurant FW in the literature (see the Introduction). The results vary depending on the type of restaurant, country of origin, measurement methods and definitions, which taken together make any attempts to aggregate the results largely unfeasible. Typically the number of participating restaurants is fairly small in these studies, which means that the choice of restaurants, i.e. type of subsector, has a considerable impact on the results. These studies can offer a glimpse of the FW situation in certain circumstances only. In contrast, there are FW studies with a top-down statistical approach and consequently broader viewpoint, that do not separate the food service sector from the rest. For example, Buzby and Hyman (2012) estimated FW in the USA only at primary, retail and consumer levels in their study. Similarly Gustavsson et al.'s (2011) study on global food losses and FW separates the losses even more strictly as production to retail and consumer levels only.

The EU FUSIONS project provided a more detailed estimation of the amount of FW in Europe with greater differentiation by sector. According to the study, 10.5 million tonnes of FW is produced yearly by the food service sector across the EU-28 countries (Stenmarck et al., 2016). This amounts to 21 kg of FW per person. Most countries produce very similar amounts of FW in kg per person, but the differences are greater when comparing produced FW in tonnes per €million of turnover in the food service sector. The comparison is presented in Table 9.2. However, these results should be regarded as tentative as they are based on a small number of measurements.

In summary it is difficult to estimate the amount of FW in the food service sector as a whole due to current literature focusing either on single restaurants in specific circumstances or on very large-scale estimates on FW in all sectors. Xue et al. (2017) also concluded that, in general, food loss and FW literature is problematic given the inconsistency of data and the narrow temporal, geographical, and food supply chain coverage. A more rigorous system for measuring FW has to be adapted by the scientific community to produce more comparable results that can be aggregated into estimates for the food service sector and its subsectors. Nevertheless, it is clear that the current amount of FW in the food service sector is high and much more effort should be made to reduce it.

For a single restaurant aiming to reduce its FW it is equally important to know the origin of FW as it is to know the total amount. Several studies that measured FW in different categories have concluded that *serving waste* from over production and buffets is typically much more significant than *kitchen waste* and *customer plate waste* (Betz et al., 2015; Silvennoinen et al., 2015; Eriksson et al., 2017). In restaurants without a buffet, customer plate waste is the most significant source of FW (Silvennoinen et al., 2015). Results from several studies on FW categories are presented for comparison in Table 9.3.

Table 9.2 FW in the food service sector in Europe in tonne/€million turnover PPP adjusted and in kg per person. Numbers were calculated using data from Stenmarck et al. (2016)

	Europe	UK	Finland	Sweden	Denmark	Germany
FW tonne/€million turnover PPP adjusted	19.6	10.1	22.4	18.7	20.9	29.9
FW kg per person	21	14.3	23.8	20.8	20.5	23.6

Table 9.3 Comparison of food waste percentages from food waste measurement studies

Study	Outlet numbers and types	Food waste %	Food waste g/ portion	Kitchen waste %	Serving waste %	Customer plate waste %
Silvennoinen et al., 2015	42 outlets, both buffet (high serving food waste %) and cooked to order restaurants (high customer plate waste %) are included.	16.9–28	58–189	1.5–6.4	3.7–17.2	4.4–9.5
Eriksson et al., 2017	30 public kitchen units, serving lunches with buffet.	23	75	0.7	14.7	7.6
Betz et al., 2015	Two buffet restaurants, top row from education sector, bottom row from business sector.	10.73 7.69	84 67	0.8 0.9	6.4 2.9	2.6 1.9
Silvennoinen et al., 2019a	51 buffet restaurants: schools, day-care centres, workplace and student canteens.	17.5	79	2.2	11.4	3.9

Similar to FW amount, the composition of FW varies depending on the type of restaurant and the country of origin. Logically there is a very strong correlation between the composition of FW and the nature of the food prepared. Therefore, to obtain more meaningful results for reducing FW, the percentage of each type of food wasted should be calculated as well (Nisonen and Silvennoinen, 2018).

As estimations for the costs of FW are dependent on results for FW amounts, their quality in current literature is similarly negligible. However, the EU FUSIONS project (Stenmarck et al., 2016) concluded that FW in the food service sector in the EU-28 was associated with costs of €20 billion. Nisonen and Silvennoinen (2018) estimate that the annual costs associated with FW in Finnish school lunches were around €69 million, with 1 kg of wasted food estimated to cost about €8. These calculations included food resource costs, transportation costs and production costs. Again, these results are based on a relatively small number of FW measurements in schools and should be regarded as tentative.

Good quality environmental impact assessments on FW in the food service sector are also scarce in the literature. In the EU FUSIONS project, a top-down approach used material flow analysis together with process life-cycle coefficients to show a result of 8,87 Mt CO_2 equivalents for the global warming potential of FW in the food service sector. Our own work with a tighter focus (Nisonen and Silvennoinen, 2018) estimated that the yearly global warming potential of waste from school meals in Finland ranged from 15,000 to 53,000 tonnes of CO_2 equivalents, depending on the served food. Lower values were achieved with vegetable-based meals with higher values attributable to meat-based meals, showing great significance according to choice of meal.

FW measurement methods and tools

Quantification of food service waste is essential for following reduction targets that have been set e.g. by the European Union (EU, 2015) and the UN. The target is to *halve per capita global food waste at the retail and consumer levels by 2030 and reduce food losses along production and supply chains* (UN, 2015). Data required by authorities, statistics and researchers can be collected by different methods, such as the use of a waste compositional analysis suitable for a specific area or country (e.g. Tostivint et al., 2016). Aggregated results can be a great source of motivation for reducing FW, but in practice every company and outlet needs to do its own measurements because more comprehensive information is needed for mitigating and managing. In this section we present different FW measurement methods and tools currently available for companies and outlets in the food service sector, as well as for researchers, and discuss their benefits and downsides.

Possible methods used in the food service sector are a FW diary, a composition study and interviews. These methods have been compared and their advantages and disadvantages are discussed in Table 9.4. Composition or sorting studies are difficult to focus on a single sector, so they are badly suited for investigating the amount of FW across the food service sector. The best results would be obtained by combining diary and interviews, as then it is possible to both obtain data on FW amounts and to understand the drivers behind the numbers. Here we focus more deeply on diary or self-reporting methods, as there are many variations in how they can be performed in the food service sector.

Measuring FW is the first step toward reductions and allows the management and staff to recognise major sources of FW and focus their reduction efforts accordingly (e.g. Eriksson et al., 2017; CEC, 2019). More accurate measurements lead to more accurate reduction measures. On the other hand, accurate measurements require more effort and work hours, which staff may be hard-pressed to find in the already busy kitchen schedule (Silvennoinen et al., 2019a). Even companies motivated to reduce their FW output want to find a compromise between more accurate measurements and the work required to perform them. The following outlines some FW measurement schemes, starting with a simple and lightweight version and progressing to those that are more accurate and work intensive.

The simplest way to measure FW is to weigh all of it in one go. One measurement and one result each day. This scheme offers a way to track the amount of FW day by day and observe how it develops over time. Measuring is simple and it does not require much time or effort. However, the types of FW (e.g. kitchen or serving food waste) cannot be identified if FW is not separated. Additionally, proper comparison with other outlets is impossible, if the amount of produced food is not measured and thus the scale of the operation is unknown.

Table 9.4 Comparing different study methods for food services: pros and cons

Food services Method	Positive aspects	Negative aspects
Diary, self-reporting method	Personnel performs measurements, exact data about food produced and discarded, data about liquids thrown to sewer and number of clients.	Time-intensive, results may have gaps in data, need education and motivation.
Composition study, sorting study	Large size of sample, data about total FW, data about packages. Data is reliable as data is collected by researchers or professionals.	No data about food produced, no possibility to analyse share of FW from food produced. Difficult to get separately collected waste samples from food service outlets.
Survey, interview	Data about FW drivers, best practices and possible reduction methods.	No data about amounts. Potential attitude–behaviour gap between reported FW disposal and actual disposal.

If FW is separated by origin before weighing, the sources of FW can be recognised and compared to each other. The inclusion of waste separation transforms the measurements from just observation into a tool of intervention. Ideally, at least FW from preparation and storing (kitchen food waste), serving (over production) and customer plate waste are all measured separately. These classes can be further divided into different food types. It is highly relevant to know if, for instance, serving waste was mainly salad, side dishes or something else (Betz et al., 2015). It is also important to separate originally inedible FW such as coffee grounds or peelings from the originally edible parts to recognise the portion of waste that could be reduced. The trade-off between finer waste categories and work intensity is fairly linear.

The next step is to include weighing of prepared or ordered food and account for the number of customers. These numbers directly describe the scale of the food service outlet's operation. In cooked to order and fast food restaurants the amount of prepared food can alternatively be calculated by first weighing different portions, then using the cash flow to obtain the number of portions sold, and finally multiplying and adding the numbers up respectively. The new information allows the calculation of how much food is wasted in proportion to produced food, or food waste percentage, which is a metric of efficiency. The major benefit from using food waste percentages is that they can be compared across different outlets of varying scales of operation, unlike absolute FW amounts. This is especially important for researchers and for companies with many outlets as it allows them to recognise how an outlet performs compared to others. With the number of customers, food waste per customer can be calculated, which is a similar metric of efficiency.

Finally, to increase the reliability of the measurements, measurement times could be increased (Eriksson et al., 2017) or they could at least be organised during different seasons. FW measurements are often performed in short campaigns, as they may be related to scientific studies or some special occasion. To get the most reliable results, long-term, permanent measurements are recommended to mitigate outside influences such as pressure from researchers or campaigning, or day to day changes in menu, and to enforce normal conditions. For example in schools, where menus are typically cycled over a certain time period, if the measurement period covered at least two identical cycles, the effects of changing menu could be eliminated and the results for the cycles would make a good comparison.

In summary there are four points that are essential for food service companies collecting data to manage and prevent FW. First and foremost is to log the amount of FW by origin: preparation (kitchen), serving (over production) and customer plate waste. Second is to calculate the share of FW from food produced and number of customers/portions. Next is to arrange separate sorting and measurement for edible and inedible parts. Finally, it is important to increase reliability with longer measurement periods, e.g. two identical menu cycles.

A barrier to more accurate measurements is the work required to perform them. Thus it is very important to encourage the development and adoption of tools that ease the process and make accurate measurement schemes more attractive. Catering companies should try to identify issues that make measurements difficult to perform. Support by management is a requirement for successful measurements, with kitchen staff requiring sufficient briefing and guidance both beforehand and during the process (Silvennoinen et al., 2019a). Easy to use scales and a well thought-out system of containers help with the process of separating and weighing FW. A modern, easy to use system for logging in the results is also recommended. Lately new software has appeared on the market allowing for logging in data from scales or mobile devices into cloud storage for easy access (e.g. Lassila & Tikanoja, 2018; Leanpath, 2018).

Best practices for reducing food waste

The conclusions about best practices for reducing FW are, for the most part, based on interviews and workshops with food service outlet staff and management from the WASTESTIMATOR and CIRCWASTE projects. This knowledge was supplemented with literature on the subject. The conclusions are presented in Figure 9.1.

Government's policies and actions have an influence on the amount of FW created in the food service sector (Chalak et al., 2018). Awareness of FW decreases wastage of food, thus information campaigns can be useful (Priefer et al., 2016; Chalak et al., 2018). Also fiscal incentives and legislative frameworks are influential, unlike legally non-binding initiatives (Chalak et al., 2018). For individual restaurants, best practices for FW reduction are

Best practices for reducing food waste

Functional and organised basic practices in kitchen

- Storage cycle
- Proper storing
- Following recipes
- Careful ordering of ingredients

Management & planning
- Work direction
- Motivation
- Improving routines
- Improving service agreement
- Communication
- Considering food waste at all stages of operations

Measurement
- The same employee can be in charge of preparing dishes (e.g. salads) and weighing them

Prediction
- Forecasting the number of customers
- Forecasting the amount of food customers will eat
- Preparing food in stages
- Using kitchen utensils and dishes of a right size

Menu
- Repurposing food
- Unifying special diet dishes

Communication with customers
- Being in contact with customers
- Prompting customers to take only as much food as they will eat at the time

Figure 9.1 Guidelines to best practices for reducing food waste, derived from interviews and workshops in the WASTESTIMATOR and CIRCWASTE projects.

Source: Silvennoinen et al. (2019a, 2019b).

not universal, as reasons behind waste generation are various (Eriksson et al., 2017). However, there are still some general instructions that are useful for every food service outlet. First of all, it is crucial that management considers FW reduction as a matter of greater importance and sets a clear goal to cut down the amount of FW. According to a study from the UK, FW is usually not seen as a priority for the management of the coffee shop sector, and a preventive approach to food waste management is rare (Filimonau et al., 2019). If the management is not committed to reducing FW, it is unlikely the employees will be either. The management must be persistent in motivating the kitchen staff to minimise FW, given the nature of the work in busy kitchen environments and the tendency to return to longstanding norms that may include wasteful actions and procedures (Silvennoinen et al., 2019a).

In addition to being motivated, the employees also need to have the professional skills to work in a kitchen without producing FW, such as ensuring recipes are followed and not making mistakes that lead to food that cannot be served (Heikkilä et al., 2016). The basic practices in the kitchen need to work well. The management is responsible for training the employees to pay attention to FW in all of their tasks (Heikkilä et al., 2016). The importance of communication should be emphasised especially in buffet restaurants: employees working in the kitchen and dining areas need to share information regarding numbers of customers and consumption of dishes (Silvennoinen et al., 2019a).

The amount of FW generated from different sources (kitchen, serving, customer leftovers) varies between food service types and individual outlets (Silvennoinen et al., 2015). This is why longer FW measurement periods are more worthwhile to conduct over shorter periods. Data based on actual measurements facilitates the dedication of the points where the majority of waste is generated and actions can be targeted to tackle identified issues (Eriksson et al., 2017). A sensible way to put measurements into practice is having the same employee that is responsible for certain dishes to do the weighing. Continuous measuring would be ideal as FW quantities and composition can change constantly. This requires measurement equipment that is easy and fast to use, and that measurements become one of the daily routines in the kitchen.

Canteens and restaurants providing buffet lunches usually have the highest proportion of waste generated as serving waste, which is food remaining from the buffet after lunch (Betz et al., 2015; Silvennoinen et al., 2015). It is not easy to predict exactly the right amount of food that should be prepared each day. Improved planning and prediction is essential in minimising serving waste. Records of the number of customers served and what was ordered are useful tools to forecast future demand (Priefer et al., 2016). Also, using smaller serving bowls especially at the end of the lunch is a good way to cut down waste while keeping the buffet attractive (Betz et al., 2015). If the kitchen has enough staff it is highly recommended to cook in stages, which means preparing more food (especially dishes that can be prepared quickly, like side dishes and salads) when needed instead of preparing it all at once before lunch (Heikkilä et al., 2016). FW minimisation should also be considered when planning the menu. For example, it is not wise to prepare dishes that often lead to a large amount of customer plate waste. Another point is that special diet dishes are often a hotspot for FW generation (Eriksson et al., 2017), and thus it would be a good option to cut down the number of different dishes by unifying them.

The most significant source for FW in à la carte restaurants is often the food left on customers' plates. Adaptation of portion sizes to customers' real need is a good way of dealing with this problem (Priefer et al., 2016; Martin-Rios et al., 2018). The staff should actively observe the quantity and composition of leftovers, and recipes should be adapted if needed. The possibility of ordering different sizes of portions and pricing the smaller ones cheaper would make customers ponder how hungry they really are. Customers can produce a lot of leftovers also in buffet restaurants if they take more food on their plates than they eat. There are several ways to influence the customer behaviour, for example getting smaller plates so customers cannot take too much food at once, or prompting the customers to take only as much food as they can eat (Kallbekken and Sælen, 2013).

If a restaurant produces a significant amount of kitchen waste it means a lot of food is spoiled in storage or the staff often makes mistakes during food preparation, such as food being burnt or too salty for consumption. Mistakes in food preparation can be reduced by ensuring that employees have sufficient professional skills and experience of working in a kitchen. Kitchen waste from storing can be prevented by improving the storage cycle, following recipes accurately, using correct package sizes and utilising ingredients near their use-by date innovatively (Silvennoinen et al., 2019a). Inedible kitchen waste can also be utilised. For example, in zero waste restaurants juices and soups can be made from peelings and broths from bones and seafood shells (Martin-Rios et al., 2018).

Keeping customers happy is important for providers of food services, and some measures to reduce FW might be unpleasant from the customers' point of view. In a Finnish study, customers were not so eager to support measures that would impact them directly, for example serving fewer dishes in a buffet or making the portion sizes smaller (Silvennoinen et al., 2013). Therefore, sensitising customers to FW issues is important in gaining their acceptance to possible changes (Betz et al., 2015).

Surplus food utilisation

A discussion of surplus food utilisation in the food service sector brings this chapter to a close. According to the FW hierarchy, the most sustainable option to deal with FW is to prevent it (Papargyropoulou et al., 2014). However, producing no FW at all is not always possible, especially in buffet restaurants. Because of this it is important to consider the second best option, which is re-using the surplus food for human consumption (Papargyropoulou et al., 2014).

There are two possible ways for food services to utilise surplus food: to sell it at a slightly reduced price after the buffet has been closed or donate it to charity or NGOs. Donating the food to people who are affected by food poverty is a socially more sustainable option (Papargyropoulou et al., 2014). On the other hand, selling the surplus food is economically smarter for the businesses. Selling can be arranged by disseminating messages via social media as well as by informal offline methods within communities. This has been implemented via mobile applications such as the 'Finnish Resq Club' app and 'Too Good to Go' in the UK.

Practical and legal issues can prevent food services from donating or selling their surplus food. The food needs to be stored and transported properly, therefore facilities with refrigeration and adequate storage are required. Preparations regarding selling or donating surplus food also require some working time. Food safety authorities can give guidance to help food services to donate and make responsibilities clear. For example, the Finnish food safety authority has introduced guidelines for foodstuffs donated to food aid (Evira, 2013). Also, according to an Italian food bank discussed in Falasconi et al. (2015), acceptance of a 'Good Samaritan Law' that protects donors from liability encouraged many schools and workplace canteens to start donating surplus food.

If selling or donating surplus food is not possible (for example, customers' plate waste or kitchen waste is not fit for human consumption) then the best option is recycling food by

Table 9.5 Food waste hierarchy in food services

	Food waste hierarchy in food services
1.Prevention	Avoid generation of surplus food and FW by adaptation of portion sizes, forecasting demand, etc.
2.Re-use	Sell surplus food or donate it to charity
3.Recycle	Recycle for animal feed or compost
4.Recovery	Recover energy e.g. via anaerobic digestion
5.Disposal	Dispose into landfills

anaerobic digestion into plants or animal feed (Papargyropoulou et al., 2014). In the EU not all foodstuffs are suitable for feed use, and the European Commission has recently published guidelines to provide further clarity on this issue (European Commission, 2018). Surplus redistribution of food forms an important part of the FW hierarchy for the food service sector, as outlined in Table 9.5, in providing an alternative where prevention and mitigation is not possible. Further to this, if food cannot be recycled into animal feed, it should be composted, or treated to recover energy and, only as a last option, disposed into a landfill (Papargyropoulou et al., 2014).

References

Betz, A., Buchli, J., Göbel, C. and Müller, C. (2015) 'Food waste in the Swiss food service industry–Magnitude and potential for reduction', *Waste Management*, vol 35, pp 218–226.

British Hospitality Association. (2015) 'Spotlight on food service management', www.bha.org.uk/word press/wp-content/uploads/2015/11/BHA-FSM-Report-2015.pdf

Buzby, J.C., and Hyman, J. (2012) 'Total and per capita value of food loss in the United States', *Food Policy*, vol 37, pp 561–570.

CEC. (2019) 'Why and How to Measure Food Loss and Waste: A Practical Guide'. Montreal, Canada: Commission for Environmental Cooperation, 60.

Chalak, A., Abou-Daher, C. and Abiad, M.G. (2018) 'Generation of food waste in the hospitality and food retail and wholesale sectors: lessons from developed economies', *Food Security*, vol 10, no 5, pp 1279–1290.

Cohen, J.F., Richardson, S., Parker, E., Catalano, P.J. and Rimm, E.B. (2014) 'Impact of the new US department of agriculture school meal standards on food selection, consumption, and waste', *American Journal of Preventive Medicine*, vol 46, no 4, pp 388–394.

Dias-Ferreira, C., Santos, T. and Oliveira, V. (2015) 'Hospital food waste and environmental and economic indicators–a Portuguese case study', *Waste Management*, vol 46, pp 146–154.

Eriksson, M., Osowski, C.P., Malefors, C., Björkman, J. and Eriksson, E. (2017) 'Quantification of food waste in public catering services–a case study from a Swedish municipality', *Waste Management*, vol 61, pp 415–422.

EU. (2015) 'Communication from the commission to the European Parliament, the council, the European economic and social committee and the committee of the regions closing the loop - An EU action plan for the circular economy', http://eur-lex.europa.eu/legal-content/EN/TXT/?qid=1453384154337&uri=CELEX:52015DC0614

European Agency for Safety and Health at Work. (2008) 'Introduction to the HORECA sector', E-Facts 21, https://osha.europa.eu/fi/tools-and-publications/publications/e-facts/efact21

European Commission. (2018) 'Guidelines for the feed use of food no longer intended to human consumption', Commission notice, https://eur-lex.europa.eu/legal-content/EN/TXT/?uri=CELEX:52018XC0416(01)

Evira. (2013) 'Foodstuffs donated to food aid', www.diva-portal.org/smash/get/diva2:902211/ATTACHMENT02.pdf

Falasconi, L., Vittuari, M., Politano, A. and Segrè, A. (2015) 'Food waste in school catering: an Italian case study', *Sustainability*, vol 7, no 11, pp 14745–14760.

Filimonau, V., Krivcova, M. and Pettit, F. (2019) 'An exploratory study of managerial approaches to food waste mitigation in coffee shops', *International Journal of Hospitality Management*, vol 76, pp 48–57.

Gustavsson, J., Cederberg, C., Sonesson, U., Van Otterdijk, R. and Meybeck, A. (2011) *Global food losses and food waste*. FAO, Rome.

Heikkilä, L., Reinikainen, A., Katajajuuri, J.M., Silvennoinen, K. and Hartikainen, H. (2016) 'Elements affecting food waste in the food service sector', *Waste Management*, vol 56, pp 446–453.

Hietala, S., Riipi, I., Välimaa, A-L. and Katajajuuri, J-M. (2018) 'Lainsäädäntötarkastelulla ruokahävikkiä pienemmäksi', Policy brief, https://tietokayttoon.fi/documents/1927382/2116852/9-2018-Lains% C3%A4%C3%A4d%C3%A4nt%C3%B6tarkastelulla+ruokah%C3%A4vikki%C3%A4+pienemm% C3%A4ksi/b0a9002e-893d-495b-9f88-bd7d15abc69e?version=1.0

HOTREC. (2018) 'Annual report 2017/2018', www.hotrec.eu/annual-report-2017-2018/

Kallbekken, S. and Sælen, H. (2013) '"Nudging"hotel guests to reduce food waste as a win–win environmental measure', *Economics Letters*, vol 119, no 3, pp 325–327.

Katajajuuri, J.M., Silvennoinen, K., Hartikainen, H., Heikkilä, L. and Reinikainen, A. (2014) 'Food waste in the Finnish food chain', *Journal of Cleaner Production*, vol 73, pp 322–329.

Lassila & Tikanoja. (2018) 'Hävikkimestari', https://havikkimestari.lassila-tikanoja.fi/

Lazell, J. (2016) 'Consumer food waste behaviour in universities: sharing as a means of prevention', *Journal of Consumer Behaviour*, vol 15, no 5, pp 430–439.

Leanpath. (2018) 'Take control of your food waste', www.leanpath.com/leanpath360/

Martin-Rios, C., Demen-Meier, C., Gössling, S. and Cornuz, C. (2018) 'Food waste management innovations in the foodservice industry', *Waste Management*, vol 79, pp 196–206.

Martins, M.L., Cunha, L.M., Rodrigues, S.S. and Rocha, A. (2014) 'Determination of plate waste in primary school lunches by weighing and visual estimation methods: a validation study', *Waste Management*, vol 34, no 8, pp 1362–1368.

Mirosa, M., Munro, H., Mangan-Walker, E. and Pearson, D. (2016) 'Reducing waste of food left on plates: interventions based on means-end chain analysis of customers in foodservice sector', *British Food Journal*, vol 118, no 9, pp 2326–2343.

Myung, E., McClaren, A. and Li, L. (2012) 'Environmentally related research in scholarly hospitality journals: current status and future opportunities', *International Journal of Hospitality Management*, vol 31, no 4, pp 1264–1275.

National Restaurant Association. (2018) 'The state of restaurant sustainability', www.restaurant.org/ research/reports/state-of-restaurant-sustainability

Nisonen, S. and Silvennoinen, K. (2018) 'Food waste in hospitality sector', Online presentation, www. luke.fi/ravintolafoorumi/wp-content/uploads/sites/4/2018/10/Results-from-WASTESTIMA TOR-project.pdf

Painter, K., Thondhlana, G. and Kua, H.W. (2016) 'Food waste generation and potential interventions at Rhodes University, South Africa', *Waste Management*, vol 56, pp 491–497.

Papargyropoulou, E., Lozano, R., Steinberger, J.K., Wright, N. and Bin Ujang, Z. (2014) 'The food waste hierarchy as a framework for the management of food surplus and food waste', *Journal of Cleaner Production*, vol 76, pp 106–115.

Parfitt, J., Barthel, M. and Macnaughton, S. (2010) 'Food waste within food supply chains: quantification and potential for change to 2050', *Philosophical Transactions of the Royal Society B: Biological Sciences*, vol 365, no 1554, pp 3065–3081.

Pirani, S.I. and Arafat, H.A. (2016) 'Reduction of food waste generation in the hospitality industry', *Journal of Cleaner Production*, vol 132, pp 129–145.

Priefer, C., Jörissen, J. and Bräutigam, K.R. (2016) 'Food waste prevention in Europe–a cause-driven approach to identify the most relevant leverage points for action', *Resources, Conservation and Recycling*, vol 109, pp 155–165.

Principato, L., Secondi, L. and Pratesi, C.A. (2015) 'Reducing food waste: an investigation on the behaviour of Italian youths', *British Food Journal*, vol 117, no 2, pp 731–748.

Silvennoinen, K., Heikkilä, L., Katajajuuri, J.M. and Reinikainen, A. (2015) 'Food waste volume and origin: case studies in the finnish food service sector', *Waste management*, vol 46, pp 140–145.

Silvennoinen, Kirsi, Hartikainen, Hanna, Katajajuuri, Juha-Matti, Nisonen, Sampsa, Pietiläinen, Oona and Timonen, Karetta (2019a) *WASTESTIMATOR : Ruokahävikin päivitetyt mittaustulokset ja ruokahävikin seurantatyökalun kehittäminen: kotitaloudet ja ravitsemispalvelut.* Luonnonvara: ja biotalouden tutkimus. 32/ 2019, p. 63.

Silvennoinen, Kirsi, Katajajuuri, Juha-Matti, Lahti, Leo, Nisonen, Sampsa, Pietiläinen, Oona, Riipi, Inkeri. 2019b. Ruokahävikin mittaaminen ja hävikin vähennyskeinot ravitsemispalveluissa: CIRCWASTE Deliverable C5.1. Luonnonvara- ja biotalouden tutkimus 49/2019: 29.

Silvennoinen, K., Lahti, L., Nisonen, S. and Pietiläinen, O. (2019b) 'Ruokahävikin mittaaminen ja hävikin vähennyskeinot ravitsemispalveluissa (*Monitoring food waste in the food service sector).* Luonnonvarakeskus, Helsinki.

Silvennoinen, K., Pinolehto, M., Korhonen, O., Riipi, I. and Katajajuuri, J.M. (2013) *Kauppakassista kaatopaikalle, ruokahävikki kotitalouksissa: kuru 2011–2013-hankkeen loppuraportti.* MTT, Jokioinen.

Smith, S.L. and Cunningham-Sabo, L. (2014) 'Food choice, plate waste and nutrient intake of elementary-and middle-school students participating in the US national school Lunch Program', *Public Health Nutrition,* vol 17, no 6, pp 1255–1263.

Sonnino, R. and McWilliam, S. (2011) 'Food waste, catering practices and public procurement: a case study of hospital food systems in Wales', *Food Policy,* vol 36, no 6, pp 823–829.

Stenmarck, Å., Jensen, C., Quested, T. and Moates, G. (2016) *Estimates of European food waste levels.* FUSIONS, Stockholm.

Tatàno, F., Caramiello, C., Paolini, T., and Tripolone, L. (2017) 'Generation and collection of restaurant waste: characterization and evaluation at a case study in Italy', *Waste Management,* vol 61, pp 423–442.

Thiagarajah, K. and Getty, V.M. (2013) 'Impact on plate waste of switching from a tray to a trayless delivery system in a university dining hall and employee response to the switch', *Journal of the Academy of Nutrition and Dietetics,* vol 113, no 1, pp 141–145.

Tostivint, C., Östergren, K., Quested, T., Soethoudt, J.M., Stenmarck, A., Svanes, E. and O'Connor, C. (2016) *Food waste quantification manual to monitor food waste amounts and progression.* FUSIONS, Paris.

UN. (2015) 'Transforming our world: the 2030 agenda for sustainable development', www.un.org/ga/ search/view_doc.asp?symbol=A/RES/70/1&Lang=E

Wang, L.E., Liu, G., Liu, X., Liu, Y., Gao, J., Zhou, B., Gao, S. and Cheng, S. (2017) 'The weight of unfinished plate: a survey based characterization of restaurant food waste in Chinese cities', *Waste Management,* vol 66, pp 3–12.

Whitehair, K.J., Shanklin, C.W. and Brannon, L.A. (2013) 'Written messages improve edible food waste behaviors in a university dining facility', *Journal of the Academy of Nutrition and Dietetics,* vol 113, no 1, pp 63–69.

Wilkie, A., Graunke, R. and Cornejo, C. (2015) 'Food waste auditing at three Florida schools', *Sustainability,* vol 7, no 2, pp 1370–1387.

WRAP. (2011) 'Food waste in schools' *Summary report.* Banbury, UK: Waste & Resources Action Programme. http://www.wrap.org.uk/sites/files/wrap/Food%20Waste%20in%20Schools%20Summary% 20Report.pdf

Xue, L., Liu, G., Parfitt, J., Liu, X., Van Herpen, E., Stenmarck, Å., O'Connor, C., Östergren, K. and Cheng, S. (2017) 'Missing food, missing data? A critical review of global food losses and food waste data', *Environmental Science and Technology,* vol 51, no 12, pp 6618–6633.

PART III

Overview of regional food waste
Research, policy, and legal approaches

Food waste is a truly global issue, with many countries, regions, and municipalities attempting to reduce, prevent, and divert food waste in their own specific way. Part III attempts to convey and review many of the (global) approaches to food waste. Each chapter highlights different (but shared) research histories, alongside policy and legal developments across the globe. In our selection of chapters we have attempted to provide a range of case studies, from both global North and South.

Stephen D. Porter's chapter 'Food waste in the UK and EU' notes the unjust reality whereby food waste is being addressed, yet poverty and food insecurity persist. He highlights alternative routes to reducing food waste beyond dominant mechanisms of voluntary agreements and consumer education campaigns. These new mechanisms include balancing power between farmers and supermarkets, and increasing retail redistribution. Porter then explores developments in EU policy. Due to the evolving nature of UK and EU policy as this book went to press, Porter was unable to cover the Delegated and Implementing Acts of 2019, which were signed into EU law. For reference: in May 2019 the European Commission has adopted a Delegated decision laying down a common food waste measurement methodology to support Member States in quantifying food waste at each stage of the food supply chain. The Implementing Act will lay down the format for reporting food waste data. Member States will be given a year to implement the necessary changes for monitoring their food waste levels, with 2020 the first year of measurement of food waste across Member States. The Delegated decision (or Act) mandates the reporting only of food waste destined to waste treatment operations (such as landfilling, composting, biogas, incineration, etc.), and food waste as sewage from households. Information on food originally intended for human consumption and then directed to animal feed or donated, and food waste drained as or within wastewater can also be reported on a voluntary basis. This means that by 2022/2023 the EU will have a comparable and comprehensive data set on food waste – a major advancement for global food waste scholarship and action.

Jean C. Buzby and Claudia Fabiano's chapter, 'Food loss and waste measurement methods and estimates for the United States', presents and compares major sources of data on food loss and waste in the United States – two federal (the US Department of Agriculture and the US Environmental Protection Agency), one collaboration, ReFED (Rethink Food Waste through Economics and Data), and two relatively simplistic calculations using existing data. It then covers the main legal incentives for food recovery, and key government actions at local, state, and federal levels relating to food waste. It concludes with a discussion about how to measure the meeting of the Sustainable Development Goal (SDG) Target 12.3, and the current feasibility of this metric – an important point to consider when this measurement is supposed to be available for any country by 2030!

In 'Estimating total and per capita food waste in Brazilian Households: a scenario analysis', Glenio Piran Dal' Magro and Edson Talamini provide an estimation of Brazilian household food waste, and contextualise this estimation through a discussion of Brazilian food waste policy. This chapter is one of the first investigations and quantifications of food waste for Brazil beyond the work of Porpino (Porpino, 2016; Porpino et al., 2015, 2016), and, with time, the issue of food loss and waste will continue to attract scholarship in Brazil.

Marlyne Sahakian, Megha Shenoy, Tammara Soma, Atsushi Watabe, Ran Yagasa, Dickella Gamaralalage Jagath Permakumara, Chen Liu, Abigail Marie Favis, and Czarina Saloma all contribute to 'Apprehending food waste in Asia: policies, practices and promising trends'. This provides an interdisciplinary perspective on food waste in Asian cities, presenting case studies from Cambodia, India, Indonesia, Japan, and the Philippines. The chapter investigates the linkages of food waste to different agendas, such as to improving nutrition or reducing negative environmental and social impacts. The chapter concludes with an overview of promising trends, and identifies recommendations for further promoting food waste policies, action, and research across the region. The learnings from these examples can be applied to many cities beyond Asia.

The food waste reduction potential of countries of the Middle East and Africa is vast. It would be impossible to do justice to the food waste situations of this region's many and diverse places within a single chapter. As a compromise, 'Food waste within South Africa and Saudi Arabia' by Suzan Oelofse, Anton Nahman, Mirza Barjees Baig, Ramy Salemdeeb, Abdul-Sattar Nizami, and Christian Reynolds, focuses on two prominent countries with differing levels of food waste research and policy. This chapter reviews current research and quantifications of food waste in both countries, listing the food waste challenges and solutions for each.

Australia and New Zealand have two of the highest per capita food waste generation rates of the global North. The chapter 'Food waste in Australia and New Zealand' by Miranda Mirosa, David Pearson, and Christian Reynolds, provides a summary of food waste research conducted in these countries, as well as future policy directions. It is notable that, at the time of press, both countries are launching major food waste policy reviews and new research activities.

References

Porpino, G., 2016. Household food waste behavior: avenues for future research. *Journal of the Association for Consumer Research* 1, 41–51.

Porpino, G., Parente, J., Wansink, B., 2015. Food waste paradox: antecedents of food disposal in low income households. *International Journal of Consumer Studies* 39, 619–629.

Porpino, G., Wansink, B., and Parente, J., 2016. Wasted positive intentions: the role of affection and abundance on household food waste. *Journal of Food Products Marketing* 22, 733–751.

10

FOOD WASTE IN THE UK AND EU

A policy and practice perspective

Stephen D. Porter

Introduction

Food loss and waste (FLW) is an issue that exists all along the food supply chain (FSC). It is not "just" a consumer problem, there are multiple stakeholders. Producers, processors, distributors, consumers, and policy-makers are all involved, though they apportion differing degrees of importance to it. It is also an issue omnipresent across the globe—though manifesting differently depending upon geographic location and political jurisdiction. While there may be conceptual similarities globally to drivers and routes to reduce the rate of occurrence, the local—"on the ground"—environment cannot be ignored. There are many lenses through which FLW can be viewed—cultural, behavioural, and economic being just a few. Here, we examine FLW and its reduction through the twin lenses of policy and practice, specifically focusing on the United Kingdom (UK) and European Union (EU). We begin with context on the continued existence of food (in)security in Europe, introduce the key stakeholders and actors in FLW discourse, and finally explore how they—and policy—have impacted levels of FLW. That the UK is due to leave the EU in early 2019 presents significant uncertainty over the policy and regulatory environments across the economy and society, not least of which is the agri-food industry. However, whether the UK remains an EU Member State or not, there are positive signs the stakeholders at all levels in the UK and its constituent home nations are serious about addressing this great societal scourge of lost and wasted food.

Wealthy, yet poverty and food insecurity remain

By many measures the UK and wider EU are wealthy. Per capita GDP in 2017 for the UK was about US$ 39,700 and US$ 33,700 for the EU, compared to the OECD and World averages of US$ 38,100 and US$ 10,700 (World Bank, n.d.).[1] The EU average is skewed lower due to Central European and Baltic Member States' relatively poorer state, whose per capita GDP is only about a third of that of the OECD (World Bank, n.d.). However, wealth of a nation extends beyond purely monetary terms, with a number of concepts existing to measure it in more qualitative terms. These examples include, Bhutan's Gross National Happiness, the EU's quality of life survey, the global World Happiness Report, and the UK's well-being index (Centre for Bhutan

Studies & GNH Research, 2016; Eurofund, 2017; Helliwell et al., 2017; Office for National Statistics, 2018a). In terms of well-being, over 80% of the UK population are highly or very highly satisfied with their lives, a figure that has risen consistently since 2012 (Office for National Statistics, 2018b). At the regional level, happiness and life satisfaction scores in the EU averaged 7.4 and 7.1 out of 10, respectively (Eurofund, 2017). The primary goal of such efforts is to obtain an objective measure on a subjective concept that is more comprehensive and holistic than simply GDP. Despite this objective, it is notable that those in the lower income brackets in the UK and EU tend to report lower scores on these "non-economic" measures.

Simply put, food is a necessary component to life. There is a sufficient global production of food in terms of calories and nutrients that food insecurity and undernourishment should not exist (Holt-Giménez et al., 2012). Coupled with the apparent wealth of EU countries and relatively cheap food,[2] it is anathema that anyone should go hungry. While the prevalence of severe food insecurity in Europe (including non-EU States) is under 2%, the UK figure is more than double at over 4%, equivalent to 2.8 million people (FAO et al., 2017; Office for National Statistics, 2018c). The proportion of the UK population experiencing persistent poverty[3] in 2015 (the most recent data) was estimated at 7.3%, or about 5 million people (Office for National Statistics, 2017). This is considerably lower than the rate of 17.3% for the EU as a whole (Eurostat, n.d.), which has a North–South and East–West divide (i.e. greater poverty in southern vs northern Europe and in eastern vs western Europe).

In light of this picture of general overall wealth yet elevated poverty rates in both the UK and EU, it is difficult to reconcile that one of the key rights to life—food—is often discarded. In Gustavsson et al. (2011), the UN's Food and Agriculture Organization (FAO) concluded that about one-third of all food produced globally is lost or wasted along the chain from farm to fork (i.e. from primary production to consumption). While it is a figure easy to recall, focusing on this value alone can cloud differences in losses between types of food, and says little about where along the chain it occurs.

Key FLW stakeholders

The following is a brief introduction to key influencing organisations and publications that have helped initiate the discourse on FLW in the UK and Europe. This is indicative rather than exhaustive—the latter would be an encyclopaedia on its own.

WRAP

The issue of food waste sits within the larger problem of overall waste reduction. From a UK perspective, food waste has been on the official agenda since 2000. This was the year of formation for WRAP (Waste and Resources Action Programme)[4] within the UK's Department for Environment, Food & Rural Affairs (i.e. Defra). In 2014, WRAP left the confines of Defra and became an independent charity—however, the majority of its funding is by government grants, with almost 80% of income provided by the EU, UK, and "home nation" administrations (WRAP, 2018a). This change in funding structure grants WRAP more freedom to pursue other revenue sources, and to be more financially sustainable itself. This organisation has been instrumental in raising the visibility of sustainable waste management in general, and food waste specifically. Campaigns have included "Love Food Hate Waste" (with its own dedicated website[5]), and driving the Courtauld Commitment, the first voluntary agreement of its kind involving all major supermarkets in the UK. The latter has recently been renewed through 2025 with a specific focus on supermarket efforts to realise SDG 12.3 of halving per capita food waste (WRAP, 2018b).

EU FUSIONS

The FUSIONS project[6] was a large-scale EU-funded research programme that ran from 2012–2016, a continuation of the initial *Preparatory Study on Food Waste Across EU 27*, a higher-level work conducted by Monier et al. (2010). FUSIONS' main objectives were: to develop a common definition of food waste and a standard methodology for data collection to better monitor it; understand the extent and drivers of food waste and how social innovation could reduce it; and, provide guidelines for EU policy development. The Council of the EU recognised this work by outlining various initiatives that would put into practice the outcomes of the FUSIONS project (European Council, 2016). One of these outline initiatives resulted in the creation of REFRESH,[7] a large-scale, multi-partner research project to fight food waste in the supply chain, and work toward achieving SDG 12.3.

UN FAO

The seminal report on food waste was published by Gustavsson et al. (2011) on behalf of the FAO. Its main contributions were to view food waste as a global issue, highlight important local differences, and to link food waste and greenhouse gas emissions. It built upon the work from many previous studies that were local and focused to ultimately claim about a third of all food produced is wasted—i.e. not consumed by humans. The resultant "Save Food" initiative[8] aims to bring together the various stakeholder groups within the agri-food network—producers, manufacturers, retailers, logistics, academics, consumers—to devise efficient and effective ways to combat food waste (Save Food Initiative, 2018).

Food loss and waste

FLW is a serious issue. Europe wastes roughly 220 Mt of food per year and, along the entire FSC, global levels have tripled since 1961 to 1.6 billion tonnes, equivalent to about 2 Gt CO_2e of embedded production-phase (i.e. pre-farm gate) emissions (Porter et al., 2016). On a per capita basis, FLW in developed countries and regions is about 95–115 kg per annum, compared to 6–11 kg in much of the developing global South (Gustavsson et al., 2011). In the UK, nearly 10 million tonnes of food, with embedded greenhouse gas (GHG) emissions of some 20 million tonnes CO_2e, is lost or wasted each year post-farm gate, more than half of which could have been avoided (WRAP, 2017a).[9] Estimates of EU food waste that also exclude on-farm losses range from 90–110 Mt per annum with about 170 Mt CO_2e of embedded emissions (Monier et al., 2010; Bräutigam et al., 2014). Not only is there an environmental cost to FLW, there is also a very real economic cost. The value of this food waste is estimated at £17 billion for the UK (WRAP, 2017a). Applying the same UK cost of £1,700 per tonne and scaling up to the EU level would equate to a value of some £374 billion (or about €425 billion[10]) of food lost each year.

The consumer stage is responsible for about a third of all lost or wasted food in Europe while on-farm losses of some commodities—such as fruits, vegetables, pulses, tubers—can be as much as 50% of all loss in the FSC (Gustavsson et al., 2011). Clearly, then, loss and waste in primary production (i.e. on farm) is an important issue. However, most policy action has been directed at the much more visible consumer/retail stages. On-farm loss and waste is relatively hidden, though this issue has been garnering attention in the UK from both the research and media communities (e.g. (WRAP, 2017b; Briggs, 2018; Feedback, 2018; Gabbatiss, 2018). Of the FLW from processing (e.g. food manufacturers, abattoirs, etc.) or distribution (e.g.

wholesale and retail markets), less than 2% is redistributed for consumption to those in need (Parfitt et al., 2016). Destruction (e.g. composting) or other non-food use (e.g. bioenergy) of such "surplus" food is by far the most common destination (Parfitt et al., 2016; Porter et al., 2018a).

Although the retail distribution channel (i.e. supermarkets) is directly responsible for just 2% of food waste (WRAP, 2017a), their power indirectly influences other actors within that chain, from farmers all the way through to the consumer (Hingley, 2005; Fulponi, 2006). On-farm production losses have not received as much attention as that of households. Unharvested produce is not defined as food under EU regulations (European Parliament and Council, 2002) and thus does not appear in national statistics. Estimates of such losses are more uncertain, though remain potentially important for economic, social, and environmental reasons. With considerable uncertainty, central estimates for the proportion of fruit and vegetables that do not enter the FSC due to purely aesthetic reasons (e.g. size, shape, visual appearance) is 20% in the UK (Porter et al., 2018b). As on-farm food loss is not included in these statistics, the avoidable loss of edible food and its economic value (about 330,000 tonnes with a value of about £87 million and embedded GHG emissions of 74,000 tonnes CO_2e)[11] is hidden and unrecognised.

Routes to reducing food waste

Balancing power between farmers and supermarkets

The economic value of the 88 million tonnes of food lost or wasted in the EU—20% of production—is estimated at €188 billion per year (EU FUSIONS, 2016). In the present food value chain, this waste occurs because it is more economically efficient than eliminating it entirely. From the farmer's perspective, why incur the added expense of harvesting produce that they know will not be sold due to being out of spec for their contracted distribution partner (i.e. usually supermarkets). These extra expenses would not be recouped, further jeopardising their already risky livelihood.[12] Due to the power differential in favour of the national supermarket chains—a small number of very large buyers versus a large number of small suppliers (i.e. farmers)—farmers are price-takers with respect to their produce (Cox and Chicksand, 2007). By banding together as voluntary producer organisations, however, it may be possible to at least partially shift power away from supermarkets (Maglaras et al., 2015). EU recognition of producer organisations brings a number of benefits under CMO (Common Organisation of Markets) regulations within the EU CAP (common agriculture policy), including access to funding for certain activities intended to benefit the organisation (European Commission, 2018a). Such benefits, however, will lapse when the UK exits the EU, unless otherwise negotiated as a part of Brexit or internally replaced by the UK or Scottish governments. With increased supplier power to negotiate more favourable terms of sale to supermarkets, more produce could potentially be available for harvest, preventing waste before it occurs.

Retail redistribution

As a proportion of sales, food waste from supermarkets is about 2% (WRAP, 2017a). However, this proportion still amounts to about 260,000 tonnes of preventable food waste in the UK (WRAP, 2018c). Redistributing this amount of food is roughly equivalent to 520 million meals (or almost 200 meals per year per person). Only a tiny proportion of surplus food is currently redistributed in this manner—some goes to animal feed but about three-quarters is destined for composting or bioenergy feedstock (WRAP, 2017a). Altering this balance in favour of redistribution may require incentives to offset additional costs such rebalancing may impose upon supermarkets (operating margins in 2016 for the "Big Four" averaged less than 3%, and were as low as 1% for Tesco) (MSCI and Colliers International, 2017).

Legislation/regulation

EU level

Food waste, and its reduction, has been a topic of discussion since at least 2011, with little achieved in the first five years of EU-level talks (European Court Auditors, 2016). There were no binding EU-level acts or policies that specifically focused on this issue, and those that existed may not have been aligned to address food waste (Porter et al., 2018a). More recently, however, the EU has initiated a number of actions with respect to food waste. These include the Action Plan for the Circular Economy, an updated Waste Directive, and clearer date marking on food; ambitions that align with the Sustainable Development Goal 12.3 on reducing food waste[13] (European Commission, 2015, 2018b; European Parliament and Council, 2018). Within the EU, the different types of legal acts include legislation, regulation, and decisions. These acts differ in to whom and how they are applied (European Union, 2018). Directives specify outcomes or goals but each Member State has the freedom to determine the means used to achieve them (e.g. Waste Framework Directive; European Parliament and Council, 2008). Regulations are binding as passed at the EU level; all Member States are expected to follow regulations in their entirety in a common manner (e.g. Common Organisation of Markets quality standards for certain fruits and vegetables; European Commission, 2011, Annex I, Part B). Decisions are binding only on specified entities in a given decision, which may be an EU Member State or private company, for example. Where conflict exists between the EU and a Member State, two entities, EU law has primacy, the adherence to which is the responsibility of the European Court of Justice (European Union, 2010).

Food and waste are highly regulated sectors of the UK and European economies, with safety seen as paramount. Both concepts have specific definitions within EU regulations, which therefore apply equally to all Member States. How waste is defined, however, does influence how food waste is monitored and managed. For example, agricultural produce only becomes "food" once it is harvested and is intended for human ingestion, and "shall not be placed on the market if it is unsafe" (European Parliament and Council, 2002, Art 2; Art 14, para 1). What is lost on the farm may therefore not be viewed as waste by the farmer (e.g. not harvested or redirected to compost or feed) and thus not accounted for in estimates of FLW. Additionally, waste is defined by the EU as "any substance or object which the holder discards or intends or is required to discard" (European Parliament and Council, 2008, Art 3, para 1).[14] Once food is deemed to be "waste", it is difficult for it to re-enter the FSC.

Perhaps the most significant set of EU acts are those wrapped up in the CAP.[15] Criticised for creating "butter mountains", "wine lakes", and widespread food destruction due to paying minimum prices for agricultural produce without reference to market impact, the policy has undergone several substantial iterations. A result has been a 90%+ reduction in the amount of food that is withdrawn from market due to overproduction. However, there remains an apparent inability to absorb a significant portion of the food into the redistribution system as almost two-thirds of such edible food is still destroyed (Porter et al., 2018a). Destruction of food in "crisis" situations—the only time the withdrawal mechanism is intended to be used under the latest CMO regulations (European Council, 2007)—remains accepted practice, which creates an inertia in the system that is difficult to offset (Peterson and Bomberg, 1999).

National level

In 2016, two EU countries (France and Italy) passed national-level legislation intended to reduce food waste from retail distribution outlets. The French law emphasises prevention, with a general ban on the practice of making unsold food unfit for consumption, punishable by fines (French Senate, 2015). French retailers with a footprint of 400 m^2 or greater are required to have agreements with charitable distributors to offtake their excess, yet still edible, food supply without charge. Italy's legislation also focuses on donation and/or redistribution as most desirable, doing so explicitly to promote the concept of "social welfare" (Italian Government, 2016). This is in contrast to the UK, where a private member's bill put forth in 2015 on this matter, has been tabled indefinitely, effectively abandoned (McCarthy, 2016).

While it is too early to evaluate the relative efficacy of either of these Continental European initiatives, they remain beacons of what is possible with sufficient support. Efforts to reduce food waste may be applied at any stage from farm to household using the waste hierarchy of value retention, which has prevention ahead of redistribution and recycling before disposal. The potential impact on existing charitable redistribution networks should not be ignored. For example, the scaling up of redistribution efforts through charitable means would lead to greater funding needs for charities to continue to operate. This will include: increased space requirements for storage; more complex logistics for distribution; and, higher overhead costs. Further, there is a risk that redistribution charities become the "dumping ground" for supermarket food waste. The result could be that the "food waste problem" is simply shifted from a few key actors, with substantial resources to address it, to many small actors that lack such resources.

Sub-national level: Scotland

The Scottish Government's 2016–17 *Programme for Scotland*[16] announced it would be consulting on a "Good Food Nation Bill" (Scottish Government, 2016). While this announcement was very light on specific detail of any consultation, grassroots organisations such as NourishScotland envisioned such a bill could explicitly institutionalise a "right to food" into Scottish law and "facilitate a just transition to a fair, healthy and sustainable food system". In the ensuing years, however, little happened. The expected consultation has not taken place and the mention of a bill was quietly left off the government's 2018–19 programme. The intended bill was downgraded to a "programme"; to brand Scotland as a "good food nation" through promoting its produce (Scottish Government, 2018a). This omission by the Scottish Government leaves only a private member's bill as a possible option.[17]

Voluntary actions by business

UK's supermarket sector

As part of the UK's policy goal of a "zero waste economy" (Defra, 2011), WRAP led the creation and launch of a voluntary agreement among the UK's largest supermarkets aimed at reducing retail food waste. Currently in its fourth phase, the Courtauld Commitment has several specific goals to be achieved by 2025, including: 20% reductions in absolute food waste and 20% reduction in relative GGH emissions intensity of consumed products (WRAP, 2018d). This may appear less ambitious than the Sustainable Development Goal of halving of retail food waste, but it must be recognised that SDG 12.3 uses a per capita (i.e. relative) metric whereas the Courtauld 2025 includes absolute reduction targets. As an exemplar of what can be achieved at the corporate level with respect to transparency—which should lead to progress on reduction—Tesco (the largest UK supermarket) is now providing details of food waste from 27 of its suppliers, in addition to the supermarket's own operations (Tesco, 2018). While it is not clear what proportion of food this group of 27 accounts for, such actions should be acknowledged as a positive step.

Private and regulated "quality" standards for fresh produce are a source of avoidable food waste (Devin and Richards, 2018). Such standards may be relaxed during times where their application could result in a lack of product availability (Silverman, 2012). More recently, sensing a bottom-up opportunity, supermarkets have launched out-of-spec (i.e. "wonky" or "ugly"[18]) ranges for fresh produce. Such action can improve food insecurity by increasing access to healthy food at lower price points. Food loss at source is reduced and may also result in increased profits and/or stability for other actors within the supply chain.

Entrepreneurship

Viewing FLW as a resource can lead to additional for-profit and not-for-profit activity. Such activity can lead to social and environmental gains such as reduced GHG emissions from landfilling of food and improved access to food for the insecure. One not-for-profit example is a community food fridge,[19] which encourages the free sharing of (safe and edible) surplus food that households/businesses/other organisations would otherwise throw away. Another similar example of reallocating surplus food is via a technological option. Users can post details of unwanted food to an app that others in the community may request.[20] Importantly, access to such food sharing initiatives is open to anyone within the community irrespective of whether they are in a position themselves to share.

Moving upstream in the FSC is loss of fresh fruit and vegetables at the farm level. It may not always be economical for a given farmer to harvest all (or, in extremes, any) available produce, due to (for example) excess yield or falling foul of "quality" regulations or similar private standards (Parfitt et al., 2010; Teuber and Jensen, 2016). Entrepreneurs have created business models that view produce that would otherwise be "walked-by" or ploughed back into the fields as a resource with value to be unlocked. For some, that could be a for-profit model (such as Imperfect Produce) or not-for-profit (e.g. FoodCloud and Olio).

Grassroots movements

Community- or private individual-led grassroots movements often predate formal policy or regulation. Parties with mutual interests can act quickly at a local level to identify relevant issues and organise to address it. Such organisations are often acting on a very limited budget and are often dependent on the volunteer's own goodwill. However, as the following examples will demonstrate, motivated private individuals and organisations can have, by acting as first-movers, a real bottom-up impact on ultimate policy development and how policy is implemented in practice.

Stop wasting food—Denmark

The consumer is at the heart of many initiatives to reduce food waste. Often, they are seen as the cause of food waste, whose behaviour needs to be changed. Such change can be influenced from the top-down through legislation, regulation, and policy. Promoting more sustainable practices can also arise from the bottom-up via grassroots efforts. An example in Europe of the latter is the Stop Wasting Food Movement[21] in Denmark, which began in 2008 (*Stop Spild af Mad* as it was originally founded and known locally). Successes in the fight against food waste claimed by this movement include: collaborations with multiple levels of Danish government, the United Nations, and the EU; a co-developer of the Food Loss & Waste Protocol;[22] an influencer to end the practice of bulk buy offers (e.g. "buy one, get one free") in food retailing; and, achieving an 83% share of mind[23] of Danes with respect to the importance of reducing household food waste (Stop Wasting Food, 2018).

Fareshare—UK

While food waste in supermarkets is quite low as a proportion of sales, only about 2% (see the 'Retail redistribution' section above), it is a major logistical exercise to move this 260,000 tonnes of food while it is still safely edible. Within the food waste hierarchy, redistribution/food rescue ranks higher than animal feed or composting, but ranks third behind these two in terms of practice, typically due to lower costs or hassle (Caplan, 2017). This is where organisations such as FareShare come in. They reside between the retailers and consumer-facing charities to organise and carry out the uplift and redistribution of surplus food from retailers to other charitable organisations. However, as a single actor, FareShare still only has capacity to handle about 5% of supermarket surplus—equivalent to some 36 million meals—to avoid it becoming food waste (FareShare, 2018). There remains a good deal of work to be done to effectively handle the remaining 95%.

Gleaning

Gleaning is an ancient practice, common in the UK and Continental Europe until the Industrial Revolution and the mechanisation of agriculture. However, through grassroots movements—such as Feedback[24] in the UK, Espigoladors[25] in Spain, Boroume[26] in Greece, and RE-BON[27] in France—gleaning is experiencing a resurgence. The practice involves the collection of unharvested produced from farmers' fields. There are many reasons produce may not be harvested—yield may be higher than the market can bear; produce may be out of specification for distribution channels; cheaper imports take market share. The end result is the same—avoidable food loss at primary production. With the permission of farmers, gleaning activity may recover at least some of this potential loss.

Brexit

The elephant in the room with respect to UK policy is its potential withdrawal from the EU in late 2019.[28] There are ramifications from this withdrawal across the entire economy, which will impact food production and manufacturing, as well as environmental protection. This will be an area ripe for future research by political and social scientists—currently, there is a distinct lack of clarity on what the impacts may be, how the UK will respond, and the duration of any response. For example, 50–60% of UK farm income is derived from EU subsidies under the CAP, a level the UK government has committed to maintain until 2020, only a year beyond the Brexit date (Miller, 2016). Prior to the Brexit referendum in 2016, the government of the day acknowledge it did not have an outline for an alternative to CAP with respect to agriculture (Downing, 2016). Since then, Westminster, the seat of the UK government and parliament, is working together with the three devolved administrations of Scotland, Wales, and Northern Ireland to deliver a solution that works for all home nations[29] (Downing and Coe, 2018). Given the sometimes fractious relationship that exists between these governments (not least on Brexit itself), a solution that is seen to work equitably across the UK may be a challenge.

The UK is nowhere near fully self-sufficient in food production—trade is necessary to fulfil the needs and diets of the country's population. In 2016, just over 50% of food consumed in the UK was imported, with 60% of imports from the EU (European Union Committee, 2018). While imports of some foods commonly consumed, such as citrus, are necessary—it is not economic to produce them in the UK—neither does the UK produce sufficient volumes of food locally to meet domestic demand (European Union Committee, 2018). Under a "no-deal" outcome of Brexit negotiations—i.e. the UK leaves the EU without a negotiated trade treaty—the Most Favoured Nation rules of World Trade Organization would come into effect (Miller, 2016). This could see consumers facing a double hit of cost increases of 7–11% for fresh fruit and vegetables and less availability due to lower imports from the EU (van Berkum et al., 2016). Paradoxically, from a food waste perspective, such an outcome could deliver a "benefit". Similar to the relative food cost to waste argument of why consumer food waste is much lower in developing as compared to developed regions (food costs are a much higher proportion of disposable income in developing regions (Gustavsson et al., 2011)), the UK could see a concomitant decrease in waste at this final stage of the FSC. However, Tiffin et al. (2011) suggest that only in the long-run would higher food prices result in lower food consumption (and thus, possibly, less food waste).

Another key issue facing the UK with respect to food production under the policy of pursuing Brexit is ensuring sufficient labour. UK farms rely heavily upon labour from non-UK EU nationals. It is estimated that only 2% of seasonal workers are UK nationals (European Union Committee, 2017). The elimination of free movement of EU Member State nationals within the EU's borders—one of the UK government's "red lines" for negotiations (Miller, 2017)—could have unintended consequences for food. The "hostile environment" policy pursued by the UK government's Home Office since 2012 to reduce net migration (Grierson, 2018) seems to be more than enough to offset the recent policy to add a paltry "extra" 2,500 non-EU seasonal workers for UK farms (Defra, 2018). Even before Brexit occurs, there are reports by mainstream media in the UK of crops not being harvested but left to rot in the field due to shortages of workers (e.g. Daneshkhu, 2017; BBC News, 2018). A cliff-edge labour shortage is looming, bringing with it the potential for domestic food supply and food loss crises.

A minor potential positive from Brexit with respect to FLW is no longer following EU regulations related to the "quality" of certain fruit and vegetables. For example, there could be more flexibility in terms of developing a wholesale ban on using cosmetic factors to decide upon the quality of fresh produce, which could reduce food loss in the on-farm and processing stages of the FSC. In practice, this is unlikely to occur as UK suppliers would still need to abide by EU standards to engage in trade with EU countries.

Conclusion

By all accounts, there is far too much avoidable FLW occurring in the UK and Europe. While there is not a complete policy vacuum, what does exist is sparse with questionable efficacy. While they may have different underlying motives, a number of civil society stakeholders have taken the initiative to address the issue. They all point to there being multiple social, environmental, and possibly economic benefits to reducing pre-consumer food waste at all levels and stages of the FSC. While there is still more to do, action has begun.

Notes

1 Values are from the World Bank data series, *GDP per capita (current US$)*.
2 Using as a definition of "cheap" the proportion of net income used by the average household for food. It is acknowledged that this metric is also flawed, as nutritious food remains out of reach for the least well-off in the UK and Europe (Statista, 2018).
3 "Persistent poverty" is defined by the ONS as currently being in relative poverty and experiencing relative poverty in at least two of the three preceding years. The ONS terminology of "relative poverty" is equivalent to the EU's "at risk of poverty", defined as a household with less than 60% of the median disposable income. Thus, relative poverty does not necessarily mean a low standard of living, and could be temporary.
4 www.wrap.org.uk
5 www.lovefoodhatewaste.com
6 http://eu-fusions.org
7 https://eu-refresh.org
8 www.save-food.org
9 The underlying data from WRAP is for the UK as a whole. The figures stated here assume pro-rata waste levels for Scotland relative to the UK (Office for National Statistics, 2018c).
10 Based upon an average Euro/Sterling exchange rate for 2017 of £0.88 (Statista, n.d.).
11 Based upon provisional 2017 Scottish agriculture production yields and values (Scottish Government, 2018b) and their on-farm central loss estimates (Porter et al., 2018b). Potatoes: 240 kt worth £43m; berries: 4 kt worth £13m; other vegetables: 90 kt worth £30m.
12 Without grants and subsidies, the average farm has run at an annual loss from the farmer's perspective each year since at least 2011 (Scottish Government, 2018c).
13 Specifically, SDG 12.3 states "By 2030, halve per capita global food waste at the retail and consumer levels and reduce food losses along production and supply chains, including post-harvest losses" (United Nations, 2015, p. 22).
14 Readers interested in greater detail on the various issues that arise with respect to how food waste is defined and perceived within the EU are directed to O'Brien (2012).
15 The CAP can trace its origins to Title II in the Treaty of Rome (United Nations, 1957). This treaty between Belgium, Germany, France, Italy, Luxembourg, and the Netherlands created the European Economic Community, the forerunner to today's European Union.
16 https://www.gov.scot/Resource/0050/00505210.pdf
17 The author is currently working alongside a Holyrood MSP on a potential private member's bill to combat pre-consumer food loss and waste.
18 For example, ASDA's "Wonky Veg" and Tesco's "Imperfectly Perfect" ranges, which are sold at lower price points than their Class I produce.
19 Hubbub is an example of a UK charity that is supporting communities that wish to implement the "food fridge" concept, which is distinct from a food bank. www.hubbub.org.uk/blog/how-are-community-fridges-different-to-food-banks
20 A specific example of such an app in the UK is Olio: https://olioex.com/about/#about
21 The movement's website is: http://stopwastingfoodmovement.org
22 Originally led by the World Resources Institute, details of the FLW Protocol may be found here: www.flwprotocol.org
23 "Share of mind" refers to the proportion of population who are aware of a particular topic. In this instance, 83% of Danes say they are more aware of household food waste as a result of the Stop Wasting Food movement's activities.

24 https://feedbackglobal.org
25 www.espigoladors.cat
26 www.boroume.gr/en/
27 www.facebook.com/rebonreseauglanagenantais
28 At time of writing, the original Brexit date of 29 Mar. 2019 has already been extended twice, to 31 Oct. 2019). There remains a great deal of uncertainty whether this date is "fixed" and what sort of Brexit will occur, if any at all.
29 The United Kingdom is comprised of four "home nations": England, Scotland, Wales, and Northern Ireland. The latter three each have their own parliament or assembly in their respective capitals of Edinburgh, Cardiff, and Belfast—i.e. some powers of Westminster have been "devolved" to these national elected bodies.

References

BBC News, 2018. Fruit ' left to rot ' due to labour shortages [WWW Document]. URL www.bbc.co.uk/news/uk-scotland-tayside-central-44884882

Bräutigam, K.-R., Jörissen, J., Priefer, C., 2014. The extent of food waste generation across EU-27: Different calculation methods and the reliability of their results. *Waste Management and Research* 32, 683–694.

Briggs, B., 2018. Third of food wasted as it's too ugly for EU and shops. *The Sunday Times*.

Caplan, P., 2017. Win-win? Food poverty, food aid and food surplus in the UK today. *Anthropology Today* 33, 17–22.

Centre for Bhutan Studies & GNH Research, 2016. *A Compass Towards A Just and Harmonious Society, 2015 Gnh Survey Report.* Gnh, Thimpu, Bhutan.

Cox, A., Chicksand, D., 2007. Are win-wins feasible? Power relationships in agri-food supply chains and markets. In Burch, D., Lawrence, G. (Eds.), *Supermarkets and Agri-Food Supply Chains Transformations in the Production and Consumption of Foods.* Edward Elgar Publishing, Northampton, MA, USA, pp. 74–99.

Daneshkhu, S., 2017. Migrant labour shortage leaves fruit rotting on UK farms. *Financial Times*.

Defra, 2011. Government review of waste policy in England 2011.

Defra, 2018. New Pilot Scheme to Bring 2,500 Seasonal Workers to UK Farms [WWW Document]. URL www.gov.uk/government/news/new-pilot-scheme-to-bring-2500-seasonal-workers-to-uk-farms

Devin, B., Richards, C., 2018. Food waste, power, and corporate social responsibility in the australian food supply chain. *Journal of Business Ethics* 150(1), 199–210.

Downing, E., 2016. EU Referendum: Impact on UK Agriculture Policy (No. CBP 7602). *House of Commons Library*.

Downing, E., Coe, S., 2018. *Brexit : Future UK Agriculture Policy (no. cbp 8218).* House of Commons Briefing Paper, London.

EU FUSIONS, 2016. *Estimates of European food waste levels.* EU FUSIONS, Stockholm.

Eurofund, 2017. *European Quality of Life Survey 2016: Quality of Life, Quality of Public Services, and Quality of Society.* Publications Office of the European Union, Luxembourg.

European Commission, 2011. Commission Implementing Regulation (EU) No 543/2011: laying down detailed rules in respect of the fruit and vegetables and processed fruit and vegetables sectors. *Official Journal of the European Union*, 163.

European Commission, 2015. *Closing the loop - An EU action plan for the Circular Economy.* Brussels: European Commision.

European Commission, 2018a. Producer Organisations and Associations of Producer Organisations [WWW Document]. URL https://ec.europa.eu/agriculture/producer-interbranch-organisations/producer-organisations-association_en

European Commission, 2018b. EU Actions Against Food Waste [WWW Document]. URL https://ec.europa.eu/food/safety/food_waste/eu_actions_en (accessed 3.9.19).

European Council, 2007. Council Regulation (EC) No 1182/2007: laying down specific rules as regards the fruit and vegetable sector. *Official Journal of the European Union*, (L 273): 1–30.

European Council, 2016. *Food Losses and Food Waste - Council Conclusions.* Council of the European Union, Brussels.

European Court Auditors, 2016. Combating Food Waste: An Opportunity for The EU to Improve The Resource-Efficiency of The Food Supply Chain. Publications Office of the European Union, Luxembourg.

European Parliament and Council, 2002. Regulation (EC) No 178/2002: laying down the general principles and requirements of food law, establishing the European Food Safety Authority and laying down procedures in matters of food safety. *Official Journal of the European Communities*, (L31): 1–24.

European Parliament and Council, 2008. Directive 2008/98/EC on waste and repealing certain directives. *Official Journal of the European Union*, (L 312): pp. 3–30.

European Parliament and Council, 2018. DIRECTIVE (EU) 2018/851 on Waste. *Official Journal of the European Union*, L150, 109–140.

European Union, 2010. Precedence of European law [WWW Document]. URL https://eur-lex.europa.eu/legal-content/EN/TXT/?uri=LEGISSUM%3Al14548 (accessed 11. 10.18).

European Union, 2018. Regulations, Directives and other acts [WWW Document]. URL https://europa.eu/european-union/eu-law/legal-acts_en

European Union Committee, 2017. *Brexit: Agriculture*. House of Lords, London.

European Union Committee, 2018. *Brexit: Food Prices and Availability*. House of Lords, London.

Eurostat, n.d. Database - Eurostat [WWW Document]. URLhttp://ec.europa.eu/eurostat/data/database

FAO, IFAD, UNICEF, WFP, WHO, 2017. *The State of Food Security and Nutrition in The World 2017: Building Resilience for Peace and Food Security*. FAO, Rome.

FareShare, 2018. What we do [WWW Document].

Feedback, 2018. Farmers Talk Food Waste: Supermarkets' Role in Crop Waste on UK Farms. Feedback Global, London.

French Senate, 2015. Proposition de Loi: La lutte contre le gaspillage alimentaire (in French). Assemblée nationale (14eme législ.).

Fulponi, L., 2006. Private voluntary standards in the food system: The perspective of major food retailers in OECD countries. *Food Policy* 31, 1–13.

Gabbatiss, J., 2018. Fruit and vegetable waste from farms 'could feed population of Birmingham or Manchester for a year', says environmental charity. Independent.

Grierson, J., 2018. Hostile environment : anatomy of a policy disaster. Guard.

Gustavsson, J., Cederberg, C., Sonesson, U., van Otterdijk, R., Meybeck, A., 2011. *Global Food Losses and Food Waste - Extent, Causes and Prevention*. FAO, Rome.

Helliwell, J., Layard, R., Sachs, J. (Eds.) 2017. World Happiness Report 2017. *Sustainable Development Solutions Network*, Sustainable Development Solutions Network, New York.

Hingley, M.K., 2005. Power to all our friends? Living with imbalance in supplier-retailer relationships. *Industrial Marketing Management* 34, 848–858.

Holt-Giménez, E., Shattuck, A., Altieri, M., Herren, H., Gliessman, S., 2012. We Already Grow Enough Food for 10 Billion People … and Still Can't End Hunger. *Journal of Sustainable Agriculture* 36, 595–598.

Italian Government, 2016. Disposizioni concernenti la donazione e la distribuzione di prodotti alimentari e farmaceutici a fini di solidarietà sociale e per la limitazione degli sprechi (in Italian). Gazz. Uff. della Repubb. Ital. 202, 1–12.

Maglaras, G., Bourlakis, M., Fotopoulos, C., 2015. Power-imbalanced relationships in the dyadic food chain: An empirical investigation of retailers' commercial practices with suppliers. *Industrial Marketing Management* 48, 187–201.

McCarthy, K., 2016. Food Waste (Reduction) Bill 2015-16 — UK Parliament. UK Parliament.

Miller, V., 2016. *Brexit : impact across policy areas (No. CBP 07213), House of Commons Briefing Paper*. House of Commons Library, London.

Miller, V., 2017. *Brexit : red lines and starting principles (No. CBP 7938), House of Commons Briefing Paper*. House of Commons Library, London.

Monier, V., Mudgal, S., Escalon, V., O'Connor, C., Gibon, T., Anderson, G., Montoux, H., Reisinger, H., Dolley, P., Ogilvie, S., Morton, G., 2010. *Preparatory Study on Food Waste Across EU 27*. Bio Intelligence Service, Paris.

MSCI, Colliers International, 2017. *UK Supermarket Investment Report 2016*. MSCI, London.

O'Brien, M., 2012. A "lasting transformation" of capitalist surplus: From food stocks to feedstocks. *Sociological Review* 60, 192–211.

Office for National Statistics, 2017. *Persistent Poverty in The UK and EU: 2015*. London.

Office for National Statistics, 2018a. *Measuring National Well-Being: Quality of life in the UK, 2018*. London.

Office for National Statistics, 2018b. *Dataset: Measuring National Well-Being: Domains and Measures (Sept 2018)*. London.

Office for National Statistics, 2018c. *Population Estimates for UK, England and Wales Scotland, and Northern Ireland: mid-2017.* London.

Parfitt, J., Barthel, M., Macnaughton, S., 2010. Food waste within food supply chains: quantification and potential for change to 2050. *Philosophical Transactions of the Royal Society B: Biological Sciences* 365, 3065–3081.

Parfitt, J., Woodham, S., Swan, E., Castella, T., Parry, A., 2016. Quantification of food surplus, waste and related materials in the grocery supply chain. *Waste & Resources Action Programme (WRAP).* URL http://www.wrap.org.uk/content/quantification-food-surplus-waste-and-related-materials-supply-chain

Peterson, J., Bomberg, E.E., 1999. The common agriculture policy. In Peterson, J., Bomberg, E. (Eds.) *Decision-Making in the European Union.* Macmillan, Basingstoke, UK, pp. 120–145.

Porter, S.D., Reay, D.S., Bomberg, E., Higgins, P., 2018a. Production-phase greenhouse gas emissions arising from deliberate withdrawal and destruction of fresh fruit and vegetables under the EU's Common Agricultural Policy. *Science of the Total Environment* 631–632, 1544–1552.

Porter, S.D., Reay, D.S., Bomberg, E., Higgins, P., 2018b. Avoidable food losses and associated production-phase greenhouse gas emissions arising from application of cosmetic standards to fresh fruit and vegetables in Europe and the UK. *Journal of Cleaner Production* 201, 869–878.

Porter, S.D., Reay, D.S., Higgins, P., Bomberg, E., 2016. A half-century of production-phase greenhouse gas emissions from food loss & waste in the global food supply chain. *Science of the Total Environment* 571, 721–729.

Save Food Initiative, 2018. SAVE FOOD INITIATIVE: Our mission and objectives [WWW Document]. URL www.save-food.org

Scottish Government, 2016. *A Plan for Scotland: The Government's Programme for Scotland, 2016–17.* The Scottish Government, Edinburgh, UK.

Scottish Government, 2018a. *Delivering for Today, Investing for Tomorrow: The Government's Programme for Scotland, 2018-19.* The Scottish Government, Edinburgh, UK.

Scottish Government, 2018b. Economic Report on Scottish Agriculture 2018 Edition [WWW Document]. URL www2.gov.scot/Resource/0053/00536695.xlsx

Scottish Government, 2018c. *Annual Estimates of Scottish Farm Business Income (FBI).* Edinburgh, UK.

Silverman, R., 2012. "Wonky" fruit and veg to return to supermarket shelves. Telegr.

Statista, 2018. Share of disposable income spent on food consumed at home in 2013, by selected countries [WWW Document]. URL www.statista.com/statistics/189227/percent-of-disposable-income-spent-on-food-at-home-2009/

Statista, n.d. The Statistics Portal [WWW Document]. URL www.statista.com

Stop Wasting Food, 2018. Our Organisation: Our Results [WWW Document]. URL: https://stopwastingfoodmovement.org/our-organization/our-results/

Tesco, 2018. Products - Food Waste: Working with suppliers [WWW Document]. URL www.tescoplc.com/little-helps-plan/products-food-waste/working-with-suppliers/

Teuber, R., Jensen, J.D., 2016. *Food Losses and Food Waste: Extent, Underlying Drivers and Impact Assessment of Prevention Approaches.* University of Copenhagen, Frederiksberg.

Tiffin, R., Balcombe, K., Salois, M., Kehlbacher, A., 2011. *Estimating Food and Drink Elasticities.* University of Reading, Reading, UK.

United Nations, 1957. The Treaty of Rome.

United Nations, 2015. Transforming our world: the 2030 Agenda for Sustainable Development. Gen. Assem. 70th Sess. Agenda items 15 116.

van Berkum, S., Jongeneel, R.A., Vrolijk, H.C.J., van Leeuwen, M.G.A., Jager, J.H., 2016. *Implications of A UK Exit from The EU for British Agriculture.* LEI Wageningen UR, Wageningen.

World Bank, n.d. World Bank Data Catalogue [WWW Document]. URL https://datacatalog.worldbank.org

WRAP, 2017a. *Estimates of Food Surplus and Waste Arisings in the UK.* Banbury, UK.

WRAP, 2017b. Food waste in primary production – a preliminary study on strawberries and lettuces. Waste & Resources Action Programme (WRAP), Banbury, UK.

WRAP, 2018a. *Annual Report and Consolidated Accounts 2017/18.* Banbury, UK.

WRAP, 2018b. The Courtauld Committment 2025 [WWW Document]. URL www.wrap.org.uk/content/courtauld-commitment-2025

WRAP, 2018c. *Courtauld Commitment 2025 Food Waste Baseline for 2015.* Banbury, UK.

WRAP, 2018d. What is Courtauld 2025? [WWW Document]. URL www.wrap.org.uk/content/what-courtauld-2025

11

FOOD LOSS AND WASTE MEASUREMENT METHODS AND ESTIMATES FOR THE UNITED STATES

Jean C. Buzby and Claudia Fabiano[1]

Introduction

As we have seen in previous chapters, food loss is an increasingly important issue that is receiving attention both domestically and internationally. As evidence of this, the U.S. Department of Agriculture (USDA) and Environmental Protection Agency (EPA) jointly announced a goal to reduce food loss and waste in the United States by 50 percent by 2030. This U.S. goal is consistent with the United Nations Sustainable Development Goal (SDG), Target 12.3 to halve per capita global food waste at the retail and consumer levels and reduce food losses along production and supply chains, including postharvest losses, by 2030. The world population is growing – the Food and Agriculture Organization (FAO) of the United Nations projects that the world population will reach almost 10 billion people in 2050 (FAO, 2018) up from the current 7.5 billion (U.S. Census Bureau, 2018). This population growth on top of the always present food insecurity is a clear signal that more food will be needed to feed people. An estimated 11.1 percent of American households (14.3 million households) were food insecure at least some time during 2018 (i.e., they lacked access to enough food for an active, healthy life for all household members) (Coleman-Jensen et al., 2019). Not only does food loss represent a loss of money and other resources (e.g., arable land, labor, and fresh water), it also implies that negative externalities (e.g., water and air pollution) were created throughout the supply chain to produce food that does not ultimately meet the intended purpose of feeding people.

With the premise that "what gets measured gets managed," estimates of food loss and waste can help decision-makers at all levels – from food producers and firms to national governments – better understand how much, where, and why food is being lost or wasted, and can provide needed information to guide the prioritization of food loss and waste reduction strategies and to monitor progress (Champions 12.3, 2018), such as to meet the SDG Target 12.3 and other goals. To this end, this chapter presents an overview of three major sources of data on food loss and waste in the United States – two federal (USDA and EPA) and one collaboration (ReFED (Rethink Food Waste through Economics and Data)), as well as two more simplistic approaches, which combined existing data sources.

For this and other comparisons of food loss and waste studies, it is important to recognize that there is a lack of common definitions for food loss and food waste worldwide, and different studies have different research goals and thus may measure different aspects of food loss or food waste. Therefore, it is difficult to precisely and meaningfully compare the data and information across studies. Not only are there different definitions of the measured variable (e.g., shrink, food loss, and food waste) but studies may also use different reference bases (e.g., volume of sales vs. food supply values vs. quantities or weight delivered; edible vs. non-edible food), and different areas of coverage (e.g., stages in the farm to fork chain, such as at the farm, retail, or consumer levels, or the specific fruits, vegetables, and mixtures covered) in the analyses (Buzby et al., 2015). Other factors may include different destinations (e.g., composting, animal feed) and the primary data sets and methods used. Additionally, data in studies may not be sufficiently disaggregated for comparison – some studies provide food loss and/or waste estimates for food groups and some for individual foods (Buzby et al., 2015).

This chapter also briefly covers some of the incentives to reduce/prevent, recover, or recycle food in the United States, including legal incentives (e.g., Good Samaritan Law), regulatory/policy incentives (e.g., statewide bans and U.S. food waste reduction goals), and financial incentives (e.g., reduce business costs, tax incentives, increase customer goodwill) spurring the private sector to measure and manage food loss and waste. The chapter concludes with new directions underway for estimating food loss and waste, both for the United States as a whole and for individual firms in specific sectors, farm to fork, and ends with some concluding thoughts.

Key food loss and waste studies and estimates in the United States

In the United States, a single comprehensive estimate of food loss and/or waste does not exist. This section covers the three major sources of national data on food loss and/or waste in the United States that enhance our understanding of the magnitude of the problem. The section also provides two relatively simplistic estimation approaches that help put the estimates into perspective. Table 11.1 is a combination and modification of the Further with Food: Center for Food Loss and Waste Solutions' (2017) table and the NRDC's Figure A1 (NRDC, 2017), each of which compared a handful of sources of U.S. food loss and/or food waste studies and estimates. Approaches varied in terms of the included food categories and the food-system stages as well as the estimation methodologies.

USDA/ERS food loss estimation method

The first data source is the Loss-Adjusted Food Availability (LAFA) data series (ERS, 2018c) produced by U.S. Department of Agriculture's Economic Research Service (USDA/ERS). It was created to measure the amounts of foods available for consumption to Americans as a proxy for actual consumption. As part of that accounting process, the secondary purpose of the series is to measure the amounts of foods that go uneaten. What goes uneaten is broader than food waste and therefore, ERS measures *food loss*, which ERS defines as the edible amount of food, post-harvest, that is available for human consumption but is not consumed for any reason. It includes cooking loss and natural moisture loss; loss from mold, pests, or inadequate climate control, and food waste, among others. In a 2014 report, ERS used the underlying food loss assumptions in the LAFA data series to estimate food loss at the retail and consumer levels for 2010, both per capita and in total for the United States (Buzby et al., 2014). This section summarizes the basic methodology behind ERS food loss estimates and then presents the estimates.

Table 11.1 Comparison of key U.S. food loss and/or waste estimates

Organization	Estimate[a]	Includes inedible parts?	Boundary: food products and food-system stages included in FLW[b] estimate	Method
Major studies				
U.S. Department of Agriculture (USDA)	66.5 million tons (133 billion lb) in 2010	No (except for some commodities at retail level, such as the inedible parts of discarded whole fresh apples)	Food categories: Approximately 215 basic commodities (no highly processed products). Food-system stages: Retail, Restaurant (consumer waste only), Foodservice/Institution (consumer waste only), Household	Estimate based on nationally representative surveys of retail inventories or shipments and household purchases and stated consumption. For details see: ERS' Loss-Adjusted Food Availability Data Series documentation (2017) and Buzby et al. (2014)
U.S. Environmental Protection Agency (USEPA)	Generated: 79.4 billion lb. (39.7 million tons). Disposed: 75.4 billion lb. (37.7 million tons) in 2015	Yes	Food categories: All food and beverage. Food-system stages: Municipal solid waste which includes: Retail, Restaurant, Foodservice/Institution, Household	Estimate of "FLW generated" equals municipal solid FLW generation, which is estimated based on existing studies of the rate of generation applied to updated census estimates of number of businesses and households. Estimate of "FLW disposed" is determined by subtracting the amount of FLW going to composting from total FLW generated. Composting estimates are based on publicly available state data EPA (2018a).
ReFED	125 billion lb. (62.5 million tons) in 2015	Yes	Food categories: All food and beverage. Food-system stages: Farm, Distribution/handling, Manufacturing, Retail, Restaurant, Foodservice/Institution, Household	Methodology applies estimates of commercial and residential FLW (from the best publicly available studies as of 2015) to 2015 U.S. Census data on manufacturing, retail, food service and households to produce national estimates of food waste going to landfills. On-farm

Relatively simplistic U.S. estimates using existing data from diverse sources

				estimates are based on extrapolation from numerous agricultural case studies. For details see: ReFED (2016a)
Natural Resources Defense Council (NRDC) with National Institutes of Health (NIH)	37 percent in 2010. NRDC (2017) applied this to USDA's food supply to estimate approx. 160 billion lb. (80 million tons) in 2010	No	*Food categories*: All food and beverage. *Food-system stages*: Distribution/Handling, Manufacturing, Retail, Restaurant, Foodservice/Institution, Household	Estimate derived by taking the percentage difference between the number of calories in the U.S. food supply (derived from FAO Food Balance Sheets) and the number of calories consumed by end consumers (estimated from the weight of the U.S. population). For details see: Hall et al. (2009)
Gustavsson et al./ FAO	206 billion lb. (103 million tons)/year	[No]	*Food categories*: Insufficient detail given. *Food-system stages*: "Production to retailing" and "Consumer"	For a validation exercise in the ReFED's technical report (ReFED, 2016b, p. 6), they took Gustavsson et al.'s (2011) estimate of 295 kg of food loss per capita in North America and applied it to the U.S. population (319 million) to roughly estimate 103 million tons of food waste/year in the United States

Source: Modified by author from the Food Loss and Waste Data Comparisons compiled by Further with Food: Center for Food Loss and Waste Solutions (January 2017) https://furtherwithfood.org/wp-content/uploads/2017/01/Food-Loss-Waste-Data-Comparisons.pdf and Gunders et al.'s (2017) figure A1.

Notes:

a For details, see EPA (2018a).

b FLW is shorthand for food loss and waste. Definitions (See the Food Loss and Waste Accounting and Reporting Standard for additional detail):

Food and Inedible Parts Food: Any substance that is intended for human consumption. It does not include crops intentionally grown for bioenergy, animal feed, seed, or industrial use.

Inedible parts: Components associated with a food that, in a particular food supply chain, are not intended to be consumed by humans (e.g., bones, rinds, pits/stones). What is considered inedible varies among users. "Inedible parts" do not include packaging.

ERS's core Food Availability (FA) data series uses a mass balance approach which compiles and compares national supply and uses for each commodity. For a given year and specific commodity (e.g., fresh apples), the supply of each commodity in the core FA data series is the sum of production, imports, and beginning inventories, and from this amount, ERS subtracts out exports, farm and industrial uses, and ending stocks. Per capita availability estimates are then calculated by dividing the total annual domestic availability for a commodity by the U.S. population for that year. The FA data series serves as the foundation for the LAFA data series, which is used to estimate both loss-adjusted food availability and food loss at the retail and consumer levels for 215 commodities (e.g., beef, canned tomatoes, fresh spinach, and eggs). The LAFA series is considered to be *preliminary* as there are initiatives underway to update and improve the data series. Buzby and Bentley (2016) provide a summary of some of the measurement issues and lessons learned from estimating food loss at the retail and consumer levels.

Unlike the core FA data series which has data back to 1909 for many commodities, the LAFA data series begins at 1970 and both series have data now available through 2017. The LAFA data series is constructed by taking the FA data for each commodity and taking into account three types of losses to more closely estimate actual intake:

1   *The loss from primary or farm weight to the retail weight* for select commodities. These conversion factors describe how a farm commodity (e.g., fresh chicken) is transformed into a consumer-ready product (e.g., boneless fresh chicken breasts).
2   *The loss at the retail level* includes loss at stores such as supermarkets, supercenters, convenience stores, mom–and–pop grocery stores, and other retail outlets (but not including restaurants and other foodservice outlets). Retail losses include dented cans, unpurchased holiday foods, spoilage, and culled blemished or misshapen foods.
3   *The loss at the consumer level* includes losses for food consumed at-home and away-from-home (e.g., fast-food and full-service restaurants, and schools) and includes "cooking loss and uneaten food" from the edible share. The "non-edible share" of certain commodities, such as fresh fruits, vegetables, and eggs are also removed at the consumer level (e.g., stems, pits, and eggshells).

The end result is that the LAFA data series more closely approximates actual food intake than the FA data series. The food loss data are expressed in per capita per day amounts, value, and calories at both the retail and consumer levels and in total. Details on the core FA data series and the LAFA series can be found on the ERS website (ERS, 2018a, 2018b).

The most recent ERS food loss study found that in the United States, food loss accounted for 31 percent – 133 billion pounds – of the 430 billion pounds of the available food supply at the retail and consumer levels in 2010 (Buzby et al., 2014) (Table 11.2). ERS does not measure the subset of food loss that is food waste (food waste is included in the ERS loss estimate). Additionally, ERS does not estimate the ultimate destination of food that goes uneaten (e.g., landfills, composting, and animal feed). Losses on the farm and between the farm and retailer were not estimated due to data limitations for some of the food groups. Had these losses been included, total postharvest loss in the United States would be over 31 percent of the food supply.

The estimated total value of food loss at the retail and consumer levels in the United States was $161.6 billion in 2010, using average retail prices for each covered commodity (Buzby et al., 2014). Buzby and Hyman (2012) provide greater detail on how ERS estimates the value of food loss using retail prices. The top three food groups in terms of share of

Table 11.2 Estimated total food loss at the retail and consumer levels in the United States, 2010

Commodity	Food supply[a]	Losses from food supply[b]					
		Retail level		Consumer level		Total retail and consumer level	
	Billion pounds	Billion pounds	Percent	Billion pounds	Percent	Billion pounds	Percent
Grain products	60.4	7.2	12	11.3	19	18.5	31
Fruit	64.3	6.0	9	12.5	19	18.4	29
Fresh	37.6	4.4	12	9.5	25	13.9	37
Processed	26.7	1.6	6	2.9	11	4.5	17
Vegetables	83.9	7.0	8	18.2	22	25.2	30
Fresh	53.5	5.2	10	12.8	24	18.0	34
Processed	30.4	1.8	6	5.3	18	7.1	24
Dairy products	83.0	9.3	11	16.2	20	25.4	31
Fluid milk	53.8	6.5	12	10.5	20	17.0	32
Other dairy products	29.1	2.8	10	5.7	19	8.5	29
Meat, poultry, and fish	58.4	2.7	5	12.7	22	15.3	26
Meat	31.6	1.4	4	7.2	23	8.6	27
Poultry	22.0	0.9	4	3.9	18	4.8	22
Fish and seafood	4.8	0.4	8	1.5	31	1.9	39
Eggs	9.8	0.7	7	2.1	21	2.8	28
Tree nuts and peanuts	3.5	0.2	6	0.3	9	0.5	15
Added sugar and sweeteners	40.8	4.5	11	12.3	30	16.7	41
Added fats and oils	26.0	5.4	21	4.5	17	9.9	38
Total	430.0	43.0	10	89.9	21	132.9	31

a Food supply at the retail level, which is the foundation for the retail – and consumer-level loss stages in the ERS LAFA data series.

b Totals may not add due to rounding.

Source: Buzby et al. (2014).

Note: Per capita losses at the retail and consumer levels for each commodity (not shown) were estimated by multiplying the quantity of that commodity available for consumption by the appropriate loss assumption. Individual loss estimates were then multiplied by the U.S. population and summed up into their respective food groups and retail or consumer levels.

total value of food loss were meat, poultry, and fish (30 percent, $48 billion); vegetables (19 percent, $30 billion); and dairy products (17 percent, $27 billion).

Per capita, food loss in 2010 totaled $522 per year at retail prices: $151 per year at the retail level and $371 at the consumer level (Buzby et al., 2014). The latter amounts to 9.2 percent of the average dollar value spent on food per consumer in 2010 ($4,016) (ERS, 2012) and 1 percent of the average disposable income ($36,016) (BLS, 2012). The yearly total of 290 pounds of food loss per capita in 2010 at the consumer level, at an estimated retail price of $371, translates into 0.8 pound or roughly $1 per day. This also translates into $1,484 for a family of four in 2010. In terms of calories of food loss, an estimated 1,249 calories per capita per day of the food supply in 2010 went uneaten at the retail and consumer levels combined.

U.S. EPA food waste methodology and estimates

The second major source of data on food loss and waste in the United States is from the U.S. EPA, which provides estimates of the amounts of *food waste* entering municipal solid waste (MSW) facilities from the residential, commercial, and institutional sectors. At this time, EPA does not include estimates of food waste generated by industrial food production (e.g., manufacturing and processing) because EPA's national waste generation estimates are focused on MSW, and these sources have been considered out of scope. However, EPA is currently expanding their methodology to include industrial food production and anticipates their updated methodology and estimates to be released in 2020.

EPA has collected and reported data on the generation and disposal of waste in the United States for more than 30 years and uses this information to measure the success of waste reduction and recycling programs across the country. EPA publishes annual national estimates of how much food waste is generated, composted, landfilled, and combusted with energy recovery (EPA, 2018): this section focuses solely on EPA's estimates of the amounts generated.

EPA currently estimates food waste generation tonnages from the residential, commercial, and institutional sectors, relying on existing studies conducted by state and municipal governments, industry groups, universities, and others. These studies generally measure food waste at the point it is ready to be managed, which excludes food that is donated to feed people, sent to feed animals, or poured down the drain. EPA estimates residential food waste generation by establishing a nation-wide per capita estimate, which is then multiplied by the United States population. The estimate is based on 25 curbside sampling studies published over the past two decades. The studies were conducted in more than one dozen cities and several states across the United States.

Commercial sector industries covered include grocery stores, full and limited-service restaurants, and hotels. Institutional sector industries include public and private elementary schools, colleges and universities, prisons, nursing homes, residential hospitals, and short-term stay hospitals. The commercial and institutional food waste generation estimates are based on dozens of industry-specific studies from across the nation that measured food waste generated at specific facilities and businesses and correlated it to facility-specific characteristics (e.g., revenue or the number of employees) to establish equations expressing generation rates (e.g., 3,000 lb. of food waste generated/employee/year in grocery stores). There are multiple studies, and therefore multiple generation rates, available for each industry. EPA scales up these rates by applying national, industry-specific business statistics (e.g., U.S. Census-reported store sales, number of employees in restaurants, number of patients in hospitals, number of inmates in prisons), which results in multiple food waste generation estimates per industry. An average annual generation estimate is then calculated for each industry, and these values are summed to calculate overall commercial or institutional sector estimates of food waste generated. The national food waste estimate in the EPA's 2018 *Facts and Figures* report is derived by adding the figures calculated for the residential, commercial, and institutional sectors (EPA, 2018a).

EPA estimates that 39.7 million tons of food waste was generated in 2015, which was 15.1 percent of total MSW generation. Of those 39.7 million tons, 22 million tons (55 percent) were from the residential sector, 14.8 million tons (37 percent) were from the commercial sector, and 2.9 million tons (7 percent) were from the institutional sector.

ReFED estimates

The third source of U.S. data on food loss and waste (FLW) is from ReFED (i.e., "Rethink Food Waste through Economics and Data"), which is a multi-stakeholder nonprofit dedicated to reducing food waste using a systems approach and economic analysis, working with decision-makers from across the food system. ReFED was formed in early 2015 to create a *Roadmap to Reduce U.S. Food Waste*, the first ever national economic study and action plan driven by a multi-stakeholder group committed to tackling food waste at scale. ReFED's vision is that implementation of its roadmap will put the United States on the path to meet the 50 percent reduction by 2030 goal.

In 2016, ReFED published a major report which used the best publicly available studies and extrapolations from agricultural case studies to develop the roadmap. The ReFED report shows the economic value of 27 solutions to food waste by analyzing their cost-effectiveness per ton of waste to provide information useful when the private sector is choosing among food loss and waste reduction actions to implement (ReFED 2016a). Of these 27 solutions, 12 fell under the category of prevention (e.g., consumer education campaigns, standardized date labeling, and waste tracking and analytics), seven were classified under recovery/redistributing food to feed people (e.g., donation tax incentives, standardized donation regulation, and donation matching software), and eight recycling solutions (e.g., centralized composting, centralized anaerobic digestion (AD), and Water Resource Recovery Facility (WRRF) with AD).

In particular, ReFED developed an economic model that performed three types of analyses on each solution: (1) a total net societal "economic value" based on their cost-effectiveness per ton of waste, (2) the business profit potential that the private sector can earn by investing in each solution, and (3) the non-financial impacts of each solution – meals saved/recovered, greenhouse gases/emissions reduced, jobs created, water conserved (ReFED, 2016b). Greater detail on ReFED's methodology can be found in their March 2016 technical appendix to their 2016 report.

Relevant here in this chapter for the U.S. comparisons, ReFED estimates a baseline of 62.5 million tons of food loss and waste in 2015 (ReFED, 2016b).

> The Roadmap U.S. food waste generation baseline of 62.5 million tons per year is the result of extensive research integrating primary and secondary data sources from specific industries. The baseline measures both food waste going to landfills (52.4 million tons per year), as well as cosmetically-imperfect produce left unused on-farm and in pack houses that can be repurposed for higher value use (10.1 million tons per year).
>
> *(ReFED, 2016b, p. 6)*

Of the estimated 62.5 million tons, approximately 27 million tons (43 percent) occurred in homes, 25 million tons (40 percent) occurred in consumer-facing businesses, 1 million tons (2 percent) occurred during manufacturing, and 10 million tons (16 percent) occurred on farms (ReFED, 2016b, p. 13). When breaking the food waste down by weight and type, ReFED found that 42 percent was fruits and vegetables, 26 percent was milk and dairy products, 19 percent was grain products, 12 percent was meat, and 2 percent was seafood. However, the estimates are not a complete picture of food waste generated.

ReFED also valued this food waste at $218 billion dollars (roughly 1.3 percent of the United States gross domestic product (GDP)) and of this amount approximately $144 billion occurred in homes, $57 billion occurred in consumer-facing businesses, $2 billion occurred during manufacturing, and $15 billion occurred on farms (ReFED, 2016b). In general, there has been a void in peer-reviewed literature and data on farm-level food loss at the national level in the United States. Previously, studies on farm-level food loss have focused on particular commodities or commodity groups. ReFED (2016b) is the first study to provide a national estimate of on-farm food loss in the United States.

More simplistic approaches that combine data

This sub-section provides two more simplistic estimates of food loss and waste in the United States, which combine data. The first is from the NRDC, which has produced two seminal reports on food waste to date by Dana Gunders (Gunders, 2012; Gunders et al., 2017): with NIH and the second uses data from a FAO contracted report (i.e., Gustavsson et al., 2011).

The foundation of the 2012 NRDC source of data on FLW in the United States is the 2009 article by Kevin Hall et al. of the NIH on the progressive increase in food waste in America and its environmental impact (Hall et al., 2009). That study used a mathematical model of human energy expenditure incorporating a range of factors. Hall et al. estimated that almost 40 percent of the U.S. food supply was wasted in 2003. This 40 percent estimate was derived by taking the percentage difference between the amount of calories in the U.S. food supply (derived from the FAO Food Balance Sheets (Food and Agriculture Organization (FAO) of the United Nations, 2017)) and the amount of calories consumed by end consumers (estimated from the average adult body weight of the U.S. population as measured by the U.S. National Health and Nutrition Examination Survey (NHANES)). Later, Kevin Hall did a preliminary update of his 2009 study, using the same methods, and estimated that the United States wasted 37 percent of the food supply in 2010. Gunders et al. (2017) used this figure to estimate that in 2010, food loss and waste in the United States totaled 160 billion pounds (80 million tons).

For a ballpark estimate using FAO data, ReFED's technical report (ReFED, 2016b, p. 6) took Gustavsson et al.'s estimate of 295 kg of food loss per capita in "North America and Oceania" (i.e., Australia, Canada, New Zealand, and the United States) and multiplied it by the U.S. population (319 million) to roughly estimate 103 million tons of food waste/year in the United States. This translates into 206 billion pounds, which is far higher than the other estimates presented here for the United States.

Other methods are available to estimate food loss and waste

There are several other methods and strategies available globally to estimate food loss and waste beyond the approaches described above and this area of research seems to be proliferating in response to the need for these estimates. Several of these methods could also be used in the United States for particular sectors and businesses from farm to fork. Three examples suffice. First, the *Food Loss and Waste Accounting and Reporting Standard* (known as the FLW Standard) produced by the multi-stakeholder partnership, Food Loss & Waste Protocol (2016), is a global standard that provides requirements and guidance for quantifying and reporting on the weight of food and/or associated inedible parts removed from the food supply chain – commonly referred to as "food loss and waste" (FLW) – generated and where it goes. Second, the Commission for Environmental Cooperation (CEC), which is an intergovernmental organization established to support cooperation among the North American Free Trade Agreement (NAFTA) partners (i.e., Mexico, Canada, and the United States) has produced a technical report (CEC, 2019a) that assesses approaches currently applied to quantify food loss and waste across the supply chain, and a companion practical guide, which has been published in English, French, and Spanish (CEC, 2019b) for users wishing to embark on quantification efforts within their own business, jurisdiction, or institution. Third, given that SDG indicator 12.3.1 covers two separate aspects of food loss and waste, a global food loss index (sub-indicator 12.3.1.b) is being developed by FAO for food loss by country for food loss prior to the retail level of the farm to fork chain and a food waste indicator is being developed by the United Nations Environment Program (UNEP) to estimate per capita food waste (kg/per year) by country (sub-indicator 12.3.1.a) for food waste at the retail level and at later stages of the farm to fork chain.

None of these methods estimate or value all of the resource costs of food loss and waste, such as the embedded land, water, nutrients, energy, agricultural chemicals, and other inputs to production, and other economic costs. Ideally, all costs should be included for use in a cost-benefit analysis for a food loss and/or food waste reduction program or regulation.

Incentives to reduce/prevent, recover, or recycle

This section introduces the fundamental principles of the legal, regulatory, and market incentives to reduce/prevent food loss and waste, recover food that is safe to eat and get it to hungry people or animals, or recycle it for another purpose other than disposing in landfills or incinerators (e.g., food waste diversion can include composting, anaerobic digestion, and feeding animals). It is important to understand these incentives as they can spur the measurement of food loss and waste by individuals and firms along the farm to fork chain and, in turn, these estimates can then encourage the adoption of strategies to reduce food loss and waste.

There are two main legal incentives in the United States for food firms to recover "apparently wholesome food" and donate it to feed hungry people, such as through feeding organizations. The first is the 1996 "Bill Emerson Good Samaritan Food Donation Act" (U.S. Code Title 42, Chapter 13A, § 1791) which standardizes food donor liability exposure at the national level and protects firms from civil and criminal liability when they donate food in good faith to a nonprofit organization and it later causes harm to the recipient (Feeding America, 2018; Legal Information Institute, 2018). The second set of legal incentives are federal and state tax incentives in the form of tax deductions or credits for charitable food donations which meet current tax laws (although these are formed by laws, they are in effect financial incentives). In general, "a taxpayer who contributes appreciated inventory or certain other ordinary income property is permitted a charitable deduction only for an amount equal to the taxpayer's basis in the contributed property, not its fair market value" (Feeding America, 2018). State tax incentives for food donations are typically broader and more tailored to small farms and businesses than federal tax incentives and they tend to vary by state (Xie and Balkus, 2016). For example, Arizona (Ariz. Rev. Stat. § 42–5074) provides restaurants a tax deduction on the gross proceeds of sales or gross income of prepared food, drink, or condiments when donated to nonprofits that regularly serve free meals to the needy and indigent at no cost, while Kentucky (Ky. Rev. Stat. Ann. § 141.392) provides taxpayers who derive income from agricultural products a tax credit of 10 percent of the fair market value of edible agricultural products donated to nonprofit food programs operating in Kentucky (Xie and Balkus, 2016).

The regulatory and policy incentives in the United States are limited and quite specific at this time – no regulations at the federal level – but rather some government actions at the local, state and federal levels. At the federal level, incentives to reduce food loss and waste are largely targets, such as the previously mentioned 16 September 2015 announcement by USDA and EPA to set the nation's first food waste goal of a 50 percent reduction by 2030 (USDA, 2015). (Prior to that in June 2013, USDA and EPA launched the U.S. Food Waste Challenge calling for both the public sector and private industry to reduce food waste but this did not give a target (USDA, 2013).) EPA and USDA joined with the private sector in November 2016 to announce the formation of the U.S. Food Loss and Waste 2030 Champions group and presented the first set of 2030 Champions (EPA, 2018b). U.S. Food Loss and Waste 2030 Champions are businesses and organizations that have made a public commitment to reduce food loss and waste in their own operations in the United States by 50 percent by the year 2030. At the state and local levels, food waste activities include organic waste bans and recycling laws, among other actions. For example, five states (California, Connecticut, Massachusetts, Rhode Island, and Vermont) and six municipalities (Austin (TX), Boulder (CO), New York City (NY), San Francisco (CA), and Seattle (WA)) have implemented organic waste bans or mandatory recycling laws (Leib et al., 2018). Additionally, Oregon Metro, the regional government for the Portland area, passed a policy in July 2018 that will require some businesses to divert food scraps (Leib et al., 2018).

Market incentives (i.e., financial incentives) to reduce food loss and waste in the United States are likely to be similar to those in other developed countries (e.g., reduce business costs, develop, enhance, and maintain customer goodwill). Under the umbrella of Corporate Social Responsibility (CSR), the food industry has developed more socially responsible initiatives in response to consumers' increasing desire for healthy options and socially responsible business practices (Wei et al., 2018). Some CSR actions relate to food waste and are displayed on their company's websites for consumers to see. For example, the foodservice chain, "*PRET*" (2018), donates unsold sandwiches and salads to food rescue organizations at the end of each business day. The airline JetBlue (2018) composted 100,000 pounds of food waste in 2016. In recent years, there has been a proliferation of companies and technologies in the United States to monitor or audit food businesses for their food loss and waste. For example, LeanPath is a food waste tracking terminal with a touchscreen user interface, built-in scale, and camera technology combined with data analytics that provides commercial kitchens with detailed information on the amount and financial and environmental impact of pre-consumer waste and on actionable insights to prevent waste and reduce costs. It is commonly believed among the food loss and waste research community that once a firm has measured food waste in their operations, they tend to move quickly to reduce it in order to reduce the cost to their business.

Looking ahead

ERS and EPA are actively improving and refining their food loss (ERS) and food waste (EPA) estimation methodologies. In 2018, ERS had a panel of experts provide recommendations on seven technical questions and seven data gaps, and adopted some of these recommendations to strengthen their LAFA data series and has plans to adopt others (Muth et al., 2019). ERS also has a contract with RTI International for a four-year study to obtain updated retail-level loss estimates for most of the 215 commodities in their LAFA data series. As previously mentioned, EPA is currently updating their methodology to include the measurement of food waste generated by industrial food production (i.e., manufacturing and processing) and include estimates for how much food waste is being sent to various destinations, beyond composting, landfill, and combustion facilities. EPA anticipates their updated methodology and estimates to be released in 2020. ReFED is also currently working with top food waste experts in both the public and private sectors to develop their next generation of data, insights, and guidance on U.S. food waste.

One question on the minds of many people in the food loss and waste research community is how we will know if we meet the SDG Target 12.3 in the United States? The answer is not so straightforward. This would require a comparison of "like" estimates from now and from after 2030, which are comparable in terms of scope and methodology. If used with proper procedures, the ERS, EPA, and ReFED estimates *could potentially* be used as a partial baseline to measure progress toward reducing food loss and waste to reach specific targets, such as reaching the 2030 goal of reducing food loss and waste by 50 percent for a particular sector of interest. However, for the ERS and EPA estimates at least, this would require continued funding for these estimates and related research. Annual budgetary priorities change over time and there is no guarantee that the administrators of these federal agencies who will be in place around the year 2030 will provide monetary support for the data and analysis needed to estimate whether or not the United States met the 2030 target. Additionally, estimation methods change over time and this could pose challenges for comparing food loss and waste estimates before and after 2030.

More broadly, *Champions 12.3*, a coalition of more than three dozen leaders worldwide to achieve SDG Target 12.3, published its third annual report on the global progress toward achieving this target. This study highlighted some of the public-private partnerships developing with the aim of reducing food loss and waste in all countries, and highlighted the U.S. Food Loss and Waste 2030 Champions, which are businesses and organizations that have made a public commitment to reduce food loss and waste in their own operations in the United States by 50 percent by 2030 (see EPA (2018) for more on these U.S. Champions). In particular, the Champions 12.3 report highlighted the U.S.-based Kroger Company's "Zero Hunger | Zero Waste" plan, which includes a $10 million innovation fund and a food rescue program, and Walmart's "Zero Waste by 2025 target" in the United States and three other countries (Canada, Japan, and the United Kingdom).

In general, the annual estimates of food loss and waste for the United States discussed here ranged from EPA's estimate of 76.8 billion pounds of food waste generated in residences, commercial establishments, and institutional sources to the simplistic application of Gustavsson et al.'s (2011) per capita estimate and the U.S. population to estimate food loss and waste of 206 billion pounds in the United States. Although it is difficult to compare the estimates because of the differences in the scope of the studies, all of the studies and estimates here suggest there is a great deal of room for improvement in preventing/reducing, recovering, and reusing/recycling uneaten food in the United States.

Note

1 Jean C. Buzby works for the U.S. Department of Agriculture's Economic Research Service and Claudia Fabiano works for the U.S. Environmental Protection Agency. The findings and conclusions in this publication are those of the authors and should not be construed to represent any official USDA, US EPA, or U.S. Government determination or policy.

References

Pret. Sustainability. www.pret.com/en-us/sustainability (accessed November 16, 2018).

Bureau of Labor Statistics (BLS). 2012. *Table 4.10 Personal Income, 1990, 2000, 2010, and Projected 2020.* Washington, DC: Bureau of Labor Statistics (BLS), 2012.

Buzby, J.C., J.T. Bentley, B. Padera, C. Ammon, and J. Campuzano. 2015. Estimated Fresh Produce Shrink and Food Loss in U.S. Supermarkets. *Agriculture*, 5, 3:626–648. http://mdpi.com/2077-0472/5/3/626

Buzby, J.C. and J. Hyman. 2012. Total and Per Capita Value of Food Loss in the United States. *Food Policy*, 37:561–570. http://ucce.ucdavis.edu/files/datastore/234-2425.pdf

Buzby, J.C., H.F. Wells, and J. Hyman. 2014. The Estimated Amount, Value, and Calories of Postharvest Food Losses at the Retail and Consumer Levels in The United States. U.S. Department of Agriculture, Economic Research Service: Washington, DC. https://ers.usda.gov/webdocs/publications/43833/43680_eib121.pdf

Buzby, Jean C. and Jeanine Bentley. Measurement Issues and Lessons Learned from Estimating Food Loss at the Retail and Consumer Levels in the USA. Invited presentation and paper for the session titled "Measuring Food Losses and Food Waste at the International Conference for Agricultural Statistics (ICAS) held at the Food and Agriculture Organization (FAO), Rome, Italy, October 27, 2016. www.istat.it/storage/icas2016/b15-buzby.pdf

CEC. 2019a. *Technical Report: Quantifying Food Loss and Waste and Its Impacts.* Montreal, Canada: Commission for Environmental Cooperation. 129. http://www3.cec.org/islandora/en/item/11813-technical-report-quantifying-food-loss-and-waste-and-its-impacts

CEC. 2019b. *Why and How to Measure Food Loss and Waste: A Practical Guide.* Montreal, Canada: Commission for Environmental Cooperation. 60. http://www3.cec.org/islandora/en/item/11814-why-and-how-measure-food-loss-and-waste-practical-guide

Champions 12.3. 2018. SDG Target 12.3 On Food Loss and Waste: 2018 Progress Report. https://champions123.org/wp-content/uploads/2018/09/18_WP_Champions_ProgressUpdate_final.pdf

Coleman-Jensen, Alisha, Matthew P. Rabbitt, Christian A. Gregory, and Anita Singh. Household Food Security in the United States in 2018. U.S. Department of Agriculture, Economic Research Service, Economic Research Report No. ERR-270, September 2019, 47. (accessed October 7, 2019).

Economic Research Service (ERS). 2012. Table 13—Per Capita Food Expenditures. http://ers.usda.gov/data-products/food-expenditures.aspx#26636.

Economic Research Service (ERS). Food Availability (LAFA) Data Documentation. ERS, U.S. Department of Agriculture. http://ers.usda.gov/data-products/food-availability-(per-capita)-data-system/food-availability-documentation.aspx (accessed July 11, 2018a).

Economic Research Service (ERS). Loss-Adjusted Food Availability (LAFA) Data Documentation. ERS, U.S. Department of Agriculture. http://ers.usda.gov/data-products/food-availability-(per-capita)-data-system/loss-adjusted-food-availability-documentation.aspx (accessed July 11, 2018b).

Economic Research Service (ERS). Loss-Adjusted Food Availability (LAFA) Data. ERS, U.S. Department of Agriculture. http://ers.usda.gov/data-products/food-availability-(per-capita)-data-system.aspx (accessed July 11, 2018c).

Environmental Protection Agency (EPA). 2018a. Food: Material-Specific Data. U.S. Environmental Protection Agency. www.epa.gov/facts-and-figures-about-materials-waste-and-recycling/food-material-specific-data (accessed August 2, 2018a).

Environmental Protection Agency (EPA). 2018b. United States Food Loss and Waste 2030 Champions. www.epa.gov/sustainable-management-food/united-states-food-loss-and-waste-2030-champions# about (accessed August 3, 2018c).

Feeding America. The Federal Bill Emerson Good Samaritan Food Donation Act. www.feedingamerica. org/about-us/partners/become-a-product-partner/food-partners (accessed November 13, 2018).

Food and Agriculture Organization (FAO) of the United Nations. 2018. The Future of Food and Agriculture: Alternative Pathways to 2050. Summary Version. Rome. www.fao.org/3/CA1553EN/ca1553en.pdf

Food and Agriculture Organization (FAO) of the United Nations. Food Balance Sheets. www.fao.org/ economic/ess/fbs/en/(accessed 25 July 2017).

Food Loss & Waste Protocol. 2016. Food Loss and Waste Accounting and Reporting Standard. www.wri.org/sites/default/files/REP_FLW_Standard_Exec_Summary_final_June27.pdf (accessed November 13, 2018).

Further with Food: Center for Food Loss and Waste Solutions. Was Initiated and Is Supported by a Public-private Partnership Composed of the Academy of Nutrition and Dietetics, Feeding America, the Food Marketing Institute, the Grocery Manufacturers Association, the Innovation Center for U.S. Dairy, the National Consumers League, the National Restaurant Association, Natural Resources Defense Council, the U.S. Department of Agriculture, the U.S. Environmental Protection Agency, the World Resources Institute, and the World Wildlife Fund. https://furtherwithfood.org/wp-content/ uploads/2017/01/Food-Loss-Waste-Data-Comparisons.pdf (accessed November 13, 2018).

Gunders, D. 2012. Wasted: How America Is Losing up to 40 Percent of Its Food from Farm to Fork to Landfill. Natural Resources Defense Council (NRDC). NRDC Issue Paper, August, IP:12-06-B. www.nrdc.org/sites/default/files/wasted-food-IP.pdf

Gunders, Dana, Jonathan Bloom, JoAnne Berkenhkamp, Darby Hoover, Andrea Spacht, and Marie Mourad. 2017. Wasted: How America Is Losing up to 40 Percent of Its Food from Farm to Fork to Landfill. Natural Resources Defense Council (NRDC). Second Edition of NRDC's Original 2012 Report. NRDC Issue Paper R: 17-05-A, April 2017. www.nrdc.org/sites/default/files/wasted-2017-report.pdf (accessed November 13, 2018).

Gustavsson, J., C. Cederberg, C., R. van Otterdijk, and A. Meybeck. 2011. Global Food Losses and Food Waste: Extent, Causes, and Prevention. Food and Agriculture Organization (FAO) of the United Nations, Rome. www.fao.org/docrep/014/mb060e/mb060e00.pdf

Hall, K.D., J. Guo, M. Dore, C.C. Chow, National Institute of Diabetes and Digestive and Kidney Diseases. 2009. The Progressive Increase of Food Waste in America and Its Environmental Impact. *PLoS ONE*, 4, 11:e7940.

JetBlue. T5's Food Trash Turns to Healthy Soils. http://responsibilityreport.jetblue.com/2016/ environment/t5s-food-trash-is-jetblues-eco-treasure (accessed November 16, 2018).

Legal Information Institute. 42 U.S. Code § 1791 - Bill Emerson Good Samaritan Food Donation Act. www.law.cornell.edu/uscode/text/42/1791 (accessed November 13, 2018).

Leib, E. Broad, K. Sandson, L. Macaluso, and C. Mansell. September 2018. Organic Waste Bans and Recycling Laws to Tackle Food Waste. *BioCycle*, 59, 8:35.www.biocycle.net/2018/09/11/organic-waste-bans-recycling-laws-tackle-food-waste/ (accessed November 13, 2018).

Muth, Mary K., Kristen Capogrossi Giombi, Marc Bellemare, and Brenna Ellison. Expert Panel on Technical Questions and Data Gaps for the ERS Loss-Adjusted Food Availability (LAFA) Data Series. Economic Research Service, U.S. Department of Agriculture, March 2019, Contractor and Cooperator Reports No. (CCR-70) 136. www.ers.usda.gov/publications/pub-details/?pubid=92408

ReFED (Rethink Food Waste Through Economics and Data). 2016a. Roadmap to Reduce Food Waste by 20 Percent. www.refed.com/downloads/ReFED_Report_2016.pdf

ReFED (Rethink Food Waste Through Economics and Data). A Roadmap to Reduce US Food Waste by 20%: Technical Appendix. www.refed.com/downloads/ReFED_Technical_Appendix.pdf [Latest revision March 2016b].

U.S. Census Bureau. U.S. And World Population Clock. www.census.gov/popclock/ (accessed November 13, 2018).

United Nations. Sustainable Development Goals: 17 Goals to Transform Our World. www.un.org/sustai nabledevelopment/ (accessed November 13, 2018).

United States Department of Agriculture (USDA). USDA and EPA Join with Private Sector, Charitable Organizations to Set Nation's First Food Waste Reduction Goals. Press release No. 0257.15, (accessed September 16, 2015a]. www.usda.gov/media/press-releases/2015/09/16/usda-and-epa-join-private-sector-charitable-organizations-set

United States Department of Agriculture (USDA). USDA and EPA Launch U.S. Food Waste Challenge. Press release No. 0112.13, www.usda.gov/media/press-releases/2013/06/04/usda-and-epa-launch-us-food-waste-challenge (accessd June 4, 2015b].

Wei, Wei, Gaeul Kim, Li Miao, Carl Behnke, and Barbara Almanza. February 7 2018. Consumer Inferences of Corporate Social Responsibility (CSR) Claims on Packaged Foods. *Journal of Business Research*, 83:186–201.

Xie, Steven and Ona Balkus. Creating a Tax Incentive for Food Donation in West Virginia. Harvard Food Law and Policy Clinic, Harvard, MA, January 20, 2016. www.chlpi.org//wp-content/uploads/2014/01/WV-Tax-Incentives-for-Food-Donation-January-2016-final-edition.pdf (accessed November 13, 2018).

12

APPREHENDING FOOD WASTE IN ASIA

Policies, practices and promising trends

*Marlyne Sahakian, Megha Shenoy, Tammara Soma, Atsushi Watabe,
Ran Yagasa, Dickella Gamaralalage Jagath Premakumara, Chen Liu,
Abigail Marie Favis and Czarina Saloma*

Introduction

Providing nutritious, safe and affordable food for all in a sustainable manner is one of the greatest challenges the world faces today, particularly in the context of Asia – where 515 million people are estimated to be undernourished, with the highest rates of food insecurity in Central and Southern Asia (FAO, IFAD, UNICEF et al., 2018). Yet an estimated one-third of the food produced for human consumption is lost or wasted worldwide (Gustavsson et al., 2011). In developing countries where national economies depend more on the agricultural sector, such as many countries in Asia, food wastage tends to occur at the post-harvest stage, also termed as "food loss" (Schneider, 2013). It is estimated that 11 kg of food per capita per year is wasted in low-income Asian countries, while 80 kg of food per capita per year is wasted in high-income Asian countries (FAO, 2013). Trends in Asia, such as rising income, dietary transition toward Westernized consumption patterns, urbanization (Teng & Trethewie, 2012), modern retail diffusion (Reardon & Hopkins, 2006), increasing obesity (Ramachandran & Snehalatha, 2010) and time scarcity (Lee, 2018), are several factors that impact food provisioning and food waste. A life cycle approach to understanding impacts across the life stages of food provisioning – from agricultural production, to sales, distribution, processing, retail, cooking, consumption and disposal – would enable "true cost" accounting of food waste, namely the inputs of fertilizers, pesticides, energy, water, as well as social issues around land access, gender and labour (Li, 2011) that go into the production of food. The paradox of wasting food in the face of global food insecurity exemplifies the failure of the global food system, and highlights the relevance of food waste prevention and reduction in sustainability efforts.

Whether related to improving nutrition or reducing environmental and social impacts, managing food waste in Asia is a relevant and timely research agenda. Globally, research on food wastage arose in the late 1980s and, since 2005, data on this issue has become more widely available (Schneider, 2013). However, there is little available data in the food waste research landscape in Asia. As we will uncover in this chapter, food waste is tied up with national, city and even community-level decision-making processes. This chapter brings together contributions by scholars involved in public management, policy analysis, waste management, sociology, planning, environmental sciences and industrial ecology, to uncover existing food waste practices in five countries, with a spotlight on urban centres, in Cambodia, India, Indonesia, Japan and the Philippines. We begin with a review of the literature on food waste in Asia, followed by an overview of the five case studies – considering countries and cities in relation to food waste management policies and practices. We then provide some insights on what lies ahead, in terms of ongoing trends and future opportunities, and conclude with a call for further research in the region.

Literature review

There is significant variation in the types and resolution of data available on food wastage across Asia. As English is not a primary language in many Asian countries, this poses two challenges: first, the inaccessibility of literature and data published in regional languages, and second, the difficulties of comparing data and problems associated with mis-interpretation, especially in the use of varying terms that are subject to cultural context: for example, the distinction between food waste, and food loss or spoilage (pre-consumer waste during harvest, transport, distribution and processing), as well as categories such as unavoidable food waste (peels, stalks, bones) and avoidable food waste (leftovers) (Schneider, 2013). Food cultures relate to different habits, rituals and preferences when it comes to preparing, eating and sharing a meal, which vary in different contexts – influencing how food is prepared and what is wasted, and what food is consumed or considered non-consumable (Sahakian et al., 2016). For example, eating meat offal, or vegetable stalks and peels, may be a part of an existing culinary tradition in some contexts but not in others.

Data on wholesale distribution, wastage during processing and transportation, treatment pathways for Municipal Solid Waste (MSW) and liquid food waste is also scarce in Asia. In industrialized countries, food wastage is identified with the post-harvest stage; one explanation might be the preference for produce with high-quality appearance, along with sales arguments and policies that align with this preference (*The Guardian*, 2013). Despite this concentration of food waste in the post-harvest stages in industrialized countries, MSW consists of less organic matter (< 50%) owing to the increased amount of packaging compared to developing countries (> 50%) (Hoornweg & Bhada-Tata, 2012). Household data on food waste is also more readily available in the West than in Asian countries, due to the lack of source segregated waste collection across Asia. While the practice of composting and, more recently, anaerobic digestion is widespread in rural areas of India and China, the management of urban food waste using these treatment options is more recent (Cheng & Hu, 2010; Sharma et al., 1997). That being said, there is a growing literature on composting in Asia, specifically community-based composting – as will be further discussed below (Pasang et al., 2007).

There is more available data on food waste in more affluent Asian countries such as Japan and South Korea, where food waste at the consumer stage is also higher – for example, for Singapore (Gustavsson et al., 2011). Japan has a detailed life cycle assessment on food wastage from households, and comprehensive data all along the food chain starting from the quantitative difference between food supply and food intake, amount of food discarded, including by-products and edible food from processing facilities, food processing industry recycling rates, information from food loss surveys, and composition of MSW (Matsuda et al., 2012; Watanabe, 2009). However, Japan imports around 60% of its food in terms of the output value of the nation's agricultural production (MAFF, 2015) and data on wastage during production, storage, processing and transport is lacking. Furthermore, 94% of food waste generated by household is incinerated or landfilled in Japan, with implementation of decentralized lower environmental impact treatment options such as anaerobic digestion and composting lacking (Liu et al., 2016). In South Korea, data is more concentrated at the end of the food chain, involving detailed information on the generation of food waste from consumers (Lee, 2018), and disposal methods (KWMN, 2001).

Given the research interest in the topic of food waste over the past decade, there has also been an increase in academic studies on this topic, leading to insightful, albeit dispersed, data from different stages of the food chain. A research project on food consumption among the middle classes in Bangalore/Bengalaru and Metro Manila resulted in a series of publications, including an edited book titled *Food Consumption in the City: Practices and Patterns in Urban Asia and the Pacific* (Sahakian et al. 2016), as well as a special issue in the *International Development Policy Journal* (Lutringer and Randeria 2017). Emerging food waste research in Asia includes Anantharaman's (2014) work in Bengalaru, where she draws on ecological citizenship theory to discuss how composting is being implemented through networks of socio-economically privileged new middle-class individuals. Based on journal keeping and weighing food, a material flow analysis among middle-class households in Bengalaru was combined with a social practice approach to understanding how and in what way food is wasted post-consumption (Leray et al., 2016). Taste preference has also been examined in the context of food provisioning and wastage in Bengaluru and Metro Manila (Sahakian et al., 2018).

For the edited collection on food consumption in Asian cities mentioned above (Sahakian et al., 2016), several authors addressed the issue of food waste: in a contribution from Japan, Watabe, Liu and Bengtsson (2016) consider uneaten food in relation to changing food consumption practices in Japanese society over time, embedded in specific cultural and social contexts, but also influenced by changing systems of provision. For Shanghai, Zhang (2016) studies the moral dimension of food waste, distinguishing frugality from thrift when it comes to consumer avoidance of food waste. Building on doctoral research in Malaysia, Papargyropoulou (2016) illustrates the question of food waste in Kuala Lumpur through the case of an upscale hotel restaurant, connecting social practices and biophysical patterns of food waste through an interdisciplinary research approach (see also Papargyropoulou et al., 2014). Lee (2016) explores food waste in Seoul's households at the interface of changing food retail systems, food practices and systems of provision (see also Lee, 2018), while Favis and Estanislao (2016) present the case of a campaign to reduce food waste in a Metro Manila private school.

Other studies have also emerged, including an early study on food waste in Turkey focused on household energy loss due to bread wastage (Gül et al., 2003; Pekcan et al., 2005), and a study on food loss in production systems in the Philippines (Mopera, 2016). Some data is available on post-harvest food losses for India (Hegazy, 2013b), and on potato storage loss in Bangladesh (Hossain & Miah, 2009). In Thailand, research was conducted on ways to reduce wastage resulting from the manual grading of fruits, specifically Javanese apples (Treeamnuk et al., 2010). In Indonesia, Soma explores the transformation of household food consumption and food wasting practices with the rise of supermarket consumption (Soma, 2017a, 2018) and critiques the ways in which low-income community members are expected to absorb the leftovers or unwanted surplus of the rich (Soma, 2017b).

Case studies in food waste management

In this section, we present case studies from Cambodia, India, Indonesia, Japan and the Philippines: first, we discuss the current context in relation to policies and practices; then, we consider points of tension and/or opportunities for interventions. Table 12.1 provides a summary of the main findings.

Cambodia (Phnom Penh)

Statistics on food loss and food waste are almost non-existent in Cambodia, save for those based on a few investigations conducted by stand-alone projects – which results in difficulty to delineate the accurate flow of food waste. Similarly, the lack of a standard definition of waste in the available data (where "organic waste" and "food waste" are often used synonymously) also poses an issue given the presumed dominance of food waste in the organic component of MSW in existing statistics.[1] Phnom Penh Capital Administration (2018) reports the dramatic increase of MSW disposal in the past five years, from 492,380 tonnes in 2012 to 808,530 tonnes in 2017 ("Phnom Penh Waste Management Strategy and Action Plan, 2018–2035"), while the organic content accounted for 70% of the disposed waste in 2009 and is considered to occupy more than 50% in the present day (Sang-Arun et al., 2011).

Policy discussions and interventions have traditionally treated food waste as organic waste under the frame of MSW management. Improvements of waste collection and disposal are given higher priority than treatment in response to weak collection and disposal systems. On the other hand, less attention has been given to the upstream considerations such as food loss at production stage, food waste reduction at consumption stage, or utilization of food waste as a resource at post-consumption stage. There is a significant potential to introduce various recycling methodologies due to the high organic content (51.9% in 2014) in the waste collected in Phnom Penh (MoEC, 2018).

National legal frameworks on waste management such as the "Environmental Guideline on Solid Waste Management in Cambodia" (2006), Sub-decree 113 on Urban Solid Waste Management (2015) and the current draft "National Strategy on Waste Management (2018–2035)" promotes source segregation, collection, and utilization of organic waste based on the 3R approach. Citizens are advised to segregate waste and sub-national governments are expected to develop legal instruments toward implementation of these policies. In addition, more recently, "Technical Guidelines on Urban Solid Waste Management" (2016) were developed with the aim of promoting local implementation, in which anaerobic digestion and composting are listed as primary methodologies for treating food waste.[2]

In Phnom Penh, the "Waste Management Strategy and Action Plan of Phnom Penh (2018–2035)" adopted in 2018 sets out the overall plan and detailed list of action to improve the city's waste management system and to promote the 3Rs. Organic waste management including food waste is positioned as a key component where the gradual development of resource utilization capacity and phased approach to the introduction of source segregation are planned (Phnom Penh Capital Administration, 2018). In the absence of effective waste collection, treatment and disposal systems, implementation of the 3Rs for food waste is still limited. Sales of food waste to livestock farmers has been a preferred choice for some waste generators (households, restaurants, hotels, etc.) although statistics are lacking to assess its impact. Seng et al. (2012) report a decline of this waste stream due to "marketable animal feed, difficulty of food waste transport and the speed of the animal production". Private initiatives for food waste reduction, albeit not large scale,

Table 12.1 Overview of food waste management strengths and weaknesses across five cities in Asia

	Data available	Focus on waste in production processes	Focus on post-consumption waste	National framework for waste management in place	Municipal governance of food waste in place and implemented	Private/citizen actions toward reducing food waste
Cambodia (Phnom Penh)	– Statistics on food waste in Cambodia including food loss in upstream life stages, during retail consumption and waste generation and treatment of food waste are almost non-existent	– Improvements of waste collection and disposal are given higher priority, as compared to upstream considerations such as food loss at production stage	+ High organic content of waste in Phnom Penh	++ Environmental Guideline on Solid Waste Management (2006), Sub–decree 113 on Urban Solid Waste Management (2015), draft National Strategy on Waste Management (2018–2035)	+ Waste Management Strategy and Action Plan of Phnom Penh Waste Management Strategy and Action Plan (2018).	+ Initiatives to curb food waste at restaurant buffets.
India (Bengaluru)	+ Data on post-harvest losses in India Composition of MSW	+ Government has invested in increasing storage capacity and food processing in production catchment	+ High organic content of waste across India	++ National-level Solid Waste Management Rules (2016)	++ BBMP rules 2012, 2013 and Amendments in 2013 to the Karnataka Municipal Corporations Act of 1976	++ Active involvement of the city corporation BBMP, and various other stakeholders including NGOs
Indonesia (Jakarta)	+ Data on MSW	– Less focus and emphasis on food waste upstream	+ More focus on post-consumption phase	++ Government Regulation No. 81/2012 toward waste segregation and management; "National Roadmap toward 2025 Clean from Waste Indonesia"; "2020 Zero Waste Indonesia" programme (2016); Integrated Waste Management Facility to Reduce-Reuse-Recycle Purpose (TPST 3R, 2017)	+ Existing municipal policy, and strategies For example a Medium-term Development Plan (RPJMD) of Surabaya City for 2010–2015	+ Various citizen-led initiatives toward household level segregation, as well as independent efforts to provide left-over food to those in need

(Continued)

Table 12.1 (Cont).

	Data available	Focus on waste in production processes	Focus on post-consumption waste	National framework for waste management in place	Municipal governance of food waste in place and implemented	Private/citizen actions toward reducing food waste
Japan (Kyoto)	+ +	+ +	+ +	+ +	+ +	+ +
	Data on food waste across the life cycle	Emphasis on waste upstream and post-consumption	Emphasis on waste upstream and post-consumption	Food Waste Recycling Law enacted in 2001, revised in 2007 and 2015. Targets have been set for different food sectors and stakeholders	Large cities and 40% of smaller cities in Japan have at least one policy tackling food waste	Awareness campaigns and initiatives among households, with involvement of private sector and NGOs
The Philippines (Metro Manila)	+	+	+ +	+ +	+ +	+ +
	Data available at MSW level on food waste as part of biodegradables (including yard waste)	Studies exist on food loss in production systems	Initiatives under way to address post-consumption waste	Republic Act 7160 (The Local Government Code of 1991) and Republic Act 9003 (The Ecological Solid Waste Management Act of 2000)	National laws give responsibility and jurisdiction to cities, municipalities, etc.	Engagement of NGOs, schools and businesses toward reduced food waste.

Legend: − − very weak; − weak; + strong; + + very strong

are emerging in Phnom Penh. For instance, many restaurants have started to charge penalties for excessive leftovers in response to wasteful consumption in buffet restaurants that are recently gaining popularity (Shafik, 2015).

Two issues prevail in relation to waste management in Cambodia: the decentralization of waste management responsibilities from provincial to municipal level can be an issue, depending on what resources are available at the municipal level. Similar to many other developing countries, including Indonesia, the amount of food waste is estimated from the total amount of solid waste. Efforts are needed to collect the necessary data on food waste and make the data accessible for decision making. In terms of opportunities for intervention, the high organic content (51.9% in 2014 [Denney, 2016]) suggests a large potential for introducing various recycling methodologies, thereby reducing organic waste entering the city's final disposal sites. There are numerous opportunities for upper-stream interventions, including efforts to reduce food loss through improving post-harvest infrastructure, as well as food waste reduction campaigns by both private and civil sectors. For instance, Seng et al. (2012) reports high willingness for source segregation and low penetration of knowledge on small-scale organic waste recycling among waste generators in Phnom Penh, suggesting an untapped potential for reduction.

India (Bengaluru)

In 2013, a study on harvest and post-harvest loss in India (except at the consumer level) estimated that the annual value of this loss for 45 crops was in the order of USD 12.60 billion[3] (Jha et al., 2015). This loss was primarily due to the lack of infrastructure for short-term storage (especially at the farm level) and the lack of processing facilities in the production catchment. To address these issues the government continues to increase storage capacity and promote new food processing technologies (GOI, 2018). At the consumer level, citizen initiatives such as The Robin Hood Army (currently active in 13 cities in India) (Vijaykumar, 2015), and the Bangalore Food Bank supported by Griffith Foods (Sinha, 2018) channel surplus food from processing industries and hotels to the homeless and hungry in urban areas.

Although Bengaluru city does not have any food waste policies per se, it has seen significant citizen action to address the problem of post-consumer food waste. In India, around 60 to 75% of MSW consists of wet-waste (food and garden waste) (Ramachandra, 2011). In response to seven public interest litigations, in 2013, the Karnataka Municipal Corporations Act of 1976 was amended to mandate the segregation of MSW at source into dry, wet and sanitary waste (GOK, 2013). This was followed by rules brought out by the city corporation Bruhat Bengaluru Mahanagar Palike (BBMP) to mandate bulk generators (any organization generating more than 10 kg of total waste per day and housing complexes with more than 50 units) to either treat segregated wet-waste onsite using composting or anaerobic digestion, or to procure the services of authorized private vendors to process segregated waste fractions (BBMP, 2013). These rules were influential in framing the 2016 national-level Solid Waste Management Rules to mandate segregation of waste at source and that bulk generators treat wet-waste onsite or use the services of authorized private vendors across the country.

In Bengaluru city, several actors are responsible for the management of food waste generated at the level of markets, households, restaurants and commercial establishments (Ziherl & Steffen, 2015a, 2015c). At the public sector level, there are elected representatives of the BBMP with its elected head and administrative staff. There are also the waste contractors who employ waste-workers or *pourakarmikas* who sweep streets and collect waste from houses, and authorized private vendors who manage segregated waste from bulk generators. From the community side, there are NGOs and social ventures, citizen groups and resident welfare associations (Ziherl & Steffen, 2015a, 2015c).

The BBMP has not been effective in ensuring the full implementation of the new Solid Waste Management (SWM) policy that mandates the segregation of waste at source and decentralized treatment of waste fractions. A corrupt nexus between contractors, BBMP elected councillors, and BBMP administrative staff holds the SWM system of the city hostage. Several times, contractors have boycotted the new tendering process that seeks to bring in transparency and accountability (High Court of Karnataka – Bengaluru Bench, 2012). Recently, due to large-scale citizen action, the BBMP is planning to do away with contractors by giving out ward-level contracts, paying *pourakarmikas* directly and giving separate contracts to those providing machinery and those supplying workforce (Bharadwaj, 2018; Joshi, 2017). Despite the widespread "Not in My Backyard" mindset, a large number of apartment and gated communities have implemented onsite community composting to treat food and garden waste (Anonymous, 2014; Yajaman, 2013).

In relation to opportunities moving forward: although in several countries source segregated wet-waste is composted in a decentralized manner, none of these cities have implemented city-wide community composting at the apartment complex level like Bengaluru has; a map based on self-reported data shows over 300 apartment complexes that segregate waste at source (2bin1bag, 2014). Case studies on apartment complexes in Bengaluru (inhabited by middle- and upper-middle-class income households) found that door-to-door collection of segregated waste and space for retrofitted composting facilities are critical prerequisites for this community-level composting (Shenoy et al., 2017).

NGOs and social enterprises organize workshops to educate residents on how to implement segregation and treatment of segregated waste. Additionally, there is access to free resources such as pamphlets, videos and documents on how to implement this system (2bin1bag; SWMRT, 2014). However, there is no systematic continuous monitoring process to ensure implementation of these rules. NGOs have been pushing the city and state government to mandate that builders of apartment complexes and gated communities plan and construct wet-waste treatment facilities such as anaerobic digesters or composting at the time of construction rather than retrofitting them later.

Indonesia

Indonesia is recognized as the world's second-largest food waste generator with about 300 kilograms of food per person each year (EIU, 2016). However, it is difficult to obtain accurate data on the current status of food waste generation at different stages of the food supply chain. The national waste management data shows Indonesia generates 175,000 tonnes of MSW per day. Out of which, about 70% is disposed in landfills with 65% as organic food waste which is the largest fraction. The issue is particularly sensitive in a country of over 266 million people, where 7.6% of the population still suffers from malnutrition and more than 36% of children under five suffer from stunting – reduced growth due to prolonged malnutrition (*Jakarta Globe*, 2017a). Like many food-exporting countries, it is estimated that a large amount of waste is caused in the pre-market stage due to defective infrastructures for transporting and storing foods. Many of the agricultural areas still have substandard roads, disorganized transport systems and a lack of access to cold storage units (*Jakarta Globe*, 2017b). However, Soma (2017b, 2018) has noted in the case of Bogor (West Java), post-harvest food waste is an important point of interest, as "buy today eat today" practices that promote smaller consumption are changing, with an increasing number of urbanites and middle/upper-income consumers stocking up and shopping at modern supermarkets. In addition, managing household food waste is also becoming problematic as traditional practices such as home composting and burying waste (which was originally biodegradable) have been made challenging with the advent of packaging waste (Soma, 2017b).

The Government of Indonesia has no specific policies, rules and regulations to address food waste. Instead, the issue is covered under the general waste management policies. Government Regulation No. 81/2012 gives direction toward waste segregation and waste management. The government issued the "National Roadmap toward 2025 Clean from Waste Indonesia," which aims to reduce waste generation by 30% and effective management of waste for at least 70% – to reduce this from being disposed of in the landfills. The Ministry of Environment and Forestry (KLHK) launched the "2020 Zero Waste Indonesia" programme in 2016 to support hundreds of communities throughout Indonesia (*The Jakarta Post*, 2016). The "Integrated Waste Management Facility to Reduce-Reuse-Recycle Purpose" (TPST 3R) is another programme of the national government to support a better waste management system in densely populated urban areas in Indonesia (UNCRD, 2017).

Following the national policies, some local initiatives have flourished, such as the collection of food waste from households and restaurants, attempts to convert these wastes into animal feed and compost. For example, Surabaya, the second-largest city in Indonesia, succeeded in reducing its MSW to landfills by more than 20% over four years (2005–2008) introducing organic waste composting in addition to its community recycling programmes for non-organic waste. Considering that food waste (organic waste), makes 57% of its waste generation, Surabaya City introduced some measures including organic waste separation (in addition to recyclables) and reduction activities in households. In addition, the city supported community-based waste collection and the promotion of composting practice by setting up composting centres and distributing thousands of home compost baskets to residents (Premakumara et al., 2011; Gilby et al., 2017).

There are also some independent efforts, such as the Green School Bali's Bio-Bus initiative (www.greenschool.org/support-us/biobus/), which operates buses that run on biodiesel from used cooking oil. The Food Bank of Indonesia is another voluntary initiative that was established in 2015 to bridge the gap between those with excess food and those who need food support. Additionally, a new programme called "A Blessing-To-Share" (https://ables singtoshare.bridestory.com/) has been implemented in Jakarta. According to its founder Astrid Paramita – this programme is trying to close the gap between the rich and needy by packing leftover food from events, especially from weddings, and delivering them to those in need in partnership with Foodbank of Indonesia (http://foodbankindonesia.org/) and others.

Points of tension remain as the issue of food waste is covered under national and MSW management. This poses two obvious challenges. First, it is difficult to measure the total volume of food waste, as waste collection is still uneven. In Bogor, for example, only 67% of the population receive waste collection services from the municipality (Soma, 2017b). Considering the importance of accurate and available data for decision making, efforts are needed to establish a data management system to collect the necessary data on food waste – in which part of the food system the food is lost and wasted and for what reasons. It is also essential to make this data and analysis up to date and accessible to the policy makers and public.

Second, as MSW management is focused on reducing or reusing the waste at the end-of-pipe stage, there is a lack of consideration on the prevention side (upstream). As is the case with many developing countries, it is essential to deal with the generation at the upper-stream stages of the food supply chain in Indonesia. The Ministry of Agriculture implements a national programme called UPSUS (Upaya Khsusus: Special Efforts in Indonesian) aimed at increasing productivity and production while at the same time reducing yield losses (2011). The programme promotes various activities such as the implementation of Good Handling Practices for reduction of post-harvest losses, extension of shelf-life, maintenance of product freshness, more effective use of resources and facilities, and so on.[4] Efforts are needed to evaluate the efficacy of these action programmes and the potential for scaling up.

Japan (Kyoto City and Oki Town)

Approximately 28.4 million tonnes of food waste is generated annually in Japan (including 10.13 million tonnes of by-products such as soybean meal and bran which have been sold commercially as animal feed or fertilizer) (MAFF, 2018). The amount of food wasted is about 34% of the annual supplies for domestic consumption. Of this amount, 20.1 million tonnes were from the food industry (processing, wholesale, retail and restaurants) while 8.32 million tonnes were from households. Among them, 6.46 million tonnes were considered edible at the moment they were discarded. This amount is virtually equivalent to the amount of the country's rice production (7.99 million tonnes in 2015), and is twice the total amount of food aid distributed worldwide (about 3.2 million tonnes in 2015) (MAFF, 2018). Although food industries contribute a large proportion to the total food waste, their reducing and recycling rate is higher than 80% (MAFF, 2018). Figure 12.1 provides an overview of food waste treatment for households and food business sectors.

The Government of Japan has strengthened its policy to tackle food waste with the Food Waste Recycling Law enacted in 2001, revised in 2007 and 2015. The objective of the law is to reduce final disposal of food waste through waste prevention and waste reduction measures, promote utilization of recycled resources in food-relevant industries to increase food waste recycling as animal feed, fertilizer and to generate energy. The usages are

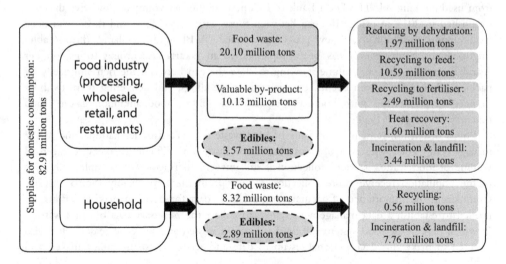

Figure 12.1 Status of food waste treatment in Japan in 2015.
Source: Chen Liu and Atsushi Watabe, based on MAFF (2018).

prioritized in the order of animal feed, fertilizers, oil and fat products, and "heat recovery" through methanation if all of the other treatments are difficult. This law mainly focuses on relevant industries (e.g. food manufacturers, wholesalers, retailers and restaurants), requiring these actors to promote the reduction and recycling of food wastes. Recycling/reduction targets have been set for each food-relevant sector. For example, the recycling targets by March 2020 are currently set to food manufacturers (95%), food wholesalers (70%), food retailers (55%) and restaurant industry (50%). Companies with large volumes of food waste generation (more than 100 tonnes per year) have to conduct mandatory regular reporting on food waste-related data (food waste generation, sales, recycled amount, recycling rates) to the ministries every year. The law also sets targets called reference generation units for the control of food waste generation (from April 2014 to March 2019) for 31 groups such as meat product manufacturers, vegetable pickles manufacturers, coffee drinks and juice manufacturers, takeout/delivery food service, hotels, school lunch and hospital food, and so on (MAFF, 2017). The revised law in 2007 encourages local governments to create a recycling loop to promote the usage of fertilizers and animal feed by the local food producers. Companies certified in the recycling loop initiative would benefit from exemption from authorized permission requirements that waste transporters need to acquire (52 certifications as of the end of April 2017) under the Public Cleansing and Waste Management Law (Denney, 2016).

At the industry level, the government also introduced the Eco-feed and Food Recycle Mark certification and registration system for businesses that produce feed and fertilizer made from food waste. As of March 2018, 28 companies have been certified for 49 products under the Eco-feed label, and 13 fertilizer production companies have been licensed under the Food Recycle Mark. The business sector has also made progress through their partnerships with government agencies. In 2012, four government agencies and private enterprises formed a working group for revising some commercial practices toward the reduction of food waste. The group first targeted the revision of the so-called one-third rule that urges manufacturers, wholesalers and retailers to discard food well before the expiration date. The group carried out pilot projects to reduce waste by mitigating this rule. Some companies also reviewed the expiration date (163 items in 2015) and the means of displaying it by month rather than a specific day (115 items in 2015) to reduce the amount of food and beverage discarded.

Local governments have made progress in targeting food waste generated by retailers, restaurants, and households. According to the Consumer Affairs Agency (2018), all prefectures and major cities and 40% of smaller cities and towns have at least one policy tackling food waste. Awareness-raising campaigns for the consumers is the most popular policy, followed by education at schools, and campaigns in restaurants and hotels to avoid leftovers. Partnerships with the food banks, usually operated by civil society organizations, are also becoming popular.

Kyoto City, the city which attracts the largest number of tourists in Japan, pioneered the local actions first by studying the waste component in 2000. The results indicated 96,000 tonnes of edible food was wasted a year. The city aims to halve the amount by 2020 and has introduced a number of actions. The city issued a certificate of "Zero-leftovers-shops and restaurants" to more than 900 shops, restaurants and hotels who promote activities to use up all food items, support customers to reduce and pack leftovers, etc. For the households, the city runs the 3-*kiri* movement comprising *Tsukai-kiri* (using-up of food items with practices of shopping, cooking and storing), *Tabe-kiri* (eating-up with proper knowledge of expiration dates, menus utilizing leftovers, etc.), and *Mizu-kiri* (drying of organic waste to reduce the amount). Additionally, the city encourages Eco-School-Excursion where students bring their toothbrushes and eco-bags and avoid left-overs during the tour.

While most of the major cities have more or less similar policies focusing on raising citizens' awareness as well as tourists', small towns in the rural areas have participated in turning food waste into resources and operating a closed loop food system. For instance, Oki town, a small town in Fukuoka Prefecture is the site of the Kururun biogas plant. The plant collects all the organic waste generated in the town (by both the household and business sectors), as well as human waste (including septic tank sludge) and produces electricity. The digestive liquid produced in the facility is used as fertilizer by farmers and in private gardens in the town. The food produced in the garden is then used for school lunches or preferentially sold to the town residents at reasonable prices. What town residents eat turns into human waste and septic tank sludge and returns to Kururun.

Civil society organizations and private companies have also run a nation-wide campaign called the NO-FOODLOSS PROJECT together with the government agencies (MAFF 2016). The campaign aims at raising public consciousness and encouraging action by supporting activities at each stage of the food chain. Food banks have also spread over the country, dealing with 7,398 tonnes of food a year (MAFF, 2014). Salvage parties, where participants bring foodstuffs and ready cooked foods that would otherwise not have been used, and prepare food together with the other participants' are also becoming common. These initiatives turn uneaten food into something valuable.

In terms of points of tension and future opportunities, all the prefectures and major cities have embarked on policies to reduce food waste, mostly through awareness-raising campaigns to consumers. Although awareness of consumers is a critical element of the issue, it is difficult to ensure changes in behaviour and achieve a substantial reduction of the waste only through the awareness campaigns (Yokohama City, 2018). Further reduction will require changes in all stages of food production, distribution, consumption and post-consumption.

Another untapped challenge is loss and wastage at the uppermost stage, namely, the farms. The data available in Japan lacks an essential part of the food waste issue for this country. While it imports 60% of the total food consumed, the statistic does not tell us the fraction of food produced overseas, to be consumed by Japanese citizens, that is lost and wasted during steps of production, storage, manufacturing and transport.

The Philippines

At the national level, several laws address MSW and food waste in the Philippines, under the overarching legislation governing waste management in the country, Republic Act 9003, or the Ecological Solid Waste Management Programme. Foremost among these is Republic Act 7160 (The Local Government Code of 1991). RA 7160 gave governing bodies of provinces, cities, municipalities and *barangays* (the smallest administrative unit in the Philippines, representing a village, ward or district) the responsibility and jurisdiction over SWM. RA 9003, provides a more holistic approach to SWM, and identifies the *barangay* as responsible for the collection of source segregated waste from the residential sector. This includes the collection of segregated food waste/yard or garden waste and recyclables which are diverted to the *barangay* composting facility or materials recovery facility, respectively. While the law downloads the responsibility to the *barangay*, the national government does not necessarily provide the local governmental units the resources to do so – one criticism of the law at the time of its ratification. The presence of a robust civil society movement in the country, including a vibrant group of environmental associations, has increased the spread of efforts in food waste management.

At the city level and for the capital region, there are different modes of food waste management in Metro Manila, a metropolitan capital region which is comprised of 16 cities and one municipality. One mode is the collection and purchase of food waste by hog raisers. In some *barangays* in Quezon City, collectors gather segregated food waste from households for free and sell these to private hog owners for a fee. Some cafeterias also sell food waste to private hog owners. Another mode relates to composting at the *barangay* or local government level. The local government unit of Marikina City organizes food waste collection through its food waste truck programme. Initially working with restaurants and other food establishments in 2014, this programme has since expanded to cover residential areas. The collected food waste is composted and then used in the city's urban gardens. Bantay Kalikasan, an NGO, is replicating the programme in other *barangays* in Marikina as part of its advocacy on waste segregation (Cahayag, 2018).

The issue of food waste became part of the mainstream media coverage in 2013, which was proclaimed the National Year of Rice. During this period, the Philippine Rice Research Institute (PRRI) launched the "Be Riceponsible Campaign" toward reducing rice wastage and increasing local yield and supply. Part of this campaign involved creating a norm around a default serving of half-cup of rice per person, leading to the passage of ordinances in Manila and Quezon city ("On Eco-Feed"). In the wake of the proclamation, the Department of the Interior and Local Government encouraged cities and municipalities to pass ordinances to address waste generated from excess servings of rice, beyond what can be consumed. Coinciding with the National Year of Rice celebration was the filing of Senate Bill 1863, the "Anti-Rice Wastage Act of 2013" on providing half-rice servings in all restaurants (Pasiona, 2016).

In certain buffet restaurants, popular in Metro Manila, awareness around food waste has increased, with messages such as "over-servings of food will be charged". Other initiatives have emerged in recent years to allow customers in restaurants to order small, medium or large plate sizes (Ziherl & Steffen, 2015b). Currently being debated is the proposed "Zero Food Waste Act" that mandates the state to develop a system to redistribute surplus edible food from restaurants, fast food chains, hotels and other food establishments to people who have less access to food (Gavilan, 2016). This legislation hopefully will end the unsafe and inhumane practice of *pagpag*, where leftover food scavenged from trash is recooked, sold and consumed by the poorest of the poor in Metro Manila.

Alongside direct food waste reduction initiatives at the city level are ordinances that penalize food establishments who improperly dispose of their used cooking oil and grease trap into the sewerage system, leading to clogged drains – a precursor to flooding. Such initiatives are usually conceptualized as flood prevention and sanitation measures, yet it should also be presented as food waste reduction and recycling methods (Chavez, 2018).

In terms of points of tension, a 2017 proposal to ban unlimited rice – which is popular in fast food chains patronized mostly by low- to middle-income groups – was met with a significant lack of public support (*The Manila Times*, 2017). The proposal was in response to data indicating an annual volume of rice wastage of roughly two tablespoons of rice per household daily and to failed attempts to achieving self-sufficiency in rice production. Culturally, rice serves as a stomach filler, especially for lower-income groups. For other diners, certain dishes are best eaten with big servings of rice. This campaign shifted the responsibility of lowering food wastage from the government, the system and the rich, to middle- and low-income individuals. In a country where thousands lack basic nutrition, this shifting of responsibility was seen as highly problematic. Citizens felt that government initiatives to measure and reduce wastage should be the main backbone of the food waste reduction efforts in the country, with individual practices being a supplement to the effort rather than the main focus.

Opportunities to reduce large-scale food wastage lie with the government as it manages production, storage and distribution of large quantities of food. For example, a 2014 audit report found that more than 7,000 family food packs intended for survivors of the Yolanda typhoon were lost due to spoilage from improper storage and mismanagement by the government (Cahayag, 2018).

Discussion and conclusion: looking ahead toward promising food waste strategies in Asia

Asia provides a rich tapestry of cultures and socio-economic dimensions where food wastage can be examined along different systems of food provisioning, and in relation to gender, class, religion and, for India, caste. With its high population, awareness building in Asia has an important role to play in reducing wastage – among the public and private sectors, and citizens alike – yet it is equally significant to examine and explore the systemic issues that exacerbate wastage. The gendered dimension of domestic work and food provisioning is one example of how food waste management post-consumption can give undue responsibility to women over men, as noted by Soma (2017a, 2016). The middle-class activism around food waste also poses issues when it comes to more inclusive and democratic forms of waste management, as underlined by Anantharaman (2014) and Upadhya (in Lutringer & Randeria, 2017). Problems of malnutrition, poverty and access to food are more acute in Asia, raising the question of food waste within the context of environmental and social justice.

As we have discussed in this chapter, food wastage is a highly contextual topic as food can be lost or wasted at different stages due to a variety of social, political, environmental and technological reasons. Solutions to these problems should also be context specific, which we have attempted to uncover through both a national and city-based case study approach. Based on this analysis, we would like to put forward the following key recommendations: First, ensuring harmonized data collection on food waste remains an issue in Asia. Toward this end, Japan has developed a system to collect and analyse statistical data on the current status of food waste generation throughout the food systems. However, in many cities and regions in Asia, the amount of food waste is estimated from the total amount of solid waste. Considering the importance of accurate and available data for decision making, efforts are needed to share best practices and encourage partnerships between cities and academic institutions to support waste audits.

Second, there is a need to better understand and improve the governance of waste in Asia, where several countries have set goals toward ambitious waste management systems recycling goals. With the current trend toward decentralization in the ongoing reform of waste sector governance, with increased responsibility placed on provincial and municipal administrations – as is the case in Cambodia and the Philippines – the question of adequate resources and political clout for implementing such strategies becomes critical. Such reforms provide an opportunity for municipal administrations to establish a waste management/ resource circulation system tailored to local needs and conditions, yet assistance is needed at the municipal level with capacity development, designing sustainable financial mechanisms for waste management, and inviting cooperation from the private and civil sectors. In a waste management and recycling marketplace, where capitalist interests are also at stake, there is also a need to tackle issues associated with corruption and unfair power balances. In Indian cities, contractor mafias are a big barrier to implementing more sustainable practices, and there is a need to ensure better monitoring of public services and transparency across the region. Promising trends are under way: this year, the Japan International Cooperation Agency (JICA) began a three-year technical cooperation project toward capacity building among select local government units (LGUs) in the Philippines, with the aim of using innovative technologies for waste management (JICA, 2017). Further research on food waste technologies such as anaerobic digesters would allow scholars and policy makers to better understand its potential efficacy in Asian countries, a technological approach that would need to be considered within the context of a largely decentralized waste management system.

The third recommendation is a call for more research and action on source reduction, not solely recycling and final waste management. While many countries in Asia tend to focus on the recycling and reuse of food waste, with economic benefits associated with both processes, there is also a need to further emphasize prevention and absolute reduction of food waste at various stages of the food chain. Tackling the issue of food waste at the source, rather than at the "end of pipe", will require engagement with different stakeholders, local to global food systems, including farmers and fisherfolk, small and medium enterprises, transnational food companies, civil society and consumer-citizens, as well as both local and national governments – specifically around issues of food distribution, exports and overproduction. There are innovative projects underway across the region – what can be termed "bottom up initiatives" – some of which have been highlighted in this chapter. These provide a clear opportunity for gathering best practices, and sharing examples of social innovation toward source reduction across cultures and contexts. The increasing popularity of the zero-waste movement in the Philippines, including zero-waste food packaging advocacies, is an example of how such an approach can gain resonance and would merit further investigation. Trends in the service sector to penalize leftovers, especially at buffets, are another example, as are the emergence of food banks for the redistribution of surplus food from hotels and restaurants to people in need.

The fourth recommendation is for scholars to better map food consumption and consumer trends across dimensions of gender and class. Eating out is an important trend in relation to food waste, no doubt related to changing and gendered household dynamics. Food preparation has been primarily the responsibility of women in most societies. Additionally, access to domestic helpers, usually female and from the lower-income groups, has become the hallmark of being a middle-class citizen across the Asian region. Provision of knowledge opportunities for women and the enlistment of men toward food waste reduction efforts can be the outcome of such gender analysis. While households have a role to play, food waste in the service industry and changes in taste preference could be prioritized in further research and policy action (Pasiona, 2016). To examine the changing role of gender and class relations, a political economy perspective could reveal how the dynamics of food acquisition, production and waste management shifts.

Ultimately, research in the area of food waste must account for economic trends: while the growing popularity in the circular economy is a promising area for research, policy and action, the ambition of reducing waste and closing loops must be understood in relation to institutional settings and social norms, or not solely ecological economic principles but also those of the social and solidarity economy (Moreau et al., 2017). If capitalist paradigms prevail, it is easy to understand how profitable recycling can be prioritized over the non-profitable reduction of food waste at source, for example. Rather than privileging profit and monetary gain, there is an increasing call for the promotion of other paradigms which put forward the importance of people and planet – such as relationship with nature, food, and more generally well-being (Kothari & Joy, 2017). Inscribing the waste management system and food waste in particular within a social and solidaristic economy may be one way forward (Sahakian & Dunand, 2015), leading to decent wages for waste-workers, penalties for food wastage in the industry sector, regulations for the safe redistribution of food to those in need, or incentives for waste reductions at source. This would require tackling the institutional frameworks and social norms that shape food waste across contexts and cultures.

Notes

1 Statistics of other dominant organic wastes such as green waste and waste textiles are often compiled as separate independent waste categories.
2 Home scale biodigesters (wet fermentation) are given higher attention based on Cambodia's unique condition (space limits and food with high moisture contents) and in line with National Biodigester Programme of the Ministry of Agriculture, Forestry and Fisheries, Cambodia.
3 1USD = INR 73.52
4 http://apec-flows.ntu.edu.tw/upload/edit/file/2%20SR_2017_C_S3-03_Indonesia-Revised2.pdf

References

2bin1bag. (2014). Green Map - Residential communities segregating waste. Retrieved 30 November, 2018, from www.2bin1bag.in/green-map.
2bin1bag. 2 bin 1 bag: divide and conquer waste. Retrieved 20 October, 2018, from www.2bin1bag.in/.
(EIU), E. I. U. (2016). Fixing food: towards a more sustainable food system.
Anantharaman, M. (2014). Networked ecological citizenship, the new middle classes and the provisioning of sustainable waste management in Bangalore, India. *Journal of Cleaner Production, 63*, 173–183.
Anonymous. (2014 24 June 2014). Six amazing groups in Bangalore that show how to manage waste in style. Citizen Matters. Retrieved from http://bengaluru.citizenmatters.in/six-amazing-groups-that-show-how-to-manage-waste-in-style-bangalore-6545.
BBMP. (2013). *Bruhat Bengaluru Mahanagara Palike Public Notice*. Bengaluru, India: Bruhat Bengaluru Mahanagar Palike.
Bharadwaj, K. V. A. (2018 2 January 2018). Direct payment won't end 'contractor mafia'. The Hindu. Retrieved from www.thehindu.com/news/cities/bangalore/direct-payment-wont-end-contractor-mafia/article22353445.ece.
Cahayag, A. (2018 10 August 2018). Bantay kalikasan to replicate Marikina's food waste management. *ABS-CBN Lingkod Kapamilya*.
Chavez, C. (2018). QC Council releases regulations penalizing restaurants contribute to flooding, in Manila Bulletin. Philippine News. Retrieved from https://news.mb.com.ph/2018/06/15/qc-council-releases-regulations-penalizing-restaurants-contribute-to-flooding/.
Cheng, H. & Hu, Y. (2010). Planning for sustainability in China's urban development: status and challenges for Dongtan eco-city project. *Journal of Environmental Monitoring, 12*(1), 119–126.
Consumer Affairs Agency. (2018). Situation of the local governments' actions to reduce food waste as of FY2017. [Online]. Retrieved from www.caa.go.jp/policies/policy/consumer_policy/information/food_loss/efforts/pdf/efforts_180703_0008.pdf. [Accessed 19 11 2018].
Denney, L. (2016). *Working Politically in Practice Series–Case Study No. 8–Reforming Solid Waste Management in Phnom Penh*. San Francisco, USA: The Asia Foundation and the Overseas Development Institute.
Favis, A. & R. D. F. Estanislao (2016). Towards sustainable consumption of rice in a private school in Metro Manila, in Sahakian et al. *Food Consumption in the City: Practices and patterns in urban Asia and the Pacific*. pp. 238–253.
FAO. (2013). The high-level multi-stakeholder consultation on food losses and food waste in Asia and the Pacific region.

FAO, IFAD, UNICEF. et al. (2018). Food security and nutrition in the world 2018: building climate resilience for food securit and nutrition. In :FAO (ed). Rome.

Gavilan, J. (2016 24 July 2016). Senate bill: restaurants must donate excess food to charities. *Rappler.*

Gilby, S., Hengesbaugh, M., Premakumara, D. G. J., Onogawa, K., Soedjono, E. S., & Fitriani, N. (2017). *Planning and Implementation of Integrated Solid Waste Management Strategies at Local Level: The Case of Surabaya City.* Hayama: IGES Centre Collaborating with UNEP on Environmental Technologies (CCET).

GOI. (2018). *Lok Sabha Unstarred Question No. 2460 on Wastage of Agricultural Products.* New Delhi: Ministry Of Agriculture And Farmers Welfare. Retrieved from www.indiaenvironmentportal.org.in/files/file/WASTAGE%20OF%20AGRICULTURAL%20PRODUCTS.pdf.

GOK. (2013). *Karnataka Municipal Corporations (Amendment) Act, 2013.* Bangalore: Karnataka Gazette Retrieved from http://dpal.kar.nic.in/ao2013/55of2013(E).pdf.

The Guardian. (2013 19 Sep). Up to two-fifths of fruit and veg crop is wasted because it is 'ugly', report finds. The Guardian. Retrieved from www.theguardian.com/environment/2013/sep/19/fruit-veget ables-wasted-ugly-report.

Gül, A., Isik, H., Bal, T., & Ozer, S. (2003). Bread consumption and waste of households in urban area of Adana province. *Electronic Journal of Polish Agricultural Universities, 6*(2), 10.

Gustavsson, J., Cederberg, C., Sonesson, U., Otterdijk, R. v., & Meybeck, A. (2011). *Global Food Losses and Food Waste: Extent, Causes and Prevention.* Rome: Food and Agriculture Organization of the United Nations.

Hegazy, R. (2013b). Post-harvest situation and losses in India. High Court of Karnataka -Bengaluru Bench: WP 24739/2012. No. WP 24739/2012, order no. 28 date of order: 18/ 06/2014 (High Court of Karnataka 2012).

Hoornweg, D. & Bhada-Tata, P. (2012). What a waste: a global review of solid waste management.

Hossain, A. & Miah, M. (2009). Post harvest losses and technical efficiency of potato storage systems in Bangladesh.

Jakarta Globe. (2017a). The Indonesia Second Largest Food Waster. 7 7 Retrieved from http://jakarta globe.id/business/indonesia-second-largest-food-waster/. [Accessed 20 11 2018].

Jakarta Globe. (2017b). The willful waste, woeful want. [Online]. Retrieved from: https://jakartaglobe. id/opinion/willful-food-waste-woeful-want/. [Accessed 20 11 2018].

The Jakarta Post. (2016). "Govt to introduce zero-waste concept," [Online]. Retrieved from www.theja kartapost.com/news/2016/03/26/govt-introduce-zero-waste-concept.html. [Accessed 20 11 2018].

Jha, S. N., Vishwakarma, R. K., Ahmad, T., Rai, A., & Dixit, A. K. (2015). *Report on Assessment of Quantitative Harvest and Post-Harvest Losses of Major Crops and Commodities in India.* (I.-C. ICAR-All India Coordinated Research Project on Post-Harvest Technology, P.O-PAU-Ludhiana- 141004, Trans.), Ludhiana, India: ICAR-All India Coordinated Research Project on Post-Harvest Technology (ICAR-CIPHET).

JICA. (2017) DENR, JICA to train LGUs on solid waste management technology. Retrieved from www.jica.go.jp/philippine/english/office/topics/news/171113.html.

Joshi, B. (2017 9 January). This is how BBMP plans to dump garbage contractor mafia menace into trash can. Economic Times. Retrieved from https://economictimes.indiatimes.com/news/politics-and-nation/this-is-how-bbmp-plans-to-dump-garbage-contractor-mafia-menace-into-trash-can/article show/56415653.cms.

Kothari, A. & Joy, K. J. (eds.). (2017). Alternative futures: India unshackled: authors upfront.

KWM Network. (2001). Korea (South) country report – Korean waste problem: the generation of the problem and civil society's counter action. Taipei, Taiwan: KWMN. Waste Not Asia 2001.

Lee, K. (2016). Convenient food, inconvenient waste: systems of provision meet social practices in Seoul, in Sahakian et al. *Food Consumption in the City: Practices and patterns in urban Asia and the Pacific.* pp. 216–237.

Lee, K. C. (2018). Grocery shopping, food waste, and the retail landscape of cities: the case of Seoul. *Journal of Cleaner Production, 172,* 325–334.

Leray, L., Sahakian, M., & Erkman, S. (2016). Understanding household food metabolism: relating micro-level material flow analysis to consumption practices. *Journal of Cleaner Production, 125,* 44–55.

Li, T. M. (2011). Centering labor in the land grab debate. *The Journal of Peasant Studies, 38*(2), 281–298.

Liu, C., Hotta Y. et al. (2016). Food waste in Japan: trends, current practices and key challenges. *Journal of Cleaner Production, 133,* 557–564.

Lutringer, C. & Randeria, S. (2017). Sustainable food consumption, urban waste management and civic activism: lessons from Bangalore/ Bengaluru, India. International development policy | Revue internationale de politique de développement 8. Retrieved from https://journals.openedition.org/poldev/2475.

MAFF (Ministry of Agriculture, Forestry and Fisheries). (2014). The survey to understand the status of activities of the food banks in Japan. Retrieved from www.maff.go.jp/j/shokusan/recycle/syoku_loss/foodbank/tachiage/pdf/25fbhk.pdf. [Accessed 19 11 2018].

MAFF (Ministry of Agriculture, Forestry and Fisheries). (2015). Shitteru? Nihon no syokuryou jijou – Nihon no syokuryou jikyuuritsu, jikyuuryoku to syokuryou anzen hosyou - (Do you know the condition of food in Japan? The ratio and capacity of food self-sufficiency and food safety in Japan). [Accessed 05 02 2019].

Ministry of Agriculture, Forestry and Fisheries. (2016). "NO-FOODLOSS PROJECT," 27 12 2016. [Online]. Retrieved from http://www.maff.go.jp/j/shokusan/recycle/syoku_loss/161227.html. [Accessed 19 11 2018].

Ministry of Agriculture, Forestry and Fisheries. (2017). "Reducing Food Loss and Waste & Promoting Recycling ~ 'MOTTAINAI' for Foods Once Again." 2017. [Online]. Retrieved from http://www.maff.go.jp/e/policies/env/attach/pdf/index-5.pdf. [Accessed 19 11 2018].

MAFF (Ministry of Agriculture, Forestry, and Fisheries, Japan). (2018). Reducing food loss and waste & promoting recycling. Retrieved from www.maff.go.jp/e/policies/env/attach/pdf/index-5.pdf.

Manila Times. (2017). The Unlimited Rice. Retrieved from www.manilatimes.net/unlimited-rice/333208/.

Matsuda, T., Yano, J., Hirai, Y., & Sakai, S. i. (2012). Life-cycle greenhouse gas inventory analysis of household waste management and food waste reduction activities in Kyoto, Japan. *The International Journal of Life Cycle Assessment*, 17(6), 743–752.

MoEC. (2018). Food waste management policy in Cambodia.

Mopera, L. E. (2016). Food loss in the food value chain: the Philippine agriculture scenario. *Journal of Developments in Sustainable Agriculture*, 11, 8–16.

Moreau, V., Sahakian, M., Griethuysen, P. V. et al. (2017). Coming full circle: why social and institutional dimensions matter for the circular economy. *Journal of Industrial Ecology*, 21, 497–506.

Papargyropoulou, E., Padfield, R., Rupani, P., & Zakaria, Z. (2014). Towards sustainable resource and waste management in developing countries: the role of commercial and food waste in Malaysia. *International Journal of Waste Resources*, 4(3), 2–7.

Papargyropoulou, E. (2016). Food waste in the food service sector: a case study from Malaysia, in Sahakian et al. *Food Consumption in the City: Practices and patterns in urban Asia and the Pacific*. pp. 199–215.

Pasang, H., Moore, G. A., & Sitorus, G. (2007). Neighbourhood-based waste management: a solution for solid waste problems in Jakarta, Indonesia. *Waste Management*, 27(12), 1924–1938.

Pasiona, S. P. (2016, 28 July 2016). Putting 'half rice' on the menu. Rappler.

Pekcan, G., Koksal, E., Kuc¸ukerdonmez, O., & Ozel, H. (2005). Household food wastage in Turkey. FAO, statistics division working paper series, No: ESS/ESSA/00be. Ankara, Turkey.

Phnom Penh Capital Administration. (2018). *Phnom Penh Waste Management Strategy and Action Plan 2018–2035*. Phnom Penh: Phnom Penh Capital Administration.

Premakumara, D. G. J., Abe, M., & Maeda, T. (2011). Reducing municipal waste through promoting integrated sustainable waste management (ISWM) practices in Surabaya City, Indonesia. *Ecosystems and Sustainable Development VIII*, 144, 457–468.

Ramachandran, Ambady. & Chamukuttan, Snehalatha. (2010). Rising burden of obesity in Asia. *Journal of obesity* 2010.

Ramachandra, T. V. (2011). Integrated management of municipal solid waste. In idbcc (Eds.), *Environmental Security: Human & Animal Health*. pp. 465–484.

Reardon, Thomas. & Rose, Hopkins. The supermarket revolution in developing countries: policies to address emerging tensions among supermarkets, suppliers and traditional retailers. *The European journal of development research*, 18.4 (2006): 522-545.

Sahakian, M., Saloma, C., & Erkman, S. (eds.). (2016). *Food Consumption in the City: Practices and Patterns in Urban Asia and the Pacific*. Oxon, UK; New York, USA: Routledge.

Sahakian, M., Saloma, C., & Ganguly, S. (2018). Exploring the role of taste in middle-class household practices. *Asian Journal of Social Science*, 46(3), 304–329.

Sahakian, M. D. & Dunand, C. (2015). The social and solidarity economy towards greater 'sustainability': learning across contexts and cultures, from Geneva to Manila. *Community Development Journal, 50*, 403–417.

Sang-Arun, J., Kim Heng, C., Uch, R., & Sam, P. (2011). *A Guide for Technology Selection and Implementation for Urban Organic Waste Utilization Projects in Cambodia.* Hayama, Japan: Institute for Global Environmental Strategies.

Schneider, F. (2013). *Review of food waste prevention on an international level.* Paper presented at the Proceedings of the Institution of Civil Engineers-Waste and Resource Management.

Seng, Bunrith, Ochiai, Satoru, Kaneko, Hidehiro (2012). Resident willingness of food waste separation in Phnom Penh, Cambodia, Proceedings of the 23rd Annual Conference of Japan Society of Material Cycles and Waste Management.

Shafik, M. (2015). Using art to reduce food waste. Retrieved from www.khmertimeskh.com/news/11100/using-art-to-reduce-food-waste/

Sharma, V., Canditelli, M., Fortuna, F., & Cornacchia, G. (1997). Processing of urban and agro-industrial residues by aerobic composting. *Energy Conversion and Management, 38*(5), 453–478.

Shenoy, M., Zhang, X., Kashyap, S., Wasdani, K. P., & Vijaygopal, A. (2017). *Decentralized Solid Waste Management Innovation in Bengaluru, South India: Mandatory Segregation and Wet-Waste Treatment at Source by Residential Bulk Generators.* Bengaluru: Ashoka Trust for Research in Ecology and the Environment.

Sinha, A. (2018 20 April 2018). Bangalore food bank providing a sustainable solution to hunger and food waste. CSR Mandate. Retrieved from www.csrmandate.org/bangalore-food-bank-providing-a-sustainable-solution-to-hunger-and-food-waste/.

Soma, T. (2016). The tale of the crying rice: the role of unpaid foodwork and learning in food waste prevention and reduction in Indonesian households. In J. Sumner (Ed.), *Learning, food, and sustainability: Sites for resistance and change.* pp. 19–34. New York: Palgrave Macmillan.

Soma, T. (2017a). Wasted infrastructures: urbanization, distancing and food waste in Bogor, Indonesia. *Built Environment, 43*(3), 431–446.

Soma, T. (2017b). Gifting, ridding and the "everyday mundane": the role of class and privilege in food waste generation in Indonesia. *Local Environment, 22*(12), 1444–1460.

Soma, T. (2018). (Re) framing the Food waste narrative: infrastructures of urban food consumption and waste in Indonesia. *Indonesia, 105,* 173–190.

SWMRT. (2014). Solid Waste Management Round Table (SWMRT). Retrieved 20 October 2018, from http://swmrt.com/#.

Teng, P. & Trethewie, S. (2012). Tackling urban and rural food wastage in Southeast Asia: issues and interventions. *Policy Brief, 17.*

Treeamnuk, K., Pathaveerat, S., Terdwongworakul, A., & Bupata, C. (2010) Design of machine to size java apple fruit with minimal damage. *Biosystems engineering, 107*(2), 140–148.

UNCRD (United Nations Centre for Regional Development). (2017). State of the 3Rs in Asia and the Pacific. Retrieved from www.uncrd.or.jp/content/documents/5689[Nov%202017]%20Indonesia.pdf. [Accessed 20 11 2018].

Vijaykumar, D. (2015 2 June 2015). The robin hood army: fighting food waste in India and Pakistan. *The Guardian.* 17.

Watabe, A, C. Liu & Bengtsson M. (2016). Uneaten food: emerging social practices around food waste in Greater Tokyo, in Sahakian et al. *Food Consumption in the City: Practices and patterns in urban Asia and the Pacific.* pp. 161–179.

Watanabe, K. (2009). Estimation of quantities of wasted food. Proceedings of the 3rd BOKU Waste Conference 2009, Wien. Facultas Verlags- und Buchhandels AG, Wien, Austria, pp. 77–84.

Yajaman, A. M. (2013 13 September 2013). A large scale composting model Bangalore's apartments can emulate. Citizen Matters. Retrieved from http://bengaluru.citizenmatters.in/a-large-scale-composting-model-bangalore-s-apartments-can-emulate-5673.

Yokohoma-City. (2018). Draft report on the directions of food waste reduction. Retrieved from: www.city.yokohama.lg.jp/shigen/sub-keikaku/shingikai/genryo-syou/h29-no5/shiryo2.pdf.

Zhang, D. (2016). From thrift to sustainability: the changing table manners of Shanghai's food leftovers, in Sahakian et al. *Food Consumption in the City: Practices and patterns in urban Asia and the Pacific.* pp. 180–198.

Ziherl, H. & Steffen, R. (Writers). (2015a). Eating out and food waste in Bangalore. Swiss Network for International Studies (SNIS) video series. Retrieved from http://foodconsumption.snis.ch/eating-out-and-food-waste-in-bangalore/.

Ziherl, H. & Steffen, R. (Writers). (2015b). Eating out and food waste in Metro Manila. Swiss Network for International Studies (SNIS) video series. Retrieved from http://foodconsumption.snis.ch/eating-out-and-food-waste-in-metro-manila/.

Ziherl, H. & Steffen, R. (Writers). (2015c). Waste management and recycling in Bangalore. Swiss Network for International Studies (SNIS) video series. Retrieved from http://foodconsumption.snis.ch/waste-management-and-recycling-in-bangalore/.

13

FOOD WASTE WITHIN SOUTH AFRICA AND SAUDI ARABIA

Suzan Oelofse, Anton Nahman, Mirza Barjees Baig, Ramy Salemdeeb, Abdul-Sattar Nizami and Christian Reynolds

Introduction

The food waste reduction potential within the countries of Middle East and Africa is vast. The FAO estimate that over 20% of most food supply chains are wasted, leading to over 210 kg/capita/year wasted across the region (Gustavsson et al., 2011). This equates to over US$60 billion a year in wasted food (FAO, 2014).

Countries in the Middle East and Africa (ME&A) region are faced with food security and sovereignty issues, with over 50% of food imported in some countries. This leads to any reductions in food supply through losses and waste being even more impactful. Likewise there are rapid structural and dynamic changes occurring throughout countries in the ME&A region that are leading to additional increases in food waste. Depending on the country within ME&A, these rapid changes include high population growth and increasing urbanisation, a scarce and fragile natural resource base, limited capacity to expand food production, high exposure to climate change impact (drought, flood, etc.), changing food preferences (which can be linked to), rising incomes, the effects of the double burden of malnutrition, sudden food price volatility, and conflicts and political instability.

As can be seen from these many generalisations it would be impossible to do justice to the food waste situations for the many countries inside the ME&A region within the space offered by this chapter. Instead, this chapter will now focus on two prominent countries in ME&A: South Africa and Saudi Arabia. Each of them with their own food waste challenges and solutions as outlined below.

Food waste within South Africa

South Africa is an interesting case study when considering food waste. It is listed as a developing country with high unemployment and poverty rates despite having an abundance of goods and natural resources and being recognised as one of the largest industrialised countries in Africa in both wealth and Gross Domestic Product (GDP) (Bakari, 2017).

South Africa is also an exception in the sub-Sahara African region in terms of the central role that modern food supply chains play in provisioning the cities (Crush and Frayne, 2011).

When comparing the average municipal solid waste composition of a sample of South African municipalities with that of sub-Saharan Africa and other countries with different income traits (Figure 13.1), it is quite clear that South Africa has a unique municipal solid waste composition. When focusing on the organic component of the municipal waste stream (garden and food waste), this comparison suggests that post-consumer food waste in South Africa is likely to be more closely aligned with that in high-income countries, despite being geographically located in sub-Saharan Africa.

South Africa is a net exporter of food (DAFF, 2017), resulting in pre-consumer food waste generation in South Africa, while post-consumer food waste will be generated in the importing country. Global estimates of food waste generation in sub-Saharan Africa are based on the assumption that food is mainly produced by small-scale farmers with inefficient farming, storage, processing and distribution systems (Gustavsson et al., 2013). The case of South Africa is, however, somewhat different. Food production in South Africa is dominated by a few powerful corporations specifically in inputs, processing and retail, and to a lesser degree in primary production (Hall and Cousins, 2015). Agriculture is dominated by large-scale commercial farming (World Bank, 2011) while food processing is dominated by four South African food giants – Tiger Brands, Pioneer, Premier and FoodCorp (Hall and Cousins, 2015). It is therefore likely that food losses and waste in the early stages of the value chain in South Africa may be more closely aligned with that of developed economies where sophisticated harvesting, storage and processing systems are in place.

This section is, therefore, a first attempt to collate the available research on food waste in South Africa with the aim to inform future research, estimates and decision making relating to food waste in South Africa. The purpose of this section is to provide an overview of food waste-related research undertaken in South Africa to date, covering the entire food value chain from agricultural production through packaging, processing, distribution and consumption.

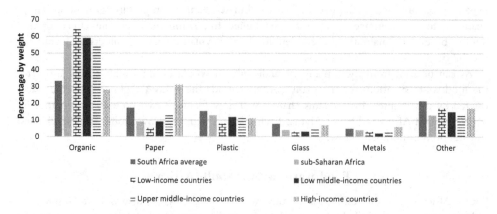

Figure 13.1 Comparing South African municipal solid waste composition with the rest of the world, values provided as percentage by weight.

Source: Adapted from Hoornweg and Bhada-Tata (2012).

Harvest and post-harvest losses

Research on food losses and waste in South Africa have traditionally focused on reducing harvest and post-harvest losses of various crops. The main causes for post-harvest losses are physiological (wilting, shrivelling and chilling injury, etc.), pathological (decay due to bacterial or fungal infestations) and physical (mechanical injury) (Mashau et al., 2012). Mechanical or physiological damage typically leads to bacterial or fungal infestations which cause decay.

A study of the post-harvest losses of fruit at the Tshakhuma fruit market in Limpopo (Mashau et al., 2012) reported no losses during transportation due to the short distance between the farm and the market (5 km). It is further reported that the produce is sourced from the commercial farms in the area and, to a limited extent, from subsistence farmers. The vendors buy stock on a weekly basis due to a lack of appropriate technology to keep fruits fresh at the market. The storage facilities at the market are in corrugated stores with no refrigerated storage containers. Vendors selling guava, avocado and pawpaw self-reported 50% losses as a result of over-ripening due to a lack of measures to control the ripening processes of the fruits. Sellers of macadamia reported no losses as dried nuts have a longer shelf life than fresh fruit and vegetables. Post-harvest fruit losses at the Tshakhuma market was 43.3% (Mashau et al., 2012). Reasons for the high losses include knowledge gaps in the use of proper packaging materials, poor procurement planning (some sellers managed to sell all their weekly stocks) and the lack of understanding of the link between transport and fruit rotting, alongside the self-reported lack of refrigeration (Mashau et al., 2012).

Munhuweyi (2012) investigated vegetable losses at the retail level in Stellenbosch. The study covered tomato, cabbage and carrots and assessed post-harvest quality and losses at the retail level and during consumer simulated storage. The environmental conditions in the supermarkets were cooler and with higher humidity than the outdoor market, but none of the outlets in this study kept the produce in the recommended optimum conditions (Munhuweyi, 2012). The losses for tomatoes at retail level averaged at 14.46%, cabbage at 21.21%, carrots at 17.93%, and apples at 10–20% but sometimes as high as 30–50%. The national loss of tomatoes at retail level is estimated at 37,207 tonnes at a value of R61.65 million (in 2012); cabbage at national level is 24,470 tonnes valued at R17.74 million; and carrots 15,250 tonnes of fresh carrots valued at R21.71 million.

Losses and waste in food supply chains

A study that investigated the motivational factors driving South African food processors to reduce food waste through recovery systems (Hayes, 2011) uncovered the following:

- Most South African retailers have policies in place to return expired and damaged stock to the suppliers for disposal. The result of this policy is that branded product is returned to the processors contributing to the waste. The data records kept by the processors are not retailer-specific but facility-specific.
- The extent of knowledge on the waste quantities was limited and less than 50% of respondents provided quantitative data on the waste generated.
- The majority of this waste (29%) is disposed of at landfill, 28% by feeding of stock, 18% is removed by third-party collections, 14% is reported to be composted, 8% is used for product recovery and 3% is donated to charities.
- Waste disposal to landfill by the meat industry is often the only option due to possible toxicity. This may occur as a result of production process failures, safety issues with raw materials and packaging or due to stock being expired.

- A change in regulation resulted in a declined market for carcass meal as it can now only be used as fertiliser due to the potential risk of spreading disease. It is reported that selling carcass meal as fertiliser is not cost effective.
- Other uses of food waste that are noted in this study include: generation of biogas; grease interceptor waste is used for the manufacture of biodiesel; apricot kernels are being exported for the production of persipan; outer hard apricot kernel shells are being used to clean jet engines; and peach kernels are used as replacement fuel for coal in the boilers.
- The reported reasons for processors to address food waste proactively are:

  - Cost of disposal is higher than handing the waste to a third-party user or even selling it to a downstream user.
  - Brand protection – if damaged or expired goods are not disposed of properly, it can damage the brand's reputation.

In 2017, Le Roux et al. estimated the wastage of carrots, cabbage, beetroot, broccoli and lettuce at each stage of the supply chain from farm to consumer as part of a water footprint determination of vegetables produced on the Steenkoppies Aquifer in Gauteng. Lettuce has higher average wastage percentages (38%) as compared to cabbage (14%) and broccoli (13%). The wastage varies depending on the season and it is noted that some of the waste is used for beneficial purposes including animal feed and composting (Le Roux et al., 2017). A summary of their findings by commodity group along the supply chain is provided in Table 13.1.

The results found that 70% of the food wastage occurred on-farm at the packhouse. The results were obtained "from a large commercial farm that uses advanced technologies" (Le Roux et al., 2017). The average calculated wastage of vegetables along the supply chain is lower than previous estimates by Oelofse and Nahman (2013). The reasons for the high wastage at the packhouse include damage as a result of pests and disease and unmarketable properties. The amount of wastage is highly variable between different vegetable types, with the highest wastage occurring in more perishable crops (lettuce) and lower wastage in less perishable crops (cabbage) (Le Roux et al., 2017).

Food waste in municipal solid waste

Adhikari et al. (2006) found a correlation between GDP, percentage urban population, municipal solid waste (MSW) generation, and food waste production on a per capita level. MSW generation is well correlated with GDP (correlation coefficient $R2 = 0.94$) whereas food waste generation demonstrated a lower ($R2 = 0.86$), but still a valid correlation. Using

Table 13.1 Summary of the wastage estimated for vegetables from the Steenkoppies aquifer

Commodity groups	Production (T/a)	Total wastage as a % of input				
		Farm	Market	Retail	Consumer	Total
Root & Tubers	49,022.9	24.3	0.7	2.3	1.5	28.8
Vegetables	47,976.6	17.9	4.6	5.5	3.6	31.6

Source: Adapted from Le Roux et al. (2017)

these correlations, Adhikari et al. (2006) calculated the urban food waste in South Africa as 5.05 million tonnes in 2005 or 48% of MSW and this is expected to increase to 7.83 million tonnes, or 45% of the total MSW fraction, in 2025 if current waste management practices are maintained (Adhikari et al., 2006).

In 2012, Nahman et al. estimated the cost of household food waste in South Africa at 1.4 million tonnes per annum, at a cost to society of R21.7 billion (approximately US$2.7 billion at 2012 exchange rates[1]) per annum (Nahman et al., 2012). More recently, there have been an increasing number of waste characterisation studies undertaken by municipalities in South Africa. Unfortunately, few of these waste characterisation studies are comparable, and food waste is still not reported as a separate waste category in most of these studies. The studies that reported food waste as a separate waste category are listed in Table 13.2. The food waste component in these studies varied between 3% in Ekurhuleni and 33% in Nelson Mandela Metropolitan municipality.

Oelofse et al. (2018) published the food waste results of comparable waste characterisation studies from two of the big metropolitan municipalities in the Gauteng Province of South Africa (Oelofse et al., 2018). The results provide an indication of the food waste disposed of to the municipal bin rather than the food waste generated at household level. These results indicated an average weekly food waste disposal rate of 0.69 kg per household in Johannesburg and 0.48 kg per household in Ekurhuleni. The household food waste disposed to landfill in these two municipalities, which are home to 25% of the South African population and

Table 13.2 Food waste percentages reported in waste characterisation studies in South Africa

Municipality	% food waste	Comment	Source
City of Cape Town	8	2011 study covering households only	CoCT IWMP, 2015
City of Tshwane		Kitchen waste from households reported as organic fraction	Komen et al., 2016
Nelson Mandela Metropolitan Municipality	33	Random sampling of trucks entering the landfill site.	Pilusa, 2017
Polokwane	31	Includes household and commercial waste	
Ethekwini	31		
Msunduzi	22	Percentage of MSW	McCarthy, 2016
Mbombela	16		
Mangaung	15		
Rustenburg	16		
Mhlatuze	23		
Emfuleni	12		
City of Johannesburg	7	Percentage of household waste	Oelofse, Muswema and Ramukhwatho, 2018
Ekurhuleni Metropolitan Municipality	3		

contribute 34% to the country's GDP, amounts to 76,661 tonnes per annum. Since these two studies are not a representative sample of metropolitan municipalities in South Africa, it is not possible to use these results for extrapolation purposes. It is, however, interesting to note that the food waste component of household waste (excluding garden waste) in these two municipalities was 3% in Ekurhuleni and 7% in Johannesburg (Oelofse et al., 2018) in contrast to the predicted 45% of MSW in 2025 (Adhikari et al., 2006).

Oelofse and Muswema (2018) estimated the food waste from domestic sources in MSW at 2.38 million tonnes per annum in 2011. They have used the food waste generation per income group from Nahman et al. (2012) and applied these to the provincial distribution of the adult population per income group in 2010.

Food waste in informal settlements

Mollatt (2014) investigated food waste flows and food production in Enkanini informal settlement in Stellenbosch using a mixed method approach including transdisciplinary, action research and participatory action research. Food waste collected from participating households was measured as, on average, 9.6 kg per household per week (Mollatt, 2014).

National estimates of food waste and cost

The first attempts to quantify food waste in South Africa beyond MSW were carried out in 2012. Oelofse and Nahman followed a similar approach to that used in the global assessment by Gustavsson et al. (2011), but using the estimated/assumed waste percentages for each commodity group in each step of the food value chain for sub-Saharan Africa and applying this to the South African production figures (Oelofse and Nahman, 2013). The calculated average per annum food waste generation figure for South Africa is reported, as a preliminary finding, at approximately 9.04 million tonnes per annum (Oelofse and Nahman, 2013). The authors caution that this is a highly aggregated result that needs to be verified through primary data collection (Oelofse and Nahman, 2013).

In 2013, Nahman and De Lange estimated the cost of edible food waste along the entire food value chain from agricultural production, post-harvest handling and storage, processing and packaging, distribution (including wholesalers, supermarkets and retailers) and consumption (waste at household level) (Nahman and De Lange, 2013). During their research, the food waste estimates of Oelofse and Nahman (2013) were updated by also accounting for food imports and exports. The new updated estimate of food waste (edible portion) generation in South Africa was 10.2 million tonnes per annum (Nahman and De Lange, 2013). Since the focus of this estimate was on the edible portion of food waste, it can be assumed that this food waste is avoidable. The total cost of the edible portion of food waste throughout the value chain amounts to R61.5 billion per annum (approximately US$7.7 billion at 2013 exchange rates), or 2.1% of the national annual GDP of South Africa (Nahman and De Lange, 2013).

However, there are also costs associated with the inedible portion of food waste, namely opportunity costs that are lost if the waste is not used as input material into other processes, such as composting, bio-energy generation, or the production of animal feed (De Lange and Nahman, 2015). De Lange and Nahman, (2015) therefore developed a methodology for the estimation of opportunity costs associated with the inedible portion of food waste.

A first step in determining the opportunity costs of inedible food waste, was to quantify it. Assuming that 81% of food waste is avoidable (based on Ventour, 2008), De Lange and Nahman (2015) calculated the total food waste in South Africa as 12.6 million tonnes per annum, of which 2.4 million tonnes (19%) are inedible. The full cost of disposing food waste to landfill (including opportunity cost and disposal costs) is estimated as a weighted average cost of R5922 (US$592 at 2015 exchange rates) per tonne. These costs should be compared to the full cost of alternative treatment options to inform decisions regarding waste management options for food waste (De Lange and Nahman, 2015).

Households' food waste behaviour

Research on household food wastage and behaviour in South Africa is limited to a few small studies in the City of Tshwane, the broader Gauteng Province and one in Kimberley in the Northern Cape. Ramukhwatho et al. (2014) reported on a survey covering 50 households in the Mamelodi Township located in the City of Tshwane Metropolitan municipality. The types of food most wasted by the respondents included pap (maize porridge, 58% of respondents), rice (26%) and bread (16%). An electronic survey covering 301 households in the broader City of Tshwane indicated that fruit and vegetables are the most wasted commodities followed by cereals and bread (including pasta, rice cakes and pastries). Dairy products (milk, yoghurt and cheese) were rated in third place followed by meat, poultry, fish and eggs (Oelofse and Marx-Pienaar, 2016). The self-reported wastage (as a percentage of purchase) was more than 30% of fruit and vegetables (31% of respondents), more than 20% of cereals and breads (34% of respondents) and more than 20% of dairy products (27% of respondents) (Oelofse and Marx-Pienaar, 2016).

The finding from the Mamelodi study is interesting from a cultural perspective as the majority of Mamelodi residents are black Africans preparing porridge as a daily staple meal and 90% of respondents indicated that they do not eat fresh fruit and vegetables (Ramukhwatho et al., 2014). An important finding from this study is the ignorance of respondents about their own household's food wastage. At the start of the interviews, 82% of respondents indicated that they did not waste food (Ramukhwatho et al., 2014).

The reported reasons for wasting food are: sell-by date indicated that the product has expired; I was concerned for the health and safety of my family, and I always prepare too much; food residues; and falling for special offers (Ramukhwatho et al., 2014; Oelofse and Marx-Pienaar, 2016). This result suggests that household food waste behaviour may be very similar to that of households in developed countries (Oelofse and Marx-Pienaar, 2016).

Marx-Pienaar and Erasmus (2014) found that bulk packs of fresh produce are preferred by nearly 70% of the 560 respondents. This preference transpired as one of the prominent causes of food waste (Marx-Pienaar and Erasmus, 2014). It is reported that 45% of respondents who purchased smaller quantities did so to avoid unnecessary wastage. Despite planning fresh produce purchases in advance (66.54%), 44.05% of respondents are reported to waste fresh produce due to slow consumption while nearly 40% admitted over purchasing when prices are low. Attractive displays are also identified as temptations that result in over purchasing (33.77%) which in turn increases wastage. This study also reported a general ignorance about sustainable disposal practices for food waste, with less than 25% of respondents recycling food waste through composting (Marx-Pienaar and Erasmus, 2014).

The consumer demand for visually appealing produce results in fresh produce with slight blemishes, but perfectly suitable for use in cooked dishes, to be discarded as waste by retailers (Marx-Pienaar and Erasmus, 2014). The consumer's perceived entitlement to superior quality produce is a critical area of concern that requires intervention if food waste is to be reduced. Another concerning finding by Marx-Pienaar and Erasmus (2014) is that almost

60% of respondents were ignorant about the climate change impacts of food wastage, not realising that food waste also generates greenhouse gases during decomposition.

Ramukhwatho (2016) conducted face-to-face interviews with 210 households in the City of Tshwane from five suburbs targeting different socio-economic groups. Participating households were requested to separate their food waste and weigh it on a weekly basis over a three-week period in order to measure actual food waste generation at household level. On average, respondents wasted 6 kg of food per week. A statistically significant difference was reported between income groups, with low-income households wasting more food than middle-income households and high-income households wasting the least food by weight (Ramukhwatho et al., 2016). Disposal to the municipal bin is the main waste management option used by 83% of respondents, while 14% of respondents feed their food waste to pets and the remaining 3% dispose of their food waste through home composting (Ramukhwatho, 2016).

A study in Kimberley (Cronje et al., 2018) revealed that 30% of respondents plan meals in advance and only 54% of those planning their meals in advance stick to their planning. More than half (52%) of respondents indicated that they bought more food than they need. The reported reasons for buying in excess (in order of importance) are: food was marked down or on special offer (68%); impulsive purchases (15%); incomplete shopping lists (14%); and influenced by a co-shopper (3%). Further findings from this study indicate that 61% of respondents discard excess food, 25% freeze surplus food, 12% donate the food, 1% dispose of the food to home composting, and another 1% store the food in the fridge for consumption on the following day. Only 21% of respondents reported that they use leftover food in additional meals. It is encouraging that 43% of respondents indicated that it bothered them a great deal when food is thrown away. The most wasted food as reported in this study is indicated in Table 13.3 (Cronje et al., 2018).

In a provincial study in the Gauteng Province, covering 1,250 households through an electronic survey, respondents rated their food wastage as more than 20% of their monthly fresh produce purchases (Marx-Pienaar et al., 2016). The reported drivers for food wastage were similar to those reported in the UK (Marx-Pienaar et al., 2016).

Chakona and Shackleton (2017) quantified food waste along a rural–urban continuum in Richards Bay, Dundee and Harrismith. A total of 554 households (183 in Richards Bay, 173 in Dundee and 198 in Harrismith) participated in the study through interviews. The majority of households are reported to eat meals as a family together at home. The findings of this study suggest that more households discard prepared food than uncooked food and drinks, but the quantities of discarded uncooked foods are significantly higher than cooked food. The estimated food waste in this study is reported to be 5–10 kg per person per annum (Chakona and Shackleton, 2017).

Table 13.3 Most wasted food items by households (% respondents) in Kimberley

Fruit	%	Vegetables	%	Other food	%
Bananas	42	Tomatoes	27	Leftovers	34
Apples	20	Potatoes	17	Milk and dairy products	30
Avocado	8	Cabbage	13	Bread	25
Oranges	5	Lettuce	12	Condiments	3
Pears	4%	Carrots	9	Convenience food	3

Source: Adapted from Cronje et al. (2018)

Venter (2017) investigated Gauteng consumers' fresh produce waste practices with a view to determining the reasons for household food wastage. The commodities wasted in order from most to least wasted are vegetables, fruit, bread, dairy products, cakes and pastries, desserts, condiments, cereals, meat, oils, beverages and sweets. The self-reported wastage as a percentage of purchase are summarised in Table 13.4. It should however be noted that the results are not representative of the demographics of the population in Gauteng (Venter, 2017).

The vegetables that are most likely to be wasted, in order from most to least, are reported as green leafy vegetables (spinach, lettuce, salad greens) followed by cucumbers, tomatoes, cabbage (cauliflower, broccoli, kale), peppers, stem and cap vegetables (mushrooms, asparagus), roots, pumpkin, peas and beans, and lastly mielie/sweetcorn on the cob. The fruits that are reportedly most likely to be wasted, in order from most to least, are soft tropical fruits (bananas, papaya, figs, guavas), hard fruit (apples and pears), avocado, melons (spanspek, watermelon), stone fruit (peaches and plums), citrus fruit, pineapple, berries and grapes. (Venter, 2017).

Universities

Food waste composition, alongside student views and behaviours have been measured at three of South Africa's universities: Stellenbosch University (Marais et al., 2017), University of Johannesburg (Sebola et al., 2014) and Rhodes University (Painter et al., 2016).

Food wastage in hospitals

Nemathaga et al. (2008) did a study on waste management practices at two hospitals in the Limpopo Province of South Africa. At the time of measurement, Tshilindzini hospital had 450 admitted patients and Elim hospital 250. The leftover food recorded at the two facilities were 70 and 48 kg/day, respectively (Nemathaga et al., 2008). This equates to 0.192 and 0.156 kg/patient per day. The reported waste management practice for leftover food is reuse or recycling, but no further detail is provided.

Table 13.4 Self-reported food waste as a percentage of purchase (N = 1,154)

Food category	% of purchase that is wasted
Vegetables	21.10
Fruit	20.14
Bread	19.22
Dairy	14.22
Cakes and pastries	13.70
Desserts	12.64
Condiments	10.55
Cereals	10.24
Meat	9.58
Oils	8.93
Beverages	8.23
Sweets	7.80

Source: Adapted from Venter (2017)

Food waste management in the hospitality sector

Mabaso (2017) conducted research on the current status of food waste management in the hospitality sector with a specific focus on an international hotel group. The research objectives covered the food waste behaviour and perceptions of hotel staff linked to food waste, and an analysis of the food waste management practices. Food waste production was measured over a six-week period. Plate waste was identified as the most common food waste, followed by production waste and serving waste. The buffet service style was identified as the service style creating the most food waste, followed by staff meals, functions, à la carte, and the hotel room service.

Marx-Pienaar et al. (2018) found that production, distribution and packaging, specifically secondary packaging used in distribution, in the quick service restaurant supply chain in South Africa warrants attention to reduce food waste. The specific concern regarding the secondary packaging is that even good quality secondary packaging does not provide the required protection to the food products, especially bakery products, during transport and distribution.

Biomass waste from food production

Oelofse and Muswema (2018) estimated the waste biomass from food processing for a number of commodities as summarised in Table 13.5. The assumptions used in the calculations were sourced from international literature and applied to available statistics on production and processing of the different commodities (Oelofse and Muswema 2018).

Environmental footprint of food waste

Mekonnen and Hoekstra determined the South African water footprint, and agriculture contributed 76% of the total footprint (Mekonnen and Hoekstra, 2011). In 2014, Oelofse calculated the water footprint of food waste (excluding fish) in South Africa using the food waste estimate of Nahman and De Lange (2013). The calculated water footprint of food waste is in the order of 12,854 Mm^3 or the equivalent of nearly 22% of the total water footprint of agricultural production in South Africa (Oelofse, 2014).

Notten et al. (2014) estimated a ballpark figure of R1 billion per year for the cost of embedded energy wasted when food is discarded. The magnitude of this wasted energy is estimated to

Table 13.5 Summary of waste biomass from food processing identified in South Africa

Source	Assumptions	Tonnes (2012/13)
Malting barley	14 to 20 kg of spent grain is produced per hectolitre of beer	584,125 to 607,490
Deciduous fruit	40% of input by weight – juice production 17.5% of input by weight – processing for preservation	184,290
Subtropical fruit	17.5% of input by weight – processing for preservation	22,980
Citrus fruit	Peels (50% of wet juiced fruit)	224,182
Vegetables (excl. potatoes)	17.5% of input by weight – processing	32,278
Potatoes	90 kg per tonne of input (56% of this is potato skins, 33% starch and 11% inert material)	33,427

Source: Adapted from Oelofse and Muswema (2018)

be enough to power the City of Johannesburg for 16 years. Fruit and vegetables account for 44% of the food waste but only 15% of the cost of wasted energy. The water (ground and surface water) used to produce food that is not consumed is estimated as 1.7 km^3 (Notten et al., 2014). This is equivalent to about 20% of the total water abstraction in South Africa at a cost of R260 million, with fruit and vegetables accounting for the largest portion. Food wastage therefore comes at a very high cost when considering the cost of energy, water and waste disposal. In addition, disposal of food waste to landfill adds opportunity cost that is lost when the valuable resources (energy, enzymes, etc.) locked in food waste are not utilised (Notten et al., 2014).

Governance issues

Harduth (2017) identified the need for legal protection for donors of surplus food in South Africa. She argues that surplus food is wasted due to potential donors' fear that they may be held liable if the donated food caused harm to beneficiaries of the donated food. It is therefore proposed that South African legislation, in line with international best practice as seen in Panama, Canada, France, Italy and the United States of America, should be developed to support and encourage surplus food donations while providing the requisite protection to the donors.

Food waste within Saudi Arabia

Research on food loss and waste (FLW) in the Arab world is scant and there is a dearth of reliable data, particularly on their magnitude, causes, sources, drivers and management, as well as the policies, interventions and initiatives directed at reducing them. This information is vital, especially in a region where reducing FLW is imperative for a sustainable food system and key for the region's food security. Three recent review papers, one by Abiad and Meho (2018) and two by Baig et al. (2018a, 2018b), have attempted to fill this literature gap. This lack of data and research is carried through to the Saudi Arabian context, with Abiad and Meho (2018) only finding four studies that examine food waste generated by different sectors in Saudi Arabia (see Table 13.6). This section summarises recent reviews as well as new developments.

The investigation made by Abiad and Meho (2018) shows interesting trends in food wastage and suggests areas of interest to be further elucidated. For example, significant waste is generated during social and religious occasions in Saudi Arabia, especially during the fasting month of Ramadan (Elmenofi et al., 2015). In that holy month, food waste is the highest in Saudi Arabia and other Gulf Cooperation Council countries (Etaam-Saudi Food Bank, 2012; CIHEAM and FAO, 2016). Furthermore, during Ramadan, 30–50% of the food prepared in Saudi Arabia is thrown away (Al-Fawaz, 2015).

The increase in food waste during Ramadan is attributed to the preparation of extravagant meals that far exceed the needs of families, and leftovers are thrown away (Zayat, 2017), although such acts do not conform with the teachings of Islam, where Muslims are asked to share excess food with the poor.

In fact, Islam prohibits wastage in every aspect of one's life, whether it is in time, energy or food, as clarified in the following verses of the Holy Quran:

> It is He Who has brought into being gardens, the cultivated and the wild, and date-palms, and fields with produce of all kinds, and olives and pomegranates, similar (in kind) and variegated. Eat of their fruit in season, but give (the poor) their due on harvest day. And do not waste, for God does not love the wasteful.
>
> *(Quran 6:141)*

Table 13.6 Published scientific research on
food waste and loss distributed across the Arab
countries

Country	Number of studies
Iraq	9
Saudi Arabia	4
Egypt	3
Lebanon	2
Morocco	2
UAE	2
Algeria	1
Jordon	1
Kuwait	1
Oman	1
Palestine	1
Tunisia	1

Source: Adapted from Abiad and Meho (2018)

O you who believe! Do not make unlawful the wholesome things which God has made
lawful for you, but commit no excess for God does not love those given to excess.

(Quran 5:87)

During social events, such as weddings, births and deaths, food is usually prepared on a large scale,
in many cases turning into lavish shows flaunting wealth and social status (Baig et al., 2018a,
2018b). For example, food wasted at an average wedding in Mecca, Saudi Arabia, can be sufficient
to feed 250 hungry people. In 2016, the amount of food wasted in Makkah was enough to feed
millions going hungry globally (Arab News, 2016). However, there is no available data on the
amount of food waste generated during such occasions across the Arab world.

The population of Saudi Arabia is expected to reach 34.4 million by 2020. Scarce arable
land and limited and diminishing natural water resources limit Riyadh's ability to meet
demand through domestic production; increasing food imports and expanding the development of alternative water resources will therefore prove critical in ensuring the country's
long-term food and water sustainability and security (Baig et al., 2018b).

With the generation of heavy oil revenues in the kingdom, rising per capita domestic
incomes and globalisation have changed Saudis' dietary patterns. A "nutrition transition" has
emerged associated with changes in diet and lifestyle; Saudis have transitioned to the consumption of more energy-dense diets. Wheat, rice, yoghurt and chicken are staple items for
Saudis, yet many are opting for a more diversified diet with greater Western influence.
Changes in lifestyle and Western-style diets are causing growing obesity issues, with 33.7%
of the adult population considered obese in 2014.

In Saudi Arabia, lack of awareness, insufficient and inappropriate planning when shopping, attitudes of young toward food, cultural norms and high income levels are the principal factors responsible for food waste (Baig et al., 2018a, 2018b).

According to a report by the country's Ministry of Environment, Water and Agriculture
(2016), Saudi citizens waste 30% of their food (around 8.3 million tons of food annually)
causing the loss of over SR49 billion annually to the national economy (*Dhaka Tribune*,

2018). Abdulfatah (2018) reports that, unfortunately, offering excessive amounts of food to guests at dinner parties is becoming a social custom, and the leftovers end up in landfills. The guests leave a significant volume of food as leftovers at dinner parties, weddings, restaurants and hotel buffets, making the kingdom number one in the world for wasting food (Baig et al., 2018a, 2018b). An average Saudi wastes 250 kg of food annually compared to the global average of 115 kg. Similarly, Saudi Arabia has the highest consumption of grains in the world, with the average citizen consuming 158 kg annually compared to the global average of 145 kg per person. Around 33.5 million people live in Saudi Arabia (Worldometers, 2018); with an average wastage of 250 kg per head, the country wastes about 8.3 million tonnes of food every year. "It's mainly due to low awareness in appreciating food, although it is embedded in our religious values."

Food waste policy

Though, at the moment, no policy exists to address the issue of food waste, several proposals have been made and are under consideration by the government and numerous initiatives have been taken in this direction. According to Abiad and Meho (2018), an action plan to reduce food losses and waste in the Kingdom of Saudi Arabia was launched in 2014. FAO has also been asked to help combat the issue.

Currently, there is no law in place that could implement fines and penalties to the food wasters at eating places (*DhakaTribune*, 2018). However, the Saudi government is considering framing laws to combat the thoughtless issue of food waste. The law would comprise penalties on individuals and organisations with regard to food waste, such as enforcing a fee on those leaving unfinished plates at the restaurant (*DhakaTribune*, 2018). Some private organisations, such as the Saudi Grains Organization (SAGO), plans to help in preparing a legislative framework to implement rules regarding wastage (*Saudi Gazette*, 2018). Saudi Arabia's Shoura Council (the apex body that runs the country) has been discussing potential legislation that will see the implementation of fines on individuals and businesses involved in wasting food. The law would primarily address the issues of food wastage in Saudi Arabia, which causes a loss of nearly $35 million in the form of food every day. Shoura Council members want to frame a law to fine organisations serving food in public and private places 38% of the total bill per serving as a punishment should they waste food (Al-Arabia, 2017). Additionally, the proposed legislation looks to impose a fine of three percent of the total bill on individuals and companies who organise private or public events without the proper licence to do so.

Other food waste reduction actions

Other initiatives taken to minimise food waste in Saudi Arabia include those in the wider food industry and the restaurant and hospitality sector.

A food bank under the name of It'aam, the Arabic word for "feeding", was established in 2010 to help feed the underprivileged by distributing excess food from hotels, banquets and wedding parties. It offers a service at 48-hours notice to individuals and organisations by either collecting leftovers in meal boxes in a hygienic manner or recycling food. It is estimated that this programme saves nearly 9,000 meals per day (6 million meals a year). In 2017, approximately 49 tons of leftover food (i.e., 144,000 meals) were collected from one site.

The General Sports Authority, represented by the Saudi Community Sports Union (SCSU), signed an agreement with the Saudi Food Bank at the authority's headquarters in Riyadh. The agreement aims to promote the conservation of food and the avoidance of food waste through the activities and programmes of the SCSU (Arab News, 2018a). The agreement also includes training for those participating in the Grace Conservation programme, in addition to teaching them the basics of food conservation and delivery. The signatories also agreed to launch a food conservation prize, in the name of the SCSU and the It'aam Association for Grace Conservation, which will target more than 100 hotels and restaurants in the kingdom (Arab News, 2018b).

Other restaurant and hospitality operators have engaged their own policies and programmes. Al-Bugamy (2015) reported that Jeddah municipality had obliged all restaurants and ceremony services to contract with the charity organisations for food distributions in order to redistribute the leftovers to the poor and needy. The municipality of Jeddah has also placed 900 containers as the second initiative for food leftovers throughout the city to preserve the blessing of food (Arab News, 2018b).

Table 13.7 Overview of identified estimates of amounts of wasted food in Saudi Arabia. National kg/capita/year estimates are highlighted in bold.

Source	Estimate	Data source for estimate
UN FAO	**21 kg/cap/year** (FLW, North Africa, West & Central Asia)	Literature search, information from local FAO offices/universities; assumptions, estimates based on comparable places/commodities/supply chain stages
COMCEC	**119 kg/cap/yr (household)** 733 kg/establishment/year (food service)	Self-report survey of 111 consumers, 94 food service establishments in Riyadh
Saudi General Authority for Statistics	14,220,000 metric tonnes household solid waste/year (equivalent to 458.5 kg/cap/year household solid waste. If this is 36% food, then waste of food = **165.1 kg/cap/year**)	
Tolba and Saab, 2008	1.5 kg/cap/day solid waste (equivalent to 547.5 kg/cap/year solid waste. If this is 36% food, then waste of food = **197.1 kg/cap/year**)	Solid waste analysis in cities such as Riyadh, Doha and Abu Dhabi
Khan and Kaneesamkandi, 2013	5.5 million tonnes/year	Solid waste experts estimate based on idea that KSA solid waste may be 36% food
Undersecretary of Saudi Arabia Ministry for Municipal and Rural Affairs	28% of Saudi waste is food 1.2–1.4 kg food waste/person/day **511 kg/capita/year**	Solid waste data
Saudi Ministry of Agriculture, unverified	**250 kg/cap/year**	NA
Eta'am (Food Bank) Director, 2016	33% (1/3) of cooked food	NA
Barilla	**427 kg/cap/yr**	Estimate from Eta'am (food bank) director
Fadal Al-Buainain, 2015	Over 50% of food wasted Over 70% of food from public events wasted	NA

Source: Baig et al. (2018b)

Many individuals are not used to filling their plate with reasonable portions (*Saudi Gazette*, 2018) so in order to minimise food waste the restaurants have started using small portions. The press have reported that this action has been taken one step further by some restaurant owners, with the establishment of a rule that people who leave food on their plates will be charged extra for wasting food (*Saudi Gazette*, 2018). The possibility of taking home a parcel made of the leftover food (i.e. a "doggy bag") is also becoming more commonplace.

Measurement of food loss and waste

Estimates of wasted food in Saudi Arabia are listed in Table 13.7. A local university in partnership with SAGO have undertaken a pilot project to reduce food waste and measure the levels of food waste in society. In order to quantify and identify the major food waster groups, the initiative was implemented in five phases. The first phase of the project was to carry out a field study to measure the levels of food waste in society in 27 cities (*Saudi Gazette*, 2018). The project involved stakeholder engagement activities from various organisations: Food and Agriculture Organization and World Resources Institute, and private companies. The initiative aims at reducing food waste, especially of wheat, rice, dates, fruits, vegetables and red and white meat. The study aims to determine the volume of food waste and measure the economic losses resulting from it. The study aims to focus on the economic, social and cultural aspects of food waste in the kingdom and will apply behavioural economics methods to curb this practice and educate the public about the best practices to minimise waste (*Saudi Gazette*, 2018). The study will also determine the food waste baseline in the kingdom and that will enable the researchers to make comparisons with the other countries in the region and around the world. The study will help the team build KPIs to measure the level of food waste up to 2020 (*Saudi Gazette*, 2018).

Note

1 Note that the US$ equivalents in these early papers were based on an exchange rate at that time of around R8 to the $. The rate now (October 2019) is closer to R14 to the $.

References

Abdulfatah, Eman (2018). Saudi Arabia ranks number one in food waste. Abdulfatah was quoted in the article written by Layan Damanhouri, published by The Daily Saudi Gazette : Available at: http://live. saudigazette.com.sa/article/536700/SAUDI-ARABIA/Saudi-Arabia-ranks-number-one-in-food-waste

Abiad, M. G. and Meho, L. I. 2018. Food loss and food waste research in the Arab world: A systematic review. *Food Security*, 1–12. doi: 10.1007/s12571-018-0782-7.

Adhikari, B.K., Barrington, S., and Martinez, J. 2006. Predicted growth of world urban food waste and methane production. *Waste Management and Research*, 24: 421–433. doi: 10.1177/0734242X06067767.

Al-Arabyia 2017. Saudi Shoura discusses law addressing food waste issue. Article appeared in Al Arabiya English Saturday, 14 January 2017 Available at: http://english.alarabiya.net/en/News/gulf/2017/01/14/ Saudi-Shoura-Council-discusses-law-addressing-food-waste-issue.html (accessed on 14 December 2019).

Al-Buainain, Fadal, 2015. Need to reduce food waste: Experts. Monday 23 March 2015. Available at: http://www.arabnews.com/saudi-arabia/news/722026 (accessed on 14 December 2019).

Al-Bugamy, Mohamed, 2015. 900 food waste containers in Jeddah. Available at: http://saudigazette. com.sa/saudi-arabia/900-food-waste-containers-in-jeddah/ (accessed on 14 December 2019).

Al-Fawaz, Nadia, 2015. Need to reduce food waste: Experts. Monday 23 March 2015. Available at: www.arabnews.com/saudi-arabia/news/722026 (accessed on 14 December 2019).

Arab News (2016). Food wasted in Makkah enough to feed millions going hungry globally. Article published on Jan 23, 2016. Available at: https://www.arabnews.com/saudi-arabia/news/869206 (accessed on 14 December 2019).

Arab News (2018a). Deal signed to reduce food waste in Saudi Arabia. Article appeared on July 13, 2018. Available at: https://www.arabnews.com/node/1338481/saudi-arabia (accessed on 14 December 2019).

Arab News 2018b . Waste not, want not: Import-reliant NENA region seeks solutions to consumption and storage issues. Kingdom's consultative Shoura Council is looking into a food waste law that could see individuals and organizations fined for excessive waste. Article written by CALINE MALEK, appeared in Arab News on October 16, 2018. Available at: https://www.arabnews.com/node/1388421/food-health (accessed on 14 December 2019).

Baig, M. B., Al-Zahrani, K. H., Schneider, F., Straquadine, G. S., and Mourad, M. 2018a. Food waste posing a serious threat to sustainability in the kingdom of Saudi Arabia—a systematic review. *Saudi Journal of Biological Sciences*, doi: 10.1016/j.sjbs.2018.06.004.

Baig, M.B., Gorski, I., and Neff, R.A. 2018b. Understanding and addressing waste of food in the kingdom of Saudi Arabia. *Saudi Journal of Biological Sciences*, doi: 10.1016/j.jbs.2018.08.030. Available online 1 September 2018 at: https://www.sciencedirect.com/science/article/pii/S1319562X1830216Xhttps://doi.org/10.1016/j.sjbs.2018.08.030 (accessed on 14 December 2019).

Bakari, S. 2017. "Why is South Africa still a developing country?" MPRA Paper 80763, University Library of Munich, Germany. https://mpra.ub.uni-muenchen.de/80763/1/MPRA_paper_80763.pdf (accessed on 7 Nov 2018).

Chakona, G. and Shackleton, C. M. 2017. Local setting influences the quantity of household food waste in mid-sized South African towns. *PLoS ONE*, 12(12): e0189407. doi: 10.1371/journal.pone.0189407.

CIHEAM, & FAO (2016). Mediterra 2016. Zero Waste in the mediterranean. Natural resources, food and knowledge. International centre for advanced mediterranean Agronomic studies and food and agriculture organization of the United Nations. Paris: Presses de Sciences Po.

CoCT (City of Cape Town). 2015. 3rd Generation integrated waste management plan. City of Cape Town. http://resource.capetown.gov.za/documentcentre/Documents/City%20strategies%2C%20plans%20and%20frameworks/Integrated%20Waste%20Management%20Plan.pdf (accessed on 14 October 2019).

Cronje, N., van der Merwe, I., and Müller, I-M. 2018. Household food waste: A case study in Kimberley, South Africa. *Journal of Consumer Sciences*, 46: 9 pages.

Crush, J. and Frayne, B. 2011. Supermarket expansion and the informal food economy in Southern African cities: Implications for urban food security. *Journal of Southern African Studies*, 37(4): 781–807. doi: 10.1080/03057070.2011.617532.

DAFF (Department of Agriculture, Forestry and Fisheries). 2017. Trends in the Agricultural Sector, 2017. Department of agriculture, forestry and fisheries, Pretoria, South Africa. www.daff.gov.za/Daffweb3/Portals/0/Statistics%20and%20Economic%20Analysis/Statistical%20Information/Trends%20in%20the%20Agricultural%20Sector%202017.pdf (accessed on 7 Nov 2018).

De Lange, W. and Nahman, A. 2015. Costs of food waste in South Africa: Incorporating inedible food waste. *Waste Management*, 40: 167–172.

DhakaTribune. 2018. Saudi Arabia Number One in Wasting Food Worldwide. An Article Published on June 12th, 2018. Available at: www.dhakatribune.com/world/2018/06/12/saudi-arabia-number-one-in-wasting-food-worldwide (accessed on 14 December 2019).

Elmenofi, A. G. G., Capone, R., Waked, S., Debs, P., Bottalico, F., and El Bilali, H. 2015. Anexploratory survey on household food wastein Egypt. Book of Proceedings of the VIInternational Scientific Agriculture Symposium"Agrosym 2015"; 15-18 October, 2015; Jahorina,Bosnia and Herzegovina. ISBN 978-99976-632-2-1. pp. 1298-1304. doi: 10.7251/ AGSY15051298E.

Etaam-Saudi Food Bank. 2012. http://saudifoodbank.com (accessed May 15, 2017).

FAO. 2014. *Food Wastage Footprint Full-Cost Accounting* (pp.1-98). Rome: FAO.

Gustavsson, J., Cederberg, C., Sonneson, U., van Otterdijk, R., and Meybeck, A. 2011. Global Food Losses and Food Waste: Extent, Causes and Prevention. Study conducted for the International Congress SAVE FOOD! At Interpack 2011, Düsseldorf, Germany. Rome: Food and Agriculture Organisation of the United Nations. www.fao.org/docrep/014/mb060e/mb060e00.pdf (accessed on 14 December 2019).

Gustavsson, J., Cederberg, C., Sonesson, U. 2013. The methodology of the FAO study: "Global food losses and food waste – Extent, causes and prevention" – FAO, 2011. SIK report No 857, January 2013

Hall, R. and Cousins, B. 2015. Commercial Farming and Agribusiness in South Africa and Their Changing Roles in Africa's Agro-food System. International Conference: Rural transformations and food systems: The BRICS and agrarian change in the global south 20-21 April 2015.

Harduth, N. 2017. *Legislation Discussion Paper: Food Donations as a Mechanism to Limit Food Waste, Food Insecurity and Malnutrition*. Unpublished.

Hayes, C. N. A. 2011. *Organic Waste Recovery: What Motivates Suppliers in the Woolworths Food Supply Chain? Dissertation Submitted in Partial Fulfilment of the Masters of Business Administration Degree.* Cape Town: University of Cape Town. http://gsblibrary.uct.ac.za/researchreports/2011/Hayes.pdf (accessed on 14 October 2019).

Hoornweg, D. and Bhada-Tata, P. 2012. *What A Waste: A Global Review of Solid Waste Management,* Washington, DC: Urban Development Series knowledge papers, World Bank.

Khan, Muhammad Sadiq Munfath., Zakariya Kaneesamkandi (2013). Biodegradable waste to biogas: renewable energy option for the Kingdom of Saudi Arabia. Internaltional Journal of Innovation Applied Studies. 4(1), 101–113. Available at: www.ijias.issr-journals.org/abstract.php?article=IJIAS-13-142-18 (accessed on 14 December 2019).

Komen, K., Mrembu, N., and van Niekerk, M.A. 2016. the role of socio-economic factors, seasonality and geographic differences on household waste generation and composition in the City of Tshwane. In: Proceedings of the 23rd WasteCon Conference, 17-21 October 2016. Emperor's Palace, Johannesburg, South Africa.

Le Roux, B., van der Laan, M., Vahrmeijer T., Annandale, J. G., and Bristow, K. L. 2017. Water footprints of vegetable crop wastage along the supply chain in Gauteng, South Africa. *Water*, 10(539): 1–15. doi: 10.3390/w10050539.

Mabaso, C. H., 2017. Food Waste Management within a Hotel Group in Gauteng. Master of Tourism and Hospitality Management. Unpublished: University of Johannesburg. Retrieved from: https://ujcontent.uj.ac.za/vital/access/manager/Repository/uj:28905/SOURCE1 (accessed on 4 January 2019).

Marais, M. L., Smit, Y., Koen, N., and Lötze, E. 2017. Are the attitudes and practices of foodservice managers, catering personnel and students contributing to excessive food wastage at Stellenbosch University?. *South African Journal of Clinical Nutrition*, 30(3): 60–67. doi: 10.1080/16070658.2017.1267348.

Marx-Pienaar, N., Du Rand, G., Viljoen, A., and Fisher, H. 2018. Food Wastage, a Concern across the South Afircan Quick Service Restaurant Supply Chain. WIT Transactions on Ecology and the Environment Vol 231. ISSN 1743-3541.

Marx-Pienaar, N. J., and Erasmus, A. C. 2014. Status consciousness and knowledge as potential impediments of households' sustainable consumption practices of fresh produce amidst times of climate change. *International Journal of Consumer Studies*, 38(4): 419–426. doi: 10.1111/ijcs.12111.

Mashau, M. E., Moyane, J. N., and Jideani, I. A. 2012. Assessment of post-harvest losses of fruits at Tshakhuma fruit market in Limpopo Province, South Africa. *African Journal of Agricultural Research*, 7(29): 4145–4150. doi: 10.5897/AJAR12.392.

McCarthy, B. 2016. The Diversion of Municipal Solid Waste Away from Landfills in 6 South African Municipalities. Waste Analysis and Composition Survey. GIZ project 81188961.

Mekonnen, M. M., and Hoekstra, A. Y., 2011. *National Water Footprint Accounts: The Green, Blue and Grey Water Footprint of Production and Consumption.* Value of Water Research Report Series No 50. UNESCO-IHE, Delft, The Netherlands.

Mollatt, M. C., 2014. Ecological Food Sense: Connections between Food Waste Flows and Food Production in Enkanini Informal Settlement, Stellenbosch. Master of Philosophy in Sustainable Development. Unpublished: University of Stellenbosch. Retrieved from: http://scholar.sun.ac.za/handle/10019.1/86550 (accessed on 8 January 2019).

Munhuweyi, K., 2012. Postharvest Losses and Changes in Quality of Vegetables from Retail to Consumer: A Case Study of Tomato, Cabbage and Carrot. Master of Science in food science. Unpublished: University of Stellenbosch. Retrieved from: https://scholar.sun.ac.za/bitstream/handle/10019.1/71946/munhuweyi_postharvest_2012.pdf?sequence=1&isAllowed=y (accessed on 7 January 2019).

Nahman, A., and De Lange, W. 2013. Cost of food waste along the value chain: Evidence form South Africa. *Waste Management*, 33: 2493–2500. doi: 10.1016/j.wasman.2013.07.012.

Nahman, A., De Lange, W., Oelofse, S., and Godfrey, L. 2012. The Costs of household food waste in South Africa. *Waste Management*, 32: 2147–2153. doi: 10.1016/j.wasman.2012.04.012.

Nemathaga, F., Maringa, S., and Chimuka, L. 2008. Hospital solid waste management practices in Limpopo Province, South Africa: A case study of two hospitals. *Waste Management*, 28: 1236–1245.

Marx-Pienaar, NJMM, Du Rand GE, van der Spuy E, Viljoen AT, and Oelofse SHH. 2016. Food Wastage: A Preliminary Study Amongst Gauteng Households in South Africa. In: Proceedings of SAAFECS 2016, Pretoria, 22-26 February 2016.

Notten, P., Bole-Rentel, T., and Rambaran, N., 2014. *Developing an Understanding of the Energy Implications of Wasted Food and Waste Disposal.* Understanding the Food Energy Water Nexus. WWF-SA,

South Africa. Available at: http://tgh.co.za/wp-content/uploads/2017/10/developing_an_ understanding_of_the_energy_implications_of_wasted_food.pdf (accessed on 10 January 2019).

Oelofse, S. 2014. Chapter 8: Food waste in South Africa: Understanding the magnitude, water footprint and cost, in Macfarlane Seth. (Ed), *The Vision Zero Waste Handbook, South Africa Volume 4.* 62–69 The essential guide to resource efficiency in South Africa. Alive2Green. ISBN 978-0-620-45067-6.

Oelofse, S., Muswema, A., and Ramukhwatho, F. 2018. Household food waste disposal in South Africa: A case of johannesburg and ekurhuleni. *South African Journal of Science*, 114(5/6): 6 pages. doi: 10.17159/sajs.2018/20170284.

Oelofse, SHH. and Marx-Pienaar, N. (2016) Household Food Wastage – A Case Study of Middle to High Income Urban Households in the City of Tshwane. In: *Proceedings of WasteCon 2016*. Emperor's Palace, johannesburg, South Africa, 17–21 October 2016. http://researchspace.csir.co.za/dspace/ handle/10204/8969 (accessed on 14 December 2019).

Oelofse, S. H. H., and Muswema, A. P. 2018. Overview of potential sources and volumes of waste biomass in South Africa, in L. Godfrey, J. F Görgens and H. Roman. (eds), *Opportunities for Biomass and Organic Waste Valorisation: Finding Alternative Solutions to Disposal in South Africa*, Pretoria: UNISA Press, 1–14.

Oelofse, S. H. H., and Nahman, A. 2013. Estimating the magnitude of food waste generated in South Africa. *Waste Management and Research*, 31(1): 80–86. doi: 10.1177/0734242X12457117.

Painter K., Thondhlana G., and Kua H. W., 2016. Food waste generation and potential interventions at Rhodes University, South Africa. *Waste Management*, 56: 491–497. doi: 10.1016/j.wasman.2016.07.013.

Pilusa, J. 2018. Estimation of the Volumes and Percentages of Absorbent Hygiene Products in South African Municipal Solid Waste (mini Waste Characterisation Report) 2017. Commissioned by the CSIR.

Ramukhwatho, F. R. 2016. An Assessment of the Household Food Waste in A Developing Country: A Case Study of Five Areas in the City of Tshwane Metropolitan Municipality, Gauteng Province, South Africa. Master of Science in Environmental Management. Unpublished: University of South Africa. Retrieved from: http://uir.unisa.ac.za/bitstream/handle/10500/21162/dissertation_ramukh watho_fr.pdf?sequence=4&isAllowed=y (accessed on 7 January 2019).

Ramukhwatho FR, Du Plessis, R and Oelofse S (2014) Household food wastage in a developing country: A case study of Mamelodi Township in South Africa. In: *Proceedings of WasteCon 2014*. Somerset West, 6–10 October 2014

Ramukhwatho, F.R., Du Plessis, R., and Oelofse, S. 2016. Household Food Wastage by Income Level: A Case Study of Five Areas in the City of Tshwane Metropolitan Municipality, Gauteng Province, South Africa. In: Proceedings of the 23rd WasteCon Conference. Emperor's Palace, 17-21 October 2016.

Saudi Gazette. (2018). National initiative to reduce food waste launched. February 19, 2018; Available at: http://saudigazette.com.sa/article/528769/SAUDI-ARABIA/National-initiative-to-reduce-food-waste-launched (accessed on 14 December 2019).

Sebola, R., Mokgatle, L., Aboyade, A., and Muzenda, E. 2014. Solid waste quantification for the university of johannesburg's waste to energy project. *International Journal of Research in Chemical, Metallurgical and Civil Engineering*, 1(1): 84–88. doi: 10.15242/IJRCMCE.E1113551.

Tolba, M. K., and Saab N. (eds). 2008. Arab environment: Future challenges. Arab Forum for Environment and Development. ISBN: 9953-437- 24-6.

Venter, N. R 2017. Consumer's Knowledge of Date Labelling and the Influence Thereof on Household Fresh Produce Waste Practices in Gauteng. Masters in Consumer Science (general). Unpublished: University of Pretoria. Retrieved from: https://repository.up.ac.za/handle/2263/65953 (accessed on 10 January 2019).

Ventour, L. 2008. The Food We Waste. Waste and Resource Action Programme (WRAP) and Exodus Market Research. ISBN 1-84405-383-0. www.lefigaro.fr/assets/pdf/Etude%20gaspillage%20alimen taire%20UK2008.pdf.

World Bank. 2011. *Missing Food: The Case of Postharvest Losses in sub-Saharan Africa* (116). Washington, D.C: The World Bank. https://siteresources.worldbank.org/INTARD/Resources/MissingFoods10_web.pdf (accessed on 14 December 2019).

Worldometers. 2018. Saudi Arabia Population. Available at: www.worldometers.info/world-population/ saudi-arabia-population (accessed on 14 December 2019).

Zayat, I. (2017). Arab countries face problem of food waste during Ramadan. An article appeared in "The Arab Weekly" on 04/06/2017. Available on https://thearabweekly.com/arab-countries-face-problem-food-waste-during-ramadan (accessed on 14 December 2019).

14

FOOD WASTE IN AUSTRALIA AND NEW ZEALAND

Miranda Mirosa, David Pearson and Christian Reynolds

Introduction

Australia and New Zealand have two of the highest per capita food waste generation rates of any developed countries. This chapter reviews existing research into food waste in Australia and New Zealand; examines the history and development of food waste policy in Australia and New Zealand; discusses drivers and composition of food waste in New Zealand, and their economic and social impacts, and suggests some potential interventions including voluntary agreements and valorisation.

Food waste in Australia

Food waste has long been a background issue for Australian citizens and government; in the last decade however, it has gained prominence. Examples of this increased attention include separate food waste collections becoming standard in many local area councils (Zero Waste SA, 2005); food rescue organisations expanding their activity (Reynolds et al., 2015b); the FOODWISE campaign (Do Something, 2013); and the Australian Broadcasting Corporation's production of two seasons of Craig Reucassel's *War On Waste* (2017 Season 1, and 2019 Season 2; www.abc.net.au/tv/programs/war-on-waste/). The remainder of this section will review the existing research and quantification of Australian food waste, and then report on recent federal policy developments.

Research and quantification

There is a history of broader waste and discards research in Australia with Hawkins (2006, 2007, 2012) publishing her foundational book on waste and ethics in 2007. Also in 2007, Edwards and Mercer (2007, 2012) published on the nascent Australian gleaning movement, examining how this youth subculture engages and reinterprets the ethics of food waste.

However, specific academic exploration and research concerning the food waste only developed after the publication of the 2009 report by The Australia Institute (Baker et al., 2009) that quantified the cost of Australia's food wastage at approximately $5.2 billion dollars a year. Adding to the interest in food waste was the *Food Waste Avoidance Benchmark Study* (NSW Environment Protection Authority, 2009). This estimated that NSW households spent approximately $2.5 billion on food that was not consumed. This evidence base was further bolstered in 2011 by the National Food Waste Assessment (Mason et al., 2011), which collated multiple waste data sources to calculate that 7.5 million tonnes of food waste was generated in 2008–2009 – the landfilling of this volume of waste generating 6.8 million tonnes of CO_2-e.

In response to a research need demonstrated by a 2009 report from the Australian Institute, the Australian Research Council funded "Zeroing in on food waste: Measuring, understanding and reducing food waste", a Linkage Project between Central Queensland University, University of South Australia and Flinders University from 2009–2013. This interdisciplinary research project engaged with food waste on many fronts. It quantified tonnages of food waste at the national level as well as economic and environmental costs of food waste in Australia (Reutter et al., 2017a; Reynolds et al., 2014a, 2014b, 2015a, 2015b, 2015c). Reynolds et al. estimated that in 2008, 7.3 million tonnes of food waste were generated in Australia, making food waste the second largest category of waste generated. Australian households formally disposed of 9 kilograms of food waste per house, per week in 2008. Households generated 56% of food waste. The service sectors produced 20%, manufacturing sectors 10%, and the agricultural sectors 7%. Using Input-Output analysis, it was determined that every tonne of waste sent to landfill created economic activity worth $2.53, whereas every tonne of waste composted creates economic activity worth $47.37. Reynolds et al. (2014a) also estimated that an additional 1.45 million tonnes of food waste per year (26% of total household food waste generated) were disposed of by informal routes such as home composting, feeding to animals, disposing via the sewer, donating to charity, or illegally dumping. This equates to an additional weekly average of 3.21 kilograms of food waste through informal methods.

The economic and environmental impacts of food rescue operations (Reynolds et al., 2015b), feeding food scraps to pets (Thompson et al., 2015), shifting to anaerobic digestion waste treatment methods (Zaman and Reynolds, 2015) and shifting to sustainable diets (Reynolds et al., 2015b, 2015c; Reynolds, 2016) to reduce food waste were all examined. The estimated impact of food rescue operations is notable with 18,105 tonnes of food waste rescued in 2008, generating approximately 6 kilograms of food waste per tonne of food rescued, at a cost of US$222 per tonne of food rescued. It was also calculated that for every US dollar spent on food rescue, edible food to the value of US$5.71 (1,863 calories) was rescued (Reynolds et al., 2015b).

As discussed in Reynolds et al. (2015b), in Australia there are four main food rescue organisations: Foodbank, Secondbite, Fareshare and OzHarvest. These food rescue organisations operate predominantly throughout the Eastern states and South Australia, but some have now expanded Australia-wide. These charities collect food "waste" that is still fit for consumption but is either close to becoming inedible (retail food that will soon reach its use-by date, and thus cannot be sold) or is surplus to requirements (food left unserved at the end of a banquet or event). Though each charity operates in its own unique manner (i.e. there are differences in the foods each operation rescues, and how it distributes this food onward), some operation generalisations are possible. The main industry sectors to donate food waste to charities are service (hospitality and events) and manufacturing. Charities receive the donated foodstuffs, transform the food into meals or food parcels and then supply these directly or through a secondary charity, non-government, or religious organisation. The recipients of this rescued food are people who are food insecure and usually live in poverty.

The "Zeroing in on food waste" project (2009–2013) also provided foundational Australian food waste research beyond quantification of food waste tonnages, economic or environmental impacts. This project developed food waste theory and methods across multiple fields to create a socio-culturally aware public education and social marketing programme to reduce food waste behaviours. The project achieved the following. It improved metrics and measurement methods for the monitoring and evaluation of household food waste prevention interventions (Høj, 2012); provided the first Australian ethnography of household food waste (Mavrakis, 2014); developed interventions to reduce household food waste based on the trans-theoretical model of behaviour change (Davison et al., 2011; Davison, 2015); established Conceptual Foundations for food rescue and redistributed food (Vlaholias et al., 2015a, 2015b); and examined how food waste was portrayed in Reality Food Television (Thompson and Haigh, 2017). Finally, the history of food waste as a policy issue in Australia was also examined by this project (Reynolds et al., 2011).

In addition to "Zeroing in on food waste", other Australian food waste research was published from 2010 onwards. Ridoutt et al. (2010) quantified the water footprint of fresh mango in Australia, and Pearson et al. (2013) provided foundation exploration into the drives of why food waste occurs in Australian households. In 2017, Reutter et al. (2017b) expanded upon the quantification of Australian food waste at the national level, finding that different estimation methods produced diverse results for food waste characterisation, and that some food waste estimates provide inconsistencies when compared. Pearson et al. (2017) also published work examining how to further improve and reframe communications that encourage individuals to reduce food waste; this took into account previous major consumer-focused communication campaigns from Australia and New Zealand. They conducted 29 60-minute qualitative interviews to provide a deep understanding of the subjective experiences and perceptions of individuals regarding food behaviours. These interviews found that though most individuals thought food discards were highly undesirable, they were not aware of the magnitude of food waste in terms of the amount discarded on a personal or a global scale. Nor are individuals knowledgeable about the impacts of food waste. Examining contemporary communications campaigns, they found that they needed to further incorporate broader context issues such as the systemic and structural issues rather than focus on individual choices alone. In 2018, Pearson and Perera (2018) then published a *Practitioner Guide for Integrated Social Marketing Communication Campaigns to Reducing Food Waste*. This provided the core advice of using headline facts; concentrating on the most impactful food waste reduction behaviour changes; identifying specific groups of individuals to target (along with their motivations); and framing messages according to these individuals and their motivations.

Also in 2018, Benyam et al. (2018) surveyed residents of two Queensland communities (Rockhampton Regional Council and Livingstone Shire Council, n = 17) on their views of their councils' domestic food waste prevention and diversion policies. Residents seemed to have knowledge of their food waste practice, but were unaware of other initiatives on food waste prevention. Interestingly, they believed that "other" groups (children) needed more education rather than themselves. Home/backyard composting was the favoured method for council-supported food waste disposal, though many participants thought that local government would make their own policy choice irrespective of feedback from residents.

In July 2018, this groundswell of research from 2008–2018 in Australia culminated in the establishment of the Fight Food Waste Cooperative Research Centre – a $130 million industry-led, government-supported 10-year research programme. Its aim is to tackle the growing international (and Australian) problem of food waste by reducing food waste throughout the supply chain, transforming unavoidable waste into innovative high-value co-products, and engaging with industry and consumers to deliver behavioural change. With around 60 industry partners across the complete food chain, this research has an ecology with the capacity to create transformative change (Fight Food Waste CRC, 2019).

Recent policy developments

Australia has a mixed historical relationship with food waste (Reynolds et al., 2011). It emerged as a public health issue before becoming an environmental issue. Food waste has traditionally been a local government and state rather than a federal policy issue in Australia; the various state-level waste or environment departments providing un-harmonised policy direction of each state; while each local government council area provides direct support and services. The few federal or national-level reports were less policy focused, and more focused on the harmonisation of data between the different states and territories (Environment Protection and Heritage Council and The Department of Environment Heritage and the Arts, 2010). Even then food waste was typically placed inside wider waste policy documents.

However, reducing food waste has recently become a priority on Australia's national agenda. The Australian government launched a national food waste reduction policy in November 2017, followed, in April 2018, by an announcement of funding for a large industry-led Fight Food Waste Cooperative Research Centre. Collectively these will assist the country in pursuit of the United Nations Sustainable Development Goal of making a significant reduction in food waste by 2030. The National Food Waste Strategy (Commonwealth of Australia and Department of the Environment and Energy, 2017) emerged from extensive consultation with industry, government (across all three tiers of federal, state and local), research community and activist organisations. It provides a framework for action across four priority areas:

1 *Policy support*: This encompasses national measurement of food waste, identifying areas to target with investment for food waste reductions, establishing a voluntary commitment programme to reduce food waste and providing enabling legislation to support these activities.
2 *Business improvements*: These cover identifying areas for improvement, supporting the adoption of technology, encouraging collaboration to identify solutions, and normalising food waste considerations into business practices.
3 *Market development*: This includes identifying food waste composition and nutritional value to develop new markets, encourage innovation, and connect food waste sources and users.
4 *Behaviour change*: This involves changing consumer behaviours and engaging the workforce to minimise food waste.

The Australian government is leading implementation of this strategy with guidance from a steering committee consisting of representatives of the food waste sector. Key to their approach is seeking a collective effort where "everyone has a role to play". Initial funding has been provided for measurement to create a National Food Waste Baseline and associated identification of areas for targeted investment (Environment Protection and Heritage Council and The Department of Environment Heritage and the Arts, 2010).

On 20 March 2019, Australia's National Food Waste Baseline was published (ARCADIS, 2019). This provided a benchmark for measuring national performance against the reduction target by establishing a consistent framework to quantify food waste generation and track progress. It estimated that in 2016–17 (the base year), Australia produced 7.3 million tonnes of food waste across the supply and consumption chain. Of this, 2.5 million (34%) was created in citizens' homes, 2.3 million tonnes (31%) in primary production and 1.8 million tonnes (25%) in the manufacturing sector. It also found that Australians recycled 1.2 million tonnes of food waste, recovered 2.9 million tonnes through alternative uses and disposed of 3.2 million tonnes. To make this estimate, more than 300 organisations were engaged through a structured consultation process. Of these, 91 submitted some level of data, while others provided anecdotal and contextual information.

It is interesting to note that this quantity of food (7.3 million tonnes) is similar to previous estimates (such as Reynolds et al. (2015a) and Reutter et al. (2017b), which reinforces the overall scale of the problem). However, this estimate apportions food waste to different parts of the supply chain than previous estimates. This could mean that Australian food waste has "flat lined", however as discussed by Reutter et al. (2017a), there are many uncertainties regarding food waste quantification. This increase in quantification efforts, research and policy action is welcome, and Australia seems to now be on a strong trajectory to address and reduce food waste.

Food waste in New Zealand

Food waste has become a major issue in New Zealand though the total volume of food lost and wasted is not yet known. As an export-orientated agricultural nation that relies heavily on its "clean green" reputation, New Zealand has every reason to be at the forefront of efforts to reduce food waste. New Zealand's large-scale primary food production sector means that a significant amount of food is likely wasted at the production end of the supply chain. Given that in medium- and high-income countries, food is wasted mainly at the later stages in the supply chain, the prospect of a "double whammy" (excess food wastage from consumerism and large-scale primary food production) may well exist in New Zealand. Though currently a lack of robust waste data, particularly in the early stages of the supply chain, make this difficult to confirm, observer reporting for example shows that cancelled export orders and crop management are causes of significant volumes of food waste in the horticultural sector (WasteMINZ TAO Forum, 2019). Furthermore, New Zealand's strong reliance on exporting has meant that food from New Zealand is subject to very high international market requirements for aesthetic product perfection – also a driver for food wastage. Culturally, New Zealand is well positioned to be taking a strong stance on food waste reduction. Te Ao Māori recognises the traditional system in which nothing was wasted – everything was able to be returned back to *Papatūānuku* (mother earth) without detriment to the *whenua* (land), *awa* (river) or *moana* (sea) (Auckland City Council, 2018). There are a number of Māori organisations working to reduce wastage. Para Kore (http://parakore. maori.nz/para-kore/what-is-para-kore/), for example, aims to empower and support organisations across New Zealand to work toward zero waste.

Research and quantification

Until 2013–2014 there was little academic research or quantification of food waste in New Zealand, nor was there any study into food waste behaviours or environmental impacts.

There were, however, government reports that discussed food waste as part of the organic waste stream (Statistics NZ, 2008; Ministry for the Environment, 2009, 2010); media reports that valued New Zealand household food waste at $750 million dollars a year (Johnston and Davison, 2011; TVNZ, 2013); audits of hospital food waste (Goonan et al., 2013, 2014); a Master's thesis that investigated household food waste with an intervention case study (Parr, 2013); a literature review by the Waiheke Resources Trust (Waiheke Resources Trust, 2013); and a consulting report for WasteMINZ, the largest representative body of the waste and resource recovery sector in New Zealand (Yates, 2013). These final three documents provide a solid review of pre-2014 New Zealand food waste knowledge and opportunities, although there are large data gaps.

In 2013, WasteMINZ launched the "National Food Waste Prevention Project". The first part of the project involved calculating estimates of nationwide household food waste. The main research methods used to collect this data were bin audits (audits of 1,402 household bins were conducted across 12 different councils; food waste was separated and weighed (WasteMINZ and Love Food Hate Waste NZ, 2015)) and a nationally representative online survey of attitudes and behaviours that led to food waste (with 1,365 households (WasteMINZ, 2014)). The audit of the formal municipal solid waste stream found that 122,547 tonnes of food waste, or the equivalent of $872 million worth of edible food, is thrown away every year. This information is now being disseminated via infographics (Love Food Hate Waste NZ, 2015a, 2015b) and council websites (Shore, 2015) as part of a nationwide "Love Food Hate Waste" campaign (www.facebook.com/lovefoodhatewas tenz). This is an application of the highly successful "Love Food Hate Waste" campaign that has been running in the United Kingdom (UK) for the last 20 years (WRAP, 2012). An evaluation of the three-year campaign was released in early 2019 which clearly demonstrated significant impact: results showed that New Zealand households are far more aware of food waste issues than they were three years ago, and many households are taking actions to reduce their food waste. Households that had heard of the "Love Food Hate Waste" campaign and engaged more deeply with food waste were able to make significant reductions to the amount of food they were throwing away (WasteMINZ, 2018).

Reynolds et al. (2016) undertook a study that aimed to estimate the tonnage, value, calories and resources wasted as a result of food waste in New Zealand during 2011. Estimates for tonnage were generated using input-output tables from the Ministry for the Environment's data on monthly landfill waste-levies. Estimates were inferred through calculations and no physical measurement of waste was undertaken. From these estimates, Reynolds et al. assumed that food waste made up 17% of total waste in New Zealand, amounting to NZ$ 568 million or $131 per person. Reynolds et al. estimated that in 2011, New Zealand households generated over 224,000 tonnes of food waste, and New Zealand industry generated over 103,000 tonnes of food waste. They disaggregated New Zealand's food waste into 14 food waste categories and found that 7% is related to "fresh" produce, and 93% "processed" food waste. Furthermore, New Zealand's food waste represents 163×10^9 calories in total, and avoidable food waste would be able to feed between 50,000 and 80,000 people a year. New Zealand food waste embodies 4.2×10^6 tonnes of CO_2-e, 4.7×10^9 m^3 of water, and 29×10^3 TJ of energy. They found that compared to other nations, New Zealanders waste less food per capita by weight, value and calorie.

Research in 2016 focused primarily on food waste in a food service setting. Mirosa et al. (2016b) examined the drivers of food left on plates through semi-structured interviews (n = 50). It was found that plate waste was created through interactions related to an individual's hedonism and self-direction – i.e. the individual's enjoyment of the meal and meeting their health goals. Linking this theory to the existing intervention literature they identified effective intervention might include pre-ordering meals, reducing food options provided, reducing plate size, removing food tray and, finally, information campaigns to raise awareness.

From a quantification perspective, researchers and WasteMINZ have jointly conducted site audits to understand how food waste is generated. They found that New Zealand's cafés and restaurants throw away 24,372 tonnes of food annually with the drivers of this related to spoilage (7%), preparation waste (70%) and plate waste (33%) (Mirosa et al., 2018b). Two Master's theses were also produced from this research project (Jones, 2017; Chisnall, 2017). Doggy bags are often touted as one of the solutions to reducing consumer food waste in this sector, but research conducted with New Zealand consumers revealed that this practice is still not commonplace: 1 in 5 people who had asked for a doggy bag were refused by staff (Mirosa et al., 2018a). This study identified barriers and benefits of consumers' current doggy bag behaviours and provided the information required to run an effective community-based social marketing campaign encouraging consumers to take their uneaten restaurant and café food home.

In addition to the above data sources, data is also available from other organisations such as food banks. Of New Zealand's 15 food rescue groups operating in 2017, 14 kept records of the tonnages of food donated, revealing that in 2017, 2,777 tonnes of food were rescued (WasteMINZ TAO Forum). In addition to the food rescue organisation's own data, there is also independent evidence available on the benefits of food rescue. For example, in 2016 and then again in 2018, the University of Otago partnered with food rescue organisation KiwiHarvest to evaluate the social value of rescuing food by nourishing communities. These analyses used a Social Return on Investment (SROI) evaluation tool to demonstrate the efficiency and effectiveness of their operation. Outcomes of food rescue for various stakeholders were detailed (Mirosa et al., 2016a), and prioritised social, economic and environmental outcomes were valued and impacts calculated, resulting in a SROI ratio (social value) of NZ$5.16 for every $1 invested (Hartshorn, 2018).

As previously mentioned, Pearson et al. (2017) published work examining how to further improve and reframe communications that encourage individuals to reduce food waste. This took into account previous major consumer-focused communication campaigns from Australia and New Zealand.

More recently there has been research into retail food waste in New Zealand (Skeaff et al., 2019; Goodman-Smith, 2018). The estimates amounted to 13 kg/capita/year for all food waste and diverted product (i.e. all food not sold or utilised at a retail level), which included 5 kg/capita/year designated as food waste (i.e. food directed to landfill, protein reprocessing and compost) and 3 kg/capita/year sent to landfill. Fresh vegetables (27%), bakery (23%), meat and fish (19%) and fresh fruit (17%) contributed the most to discarded product. Interviews with 16 retail staff identified the following motivators for encouraging food waste reduction: concern for the environment; making profit; caring for the community; and doing the "right" thing. The key barriers identified to food waste reduction included: training and educating staff; food safety concerns; quality standards; availability of waste diversion avenues and capacity; and lack of available resources.

Like many retailers elsewhere in the world, New Zealand supermarkets have started selling misshapen or "ugly" fruit and vegetables. In response to this, researchers have started to explore New Zealanders' perceptions of this suboptimal produce. For example, using two qualitative research methods, researchers investigated children's edibility perceptions of suboptimal produce with varied appearance defects. The results show that unlike adult samples previously studied, children are more accepting of suboptimal produce reflecting retailers' opportunities in marketing suboptimal produce to children, who by their familial influence may also be able to get families to buy and consume suboptimal produce (Makhal et al., 2019).

Most recently, the government has invested significant funding into research into improved packaging with a three-year research project under way investigating consumer understanding of the importance of smart packaging for consumer confidence, food safety and reduced food loss and waste (Mirosa et al., New Zealand-China Strategic Research Alliance Joint Research (2018–21)). Another area where significant public and private investment has been made is in converting unmarketable crops that would have been wasted into value-added products for export. The Bioresource Processing Alliance (BPA, https://bioresourceprocessing.co.nz/) is a programme funded by the Ministry for Business, Innovation and Employment which is a collaborative R&D programme involving research institutes and universities. To date (2018), they have conducted 147 research projects, have had ten products enter the market, which have generated over NZ$2.7m in revenue for companies and have diverted over 2,500 T of material into higher value uses.

Recent policy developments

Food waste policy has been primarily developed through general waste policy, with the key legislation being the Waste Minimisation Act 2008 (WMA) which enables the government's resource efficiency and waste portfolio. The WMA provides funding opportunities for waste minimisation initiatives which the Ministry for the Environment distributes via the Waste Minimisation Fund, including projects focused on reducing food waste, such as the "Good Neighbour Food Rescue" project (https://goodneighbour.co.nz/food-rescue/), the aforementioned "Love Food, Hate Waste" campaign, and several composting projects that recycle food waste into compost products. In addition to central government, New Zealand territorial authorities play a key role in waste minimisation and management at the local level. However, despite engagement from both central and local government, there has not yet been a single national strategy document on food waste.

In 2018–2019, the New Zealand Parliament's Environment Select Committee carried out a briefing to look into ways to prevent the wastage of food in New Zealand. Though not a formal inquiry, the briefing focused on learning and understanding what the challenges are and what solutions might exist to prevent and reduce food loss and waste in New Zealand. Over this briefing, the committee received written evidence from over 30 organisations and individuals that are involved in some way with the food sector, or with food waste (New Zealand Parliament, n.d). The Environment Select Committee then invited oral evidence from multiple groups. Videos of the oral evidence submissions are archived on the Environment Select Committee's Facebook website (Environment Committee, 2019a, 2019b, 2019c, 2019d).

General optimism around the potential to reduce food waste in New Zealand is high, with significant interest in the issue in both the public and private sectors. Moving forward, a collaborative whole supply chain approach to food waste prevention is going to be a key determinant of success.

Possible actions and interventions for Australia and New Zealand

Although a high level of policy attention is now being given to food waste in Australia and New Zealand, there are gaps between translating this into action and interventions to reduce and prevent food waste. The remainder of this section will highlight these possible actions.

There are different actions that can be deployed in different parts of the food system. Reynolds et al. (2019) reviewed existing academic literature on the effectiveness of different consumer food waste interventions, finding that changing the size or type of plates was effective (up to 57% food waste reduction) in hospitality environments (see Chapter 24 for further information); information campaigns were also shown to be effective, with up to 28% food waste reduction (in a small sample size intervention). Other actions for reduction have limited evidence of effectiveness at reducing food waste (e.g. though there is anecdotal/self-reported evidence that cooking classes, fridge cameras, food sharing apps, advertising and information sharing all work to reduce food waste, none of these methods have measured evidence of food waste reductions). Many of these interventions could be tested in Australia and New Zealand.

Australia and New Zealand are currently running information campaigns ("Love Food Hate Waste"), beginning to actively measure food waste, and also have some industry support for food waste reduction. One logical step would be to expand upon these existing actions through the establishment of a voluntary agreement in each country. In the context of environmental sustainability, voluntary agreements are schemes in which public and private sector organisations make commitments to improve their environmental performance, without the need for legislation or sanctions. They cover arrangements such as public voluntary programmes, negotiated agreements or unilateral commitments (Boulding and Devine, 2019). One example of an existing food waste voluntary agreement is the Courtauld Commitment in the UK (see Chapter 12). With strong governmental leadership and industry support, a food waste voluntary agreement has the potential to create the right environment to reduce food waste in Australia and New Zealand. These voluntary agreements could also include the creation of food waste reduction targets for the government and industry.

One further action for food waste reduction in Australia and New Zealand would be to increase the amount of valorisation and investment in the bio economy (see Chapter 25). In both countries, valorisation is still in its infant stage. The growth of the bio economy will lead to greater amounts of unavoidable food waste being transformed into higher value products.

References

ARCADIS. 2019. National food waste Baseline - Final assessment report, ARCADIS. www.environ ment.gov.au/protection/waste-resource-recovery/food-waste

Auckland City Council. 2018. Written submission for the New Zealand Parliament Environment Committee on the briefing to investigate food waste in New Zealand. www.parliament.nz/en/pb/sc/sub missions-and-advice/document/52SCEN_EVI_78944_EN4319/auckland-council

Baker, D., Fear, J., and Denniss, R., 2009. What a waste: An analysis of household expenditure on food | The Australia Institute. The Australian Institute, 1–25.

Benyam, A., Kinnear, S., and Rolfe, J., 2018. Integrating community perspectives into domestic food waste prevention and diversion policies. *Resources, Conservation and Recycling* 134, 174–183. doi: 10.1016/j.resconrec.2018.03.019

Boulding, A., Devine, R., 2019. Evaluation FA Pilots - Final Synthesis Report. REFRESH Deliverable D2.8

Chisnall, S. J., 2017. A taste for consumption:' Food waste generation in New Zealand cafés and restaurants, Doctoral dissertation. University of Otago.

Davison, S., 2015. Developing, delivering and evaluating a psychology based informational intervention for reducing food waste in households.

Davison, S., Thompson, K., Dawson, D., and Sharp, A., 2011. Reducing Wasteful Household Behaviours: Contributions from Psychology and Implications for Intervention Design, in: Lehmann, S., and Crocker, R.. (Eds.), *Consumption, Zero Waste and Sustainable Design*. London: Earthscan, pp. 67–88.

Do Something. 2013. Food waste fast facts. [WWW Document]. http://foodwise.com.au/foodwaste/food-waste-fast-facts/ (accessed 7.8.19).

Edwards, F., and Mercer, D., 2007. Gleaning from Gluttony: An Australian Youth Subculture Confronts the Ethics of Waste. *Australian Geographer* 38, 279–296.

Edwards, F., and Mercer, D., 2012. Food waste in Australia: the freegan response. *The Sociological Review* 60, 174–191.

Environment - New Zealand Parliament - Submissions to Food Waste Briefing [WWW Document]. n.d. www.parliament.nz/en/pb/sc/scl/environment/tab/submissionsandadvice?criteria.Keyword=food&criteria.Timeframe=&criteria.DateFrom=&criteria.DateTo=&criteria.DocumentStatus=Current&fbclid=IwAR0O755QEqtUnCKTGoXZmiqmCTcqUyXVwsmAFJwUbfjLkB0sFjDLVPVAkQ8 (accessed 7. 8.19).

Environment Committee - Briefing to Investigate Food Waste - Hearing of evidence (14.03.19) | Facebook [WWW Document]. n.d. www.facebook.com/watch/?v=433082927428589 (accessed 7. 8.19).

Environment Committee - Briefing to investigate food waste in New Zealand (02.05.2019) | Facebook [WWW Document]. n.d. https://www.facebook.com/environmentSCNZ/videos/2165756716826903/ (accessed 7.8.19).

Environment Committee - Briefing to investigate food waste in New Zealand (07.03.2019) | Facebook [WWW Document]. n.d. www.facebook.com/environmentSCNZ/videos/613323705794894/(accessed 7. 8.19).

Environment Protection and Heritage Council, The Department of Environment Heritage and the Arts. 2010. National Waste Report 2010.

Fight Food Waste CRC. (2019). Fight food waste CRC | Fight food waste cooperative research centre. [WWW Document]. https://fightfoodwastecrc.com.au/ (accessed 7.8.19).

Goodman-Smith, F., 2018. A quantitative and qualitative study of retail food waste in New Zealand (Doctoral dissertation). University of Otago.

Goonan, S., Mirosa, M., and Spence, H., 2013. Hospital food waste: a qualitative study of food production and pre-consumption food waste. *Nutrition & Dietetics* 70, 13–14.

Goonan, S., Mirosa, M., and Spence, H., 2014. Getting a taste for food waste: a mixed methods ethnographic study into hospital food waste before patient consumption conducted at three New Zealand foodservice facilities. *Journal of the Academy of Nutrition and Dietetics* 114, 63–71. doi: 10.1016/j.jand.2013.09.022

Hawkins, G., 2006. *The Ethics of Waste*, $39.95 ed. UNSW Press, Sydney: UNSW Press, 2006.

Hawkins, G., 2007. Waste in Sydney: Unwelcome returns. PMLA.

Hawkins, G., 2012. The performativity of food packaging: market devices, waste crisis and recycling. *Sociology Review* 60, 66–83. doi: 10.1111/1467-954X.12038

Høj, S. B., 2012. Metrics and measurement methods for the monitoring and evaluation of household food waste prevention interventions.

Johnston, M., and Davison, I., 2011. Study: $750m a year wasted on food. NZ Herald.

Join the Environment Committee as they … - Environment Committee [WWW Document]. n.d. www.facebook.com/environmentSCNZ/videos/820693414959171/ (accessed 7. 8.19).

Jones, E., 2017. An investigation into food waste produced in New Zealand restaurants and cafes. University of Otago.

Love Food Hate Waste NZ. 2015a. Environmental Infographic.

Love Food Hate Waste NZ. 2015b. How did you calculate that? Explanations for the statistics in food waste infographics.

Hartshorn. 2018. MSc thesis: 'Evaluating the social value of a New Zealand food rescue organisation using Social Return on Investment analysis', Supervised by Mainvil, L and Mirosa M. University of Otago.

Makhal, A., Thyne, M., Robertson, K., and Mirosa, M., 2019. "I don't like wonky carrots": an exploration of children's perceptions of suboptimal fruits and vegetables. *Journal of Retailing and Consumer Services*. in press. Doi: 10.1016/j.jretconser.2019.101945. Available online 17 September 2019.

Mason, L., Boyle, T., Fyfe, J., Smith, T., and Cordell, D., 2011. National food waste data assessment: Final report.

Mavrakis, V., 2014. The generative mechanisms of "food waste" in South Australian household settings, (Doctoral dissertation). Flinders University.

Ministry for the Environment. 2009. Solid waste composition, environmental report card.

Ministry for the Environment. 2010. The New Zealand waste strategy.

Mirosa, M., Bremer, P., Oey, I., Billington, C., Young, E. Research grant (2018-21), Understanding the importance of smart packaging for consumer confidence, food safety and an improved supply chain, New Zealand-China strategic research alliance joint research.

Mirosa, M., Liu, Y., and Mirosa, R., 2018a. Consumers' behaviors and attitudes toward doggy bags: identifying barriers and benefits to promoting behavior change. *Journal of Food Products Marketing* 24 (5), 563–590. doi: 10.1080/10454446.2018.1472699

Mirosa, M., Mainvil, L., Chisnall, S., Jones, E., and Marshall, J., 2018b. *Foodwaste in the Cafe & Restaurant Sector in New Zealand*, Auckland: WasteMINZ.

Mirosa, M., Mainvil, L., Horne, H., and Mangan-Walker, E., 2016a. The social value of rescuing food, nourishing communities. *British Food Journal* 118 (12), 3044–3058. www.emeraldinsight.com/doi/full/10.1108/BFJ-04-2016-0149;

Mirosa, M., Munro, H., Mangan-Walker, E., and Pearson, D., 2016b. Reducing waste of food left on plates. *British Food Journal* 118, 2326–2343. doi: 10.1108/BFJ-12-2015-0460

National Food Waste Strategy |Department of the Environment and Energy [WWW Document]. n.d. www.environment.gov.au/protection/waste-resource-recovery/publications/national-food-waste-strategy (accessed 7.8.19).

NSW Environment Protection Authority. 2009. Food waste avoidance benchmark study.

Parr, H., 2013. Food waste New Zealand : A case study investigating the food waste phenomenon.

Pearson, D., Minehan, M., and Wakefield-Rann, R., 2013. Food waste in Australian households: why does it occur. *Australasian-Pacific Journal of Regional Food Studies* 3, 118–132.

Pearson, D., Mirosa, M., Andrews, L., and Kerr, G., 2017. Reframing communications that encourage individuals to reduce food waste. *Communication Research and Practice* 3, 137–154. doi: 10.1080/22041451.2016.1209274

Pearson, D., and Perera, A., 2018. Reducing Food Waste. *Social Marketing Quarterly* 24, 45–57. doi: 10.1177/1524500417750830

Reutter, B., Lant, P., Reynolds, C., and Lane, J., 2017a. Food waste consequences: Environmentally extended input-output as a framework for analysis. *Journal of Cleaner Production* 153, 506–514. doi: 10.1016/j.jclepro.2016.09.104

Reutter, B., Lant, P. A., and Lane, J. L., 2017b. The challenge of characterising food waste at a national level—An Australian example. *Environmental science and policy* 78.

Reynolds, C., 2016. A comparison of the socio-economics of food waste in the United Kingdom and Australia.

Reynolds, C., Geschke, A., Piantadosi, J., and Boland, J., 2015a. Estimating industrial solid waste and municipal solid waste data at high resolution using economic accounts: an input–output approach with Australian case study. *Journal of Material Cycles and Waste Management* 18, 677–686. doi: 10.1007/s10163-015-0363-1

Reynolds, C., Piantadosi, J., and Boland, J., 2015b. Rescuing food from the organics waste stream to feed the food insecure: an economic and environmental assessment of australian food rescue operations using environmentally extended waste input-output analysis. *Sustainability* 7, 4707–4726. doi:10.3390/su7044707

Reynolds, C. J., Piantadosi, J., Buckley, J. D., Weinstein, P., Boland, J., 2015c. Evaluation of the environmental impact of weekly food consumption in different socio-economic households in Australia using environmentally extended input–output analysis. *Ecological Economics* 111, 58–64. doi: 10.1016/j.ecolecon.2015.01.007

Reynolds, C., Goucher, L., Quested, T., Bromley, S., Gillick, S., Wells, V. K., Evans, D., Koh, L., Kanyama, A. C., Katzeff, C., and Svenfelt, Å., 2019. Consumption-stage food waste reduction interventions–What works and how to design better interventions. *Food policy* 83, 7–27.

Reynolds, C., Mirosa, M., and Clothier, B., 2016. New zealand's food waste: estimating the tonnes, value, calories and resources wasted. *Agriculture* 6, 9. doi: 10.3390/agriculture6010009

Reynolds, Christian J., Mavrakis, V., Davison, S., Høj, S. B., Vlaholias, E., Sharp, A., Thompson, K., Ward, P., Coveney, J., Piantadosi, J., Boland, J., and Dawson, D., 2014a. Estimating informal household food waste in developed countries: the case of Australia. *Waste Management & Research* 32, 1254–1258. doi: 10.1177/0734242X14549797

Reynolds, C. J., Piantadosi, J., and Boland, J., 2014b. A waste supply-use analysis of Australian waste flows. *Economic Structures* 3. doi: 10.1186/s40008-014-0005-0

Reynolds, C. J., Thompson, K., Boland, J., and Dawson, D., 2011. Climate Change on the Menu? A retrospective look at the development of South Australian municipal food waste policy. *The International Journal of Climate Change: Impacts and Responses* 3 (3), 101–112.

Ridoutt, B. G., Juliano, P., Sanguansri, P., and Sellahewa, J., 2010. The water footprint of food waste: case study of fresh mango in Australia. *Journal of Cleaner Production* 18, 1714–1721. doi: 10.1016/j.jclepro.2010.07.011

Shore, M., 2015. Food waste - waitaki resource recovery park. [WWW Document].

Skeaff, S., Goodman-Smith, F., and Mirosa, M., 2019. A quantitative and qualitative study of retail food waste in new zealand. *Proceedings* 8, 18. doi: 10.3390/proceedings2019008018

Statistics NZ. 2008. Statistics NZ sustainable development report 2008.

Thompson, K., and Haigh, L., 2017. Representations of food waste in reality food television: an exploratory analysis of ramsay's kitchen nightmares. *Sustainability* 9, 1139. doi: 10.3390/su9071139

Thompson, K., O'Dwyer, L., Sharp, A., Smith, B., Reynolds, C., Hadley, T., and Hazel, S., 2015. What's in a Dog's breakfast? Considering the social, veterinary and environmental implications of feeding food scraps to pets using three Australian surveys. *Sustainability* 7, 7195–7213. doi: 10.3390/su7067195

TVNZ. 2013. Up to half of world's food goes to waste, report says.

Vlaholias, E., Thompson, K., Every, D., and Dawson, D., 2015a. Charity starts ... at work? Conceptual foundations for research with businesses that donate to food redistribution organisations. *Sustainability* 7, 7997–8021. doi: 10.3390/su7067997

Vlaholias, E. G., Thompson, K., Every, D., and Dawson, D., 2015b. Reducing Food Waste through Charity: Exploring the Giving and Receiving of Redistributed Food, in: San-Epifanio, L. E., and De Renobales Scheifler, M. (Eds.), *Envisioning a Future Without Food Waste and Food Poverty*. Presented at the Envisioning a Future without Food Waste and Food Poverty: Societal Challenges., The Netherlands: Wageningen Academic Publishers, pp. 271–278. doi: 10.3920/978-90-8686-820-9_33

Waiheke Resources Trust. 2013. Food waste : Food waste : A literature review.

WasteMINZ. 2014. National food waste prevention study.

WasteMINZ, Love Food Hate Waste NZ, 2015. New Zealand Food Waste Audits.

WasteMINZ. 2018. New Zealand food waste research love food hate waste campaign evaluation. https://lovefoodhatewaste.co.nz/wp-content/uploads/2019/02/Love-Food-Hate-Waste-Research-Results-Summary-February-2019.pdf

WasteMINZ TAO Forum. 2019. Written submission for the New Zealand parliament environment committee on the briefing to investigate food waste in New Zealand. www.parliament.nz/en/pb/sc/submissions-and-advice/document/52SCEN_EVI_78944_EN4329/wasteminz-and-wasteminz-territorial-authorities-officers

WRAP. 2012. Welcome to love food hate waste an introduction welcome to love food hate waste.

Yates, S., 2013. Summary of existing information on domestic food waste in New Zealand.

Zaman, A., Reynolds, C., 2015. The economic and bio-energy production potential of South Australian food waste using Anaerobic digestion, in: Unmaking Waste 2015 Conference Proceedings.

Zero Waste SA. 2005. Zero waste events : Event waste Composting Trials Zero Waste SA Zero Waste events : Event waste composting trials. Zero Waste SA.

15

ESTIMATING TOTAL AND PER CAPITA FOOD WASTE IN BRAZILIAN HOUSEHOLDS

A scenario analysis

Glenio Piran Dal' Magro and Edson Talamini

Introduction

Rapid urbanization, population growth, and food loss and waste (FLW) have become a trending concern for developed and developing countries (Dubbeling et al., 2016). The FLW stems from factors that connect from land use, processing or transportation, and even the frequency of food purchase. It refers to a decrease in food originally intended for human consumption (HLPE, 2014).

Food waste is produced throughout the food supply chain (FSC): during production, storage, transportation, and processing, including retailers and restaurant and residential kitchens (Lundqvist et al., 2008). It is estimated that between 30% and 50% of all foods produced do not reach the human stomach (Lipinski et al., 2013; IME-Institution of Mechanical Engineers, 2018), and up to 60% of food released into landfills is still considered fresh edible food (WRAP, 2011; Mason et al., 2011).

At the consumption stage, FLW represents food items intended for human consumption, but not consumed, such as preparations, fresh or processed foods, and ready meals, which are lost or wasted in retail, restaurants or at home. The amount of food available for consumption varies by country. Generally, developed countries have larger food surpluses, which exceed the minimum requirements required by their populations, and tend to waste more than developing countries (Stuart, 2009). According to FAO, enough food is already produced for every person in the world to have approximately 2,700 calories per day (FAO, 2013).

On a per capita basis, FLW is higher in the industrialized world than in developing countries (Halloran et al., 2014). Therefore, it directly affects the availability of food. Globally, it translates into reduced food availability (in mass, calories or nutrients), but with more diversified and indirect effects on food security at the local level (Pinstrup-Andersen, Gitz, and Meyback, 2016).

In general, the highest amount of FLW occurs in the FSC consumption stage (Monier et al., 2010; Parfitt et al., 2010; Gustavsson et al., 2011; Kranert et al., 2012), mainly derived from food with short shelf life (Vanham et al., 2015). According to Evans (2012), consumers do not plan to generate waste, and some even feel guilty when it occurs. According to Evans (2012) consumers do not plan to generate waste and some even feel guilty when it occurs. Different interaction activities influence the amount of FLW generated in households (Mondejar-Jiménez et al., 2016; Quested et al., 2013), such as business transactions, daily interactions and inappropriate domestic practices, which makes the food to end up in the trash (Evans, 2012). Besides, in households, the food is wasted mainly during the preparation or serving (Pekcan et al., 2006).

In this sense, the FLW becomes problematic due to different peculiarities:

- *nutritionally*, because part of the wasted food remains edible (Oelofse and Nahman, 2013);
- *economically*, food waste costs are undervalued, particularly in countries where food accounts for a small proportion of consumers' budgets (Gunders, 2012);
- *environmentally*, because it implies the consumption of environmental resources used for food production, such as water and fossil fuels, aiding in global climate change (Hall et al., 2009; Gustavsson et al., 2011);
- *politically*, because it implies costs in the proper disposal of potentially edible foods, representing values commonly ignored by policymakers (Nahman and Lange, 2013); and
- *socially* because hunger and waste represent a moral and ethical paradox in society.

Minimizing FLW is directly related to the possibility of providing economic benefits, improving the efficiency of natural resource use, reducing environmental impacts, and minimizing food insecurity (FLW, 2016). However, currently, there is no satisfactory understanding of how, why, and where food or its edible parts are removed from the FSC (FLW – Food Loss and Waste Protocol, 2016). Thus, to do this, a consistent set of information and reports are necessary to define planning actions.

Estimates are an important part of the planning process, as they guide decision making. For this, technical studies on the problem can contribute in the direction and optimization of actions, tools, planning, and applied resources. Therefore, the scenario technique can be considered an important methodological resource, incorporated as a tool in strategic planning processes (Buarque, 2003).

"The scenarios seek to describe alternative futures to support the decision and stand out, therefore, as planning tools in reality loaded with risks, surprises, and unpredictability" (Buarque, 2003, p. 21). Moreover, in developing countries, there is a lack of historical data, which makes planning difficult (Dyson and Chang, 2005). Therefore, the scenario technique is a tool that can be used in strategic planning in several areas, including the management of FLW. The possibility of estimating scenarios of FLW can contribute to the planning and development of management strategies (Daskalopoulos, Badr, and Probert, 1998) and mitigation.

In this context, the present text makes use of different scenarios with the objective of estimating FLW values in the consumption stage, more precisely household consumption. Estimates are based on the quantification of household food purchases and their respective expenditures for Brazil. The data used correspond to the year 2008; the last data made available by the official body of the Brazilian government.

Contextualizing food waste policy in Brazil

In Brazil, issues that involve FLW involve several stakeholders and work fronts. The generation of FLW is a matter of concern. Law 12,305/2010 was instituted by the Solid Waste National Policy (Brazil, 2010), which in its second chapter defines recycling as the process of transformation of the solid waste that involves the alteration of its physical, physical-chemical or biological properties, aiming to transform this waste into inputs or new products. It is important to take note of the conditions and standards established by the competent bodies of the Environment National System (Sisnama) and, if applicable, by the National Health Surveillance System (SNVS) and the Unified System of Attention to Agricultural and Livestock Health (Suasa).

Data from the Brazilian Association of Public Cleaning and Special Waste Companies (Albrepe) show that, in 2017, 40% of the gathered solid waste is still dumped in inadequate places, such as dumping grounds and landfills that do not have in place the systems and measures needed for environment protection (Abrelpe, 2018). In addition, urban solid waste consists of more than 50% of organic matter and, therefore, needs suitable treatment.

An important strategy on the FLW thematic is the Technical Committee on Food Loss and Waste, a government agency that, in 2017, developed the Intersectoral Strategy for Food Loss and Waste Reduction, complying with the recommendations of the FAO Panel of Experts. The main axes of strategy are (Bocchi, 2018): (1) research, knowledge, and innovation (methodology development for FLW quantification, fostering research and technological innovations that aim at understanding the causes and solutions for their mitigation); (2) communication, education, and training (dissemination of good practices and education for FLW reduction); (3) public policy fostering (including food banks and the incentive to short-circuit commercialization, for example, farmers selling produce directly to the consumer); and (4) legislation – civil liability for food donation, tax exemption for donor companies, food labeling, etc.

In terms of legislation, there are in process more than 30 bills on FLW in the Brazilian National Congress (PEIXOTO, 2018). Most of the items address ways and strategies to mitigate FLW in the distribution and consumption steps. Specifically, these initiatives aim to (PEIXOTO, 2018):

- establish a national policy to fight FLW;
- create food surplus redistribution programs and the Food Gathering and Donation Program;
- reuse prepared foods, for donation;
- regulate food donations to charity institutions;
- oblige establishments that market food to properly dispose of foods that have not been sold; and
- permit establishments that provide meals to donate what has not been sold.

More strictly there are bills that establish the obligation to donate food when it is not sold. However, the logistics to promote this donation are not simple and its costs may make it impractical. In addition, it can be understood that food donation can be done through other agents, such as food banks, rather than direct to the final receiver. Other projects, more meticulous, only impose the obligation to donate on establishments of a certain minimum area, determined in square meters.

Although there is a clear understanding and agreement on food donation, the Brazilian legislation still needs to clarify the possible legal risks of the food donor being blamed in case there are possible damages caused to the health of the grantee. To avoid the burden of civil responsibility, the donor, in most cases, prefers to discard the food rather than donating it and assuming the possible risks of indemnity to the grantee.

To regulate food donations, the oldest proposal is PL No. 4,747/1998 (Senate Bill – PLS No. 165/1997, originally), known as the Good Samaritan project. The project aims to exempt the food donor from civil or criminal liability, in case of possible damage or death caused to the beneficiary by the consumption of the donated food, provided that the donation is not characterized by bad intent or negligence of the donor. Analyzing the legislative proposals in the Chamber of Deputies and the Federal Senate, a gap can be seen and the consequent need to institute in law a set of actions aiming at the development of awareness about adequate and responsible food consumption, targeting the mitigation of FLW in Brazil and its real implications for society.

On the other hand, actions aiming at mitigation of FLW are developed by civil society. The engagement of organizations in campaigns and movements to reduce FLW has increased in recent decades. In Brazil there are two main groups of food banks (Grisa and Fornazier, 2018): (1) the public ones, supported by the Ministry of Social Development, of which there are 84 installed and 24 under construction; and (2) the private ones, composed by 87 units linked to the Social Service of the Market (SESC).

The structuring of food banks throughout the country has been of fundamental importance. Food banks are physical and/or logistical structures that offer the service of gathering and/or reception, storage, and free distribution of food from donations coming from private and/or public sectors. The donations are directed to several institutions of social assistance, education, and health, among other registered beneficiaries. Food banks are strategic organizations that act to reuse food that is still fit for human consumption and, when this is not possible, this food is redirected toward the animal consumption chain.

Following this idea, the Mesa Brasil Sesc project is responsible for collecting and distributing surplus or food that does not meet marketing standards, but which is still fit for human consumption. It differs from food banks by developing procedures of collection and immediate distribution of food to organizations, the so-called urban harvest. The urban harvest is characterized by being agile and requiring less resources to be established and maintained, because the food is not stored. Mesa Brasil Sesc is distributed in all the states of the Brazilian territory, currently covering about 500 cities in Brazil. Another civil society initiative, Save Food, was launched in Brazil in 2016. The initiative is part of the international effort to reduce FLW. It aims to form a national network of experts from the public and private sectors to work collaboratively and execute projects, while at the same time making civil society aware of its actions.

The construction and analysis of wasteful scenarios in Brazilian households

Description of the study

The objective of this study was to estimate the average household food waste in Brazil, based on food acquisition values. The data used correspond to the Family Budget Survey – POF, for the year 2008, published by the Brazilian Institute of Geography and Statistics (IBGE, 2010). Based on these data, four alternative scenarios of waste were constructed at the household level for Brazil in 2008.

Data used and scenario description

The data used correspond to the average household per capita food intake (in kilograms) and the average household monetary expenditure per capita (in R\$[1]) for Brazil, its regions, and states,[2] by product group. The exchange rate used is that for January 2009: R1 = US\$ 2.38.

Foods purchased by Brazilian families were organized into groups, which corresponded to: (1) Cereals, legumes, and oilseeds; (2) Vegetables; (3) Fruits; (4) Flours, starches, and dough; (5) Bakery products; (6) Meat, fish, and offal; (7) Poultry and eggs; (8) Dairy products; (9) Sugars, sweets, and confectionery; (10) Salts and condiments; (11) Oils and fats; (12) Drinks and infusions; (13) Prepared foodstuffs, industrial mixtures, canned goods, and preserves; (14) Other products.

Furthermore, four hypotheses of waste behaviors were considered to construct the scenarios. Three behaviors were identified by Gustavsson et al., (2011) from the analysis of global data of different food groups in different global regions. The assumptions correspond to 5%, 11%, and 40% of waste and represent, respectively, determining FLW at the consumption stage for sub-Saharan Africa, Latin America, and the industrialized countries of Europe and North America. The fourth hypothesis of 25%, taken as an intermediate value, was added. This alternative scenario corresponds to the intermediate behavior of waste in the consumption stage, between Latin America and the industrialized countries of Europe and North America.

Data collection and analysis

The average acquisition costs (kilograms/per capita/year) and average expenditures (real/per capita/year) of the food were collected from the 2008/2009 POF samples (www.ibge.gov.br/home/XML/pof_2008_2009.shtm) for Brazil, its regions, and federal units.

The annual per capita household food acquisition values were collected from the POF and are organized into 14 categories, previously described. The quantities of products purchased in liquid form were converted into kilograms, by volume being equal to the weight.

The monthly average household monetary expenditure amounts were organized in the same 14 categories, being transformed into annual per capita monetary expenditure (Equation 1). From the values of the sample, the total values for the Brazilian population and each region in 2008 were inferred.

$$\bar{x}_{Mon\ per\ capita} = \frac{(\bar{x}a * 12)}{\bar{x}b} \tag{1}$$

Where:

$\bar{x}_{Mon\ per\ capita}$ = per capita annual monetary average, in Real
$\bar{x}a$ = monthly average household monetary expenditure for the respective group, in Real
12 = months of the year
$\bar{x}b$ = average of the number of residents in a family by state, region, and in Brazil[3]

The descriptive analysis of the data was performed to evaluate the behavior in the four different scenarios. Therefore, the values representing the quantitative estimates of waste at 5%, 11%, 25%, and 40% were calculated from the acquisition values for each food group (Equation 2). We also used the estimates of wastage, to calculate the representative monetary values for each group, in each scenario (Equation 3).

$$\bar{x}_{Des\ per\ capita/kg} = (\bar{x}d * p) \tag{2}$$

Where:

$\bar{x}_{Des\ per\ capita/kg}$ = average per capita household food waste for the respective group, in kilograms

$\overline{x}_d$ = average per capita household food acquisition for the respective group, in kilograms

p = scenario of the percentage of waste (5%, 11%, 25%, or 40%)

$$\overline{x}_{Des\ per\ capita/R\$} = (\overline{x}_{Mon} * p) \tag{3}$$

Where:

$\overline{x}_{Despercapita/R\$}$ = monetary average of the per capita household food waste for the respective group, in Real

$\overline{x}_{Mon}$ = average per capita household food expenditure for the respective group, in Real

p = scenario of the percentage of waste (5%, 11%, 25%, or 40%)

Moreover, due to the amount of food estimated as waste in the four scenarios, and the monetary value it represents, it was extrapolated to the Brazilian population. The amount of food waste generated for Brazil and each region was calculated (Equation 4), with the average values representing the amount of food per capita wasted per year. Also, with the monetary value per capita/year, also generated in the consumption stage, the monetary amount that represents the waste in the household consumption stage in Brazil and its regions (Equation 5) was calculated.

$$Ktotal = \sum \overline{x}_{Des\ per\ capita/kg} * P \tag{4}$$

Where:

K_{total} = total quantity of household food waste in Brazil or its regions, in kilograms

$\overline{x}_{Des\ per\ capita/kg}$ = sum of the average per capita household food waste of all groups for Brazil or region, in kilograms

P = population of Brazil or region[4]

$$Dtotal = \sum \overline{x}_{Des\ per\ capita/Mon} * P \tag{5}$$

Where:

D_{total} = total quantity of household food waste in Brazil or its regions, in Real

$\sum \overline{x}_{Des\ per\ capita/Mon}$ = sum of the average per capita household food waste of all groups for Brazil or region, in Real

P = population of Brazil or region

The physical and monetary dimensions of FLW in Brazilian households

The food acquisition for household consumption by product groups in Brazil and its regions in 2008 is represented in Figure 15.1(a). Food groups are constituted by the annual per capita average. In 2008, the groups most acquired by Brazilians were beverages and infusions, followed by cereals, legumes, and oilseeds, dairy products, and meat, fish, and offal.

When analyzing the annual averages of each food group by region, the per capita acquisition in 2008 was higher for the groups of beverages and infusions (64.1 kg), dairy products (67.41 kg), vegetables (38.60 kg) and fruits (36.53 kg) in the South region, when compared with the other regions. On the other hand, for the cereal, legumes, and oilseed groups (54.02 kg) and meat, fish, and offal (50.20 kg) the Northern region acquired the highest quantities per capita. It should be noted that the Southern region was the one that acquired

a)

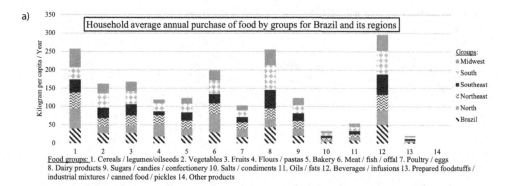

Food groups: 1. Cereals / legumes/oilseeds 2. Vegetables 3. Fruits 4. Flours / pastas 5. Bakery 6. Meat / fish / offal 7. Poultry / eggs 8. Dairy products 9. Sugars / candies / confectionery 10. Salts / condiments 11. Oils / fats 12. Beverages / infusions 13. Prepared foodstuffs / industrial mixtures / canned food / pickles 14. Other products

b)

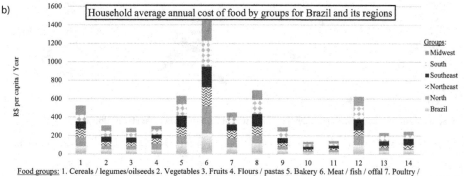

Food groups: 1. Cereals / legumes/oilseeds 2. Vegetables 3. Fruits 4. Flours / pastas 5. Bakery 6. Meat / fish / offal 7. Poultry / eggs 8. Dairy products 9. Sugars / candies / confectionery 10. Salts / condiments 11. Oils / fats 12. Beverages / infusions 13. Prepared foods / industrial mixtures / canned food / pickles 14. Other products

Figure 15.1 Purchase and household average food cost in 2008.

the least food from the group of cereals, legumes, and oilseeds (32.61 kg), and the Southeast region, acquired the least from the meats, fish, and offal group (28.03 kg).

The food expenditure corresponding to household consumption by food groups (in R$ per capita per year), for Brazil and its regions in 2008, is represented in Figure 15.1(b). It shows that the highest household expenditure in the Brazilian population in 2008 was on meat, fish, and offal, followed by dairy products, bakery, and beverages and infusions. In contrast, salts and condiments, and the group of oils and fats represented the lowest expenditure per capita for domestic consumption.

When analyzing the annual averages of each region for each food group, it was observed that among the groups with the highest per capita expenditure, the North region was highlighted in the meats, fish, and offal (R$ 295.75), cereals, legumes, and oilseeds (R$ 100.80), and poultry and eggs (R$ 101.97). On the other hand, the South region had the highest expenditure per capita for the bakery groups (R$ 129.35), dairy products (R$ 153.6), and the beverages and infusions group (R$ 145.32).

From the quantification of averages of food purchased for home consumption, four scenarios of household food waste were created with 5%, 11%, 25%, and 40% of wastage (Figure 15.2). Each scenario used the volume in kilograms and the monetary value, in reals, to calculate the waste per food group for Brazil and its respective regions.

Figure 15.2 (a) shows the amounts of household food waste, in kilograms, calculated for each scenario. Due to the methodology used, the groups that contribute most to the

(a) Scenarios of the estimation of Brazilian household food waste in kilogram

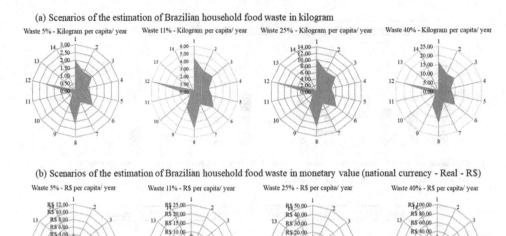

(b) Scenarios of the estimation of Brazilian household food waste in monetary value (national currency - Real - R$)

(c) Scenarios of the amount of monthly family income wasted in Brazilian households (in kilogram)

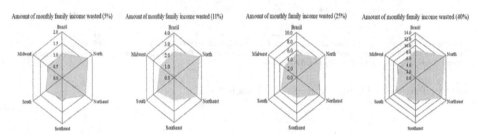

Figure 15.2 Scenarios of the estimation of Brazilian household food waste (a) in kilograms and (b) in monetary value, for the 14 food groups in 2008. (c) Scenarios of the amount of monthly family income wasted in Brazilian households due to wasted food.

Note: Average monthly family income: Brazil – R$2,641.63; North – R$2,011.72; Northeast – R$1,712.88; Southeast – R$3,193.05; South – R$2,873.52; Midwest – R$2,731.14.

generation of household waste of food correspond to the groups with the highest amount of food purchased. In this sense, the groups of beverages, dairy products, and cereals, legumes and oilseeds contributed the most to the generation of food waste at the household consumption level.

The amounts vary between groups analyzed. They are between 0 kg/per capita/year, which is in the group called other products for the scenario with 5% of waste, up to 20.29 kg/per capita/year for the beverages and infusions group, corresponding to the scenario with 40%. Among the regions, the South contributes the largest quantities of waste from the beverage and dairy groups, while the North and Northeast regions contribute the largest amounts of waste in the group of cereals, legumes, and oilseeds.

Figure 15.2(b) shows the monetary values, in Real, corresponding to the calculated proportions of waste for each scenario. In the same way as with quantity, the groups with the highest expenditure values represent the highest monetary values in the generation of food waste at the stage of household consumption. In this sense, the groups of meat, fish and offal, dairy products, bakery, and beverages were the ones with the highest monetary value among the analyzed groups.

The monetary values, which correspond to the generation of food waste, identified in the calculations are between R$ 1.11/per capita/year, for the group of sugars, sweets, and confectionery, calculated in the scenario with 5% of waste, and R$ 89.72/per capita/year for the meats, fish, and offal group corresponding to the scenario with 40%. The North and South regions contribute to the highest monetary values in the generation of waste for the meats, fish, and offal group. Also, the South region presents the highest monetary values regarding household food waste for dairy products, bakery, and beverages.

Figure 15.2(c) shows the proportion of monthly family income that corresponds to the household food waste generated in each family. For each scenario, the monetary amounts of waste were converted into percentages. The North and Northeast regions have the lowest monthly family income, resulting in higher percentages of income being wasted due to household food waste. The waste in the North region can represent between 1.7% and 13.6% of monthly income, according to the scenario. On the other hand, the waste in the Southeast region represents between 0.9 and 7.3% of the family income. The low representation is related to a higher family income in the Southeast region.

Table 15.1 shows the average values (in kilograms and monetary value) of the food groups purchased for domestic consumption in Brazil in 2008. The scenarios of waste (5%, 11%, 20%, and 40%) are presented with the Brazilian estimates of the annual average per capita generation for each food group and the corresponding monetary values. It was identified that in the year 2008 the average household per capita food wastage of the Brazilian population was 336.72 kg, corresponding to a monetary expense of R$ 1,024.91. This value corresponds to US$ 430.58.

Based on the analysis of possible scenarios of behavior at the consumption stage and consequent generation of waste, different values were identified at the household level. With 5% of food waste, a quantity of waste generation in the consumption was identified, at the household level, of 15.76 kg per capita/year. This quantity means that if Brazil produces waste in the consumption phase analogous to that of sub-Saharan Africa, it will represent R$ 51.25 per capita/year, which corresponds to US$ 21.53.

With the scenario of 11%, a percentage identified as the amount of food waste in the consumption stage for the Latin American countries, the amount of waste generated at the household consumption level was estimated at 34.67 kg/per capita/year. Therefore, if Brazil has a waste behavior corresponding to the value identified for Latin America, it would represent R$ 112.74 per capita/year, corresponding to US$ 47.36.

If the Brazilian population shows the same level of consumption as that identified in the industrialized countries of North America and Europe, the amount of household-level waste generated would be 126.08 kg/capita/year. Moreover, that is, the 40% waste percentage represents R$ 409.96, corresponding to US$ 172.23 per capita/year. Also, considering a waste behavior at the household consumption level of 25%, the amount generated in the household would be 78.80 kg/per capita/year, corresponding to R$ 256.23, equivalent to US$ 107.65 in 2008.

In recent research developed to directly estimate the amount of food wasted by Brazilian households, Porpino et al. (2018) detected the amount of 128.8 kg of food wasted per year. According to the authors, the identified value positions Brazil among the countries that waste the least food in the world, a characteristic usually associated with more developed

Table 15.1 Per capita estimate of food waste in Brazilian household consumption in 2008

| Food groups | Total food purchase | | | Scenarios of food waste per capita | | | | | | | | | | | |
| | | | | 5% | | | 11% | | | 25% | | | 40% | | |
	kg	R$	US$*	kg	R$	US$*	kg	R$	US$*	kg	R$	US$*	kg	R$	US$*
Cereals/legumes/oilseed	40.23	81.92	34.42	2.01	4.1	1.72	4.42	9.01	3.79	10.06	20.48	8.60	16.09	32.77	13.77
Vegetables	27.08	49.80	20.92	1.35	2.49	1.05	2.98	5.48	2.30	6.77	12.45	5.23	10.83	19.92	8.37
Fruits	28.86	47.40	19.91	1.44	2.37	1.00	3.17	5.21	2.19	7.22	11.85	4.98	11.55	18.96	7.97
Flours/ pastas	18.09	46.87	19.69	0.90	2.34	0.98	1.99	5.16	2.17	4.52	11.72	4.92	7.24	18.75	7.88
Bakery	21.51	106.76	44.85	1.08	5.34	2.24	2.37	11.74	4.93	5.38	26.69	11.21	8.60	42.71	17.94
Meat/fish/offal	30.17	224.29	94.23	1.51	11.21	4.71	3.32	24.67	10.36	7.54	56.07	23.56	12.07	89.72	37.69
Poultry/eggs	16.42	70.80	29.74	0.82	3.54	1.49	1.81	7.79	3.27	4.10	17.7	7.44	6.57	28.32	11.90
Dairy products	43.71	117.42	49.33	2.19	5.87	2.47	4.81	12.92	5.43	10.93	29.36	12.33	17.48	46.97	19.73
Sugars/sweets/confectionery	20.52	47.47	19.94	1.03	2.37	1.00	2.26	5.22	2.19	5.13	11.87	4.99	8.21	18.99	7.98
Salts/condiments	5.44	22.27	9.36	0.27	1.11	0.47	0.60	2.45	1.03	1.36	5.57	2.34	2.17	8.91	3.74
Oils/fats	8.93	23.26	9.77	0.45	1.16	0.49	0.98	2.56	1.08	2.23	5.81	2.44	3.57	9.3	3.91
Beverages/infusions	50.71	99.04	41.61	2.54	4.95	2.08	5.58	10.89	4.58	12,68	24.76	10.40	20.29	39.61	16.64
Prepared foodstuffs/industrial mixtures/canned food/pickles	3.51	39.18	16.46	0.18	1.96	0.82	0.39	4.31	1.81	0.88	9.79	4.11	1.40	15.67	6.58
Other products	0.04	48.42	20.34	0.00	2.42	1.02	0.00	5.33	2.24	0.01	12.11	5.09	0.02	19.37	8.14
Total	336.72	1.024.91	430.58	15.76	51.25	21.53	34.67	112.74	47.36	78.80	256.23	107.65	126.08	409.96	172.23

Source: Available at: www.bcb.gov.br/
Notes: The minimum reference salary of the survey was R$ 415.00, effective January 15, 2009.
* The exchange rate used is that for January 2009: R1 = US$ 2.38.

countries. Also, this corresponds to a proportion of per capita food waste between the 11% and 25% scenarios.

It should be noted that although the meats and fish group did not contribute the highest quantitative value of household food waste in Brazil, it presented higher monetary value compared to other groups of food items. This question corroborates Nahman and Lange's (2013) finding that meat, fish, and seafood represent only 9% of the total amount of waste in the South African FSC, but the highest price of these products represents 41% of the monetary waste.

Other relevant research on FLW was carried out in the United States of America. In order to identify values of food waste over the analyzed period, in 1974 approximately 900 kcal per capita/day was wasted, whereas in 2003 the Americans wasted 1,400 kcal per capita/day (Hall et al., 2009). According to the authors, this represents 150 trillion kcal/year.

It is worth mentioning that although Brazil is among the largest food producers and the second largest agricultural exporter in the world (OECD/FAO, 2015), the Brazilian population has sometimes presented levels of food insecurity (IBGE – Instituto Brasileiro de Geografia e Estatística, 2010). Food and nutritional insecurity have always been linked to the inaccessibility of sufficient food for an active and healthy life permanently (Hoffman, 1995). Socioeconomic aspects are among the main limits that make it impossible for the population, especially from developing countries, to obtain access to food (Abreu et al., 2001).

Currently, Brazil coexists with a double nutritional epidemiological conjuncture related to food insecurity. Situations of hunger coexist with situations of the population obesity, the so-called Nutritional Epidemiological Transition, which is a phenomenon characterized by the increase in overweight and obesity rates in the population. According to the Brazilian Institute of Geography and Statistics, 65.6 million Brazilians do not have sufficient food, 40.1 million of whom live with the mild form of food insecurity, claiming to be hungry occasionally; 14.3 million are in a moderate situation, able to eat properly but in food insecurity in the period of three months prior to the survey; and 11.2 million go through food deprivation, or severe food insecurity (BRAZIL, 2013). On the other hand, data from the same research indicate that currently 50.8% of Brazilians are overweight, and more men are overweight than women.

Generally, these distinctions also occur: overeating, and there may be consumer food waste (Eshel and Martin, 2006), coexists with malnutrition, also caused by inequalities in distribution (Porkka et al., 2013). Thus, food insecurity, obesity, and overweight, which are also associated with poverty and growth in developed and developing countries (James et al., 2001; Abelson and Kennedy, 2004), are observed.

The precarious distribution and supply situation, based on a high loss pattern, are responsible for subtracting a considerable portion of food from the productive effort and exacerbating the world's availability of food (Belik, Cunha, and Costa, 2012). Still, these authors argue that the highest rates of food loss are in the distribution phase and are considered significant on a global scale, but with few diffused efforts to combat this phenomenon. In developing countries, food waste arises mainly due to financial, managerial, and technical constraints ranging from harvesting, storage, facilities, infrastructure, processing, packaging, and marketing systems, leading to the loss of over 40% of post-harvest food (Parfitt et al., 2010).

Table 15.2 presents estimates of total quantification of household food waste in Brazil and its regions in 2008. Estimates range from 2 million to 23 million kilos of food wasted at

Table 15.2 Estimates of total Brazilian household food waste in 2008

Brazil and regions	Scenarios of food waste total											
	5%			11%			2.5%			40%		
	kg	R$	US$*	kg	R$	US$*	kg	R$	US$*	kg	R$	US$*
Brazil	2,993,763.75	9,734,197.35	4,089,483.41	6,586,280,259	21,415,234.18	8,996,863.50	14,968,818.77	48,670,986.77	20,447,417.04	23,950,110.03	77,873,578.83	32,715,867.26
North	247,253.63	804,950.46	338,171.85	543,957.99	1,770,891.01	743,978.07	1,236,268.16	4,024,752.30	1,690,859.26	1,978,029.05	6,439,603.68	2,705,374.82
Northeast	769,729.50	2,392,719.29	1,005,217.53	1,693,404.90	5,263,982.43	2,211,478.57	3,848,647.50	11,963,596.44	5,026,087.65	6,157,836.00	19,141,754.30	8,041,740.24
Southeast	1,245,338.85	4,441,403.69	1,865,900.81	2,739,745.47	9,771,088.13	4,104,981.78	6,226,694.25	22,207,018.47	9,329,504.04	9,962,710.80	35,531,229.55	14,927,206.47
South	529,601.52	1,740,828.08	731,348.18	1,165,123.34	3,829,821.77	1,608,966.00	2,648,007.60	8,704,140.39	3,656,740.91	4,236,812.16	13,926,624.62	5,850,785.46
Midwest	201,898.49	666,658.57	280,073.34	459,438.98	1,466,648.85	616,161.35	1,009,492.45	3,333,292.83	1,400,366.69	1,615,187.93	5,333,268.53	2,240,586.70

Note: The minimum reference salary of the survey was R$ 415.00, effective January 15, 2009.
* The exchange rate used is that for January 2009: R1 = US$ 2.38.
Available at: www.bcb.gov.br/

the household consumption level. The most populous regions, the Southeast and Northeast, are those that contribute the largest amounts.

Nationally, these amounts range from R\$ 9 billion (US\$ 4,089,483.41) to R\$ 77 billion (US\$ 32,715,867.26) that circulated in the Brazilian economy and were wasted. A study carried out in South Africa in 2012 showed that the total cost of food wastage in the country's food value chain was approximately \$ 7.7 billion per year, with 9.75% of this value occurring at the consumption level (Nahman and Lange, 2013).

Final considerations

In this research, estimates of food waste at the consumption level for Brazil and its regions were calculated for the year 2008. A summary of food waste policy in Brazil was provided to give context to this quantification.

It was also identified that the beverage and infusions; dairy; cereals, legumes, and oilseeds product groups; and the meat, fish, and offal group were the most acquired by Brazilians in 2008. The Southern region purchased the largest amounts of most food groups.

In relation to expenditure, the groups identified with the highest values were meat, fish and offal; dairy products; beverages and infusions; baked goods; and cereals, legumes, and oilseeds. The North region and the South region were the ones that spent the most on the food groups surveyed.

The regions with the largest acquisition and largest population, consequently, have the highest values, in kilograms and monetary, of waste. Therefore, the estimates in the waste scenarios presented values between 2 million and 23 million kilograms of food wasted at the household consumption level for the year 2008. These values ranged from R\$ 9 billion (US\$ 4,089,483.41) to R\$ 77 billion (US\$ 32,715,867.26) according to the specific scenario.

The quantification of food waste in Brazil requires more detailed information, especially regarding the different links in the FSC. Therefore, this work adds general results and contributes as a basis for future research and raises the importance of developing governmental actions to mitigate food waste.

The method used to estimate household food waste was based on scenarios, assuming that the waste is uniform among the Brazilian regions. By assuming this method, it is considered that all the different regions waste their food proportionally equally. This statement represents a limitation for the research, since it does not consider other possible factors that can determine the quantities of food wasted in each region.

Also, it can be highlighted as a limitation that the scenario constructed by a fixed percentage value, makes the regions and states that have the highest per capita values of acquisition and household expenditure, consequently, contribute to the higher values of waste.

The issue of FLW is still a challenge for Brazil. It is necessary to broaden knowledge and increase discussion on the subject, as well as to include civil society in the debate, as well as improving legislation to guide this process in a sustainable way and with minimal losses to the productive process and the environment.

Notes

1 The symbol R\$ corresponds to the Brazilian currency, the Real.
2 Regions and their respective states: North (Acre – AC; Amazonas – AM; Rondônia – RO; Roraima – RR; Amapá – AP; Pará – PA; Tocantins – TO); Northeast (Maranhão – MA; Piauí – PI; Ceará – CE; Rio Grande do Norte – RN; Paraíba – PB; Pernambuco – PE; Alagoas – AL; Sergipe –

SE; Bahia – BA); Midwest (Mato Grosso – MT; Goiás – GO; Distrito Federal – DF; Mato Grosso do Sul – MS); Southeast (Minas Gerais – MG; Espírito Santo – ES; Rio de Janeiro – RJ; São Paulo – SP); South (Paraná – PR; Santa Catarina – SC; Rio Grande do Sul – RS).

3 Average number of residents per family: Rondônia 3.34; Acre 3.75; Amazonas 4.15; Roraima 3.84; Pará 4.05; Amapá 4.14; Tocantins 3.59; Maranhão 3.81; Piauí 3.67; Ceará 3.71; Rio Grande do Norte 3.55; Paraíba 3.43; Pernambuco 3.38; Alagoas 3.6; Sergipe 3.54; Bahia 3.53; Minas Gerais 3.21; Espírito Santo 3.14; Rio de Janeiro 3.05; São Paulo 3.14; Paraná 3.23; Santa Catarina 3.1; Rio Grande do Sul 3.03; Mato Grosso do Sul 3.2; Mato Grosso 3.11; Goiás 3.13; Distrito Federal 3.36; Região Norte 3.9; Região Nordeste 3.55; Região Sudeste 3.14; Região Sul 3.1; Região Centro-Oeste 3.16; Brasil 3.4.

4 Population data: Brazil: 189,953,000; North: 15,327,000; Northeast: 53,493,000; Southeast: 79,800,000; South: 27,556,000; Midwest: 13,777,000 (IBGE – Instituto Brasileiro de Geografia e Estatística, 2010).

References

Abelson, P. and Kennedy, D. (2004) The obesity epidemic, *Science*, vol 304, pp 1413.

ABRELPE - Associação brasileira de empresas de limpeza pública e resíduos especiais (2018) 'Panorama dos Resíduos Sólidos no Brasil – 2017', http://abrelpe.org.br/pdfs/panorama/panorama_abrelpe_2017.pdf, acessed 14 February 2019.

Abreu, E. S. et al. (2001) 'Alimentação mundial: uma reflexão sobre a história", *Saúde e Sociedade*, vol 10, no 2, pp 03–14.

Belik, W., Cunha, A. R. A. A. and Costa, L. A. (2012) Crise dos alimentos e estratégias para a redução do desperdício no contexto de uma política de segurança alimentar e nutricional no Brasil, *Planejamento e políticas públicas*, vol 38, no 1, pp 107–132.

Bocchi, C. P. (2018) 'Perdas e desperdício de alimentos no contexto da política e do sistema nacional de segurança alimentar nutricional do Brasil' in Melo, E. V. (ed) Perdas e desperdício de alimentos [recurso eletrônico]: estratégias para redução. Edições Câmara; Brasília.

BRASIL - Lei 12.305/2010. (2010) 'Institui a Política Nacional de Resíduos Sólidos; altera a Lei 9.605, de 12 de fevereiro de 1998; e dá outras providências', www.planalto.gov.br/ccivil_03/_ato2007-2010/2010/lei/l12305.htm, acessed 14 February 2019.

BRASIL – Ministério da Saúde. (2013) 'Brasil estabiliza taxas de sobrepeso e obesidade', www.brasil.gov.br/saude/2014/04/brasil-estabiliza-taxas-de-sobrepeso-e-obesidade, acessed 02 September 2018.

Buarque, C. S. (2003) *Metodologia e técnicas de construção de cenários globais e regionais*. IPEA, Brasília.

Daskalopoulos, E., Badr, O. and Probert, S.D. (1998) Municipal solid waste: a prediction methodology for the generation rate and composition in the European Union and the United States of America, *Resources, Conservation and Recycling*, vol 24, no 1, pp 155–166.

Dubbeling, M. et al. (2016) *City region food systems and food waste management*. Germany: GmbH/RUAF Fundatuion/FAO, pp 186.

Dyson, B. and Chang, N. B. (2005) Forecasting municipal solid waste generation in a fast growing region with system dynamics modeling, *Waste Management*, vol 25, no 7, pp 669–679.

Eshel, G. and Martin, P. A. (2006) Diet, energy, and global warming, *Earth Interact*, vol 10, pp 1–17.

Evans, D. (2012) Beyond the throwaway society: ordinary domestic practice and a sociological approach to household food waste, *Sociology*, vol 46, pp 41–56.

FAO – Food and Agriculture Organization of the United Nations. (2013) *Food Wastage Footprint. Impacts on Natural Resources*. Rome: FAO.

FLW – Food Loss and Waste Protocol. (2016) *Food Loss and Waste Accounting and Reporting Standard*. World Resources Institute. USA:Washington, www.wri.org/sites/default/files/REP_FLW_Standard.pdf, acessed 10 June 2018.

Grisa, C., and Fornazier, A. (2018) 'O desperdício de alimentos e as políticas públicas no Brasil: entre ações produtivistas e políticas alimentares' in Zardo, M. (ed) Desperdício de alimentos [recurso eletrônico]: velhos hábitos, novos desafios. Educs; Caxias do Sul.

Gunders, D. (2012) *Wasted: how America is losing up to 40 percent of its food from farm to fork to landfill*. NRDC, New York City: Natural Resources Defense Council, pp 26.

Gustavsson, J. et al. (2011) *Global Food Losses and Food Waste— Extent, Causes and Prevention*, Gothenburg, Rome: Swedish Institute for Food and Biotechnology (SIK), FAO.

Hall, K.D. et al. (2009) The Progressive Increase of Food Waste in America and Its Environmental Impact, *PLoS ONE*, vol 4, pp 7940.

Halloran, A. et al. (2014) Addressing food waste reduction in Denmark, *Food Policy*, vol 49, pp 294–301.

HLPE. (2014) *Food losses and waste in the context of sustainable food systems*. A report by the High Level Panel of Experts on Food Security and Nutrition of the Committee on World Food Security. Rome: FAO.

Hoffman, R. (1995) Pobreza, insegurança alimentar e desnutrição no Brasil, *Estudos Avançados*, vol 9, no 24, pp 159–172.

IBGE – Instituto Brasileiro de Geografia e Estatística. (2010) 'Pesquisa de Orçamentos Familiares 2008–2009: aquisição alimentar domiciliar per capta', www.sidra.ibge.gov.br/bda/pesquisas/pof/, acessed 23 May 2018.

IME-Institution of Mechanical Engineers. 'Global Food -Waste Not, Want Not', www.imeche.org/knowledge/themes/environment/global-food, accessed on 29 September 2018.

James, P. T. et al. (2001) The worldwide obesity epidemic, *Obesity Research*, vol 9, pp 228–233.

Kranert, M. et al. (2012) 'Ermittlung der weggeworfenen Lebensmittelmengen und Vorschläge zur Verminderung der Wegwerfrate bei Lebensmitteln in Deutschland', www.bmelv.de/SharedDocs/Downloads/Ernaehrung/WvL/Studie_Lebensmittelabfaelle_Langfassung.pdf?__blob=publicationFile, accessed 17 November 2018.

Lipinski, B. et al. (2013) *Reducing Food Loss and Waste*. Instalment 2 of "Creating a Sustainable Food Future"; World Resources Institute: Washington, DC, USA.

Lundqvist, J., Fraiture, C. and Molden, D. (2008) *Saving Water: From Field to Fork – Curbing Losses and Wastage in the Food Chain, SIWI Policy Brief*. Stockholm International Water Institute (SIWI): Sweden:Stockholm.

Mason, L. et al. (2011) *The Department Of Sustainability Water, Population and Communities (DSEWPC) E. National Food Waste Assessment: Final Report*. Institute For Sustainable Futures (UTS), and The Department Of Sustainability, Environment, Water, Population and Communities (DSEWPC): Sydney, Australia, 2011.

Mondejar-Jiménez, J.A. et al. (2016) From the table to waste: an exploratory study on behaviour towards food waste of Spanish and Italian youths, *Journal of Cleaner Production*, vol 138, no 1, pp 8–18.

Monier, V. et al. (2010) 'Preparatory Study on Food Waste Across EU 27, Final Report', http://ec.europa.eu/environment/eussd/pdf/bio_foodwaste_report.pdf, accessed 17 November 2018.

Nahman, A. and Lange, W. (2013) Costs of food waste along the value chain: Evidence from South Africa, *Waste Management*, vol 33, no 11, pp 2493–2500.

OECD/FAO. (2015) 'Brazilian agriculture: prospects and challenges1, in OECD-FAO Agricultural Outlook 2015-2024. OECD Publishing, Paris, http://dx.doi.org/10.1787/agr_outlook-2015-en, accessed 27 July 2016.

Oelofse, S. and Nahman, A. (2013) Estimating the magnitude of food waste generated in South Africa, *Waste Management and Research*, vol 31, no 1, pp 80–86.

Parfitt, J., Barthel, M. and Macnaughton, S. (2010) 'Food waste within food supply chains: quantification and potential for change to 2050⊠, *Philosophical Transactions of The Royal Society B Biological Sciences*, vol 365, no 1554, pp 3065–3081.

PEIXOTO, M. (2018) 'Perdas e desperdício de alimentos: panorama internacional e proposições legislativas no Brasil', in Zardo, M. (ed) Desperdício de alimentos [recurso eletrônico]: velhos hábitos, novos desafios. Educs; Caxias do Sul.

Pekcan, G. et al. (2006) *Household food wastage in Turkey*. FAO Statistics Division, Working Paper Series, No: ESS/ESSA/006e, www.fao.org/docrep/013/am063e/am063e00.pdf, accessed 19 September 2018.

Pinstrup-Andersen, A., Gitz, V. and Meyback, A. (2016) Food losses and waste and the debate on food and nutrition security, in B. Pritchard, R. Ortiz and M. Shekar (eds.), *Routledge handbook of food and nutrition security*, pp. 169–196. London; New York.

Porkka, M. et al. (2013) From food insufficiency towards trade dependency: a historical analysis of global food availability, *PLoS One*, vol 8, no 12, pp 1–12.

Porpino, G. et al. (2018). *Intercâmbio Brasil – União Europeia sobre desperdício de alimentos*. Relatório final de pesquisa. Brasília: Diálogos Setoriais União Europeia – Brasil, www.sectordialogues.org/publicacao. accessed 19 January 2019.

Quested, T.E. et al. (2013) Spaghetti soup: the complex world of food waste behaviours, *Resources Conservation and Recycling*, vol 79, pp 43–51.

Stuart, T. (2009) *Waste: uncovering the global food scandal*. W.W. Norton Co, London.

Vanham, D. et al. (2015) Lost water and nitrogen resources due to EU consumer food waste, *Environmental Research Letters*, vol 10, pp 1–15.

WRAP. (2011) The Composition of Waste Disposed of by the UK Hospitality Industry. WRAP: Banbury, UK.

PART IV

Methodologies in food waste studies

Part IV of this Handbook turns to the repertoire of research approaches open to food waste researchers. The chapters present different ways of studying food waste through both qualitative and quantitative methods. Authors not only offer instructions to employ such methods but also present key debates currently unfolding on the merits and drawbacks of their usage.

Part IV opens with Sally Geislar's fundamental work of quantifying and measuring food waste in her chapter 'Quantifying food waste: food waste audits, surveys, and new technologies'. The premise of this chapter is that first there is a lack of shared resources with regard to how food waste can be best measured at the household level. There is an increasing demand for a detailed explanation of quantitative methods, such as auditing and surveys, their strengths and limitations, and how they can be best implemented in both practitioner and academic settings. This chapter meets all these demands by focusing on the retail and consumption areas of the supply chain drawing upon a number of real-world examples. Quantitative methods play an important role in tackling food waste by providing clear and consistent measures to account levels of waste against targeted reductions and compliance. The chapter gives detail around how food waste should be conceptualised in this context such as what sources of food waste to include, how edibility should be approached, and the differences between food waste and food loss. Following this, the chapter explains the Food Loss and Waste Protocol, attributable data collection methods, and waste composition analysis which includes a discussion of sampling, sorting, and weighing. The chapter concludes by detailing surveys in further detail as well as more recent emerging methods.

The second chapter moves beyond the 'what' and the 'how much' to the 'why' in researching food waste at the consumer level. In this chapter, Laura C. Moreno, Jordon Lazell, Vicki Mavrakis, and Belinda Li begin by looking at how different disciplines have approached this. The chapter then gives a critique of the popular theories of the planned behaviour approach and puts forward theories of practice as an alternative. The merits of this theoretical lens are outlined, such as the ability to move beyond understandings of attitudes and motivations to properly account for the consumption habits of consumers and how these are interconnected with the passage of food into waste. Specific considerations are then given with regard to using this approach to researching food waste behaviours. Ethnography is then discussed as an appropriate methodology with diaries further detailed as

253

one of the many methods that make up an ethnographic research procedure. This chapter is a useful toolkit and primer for qualitative food waste research. In particular the chapter is attentive to a number of things to consider when employing ethnography and the lens of theories of practice as an approach to investigating food waste.

Part IV then turns to look at psycho-social models in further detail. Sandra Davison, Lisanne van Geffen, Erica van Herpen, and Anne Sharp's chapter, 'Applying behaviour change methods to food waste', compares the Motivation, Ability and Opportunity Model (MOA) and the Transtheoretical Model (TTM) to understand householders' wasteful food behaviours. The chapter expands discussion on the ability and opportunity to undertake more desirable food behaviours to mitigate food waste. Through the two models, opportunities, interactions and interventions are interrogated. Five stages of behaviour change are further elaborated upon: pre-contemplation, contemplation, preparation, action, and maintenance. An example is then shown using data on Australian households' food management behaviours. The chapter draws to a close by explaining the workings of message campaigns as an intervention.

Tammara Soma, Belinda Li, Adrianne Lickers Xavier, Sean Geobey, and Rafaela F. Gutierrez introduce the role of social innovation in addressing the complex issue of food waste in 'All my relations: applying social innovation and Indigenous methodology to challenge the paradigm of food waste'. This chapter presents findings from the Food Systems Lab, a one-year social innovation lab to address the issue of food waste piloted in the City of Toronto. This chapter also explores alternative conceptual frameworks, which emerged from the participation of Indigenous stakeholders. Together these offer a unique perspective on food waste that should enrich and broaden the perspectives of students, researchers, and practitioners, and make us ask ourselves how we can engage with these new outlooks and methodologies.

Finally, Cansu Kandemir, Christian Reynolds, Monika Verma, Matthew Grainger, Gavin Stewart, Simone Righi, Simone Piras, Marco Setti, Matteo Vittuari, and Tom Quested, provide an overview of four modelling methodologies in 'Modelling approaches to food waste: discrete event simulation; machine learning; Bayesian networks; agent-based modelling; and mass balance estimation'. These different computational and mathematical models provide ways to simulate, diagnose, and predict different dimensions of complex food waste generation and prevention. For instance, 'discrete event simulation' is currently used to understand the different impacts of shelf life and portion size, while 'mass balance estimation' helps to estimate global food waste quantities when no physical measurements are available.

16

QUANTIFYING FOOD WASTE

Food waste audits, surveys, and new technologies

Sally Geislar

Introduction

The study of food waste has garnered increased attention by scholars, practitioners, commercial, and non-governmental organizations in recent years. As Porpino (2016) points out, peer-reviewed journal articles on household food waste saw a dramatic increase beginning near the end of the last decade. Yet the literature still lacks shared measures to quantify household food waste. As researchers prepare to fill this demand, an understanding of the various conceptualizations of food waste and the available methods can help guide study-design decisions.

This chapter will provide an introduction to the use of quantitative methods in food waste research with special attention to audits, surveys, and new technologies. Several examples from academic and practitioner settings will be discussed to highlight the strengths and limitations of each method. Furthermore, this chapter will focus heavily on retail and consumption stages of the food system in developed economies. Further discussion on qualitative approaches (Li, Moreno, and Lazell), developing economies (Papargyropou; Oelofse), and other food system stages (Bennett; Gooch) can be found in this volume.

Why quantify?

Quantitative methods generally help food waste researchers answer questions of 'what' and 'how much', while qualitative methods such as ethnographic observation are typically best-suited to answer questions of 'how' or 'why'. Food waste studies, as with other fields, will benefit from continued conversation between these two approaches. Qualitative research can identify new hypotheses and uncover new processes that quantitative researchers can use to improve predictive models. In turn, quantitative research can leverage large amounts of data to identify hotspots of food waste generation that demand in-depth qualitative attention to better understand how food waste occurs.

Quantifying food waste is an important step in meeting goals set by entities at scales ranging from a single company or city to the United Nations Sustainable Development Goals (UN SDG). For instance, in order to track progress in achieving UN SDG (2018) to 'halve per capita global food waste at the food retail and consumer levels and reduce food losses along production and supply chains', there must be clear and consistent measures of food loss and waste. At the opposite scale, a single company may conduct food waste measurements to ensure compliance, meet corporate responsibility goals, or reduce costs. The next section discusses points of contention in establishing consistent food waste measures.

Conceptualizing food waste

Having a clear and consistent definition of the subject to be measured enables a field to develop valid and reliable measures, and to generate understanding about the issue beyond a single case. Yet the measures used by organizations and governmental agencies around the world differ greatly, resulting in disparate conclusions of food waste estimates, contributors and appropriate interventions.

Decisions about what to include when we measure food waste reflect the values and goals of the researcher and often those of the funding entity. For instance, entities addressing health and hunger issues may quantify the caloric value of food waste or portion of edible food wasted. Measuring the greenhouse gas emissions similarly reflects goals to reduce the environmental degradation stemming from wasted food. The data and results of such studies, consequently, can be used to motivate or design appropriate interventions to address the issue(s) of interest. Indeed, Bellemare et al. (2017) argue that 'sound measures [are] the basis of sound policy-making'. However, divergence in food waste quantification risks producing incommensurable studies of food waste.

Several conceptual ambiguities serve as potential sources for such divergence. First, some measures exclude inedible food parts such as egg shells and pineapple skins because they do not represent missed opportunities to provide human sustenance. By contrast, researchers may include inedible food materials when interested in avoiding the environmental and economic costs of landfilling organic materials (WRI, 2016a). Rather than this distinction between inedible versus edible, WRAP (Quested and Murphy, 2014) conceptualized food waste in terms of avoidability; 'avoidable', 'possibly avoidable', and 'unavoidable'. The first reflects food that was edible when it reached the consumer, the second allows for different cultural understandings of what is edible (e.g., fish heads, carrot greens), and the third aligns with 'inedible' food parts such as our aforementioned pineapple skins.

A recent report that surveyed more than 500 Danish households underscores the importance of measures that account for consumer perceptions of edibility. Fish skins were considered 'never edible' by 62% of Danes (Stancu and Lähteenmäki, 2018, p. 40) even though a litany of recipes for crisp fish skins are readily available online, and mackerel, sardines, and even anchovies can be eaten whole. Further, there was no convergence on the perceived edibility of several vegetable parts including the upper part of leaks, broccoli stalks, and apple skins; no majority emerged on whether these foods were 'always edible', 'edible only in specific recipes', or 'never edible'.

Nicholes et al. (2019) argue that perceived edibility only paints part of the picture for food waste measures, for it says nothing of whether respondents personally eat that food. In a nationally representative survey in the UK, the authors found that despite a majority indicating a food item's edibility, most respondents indicated they 'never' or 'only occasionally' ate items such as parsnip and carrot skins, outer cabbage leaves, and stalks of broccoli and cauliflower (Nicholes et al., 2019). Put another way, just because people intellectually understand a food part as edible, doesn't mean it will make it to their dinner plate. Indeed extreme responses ('I never' or 'I always eat part') comprised two-thirds of all responses about what people actually eat, compared to a much more nuanced field of foods perceived as technically edible.

A second conceptual ambiguity arises from disagreement over whether food waste measures should exclusively focus on food produced for human consumption (FAO, ERS, FUSIONS) or include food grown for animal feed or energy production (US EPA). One important consequence of this is that when food produced for human consumption is removed from the supply chain and ultimately recovered for non-food use (e.g., animal feed, fertilizer), the former set of organizations consider this 'food waste' while the latter does not (Bellemare et al., 2017).

Bellemare et al. (2017) propose a food waste measure in which only landfilled food is classified as 'food waste', omitting food that has 'any kind of productive use, whether it is food or nonfood' (p. 1152). While this approach is consistent with tracking the goals of landfill diversion, measures like this are inadequate for researchers and practitioners who value a 'highest and best use' ethos embodied in food waste hierarchies (US EPA, 2016a). Landfill-focused conceptualizations of food waste fail to track progress toward preferred alternative processing methods (Geislar, forthcoming).

The stage at which food waste generation occurs also serves as an important demarcation for some measures. For instance, the US EPA does not consider waste that occurs prior to retail and household consumption to be 'food waste' (US EPA, 2017). Zero Waste Scotland and others adopted the term 'food loss' to capture food waste at these pre-consumption stages including production, distribution, or storage. Food loss exclusively pertains to food intended for human consumption that became unfit to eat prior to retail or household consumption (Parfitt et al., 2015).

Even food that is consumed may be considered food waste by some measures. Blair and Sobal (2006) conceptualize luxus consumption as a source of food waste through the consumption of calories in excess of the metabolic needs of the body. Perhaps most obviously pertinent to studies of obesity and nutrition, the authors explicitly link luxus consumption to the unnecessary social, environmental, and economic costs of the food system.

Overall, these disparate conceptualizations not only obscure the magnitude of food wastage, they also thwart efforts to identify the sources of food waste and to design appropriate interventions.

Quantitative food waste measures

Clear definitions of food waste will aid researchers in developing valid and reliable measures; that is, measures that are accurate and consistent. In quantitative research, a measure is thought to be valid when it reflects the relevant social and material reality of food waste. The measure should capture what we think of when we think of food waste (i.e., face validity) and, to the extent possible, it should capture all important factors pertaining to food waste (i.e., content validity). To be consistent, quantitative measures should be applied in the same fashion across time, populations, studies, and research entities.

Though validity and reliability are both important, efforts to increase one may come at the expense of the other. Specifically, adopting a uniform (i.e., consistent) measure may ultimately overlook important elements of food waste in particular food system contexts or toward particular goals, whereas efforts to capture all relevant aspects of a given context threaten commensurability, and indeed feasibility. Truly, while growers, grocers, and households may report food waste with the same reliable metric (e.g., weight), the types of food waste generated, sites of investigation, and approaches to measurement will differ greatly. For instance, a grower may estimate food waste by including the portion of food unfit for retail specifications, or damaged during harvest. These measures are rendered meaningless at the household level. Conversely, measuring food waste in terms of weight alone obscures important patterns in food waste generation particular to a site or to the food system stage. Where possible, researchers should obtain estimates both for food waste weight and the contextual factors contributing to food waste generation.

The food loss and waste protocol

International efforts are under way to develop more consistent, or reliable, measures of food waste. In 2013, the World Resources Institute (WRI) launched the Food Loss and Waste Protocol (FLWP) as a multi-stakeholder partnership to standardize the quantification of food loss. The FLWP supports entities to develop food loss and waste inventories and to render the data and results consistent across inventories.

The FLWP defines ten quantification methods and guides users step-by-step through the application thereof. While the protocol is designed to be accessible to a wide range of purposes and educational backgrounds, it does identify tools that demand more expertise. Best practices for data collection and the relevant advantages and disadvantages are also outlined. The FLWP further instructs readers on determining the scope of their study, developing a sampling strategy, conducting measurement, and scaling up the data (i.e., how to use sample results to derive estimates for the target population).

The protocol differentiates inferential methods (i.e., mass balance, modeling, and proxy data) from those that rely on measurement in some form (i.e., direct weighing, counting, assessing volume, waste composition analysis (WCA), records, diaries, surveys (WRI, 2016b)). The current chapter will focus on WCAs and surveys as well as new technologies not discussed in the protocol. For further discussion on diaries see Li, Moreno, and Lazell (this volume) and for inference-based measures see Reynolds (this volume).

The different methods described in the protocol capture only three unique variables (i.e., weight, quantity, and volume), and the latter two are typically converted to weight when reported. Of course, converting all measures to the same unit is in fulfillment of the protocol's goal to provide a unified and consistent measure for food waste. These measures are explored in greater detail in the following section.

In addition to weight, volume, and quantity, food waste is often reported in terms of cost (Buzby and Hyman, 2012), number of meals lost, 'calorific value, quantification of greenhouse gas impacts and lost inputs (e.g., nutrients and water)' (Parfitt et al., 2010, p. 1). Measures may be further classified by food item type (e.g., dairy, meat, grain), food system stage, meals vs. snacks, preparation site (e.g., at-home, take-out, pre-prepared), level of processing (e.g., fresh, packaged, frozen), retail source (e.g., big-box stores, corner stores; Lee, 2018). Ultimately, the FLWP would urge researchers to report food waste weight alongside such measures.

It should be noted that while capturing data that renders one's results comparable to others is desirable, it should not dissuade researchers from capturing additional factors or developing new measures that are relevant to the research question or that improve our understanding of the relationship between food waste and the world. Indeed, the protocol itself includes an appendix to support researchers interested in expressing food waste in terms beyond (and including) weight (WRI, 2016a, p. 128).

Fields such as public health, for instance, have long collected data on portion size, caloric intake, and nutritional value to understand issues of obesity, hunger, and malnutrition. This data may help unlock processes by which food waste occurs and reveal opportunities for policy intervention. Other measures may expand our ability to link food waste effects across the food system. A measure of embodied resources, for instance, captures the water, energy, and labor used to produce, transport, store, and prepare food that ultimately became waste (UN FAO, 2014). A recent food-systems measure called 'net yield efficiency' incorporates food waste at later stages of the food system (e.g., distribution and consumption) to estimate the efficiency of different farming methods (Baker et al., 2019). These variables are often reported alongside weight measures and can already be found in several multi-disciplinary food waste studies (Visschers et al., 2016; Cuéllar and Webber, 2010; Roe et al., 2018).

Data collection methods

The FLWP suggests several considerations for researchers choosing a quantification method, including level of accuracy, access to waste materials, logistical support, and study resources and goals. The protocol includes a link to WRI's method-ranking tool that ranks available methods along with rationale for the ranking (WRI, 2016a, p. 63). While new technologies are transforming the means by which weight, count, and volume variables are measured (see the 'Emergent methods' section, below), I will here briefly discuss conventional methods.

The most straightforward measure of food waste involves direct weighing with a scale. By contrast, quantity can be captured by counting and is most appropriate when food waste occurs in discrete units (e.g., watermelons, cans, bags, pallets). Count measures typically estimate weight by measuring the weight of a single unit, and then multiplying by the number of units (WRI, 2016b). Volume-based measures are often used where weighing or counting is not feasible. First, researchers determine the approximate space occupied by food waste and then convert this to a weight estimate. However, not all food items fill space with equal density. For example, a bowl of strawberries clearly has more empty space or 'void' than the same bowl filled with sugar. While the FAO and others have established density factors to estimate volume-based weight measures (kg/l) for different types of food waste, the FLWP encourages researchers to develop their own density factor based on a sample of the waste being studied.

The remaining tools described in the protocol use at least one of these measures. For instance, surveys may ask respondents to weigh or estimate volume. The following sections describe basic procedures for waste composition analyses and surveys, followed by new technologies not discussed in the FLWP. For each, I present examples from the literature to demonstrate their application.

Waste composition analysis

WCA involves separating food waste from other waste streams, sorting food items by category, and finally weighing each category (WRI, 2016b). WCAs can be conducted for a range of entities, including households, communities, schools, or businesses.[1] In residential settings, WCAs are typically done to evaluate existing sorting behaviors, provide baseline data from which to design and test waste management policies and schemes, or to calculate environmental impact (Parfitt et al., 2015). Businesses may conduct WCAs to avoid waste generation by identifying cost-saving measures, whereas schools may do so in line with educational goals.

WCAs are costly and demand significant resources in terms of staff time, materials, logistics, and facilities. However, the strength of WCAs is in the accuracy of measurement, especially by avoiding under-reporting, a problem common to survey and diary methods (WRI, 2016b). Combining WCAs with the latter methods can reveal not only the quantity and types of food waste, but why and how they are produced (see Parizeau et al., 2015).

The WCA can be used in a cross-sectional study design that provides a snapshot of food waste, or in longitudinal and experimental designs. For instance, Bernstad (2014) collected and analyzed waste materials at five different time points to test the effect of two interventions on waste composition. The team examined the amount of separated food waste, portion of total waste, contamination, and typology of food wasted. To reduce costs, WCAs can be conducted for a sub-sample of the study population, as when Bernstad surveyed 1,633 residents but only analyzed materials for 30% of the study sample. Sampling strategies for WCAs are discussed in the next section, and the WCA process is described in greater detail in the 'Sorting and weighing' section below.

Sampling

Three common sampling strategies for WCAs include bulk, small-area, and individual-producer sampling (WRI, 2016a, 2016b; for a detailed sampling guide see Parfitt et al., 2015). Bulk sampling relies on a regular collection vehicle to transport aggregated waste from several individual-producer sites (e.g., residences or businesses) to a single location where the contents will be sorted by food type. Small-area sampling uses the same process except that researchers select a particular neighborhood or business cluster from which to sample because they exhibit some characteristic of interest (e.g., low- or high-income neighborhood, proximity to transit). Finally, individual-producer sampling collects food waste directly from producers, applies a unique identifier to each unit's waste bag, and keeps the contents from each unit separate from the others throughout the WCA process. If the producer does not secure the materials in a bag, the research team does so.

Individual-producer sampling presents additional factors including logistical and legal issues that should be considered. Because this method does not rely on regular collection vehicles, researchers should collect the materials on the normal collection day close to the normal time of collection (WRI, 2016b). This approach not only increases the likelihood that participants will make their waste materials available to researchers at the correct time, but also ensures that researchers know the period of food waste generation (i.e., waste produced since the previous collection day). However, researchers should be sure to collect the materials at least one hour prior to collection time to avoid having their sample accidentally collected by the waste hauler. Researchers should consult local laws to determine whether a permit is required for transporting and storing waste and whether consent from individual producers is required for 'snooping' through the waste of others (WRI, 2016b).

Sampling method should be selected based on appropriateness to study goals and available resources. Bulk and small-area sampling tend to be cheaper than sampling individuals but also require researchers to work closely with relevant waste hauler(s) to collect and divert the sample. These methods produce a lower level of data granularity compared to individual sampling, limiting the claims that can be made about causal factors and the ability to identify appropriate interventions.[2]

Sampling procedures and data analysis should account for factors that may produce skewed data on the type and amount of waste placed in the bin. Zero Waste Scotland highlights socio-economic and demographic factors, housing type, season, climate, and existing waste schemes (Parfitt et al., 2015). Furthermore, location of the waste container, holidays, and frequency and cost-scheme of collection are important factors shaping what households and businesses place in the bin. WCAs in businesses require further attention to business days, economic sector, level of mechanization, and staff education level (WRI, 2016b).

Using a sampling method to conduct a WCA requires a final step to scale up the data. Scaling up refers to the process of using the data collected from the sample to make claims about the larger population to which one aims to generalize (i.e., target population). For instance, if a small-area sample collected food waste from several blocks in a low-income community, a well-designed study can generalize the results of this sample to make claims or predictions about all blocks in the low-income community, and perhaps, though with greater limitations, to the municipality and to low-income blocks more generally. Failing to consider the aforementioned factors in sampling procedures, however, may produce non-representative results and so threaten the generalizability of the study.

Sorting and weighing

Prior to collecting any materials, researchers should decide which categories are appropriate for sorting waste materials.[3] Categories of food waste should be clearly defined, avoid overlap, and capture all possible classes of food relevant to the study site and population (Parfitt et al., 2015; WRI, 2016b). Food and meals that are composite or unidentifiable may be difficult to classify. In such cases, the FLWP suggests assigning the meal based on the main ingredient. A casserole, for instance, may comprise noodles, several vegetables, bread crumbs, meat, and sauce, but with pasta being the dominant ingredient, it would be placed in the 'grain' category. For unidentifiable foods, researchers should create a separate category for this and sort accordingly (WRI, 2016b).

By aligning food waste categories with existing standards, researchers can ensure comparability of data (Parfitt et al., 2015; WRI, 2016b). However, this should not discourage the measurement of sub-categories of interest to a particular study as long as the data can be aggregated to estimate the standard measure. Consider a study examining grocery store discards of fruit with short shelf-lives (e.g., raspberries, blackberries), but the hypothetical standard measure only considers 'fruit' as a single category. The study could proceed in measuring raspberries and blackberries as sub-categories of fruit so long as all fruit is captured in the measures, perhaps by using an 'all other fruit' category. By contrast, if the study only measures 'fruit' but the hypothetical standard uses sub-'fruit' categories, the study results would be incommensurable with others because the study's 'fruit' measure cannot be disaggregated.

Once categories have been determined, researchers should prepare a sorting area by arranging several bins, one for each category of food waste, around a raised screen with a tarp underneath to catch fine particles (WRI, 2016b). A small amount of collected materials are subsequently placed onto the screen from where researchers evaluate materials and place them in the appropriate bin without forcing items through the screen. The material that is small enough to fall through the screen onto the tarp should be subsequently placed in a separate bin and weighed. Furthermore, some amount of liquid may have collected in the bins, and researchers should keep absorbent materials (e.g., cloths, mop) for safety and hygiene purposes.

A single study may need several such sorting stations operating simultaneously to accommodate the study team or the sampling unit. Once all materials have been sorted, the bins are weighed and weight totals for each category are recorded. If an individual-producer sampling method was used, researchers should be careful to keep producers' materials separated and carefully identified throughout the WCA.

Zero Waste Scotland (2015) outlines best practices when weighing waste. These include using scales with an appropriate range of weights for the scope of waste measured, regularly calibrating scales, and omitting from final measures the weight of food packaging or any container used to hold materials on scales. Researchers should also ensure that sorting containers do not fill beyond the ability to move them or support their weight on the scale. Both the FLWP and Zero Waste Scotland stress the importance of ensuring that work spaces adhere to safety and health codes including adequate lighting, restrooms for sorters, and hygienic practices (Parfitt et al., 2015; WRI, 2016b).

Surveys

Surveys are a widely used tool to estimate food waste across the food system (e.g., farmers, grocers, caterers), especially at the level of household consumption. Generally, surveys use structured questions to collect information from a large number of subjects (e.g., individuals, companies, schools). Questions may be open-ended to allow free-response or closed-ended with continuous or discrete response categories. Surveys typically collect data on attitudes and beliefs, but may also be used to record self-reported behavior and self-collected measurements. Because surveys measure characteristics of food waste materials and the producers thereof, correlates and predictors of food waste can be identified.

Instructions typically specify who should complete the survey, and when measurement should take place. For example, a study may instruct the household member primarily responsible for grocery shopping to record weights only when the kitchen food waste collection container is full, at the end of each day, or at the end of each meal event. Incentives and feedback are often used to recruit and retain participants.

Measuring food waste with surveys

To quantify food waste, surveys can instruct respondents to report the weight, quantity, or volume by estimating or even collecting measurements. In all cases, calibrated devices and clear instructions, using graphics where possible, can increase respondents' accuracy. To measure weight directly, respondents will need a scale of some kind. Ideally, all participants use the same scale type and food waste container (e.g., kitchen caddy, compostable bag) to reduce errors. Consistency can be improved by distributing scales (e.g., handheld), or sending researchers to the sites to weigh the waste. While these procedures yield gains in accuracy, both methods add significant costs to a study.

Volumetric measurements are less costly than direct weighing, and may be achieved with a variety of strategies. Participants may be asked to report volume and count of bags or containers used. Utilizing containers or bags with a known volume can improve accuracy. For instance, several campaigns in the US EPA's Food Too Good to Waste Challenge (US EPA, 2016b) instructed participants to collect food waste using a common paper grocery bag with a printable template marking volume affixed to the bag (e.g., 1/8 ... 7/8, Full). Participants were asked to record the volume once per week. If the bag filled prior to the week's end, they recorded how many days it was used, began a new bag, and reported weekly bag quantity.

Volume estimates are simplified in communities with volume-based fees for food waste collection. Some fee systems, for example, require residents to purchase a particular bag for food waste disposal, providing a ready standard for volume estimates. In a residential survey, Lee (2018) tailored data collection approaches to each community's collection method across Seoul, South Korea. For those using standardized food waste bags, Lee requested an estimate of the number and fullness of bags that week. In communities using RFID technology (see 'Emergent methods' section, below), the survey requested the recent food waste bill. Lee could then calculate the weight by dividing the billed amount by the local rate.

Research design in surveys

Like WCAs, surveys may be used in cross-sectional, longitudinal, and experimental designs. Longitudinal approaches are used to detect changes in the variable(s) of interest over time by administering the same survey at two or more time points. Surveys in experimental designs are administered before and after some treatment or intervention received by the treatment group. When using a case-control experimental design, the sample is randomly assigned to treatment or control groups, and the latter does not receive the intervention. Randomization should ensure that each individual in the sample has an equal chance of receiving the treatment as not, thus strengthening claims that any differences between the groups result from the intervention.

Experiments may be lab-based (Qi and Roe, 2017) or in-situ (Geislar, 2017). Qi and Roe (2017) conducted a laboratory experiment (n = 251) testing whether consumers would waste more food if they knew it would be composted rather than landfilled, even when they were aware of the social and environmental harms of wasted food. Participants were given a meal and randomly assigned to one of four groups who either received information about the harms of food waste or about financial literacy (i.e., control group), and were either informed that their food waste would be landfilled or composted. This complex design enabled the authors to detect that while information about social and environmental harms motivated food waste prevention, knowing that food waste would be composted mitigated this effect.

By contrast, Geislar (2017) conducted a field experiment (n = 364) to improve a new curbside organics program. A random selection of all households in the program were surveyed before and after receiving the new bins. Participants were then randomly assigned to treatment and control groups in a second intervention testing whether norm communication improved participation, followed by a third and final survey. Respondents were asked to report how much of their food waste was separated into the new organics bin from 'none' to 'all' on a five-point scale. The results indicated that while supportive infrastructure (i.e., curbside bins) increased food waste separation, residents receiving normative messages about neighborhood participation further increased separation behaviors, retention, and policy support beyond the control group.

Field experiments tend to be more costly than those in labs and must account for more potentially confounding factors. However, the highly controlled, artificial setting of lab-based experiments is thought to create behavioral responses that differ from participants' everyday experience. Results of field experiments are thought to better reflect real-world responses to interventions. For more examples of experimental designs, see van Geffen and Davison (this volume).

Survey administration and access

Surveys may be administered in-person by a researcher, or completed by the respondent on their own time. In-person surveys occur in laboratory or public settings such as a grocery entrance, farmer's market, or park. They may be printed and mailed (Visschers et al., 2016), digitally distributed through email, websites, mobile applications, or in both print and digital formats within a single study (Geislar, 2017).

Contact information may be sampled from telephone directories (Visschers et al., 2016); however, significant concerns arise over the representativeness of such samples as younger residents are increasingly disproportionately unlikely to have a landline phone. Contacts may be purchased from private research firms (Lee, 2018), but tend to be costly. Instead, many researchers partner with interested organizations or agencies that already have access to contacts. Russell et al. (2017) designed a survey that the collaborating grocer administered digitally to their existing customer database. Geislar (2017) received a complete list of addresses enrolled in the new curbside organics program from the public agency overseeing residential waste management.

Careful attention should be paid to whether the survey mode (e.g., phone, mail, email, website, mobile application) threatens the response rate and representativeness of the sample. Researchers often must weigh trade-offs between cost and response rates in selecting survey mode. Response rates tend to be highest with in-person surveys, but so are costs. Phone surveys require a great deal of staff and training time, making them similarly costly to administer. Residents are also increasingly screening unknown numbers to avoid telemarketers and scams, driving up the number of contacts needed at the outset to obtain the desired sample. Mail-based and digital surveys similarly suffer from the onslaught of junk mail. Moreover, mail can be costly due to initial postage and provision of a postage-paid return envelope to increase response rates.[4] While digital surveys have no postage costs, they threaten representativeness as those without internet access are excluded.

Digital surveys may also threaten response rates. For instance, a trial recruitment found that recruitment materials providing both print and digital survey options rather than only a digital option resulted in a five-fold increase in the response rate (15% and 3%, respectively; Geislar, 2017). The population recruited with both print and digital response options were also more representative of the general population in terms of age and education. Researchers conducting probability sampling should estimate the appropriate recruitment sample by accounting for desired power (UCSF, 2015), anticipated response rates (ideally based on a trial recruitment), and expected attrition during the study period, especially in longitudinal studies. See Geislar (2016) for details about the process.

In-person survey collection should consider carefully how various environmental factors may result in selection bias in their sample. Positioning survey administrators at farmer's markets, for instance, would be an excellent approach if one's research question pertained to market-goers in particular. However, the generalizability of such a study beyond farmer's market patrons is limited as they tend not to be representative of the broader population. By contrast, grocery stores remain the conventional means of food procurement in most developed countries, providing comparatively lower risk of selection bias. Nevertheless, other factors may introduce bias into the sample; time of day, economic and racial integration of neighborhood and clientele, even the appearance, demeanor and linguistic compatibility of survey administrators. The increasing use of grocery-delivery services may add further selection risk.

Emergent methods

In this section, I provide a brief overview of technology use in quantifying food waste, especially digital photography methods. In a recent systematic review, Hannan et al. (2015) discuss spatial, sensory, and radio frequency technologies being used to optimize waste management. They found that spatial technologies such as GIS and GPS have been used in estimation, route optimization, and billing. Sensors and imaging technologies measure sorting accuracy, bin-fill levels, moisture, energy, and odors. Some sensors automatically weigh and transmit food waste data. For instance, 'load cells' on collection vehicles (Hannan et al., 2015) and kitchen bins with built-in scales (Gartland and Piasek, 2009) capture and transmit waste weight. Others used infrared LED lights in the bin lids that trigger a collection request when one of the beams is broken, indicating desired bin-fill level (Johansson, 2006 as cited by Hannan et al., 2015).

Other technologies such as radio frequency identification (RFID) are already in use in some cities to support volume-based fee systems (Lee, 2018). RFIDs use 'a tag equipped with a wireless microchip and antenna which communicates directly to a reader,' typically affixed to the collection vehicle (Gnoni et al., 2013, p. 28). This technology can be used to trace not only information on waste generators (e.g., address), but weight, volume, and type of food. Gnoni et al. (2013) used an RFID reader and weight platform affixed to the collection vehicle to provide immediate feedback and bill calculation while reducing the labor needed in manually recorded pay-as-you-throw systems.

While many of these studies rely on technologies still foreign to most people, others are using more commonplace technology to quantify food waste. Namely, digital photography methods capture a photograph of food and or food waste that researchers use to derive estimates of quantity, weight, or type. Williamson et al. (2003) and others validated the use of digital photography to estimate portion size of food selection, plate waste, and food intake. When combined with data transmission technology such as smart phones, digital photography methods reduce participant burden and error from self-report estimates, while increasing the granularity of data and the speed of collection, analysis, and feedback compared to survey or audit methods.

For instance, Roe et al. (2018) used the Remote Food Photography Method (RFPM) asking participants to photograph their selected food prior to eating, and then their plate remains after eating for each serving. Participants then transmitted photographs via smart phone. Finally, researchers derive portion size and waste estimates using the difference of food left on the plate from food selected and converting each to grams. Ultimately the authors derived caloric intake and nutrition by referencing the USDA's Food and Nutrient Database for Dietary Studies using the difference of food waste from portion size. When participants failed to collect photographs (about 10% of days), Roe et al. requested paper diaries. When a photographed item was unidentifiable by researchers, participants were asked to classify it using the aforementioned USDA database.

The RFPM allows researchers to identify which types of food items are wasted in the greatest quantity and frequency, much like a WCA, but at a fraction of the cost. The RFPM can also be used to distinguish which meals generate the most food waste, a granularity often out of reach of WCAs with an accuracy superior to surveys. However, most photography-based studies have used the lunch-time meal despite recent research identifying a greater amount of food waste generated at the evening meal (Quested and Murphy, 2014). Collecting granular data on food waste types and sites can aid in appropriately targeting behavioral and infrastructural interventions.

Furthermore, the current scope of RFPM use is somewhat narrow as it has largely been used to capture plate waste, omitting household food waste arising from over-preparation or poor storage for instance. Similarly, few have used RFPM to examine what is done with food once it becomes waste (e.g., fed to pets, in-sink disposal, compost, garbage). One exception is the use of photography inside the bin. Comber and Thieme (2013) used a 'bincam' to automatically capture photos of each waste-bin deposit in participants' homes. The mini-smartphone installed on the underside of the lid detects each time the lid opens and closes, then snaps a photo of the bin contents. In this study, the photos were then coded and tagged by workers at Amazon's crowd-sourcing service Mechanical Turk (Mturk) who identified the 'total number of items, the number of recyclable items, and the number of food items in each image' (Comber and Thieme, 2013, p. 1202).

This method significantly reduces participant burden and reduces lag-time for feedback; however, added costs for coding and tagging photos may prove prohibitive. Future research should adapt RFPM and other digital photography methods to examine processes outside of meal events and to quantify food waste as it moves into, through, and out of the household.

Comparing quantitative methods

This chapter set out to summarize a suite of quantitative data collection methods. Recent research has tested several of these methods for accuracy, consistency, completeness, and effort on the part of respondents and researchers (van Herpen et al., 2019). The researchers compared food waste estimates from surveys, food diaries, photo-coding, and kitchen caddies. The lattermost were collected and weighed by researchers. Participants were assigned to one of three groups; each completed surveys and diaries, and one group was also asked to record their food waste using photos and caddies.

The four methods revealed low variation in food waste estimates within subjects over time, providing some evidence for reliability; however, the study revealed significant differences between the estimates from the different methods. Indeed, food waste estimates from surveys were significantly different from all other methods, and demonstrated the greatest underestimation of food waste compared to measures that estimated weight (i.e., photos and caddies). In fact, survey underestimation persisted across all states of food waste (i.e., 'unused', 'partly used', 'meal leftover', and 'stored leftover') and was especially pronounced for fruits, vegetables, and breads and cereals.

Conclusion

The quantification of food waste is a necessary tool to reach policy goals intended to reduce and recover food waste across the food system. Shared meaning around what constitutes food waste will be necessary to render international efforts commensurable. This shared meaning can support uniform measures and reliable methods for quantitative data collection like those proposed by the World Resources Institute (WRI, 2016b). Uniform measures should stand independent of what may be divergent goals and values embodied in policies targeting food waste, be they health, environment, economy, or justice. However, uniform measures should not discourage innovations in measuring food waste.

In choosing the appropriate method, researchers have several factors to consider including available resources, desired level of accuracy, expertise needed, and access to food waste materials and participants. In general costs increase as the desired granularity of data or expected response rates increase. Yet this positive association is no natural law. New technologies are already transforming how food waste is measured and monitored, reducing per unit costs of collecting household-level data. This emerging era of metered food waste presents new opportunities for understanding and preventing food waste generation.

Notes

1 Special considerations are needed for conducting WCAs at a school, and the interested reader should consult Terry et al. (2017).
2 It should be noted that to avoid an ecological fallacy, analysts should avoid making claims about food waste generation at a unit smaller than that at which the data was collected. Specifically, small-area samples cannot inform us about individual households within the sample.
3 See 'Food waste measures' section for examples including food item type or edibility.
4 Business-Reply Mail through the US Postal Service offers special rate systems that only charge postage for envelopes that respondents actually mail. This service may be available to universities, companies, or agencies in the US.

References

Baker, N., Popay, S., Bennett, J., & Neafsey, M. (2019). Net yield efficiency: Comparing salad and vegetable waste between community supported agriculture and supermarkets in the UK. *Journal of Agriculture, Food Systems, and Community Development, 8*(4), 179–192. doi: 10.5304/jafscd.2019.084.013.

Bellemare, M., Çakir, M., Peterson, H., Novak, L., & Rudi, J. (2017). On the measurement of food waste. *American Journal of Applied Economics, 99*(5), 1148–1158. doi: 10.1093/ajae/aax034.

Bernstad, A. (2014). Household food waste separation behavior and the importance of convenience. *Waste Management, 34*(7): 1317–1323.

Blair, D., & Sobal, J. (2006). Luxus consumption: Wasting food resources through overeating. *Agriculture and Human Values, 23*(1), 63–74. doi: 10.1007/s10460-004-5869-4.

Buzby, J.C., & Hyman, J. (2012). Total and per capita value of food loss in the United States. *Food Policy, 37*(5): 561–570.

Comber, R., & Thieme, A. (2013). Designing beyond habit: Opening space for improved recycling and food waste behaviors through processes of persuasion, social influence and aversive affect. *Perspectives on Ubiquitous Computing, 17*, 1197–1210. doi: 10.1007/s00779-012-0587-1.

Cuéllar, A., & Webber, M. (2010). Wasted food, wasted energy: The embedded energy in food waste in the US. *Environmental Science & Technology, 44*(16), 6464–6469. doi: 10.1021/es100310d.

Gartland, A., & Piasek, P. (2009). Weigh you waste: A sustainable way to reduce waste. *Computer Human Interactions*, 2853–2858. doi: 10.1145/1520340.1520414.

Geislar, S. (2016). Closing the food systems loop: Leveraging social sciences to improve organic waste policy (Doctoral Dissertation). Irvine: University of California..

Geislar, S. (2017). The new norms of food waste at the curb: Evidence-based policy tools to address barriers and benefits. *Waste Management, 68*, 571–580. doi: 10.1016/j.wasman.2017.07.010.

Geislar, S. (forthcoming). The problem with food waste: A comparative case study of organic waste policy in the U.S. and The Netherlands. In Y. Rollins, & C. Kuyvenhoven, *Throw Away Societies: People, Places and Waste*. London: Routledge.

Gnoni, M., Lettera, G., & Rollo, A. (2013). A feasibility study of a RFID traceability system in municipal solid waste management. *International Journal of Information Technology and Management, 12*(1), 27–38.

Hannan, M., Al Mamun, M., Hussain, A., Basri, H., & Begum, R. (2015). A review on technologies and their usage in solid waste monitoring and management systems: Issues and challenges. *Waste Management, 43*, 509–523. doi: 10.1016/j.wasman.2015.05.033.

Lee, K.C. (2018). Grocery shopping, food waste, and the retail landscape of cities: The case of Seoul. *Journal of Cleaner Production, 172*, 325–334.

Nicholes, M. J., Quested, T. E., Reynolds, C., Gillick, S., & Parry, A. D. (2019). Surely you don't eat parsnip skins? Categorising the edibility of food waste. *Resources, Conservation, and Recycling, 147*, pp.179–188.

Parfitt, J., Barthel, M., & Macnaughton, S. (2010). Food waste within food supply chains: Quantification and potential for change to 2050. *Philosophical Transactions of the Royal Society Biological Sciences, 365*(1554), 3065–3081.

Parfitt, J., Griffiths, P., & Reid, T. (2015). *Guidance on the Methodology for Waste Composition Analysis.* Stirling: Zero Waste Scotland.

Parizeau, K., von Massow, M., & Martin, R. (2015). Household-level dynamics of food waste production and related beliefs, attitudes, and behaviors in Guelph, Ontario. *Waste Management*, 35, 207–217.

Porpino, G. (2016). Household food waste behavior: Avenues for future research. *Journal of the Association for Consumer Research, 1*, 41–51. doi: 10.1086/684528.

Qi, D., & Roe, B. (2017). Foodservice composting crowds out consumer food waste reduction behavior in a dining experiment. *American Journal of Agricultural and Applied Economics, 99*(5), 1159–1171. doi: 10.1093/ajae/aax050.

Quested, T., & Murphy, L. (2014). *Household Food and Drink Waste: A Product Focus.* Banbury, UK: UK Waste and Resources Action Programme.

Roe, B., Apolzan, J., Qi, D., Allen, H., & Martin, C. (2018). Plate waste of adults in the United States measured in free-living conditions. *PLoS ONE, 13*(2), 1–16. doi: 10.1371/journal.pone.0191813.

Russell, S. V., Young, C. W., Unsworth, K. L., & Robinson, C. (2017). Bringing habits and emotions into food waste behavior. *Resources, Conservation, and Recycling*, 125, 107–114.

Stancu, V., & Lähteenmäki, L. (2018). *Consumer Food Waste in Denmark.* Aarhus University: Denmark Centre for Food and Agriculture.

Terry, M., Sturdivant, S., & Nguyen, J. (2017). *Guide to Conducting Student Food Waste Audits: A Resource for Schools.* Washington, DC: United States Department of Agriculture.

U.S. EPA. (2016a). Food recovery hierarchy. Retrieved Apr 2016, from Sustainable Management of Food: www.epa.gov/sustainable-management-food/food-recovery-hierarchy

U.S. EPA (2016b). *Food: Too good to waste: An Evaluation Report.* Washington, DC: US Environmental Protection Agency.

U.S. EPA. (2017, Feb). United States 2030 food loss and waste reduction goal. Retrieved from Sustainable Management of Food: www.epa.gov/sustainable-management-food/united-states-2030-food-loss-and-waste-reduction-goal

UCSF. (2015, Jan). *Sample Size Calculators.* Retrieved from Clinical & Translational Science Institute: www.sample-size.net/sample-size-means/

UN FAO. (2014). *Food Wastage Footprint: Full-Cost Accounting.* Rome: Food and Agriculture Organization of the United Nations.

UN SDG. (2018, Sept). Goal 12: Sustainable consumption and production. Retrieved from United Nations Sustainable Development Goals: www.un.org/sustainabledevelopment/sustainable-consumption-production/

van Herpen, E., van der Lans, I., Holthusysen, N., Nijenhuis-de Vries, M., & Quested, T. E. (2019). Comparing wasted apples and oranges: An assessment of methods to measure household food waste. *Waste Management, 88*, 71–84. doi: 10.1016/j.wasman.2019.03.013.

Visschers, V. H., Wickli, N., & Siegrist, M. (2016). Sorting out food waste behavior: A survey on the motivators and barriers of self-reported amounts of food waste in households. *Journal of Environmental Psychology*, 45, 66–78. doi: 10.1016/j.jenvp.2015.11.007

Williamson, D., Allen, H., Martin, P., Alfonso, A., Gerald, B., & Hunt, A. (2003). Comparison of digital photography to weighed and visual estimation of portion sizes. *Journal of the American Dietary Association, 103*(9), 1139–1145. doi: 10.1053/jada.2003.50567.

WRI (2016a). *Food Loss and Waste Accounting and Reporting Standard.* Washington, DC: World Resources Institute.

WRI (2016b). *Food Loss and Waste Protocol: Guidance on Flw Quantification Methods.* Washington, DC: World Resources Institute. Retrieved from www.flwprotocol.org

17

MOVING BEYOND THE 'WHAT' AND 'HOW MUCH' TO THE 'WHY'

Researching food waste at the consumer level

Laura C. Moreno, Jordon Lazell, Vicki Mavrakis and Belinda Li

Introduction

Globally, it is estimated that approximately one-third of food intended for human consumption is lost or wasted. The consumer level of the food supply chain has been identified as one of the largest contributors to food waste generation, especially for more developed and affluent countries (Gustavsson et al., 2011). As a result, there is an increasing focus on wasted food at the consumer level, particularly in households (see Chapter 8 in this Handbook). Previously, efforts to mitigate the impacts of food waste largely focused on diverting food materials from landfill and incinerators to compost or other diversion options (Papargyropoulou et al., 2014; Thyberg & Tonjes, 2016). However, there is an increasing acknowledgement that waste prevention or source reduction, rather than diversion, is the optimal solution to reduce the negative environmental and social impacts of food waste (Papargyropoulou et al., 2014; Thyberg & Tonjes, 2016; Salemdeeb et al., 2017).

Beyond methane emissions from landfills, the impacts of wasted food are many. The resources and pollutants associated with food production, including energy, water, and greenhouse gas emissions, are essentially 'wasted' when food goes uneaten (FAO, 2013). Prevention addresses the impacts of wasted food by maximising the amount of food eaten by people and minimising the generation of food waste. As such, prevention interventions tend to focus on the 'avoidable' or 'edible' portions of food waste. Common suggestions for food waste prevention in households include improving storage practices, better planning, and using all parts of food items (e.g. the broccoli stalk). Other suggestions, including reformatting date labels or offering smaller portion sizes, aim to change practices in other stages of the food supply chain to influence consumer-level food waste (Papargyropoulou et al., 2014; Thyberg & Tonjes, 2016).

Food waste prevention at the individual (person, household, or business) level requires changes in behaviours that contribute to wasted food, such as food provisioning, storage, and cooking (Watson & Meah, 2013; Quested et al., 2013; Papargyropoulou et al., 2014; Thyberg & Tonjes, 2016). These behaviours are often difficult to change because they are rooted in habit or engrained in a person's culture or identity (Stefan et al., 2013; Devaney & Davies, 2017). To understand how to design policies, consumer outreach programmes, or other interventions that target food waste prevention, a deeper understanding of *why* food is wasted is necessary. Despite the growing body of literature on the causes of wasted food, there is relatively limited knowledge about the underlying determinants of consumer-level food waste (Graham-Rowe et al., 2014; Schanes et al., 2018). Given the complexity and diversity of behaviours, experiences, meanings, values, and contexts related to wasting food, a research approach that is flexible and iterative is needed. Many qualitative research methods fit these needs because they allow for behaviours to be studied within social, cultural, and local contexts. It is within these contexts that values, attitudes, and beliefs acquire particular cultural meaning that allow for a better understanding of how and why food is discarded.

Qualitative methods are commonly used in research eliciting information on human behaviour. In the context of food waste, qualitative methods reveal how people perceive discarding food within their homes and why they do it, beyond the often-quoted answer, 'because we buy too much!' (Koivupuro et al., 2012; Roodhuyzen et al., 2017). Qualitative methods provide tools for researchers to talk to participants and observe them in such a way that participants do not feel pressured to change their behaviour. This is important as people may act in ways that are contrary to the attitudes and knowledge they hold toward an issue. For example, most people report that wasting food makes them feel guilty. In a national survey of U.S. consumers, 52% of respondents indicated that throwing food away 'bothers them a lot' (Neff et al., 2015). However, presence of guilt has not been correlated with amount of food waste generated in a household (NRDC, 2017a). Qualitative research is suited to not only provide explanations of how people may not act in accordance with their stated beliefs, but also how someone's perception of their behaviours (stated behaviour) compares to their actual, or revealed, behaviour (Barr, 2006).

While modelling, auditing, and quantification can provide important information about the food waste problem, namely *what, how much,* and *where,* it does not tell us *why* food is wasted. Food waste comes about as an often overlooked result of the mundane, routinised nature of people's lives (Evans, 2011a, 2014). Understanding why food is wasted involves exploring not just the food material itself, but also people and the flow of actions that make up their everyday lives (Spaargaren, 2011). There are many behavioural theories in sociology, psychology, and economics that can be used to explain consumer-level food waste. However, theories of practice has proven theoretically and analytically beneficial for studying unsustainable behaviours, such as wasted food (Evans, 2014).

In this chapter, a theories of practice approach is presented as a means of framing methods to study why food is wasted. The discussion highlights the capacity of theories of practice to overcome the drawbacks of other approaches that have a narrow focus on the responsibility of individuals that subsequently preclude wider contextual aspects of society and culture (Wahlen & Dubuisson-Quellier, 2018). Critically, a 'practice lens' re-characterises the problem of wasted food away from one that is understood and solved via the pursuit of individual control, to one that considers the routines and habits of consumers within a larger set of social, cultural, and structural contexts. Instead of piecemeal change by individual behaviour in isolation, insight derived from theories of practice can provide structure and guidance to help create transformative, socio-technical change (Shove & Walker, 2010; Spurling et al., 2013; Shove, 2014; Welch & Yates, 2018).

The following section gives a brief overview of behavioural theories used in consumer food waste research followed by a more detailed introduction to theories of practice. The remainder of the chapter outlines two sets of methodologies that can be used to explore 'why' food is wasted: ethnography and kitchen diaries. Broadly, ethnography is a toolkit of qualitative methods for understanding lived experiences in a 'natural' setting within cultural context. Diaries can be used to capture both qualitative and quantitative information about routines and habits that might otherwise be overlooked. As a whole, this chapter puts forward and discusses theoretical underpinnings and methodologies that can be applied to research to help answer the question of why food is wasted at the consumer level.

Understanding the *why*: an introduction to theories of consumer behaviour

Increasing interest in food discarded by consumers has led to an uptick in research related to behaviour, with a specific focus on how food is wasted in households (Stangherlin & de Barcellos, 2018). It is widely accepted that the single act of throwing food away is not the only behaviour of interest that allows researchers to understand why and how food is discarded in households. Rather, food-related household practices and routines within the food activity stages, including planning, shopping, storing, cooking, and eating, are also studied in order to understand how these stages contribute to excess or discarded food (Quested et al., 2013; Setti et al., 2018). From the point of view of participants, the purpose of participating in these activities is to produce and consume food, not to discard it. However, food can be discarded at many points within and between these activity stages. For example, leftovers from dinner can be discarded immediately after eating or stored in the refrigerator to be either eaten or discarded at a later date. Understanding how people engage with food is critical to understanding how food is transformed into waste within households as well as allowing for intervention opportunities to be identified. Thus, to fully define the act of wasting food, behavioural models must capture factors related to both waste *and* food.

Many studies use a psychology- or sociology-based lens for framing how people act and why they waste food. Psychology-based approaches, such as the Theory of Planned Behaviour (TPB) or the Transtheoretical Model of Behaviour Change, tend to identify and measure specific factors and processes that either serve as barriers or motivators for pro-environmental behaviours (Schanes et al., 2018). Additionally, the dominant ways of characterising behaviour places the individual/consumer/eater at the centre of the analysis (Hargreaves, 2011; Southerton & Yates, 2015) either as a rational actor making independent choices or as a simple follower of social norms and expectations (Warde, 2005). Studies utilising these psychology-based theories tend to mainly focus on the predicting determinants, such as:

* planning and shopping being important predictors (Stefan et al., 2013);
* intentions being potentially linked with waste reduction (Graham-Rowe et al., 2015);
* perceived behavioural control, or a person's perception of what they can and cannot change, being somewhat insignificant in predicting behaviour (Stancu et al., 2016).

The TPB is one of the dominant psychological theories applied to consumer-level food waste. TPB assumes that: (1) the majority of human behaviour is goal-directed; (2) someone's intention is the closest precursor to behaviour and can be used to determine what they do; and (3) intention is mostly influenced by attitudes and social norms about that behaviour (Ajzen, 1985). One of the strengths of TPB is that it provides a somewhat linear model of behaviour that is easily applied to quantitative modelling. However, TPB has many shortcomings that make it less than ideal for food waste research. First, TPB focuses on one specific behaviour; the behaviour of wasting food is often intertwined with many food-related behaviours which are omitted from the analysis. Second, to effectively use TPB, the variables (e.g. social norms, attitudes) must be compatible in terms of time and context. Behaviours associated with wasting food often vary significantly both spatially and temporally, thus limiting the TPB model to very specific times and contexts (Hargreaves, 2011). Additionally, TPB does not consider the attitude–behaviour gap whereby the attitudes of individuals, such as their values and motivations (often used as measures in TPB), do not always represent their actual, performed behaviour (Boulstridge & Carrigan, 2000; Moraes et al., 2012). With the focus on the individual as the main agent of change in TPB, there has been a tendency to categorise wasting food as a behaviour that is a result of an individual's laziness, apathy, or lack of knowledge (Evans, 2011b; Meah, 2014). Researchers have questioned the accuracy and usefulness of understandings of wasteful behaviours derived from individually based attitudes, motivations, and beliefs (Lazell, 2016). Furthermore, it is questionable whether the long-term behaviour changes required to significantly lower the amount of food wasted can be achieved through relying on individual behaviour changes (Evans, 2011a).

In contrast, sociology-based approaches, such as theories of practice, look beyond the individual to include social, cultural, and contextual factors. This approach involves seeking an understanding of the underlying social norms, the materials and objects involved in behaviour, and how these are organised over the course of daily life. Here, 'behaviours' are called 'practices', and are considered to be representative of factors that exist and are constructed beyond the individual. Shove et al. (2012: 14) state that practices are made up of three elements: meanings, which refers to 'symbolic meanings, ideas and aspirations'; materials, which refers to the objects and the components of these objects that are involved in practices; and finally competencies, which are the skills and knowledge of knowing how to do something. In some ways, the process of behavioural influence can be considered cyclical and continuous; behaviours are situated and distributed in social norms which, in turn, hold influence over the conduct and behaviour of others (Evans, 2018). In other words, practices here are positioned as the vehicles through which behaviour can be understood, including how they are employed in the flow of everyday life.

Theories of practice represent an increasingly used theoretical frame for both sustainable consumption and food waste research (Evans et al., 2012; Southerton & Yates, 2015). There is no single theory of practice, rather this approach draws upon a heterogeneous group of theoretical contributions that situate practices and their dynamics at the centre in systems and structures of society. Using this as a theoretical underpinning, wasting food is not seen as an individual phenomenon, but rather a social phenomenon arising from shared meanings, things and their uses, bodily and mental activities, knowledge, and understanding (Evans, 2014; Lazell, 2016). Individuals are considered 'carriers of practice' meaning that the behaviours they participate in are not qualities of the individual, but are qualities of the practice (Reckwitz, 2002; Hargreaves, 2011). A key difference between this practice approach and a psychology-based theory is that rather than characterising all individuals' behaviours as a result of deliberation and weighing possible options, a practice approach is able to consider the automated or unconscious nature of behaviours that are difficult to explain through people's rational accounts of their actions (Warde, 2016). While theories of practice has the advantage of capturing the complexity of behaviour, it is less easily translatable to quantitative modelling because it has no pre-established structure.

Theories of practice takes into account many of the complexities in behaviour that TPB does not effectively address. It allows for multiple practices to be linked and to incorporate the spatio-temporal component of food-related behaviours (Shove et al., 2012). To give an example, TPB can capture the pro-environmental beliefs and intentions to not waste food by a parent and their children. However, it cannot capture how the parent's routine, such as their work schedule, may influence if meal plans were followed or how changes in that routine may subsequently affect how meals are prepared, potentially leading to waste through uneaten food. During a particularly stressful week at work, a parent may choose to order pizza instead of following through with their week's plan of cooking a healthier meal from scratch. The fluctuating dynamics of daily life intertwined with many other factors and contexts all influence how much food is eventually discarded in that household.

The following outlines a version of theories of practice for research on food waste, encapsulating the need to look at wider consumption behaviours within everyday life.

A practice-based approach to research food waste

What is a practice?

'Practices' are the core analytical unit for theories of practice that encompass expressions of behaviour. There are many different definitions of a practice. However, a practice is generally accepted as a set of repeated actions or activities that occur in different contexts across time and space, with specific components of what happened ('doings') and how it was perceived ('sayings') (Schatzki, 1996). A practice represents the generally accepted norms of how people go about activities, such as how the practice of driving a car features a number of doings (e.g. moving the steering wheel or stopping at a red light) and sayings (e.g. feeling impatient in traffic). Reckwitz (2002) expands this definition further to explain:

> A practice is thus a routinized way in which bodies are moved, objects are handled, subjects are treated, things are described, and the world is understood ...
> A practice is social, as it is a 'type' of behaving and understanding that appears at different locales and at different points in time and is carried out by different body/minds.
>
> *(Reckwitz, 2002: 250)*

By de-centring the individual and making the practice the focal point, there is a broader focus on how a 'combination of material objects, practical know how, and socially sanctioned objectives [are] deployed' (Southerton & Yates, 2015: 138). Various authors have presented a framework of elements that constitute a practice which typically include:

- *Objects, tools, and their materiality* which can include physical objects and their use (Reckwitz, 2002), including tools and technologies. For instance, in food waste research, the food item itself is a key factor in terms of its putrescibility and freshness which prompts a visceral response. Other key objects and tools include packaging, refrigerators, and grocery stores. These 'things' are not just important as physical objects or technologies, but also in how they create and carry social meanings and script actions.
- *Competencies and practical know-how* signifies the skills and techniques, knowledge, and understanding required to perform a practice (Reckwitz, 2002; Shove et al., 2012).

For example, this might include cooking abilities or knowledge of how to store food.

* *Socially negotiated meanings* which includes 'symbolic meanings, ideas and aspirations', mental activities, motivations, and emotions (Shove et al., 2012: 14). For instance, the act of showing love and care by providing food or cooking for someone (Evans, 2011a).

Theories of practice outline the workings of practices in the social world. A first wave of theoretical work by Giddens and Bourdieu, among other theorists, established how habits and routines are a basis for knowledge. Gidden's (1984) and Bourdieu's (1977, 1990) works were critical in explaining how society can be interpreted as a series of recurring practices that represent the automated, mundane, and dispositional actions in everyday life. A second wave of work by Schatzki (1996, 2001, 2010) and Reckwitz (2002) brought together, clarified, and further developed a range of practice-based theories, known as a 'practice-based approach' (for a more comprehensive overview of theories of practice see David Nicolini's (2012) book *Practice Theory, Work, & Organization*).

Schatzki (1996, 2010) explains that a practice can be viewed not only as a coordinated entity, as described above, but also as a performance. This gives an important clarification of how practices can be studied as the main unit of analysis in research. In simpler terms, the 'performance' of a practice are the actions performed by individuals. For example, observing household members interact with and eventually discard food is documenting the 'performance' of wasting food. These observed actions are theorised as practices by interrogating the routine habitual nature of the actions as well as their meaning, competence, and/or material elements. People participate in a practice in different ways, depending on varying contexts and characteristics (for instance, household organisation or eating preferences) (Reckwitz, 2002). These differences can be explored to better understand how people engage in a practice as well as the structure of the practice (Warde, 2005). These differences exist because the individual is a skilled performer (neither autonomous nor a thoughtless conformer) who actively negotiates and enacts a wide range of practices within daily life (Hargreaves, 2011). At the same time, the performer reproduces, negotiates, and shapes practices through their repeated performances (Warde, 2016).

A practice lens can help achieve societal transformation toward more sustainable forms of consumption. It offers an alternative form of environmental governance from strategies that rely on change via the consumer's moral conscious or responsibility of doing the 'right' thing (Spaargaren, 2011). Rather, policy interventions should seek to address sets or bundles of practices that are representative of different domains of everyday life (Shove, 2014). Food waste is inherently linked to wider food practices such as food provisioning and preparation. Instead of focusing narrowly on changing the behaviour of wasting food, change should be pursued for the 'bundle' of interlinked practices, also called 'regimes'. A 'regime' describes the shared understandings or ways of living actioned through bundles of practices (Crivits & Paredis, 2013; Evans, 2014). For example, a 'bundle' of practices for wasting food may include components of planning for meals, transportation to purchase food, shopping, preparing and storing food, interactions with family or friends, and eventually discarding any leftovers. Regimes of food practices are based on socio-cultural understandings and interconnected with the practices of everyday life. Halkier et al. (2011) explain that a focus on multiple intersecting practices is required, rather than single practices, in order to achieve an understanding of consumption practices. A practice approach incorporates such factors into research and therefore into designing policy interventions. Using a practice lens, interventions might include modernising a practice, modifying the materials involved through technological change, or laying out new ways of doing a practice. The next section discusses application of theories of practice in the area of food waste at consumer level in more detail.

Application of theories of practice in consumer food waste research

A small but ever-evolving field has started to emerge in the food waste literature that utilises a practice-based approach. The prominent work of David Evans has made a distinct case for moving away from blaming food wastage on the individual (Evans, 2011a) and shifting consumer-focused studies toward practice approaches. His work is an established marker for knowledge of domestic consumption and material culture (Evans, 2014), in particular the socially and materially organised practices present in the passage of food into waste (Evans, 2012). This knowledge is set against a backdrop of behavioural dimensions of sustainable consumption, such as the social and cultural conventions of everyday life (Evans, 2011a, 2011b).

A number of authors have also utilised a similar approach. Practice-based studies of domestic food and waste have examined the provision of food (Watson & Meah, 2013), eating of food (Southerton & Yates, 2015), devices such as fridges and freezers (Hand & Shove, 2007; Waitt & Phillips, 2016), food preparation and cooking (Foden et al., 2017), household organisation (Evans, 2011a; Hebrok & Heidenstrøm, 2019), work and school routines (Revilla & Salet, 2018), and food waste bins (Metcalfe et al., 2012) among other factors yet to be explored (Hebrok & Boks, 2017; Schanes et al., 2018).

Methodological considerations for practice-based food waste behaviour research

In the field of consumption, literature provides mixed guidance on methodological and analytical questions of practice (compare Halkier & Jensen (2011) and Crivits & Paredis (2013), for example), and this has yet to trickle down to sub-themes, such as food waste. Nevertheless, this can be viewed as an advantage in enabling the researcher or practitioner to tailor aspects of the field of theories of practice to suit their study or programme, with this chapter illustrating the ways in which theories of practice can be employed to study why food goes to waste at consumer or household level.

The choice of methods and their implementation must 'get at the heart' of practices. Observational methods to understand both the doings and sayings of a practice are ideal as they overcome limitations of methods that rely on stated behaviours, which can be different from actual lived behaviours (Vermeir & Verbeke, 2006). Studies of food waste using a practice-based lens have utilised ethnographic and mixed method approaches, including interviews, material collation (e.g. collecting receipts and recipes), participant observation (e.g. shop-alongs), and participant-generated resources, such as kitchen diaries. These methods allow researchers to better understand wasting food within the lived, mundane, everyday experience by triangulating the participants' reflections on their practices with both researcher- and participant-generated accounts of actions (Pink, 2012). Researchers are seeking data on what people consider normal day-to-day habits; the 'shared understandings of normality' as represented in the practices participants both engage in and coordinate (Evans et al., 2012: 116).

Studies of practices should also take into account the aspects that order, shape, condition, and contextualise these practices. These may extend across practices of acquisition, appropriation, appreciation, disposal, divestment, and devaluation in the case of consumption (Evans, 2018). For example, understanding the practice of wasting food requires researchers and practitioners to also explore aspects such as how food is purchased, how people communicate or express love by cooking and eating food, if people are concerned about health, and daily routines. Questions can be raised over where the study of practice begins and ends. Which adjacent practices are relevant and which are not is not always clear, including which details of which elements should be considered (Warde, 2005; Southerton & Yates, 2015). Nicolini's (2012) chapter 'Bringing it all together: a toolkit to study and represent practice at work' is an excellent account of approaching this problem. Nicolini explains a process of 'zooming in' to look at the performative intricacies and outcomes of a practice then 'zooming out' to explore how practices relate to each other in space and time. Understanding of the practice is accomplished by translating the doings and sayings of participants using descriptive and contextualised accounts of their performances (Nicolini, 2012: 211–242).

When studying food waste behaviours and related practices, there are three key things to consider in order to ensure practices are placed centrally in the data collection and analysis procedure. First, methods should be able to record performances and their embodied nature (such as the visceral nature of interactions with food and waste). Second, participants are not always able to explain their actions, particularly in the case of habits and routines. For some participants, practice relevant details may seem obvious and overlooked, such as the banalities of preparing food or organising food in the home. Third, there are potential challenges in the invasiveness of methods, especially since many of the performances of interest happen behind closed doors, in a household. Ideally, a practice-based account is produced from a fully immersive position, being present during the participant's performances of practices to break down boundaries between the participant's account of the practices they engage in and their actual lived behaviour. However, a fully immersive experience in a household can be difficult to achieve. Options such as material collation and voluntarily recorded photography/video with a follow-up interview can mitigate such concerns.

In the following two sections, ethnography and diaries are explored as two common methodologies to explore consumer-level food waste using a practice-based lens. Each section will briefly describe the methodology, including how it can be specifically tailored to a study food waste.

Ethnography: a toolkit of observation methodologies

What is ethnography?

Ethnography, from the Greek words *ethnos* meaning folk or people and *grapho* meaning to write, is the systematic study of people and cultures. It can help us understand human behaviour by discovering its meanings in a socio-cultural context (Hammersley & Atkinson, 2007). Ethnography is a set of qualitative methods used in social sciences that focuses on the observation of social practices and interactions. The goal is to observe without imposing any structure or framework upon the situation, or as Spradley (1979) states, the researcher must 'get inside their heads'. This reference is made with regard to the researcher understanding the culture and values of the participants, or in this case, of how they construct their world and what they are saying and doing about food waste. Several different types of ethnography exist based on different approaches and contexts (see Hammersley & Atkinson, 2007 in further reading for an extensive account of ethnography approaches).

Studies of food waste using ethnography allow researchers to provide a socially and culturally contextualised account of the passage of food into waste as part of the lived experience of the individual. Ethnography allows for thick descriptions of behaviour and its framing in naturally occurring settings (Brewer, 2000; Elliott & Jankel-Elliott, 2003). How and why food becomes wasted by consumers is wrapped up in myriad practices, objects, tools, and meanings related to consumption (Schanes et al., 2018). An ethnographic approach allows researchers to capture such aspects of the food waste phenomenon to more fully understand it.

Evans' (2014) ethnographic work exploring food consumption and waste in the home featured methods such as shop-alongs and observing meal preparation. His research outlined the benefits of 'hanging out' with participants to understand their consumption habits. Another example is Cappellini and Parsons' (2013) work on interpersonal family relationships and food waste showing how food can be a point of contention between family members. Farr-Wharton et al. (2014) used ethnography to understand the reasons leading to food being wasted due to not being eaten before its expiry. Ganglbauer et al. (2013) showed how food waste arose from multiple moments and how those moments were integrated with other practices by using interviews and in-home tours alongside a fridge camera. Work exploring kitchen practices has also utilised visual ethnographies to enable participants to present stories of their use of kitchens through tours, photography, diaries, scrapbooks, interviews, and video footage (Wills et al., 2015).

Methodological considerations for ethnography

Ethnographic methods are field-based, personalised, use more than one data-collection technique, require a long-term commitment (from several weeks to a year or more), and are inductive. In other words, research is performed without prior assumptions or hypotheses. Instead, it is more exploratory in nature, accumulating descriptive detail to build toward general patterns or explanatory theories. Ethnography relies heavily on storytelling and presenting the critical incidents being studied (selectively), which is viewed as a weakness by those using quantitative methods. However, ethnography can uncover experiences and knowledge that other research methods do not, and it can highlight those things that are taken for granted.

Employing ethnography with a practice lens must place performances at the centre of its data-collection procedure. This means seeking to collate accounts of performances through different means, for example through observation, interviewing, visually through photography or video, through participant-generated materials such as diaries and images, and also drawing upon researcher reflections of the research progress. Each of these has its merits as a method. Hitchings (2012) and Martens (2012) discuss the extent to which aspects of practice can be uncovered through 'talk' highlighting some limitations of how actions are translated into words. Martens and Scott (2017) explain a three-spurred ethnographic practice-based strategy of looking 'at' and 'into' performances to supplement understanding of everyday kitchen practices. Kendall et al. (2016) presents a similar multifaceted approach as a 'tool kit' that aligns well with a practice theoretical lens. These methods are able to move the research premise along from individualistic accounts that solely consider attitudes and motivations to properly account for how food comes to be wasted. Depending upon the nature and context of study, certain tools will be more applicable than others in unearthing participants' actions.

Three methodological considerations are now outlined in the context of studying why food is wasted through ethnographic means. First, ethnography seeks an insiders' view of a study group and the dynamics of their activities. Naturally, the researcher is an integral part of the research, often bringing their own views and subjectivities. It is therefore important to take into consideration the researcher's background in order to properly account for any subjectivities (Eberle & Maeder, 2011; Creswell & Creswell, 2017). Max Weber stated that all research is influenced to some extent by the values of the researcher and through those values certain problems are identified and studied in particular ways (Weber, 1946). The conclusions and implications drawn from a study are largely grounded in the moral and political beliefs of the researcher. As a way of acknowledging this potential limitation, Layder (2006) explains that stating the researcher's own assumptions at the start facilitates the production of more powerful and adequate interpretations of data.

Second, it is critical to define the field of study and social environment within which behaviours are being observed and researched. When making observations, the actual event of interest, in this case discarding food, should not be the only information recorded. Contextual information about the physical and social environment as well as other relevant practices should also be recorded. Given there are several different methods that represent an ethnographic approach, important information to adequately record might include: the location, time, or other relevant information about where the observation is taking place, including spatial and material characteristics (e.g. size of kitchen or type of supermarket); usage of objects and typical behaviours that represent the place or event (e.g. size of refrigerator and how full it is) (Pink, 2012); level of participation and involvement of study subjects; the level of formality of the interview; whether the discussion took place as a separate action or while the participant was engaged in activities; and a description of other relevant practices and activities that were observed (e.g. cooking).

Third, ethnographic research is time consuming, as it is carried out over significant periods of time in order to accumulate in-depth knowledge of the group or culture being observed. In order to obtain rich data, the ethnographer must build up trust with participants and, as an outsider, must be able to exercise discretion to avoid offending, alienating, or harming those being observed. It can also be costly to have a researcher in situ for extended periods of time. Factors such as the combination of the methods to be used and the length of deployment in the study site should be jointly considered in context with the study goals, resources, and intended location of observation.

Diaries as a research method

Diaries are a commonly used research method to gather information about behaviours and experiences, especially for situations that are difficult to observe or routine events, such as eating or discarding food (Shelbe et al., 2017). Generally, participants are asked to record specific information in a 'diary' based on the specific goals of the research. Used in many disciplines including public health, urban planning, and sociology, diaries can be designed to capture both quantitative and qualitative information. The information collected can range from counts or weights of objects to feelings about events or happenings. Diaries can be considered a part of an ethnographic study or a substitute for ethnography or other more detailed observations (Reid et al., 2011).

Diaries allow researchers and practitioners to look at the set of behaviours related to wasting food, including what, how, and why food is wasted. Diaries can capture performances of other practices related to wasting food that are important to understanding the practice of disposal, including shopping, storage, preparation of food, and eating. They can also take spatiality and temporality into account. By studying and comparing performances by different people or households, diaries allow for the individualised differentiation of performances.

There are four main types of diaries that can be used individually or together to study wasted food:

1   *Kitchen diaries*: Kitchen diaries are a quantitative or quasi-quantitative self-reporting tool involving individuals or a group of individuals (e.g. all members of a household) recording a daily log of food waste and other information (Hanson et al., n.d-a). The objective of using kitchen diaries as a data-collection tool is to record both the quantity (or estimate of the quantity) of food waste and the associated behaviour that led to each occurrence. While kitchen diaries are used to estimate the amount of food discarded, they are also used to capture information on the larger performance of wasting food. They can be used to record more detailed information about the performance, such as the reason that food was discarded, the meal the food was associated with, or the discard destination. This tool is primarily used to gather data on household food waste, although similar methods are used in commercial settings.

2   *Purchasing/storage diaries*: Similar to kitchen diaries, purchasing/storage diaries seek to quantitatively or quasi-quantitatively capture food purchasing and storage behaviours. Storage diaries require respondents to catalogue the food in their refrigerators, cupboards, and other storage locations and sometimes indicate when and why food is used or discarded from the storage locations. In purchasing diaries, respondents quantify and describe their purchasing decisions, often including reasons for purchasing an item. These two types of diaries can also be used in conjunction with a food intake and kitchen diary to capture the flow of food in and out of a household.

3   *Time diaries*: Time diaries can be used to capture information on a variety of activities including food disposal, eating, and food preparation. This type of diary tracks the activities of the person(s) of interest, including when and where the activities happen, sequencing with other activities, and social interactions. The purpose of the time diary method is to allow for activities to be identified into clusters that form practices and to record them chronologically (Southerton & Yates, 2015). Southerton and Yates performed a study that asked 2,784 consumers to record their eating activities in a time diary. Respondents were asked to describe their eating events including information on what they ate, where they ate, who they ate with, what was eaten, how long the meal lasted, how the food was prepared, how much food was leftover, and whether the excess food was saved or discarded. Time diaries can also be used to collect other information on experiences such as their understanding of, or feelings toward, the experience.

The remainder of this section will focus on kitchen diaries, though many of the benefits and limitations of kitchen diaries apply to the other types of diaries as well.

What are kitchen diaries?

A kitchen diary is a method that typically involves participants (or in some cases practitioners) recording the contents and weight of food consumed and/or discarded. A paper-based or online template provides a 'form' for participants to complete with the requested information. For quantitative research this has been considered a core methodology and used in many large-scale studies such as those done by the UK Waste & Resources Action Programme (WRAP, 2013), the Natural Resources Defense Council (NRDC, 2017a),

Metro Vancouver (2018), and Oregon Department of Environmental Quality (McDermott et al., 2019) (see Table 17.1 for further details on previous kitchen diary studies).

The type of information recorded in a kitchen diary varies depending on the specific goals of the study, but generally includes at least a short description of the food item being discarded accompanied by a quantitative measure such as the weight, volume, or item counts. Additional information captured in a kitchen diary can include the time of discard, discard destination, which meal the food is associated with, state of the food (e.g. cooked, prepared, or inedible parts), and reason for disposal. A comment section can also be provided to capture any additional information or reactions from the participants. Kitchen diaries are normally recorded for a one- to two-week duration, either consecutively or a minimum number of days within a time period (e.g. seven days within two weeks). The methods of recording data for kitchen diaries are further discussed in the section on types of kitchen diaries.

Kitchen diaries are normally recorded by recruited participants in a voluntary study. The total number of participants in a study mostly depends on available budget and resources, as well as the goal of the study. Some studies may use the diary method to explore potential themes, but do not need statistical representativeness for extrapolating to a larger population. For studies that seek representative data, it is estimated that statistical representativeness is typically achieved with between 300 to 500 participants for a population of 10,000 people or greater when looking at edible food waste generated in households. After data collection and analysis, the Natural Resources Defense Council (NRDC) study back-calculated the ideal sample size (using 10% margin of error and 95% confidence interval) for the study when focusing on edible food waste generated in households. They found that the ideal sample sizes for New York City and Denver, respectively, were 573 and 405 households (NRDC, 2017b). Recruitment, especially for studies seeking statistical representation, can be resource-intensive and difficult to correct for self-selection bias (see section on limitations for more information on bias in diary studies). For these studies, participants can be recruited using random or stratified-random sampling techniques or through pre-selected samples identified by research firms (e.g. omnibus surveys). Participants can be recruited via door-to-door engagement, by phone, web service, or survey panels. In some cases, open recruitment is used, but may generate results that are not representative. Participants are normally compensated with a small honorarium for completing the study and supplied with any materials needed to complete the study, such as scales for weighing food. It is important to consider an honorarium that would be adequate to mitigate attrition, which may be as high as half of the participants if the compensation is too low.

Kitchen diaries are often used alongside other research tools such as surveys or waste audits. Combining the results of kitchen diaries with information collected from surveys is used to connect food waste generation with information such as demographics and behaviours to better understand the waste patterns of different types of people. Guides and methodology documents with details on implementing kitchen diaries have been published by WRAP (2013), NRDC (2017b), Oregon Department of Environmental Quality (McDermott et al., 2019), and the National Zero Waste Council (2018).

Types of kitchen diaries

There are three main types of kitchen diaries that are currently being used: (1) paper; (2) digital; and (3) automatic. Each of these types has the same overall outputs, however, the data is collected differently, with different levels of participation required from the respondent.

Table 17.1 Select kitchen diary studies focused on household food waste

Research organisation/source	Location	Number of households sampled	Method of recording data	Food waste metric	Qualitative information captured
Waste & Resources Action Programme (WRAP, 2013)	Various cities in England and Wales, United Kingdom	948	Paper	Weight, volume, number or amount	• Description of food • How food was purchased • Pack size • State of food • Where food waste was disposed • Reason for wasting
Natural Resources Defense Council (NRDC, 2017a)	Nashville, TN, USA Denver, CO, USA New York, NY, USA	613	Paper	Weight	• Time • Description of food • Meal • Type of packaging • Where food waste was disposed • State of food • Reason for wasting
Metro Vancouver (via email communication, 2018)	Metro Vancouver, BC, Canada	501	Paper	Weight	• Description of food • State of food • Where food waste was disposed • Reason for wasting
Oregon Department of Environmental Quality, 2017 (McDermott et al., 2019)	OR, USA	299	Digital (via website)	Weight	• Description of food • Meal • Where food waste was disposed • Origin of food • State of food • Reasons for wasting

Paper

Participants are given a paper diary with a data entry form to complete each day of the diary recording period. Instructions on how to complete the diary are also included. See Figure 17.1 for an example of a kitchen diary page. Participants record descriptions of food items that they discard along with the quantity (as weight, estimated volumes, or counts depending on the recording method used) and other relevant information. Weight-based recording is considered the best method as it reduces the level of subjectivity for the participant while reducing analysis time by researchers to convert volumes to weights. Participants are instructed to record separate weights for each type of food item (e.g. weigh potato peels separate from onion skins).

To compile and analyse results, coding of food descriptions into categories is conducted by research staff for consistency and to make analysis easier. Kitchen diary data is entered using a standardised food list to allow for analysis of food by type. For example, participants may write 'Granny Smith apple', 'apple', 'red apple', or 'apples' in their diary. These entries would all be coded as 'apple'. Additionally, mistakes in self-categorisation by participants are corrected (e.g. participant indicated that they discarded 'mouldy pizza' because it is 'inedible parts', however, it should be corrected to 'spoiled/mouldy' for the loss reason based on the description). If participants recorded quantities as volumes or item counts, at this stage the researchers also convert the volumes or item counts to weights. Some research seeks to identify which portion of the food discarded is 'edible'. Using the project definition of edibility, research staff will also classify what items or portions of items are edible.

One of the benefits of a paper-based method is that the kitchen diary can be left in the kitchen near the place of disposal to best capture food wasted by all members of the household at the time of disposal. Web-based and app-based methods have the potential to introduce a barrier for all household members to equally participate and may increase risk of an item not being recorded if the computer or phone is not close at hand at the time of discard. However, the paper-based method is generally the most time consuming, with the need to hand write most of the information. Additionally, the handwritten method is the most time consuming for the research staff to digitise the information from the paper form.

Digital kitchen diaries

'Digital' kitchen diaries are essentially the paper kitchen diary in a digital form. A survey tool or other online form can be used to collect the information from the respondent using a computer-based or a phone-based online interface. For digital kitchen diaries, the respondent is still generally asked to measure the food at the time of disposal either using a scale, container, or by providing counts. Digital kitchen diaries can include tools, such as photos or drop-down menus, to streamline data entry and reduce errors and omissions. Additionally, digital kitchen diaries reduce costs by eliminating the need to convert paper kitchen diaries to digital form for data analysis.

Automatic kitchen diaries

'Automatic' kitchen diaries are currently in development to eliminate the need for measurement by the respondent. Instead, an automatic kitchen diary can estimate quantities of discarded food using a photo, generally taken using a phone app. Reducing the step of measurement has the potential to both increase accuracy and decrease omissions by reducing effort needed by the respondent. The respondent would still be required to fill in any additional information such as the reason for discard.

Participant ID:	Use a separate row for each type of food or drink discarded – even if it is for the same meal						If nothing is recorded in the table for the day – please indicate why:																				
What? Give a detailed description of any food or drink including inedible parts	Which meal? Check the box in the column that best describes the meal associated with the discarded food or drink					How much? Weight in kilos or ounces (delete as appropriate)	Where? Check the box that best describes where you discarded the food or drink							State of Food? Check the box that best describes the state of the food or drink when discarded					Why? Check the box that best describes why you discarded the food or drink								
	Breakfast	Lunch	Dinner	Snacks	Other		Trash/ rubbish bin	Down the drain	Fed to pets or animals	Home compost	Local compost collection	Other compost	Other (write in)	Whole	Prepared, not cooked	Cooked/ leftover	Inedible parts	Other (write in)	Past date on label	Mouldy or spoiled	Did not taste good	Left out too long	Improperly cooked	Too little to save	Did not want as leftovers	Inedible parts	Other (write in)

Figure 17.1 A sample page of a kitchen diary.

The Remote Food Photography Method ® (RFPM) or SmartIntake ® app is an example of a type of automatic kitchen diary. RFPM estimates plate waste over a period of many days, including multiple meals. Participants use a smartphone app to take photos of their plate of food before and after each meal or serving. Benefits of this technology include that information is recorded in 'real-time' and reminders can be sent to the participant's phone if a period of time elapses without pictures being taken. Using validation of doubly labelled water (a technique used in dietary assessment to compare reported food consumption with actual consumption), it was found that the error in reporting was less than 4% (Roe et al., 2018). While this method is currently being used to measure plate waste, there is potential for it to be expanded to other types of wasted food. Additionally, this method currently tracks food at the individual level, whereas household-level data is often desired to best understand why food is wasted in households.

Table 17.2 provides a summary of the benefits and drawbacks of paper, digital, and automatic kitchen diary methods.

Benefits of kitchen diaries

Other than kitchen diaries, the two other main food waste quantification techniques for the household level are waste composition studies and waste recalls/estimations. Waste composition studies collect municipal solid waste, generally either collected at the kerbside or at a waste transfer station, and divides the material into set categories by material type (see Chapter 16 in this volume for more information). Waste recalls or estimations retrospectively ask respondents to estimate or remember how much they wasted over a given period of time.

One of the major benefits of kitchen diaries compared to waste composition studies and waste recalls/estimations is that they provide a more accurate estimate of *total* generation of household food waste. Many of the methods used in food waste studies are based on dietary assessment methodologies that have been used for decades in public health. Research has shown that dietary recalls (analogous to waste recalls/estimations) are generally more inaccurate than dietary records (analogous to kitchen diaries) because dietary records are completed at the time of food intake rather than relying on memory (Thompson & Subar, 2013). Additionally, people have been shown to generally underestimate how much food they waste (Neff et al., 2015). Kitchen diaries also provide information of food discarded to destinations that are generally missed by waste composition studies, such as drain disposal, feeding pets, and backyard composting. Thus, waste composition studies also do not capture *total* generation.

Another significant benefit of kitchen diaries is that they provide more detailed information on the type of food items discarded, since they generally require the respondent to identify exactly what types of food are discarded, the state of the food, and the discard destination. Specifically, in waste composition studies, identifying the type of food discarded can be difficult especially if it has been in the waste bin for a long period of time or the waste has been tossed, compacted, or altered in another way. Furthermore, waste composition studies are not usually directly linked with individual households, rather the material sorted is an aggregate of many households, thus specific characteristics and contexts of how and why food is discarded are lost. Kitchen diaries, however, are generally linked to a specific household and coupled with a survey to collect information about the household. Given that the context and who is discarding the food are important to understanding the larger set of behaviours and factors, this coupling of methods allows researchers to understand the larger practice of wasting food.

Last, a major benefit of kitchen diaries is the ability to use the information to develop relevant messages for interventions. Solid waste managers may continue to use waste

Table 17.2 Summary of benefits and drawbacks by type of kitchen diary

	Paper	Digital	Automatic
Ease of use	• Literacy is a basic requirement • Participant must learn to operate a scale or follow a measurement scheme • Does not require use of computer or cell phone	• Literacy is a basic requirement • Participant must learn to operate a scale or follow a measurement scheme • Requires use of computer or cell phone	• Literacy is a basic requirement • Participant is not required to operate a scale • Requires use of computer or cell phone
Time	• Most time required by participants to complete this type of diary because of need to hand write all information • Most time required for researchers to convert information on paper to digital form	• Reduces time needed by participant to record items, especially if tools are used to streamline data input • Reduces time needed by researchers because information does not need to be converted from paper to digital	• Reduces time needed by participant to record items, especially if tools are used to streamline data input • Reduces time needed by researchers because information does not need to be converted from paper to digital
Accuracy	• Potential omissions due to effort needed to record items • Diary can be kept in the kitchen area to facilitate reporting and participation of all family members	• Fewer potential omissions in terms of ability to take picture and submit items at later time • Fewer omissions due to reduced effort needed to record items • More omissions due to lack of accessibility of phone or computer in kitchen or by all members of household • Potentially fewer errors for recording weight and other information via picture	• Fewer potential omissions in terms of ability to take picture and submit items at later time • Fewer omissions due to reduced effort needed to record items • More omissions due to lack of accessibility of phone or computer in kitchen or by all members of household • Potentially fewer errors for recording weight and other information via picture

composition studies to estimate generation of food waste, but kitchen diaries have additional benefits for government and other organisations focusing on consumer education and other interventions. Kitchen diaries can give more detailed information on how and why food is wasted. Are certain food items frequently discarded for the same reason? Are people discarding items because they think they are inedible when, in fact, they can be safely eaten (e.g. broccoli stalks)? For example, a common finding across the studies conducted by WRAP, NRDC, and Metro Vancouver was that leftovers and prepared food were thrown out frequently because they were spoiled. Therefore, in all three campaigns, some of the main messages were on how to keep food fresher for longer, how to incorporate leftovers into new meals, and how to get people to prioritise eating leftovers before they spoil.

Limitations of kitchen diaries

While kitchen diaries have many benefits compared to waste composition studies and waste recalls/estimations, they also have drawbacks. Some of the drawbacks are unique to kitchen diaries while others are limitations of all three methods. When designing a research study, actions should be taken to minimise these limitations, however, eliminating all bias might not be possible. The major limitations of kitchen diaries are:

- *Recruitment bias*: If the goal of the study is to provide a representative sample of households, then recruitment bias should be considered. Due to the time-intensive nature of the kitchen diary, as well as the requirement for literacy, certain populations might be systematically excluded from the study. For instance, participants that are already interested in issues of food waste may oversubscribe while participants without previous interest may drop out. Additionally, people that consider themselves time-constrained might not agree to participate.
- *Self-reporting/response bias*: The self-reporting nature of the diary may lead to underreporting through intentional or unintentional omissions of occurrences of food waste or changes in behaviour that result from the act of completing a diary (e.g. participants want to show they do not waste food and so alter their food consumption patterns for that week). In dietary assessment studies, respondent fatigue has been shown to result in less accurate reporting as the study progresses. Recording periods of greater than four days in dietary assessment studies are shown to yield unsatisfactory results (Thompson & Subar, 2013).
- *Resource constraints*: Cost to implement studies with kitchen diaries with statistical representation is high. Significant resources are needed for recruitment, support, and incentives during measurement, especially if waste audits are being used in the study to corroborate what is recorded in the kitchen diary and to estimate underreporting. Resources needed to standardise and interpret data can be high, even for digital kitchen diaries because of how food is described.
- *Accounting for edibility*: Many studies are often interested in only the 'edible' portion of food discarded, or want to distinguish between the edible portion and associated inedible parts. This is particularly relevant for studies focusing on food waste prevention because they tend to focus on the 'avoidable' or 'edible' portions of food waste. However, edibility is a socioculturally constructed concept and not an innate characteristic of a material (Papargyropoulou et al., 2014; Gillick & Quested, 2018; Nicholes et al., 2019; Hanson et al., n.d.-b), thus there is no universally agreed-upon definition of edibility, even within a country or culture. USDA National Nutrient Database for Standard Reference (USDA, 2018), UK WRAP (Gillick & Quested, 2018; Nicholes et al., 2019), and NRDC (NRDC, 2017b) have different classifications of edibility that can be used. Unfortunately, digestibility or ingestibility cannot be used as a measure of edibility because most parts of food are digestible with enough treatment (Gillick & Quested, 2018). Additionally, respondents may have very different definitions of edibility (that may or may not align with the definition in the study). Consistently accounting for edibility can be difficult given the respondents' varying definitions (e.g. pizza crusts defined as 'inedible parts' by respondent). However, it is important to transparently report edibility for easier comparison to other studies.
- *Logistics*: To make measurement easier, respondents often include packaging in the measurement. Information can be collected to remove the weight of packaging as part

of the data analysis. Even with simple and straightforward instructions, respondents might not follow directions, even with respondent support. Incomplete or incorrect data will either need to be omitted or corrected using suitable assumptions.

- *Hard-to-capture items*: Some food items are harder to capture in a kitchen diary format than others. For instance, food wasted outside of the household is difficult to measure if a quantitative estimate is desired, because a respondent is unlikely to carry a measuring implement around with them and measure in public places. Additionally, purges, such as refrigerator cleanouts, are unlikely to be captured due to lack of frequency as well as respondent decisions to postpone purges due to the work required to record in the kitchen diary. To still capture this information, a qualitative measure can be used or an automatic kitchen diary may also overcome the limitation of needing to carry around a measuring instrument.
- *Representativeness of measured time frame*: A kitchen diary records a snapshot in time and might not be representative of a 'typical' week for a household. Additionally, seasonal differences as well as lack of consistency in household habits and behaviours can make it questionable to extrapolate kitchen diary data to a whole year.

Despite the limitations of the kitchen diary, it is still one of the most used methods for quantitatively and qualitatively capturing detailed information on food discarded in households. For studies only needing quantity of food discarded and collected as municipal solid waste without additional information, a waste audit may be a better option. However, for studies wanting more detailed information, there are currently no other mainstream methods with fewer limitations. Additionally, techniques can be used, and new technologies are being developed, to help reduce the impacts of the limitations described above.

Ways to overcome limitations

Using computer or app-based technologies as well as careful planning in study design can help reduce the impacts of the biases and limitations described previously. Dietary assessment to measure food intake has many analogies to measuring discarded food, thus strategies from public health can potentially be used to overcome some of the outcomes above. One method to improve the representativeness of dietary records (or kitchen diaries) is to measure non-consecutive days. Another is to have a trained interviewer review the record to clarify entries and probe for food items that might have been omitted (Thompson & Subar, 2013). The development of digital and automatic kitchen diaries also provides the opportunity to reduce resources needed for research staff to transcribe paper kitchen diaries into digital form. Automatic kitchen diaries take it a step further by reducing the need for the respondent to measure the quantity of food wasted themselves. This reduces significant burdens of time, effort, and user error which could both increase participation across more populations as well as reduce omissions and errors. Additionally, eliminating the need for user measurement would allow for food discarded outside of the household to be more easily captured.

If trying to estimate the amount of underreporting in a kitchen diary study, a waste composition study can be used to determine the level of underreporting in the municipal solid waste stream. UK WRAP, NRDC, and Oregon Department of Environmental Quality used this method to estimate the underreporting rate for kitchen diaries. Interestingly, all three studies resulted in an underreporting rate of around 40% (WRAP, 2013; Natural Resources Defense Council (NRDC), 2017a; McDermott et al., 2019). While this is the most used method to determine underreporting in kitchen diaries, it is untested whether the underreporting factors for materials reaching kerbside collection are the same as those for other disposal destinations (e.g. drain disposal, feeding animals, and backyard composting). Additionally, the type of error from underreporting would be systematic between repeated studies as long as they have the same approximate sample characteristics. Therefore, any difference between the two studies represents a valid difference.

Suggested further reading

- Evans, D. (2014). *Food Waste: Home Consumption, Material Culture and Everyday Life*. London: Bloomsbury.
- Evans, D., McMeekin, A., & Southerton, D. (2012). *Sustainable consumption, behaviour change policies and theories of practice*. Helsinki Collegium 2012. Available at: http://hdl. handle.net/10138/34226.
- Hammersley, M. & Atkinson, P. (2007). *Ethnography: Principles in Practice*. London: Routledge.
- Nicolini, D. (2012). Bringing it all Together: A Toolkit to Study and Represent Practices at Work. In *Practice Theory, Work, & Organization* (pp. 213–242). London: Oxford University Press.
- Pink, S. (2012). *Situating Everyday Life*. London: SAGE Publications.
- Pink, S. (2015). *Doing Sensory Ethnography*. Los Angeles, CA: SAGE Publications Ltd.
- Shove, E., Pantzar, M., & Watson, M. (2012). *The Dynamics of Social Practice: Everyday Life and How it Changes*. London Sage Publications Ltd.
- Southerton, D. & Yates, L. (2015). Exploring Food Waste through the lens of Social Practice Theories: Some Reflections on Eating as a Compound Practice. In K. Ekstrom, (ed.) *Waste Management and Sustainable Consumption: Reflections on Consumer Waste* (pp. 133–149). London: Routledge.
- Warde, A. (2005). 'Consumption and theories of practice,' *Journal of Consumer Culture*, 5(2), 131–153. doi: 10.1177/1469540505053090.
- Warde, A. (2014). 'After taste: culture, consumption and theories of practice', *Journal of Consumer Culture*, 14(3), 279–303. doi: 10.1177/1469540514547828.
- Warde, A. (2016). *The Practice of Eating*. London: Polity Press.

References

Ajzen, I. (1985). From Intentions to Actions: A Theory of Planned behaviour. In J. Kuhl & J. Beckmann (Eds.), *Action Control: From Cognition to Behaviour* (pp. 11–40). Berlin, New York: Springer, Verlag https://www.worldcat.org/title/action-control-from-cognition-to-behavior/oclc/12234134.

Barr, S. (2006). 'Environmental action in the home: Investigating the "value-action" gap,' *Geography*, 91(1), 43–54.

Boulstridge, E., & Carrigan, M. (2000). 'Do consumers really care about corporate responsibility? Highlighting the attitude—behaviour gap,' *Journal of Communication Management*, 4(4), 355–368. doi: 10.1108/eb023532.

Bourdieu, P. (1977). *Outline of a Theory of Practice*. Cambridge, UK: Cambridge University Press.

Bourdieu, P. (1990). *The Logic of Practice*. Cambridge, UK: Polity Press.

Brewer, J. (2000). *Ethnography*. Buckingham: Open University Press.

Cappellini, B., & Parsons, E. (2013). 'Practising thrift at dinnertime: Mealtime leftovers, sacrifice and family membership,' *The Sociological Review*, 60(S2), 121–134. doi: 10.1111/1467-954X.12041.

Creswell, J.W., & Creswell, J.D. (2017). *Research Design: Qualitative, Quantitative, and Mixed Methods Approaches*. Thousand Oaks, CA: Sage Publications https://us.sagepub.com/en-us/nam/research-design/book255675.

Crivits, M., & Paredis, E. (2013). 'Designing an explanatory practice framework: Local food systems as a case,' *Journal of Consumer Culture*, 13(3), 306–336. doi: 10.1177/1469540513484321.

Devaney, L., & Davies, A.R. (2017). 'Disrupting household food consumption through experimental HomeLabs: Outcomes, connections, contexts,' *Journal of Consumer Culture*, 17(3), 823–844. doi: 10.1177/1469540516631153.

Eberle, T.S., & Maeder, C. (2011). Organizational ethnography. Qualitative research. In D. Silverman (Ed.), *Qualitative Research: Issues of Theory, Method, and Practice*. Los Angeles, California: SAGE Publications https://www.worldcat.org/title/qualitative-research-issues-of-theory-method-and-practice/oclc/894993980.

Elliott, R., & Jankel-Elliott, N. (2003). 'Using ethnography in strategic consumer research,' *Qualitative Market Research: An International Journal*, 6(4), 215–223. doi: 10.1108/13522750310495300.

Evans, D. (2011a). 'Blaming the consumer – once again: The social and material contexts of everyday food waste practices in some English household,' *Critical Public Health*, 21(4), 429–440. doi: 10.1080/09581596.2011.608797.

Evans, D. (2011b). 'Thrifty, green or frugal: Reflections on sustainable consumption in a changing economic climate,' *Geoforum*, 42(5), 550–557. doi: 10.1016/j.geoforum.2011.03.008.

Evans, D. (2012). 'Beyond the throwaway society: Ordinary domestic practice and a sociological approach to household food waste,' *Sociology*, 46(1), 41–56. doi: 10.1177/0038038511416150.

Evans, D. (2014). *Food Waste: Home Consumption, Material Culture and Everyday Life*. London: Bloomsbury.

Evans, D., Mcmeekin, A., & Southerton, D. (2012). Sustainable Consumption, Behaviour Change Policies and Theories of Practice. In A. Warde & D. Southerton (Eds.), *The Habits of Consumption COLLeGIUM: Studies across Disciplines in the Humanities and Social Sciences* (pp. 113–129). Helsinki: Helsinki Collegium for Advanced Studies.

Evans, D.M. (2018). 'What is consumption, where has it been going, and does it still matter?' *The Sociological Review*, 36(3), 499–517. doi: 10.1177/0038026118764028.

Farr-Wharton, G., Foth, M., & Choi, J. (2014). 'Identifying factors that promote consumer behaviours causing expired domestic food waste,' *Journal of Consumer Behaviour*, 12(4), 393–402. doi: 10.1002/cb.

Foden, M., Browne, A., Evans, D., Sharp, L., & Watson, M. (2017). *Food Waste and Kitchen Practices: Implications for Policy and Intervention*. UK: University of Sheffield. doi: 10.13140/RG.2.2.13146.24005.

Food and Agriculture Organization of the United Nations (FAO). (2013). *Food Waste Footprint: Impact on Natural Resources*. Retrieved from www.fao.org/docrep/018/i3347e/i3347e.pdf

Ganglbauer, E., Fitzpatrick, G., & Comber, R. (2013). 'Negotiating food waste: Using a practice lens to inform design,' *ACM Transactions on Computer-Human Interaction*, 20(2), 1–25. doi: http://doi.org/http://dx.doi.org/10.1145/2463579.2463582.

Giddens, A. (1984). *The Constitution of Society*. Cambridge, UK: Polity Press.

Gillick, S., & Quested, T. (2018). *Household Food Waste: Restated Data for 2007-2015*. Retrieved from Waste and Resources Action Programme (WRAP).

Graham-Rowe, E., Jessop, D.C., & Sparks, P. (2014). 'Identifying motivations and barriers to minimising household food waste,' *Resources, Conservation and Recycling*, 84, 15–23. doi: 10.1016/j.resconrec.2013.12.005.

Graham-Rowe, E., Jessop, D.C., & Sparks, P. (2015). 'Predicting household food waste reduction using an extended theory of planned behaviour,' *Resources, Conservation and Recycling*, 101, 194–202.

Gustavsson, J., Cederberg, C., Sonesson, U., van Otterdijk, R., & Meybeck, A. (2011). *Global Food Losses and Food Waste: Extent, Causes, and Prevention*. Rome: Food and Agriculture Organization (FAO).

Halkier, B., Katz-Gerro, T., and Martens, L. (2011) 'Applying Practice Theory to the Study of Consumption: Theoretical and Methodological Considerations,' *Journal of Consumer Culture*, 11(1), 3–13.

Halkier, B., & Jensen, I. (2011). 'Methodological challenges in using practice theory in consumption research. Examples from a study on handling nutritional contestations of food consumption,' *Journal of Consumer Culture*, 11(1), 101–123. doi: 10.1177/1469540510391365.

Hammersley, M., & Atkinson, P. (2007). *Ethnography: Principles in Practice*. 3rd edn. London: Routledge.

Hand, M., & Shove, E. (2007). 'Condensing practices: Ways of living with a freezer,' *Journal of Consumer Culture*, 7(1), 79–104. doi: 10.1177/1469540507073509.

Hanson, C.Lipinski, B.Robertson, K.Dias, D.Gavilan, I.Gréverath, P., ...Quested, T. (n.d.-a). *Guidance on FLW Quantification Methods*. Retrieved from http://flwprotocol.org/wp-content/uploads/2016/05/FLW_Protocol_Guidance_on_FLW_Quantification_Methods.pdf

Hanson, C., Lipinski, B., Robertson, K., Dias, D., Gavilan, I., Gréverath, P., ... Quested, T. (n.d.-b). *Food Loss and Waste Accounting and Reporting Standard*. Retrieved from http://flwprotocol.org/wp-content/uploads/2017/05/FLW_Standard_final_2016.pdf

Hargreaves, T. (2011). 'Practice-ing behaviour change: Applying social practice theory to pro-environmental behaviour change,' *Journal of Consumer Culture*, 11(1), 79–99. doi: 10.1177/1469540510390500.

Hebrok, M., & Boks, C. (2017). 'Household food waste: Drivers and potential intervention points for design – An extensive review,' *Journal of Cleaner Production*, 151, 380–392. doi: 10.1016/j.jclepro.2017.03.069.

Hebrok, M., & Heidenstrøm, N. (2019). 'Contextualising food waste prevention-decisive moments within everyday practices,' *Journal of Cleaner Production*, 210, 1435–1448. doi: 10.1016/j.jclepro.2018.11.141.

Hitchings, R. (2012). 'People can talk about their practices,' *Area*, 44(1), 61–67. doi: 10.1111/j.1475-4762.2011.01060.x.

Kendall, H., Brennan, M., Seal, C., Ladha, C., & Kuznesof, S. (2016). 'Behind the kitchen door: A novel mixed method approach for exploring the food provisioning practices of the older consumer q,' *Food Quality and Preference*, 53, 105–116. doi: 10.1016/j.foodqual.2016.06.005.

Koivupuro, H.-K., Hartikainen, H., Silvennoinen, K., Katajajuuri, J.-M., Heikintalo, N., Reinikainen, A., & Jalkanen, L. (2012). 'Influence of socio-demographical, behavioural and attitudinal factors on the amount of avoidable food waste generated in Finnish households: Factors influencing household food waste,' *International Journal of Consumer Studies*, 36(2), 183–191. doi: 10.1111/j.1470-6431.2011.01080.

Layder, D. (2006). *Understanding Social Theory*. London ; Thousand Oaks, California: SAGE Publications https://www.worldcat.org/title/understanding-social-theory/oclc/297462576.

Lazell, J. (2016). 'Consumer food waste behaviour in universities: Sharing as a means of prevention,' *Journal of Consumer Behaviour*, 15(5), 430–439. doi: 10.1002/cb.1581.

Martens, L. (2012). 'Practice "in talk" and talk "as Practice": Dish washing and the reach of language,' *Sociological Research Online*, 17(3), 22. doi: 10.5153/sro.2681.

Martens, L., & Scott, S. (2017). Understanding Everyday Kitchen Life: Looking at Performance, into Performances and for Practices. In M. Jonas, B. Littig, & A. Wroblewski (eds.), *Methodological Reflections on Practice Oriented Theories* (pp. 177–191). Cham, Switzerland: Springer. doi: 10.1007/978-3-319-52897-7.

McDermott, C., Elliott, D., Moreno, L.C., Broderson, R., & Mulder, C. (2019). *Oregon Wasted Food Study: Summary of Findings (2019)*. Institute for Sustainable Solutions/Oregon Department of Environmental Quality.

Meah, A. (2014). 'Still blaming the consumer? Geographies of responsibility in domestic food safety practices,' *Critical Public Health*, 24(1), 88–103. doi: 10.1080/09581596.2013.791387.

Metcalfe, A., Riley, M., Barr, S., Tudor, T., Robinson, G., & Guilbert, S. (2012). 'Food waste bins: Bridging infrastructures and practices,' *Sociological Review*, 60, 135–155. doi: 10.1111/1467-954X.12042.

Moraes, C., Carrigan, M., & Szmigin, I. (2012). 'The coherence of inconsistencies: Attitude – behaviour gaps and new consumption communities,' *Journal of Marketing Management*, 28(1–2), 103–128. doi: 10.1080/0267257X.2011.615482.

National Zero Waste Council. (2018) *How to Measure: A Guide for Measuring Food Waste from Households in Canada*. www.nzwc.ca/focus/food/Documents/LFHW_HowToMeasureFoodWaste_English.PDF

Natural Resources Defense Council (NRDC). (2017a). *Estimating Quantities and Types of Food Waste at the City Level*. Retrieved from www.nrdc.org/sites/default/files/food-waste-city-level-report.pdf

Natural Resources Defense Council (NRDC). (2017b). *Estimating Quantities and Types of Food Waste at the City Level: Technical Appendices*. Retrieved from www.nrdc.org/sites/default/files/food-waste-city-level-technical-appendices.pdf

Neff, R.A., Spiker, M.L., & Truant, P.L. (2015). 'Wasted food: U.S. consumers' reported awareness, attitudes, and behaviours,' *PLoS ONE*, 10(6), 1–16. doi: http://doi.org/10.1371/journal.pone.0127881.

Nicholes, M.J., Quested, T.E., Reynolds, C., Gillick, S., & Parry, A.D. (2019). 'Surely you don't eat parsnip skins? Categorising the edibility of food waste,' *Resources, Conservation, and Recycling*,147, 179–188. https://doi.org/10.1016/j.resconrec.2019.03.004.

Nicolini, D. (2012). *Practice Theory, Work, & Organization*. Oxford: Oxford University Press.

Papargyropoulou, E., Lozano, R., J.K. Steinberger, Wright, N., & Ujang, Z. (2014). 'The food waste hierarchy as a framework for the management of food surplus and food waste,' *Journal of Cleaner Production*, 76, 106–115. doi: 10.1016/j.jclepro.2014.04.020.

Pink, S. (2012). *Situating Everyday Life*. London: SAGE Publications Ltd.

Quested, T.E., Marsh, E., Stunell, D., & Parry, A.D. (2013). 'Spaghetti soup: The complex world of food waste behaviours,' *Resources, Conservation and Recycling*, 79, 43–51. doi: http://doi.org/10.1016/j.resconrec.2013.04.011.

Reckwitz, A. (2002). 'Toward a theory of social practices: A development in culturalist theorizing,' *European Journal of Social Theory*, 5(2), 243–263. doi: 10.1177/13684310222225432.

Reid, L., Hunter, C., & Sutton, P.W. (2011). 'Rising to the challenge of environmental behaviour change: Developing a reflexive diary approach,' *Geoforum*, 42(6), 720–730. doi: http://doi.org/10.1016/j.geoforum.2011.04.011.

Revilla, B.P., & Salet, W. (2018). 'The social meaning and function of household food rituals in preventing food waste,' *Journal of Cleaner Production*, 198, 320–332. doi: 10.1016/j.jclepro.2018.06.038.

Richter, B., & Bokelmann, W. (2017). 'Explorative study about the analysis of storing, purchasing and wasting food by using household diaries,' *Resources, Conservation and Recycling*, 125 (June), 181–187. doi: http://doi.org/10.1016/j.resconrec.2017.06.006.

Roe, B.E., Apolzan, J.W., Qi, D., Allen, H.R., & Martin, C.K. (2018). 'Plate waste of adults in the United States measured in free-living conditions,' *PLOS ONE*, 13(2). doi: 10.1371/journal.pone.0191813.

Roodhuyzen, D.M.A., Luning, P.A., Fogliano, V., & Steenbekkers, L.P.A. (2017). 'Putting together the puzzle of consumer food waste: Towards an integral perspective,' *Trends in Food Science & Technology*, 68, 37–50. doi: 10.1016/j.tifs.2017.07.009.

Salemdeeb, R., Font Vivanco, D., Al-Tabbaa, A., & Zu Ermgassen, E.K.H.J. (2017). 'A holistic approach to the environmental evaluation of food waste prevention,' *Waste Management*, 59, 442–450. doi: 10.1016/j.wasman.2016.09.042.

Schanes, K., Dobernig, K., & Gözet, B. (2018). 'Food waste matters - A systematic review of household food waste practices and their policy implications,' *Journal of Cleaner Production*, 182, 978–991. doi: 10.1016/j.jclepro.2018.02.030.

Schatzki, T.R. (1996). *Social Practices: A Wittgensteinian Approach to Human Activity and the Social*. Cambridge, UK: Cambridge University Press.

Schatzki, T.R. (2001). Introduction: practice theory. In T.R. Schatzki, K. Cetina, & E. von Savigny (Eds.), *The Practice Turn in Contemporary Theory* (pp. 1–15). London: Routledge.

Schatzki, T.R. (2010). *The Timespace of Human Activity: On Performance, Society, and History as indeterminate Teleological events*. Maryland: Lexington Books.

Setti, M., Banchelli, F., Falasconi, L., Segrè, A., & Vittuari, M. (2018). 'Consumers' food cycle and household waste: When behaviours matter,' *Journal of Cleaner Production*, 185, 694–706. doi: 10.1016/j.jclepro.2018.03.024.

Shelbe, L., Thomson, L., & Wildemuth, B.M. (2017). Research Diaries. In B.M. Wildemuth (Ed.), *Applications of Social Research Methods to Questions in Information and Library Science* ((Second)) (228–238). Santa Barbara, California: Libraries Unlimited.

Shove, E. (2014). 'Putting practice into policy: Reconfiguring questions of consumption and climate change,' *Contemporary Social Science*, 9(4), 415–429. doi: 10.1080/21582041.2012.692484.

Shove, E., Pantzar, M., & Watson, M. (2012). *The Dynamics of Social Practice: Everyday Life and How It Changes*. London: Sage Publications Ltd.

Shove, E., & Walker, G. (2010). 'Governing transitions in the sustainability of everyday life,' *Research Policy*, 39(4), 471–476. doi: 10.1016/j.respol.2010.01.019.

Southerton, D., & Yates, L. (2015). Exploring Food Waste through the lens of Social Practice Theories: Some reflections on eating as a compound practice. In K. Ekstrom (Ed.), *Waste Management and Sustainable Consumption: Reflections on Consumer Waste* (132–149). London: Routledge.

Spaargaren, G. (2011). 'Theories of practices: Agency, technology, and culture,' *Global Environmental Change*, 21(3), 813–822. doi: 10.1016/j.gloenvcha.2011.03.010.

Spradley, J. (1979). *The Ethnographic Interview*. New York: Holt, Rinehart, and Winston.

Spurling, N., Mcmeekin, A., Shove, E., Southerton, D., & Welch, D. (2013). *Interventions in practice: re-framing policy approaches to consumer behaviour*. Sustainable Practices Research.

Stancu, V., Haugaard, P., & Lähteenmäki, L. (2016). 'Determinants of consumer food waste behaviour: Two routes to food waste,' *Appetite*, 96, 7–17. doi: 10.1016/j.appet.2015.08.025.

Stangherlin, I., & de Barcellos, M.(2018). 'Drivers and barriers to food waste reduction,' *British Food Journal*, 120(10), 2364–2387. doi: 10.1108/BFJ-12-2017-0726.

Stefan, V., van Herpen, E., Tudoran, A.A., & Lähteenmäki, L. (2013). 'Avoiding food waste by Romanian consumers: The importance of planning and shopping routines,' *Food Quality and Preference*, 28 (1), 375–381. doi: 10.1016/j.foodqual.2012.11.001.

Thompson, F.E., & Subar, A.F. (2013). 'Dietary assessment methodology,' *Nutrition in the Prevention and Treatment of Disease*, 4th Edition. doi: http://doi.org/10.1016/B978-0-12-391884-0.00001-9.

Thyberg, K.L., & Tonjes, D.J. (2016). 'Drivers of food waste and their implications for sustainable policy development,' *Resources, Conservation and Recycling*, 106, 110–123. doi: 10.1016/j.resconrec.2015.11.016.

United States Department of Agriculture. (2018). *National Nutrient Database for Standard Reference Legacy Release*. Retrieved from https://ndb.nal.usda.gov/ndb/

Vermeir, I., & Verbeke, W. (2006). 'Sustainable food consumption: Exploring the consumer "attitude - behavioural intention" gap,' *Journal of Agricultural and Environmental Ethics*, 19(2), 169–194. doi: 10.1007/s10806-005-5485-3.

Wahlen, S., & Dubuisson-Quellier, S. (2018). 'Consumption governance toward more sustainable consumption,' *Journal of Family & Consumer Sciences*, 110(1), 7–12. doi: 10.14307/JFCS110.1.7.

Waitt, G., & Phillips, C. (2016). 'Food waste and domestic refrigeration: a visceral and material approach,' *Social & Cultural Geography*, 17(2), 359–379.

Warde, A. (2005). 'Consumption and theories of practice,' *Journal of Consumer Culture*, 5(2), 131–153. doi: 10.1177/1469540505053090.

Warde, A. (2016). *The Practice of Eating*. Cambridge, UK: Polity Press.

Waste & Resources Action Programme. (2013). Methods used for the household food and drink waste in the UK 2012. www.wrap.org.uk/sites/files/wrap/hhfdw-2012-main.pdf.pdf

Watson, M., & Meah, A. (2013). 'Food, waste and safety: Negotiating conflicting social anxieties into the practices of domestic provisioning,' *Sociological Review*, 60(S2), 102–120. doi: 10.1111/1467-954X.12040.

Weber, M. (1946). Science as a vocation. In Tauber, A. (Ed.), *Science and the Quest for Reality* (382–394). New York: Oxford University Press.

Welch, D., & Yates, L. (2018). 'The practices of collective action: Practice theory, sustainability transitions and social change,' *Journal for the Theory of Social Behaviour*, 48(3), 288–305. doi: 10.1111/jtsb.12168.

Wills, W.J., Dickinson, A.M., Meah, A., & Short, F. (2015). 'Reflections on the use of visual methods in a qualitative study of domestic kitchen practices,' *Sociology*, 50(3), 470–485. doi: 10.1177/0038038515587651.

18

APPLYING BEHAVIOUR CHANGE METHODS TO FOOD WASTE

*Sandra Davison, Lisanne van Geffen, Erica van Herpen and
Anne Sharp*

Changing food waste preventing behaviours

All human behaviour is complex and this includes behaviours related to food waste where a diversity of factors have been related to household food wasting behaviours (Quested *et al.*, 2013; Parizeau, von Massow and Martin, 2015; Thyberg and Tonjes, 2016). Consequently, it is unlikely that any one theory or model could fully explore, explain or predict household food waste. However, models such as the Motivation Abilities and Opportunities (MOA) framework and the Transtheoretical Model of Behaviour Change (TTM), which are introduced in this chapter, have important roles to play. Further, the models can also provide frameworks for the development of interventions to change wasteful food behaviours. Each model is introduced and its application illustrated in the context of food waste, with overall conclusions for both models' contributions finishing the chapter.

Motivation abilities and opportunities framework

According to the MOA framework, people perform desirable behaviours when these are in their self-interest and can be performed easily and effectively (Olander and Thøgersen, 1995; Rothschild, 1999). If the behaviours are not in their self-interest or if these are too difficult to be performed, people are resistant or simply unable to perform them. In the MOA framework, factors influencing self-interest are referred to as motivation, and factors influencing the easiness and effectiveness of the behaviours are referred to as opportunities and abilities (see Figure 18.1). This division of the multitude of factors into the three parts successfully guides intervention selection, as different interventions are likely to be required for the different MOA defined parts. This section discusses factors influencing food waste reduction and intervention selection, from the perspective of the MOA framework.

Motivation

Motivation refers to a person's self-interest in performing a behaviour voluntarily. People are considered to be goal-driven, implying that behaviours are in their self-interest when

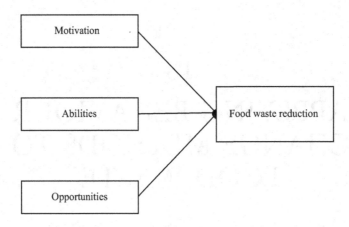

Figure 18.1 MOA framework.

these contribute to goal fulfilment. Setting a goal to reduce waste levels is determined by a person's awareness about the consequences of – and attitudes toward – wasting food as well as the social norms surrounding in-home food waste reduction.

To consider setting a goal to reduce food waste levels, people need to be aware that food waste has negative consequences. Most people, indeed, believe that food waste is negative for the environment and food distribution (Eurobarometer, 2014; Secondi, Principato and Laureti, 2015), but underestimate the actual scope of the issue and the impact of its consequences (Principato, Secondi and Pratesi, 2015; Fox *et al.*, 2018). Also, they are likely to underestimate how much they waste themselves (Abeliotis, Lasaridi and Chroni, 2014). As a result, reducing food waste levels is often not considered relevant enough to be a goal to strive for.

It is not only awareness of the behavioural consequences that influences goal-setting, but also the importance given to these consequences. The importance given to an issue is reflected in people's attitudes, that is, their thoughts and feelings toward wasting food. Research consistently finds that people have strong negative thoughts and feelings toward wasting food (Stefan *et al.*, 2013; Stancu, Haugaard and Lähteenmaki, 2016; Roodhuyzen *et al.*, 2017). They consider it to be morally wrong and this makes them feel guilty. However, this is often a reflection of people's attitude toward global food waste or their own food waste on an abstract level. When discussing their food waste levels in a more practical and day-to-day manner, people's responses are usually nuanced or more neutral toward the issue (Van Geffen, Van Herpen and Van Trijp, 2016), and people appear to trivialize their day-to-day food waste. This neutral attitude seems to stem from the feeling that the dynamics of life make food waste inevitable and, therefore, it is needless to feel guilty each time food is wasted.

Behaviour is further known to be strongly influenced by social norms (Cialdini, Kallgren and Reno, 1991). Therefore, it is unsurprising that social norm beliefs also influence people's motivation to reduce their waste levels. More precisely, people's beliefs of how others who are important to them think about food waste, do not convincingly influence household management behaviours (Stefan *et al.*, 2013; Visschers, Wickli and Siegrist, 2016) or waste levels (Van Geffen, Van Herpen, and Van Trijp, 2017), but can influence setting an intention to reduce waste (Graham-Rowe, Jessop and Sparks, 2014; Stancu, Haugaard and Lähteenmaki, 2016; Russell *et al.*, 2017). However, people's beliefs about whether others important to them waste very little or no food can strongly influence their behaviour, such that they want to match the behaviours of these others (Van Geffen, Van Herpen and Van Trijp, 2017).

Often overlooked in current food waste literature, is the influence of other goals on the motivation to reduce waste levels. People have multiple valued goals they aim to act upon when handling food. These goals include ensuring consumption of safe foods (Watson and Meah, 2012), and achieving efficiency in preparation (Evans, 2012). Therefore, in order to set a goal to reduce waste levels, people should not only find food waste reduction important, but also more important than these other goals. Yet, food waste reduction, in contrast to some of the other goals, has few direct personal benefits, while people are known to act most easily on goals that have such benefits (Steg *et al.*, 2014). Food waste reduction is considered important due to its financial consequences and impact on the environment, but food prices are relatively low and the environmental impact is distant. In contrast, some of the other goals have personal and direct benefits, such as ensuring health, pleasure or saving time. These other goals are, therefore, more easily acted upon than waste reduction. This can steer toward waste generation, certainly in cases where goals are in conflict (Nielsen, 2017), for instance when distasteful food is left and people need to decide if they will eat it to reduce waste or discard it to ensure food enjoyment. To circumvent such situations, it is beneficial if people are able to handle their food such that they can reduce waste while also acting upon important other goals.

Abilities

The MOA framework states that motivation to perform certain behaviours is not sufficient to actually perform them (Olander and Thøgersen, 1995; Rothschild, 1999). Rather, the right skills and knowledge sets are required to ensure that the behaviours can be performed effectively and easily. Research on objective abilities has shown that people often have incorrect knowledge on date labels (Quested *et al.*, 2011) and suboptimal storage knowledge (Plumb and Downing, 2013; Aschemann-Witzel *et al.*, 2015), which increases the likelihood to waste as it shortens the time in which foods will be eaten. Other research lines have examined subjective abilities, that is, people's belief that they are able to effectively perform certain household management practices. Results have shown that subjective abilities influence behaviour and actual waste levels (Stefan *et al.*, 2013; Van Geffen, Van Herpen and Van Trijp, 2017). These subjective abilities include people's ability to plan accurately, to prolong products' shelf-life, to store foods safely and to cook (tasty) dishes with left-overs.

Opportunities

The MOA framework further states that next to motivation and abilities, opportunities need to be present in order for the behaviours to be performed. People only have so much time, energy and money to allocate in their daily life and opportunities influence how much of these resources need to be used in order to effectively reduce waste levels. If the performance of the desired behaviours is (perceived as) impossible or at the least inconvenient then they are unlikely to be performed. In terms of food waste, the opportunities refer to several aspects of the food-handling process, namely fluctuations in daily schedules (e.g., number of people joining for dinner, unexpected work or social appointments), food supply availability, (super)markets accessibility, and equipment at home (Van Geffen, Van Herpen and Van Trijp, 2017). In cases of highly dynamic lives and fluctuating daily schedules, the amount of time and energy needed to correctly adjust the food-handling behaviours (e.g., the planning) increases. The availability of the products in the stores determines how easily the right packaging sizes and quality can be bought to avoid spoilage and the amount of money required for it. The accessibility of stores determines the amount of time needed to shop for food, and the amount of equipment at home how easily this food can be stored. Interestingly, the direction of the influences of these latter two opportunities is not yet clear; shops that are located closer to the home (thus requiring less time to visit and higher visit frequency), and more storage space at home, can be linked to more accurate planning and better storage practices in terms of shelf-life, but also to a lack of planning or over-purchasing and stocking up products. In any case, opportunities determine how easily people can reduce food waste levels while also acting upon their other valued goals. The better the opportunities, the more likely people will perform food waste reducing behaviours.

Interactions

The MOA framework is a social marketing tool, particularly intended for practical application in terms of intervention selection. Nevertheless, several theoretical investigations have taken place. These predominately investigated if and how the MOA parts interact (Binney, Hall and Shaw, 2003; Brug, 2008; Siemsen, Roth and Balasubramanian, 2008). So far, there is no clear consensus on this (Brug, 2008). Some suggest that abilities and opportunities are moderators between motivation and behaviour (Binney, Hall and Shaw, 2003), others that there is a bottleneck structure, meaning that it is the constraining factor among the three of motivation, ability and opportunity that determines behaviour (Siemsen, Roth and Balasubramanian, 2008). Regardless, the MOA framework has proven suitable for intervention selection. It states that the motivation, abilities and opportunities can be either present or absent (to a more or lesser extent), which implies that there are eight different segment possibilities (i.e., combinations of motivation present/absent, abilities present/absent and opportunities present/absent) (Binney, Hall and Shaw, 2003). For each possibility different types of intervention are most suited. The interventions corresponding to each MOA part will be discussed in turn.

Interventions based on the MOA framework

Motivation, abilities and opportunities determine if people are prone, unable or resistant to perform food waste reducing behaviours (MacInnis *et al.*, 1991; Binney, Hall and Shaw, 2003). The MOA framework suggests that different types of social interventions should be used in each case. When motivation, abilities and opportunities are present, reminders in the form of informational campaigns may be enough to encourage people to continue performing the behaviours. Yet, when (at least) one of the three aspects is lacking, other types of interventions are more promising.

When motivation is absent, changes in the regulatory environment (laws and regulations) can encourage people to reduce their waste levels. Changing the costs and benefits of food waste related behaviours can strengthen the importance given to waste reduction, also in relation to other valued goals. For example, high waste levels can be discouraged by introducing (monetary) penalties (Jereme *et al.*, 2018) and low waste levels can be encouraged by subsidizing, providing special privileges or praise (Reisch, Eberle and Lorek, 2013). Alternatively, one can make changes in the choice structure of people to make behaviours that will reduce waste levels most likely to be performed, without eliminating choice options (von Kameke and Fischer, 2018). These nudges can gently steer people toward food waste reducing behaviours so that motivation does not need to be present to still perform the behaviours. Regulatory interventions or nudges are promising techniques to overcome lacking motivation to reduce waste levels (Reisch, Eberle and Lorek, 2013; Reisch and Zhao, 2017). Yet, a downside is that the interventions improve externally, and not the internally, regulated motivation (Steg *et al.*, 2014) and consequently, people are likely to fall back into their old behaviour as soon as the interventions are dropped.

When motivation to reduce waste levels is present, but not easily prioritized over other goals, interventions that reinforce people's motivation seem best suited. These include interventions such as prompts, affective campaign appeals (Peter and Honea, 2012), social influences (Osbaldiston and Schott, 2012), competition (Abrahamse and Matthies, 2013) or commitment (Abrahamse and Matthies, 2013; Stöckli, Niklaus and Dorn, 2018). These types of interventions have in common that they do not necessarily change people's beliefs concerning food waste (Whitehair, Shanklin and Brannon, 2013) and consequently will only be successful for people who already intend to reduce their waste levels (Peter and Honea, 2012; Wonneberger, 2018).

In cases where abilities are lacking, people can best be helped by interventions that improve their food handling. One can think of educational campaigns to teach efficient food-handling skills and improve knowledge (Terpstra *et al.*, 2005; Dyen and Sirieix, 2016; Schmidt, 2016; Romani *et al.*, 2018). Providing instructions has been shown to be successful when used in isolation (Romani *et al.*, 2018), but more effective when used in combination with other interventions, such as commitment and prompts (Osbaldiston and Schott, 2012; Schmidt, 2016). Additionally, interventions can provide feedback on the level of food wasted and/or efficiency of certain food-handling behaviours (e.g., planning). This feedback can subsequently be used to improve food-handling behaviours. General pro-environmental literature has shown that feedback seems to be most effective for people who are already motivated (McKenzie-Mohr and Schultz, 2014).

When opportunities are lacking, marketing may be sufficient to achieve appropriate behaviour by introducing a product or service into the environment that enables people to manifest their motivation and utilize their abilities. Examples include the introduction of appropriate packaging sizes (and corresponding prices), or automation of certain food-handling behaviours to save time (e.g., online shopping). These products or services can make it easier to perform food waste reducing behaviour, such that fewer resources (e.g., time, energy or money) are needed.

Transtheoretical model (TTM)

The TTM (Prochaska, DiClemente and Norcross, 1992; Prochaska, 2013) is a well-established, psychology-based behaviour change model that offers methods to assess and evaluate behaviours, and many underlying psycho-social influences. The TTM has been widely used to guide and evaluate interventions that target the prevention or reduction of unwanted behaviours (e.g., smoking), or the introduction of a new behaviour (e.g., exercise). The model is very adaptable, having been shown to successfully measure, manage or change a range of behaviours from fruit consumption (de Vet *et al.*, 2008); childhood obesity (Ham et al., 2016); smoking cessation (Prochaska and Norcross, 2001); increasing physical exercise (Hellsten *et al.*, 2008); increasing green eating behaviours (Monroe *et al.*, 2015); to the promotion of cycling (Rose and Marfurt, 2007; Forward, 2014). Yet, the use of the TTM has not yet spread to the context of household food waste, although it would seem applicable to household food management behaviours, and behaviour changes that could reduce the large amounts of food that are currently wasted in homes (Davison *et al.*, 2012).

The TTM consists of four main concepts, all related to behaviour change:

1   Five 'stages of change' (from when a person is not thinking about changing a behaviour to the stage where a person has changed and is maintaining a new behaviour).
2   Decisional balance (the pros and cons a person perceives as being related to changing a behaviour).
3   Ten processes of change (the use of underlying psycho-social factors that can influence behaviour change).
4   Self-efficacy (belief in one's ability to perform a specific behaviour).

Briefly, the principles of the TTM (Prochaska, DiClemente and Norcross, 1992) are that within any community, different people will be in different stages of change, with people in different stages of change perceiving different costs and benefits (pros and cons) related to altering their behaviour. Differences in the type and frequency of use of various psycho-social processes (processes of change) will also be occurring at different stages of change. In addition, people will have differing degrees of self-confidence about their ability to make a change to a specific behaviour (self-efficacy). Consequently, there is a need to develop different messages and interventions for different people in different stages of change. It is unlikely that people in different stages will all respond to, or be motivated by, the same type of message. These principles would also apply to householders in the community. Therefore, using the TTM can help identify, measure and encourage change in behaviours related to the wasting of food.

Each of the four main concepts of the TTM will now be explained in detail. First, examples are provided to explain how these concepts could be related to food management behaviours and household food waste. Second, examples are provided to explain how the concepts can be used in food waste avoidance campaigns and behaviour change interventions.

Stages of change, household food management behaviours and food waste

Five stages of change can be passed through on the way to making changes and developing a new behaviour, or eliminating an old unwanted behaviour. Using similar stage descriptions that have been noted for the uptake of regular exercise (Reed *et al.*, 1997), the stages of change for food management behaviours could be described as:

1.   *Pre-contemplation.* No thought about changing any usual behaviour. For example, a householder might have no thoughts about changing current behaviours such as ceasing to purchase more food than needed, or making better use of left-overs.
2.   *Contemplation.* A change is considered, but at this stage there is no clear intention to make any changes in the near future. Here a householder might notice that too much food has been purchased, or that too much food remains uneaten and is discarded. Thoughts might begin to emerge about the possibility of not wasting food. However, at this stage the routine behaviours do not change.
3.   *Preparation.* Having considered the possibility of change, a householder in this stage will usually start to make some plans or make a commitment to change. For example, consider purchasing food online to avoid the temptation of purchasing extra food that is being displayed in supermarkets, or seeking out recipes to reuse left-over food. Here a new behaviour could even be trialled; such as sometimes making a new meal from left-overs.

4. *Action.* At this stage, a householder commences to regularly perform a new food management behaviour, for example regularly using left-over food for another meal.
5. *Maintenance.* At this stage the person has been regularly performing a new behaviour, or has ceased to perform an unwanted behaviour, for some time. Maintenance is usually achieved when the wanted behaviour has been performed for six months or more. Householders in a maintenance stage would, for example, now be in a routine of always using left-overs; or always planning menus and purchasing food accordingly.

Figure 18.2 illustrates the stages of change, and shows how the TTM stages also accommodate the possibility of relapse, helping to understand how people may slip back to an old behaviour for a time, and then later once again contemplate changing back to the new behaviour. This seems to be a realistic approach as it can take time for people to completely give up an old behaviour, especially if that behaviour has become habitual, as habits are difficult to control (de Vries, Aarts and Midden, 2011). Therefore, householders could take time to fully establish a new behaviour, and could perhaps slip back to some old, previously habitual food management behaviours. For example, it may appear easier, and save time, to once again simply discard left-over food rather than think about re-using it.

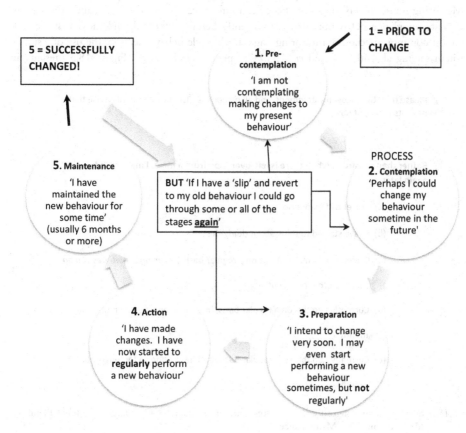

Figure 18.2 The TTM stages of change.

Source: Adapted with permission from Davison, 2015; based on Prochaska and DiClemente, 1983.

Movement through the stages of change is likely to be cyclic, as changing any well-established behaviour will usually be difficult. This is because a behaviour that is being regularly performed brings with it some type of payoff (Skinner, 1953), or reward, for the person performing that behaviour – otherwise there would be no point in the behaviour being performed. For example, over-purchasing food in the supermarket may result in positive feelings and answer a householder's thoughts that it is better to have too much, rather than just enough, to feed the family. Or it may be easier, or even work in better with other household schedules and household members, to stop planning meals and therefore stop purchasing only what is needed for meals. Thus, convenience can be a motive for someone to stop considering a new behaviour for a while (or even permanently), or for someone to slip back to an old behaviour, even after performing a new behaviour for some time. So a cyclic movement of the stages allows for the possibility of movement in and out of the stages before a person finally establishes, and maintains, a new behaviour. This means that a householder who, for example, stopped planning meals (relapse) may at some future time again start noticing the amount of food remaining unused and discarded, feel some concern or guilt about this, and again start considering how to avoid this waste (contemplation stage). The householder may start again to move through the stages, and maybe this time will ultimately reach a stage of consistently planning meals and reducing food that previously remained unused (maintenance stage).

Measuring householders' stages of change can inform campaign developers and others about food waste avoidance behaviours that are currently being performed, and those that are not. The most common method of measuring stages for lifestyle behaviours is by the use of a simple five-item staging algorithm (Reed *et al.*, 1997; Spencer *et al.*, 2006). Figure 18.3 presents an

Please read the following statement, and all responses. Then circle the response that best fits you right now.

Rather than discard it, when there is left-over food from a meal, I make sure I use it again later

      (a) Currently I do not do this

      (b) I have started to think about doing this

      (c) Currently I do this, but **not** on a regular basis (*meaning sometimes you do this, but other times not*)

      (d) Currently I do this on a regular basis, but I have only begun in the past month

      (e) Currently I do this on a regular basis, and have done so for longer than 6 months.

Figure 18.3 Stage of change algorithm. (a) = Pre-contemplation; (b) = Contemplation; (c) = Planning; (d) = Action; (e) = Maintenance.

Table 18.1 Stage of change: Australian householders' food management behaviours

Food management behaviour	Number of participants				
	PC	C	P	A	M
Checking food stocks prior to shopping	83 (10%)	14 (2%)	269 (32%)	58 (7%)	426 (50%)
Planning meals at least 2 days in advance	255 (30%)	42 (5%)	242 (28%)	56 (7%)	255 (30%)
Know exactly what intend to buy because have a written or mental shopping list	62 (7%)	15 (2%)	192 (23%)	63 (7%)	518 (61%)
Adhere to planned purchases and do not buy more	287 (34%)	20 (2%)	281 (33%)	49 (6%)	213 (25%)
Cook right amount of rice	229 (28%)	7 (9%)	88 (11%)	30 (4%)	453 (56%)
Cook right amount of pasta	213 (27%)	8 (1%)	100 (12%)	35 (4%)	445 (56%)
Use left-over food from one meal for another meal or snack	53 (6%)	14 (2%)	121 (14%)	41 (5%)	621 (73%)
Place majority of fresh fruit in the fridge	298 (35%)	15 (2%)	79 (9%)	26 (3%)	432 (51%)

Source: From Davison (2015)
Note: PC = Pre-contemplation; C = Contemplation; P = Planning; A = Action; M = Maintenance.

example of an algorithm measuring one food management behaviour, where a single response can identify a person's stage of change. Algorithms of this type can also be formatted to assess multiple behaviours, one by one. This is a useful way to measure several different food management behaviours related to food waste, as householders are unlikely to be in the same stage of change for all their food management behaviours.

Knowing which desirable food management behaviours are frequently being performed by householders, and which are not, can help guide the development of messages and strategies for food waste avoidance campaigns. For example, if a TTM algorithm, related to the behaviour of storing fresh fruit, indicated that a large portion of a population were not storing their fresh fruit correctly, then information and messages in campaigns could focus more on targeting this behaviour. Whereas, if a TTM algorithm related to storing bread indicated most of the population were already freezing their bread and storing it in the correct manner, then bread storage could receive less focus.

A hypothetical application of the TTM to food waste was presented by Davison *et al.* (2012). This was later followed by a trial application to food waste (Davison, 2015), where prior to developing an informational intervention, several key food management behaviours being performed by Australian householders (n = 926) were measured by stage of change algorithms (Davison, 2015). Results, presented in Table 18.1, showed wide variations in the number of householders performing the measured food behaviours, with this information then helping to guide the direction of a later food waste avoidance intervention.

Decisional balance

Decisional balance is the weighing up of the benefits (pros) and the costs (cons) of changing to a new behaviour. People in the lower stages of change are likely to see more cons related to making a behaviour change, whereas people in the higher stages will have come to see more pros. Across many behaviours, including those related to sunscreen use, smoking and

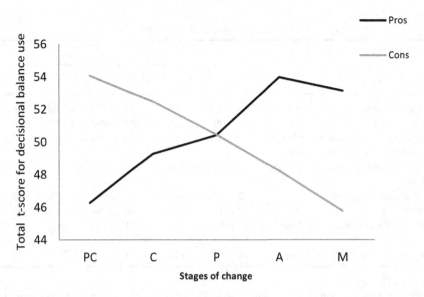

Figure 18.4 Decisional balance: crossover of pros and cons scores.
Source: Davison (2015).

exercising (Prochaska *et al.*, 1994), research has been able to show a clear crossover, whereby people in the middle stages of change reduce their perception of cons, and increase their perception of pros related to a new behaviour. This crossover has also been evident after measuring Australian householders' pros and cons related to the behaviour of discarding edible food to the household garbage bin (Davison, 2015), as shown in Figure 18.4.

Key: PC = Pre-contemplation; C = Contemplation; P = Planning; A = Action; M = Maintenance.

Logically, when more benefits can be related to a new behaviour, there is more likelihood that a householder will be motivated to use the new behaviour. Therefore, measuring the TTM concept of decisional balance can inform programme developers, as knowing what is specifically hindering or helping householders to change one of their food management behaviours can then be targeted in campaigns.

Decisional balance can be measured using a ten- or 20-item scale, with half the items relating to cons and half to pros. The creation of items is somewhat arbitrary and will differ for different behaviours but the underlying theme that was developed in early TTM research should be maintained. For example, a high loading decisional balance scale item related to exercise (Marcus, Rakowski and Rossi, 1992) was 'I would feel good about myself if I kept my commitment to exercise'. This statement can be adapted to 'I would feel better about myself if I discarded less edible food'. An example of a food management related pro and con item, drawn from recent research (Davison, 2015) is:

PRO: Learning more about how to best manage my food at home could help me reduce the amount of money I now spend on food.
CON: Making any changes to the way I usually manage the household food would take too much of my time and/or effort.

Self-efficacy

When evaluating food management behaviours it may also be helpful to assess the TTM concept of self-efficacy, described as belief in one's ability to perform a specific behaviour. The higher one's self-efficacy the more likely a specific behaviour will be performed successfully (Bandura, 1982) and self-efficacy has been noted as a significant predictor of household general waste management in a UK population (Barr, 2007). Stefan *et al.* (2013) related perceived behavioural control (which has been linked to self-efficacy) to the shopping routines of Romanian consumers, and noted a lack of control was highly related to shopping for food and food waste. Self-efficacy has been measured using simple Likert-type scales (Schorr *et al.*, 2008).

If self-efficacy is shown to be low, then strategies may be included in a campaign or intervention to help improve levels of confidence. Increasing skills is one method of increasing self-efficacy (Watson and Tharp, 2007); for example, encouraging attendance at workshops that show how to use left-overs or showing how to efficiently store food. Being shown how a new behaviour can reduce a problem, and then actually performing that new behaviour, could also help increase householders' beliefs about their ability to change.

Processes of change, household food management behaviours and food waste

As already noted, people do not usually move through the stages of change in a quick or simple manner. A variety of external and internal factors can influence progression toward a new behaviour. Drawing on other influential behaviour change theories, the TTM concept of processes of change includes ten psycho-social processes related to changing a behaviour (five experiential or cognitive-type processes, and five behavioural-type processes), as illustrated in Table 18.2.

Table 18.2 The TTM processes of change

Process	Description
Experiential/cognitive processes	
Consciousness raising	Efforts by an individual to seek new information and gain understanding about a problem
Dramatic relief	Experiencing and expressing feelings about one's problems
Environmental reevaluation	Assessing how a problem affects the physical environment
Self-reevaluation	Assessing how one thinks and feels about a problem
Self-liberation	Choosing and committing to act, or believing personal change is possible
Behavioural processes	
Social liberation	Awareness of availability and acceptance of alternative non-problem behaviours; influences from others or the environment
Counter conditioning	Finding alternatives. Substitution of alternative behaviour for a problem behaviour
Helping relationships	Accepting, utilizing the support of others
Stimulus control	Restructuring one's physical environment, controlling a situation and other causes that trigger a situation, using prompts
Reinforcement management	Being rewarded for making changes, changing the contingencies that control or maintain the problem

The processes describe how people change Norcross, Krebs and Prochaska (2011), and that their use, especially the frequency of use, will differ according to a person's stage of change. For example, for smoking cessation (Prochaska *et al.*, 1988) and mammography screening (Pruitt *et al.*, 2010), people in the early stages of change were found to mostly use the five experiential/cognitive type of processes, while the behavioural processes were mostly used in later stages. However, for some behaviours the use of the processes is not so clearly defined by each stage.

For a variety of health behaviours (Rosen, 2000) and for people who were increasing the fruit intake in their diets (de Vet *et al.*, 2008), both experiential and behavioural processes have been used in all stages, with the use of all processes increasing as stage of change increased. Results of pre-intervention and post-intervention surveys have found somewhat similar use of processes for household food management (Davison, 2015). Figure 18.5 highlights the pattern of processes used by householders at the pre-intervention survey (S1) and the post-intervention survey (S2). Those in a preparation stage of change (intending to stop placing edible food in their home garbage bins in the near future) or higher stages (not placing edible food in the bin) all increased their use of processes following a food waste prevention intervention. The experiential processes also remained the most frequently used processes across all the stages of change, although this cognitive-type process use did decrease for those who were maintaining the desirable behaviour of not discarding edible food. This would seem a logical result as once a new food behaviour was well established then less on-going cognitive processing would be required, and a similar result for the use of experiential processes has also been found in some past exercise research (Marshall and Biddle, 2001).

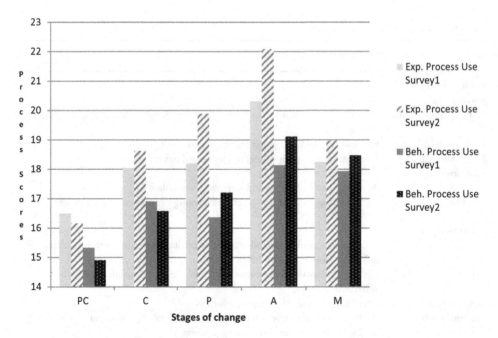

Figure 18.5 Processes of change: frequency of use.
Source: Davison (2015).

Using the TTM processes of change to develop campaign messages

Campaign messages that encourage the use of the processes of change can help increase readiness to change, and also help motivate people to change. Table 18.3 illustrates how messages and strategies can be developed in the context of household food waste, for an experiential process (consciousness raising) and a behavioural process (counter conditioning).

The TTM advocates that different messages for change, relating to different processes, should be delivered to different people at different times, according to their various stages of change. However, from the perspective of an economical intervention to reduce food waste in a large population, it would seem practical, and just as useful, to deliver a single intervention that encourages the use of all ten processes of change. As all processes are used to some extent at any one time, all process-related messages and strategies could be delivered at the one time – with the expectation that as different householders will be in different stages of readiness, the appeal and the frequency of use of the strategies will differ somewhat, but everyone should pay attention to at least some of the delivered messages and strategies. This method was adopted when groups of Australian householders were presented with food waste avoidance information, in either a paper calendar carefully designed to include messages relating to all TTM processes which was posted to householders; or similar information in emails that were delivered online to some householders (Davison, 2015). The TTM can then be used at a population level to gain a snapshot of a population and the spread of its behaviours across the desired behaviour spectrum.

In the TTM food waste trial, after four months Australian householders who received and were reading the calendar reduced self-reported discarded food by 47 per cent, and those who accessed the online information reduced their discarded food by 40 per cent (Davison, 2015). Interestingly, results were not statistically significant with a control group also reducing their discarded food by 30 per cent. All the householders had been exposed to the TTM concepts in items they responded to in a pre-intervention survey. To some extent, this may have also

Table 18.3 Examples of strategies based on processes of change

Process of change	Food waste avoidance, strategy examples
Consciousness raising	Being interested in information about household food waste. Being aware of own food management behaviours. *Strategy:* Messages to attract attention to amount of food that is wasted in households; messages that highlight that almost all households do waste some food – even though they think they don't. Where possible, keep questions and statements personal. E.g. 1. Ask 'Do **you** know what food went in **your** bin today?' 2. Highlight statistics for amounts of wasted edible food. 3. Note the environmental and personal costs of wasting food.
Counter conditioning	Rearranging or changing usual household procedures in order to avoid food being discarded. *Strategy:* Encourage a new behaviour. E.g. 1. This could be as simple as explaining that bread will keep fresher if frozen, rather than if stored in containers or if stored in the fridge. 2. Encourage rotation of refrigerated food. 3. Suggest any smaller portions of refrigerated food be grouped in larger trays that can be easily moved forward for inspection (to avoid forgetting about them).

increased the control group's awareness about their discarded food (the TTM process of con-sciousness raising). The pre-intervention survey may have also encouraged some self-monitoring which may also contribute to positive behaviour changes (Watson and Tharp, 2007). Regardless, the trial was able to show that the TTM can be successfully applied to food waste and to success-fully capture a population's behaviour change as a result of marketing intervention.

A further point of interest from the Australian research is that prior to any intervention, all householders believed they only discarded between two and three cups of edible food weekly – discarded amounts that appear much smaller than the weekly 2.2 kilograms of edible food an independent household garbage bin audit had previously revealed for Australian households (Sustainability Victoria, 2014). Thus, although information and messages appeared to be able to reduce amounts of wasted food, householders still appeared to be under-estimating the amount of their waste – highlighting one of the challenges that still needs to be addressed by campaign developers and people working in food waste in general.

Conclusion

This chapter has introduced the MOA and the TTM, two models that can be used to help understand householders' motives and the influences related to the way they manage their food in the home. Both models help to identify barriers, including important internal bar-riers, that can prevent householders from reducing amounts of food they currently discard. The MOA and the TTM address also householders' readiness to change, and offer clear guidelines to help increase motivation to change. The models can also guide interventions or campaigns aimed at household food waste avoidance.

The MOA framework stresses that desirable behaviours will be performed when motiv-ation, abilities and opportunities are present. For food waste reducing behaviours to be per-formed, people should consider it to be in their self-interest, and thus that it is important in itself and in comparison to other valued goals. Additionally, people should have the right skills and knowledge sets to be able to perform food waste reducing behaviours. Also, people should have the opportunities to perform the behaviours without needing to spend too much time, energy or money to do so. In cases where one of the three elements is lacking, different interventions may be used to overcome this. Lacking motivation can be overcome by introducing regulatory incentives, nudging, or interventions that reinforce motivation such as prompts, affective campaign appeals, competition, social influences or commitment. Lacking abilities can be overcome by providing informational campaigns that consist of tips and tricks to improve people's food-handling habits. Finally, new products or services can be introduced in cases where opportunities are lacking.

Using the TTM concept of the stages of change, desirable food management behaviours that householders are performing, or not performing, can be identified in large populations. With additional knowledge gained from the TTM concepts of decisional balance, processes of change, and self-efficacy, appropriate strategies can be created to help householders become more aware of their own food management behaviours, to ready themselves for change, and to ultimately perform more of the key behaviours that research has already related to food waste avoidance. Raising levels of awareness about householders' own contributions to food waste is always an important first step toward reducing the amount of discarded food. Unless a householder believes some food is discarded in his or her home, and sees this as waste, no attention will be paid to messages that show how to avoid food waste in homes.

Both behaviour change models discussed in this chapter offer fruitful avenues to further explore for people who are in the position of creating interventions to reduce food waste.

References

Abeliotis, K., Lasaridi, K. and Chroni, C. (2014) 'Attitudes and behaviour of Greek households regarding food waste prevention', *Waste Management & Research*, vol. 32, no. 3, pp. 237–240.

Abrahamse, W. and Matthies, E. (2013) 'Informational strategies to promote pro-environmental behaviour: changing knowledge, awareness and attitudes', in Steg, L., van der Berg, A. and de Groot, I. (eds) *Environmental psychology: An introduction*, pp. 223–232. Chichester: Wiley-Blackwell.

Aschemann-Witzel, J., de Hooge, I., Amani, P., Bech-Larsen, T. and Oostindjer, M. (2015) 'Consumer-related food waste: Causes and potential for action', *Sustainability*, vol. 7, no. 6, pp. 6457–6477. doi: 10.3390/su7066457.

Bandura, A. (1982) 'Self-efficacy mechanism in human agency', *American Psychologist*, vol. 37, pp. 122–147.

Barr, S. (2007) 'Factors influencing environmental attitudes and behaviors: A U.K. case study of household waste management', *Environment and Behavior*, vol. 39, no. 4, pp. 435–473.

Binney, W., Hall, J., & Shaw, M. (2003) 'A further development in social marketing: application of the MOA framework and behavioral implications', *Marketing Theory*, vol. 3, no. 3, 387–403.

Brug, J. (2008) 'Determinants of healthy eating: motivation, abilities and environmental opportunities', *Family practice*, vol. 25, no. suppl_1, pp. i50–i55.

Cialdini, R. B., Kallgren, C. A. and Reno, R. R. (1991) 'A focus theory of normative conduct: A theoretical refinement and reevaluation of the role of norms in human behavior', *Advances in Experimental Social Psychology*, vol. 24(C), pp. 201–234. doi: 10.1016/S0065-2601(08)60330-5.

Davison, S. (2015) 'Developing, delivering and evaluation a psychology based informational intervention for reducing food waste in households', PhD thesis, University of South Australia, Adelaide.

Davison, S., Thompson, K., Sharp, A. and Dawson, D. (2012) 'Reducing wasteful household behaviours; contributions from psychology and implications for intervention design', in S. Lehmann and R. Crocker (eds) *Designing for Zero Waste: Consumption, Technologies and the Built Environment*, (pp.67–88). London: Earthscan.

de Vet, E., De Nooijer, J., De Vries, N. K. and Brug J. (2008) 'Do the transtheoretical processes of change predict transitions in stages of change for fruit intake?' *Health Education & Behavior*, vol. 35, pp. 603–618.

de Vries, P., Aarts, H. and Midden, C.J.H. (2011) 'Changing simple energy-related consumer behaviors: How the enactment of intentions is thwarted by acting and non-active habits', *Environment and Behavior*, vol. XX, no. X, pp. 1–22.

Dyen, M. and Sirieix, L. (2016) 'How does a local initiative contribute to social inclusion and promote sustainable food practices? Focus on the example of social cooking workshops', *International Journal of Consumer Studies*, vol. 40, no. 6, pp. 685–694. doi: 10.1111/ijcs.12281.

Eurobarometer. (2014) *Attitudes of Europeans towards Resource Efficiency. Flash Eurobarometer 388*. Available at: http://ec.europa.eu/public_opinion/flash/fl_316_en.pdf

Evans, D. (2012) 'Beyond the throwaway society: Ordinary domestic practice and a sociological approach to household food waste', *Sociology*, vol. 46, no. 1, pp. 41–56. doi: 10.1177/0038038511416150.

Forward, S.E., (2014). 'Exploring people's willingness to bike using a combination of the theory of planned behavioural and the transtheoretical model', *Revue Européenne de Psychologie Appliquée/ European Review of Applied Psychology*, vol. 64, no. 3, pp.151–159.

Fox, D., Ioannidi, E., Sun, Y. T., Jape, V. W., Bawono, W. R., Zhang, S. and Perez-Cueto, F. J. A. (2018) 'Consumers with high education levels belonging to the millennial generation from Denmark, Greece, Indonesia and Taiwan differ in the level of knowledge on food waste', *International Journal of Gastronomy and Food Science*, vol. 11(February 2017), pp. 49–54. doi: 10.1016/j.ijgfs.2017.11.005.

Graham-Rowe, E., Jessop, D. C. and Sparks, P. (2014) 'Identifying motivations and barriers to minimising household food waste', *Resources, Conservation and Recycling*, vol. 84, pp. 15–23.

Ham, O.K., Sung, K.M., Lee, B.G., Choi, H.W. and Im, E.O., (2016) 'Transtheoretical model based exercise counseling combined with music skipping rope exercise on childhood obesity', *Asian nursing research*, vol. 10, no.2, pp.116–122.

Hellsten, L., Nigg, C., Norman, G., Burbank, P., Braun, L., Breger, R., Coday, M., Elliot, D., Garber, C., Greaney, M. M. and Lees, F. (2008) 'Accumulation of behavioral validation evidence for physical activity stage of change', *Health Psychology*, vol. 27, no. 1, pp. S43-S53.

Jereme, I. A., Siwar, C., Begum, R. A., Talib, B. A. and Choy, E. A. (2018) 'Analysis of household food waste reduction towards sustainable food waste management in Malaysia', *Journal of Solid Waste Technology and Management*, vol. 44, no. 1, pp. 86–96. doi: 10.5276/JSWTM.2018.86.

MacInnis, D. J., Moorman, C., & Jaworski, B. J. (1991) 'Enhancing consumers' motivation, ability, and opportunity to process brand information from ads: conceptual framework and managerial implications', *Journal of Marketing*, vol. 55, no. 1, pp. 32–53.

Marcus, B. H., Rakowski, W. and Rossi, J. S. (1992) 'Assessing motivational readiness and decision making for exercise', *Health Psychology*, vol. 11, pp. 257–261.

Marshall, S. J. and Biddle, S. J. H. (2001) 'The transtheoretical model of behaviour change: A meta-analysis of applications to physical activity and exercise', *Annals of Behavior Medicine*, vol. 23, no. 4, pp. 229–246.

McKenzie-Mohr, D. and Schultz, P. W. (2014) 'Choosing effective behavior change tools', *Social Marketing Quarterly*, vol. 20, no. 1, pp. 35–46. doi: 10.1177/1524500413519257.

Monroe, J. T., Lofgren, I. E., Sartini, B. L. and Greene, G. W. (2015) 'The green eating project: Web-based intervention to promote environmentally conscious eating behaviours in US university students', *Public Health Nutrition*, vol. 18, no. 13, pp. 2368–2378.

Nielsen, K. S. (2017) 'From prediction to process: A self-regulation account of environmental behavior change', *Journal of Environmental Psychology*. Elsevier Ltd, vol. 51, pp. 189–198. doi: 10.1016/j.jenvp.2017.04.002.

Norcross, J. C., Krebs, P. M. and Prochaska, J. O. (2011) 'Stages of change', *Journal of Clinical Psychology: In Session*, vol. 67, no. 2, pp. 143–154.

Olander, F. and Thøgersen, J. (1995) 'Understanding of consumer behaviour as a prerequisite for environmental protection', *Journal of consumer policy*, vol. 18, no. 4, (1994), pp. 345–385.

Osbaldiston, R. and Schott, J. P. (2012) 'Environmental sustainability and behavioral science: Meta-analysis of proenvironmental behavior experiments', *Environment and Behavior*, vol. 44, no. 2, pp. 257–299. doi: 10.1177/0013916511402673.

Parizeau, K., von Massow, M. and Martin, R. (2015) 'Household-level dynamics of food waste production and related beliefs, attitudes, and behaviours in Guelph, Ontario', *Waste Management*, vol. 35, pp. 207–217.

Peter, P. C. and Honea, H. (2012) 'Targeting social messages with emotions of change: The call for optimism', *Journal of Public Policy & Marketing*, vol. 31, no. 2, pp. 269–283. doi: 10.1509/jppm.11.098.

Plumb, A. and Downing, P. (2013) *Consumer Attitudes to Food Waste and Food Packaging*. WRAP.

Principato, L., Secondi, L. and Pratesi, C. A. (2015) 'Reducing food waste: An investigation on the behaviour of Italian youths', *British Food Journal*, vol. 117, no. 2, pp. 731–748.

Prochaska, J. O. (2013) 'Transtheoretical model of behavior change', in Gellman M.D. and Turner J.R. (eds) *Encyclopedia of Behavioral Medicine*, pp. 1997–2000. New York, NY: Springer.

Prochaska, J. O. and DiClemente, C.C. (1983) 'Stages and processes of self-change of smoking: Toward an integrative model of change', *Journal of Consulting and Clinical Psychology*, vol. 51, pp. 390–395.

Prochaska, J. O., DiClemente, C. C. and Norcross, J. C. (1992) 'In search of how people change: Applications to addictive behaviors', *American Psychologist*, vol. 47, pp. 1102–1114.

Prochaska, J. O. and Norcross, J. C. (2001) 'Stages of change', *Psychotherapy: Theory, Research and Practice*, vol. 38, no. 4, pp. 443–448.

Prochaska, J. O., Velicer, W. F., DiClemente, C. C. and Fava, J. (1988) 'Measuring processes of change: Applications to the cessation of smoking', *Journal of Consulting and Clinical Psychology*, vol. 56, no. 4, pp. 520–528.

Prochaska, J. O., Velicer, W. F., Rossi, J. S., Goldstein, M. G., Marcus, B. H., Rakowski, W., Fiore, C., Harlow, L. L., Redding, C. A., Rosenbloom, D. and Rossi, S. R. (1994) 'Stages of change and decisional balance for 12 problem behaviors', *Health Psychology*, vol. 13, no. 1, pp. 39–46.

Pruitt, S., McQueen, A., Tiro, J., Rakowski, W., DiClemente, C. and Vernon, S. (2010) 'Construct validity of a mammography processes of change scale and invariance by stage of change', *Journal of Health Psychology*, vol. 15, no. 1, pp. 64–74.

Quested, T., Marsh, E., Stunell, D. and Parry, A. D. (2013) 'Spaghetti soup: The complex world of food waste behaviours', *Resources, Conservation and Recycling*, vol. 79, pp. 43–51.

Quested, T. E., Parry, A. D., Easteal, S. and Swannell, R. (2011) 'Food and drink waste from households in the UK', *Nutrition Bulletin*, vol. 36, no. 4, pp. 460–467. doi: 10.1111/j.1467-3010.2011.01924.x.

Reed, G. R., Velicer, W. F., Prochaska, J. O., Rossi, J. and Marcus, B. H. (1997) 'What makes a good staging algorithm: Examples from regular exercise', *American Journal of Health Promotion*, vol. 12, no. 1, pp. 57–66.

Reisch, L., Eberle, U. and Lorek, S. (2013) 'Sustainable food consumption: An overview of contemporary issues and policies', *Sustainability: Science, Practice, and Policy*, vol. 9, no. 2, pp. 7–25. doi: 10.1080/15487733.2013.11908111.

Reisch, L. and Zhao, M. (2017) 'Behavioural economics, consumer behaviour and consumer policy: State of the art', *Behavioural Public Policy*, vol. 1, no. 2, pp. 190–206. doi: 10.1017/bpp.2017.1.

Romani, S., Grappi, S., Bagozzi, R. P. and Barone, A. M. (2018) 'Domestic food practices: A study of food management behaviors and the role of food preparation planning in reducing waste', *Appetite*. Elsevier Ltd, vol. 121, pp. 215–227. doi: 10.1016/j.appet.2017.11.093.

Roodhuyzen, D. M. A., Luning, P. A., Fogliano, V. and Steenbekkers, L. P. A. (2017) 'Putting together the puzzle of consumer food waste: Towards an integral perspective', *Trends in Food Science and Technology*. Elsevier Ltd, vol. 68, pp. 37–50. doi: 10.1016/j.tifs.2017.07.009.

Rose, G. and Marfurt, H. (2007) 'Travel behaviour change impacts of a major ride to work day event', *Transportation Research Part A*, vol. 41, no. 4, pp. 351–364.

Rosen, C. S. (2000) 'Is the sequencing of change processes by stage consistent across health problems? A meta-analysis', *Health Psychology*, vol. 19, no. 6, pp. 593–604.

Rothschild, M. (1999) 'Promises: And carrots, sticks, the a conceptual framework for and health of public management Behaviors Issue Social', *Journal of Marketing*, vol. 63, no. 4, pp. 24–37.

Russell, S. V., Young, C. W., Unsworth, K. L. and Robinson, C. (2017) 'Bringing habits and emotions into food waste behaviour', *Resources, Conservation and Recycling*. Elsevier, vol. 125(May), pp. 107–114. doi:10.1016/j.resconrec.2017.06.007.

Schmidt, K. (2016) 'Explaining and promoting household food waste-prevention by an environmental psychological based intervention study', *Resources, Conservation and Recycling*. Elsevier B.V., vol. 111, pp. 53–66. doi: 10.1016/j.resconrec.2016.04.006.

Schorr, G., Ulbricht, S., Schmidt, C. O., Baumeister, S. E., Ruge, J., Schumann, A., Rumpf, H., John, U. and Meyer, C. (2008) 'Does precontemplation represent a homogeneous stage category? A latent class analysis on German smokers', *Journal of Consulting and Clinical Psychology*, vol. 76, no. 5, pp. 840–851.

Secondi, L., Principato, L. and Laureti, T. (2015) 'Household food waste behaviour in EU-27 countries: A multilevel analysis', *Food Policy*, vol. 56, pp. 25–40.

Siemsen, E., Roth, A. V., & Balasubramanian, S. (2008). 'How motivation, opportunity, and ability drive knowledge sharing: The constraining-factor model', *Journal of Operations Management*, vol. 26, no. 3, pp. 426–445.

Skinner, B. F. (1953) *Science and Human Behaviour*. Cambridge: B.F. Skinner Foundation, 2005.

Spencer, L., Adams., T. B., Malone, S., Roy., L. and Yost, E. (2006) 'Applying the transtheoretical model to exercise: A systematic and comprehensive review of the literature', *Health Promotion Practice*, vol. 7, no. 4, pp. 428–443.

Stancu, V., Haugaard, P. and Lähteenmaki, L. (2016) 'Determinants of consumer food waste behaviour: Two routes to food waste', *Appetite*, vol. 96, pp. 7–17. doi: 10.1016/j.appet.2015.08.025.

Stefan, V., van Herpen, E., Tudoran, A. A. and Lähteenmaki, L. (2013) 'Avoiding food waste by Romanian consumers: The importance of planning and shopping routines', *Food Quality and Preference*, vol. 28, pp. 375–381.

Steg, L., Bolderdijk, J. W., Keizer, K. and Perlaviciute, G. (2014) 'An integrated framework for encouraging pro-environmental behaviour: The role of values, situational factors and goals', *Journal of Environmental Psychology*. Elsevier Ltd, vol. 38, pp. 104–115. doi: 10.1016/j.jenvp.2014.01.002.

Stöckli, S., Niklaus, E. and Dorn, M. (2018) 'Call for testing interventions to prevent consumer food waste', *Resources, Conservation and Recycling*. Elsevier, vol.136(March), pp. 445–462. doi:10.1016/j.resconrec.2018.03.029.

Sustainability Victoria. (2014). '*Food waste in the garbage bin 2013.*' Available at: http://www.sustainability.vic.gov.au/~/media/resources/documents/publications%20and%20research/research/bin%20audits/bin%20audit%20report_food%20waste.pdf

Terpstra, M. J., Steenbekkers, L. P. A., Maertelaere, N. C. M. De and Nijhuis, S. (2005) 'Food storage and disposal: Consumer practices and knowledge', *British Food Journal*, vol. 107, no. 7, pp. 526–533. doi: 10.1108/00070700510606918.

Thyberg, K. L. and Tonjes, D. J. (2016) 'Drivers of food waste and their implications for sustainable policy development', *Resources, Conservation and Recycling*, vol. 106, pp. 110–123.

Van Geffen, L., Van Herpen, E. and Van Trijp, H. (2016) 'Causes & determinants of consumers food waste - A theoretical framework', *EU Refresh Project*, (641933). Available at: https://eu-refresh.org/causes-determinants-consumers-food-waste

Van Geffen, L., Van Herpen, E. and Van Trijp, H. (2017) 'Quantified consumer insights on food waste Pan-European research for quantified consumer food waste understanding', *EU Refresh Project*,

(641933). Available at: http://eu-refresh.org/sites/default/files/REFRESH 2017Quantified con sumer insights on food waste D1.4_0.pdf

Visschers, V. H. M., Wickli, N. and Siegrist, M. (2016) 'Sorting out food waste behaviour: A survey on the motivators and barriers of self-reported amounts of food waste in households', *Journal of Environmental Psychology*. Elsevier Ltd, vol. 45, pp. 66–78. doi: 10.1016/j.jenvp.2015.11.007.

von Kameke, C. and Fischer, D. (2018) 'Preventing household food waste via nudging: An exploration of consumer perceptions', *Journal of Cleaner Production*. Elsevier Ltd, vol. 184, pp. 32–40. doi: 10.1016/j.jclepro.2018.02.131.

Watson D. L. and Tharp, R. G. (2007) *Self-directed Behavior: Self-modification for Personal Adjustment*. (9th ed.). Pacific Grove, CA: Brooks/Cole Publishing Company.

Watson, M., & Meah, A. (2012). 'Food, waste and safety: negotiating conflicting social anxieties into the practices of domestic provisioning', *The Sociological Review*, vol. 60, no. S2, pp. 102–120.

Whitehair, K. J., Shanklin, C. W., & Brannon, L. A. (2013). 'Written messages improve edible food waste behaviors in a university dining facility', *Journal of the Academy of Nutrition and Dietetics*, vol. 113, no. 1, pp. 63–69.

Wonneberger, A. (2018) 'Environmentalism—A question of guilt? Testing a model of guilt arousal and effects for environmental campaigns', *Journal of Nonprofit and Public Sector Marketing*. Routledge, vol. 30, no. 2, pp. 168–186. doi:10.1080/10495142.2017.1326873.

19

ALL MY RELATIONS

Applying social innovation and Indigenous methodology to challenge the paradigm of food waste .

Tammara Soma, Belinda Li, Adrianne Lickers Xavier, Sean Geobey and Rafaela F. Gutierrez

Introduction

The issue of food waste is now widely established as a key research agenda and as an urgent problem to be addressed by international institutions such as the Food and Agriculture Organization (2011), the World Bank (2018) as well as by various scholars in the fields of sociology (Evans, 2014), planning (Soma, 2018a), environmental studies (MacRae, 2016), and geography (Parizeau et al., 2015). In popular culture, celebrity chefs are also contributing to the "food waste fight." UK celebrity chef Jamie Oliver recently launched a "food waste" themed pop-up shop serving repurposed surplus food and recipes with the most commonly wasted ingredients, such as stale bread. The 2017 documentary *Wasted*, produced by the late Anthony Bourdain, explored diverse solutions to address food waste based on the food recovery hierarchy framework (for more on the food recovery hierarchy framework, see Papargyropoulou et al. (2014)). As evidenced by the growing mainstream interest in this issue, no longer is this field restricted to technical concerns around waste management.

The search for solutions to address food waste has brought innovative collaborations across sectors, as well as critical debates. One particularly significant and critical debate around food waste solutions has centred around the pairing of the food waste issue with issues of food insecurity. More specifically, in aiming to reduce food waste, scholars and activists have critiqued the idea that it is acceptable to feed low-income communities with corporate food waste (Caplan, 2017; Fisher, 2017; Riches, 2018). Scholars have noted that approaches to reduce food waste that is focused on shifting unwanted food from retailers or corporations to low-income communities does not actually offer a long-term solution to the problem of food insecurity. This solution also does not address the root causes of food waste, and may in fact, as Fisher (2017) argues, reward wasteful behaviours financially through tax incentives, as well as providing these corporations with a "halo" of doing good for simply maintaining the status quo. While it may be argued that said solution is a necessary stop-gap measure, increasingly, more and more scholars are calling out for more systemic solutions to address food waste (Gille, 2012; Cloke, 2013; Soma, 2018b), as well as solutions that are embedded in social justice.

To better understand the ways in which systemic approaches can be developed, this chapter will first explore the theoretical underpinnings of the social innovation method with respect to aspects of complexity, uncertainty, and knowledge creation. The chapter will identify the potential role of social innovation methodology and some of the barriers to solving a complex problem such as food waste. To do so, we will showcase findings from the Food Systems Lab, a Canadian social innovation lab focused on tackling food waste in the Greater Toronto Area through the principles of Indigenous reconciliation and decolonization (see: 2015 Truth and Reconciliation Commission of Canada Call to Action). It will also share a vignette from one of the authors (an Indigenous scholar from Six Nations) to illustrate an alternative paradigm that challenges the commodification of food and the unjust relationships that lead to waste. The Indigenous paradigm and teaching of "All My Relations" informed the methodology and the facilitation of the lab workshops. The lab included the co-creatión of knowledge and collaboration with participants (both Indigenous and non-Indigenous), the incorporation of Indigenous ceremonies, stories, teachings as well as learning circles. Social innovation labs typically aim to generate disruptive innovations and systemic change. Without a systems approach to addressing food waste, deeply held assumptions might not be challenged, critical features of the broader system might go unnoticed, and opportunities for innovation and collaboration might be missed.

What is social innovation and why apply this to food waste?

A social innovation lab strategically brings together a variety of stakeholders to develop a common understanding of a problem. The stakeholders then work together on innovative solutions through iterations of information collection, analysis, creative engagement, and prototype development (Westley et al., 2012). A social innovation lab is useful for working on complex social problems such as food waste because it takes a whole systems approach and uses a data-oriented evidence base for testing hypotheses, rigorous tracking, and analysis. There is no single agreed-upon definition for social innovation. However, the general idea of social innovation is something that causes a profound and permanent shift in the social system. Westley and Antadze (2010) define social innovation as a complex process of introducing new products, processes or programmes that profoundly change the basic routines, resource and authority flows, or beliefs of the social system in which the innovation occurs. Such successful social innovations have durability and broad impact. Social innovation can take different forms and is generally categorized into three types: (1) incremental innovations; (2) institutional innovations; and (3) disruptive innovations (see Table 19.1).

The types of disruptive innovations that would facilitate systems change and enable long-term solutions to the food waste problem are of interest in this chapter. According to Westley and Antadze (2010), the potential for social innovation is significant considering the innovations that have the potential to disrupt and change the broader system. To disrupt an unjust or wasteful system, diverse and cross-sectoral participation are important. As Westley and Antadze argue (2010, np), "a social innovation must cross multiple social boundaries to reach more people and different people, more organizations and different organizations, organizations nested across scales (from local to regional to national to global) and linked in social networks." In light of Gille's (2012) caution, she noted that the risks and the complexity of food waste (both from a geographical and scalar perspective) will mean that "solutions to the 'food waste problem' limited to technological innovation and a few sites or even countries will prove insufficient and will likely exacerbate existing inequalities."

Table 19.1 Categories of social innovation

Categories of social innovation	Description
Incremental innovations	Goods and services to address social need more effectively or efficiently
Institutional innovations	Harness or retool existing social and economic structures to generate new social value and outcomes
Disruptive innovations	Aim at systems change and can result in changes to power relations, alter social hierarchies, and reframe issues to the benefit of otherwise disenfranchised groups

Source: Adapted from Nicholls et al. (2015)

In addressing the issue of food waste, stakeholders ranging from consumers and producers to policymakers and investors each have their own perspectives on identifying the most difficult challenge in the food systems. There are also different interests with respect to desirable outcomes for the system. While there is some capacity to experiment within the food waste system, at a large scale, experimentation often involves bets with large stakes, be they economic, social, cultural, environmental, or health-related. Bringing these elements together suggests that food waste is a wicked problem domain (Rittel and Webber, 1973; see Table 19.2).

By existing in a space where different actors disagree about the objectives of the system and have a relatively high degree of uncertainty about the system, there is an inherent complexity to this system. In line with Gille's (2012) argument that developing technological innovation in a few sites or even countries to address a complex systemic problem such as food waste will prove insufficient and will likely exacerbate existing inequalities, in these complex systems, straightforward planning and policy approaches tend to fail. Instead, approaches that involve the co-creation of approaches with a variety of system actors, namely via social innovation, are more likely to succeed (Zimmerman, 1998). Doing so

Table 19.2 Defining characteristics of a wicked problem

	Defining characteristics
Wicked problem	They have no definitive formulation
	There is no stopping rule to determine when the problem is solved
	Solutions are not true-or-false but are, instead, better-or-worse
	There is no ultimate solution
	Trial-and-error processes do not work because the problem changes its nature
	There is no exhaustive set of possible solutions
	Each one is effectively unique
	They are nested within and also contain other wicked problems
	How the problem is defined will determine the range of possible solutions
	Those who plan or intervene in the problem are responsible for the consequences of the intervention

Source: Information adapted from Rittel and Webber (1973)

increases the variety of possible solutions that those in the system can use to respond to increasing complexity (Ashby, 1957, 1991), each of which in turn also produces additional information about the system that can then in turn be used to better understand the system itself (Arthur, 1994).

Given the complexity and the uncertainty of food systems, it is critical that research be brought into decision-making. However, doing so requires moving outside the realm of value-free and highly certain knowledge creation in "normal" science. Moreover, this also requires moving beyond "normal" decision-making where a policymaker is assumed to have the knowledge and authority needed to make their decisions. High-stakes, high-uncertainty decisions are ubiquitous and both "normal science" and "normal policymaking" are incapable of responding to these often highly contextual decisions, yet these challenges do not negate the need for evidence to guide decision-making. Post-normal science moves beyond basic science, applied science and research-based consulting to bring in a broader set of stakeholders for both knowledge creation and knowledge use (Funtowicz and Ravetz, 1994; Ravetz, 1999). Biggs et al. (2010) argue that triggers for fostering social innovation in ecosystem management are an impetus for innovation, bricolage, and opportunities for the spread of new ideas and processes. Tied to this, crises in the system, fragmentation, a reframing of perspectives, engagement with stakeholders, leadership, and social entrepreneurship all facilitate system transformation (Biggs et al., 2010).

Processes that support both the emergence of opportunities for social innovation and the facilitation of system transformation can enable social innovation to occur, though doing so is not without risk as the co-creative, exploratory nature of such supports is difficult to direct in a desired direction by those providing the support. This deep co-creation of knowledge forms the research basis of directed social innovation processes and when brought into an operational form with design (or prototypes) offers opportunities to operationalize co-creation in complex systems. Design thinking provides systematic creative processes to develop prototypes that can be used to quickly test solutions to problems (Martin, 2009a; Brown and Barry, 2009). A wide range of design thinking tools and processes exist and in the space of wicked problems. A great deal of experimentation in the development of these prototypes can be used to help different stakeholders work through an understanding of their wicked problem and also to translate between their different ways of thinking. The prototypes can be viewed as boundary objects, which are malleable enough to be adaptable to their localized contexts and the needs of different stakeholders, but also stable enough to hold some consistency between the ways different stakeholders refer to and use them (Star and Griesemer, 1989). In doing so, the prototypes can assist stakeholders in communicating with each other and building common understandings of the problem in addition to providing early models of complex systems intervention.

There are numerous social innovation labs tackling various issues from environmental, health, housing and homelessness, to employment, Indigenous food sovereignty, and arts. The Ontario Tender Fruit Lab is one example of a social innovation lab—a partnership between the MaRS Solutions Lab and the Waterloo Institute for Social Innovation and Resilience (WISIR)—to ensure a thriving and resilient tender fruit industry in Ontario (Tjornbo et al., 2014). There were several initiatives developed and launched through the lab. For example, one of the participants of the lab, the Ontario Tender Fruit Growers was awarded approximately $355,000 in a Growing Forward 2 Funding from Agriculture and Agri-Food Canada to better develop infrastructure and practices to manage the transport and handling of tender fruit products (MaRS, 2015). Another participant (Vineland Growers Cooperative) developed a more sustainable packaging alternative to minimize waste, and to save on packing and labour costs (MaRS, 2015). In line with food-related social innovation labs, we will now explore the role of social innovation in food waste prevention and reduction through the case of the Food Systems Lab.

Case study: Food Systems Lab

The Food Systems Lab was a one-year pilot social innovation lab that sought to develop collaborative and systemic solutions to reduce food waste in Toronto, Ontario, Canada. The intent of this pilot was to apply social innovation methodology to bring together diverse stakeholders across the food system to generate ideas for systemic solutions to reduce food waste in the city. The lab process included a combination of qualitative and quantitative research such as interviews with stakeholders and experts to harvest current knowledge about food waste, analysis of archival records, and collaborative activities. Stakeholders were engaged in a series of three workshops to gain a deeper understanding of the system, identify and prototype innovations, and develop opportunities to address root causes of food waste. The stakeholders included farmers, food businesses, Indigenous leaders, retailers, food processors, consumers, schools, industry associations, civil society groups, faith organizations, charitable foundations, and government representatives (municipal and provincial). The Food Systems Lab generally followed the methodology from the Social Innovation Lab Guide (Westley and Laban, 2015) developed by the Waterloo Institute for Social Innovation and Resilience with minor modifications based on the need to adapt to changing circumstances. The methodology included a variety of tools and processes such as: recruiting participants, conducting research (including setting the challenge brief), working with system modellers or simulators, preparing logistics, designing and delivering workshops, and conducting additional research. The following are phases of the lab process which included: (a) Preliminary research; (b) Workshop 1: Seeing the System; (c) Workshop 2: Designing Solutions; (d) Workshop 3: Prototyping Interventions.

Lab methodology: Preliminary research

The lab team conducted three months of research to develop a challenge brief and a "convening question" for the lab. The convening question is the primary problem that the lab aims to solve and provides specificity to the challenge and system boundaries that the lab will work in (Westley and Laban, 2015). It is important to create a well-defined convening question to provide clarity to lab participants and set an appropriate scale for potential solutions. The risk of selecting a convening question that is too broad is that the problem becomes too overwhelming to solve or participants are not able to find common ground to work toward a solution. As we have previously mentioned, the "Wicked Questions" framework is recommended to develop a convening question. A wicked question does not have obvious answers or solutions embedded within it and is centred around a paradox or trade-offs that reflect contraindications of a variety of perspectives (Westley and Laban, 2015).

Research activities included 47 semi-structured key informant interviews and a literature review. Key informants were selected from a cross-section of stakeholder groups to be representative of the food system in Toronto. Stakeholders were grouped as follows: Academic, Consultant, Education, Faith Institution, Food Recovery, Food Service, Foundation, Government, Indigenous, Association, Non-Profit, Processor, Producer, Retail and Tech Start-Up.

Most key informant interviews were conducted over the phone with an interviewer and occasionally a note-taker. When a note-taker was not present, key informants were asked for permission to record the interview. By recording interviews, the lab team was able to gather more details that might have been missed while taking notes, and more closely observe changes in voice tonality to capture emotions and reactions as interviewees answered questions. Preliminary research findings were summarized into a design brief that would be used to share the findings from the interview and to set the context of the problem. The research findings were used to shape the first workshop and to propose a convening question. Note that while the convening question itself was still a work in progress, it was used as a starting point of conversation and debate. The convening question that was introduced to the participants at the first workshop was the following:

How can we reduce food waste while ensuring that food is accessible, affordable, and that we support a vibrant food sector?

Workshop 1: Seeing the System

The goal of Workshop 1 entitled "Seeing the System" held in November 2016 was to gain a broad and deep understanding of the issue of food waste in the Greater Toronto Area and open new possibilities for interpretation. An invitation to apply and attend the social innovation lab was sent through food listserves such as the Canadian Association of Food Studies mailing list. The research team also connected with individuals who were involved in food systems issues through the collective network that has been cultivated by the lead author Tammara Soma. At the first workshop, 30 individuals representing different parts of the food system attended. In contrast to dominant consultation processes in the food waste field, unique to the lab is the inclusion of stakeholders who are usually left out of the food waste policy conversation and consultation. It is these typically excluded stakeholders who are actually directly impacted by food waste related interventions such as interventions that focus on food redistributions, or interventions at the farm. For example, participants from low-income community members and organizations that supported low-income community members were included. At the production stage, we included farmers as stakeholders but also made sure to include small-scale urban farmers and a migrant farm worker. Participation in the lab workshops for two full days, which includes all meals, costs participants $100. To ensure accessibility, full or partial bursaries were provided to whomever indicated need in their application. In addition, those requesting income support to attend the workshop were provided an honorarium, as well as the cost of transportation.

We used a variety of whole system thinking tools to uncover assumptions and bring together a diversity of viewpoints. The workshop began with an opening by an Indigenous elder to bring lab participants into a space that values reconciliation and Indigenous learning to solve complex problems. Participants then explored issues related to food waste through systems mapping and a timeline exercise to identify historical events that contributed to shifting the food system toward wasting more food. During the first day the participants worked with the convening question. The participants identified key issues and concerns with this question. The top issues identified by participants were related to food literacy, food access and prices, issues around scaling up sustainable food in the market, and the term waste. Participants noted that people lack food skills and a connection to how food is produced. Participants also questioned the use of the term affordable food as some mentioned issues with current food prices and pointed to the problem of lack of income, the ability for local and more sustainably produced foods to compete in the marketplace and viewing food waste as waste instead of a resource.

Another activity was to answer a timeline activity of "How did we get here?" From a combination of intergenerational lab participants, key events were charted on a timeline including input and background research and global and regional food trends over the past century. The timeline exercise allowed the participants to look for patterns and it was an effective way to open up thinking about how food waste has been addressed in the past. Table 19.3 provides a summary of the outputs from Workshop 1 with additional research conducted by the team.

On the second day, one of the activities of Workshop 1 was identifying the "horns of the dilemma" of food waste in Toronto, two desirable alternatives that appear to oppose each other. Lab participants were first asked to describe the current system (status quo) of food waste management and generation in Toronto. Then, in contrast, they described the ideal system. After the group identified that most of the current system descriptions were defined in a negative sense (for example: the current food system does not pay a living wage for most food workers), lab participants then identified some of the positive values of the current system. Defining both horns by their positive value was an exercise to stimulate innovation. Table 19.4 offers a summary of some of the horns of the dilemma developed by participants.

Table 19.3 Summary findings of "How did we get here?" activity

Decade	Beyond Toronto	Toronto
1950s	Surplus food from US re-routed as food aid as Cold War strategy Post-World War II Baby Boom generation	1954 Ontario Food Terminal established City of Toronto and 12 municipalities federated into Metro Toronto
1960s	Increased agricultural production through "Green Revolution" via hybrid seeds, pesticides, and synthetic fertilizers Second-wave feminism (1960s–1980s)	Housing revolution, suburbanization and urban sprawl consuming Canada's prime farmland; social housing projects Regent/Moss/Alexandra parks Toronto's food came from 350 km radius of the city
1970s	1970 "Father of Green Revolution" Norman Borlaug won Nobel Peace Prize 1971 Frances Moore Lappé *Diet for a Small Planet*	1971 Toronto's population doubled to two million Average house price in 1971 was $30,426
1980s	"Supermarket Revolution" 1981 First food bank established in Alberta	Blue Box (recycling system) established Number of impoverished families in Toronto increased
1990s	1994 North American Free Trade Agreement 1995 World Trade Organization established 1996 Food Sovereignty Movement	1991 Toronto Food Policy Council founded 1998 Amalgamation of Toronto
2000s	80% of Canada's population reside in urban areas	May 2000 Toronto City Council voted to become a food-secure city (Toronto Food Charter) 2002 Green bin programme began
2010s	Food Waste Report by Value Chain Management Centre food waste at $27billion, revised to $31 billion in 2014	2014 According to Household Food Insecurity in Canada, 1 in 8 Toronto households are food insecure 2015 Toronto Poverty Reduction Strategy

Table 19.4 Summary of the "horns of the dilemma" exercise

How do we ...?		
produce food efficiently, using the latest industrial technology	while	maintaining traditions, culture, and environmental sustainability?
have a wide selection of convenient and culturally appropriate food available throughout the year	while	minimizing food miles and ensuring resilience in the local food system for times when food cannot be imported?
keep food and disposal of waste affordable for everyone	while	compensating food producers and labourers fairly to maintain a living wage?
maintain high food quality and safety standards	while	maximizing the use of food and food by-products?
optimize economies of scale and infrastructure developed for a centralized supply chain	while	supporting locally owned small and medium enterprises?

During the second day, the participants went on a research mission to observe everyday practices of food consumption and food waste generation in downtown Toronto to gain first-hand experience.

Workshop 2: Designing Solutions

The second workshop was conducted in March (approximately four months after the first workshop). The participants were recruited in the same way as for the first workshop. Approximately two-thirds of the participants of Workshop 2 were present at Workshop 1 with new participants joining through invitation or a new round of applications for a total of 30 participants. At each of the workshops we made efforts to ensure that there were participants representing the entire food supply chain. The goal of the first day was to generate divergent ideas, push our thinking, and select ideas for bricolage. We looked back at our outputs from Workshop 1 and case studies of current food waste solutions. Through these reflective exercises, we identified elements of solutions that help or hinder systemic change to reduce food waste. Through a rapid brainstorming, ranking, and clustering process, we generated more than 30 ideas and identified 19 ideas for bricolage. Participants then selected ideas they wanted to work on and ten bricolage groups were created. The group first identified patterns from existing innovations, then created a long list of over 30 solution ideas. These ideas were ranked, and further developed with a bricolage exercise where teams "sculpted" their ideas using found objects to turn these ideas from theory into a tangible working model. Seven ideas were mapped onto a Rhizome Impact Canvas (based on a business model canvas) developed by a lab member.

Workshop 3: Prototyping Interventions

The third workshop, attended by 35 participants (some of whom were a mix of participants from Workshops 1 and 2 and new participants), was focused on refining business concepts and/or interventions that could be developed into pitches to stakeholders and potential supporters. This workshop used rapid prototyping tools to redesign ideas based on feedback through various mechanisms. Among seven business ideas for reducing food waste created in Workshop 2, five pitches were further developed at the third workshop which included the following:

- *App C*: Matching food vendors or urban growers to community food organizations, the private sector, and general public so surplus food can be sold at below-market prices. Community food organizations have a preferred window to purchase food before it becomes available to everyone else.
- *Brother Nature's Food Waste Pick-Up*: A bicycle-powered delivery service to bring food scraps from restaurants to community gardens/urban growers. The compost can be used to grow food and this food delivered back to the restaurants using bicycles.
- *Mosaic Campaign*: A friendly neighbourhood education campaign combined with a competition to waste less food. Residents learn skills such as preparing meals from different cultures, using leftovers or parts of food that usually are not eaten, and meal planning at community workshops.
- *Our Food, Our Future*: A coalition to align the efforts of organizations working on sustainable food in education and build a standard guideline for increasing awareness of food waste and food issues in schools, support schools to implement change and policies, and reduce the amount of food wasted in schools. The behaviours that students adopt from school to reduce food waste may then be adopted by their families, leading to less food waste in homes as well.
- *Technology for Change*: Introduce food processing technology at the farm level to decrease perishability while increasing revenue by capturing more of the value chain through selling preserved crops throughout the year.

The participants were engaged in different activities to redesign ideas based on feedback through various mechanisms. These included sensitivity testing, pitching in a "Regenerative Food Den" (a mock *Dragons' Den*-style investment pitching session), and minimum viable product testing. In small groups, the participants created a mind map with the central idea, best practices, and purpose. They had the opportunity to test scenarios by interviewing possible customers and finally pitched the idea to all the other groups. As a result, some of the business ideas were explored further and are currently in the process of being implemented. In addition, considering that the Food Systems Lab aims to explore new opportunities for interpreting the issue, and as one of the goals of the lab is to contribute to the process of reconciliation, it is critical to incorporate Indigenous knowledge and learning within this chapter through a vignette of the lived experience of an Indigenous scholar. Indigenous ecological knowledge offers an alternative view of food that challenges the underpinning of the neo-liberal, commodified, and industrial food system. This vignette offers an alternative framework to address the issue of food waste. While this format might not seem conventional in the context of Western academic practices, stories are key to Indigenous methodology (McGregor, 2004) and it is therefore applicable to this chapter.

Adrianne Lickers Xavier vignette: food as relations

When I think of food, I most often think of family and I think of the gathering together of people. The context of this chapter is food waste. However, food waste is not an inherent part of my Indigenous worldview. In order to discuss food waste, we need to unpack the paradigm that has categorized food as a commodity. As such, coming from an Indigenous place and space, the first question I pose is, "How do we see food?" I will begin this exploration with a story and I do this for many reasons. First and foremost, sharing is about being able to understand someone else's perspective and my Haudenosaunee roots have provided me with a voice to tell stories. There are many perspectives on food and what it means for various cultures (Coveney, 2006); however, I relate mostly to the perspective offered by Indigenous scholar Robin Wall Kimmerer (a citizen of Potawatomi Nation):

> In the Western tradition there is a recognized hierarchy of beings, with, of course, the human being on top—the pinnacle of evolution, the darling of Creation—and the plants at the bottom. But in Native ways of knowing, human people are often referred to as "the younger brothers of Creation." We say that humans have the least experience with how to live and thus the most to learn—we must look to our teachers among the other species for guidance. Their wisdom is apparent in the way that they live. They teach us by example. They've been on the earth far longer than we have been, and have had time to figure things out. They live both above and below ground, joining Skyworld to the earth. Plants know how to make food and medicine from light and water, and then they give it away.
>
> *(Kimmerer, 2013, p. 9)*

To be clear, as with Kimmerer, I can only speak from my own perspective, as I do not represent the voices of every Indigenous group. While I recognize the importance of understanding the technicality of measurements and the logistics of the food supply chain, I will primarily speak about how I was taught to see food, and how these teachings have shaped my identity as an Indigenous woman. The story that informs my paradigm is a creation story of the Mohawk[1] (Kanien'keh.:ka) people or rather, their telling of the story. The story of the Sky Woman is particularly relevant to this topic as it touches upon the genesis of the reciprocal relationship between food relations and human relations (for a detailed story see Horne-Miller (2016)). The story opens in the beginning of time when Sky Woman falls from the Sky World to an earth world that was filled by water. She was greeted by various creatures, water birds such as herons and loons, otters, beavers, and muskrats, all of whom shared, sacrificed, and saved Sky Woman and her baby in the earth world. Sky Woman sang songs and danced to share her gratitude, spreading the earth on a back of a Turtle being, placing tobacco and strawberry plants and seeds brought by her from Sky World. The shell of the Turtle being continued to grow and spread out in all directions to form "Turtle Island" also known as the continent of North America. Horne-Miller described Sky Woman's experience:

> I looked down and around me in wonder at the new life growing. Corn stalks began to appear, growing taller and forming silken hair that peered from their crowns. As the minutes went by, beans and squash also appeared. I could see all kinds of herbs, fruits, medicines in the ground around me. The air started to smell of the fragrant aromas of rich black soil and lush plant growth. I could see bright red strawberries and large flat tobacco leaves as well. I knew that as long as I had the sacred medicines, along with the corn, beans, and squash to eat, my baby and I would be fine.
>
> *(2016, 22)*

The first action after growing the plants is for Sky Woman to offer the harvest to all the animals, "Come and eat! I have planted all the things we will need on this earth to survive" (Horne-Miller, 2016, p. 22). This act signifies the beginning of the reciprocal relationship. When Sky Woman's offspring hunt the animals to eat, they have fed each other and have both contributed to the reciprocal relationship. The story is a basis for understanding culture and belief around food. Sky Woman is helped by the plants and animals. She then feeds them and knows they will in turn feed her. When her daughter Iakotsitionteh died, she was buried in the ground and Sky Woman recognized that her daughter's "body will nourish the earth and give life to the new plants and animals" (Horne-Miller, 2016, p. 22). The stories of relationship and reciprocity are integral to the All My Relations principle. The All My Relations teaching is based on the perspective that we are all here together and that we are all in this together. It is therefore our duty to ensure that we maintain a reciprocal relationship of caring for all of creation.

This paradigm influenced my work at a community food access programme; a programme that has focused on food security and ensuring the people in my community had enough to eat, or at least knew how to grow food to help make sure their family had enough. In my community at Six Nations, the Farmer's Association in partnership with the local government grows our community's traditional white corn. When I think about food and what is considered "appealing" I think about that white corn. Each year, the community is welcome to go and pick as much of it as they want. Inevitably, the conversation would turn to growing, planting, and saving food for winter. I was taught, by a late-friend of mine who was a seed saver and food educator that the best corn is the corn we dry and save for seed, because we hope that next year we can grow more corn just like it. Those of lower quality are the ones we eat. This is an important reminder as the current scale of industrial food production is fixated with aesthetic perfection and, as a result, food products that are considered "odd" or do not fit aesthetic standards are usually wasted.

To return to the conversation started by Kimmerer (2013), namely the idea that plants share knowledge with people themselves, this is a perspective that is unique to Indigenous belief. This idea of humans and the non-human world sharing knowledge with each other is represented in many ways within Indigenous culture. As I have noted, the Haudenosaunee creation story tells of Sky Woman falling and animals offering support to help her, and in turn she helps form Turtle Island or North America. When her daughter dies, in turn, foods and medicines grow from her body which is then consumed by animal and plant beings (Haudenosaunee Confederacy, 2018). The idea that knowledge is not the exclusive domain of people is based on respect for the knowledge and contributions of the non-human. Another example is the "All My Relations" teaching. When we started discussing food waste, and the relationship to food that we each hold, it is deceptively simple to use a pan-Indigenous approach. The truth is, there are similarities, and there are differences in each Nation's approach to food and ideas around it. However, in this case, we have been discussing the threads of similarity that in the context of this chapter are important to consider. Key to many Indigenous cultures is the view that plants, animals, and humans share a social dynamic.

The story of the three sisters is another example that is important for Haudenosaunee communities (Eames-Sheavly, 1993). The story is of three sisters who lived in a field together. They had unique characteristics: a young girl who barely crawls along the ground, a middle sister who wears a bright green shawl, and the oldest sister who stands tall and has long golden hair who watches over the other two. These sisters in this Haudenosaunee story also represent the foods that sustain us. The corn who is the oldest sister, the beans who are the youngest and the squash the middle sister. The legends say that they disappeared one by one after a young boy was seen in the field. Having their "heads turned" by this young man, they each in their turn went away, beans first, then squash and finally late in the year, corn. When the young boy comes to get the corn and brings her back to his home, she is reunited with her sisters who have been at the longhouse providing for the people. The story is multifaceted and inherently indicative of the Haudenosaunee traditions. The sisters are given a life force, and a humanism that we acknowledge and respect. The story ends with the three sisters in the Longhouse, drying, and being stored to be able to help feed the people for the winter. The resulting legend does two things, it reinforces the food and plant life cycle of growing, harvesting, and preserving food. In addition, it also demonstrates the care with which the culture reveres and respects these plants for their ability to nourish us.

The "more than human" connection and relationship between the Haudenosaunee and the three sisters also exists in other Indigenous communities. The Inuvialuit of Paulatuuq have a relationship with fish that extends beyond regarding the fish as a "simple" food source (Todd, 2016). Their relationship is a complex representation of the connection of the Inuvialuit to non-human beings as part of their understanding of the world. The Western definition of hunting emphasizes the pursuit and slaughter of an animal (Bodenhorn, 1990 in Todd, 2016); on the other hand, the Iñupiat perspective on hunting is much more complex. For Iñupiat whale hunters, there are protocols and rituals including the use of certain tools, and proper treatment of the animal's body and soul to ensure the continuation of amicable animal and human relations (Bodenhorn, 1990 in Todd, 2016). Kimmerer (2013, p. 22) recounts the story of a Gwi'chin man who says he was "raised by a river", signifying gratitude for the life-giving abilities of the river. The story of the Gwi'chin man led her to state that she was raised by strawberries, as food is considered to provide life lessons, is a personal guide by which to live, and also offers sustenance. This connection to the food, place, and things that are not human all are examples of the relationships that many Indigenous communities have with their world. To further illustrate, the concept that permeates through Indigenous methodology is to consider the impact of our actions for other relations. We would pick enough berries to make medicine especially with the first berries of the season, but we would not pick so much that the animals would have none. The ability to be respectful of both the plant, and its need to survive and thrive, and to consider the needs of other animals who might eat of those foods is part of the often-unspoken thought process that relates to these foods and Indigenous relationships to it.

In my culture, corn holds a very important place. White corn can be picked at different times in the season. The small green corn is picked earlier, but the mature white corn, just like the three sisters story, is harvested late in the summer. In the Fall, the corn is picked and taken home to be hung and dried. The larger outer husks are pulled off and the inner ones are pulled back to reveal the corn. They are not removed because the husks, still attached, are then used to braid the corn into a long hanging bunch. It takes a strong hand and patience to carefully braid that corn. You need to make it tight enough to allow the husks to dry and not lose them or have your braid fall apart. When the corn is braided, it can be hung up to dry, so that it is lyed, or roasted as needed. The husks can be washed, and used to make cornhusk dolls or mats, or woven together to make up masks or baskets. Every part of the corn is used in some way. In Anishinaabe teachings, the lessons, stories and knowledge are shared with a goal in mind, namely, to instil the reciprocity of sharing.

The Anishinaabe story talks of many things but one part in particular tells of community and wild rice (Mills, 2017). The story explains that wild rice (*manoomin*) harvesting is a process and a shared venture with families, requiring several stages including harvesting, roasting, cleaning, dancing (which helps loosen the hull), and then finally sharing (Mills, 2017, p. 183). Before it can be shared to eat, the (wild rice) is prepared, and then thanks are given, to remind of everyone who helped including the Creator, and all parts of creation that are able to be sustained with it, including the ducks and water animals who feast upon the rice that falls back into the water as it is being harvested. Every grain of rice has a purpose, it feeds, grows, and reseeds. It feeds the people, leads them in a dance, and offers them sustenance. A respectful relationship, and not taking advantage or overconsuming is exactly what allows for our community to continue to fish, hunt, and sustain ourselves. Always take what you need, but never more, and never take so much that you will harm that plant, or animal family or it will not be there for you in the future.

Conclusion

The social innovation process at the Food Systems Lab has resulted in more research and iteration of the ideas developed during the workshops. The lab was invited to contribute a food waste commentary to the National Food Policy consultation in Canada and submitted a discussion paper with key findings and policy recommendations. Through communication with participants on the role of education and food literacy, the lab is currently conducting more research on the innovative potential of gamifying food waste prevention and reduction in the city of Toronto. It is also exploring systemic and spatial nudges that can help households prevent and reduce their food waste. Collaborating with some of the workshop participants and other experts in North America, the lab has been hired to develop a North American toolkit to engage youth in a collective movement to prevent, reduce, and recover food loss and waste. This toolkit includes activities and lessons that emphasize Indigenous food traditions and cultures across the three countries (Mexico, United States, and Canada). To end this chapter, we feel it poignant to close with the words of Anishinaabe Indigenous scholar Melanie Goodchild (Special Advisor to the Food Systems Lab), who noted in her worldview that "food sources are our relatives" and, accordingly, we conclude with a call for current and future scholars in the field of food waste studies to consider this alternative approach and to explore the implication of applying the paradigm of "food as our relatives" to challenge the commodification of our food system.

Note

1 The Mohawk are one of the six nations from my community, though there are communities of those nations individually, such as Kahnawake or Akwesasne, so I want to be clear this is a Mohawk incarnation of the creation story.

References

Arthur, W. B. (1994). Inductive reasoning and bounded rationality. *The American Economic Review*, *84* (2), 406–411.

Ashby, W. R. (1957). *An introduction to cybernetics.* Chapman and Hall Ltd. Retrieved from: http://dspace.utalca.cl/handle/1950/6344

Ashby, W. R. (1991). Requisite variety and its implications for the control of complex systems. In George Klir (Ed.). *Facets of systems science.* 405–417. Boston, MA: Springer.

Biggs, R., Westley, F. R., & Carpenter, S. R. (2010). Navigating the back loop: Fostering social innovation and transformation in ecosystem management. *Ecology and Society, 15* (2), 9. Retrieved from: http://ecologyandsociety.org/vol15/iss2/art9/ ecologyandsociety.org/vol15/iss2/art9/

Bodenhorn, Barbara. (1990). I'm not the great hunter, my wife is': Inupiat and anthropological models of gender. *Études/Inuit/Studies, 14* (1–2), 55–74.

Brown, Tim, & Barry, Kātz. (2009). *Change by design: How design thinking transforms organizations and inspires innovation.* New York: Harper Business.

Caplan, P. (2017). Win-win?: Food poverty, food aid and food surplus in the UK today. *Anthropology Today, 33* (3), 17–22.

Cloke, J. (2013). Empires of waste and the food security meme. *Geography Compass*, 7 (9), 622–636.

Coveney, J. (2006). *Food, morals and meaning: The pleasure and anxiety of eating*. London: Routledge.

Eames-Sheavly, M. (1993). The three sisters; Exploring an Iroquois garden. *4-H Leaders/Members guide*, 28. NY: Cornell Cooperative Extension.

Evans, D. (2014). *Food waste: home consumption, material culture and everyday life*. 50 Bedford Square London WC1B 3DP UK: Bloomsbury Publishing.

Fisher, A. (2017). *Big hunger: The unholy alliance between corporate America and anti-hunger groups*. Cambridge, MA: MIT Press.

Food and Agriculture Organization. (2011). *Global food losses and food waste. Extent, causes and prevention*. Rome. Retrieved December 11th 2018 from: www.fao.org/3/a-i2697e.pdf

Funtowicz, S. O., & Ravetz, J. R. (1994). Uncertainty, complexity and post-normal science. *Environmental Toxicology and Chemistry: An International Journal*, 13 (12), 1881–1885.

Gille, Z. (2012). From risk to waste: global food waste regimes. *The Sociological Review*, 60, 27–46.

Haudenosaunee Confederacy. (2018, January 1). *Historical life as a Haudenosaunee*. Retrieved August 5, 2018, from Haudenosaunee Confederacy: www.haudenosauneeconfederacy.com/historical-life-as-a-haudenosaunee/

Horne-Miller, K. (2016). Distortion and healing; finding balance and a "good mind" through the rearticulation of Sky Woman's journey. In N. & J. Kermoal ed. *Living on the land; Indigenous women's understanding of place*. 19–38. Edmonton, AB: AU Press.

Kimmerer, R. W. (2013). *Braiding sweetgrass*. Minneapolis, MN: US: Milkweeds Editions.

Macrae, R., Siu, A., Kohn, M., Matsubuchi-Shaw, M., McCallum, D., Cervantes, T. H., & Perreault, D. (2016). Making better use of what we have: Strategies to minimize food waste and resource inefficiency in Canada. *Canadian Food Studies/La Revue canadienne des études sur l'alimentation*, 3 (2), 145–215.

Martin, R. L. (2009a). *The design of business: Why design thinking is the next competitive advantage*. Boston, Massachussets: Harvard Business Press.

McGregor, D. (2004). Coming full circle: Indigenous knowledge, environment, and our future. *American Indian Quarterly*, 28 (3/4), 385–410.

Mills, A. (2017). Driving the gift home. *Windsor Yearbook of Access to Justice*, 33 (1): 167–186.

Nicholls, A., Simon, J., Gabriel, M., & Whelan, C. (Eds.) (2015). *New frontiers in social innovation research*. New York, NY: Springer.

Papargyropoulou, E., Lozano, R., Steinberger, J. K., Wright, N., & Bin Ujang, Z. (2014). The food waste hierarchy as a framework for the management of food surplus and food waste. *Journal of Cleaner Production*, 76, 106–115.

Parizeau, K., von Massow, M., & Martin, R. (2015). Household-level dynamics of food waste production and related beliefs, attitudes, and behaviours in Guelph, Ontario. *Waste Management*, 35, 207–217.

Ravetz, I. R. (1999). What is post-normal science. *Futures-the Journal of Forecasting Planning and Policy*, 31 (7), 647–654.

Riches, G. (2018). *Food bank nations: Poverty, corporate charity and the right to food*. New York, NY: Routledge.

Rittel, H. W., & Webber, M. M. (1973). Dilemmas in a general theory of planning. *Policy Sciences*, 4 (2), 155–169.

Soma, T. (2018a). (Re) framing the food waste narrative: Infrastructures of urban food consumption and waste in Indonesia. *Indonesia*, (105), 173–190.

Soma, T. (2018b). Closing the loop on Canada's national food policy: A food waste agenda. *Canadian Food Studies/La Revue canadienne des études sur l'alimentation*, 5 (3), 273–278.

Star, S. L., & Griesemer, J. R. (1989). Institutional ecology,translations' and boundary objects: Amateurs and professionals in Berkeley's museum of vertebrate zoology, 1907-39. *Social Studies of Science*, 19 (3), 387–420.

Tjornbo, O., Chung, H., Laban, S., Buré, C. (2014). *Design Brief Ontario Tender Fruit Lab*. Retrieved October 23rd 2019 from: https://www.marsdd.com/wp-content/uploads/2014/12/DesignBrief_Ontario-Tender-Fruit-Lab_web.pdf

Todd, Z. (2016). This Is the Life. In Kermoal, N., & Altamirano-Jiménez, I. (eds.). *Living on the land: Indigenous women's understanding of place*. 191–212. Edmonton, AB: Athabasca University Press.

Westley, F. & Antadze, N. (2010). Making a difference: Strategies for scaling social innovation for greater impact. *The Innovation Journal: The Public Sector Innovation Journal*, 15 (2), 1–19.

Westley, F., Goebey, S., & Robinson, K. (2012). *Change lab/design lab for social innovation. Waterloo Institute of Social Innovation and Resilience.* http://sigeneration.ca/documents/Paper_FINAL_LabforSocialInnovation.pdf

Westley, F., Laban, S. (2015). *Social Innovation Lab Guide.* Retrieved October 23rd 2019 from: https://uwaterloo.ca/waterloo-institute-for-social-innovation-and-resilience/sites/ca.waterloo-institute-for-social-innovation-and-resilience/files/uploads/files/10_silabguide_final.pdf

World Bank. (2018). *What a waste 2.0: A global snapshot of solid waste management to 2050.* Retrieved November 29th 2018 from: https://openknowledge.worldbank.org/bitstream/handle/10986/30317/9781464813290.pdf?sequence=10&isAllowed=y

Zimmerman, B., Lindberg, C., & Plsek, P. (1998). Edgeware. *VHA, Irving, TX.*

20

MODELLING APPROACHES TO FOOD WASTE

Discrete event simulation; machine learning; Bayesian networks; agent-based modelling; and mass balance estimation

Cansu Kandemir, Christian Reynolds, Monika Verma, Matthew Grainger, Gavin Stewart, Simone Righi, Simone Piras, Marco Setti, Matteo Vittuari and Tom Quested

Introduction

Food waste is a complex phenomenon. Food gets wasted for a range of different reasons, which are affected by a range of factors: to give a few examples at the household level, how people shop, what they buy, how those items are packaged, the time devoted to food-related activities, skills and capabilities relating to cooking and food management in the home, and attitudes to food safety (Quested et al., 2013). Given this complexity, there are many challenges and questions that need answering for those wishing to prevent food from being wasted or estimating the quantity of food being wasted. Ideally, empirical data would be obtained, but this is currently lacking, mainly due to the monetary and time cost of obtaining such data. Therefore, system-based simulation methods and modelling approaches are being developed using currently available data, as they can incorporate these complexities and allow these challenging questions to be answered.

Numerous methods have been used to infer the amount of food loss, waste or surplus. This chapter introduces four of the most exciting contemporary food waste prediction and prevention approaches including discrete event simulation (DES), agent-based modelling, machine learning and Bayesian networks, and mass balance estimation (quantification of food waste using food availability, metabolism and calories consumed).

These models are useful for answering different types of question related to food waste. These can include: (1) quantifying the generation of food waste in specific geographies, industries or households; (2) understanding relationships between different causal factors of food waste; and (3) assisting with the prioritising of potential initiatives for reducing food waste. For instance, for a research question around "how will the food waste reduction potential compare between providing a longer shelf life for a given product and deploying a behaviour change campaign to encourage people to store foods optimally?", different models will produce different insights.

Discrete event simulation

DES is a system-based approach that models a system as a sequence of events over time (Delaney and Vaccari, 1989). In DES, each event marks a change of state in the system. In household food waste simulation, events are specific instances of purchasing, consumption and disposal and each event is controlled by a series of rules that are specified by the user. The fact that the generation of waste (and attempts to prevent this waste) are influenced by decisions relating to purchasing, storage and their use lends itself to modelling the journey of the item through the home and the influence of various decisions.

A key element of DES is the ability to model processes stochastically, i.e. using probabilities to guide decisions, so that the outcome of each decision is not always the same. For example, the amount of milk drunk in a household each day is not constant but varies from day to day (Evans, 2012). DES allows a model to reflect this probabilistic nature. This is achieved by using random numbers to sample from a distribution of realistic values to determine which events happen and their extent. Many instances of food wastage are related to "unexpected" and "unusual" events: buying a product with an unusually short shelf life, an unplanned social engagement, or a work commitment leading to dinner being bought and eaten on the way home, rather than in the home (WRAP, 2007). Therefore, to understand the generation of food waste, it is important to model each day as different from the last to understand the impact of this variability. Methods that only include an average level of consumption (e.g. system dynamics) and do not include variation over time would omit an important dynamic within the system and, consequently, the modelling results would be less realistic.

Another aspect of DES models is that they are constructed for a specific system, in this case a single household (rather than an "average" household). This means that each household modelled has an integer number of people, rather than the national average of 2.4 people per household. Additionally, different variants of the model can be constructed for different household sizes and other household characteristics.

The successful application of DES to food waste in the home opens up the possibility of using such modelling for other waste streams in the home, and possibly waste generated from businesses. To the best of the authors' knowledge, this has not been done to date, so could be a new area for operational researchers to investigate, leading to many new insights for those working in the area of waste generation and human behaviour.

Milk model and key findings

The initial application of DES to household food waste was *The Milk Model*. This project developed a simulation for one product (milk) and sought to replicate the purchasing, consumption, and waste of milk in real homes. The model contains parameters relating to the shelf life of milk and many actions taken around shopping and using the milk (Figure 20.1). Data from both quantitative and qualitative social research were used as inputs into The Milk Model. In addition, other survey information relating to milk was included, such as purchasing levels and available shelf life. In such a way, the model acts as a framework in which different types of information are combined to assess waste levels. The model has several inter-dependencies and feedback loops. For example, the number of top-up shops

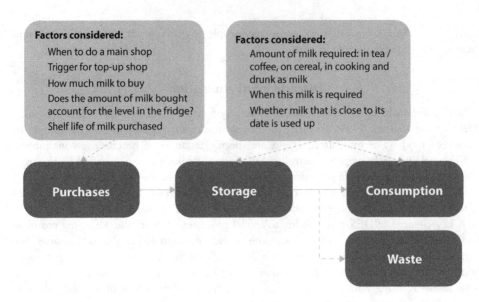

Factors considered:

When to do a main shop
Trigger for top-up shop
How much milk to buy
Does the amount of milk bought
account for the level in the fridge?
Shelf life of milk purchased

Factors considered:

Amount of milk required: in tea /
coffee, on cereal, in cooking and
drunk as milk
When this milk is required
Whether milk that is close to its
date is used up

Purchases   **Storage**   **Consumption**

Waste

Figure 20.1 Simplified schematic of the system being modelled.

depends on the amount of milk in the fridge, which links back to both consumption and purchasing decisions. This means that the household being modelled can adapt to what is going on in the home in a pseudo-intelligent way.

The model has been able to replicate many results that have been observed empirically including the trend in milk (and food) waste with household size (Quested, 2013). It also has a similar degree of variation over time to that observed between households in survey work. Both similarities with empirical evidence build confidence in the model.

Table 20.1 summarises the changes that could lead to lower levels of milk waste, which are grouped into those relating to the product, those relating to purchasing activities and those relating to how the milk is consumed. The table also highlights some unintended consequences of making changes to reduce waste. Some of these consequences are positive: if the shelf life of milk is extended, not only is there less waste but there are also fewer incidents of milk requirements being unfulfilled due to insufficient milk in the fridge. However, some waste-prevention measures involve trade-offs including increased amount of packaging (if a given amount of milk is bought in more bottles) and increased frequency of top-up shops (if less milk is bought in shopping trips). There are also potential impacts – both positive and negative – on the supply chain: for instance, increasing the shelf life of milk for the public may have implications for logistics and storage for milk producers and retailers.

Machine learning and Bayesian networks

Robust analysis is dependent on multiple methods providing confirmation of results. Two types of analytical method that allow the identification of the "importance" of variables in explaining food waste generation (both self-reported and objectively measured) may be two machine learning algorithms (Random Forest and Hill-climbing). These methods can be used to develop regression and classification trees as well as Bayesian networks.

Table 20.1 Changes that could lead to lower milk waste

		Impact on …		
	Change leading to waste reduction	Waste	Unfulfilled milk requirements	Notes
Product	Increasing average shelf life of milk	↓↓	↓	This reduces the number of bottles with a short shelf life.
	Decreasing variability in shelf life of milk	↓	↓	This reduces the number of short shelf life bottles available for purchase.
	Increasing time limit in "once opened use within x days"	↓↓	↓	This has greater impact when milk is bought in large bottles.
Purchasing	Checking milk stocks in fridge and adjusting purchases accordingly	↓↓	↑	This has a large waste-prevention effect. There is a slight increase in running out of milk if purchases are adjusted by stock levels.
	Decreasing the amount of milk purchased in a main or top-up shop	↓↓	↑	This has a direct effect on waste. It can increase the number of top-up shops, which can have an environmental impact.
	Decreasing the amount of milk that triggers a top-up shop	↓	↑	There is a large trade-off in when to do a top-up shop between waste and running out of milk.
	Buying milk in more, smaller bottles	↓	↑↑	Effect on waste is highly context dependent: large effect if milk purchased infrequently and by the households following "once open, used within x days" advice. However, this could increase total packaging used.
Consumption and Miscellaneous	Using up milk which is approaching its date	↓	→	This could potentially lead to overconsumption.
	Decreasing variability in consumption	↓↓	↓	This is dictated by lifestyle. It has more of an impact on waste in smaller households.
	Increasing household size	↓↓	↓	Fixed by circumstance.

Note: intensity of effect, indicated by arrows, represents authors' view using model results. Source: Quested (2013)

Machine learning is a subfield of computer science that is related to the study of pattern recognition and artificial intelligence. The two algorithms used are designed to recognise relationships between variables and to show how important each variable is to the response (in this case food waste). Random Forests creates many regression and classification trees (minimum 500) where the data are split into different branches of the tree to best explain the response variable. The user can then explore these different branches to examine the relationships between variables.

Bayesian networks are a graphical representation of a network of variables whereby related variables are joined by an arc (or arrow) and a set of conditional probabilities (where the state of one variable is conditional on the state of another). Machine-learned Bayesian networks can recognise relationships between variables but not the direction of the relationship, so arrow heads are added at random. Machine learning is much more robust to highly correlated variables than previous regression analysis methods.

These different models allow the investigation into relationships that drive food waste in a variety of settings. Below we highlight some examples of machine learning and Bayesian networks being used to investigate household food waste.

The use of systems models to identify food waste drivers: Grainger et al. (2018a)

Grainger et al.'s paper investigated the drivers of household food waste using Bayesian networks to identify the impact of household characteristics and other variables on self-assessed food waste. Using EU-level Eurobarometer data from 2013, the study confirmed that the country, the age of the respondent, the status (student/non-student), and a belief that the family wastes too much are related to the level of self-assessed food waste. In addition, households from lower-income EU countries (e.g. Portugal, Greece, Bulgaria, Cyprus and Latvia), as well as students and young adults, tend to report higher levels of food waste.

However, the analysis found no evidence that food waste behaviours differ between people living in urban and rural areas, and little support of a difference between genders. These geographical and gender differences had been identified in previous literature as potential drivers of food waste (Wenlock and Buss, 1977; Sonesson et al., 2005; Barr, 2007; Koivupuro et al., 2012; Canali et al., 2014; Parizeau et al., 2015; Setti et al., 2016; Stancu et al., 2016). The additional insight provided by the application of Bayesian networks provides clarity to the researcher to understand which relationships have evidence within the currently available data. This insight can then be acted upon by the policy maker. In this case, the researchers suggested country-level policy measures targeting different age groups.

Model selection and averaging in the assessment of the drivers of household food waste to reduce the probability of false positives: Grainger et al. (2018b)

This paper used machine learning algorithms (Random Forests and "Boruta") along with Generalised Linear Models to identify the key drivers of household food waste, while also reflecting the uncertainty inherent in the analysis of complex observational multidimensional data. The data investigated was household food waste data collected by WRAP (2012) which consisted of face-to-face in-home interview responses (categorical data) on socio-demographic aspects of households and behavioural responses to food waste, along with data on the amount of waste collected from the kerbside for 1,770 households.

As the data set has over 50 variables, there would be over a quadrillion possible Generalised Linear Models to run. To simplify this, the "Boruta" and random machine learning algorithms were first used to refine and reduce the variable list. The "Boruta" algorithm adds randomness to the variable set by creating shuffled copies of all variables (these are called "shadow features"). It then runs a Random Forest classifier on the extended dataset, and assesses the mean decrease in accuracy to evaluate the importance of each variable (higher means are more important). At each iteration, "Boruta" assesses if each variable has a higher Z-score than the maximum Z-score of its shadow features. Variables with scores lower than shadow features are deemed highly unimportant, and removed from the set. The algorithm runs until all variables are confirmed or rejected (or it reaches a specified limit of runs – here, we used 500 trees maximum). The variables retained after applying the "Boruta" algorithm were then processed using a Generalised Linear Model to assess correlations between "avoidable household food waste" and the socio-demographic and behavioural variables.

The "Boruta" algorithm consistently identified household size, home ownership status, household composition, employment status and the presence of fussy eaters as significant drivers of food waste in all sets of variables. Household size was always the most important variable.

The final model contained household size, local authority, household composition, house type, home ownership status, employment status, the presence of fussy eaters, the presence of children aged between 3 and 11, age of the respondent, social grouping, checking cupboards for tinned food prior to shopping, and discard behaviours related to vegetables, cheese and food past its sell-by date. The variables with the largest positive effect (greater amounts of food waste) included the presence of fussy eaters, household size, and one particular local authority (individual local authority identity was anonymised). Variables with the largest negative effect (reductions in food waste) included discard behaviours interacting with the presence of fussy eaters, employment status interacting with the presence of fussy eaters, four specific local authorities and home ownership status (owning a house outright).

As with Grainger et al. (2018a), the application of the machine learning algorithms has enabled new insight into the drivers of household food waste. Again, it is interesting to note that some of the drivers identified as important by previous literature, such as awareness of the food waste problem and shopping habits, here are found as not important.

Agent-based modelling

Agent-Based Models (ABMs) are computational systems that simulate the individual decision-making process of a large number of agents acting and interacting through a set of prescribed rules (Farmer and Foley, 2009). The output of an ABM are the emerging phenomena resulting from the interaction among agents' choice on a large scale, both temporal and dimensional. The characteristics of ABMs lead to several advantages. On the one hand, they allow for a large degree of heterogeneity in agents' characteristics and interaction rules; on the other hand, they allow for the introduction of a well-defined institutional structure. Nevertheless, it is important to constrain the additional complexity to avoid generating models as difficult to understand as the reality studied.

The main tool to analyse ABMs are Monte-Carlo computer simulations, where a set of inputs is provided to the model, and the dynamics of the model are iterated many times with different sequences of random numbers. This allows the study of the statistical characteristics of the simulation output (means and standard deviations of the results, their distribution, and the occurrence of rare extreme events), separating random events from proper emerging properties of the simulated system. By modifying the parameter sets, it is possible to *check the robustness* of the results and to assess the implications of a shift in one of the parameters. A well-developed model can be used as a virtual laboratory, as it allows the generation of alternative time-series under controlled "quasi-experimental" conditions. As such, ABMs can also be studied with *regression* techniques, exploring the correlations between different parameters and outcomes and the impact of different types of heterogeneity. Given that many relationships among variables are typically hard-wired, causation structures can also be studied. An alternative method of analysis frequently used to assess ABMs is the *comparison of scenarios*. Within this method, different initialisations and sets of rules are created to simulate specific known cases (such as two countries), or to study the expected impact of a policy intervention. Both the aggregate outcomes and the individual trajectories of the agents are then assessed comparatively. The analysis of the results frequently relies on *graphs*, such as plots and figures.

To design and develop an ABM, it is necessary to specify at least three elements: the *entities (agents)*; their *interaction rules*; and the *environment and institutions* within which agents interact. The *agents* are the autonomous and discrete decision-making units whose behaviour is modelled. In socio-economic simulations, they are typically individuals, companies, or even nations. Their characteristics usually include: *attributes* (idiosyncratic or group-specific properties); *rules of behaviour* (assumptions made about their decision-making processes); *memory* (the possibility of recalling past actions and interactions and their results); and *perception of the environment*. The *interaction rules* are the constraints on how agents can interact. Depending on the type of model, they can be represented in game theoretical form (agents receive a payoff that depends on their actions and on those of other players), as economic exchanges (one or more individuals buy something that someone else sells in exchange for something else), or as exchanges of information. Exchanges typically happen on a defined *interaction space*. Finally, the *environment and institutions* define the external constraints that influence all agents (or groups of them), and their interactions.

Both ABMs described below (Grainger et al., 2018d), were developed in MatLab R2017a, while the Bayesian network of consumer food waste generation was developed in R. The integration of the two models was achieved through C++ in DOS, with externally controlled processes in both R and MatLab to allow the sharing of inputs and outputs.

An ABM of retail food waste

The retail ABM developed by Grainger et al. (2018d) aimed at simulating the interaction between the adoption of an innovation reducing food waste by retailers and resulting food waste levels. The challenge of this setting is represented by the fact that retailers earn a profit from the food wasted at home by consumers, thus profit-maximising retailers are not willing to innovate to reduce it. However, behavioural economics theory points out that additional concerns, such as reputation, can lead to non-trivial outcomes.

The ABM considers the market for a single food commodity, namely fresh fruit and vegetables, due to their high perishability. The introduction of a waste-reducing technology has an impact on the purchasing behaviour of consumers and on retailers' marketing strategies. The market operates in imperfect conditions (e.g. asymmetric information and concentration).

Retail agents are modelled as belonging to three different groups: small shops, discounts and large-scale companies. Each agent can adopt only one of two different technologies: a baseline that generates a high amount of food waste (initially adopted by all retailers) or an innovative technology that reduces the amount of food waste generated either in store or by customers at home. Retailers decide whether to adopt the low-waste innovation based on a utility function which includes three main elements: (1) the profit earned, which depends on selling prices, innovation costs and the share of food wasted in store and by consumers after purchase; (2) environmental concerns, and reputational concerns linked to pro-environmental behaviours; (3) other retailers' decisions.

To reduce complexity, consumers are modelled as homogeneous masses with shared attributes, or with attributes varying within a certain range, who at the onset of each simulation purchase from the same typology of retailers. Three groups of consumers are considered: (1) quality-oriented ones, who purchase from small shops, characterised by a low price elasticity; (2) unsophisticated ones, who purchase from large-scale companies, characterised by an average elasticity; (3) convenience-seeking consumers, who purchase from discounts, characterised by a high elasticity. Consumers choose the retailer from which to purchase based on a set of parameters that do not vary *inside* groups, but may change *between* groups: elasticity to price; environmental concerns; their state of information about the existence of retailers which adopted the low-waste technology; and a satiation quantity, which is the same for all of the consumers and is technology-dependent (the quantity of food necessary to achieve satiation is lower if the retailer a consumer purchases from has adopted the low-waste technology).

Within the model, time is divided into ticks during which decisions are assumed to be taken parallelly by all agents according to a set of steps. The intra-period steps of the retail model are the following:

1. Each retailer (with a given probability) can decide to change the technology adopted, maximising its utility function.
2. Given the previous decision, each retailer can change its selling price (small shops base the pricing decision on the behaviour of similar companies in their network, large and discount companies on the market share of adopting retailers).
3. The consumers purchasing from a retailer that changes technology are assigned to the same retailer.
4. A share of consumers becomes informed about the existence of the low-waste technology – according to the literature on innovation diffusion (Rogers, 2010), this share depends on information from external sources (e.g. advertising from retailers) and information circulating among consumers (e.g. word of mouth).
5. A mass of consumers with similar characteristics decides to move to a different retailer based on the parameters listed previously, including their utility and information status.
6. The market shares of each retailer are recalculated, and a new step can start.

Outputs and applications

The final output consists in the market shares of retailers that adopted the low food waste technology, as well as in the total food waste generated in the market. Examples of technologies whose adoption can be simulated are a storage system prolonging the shelf life of fruits and vegetables, a bag allowing consumers to reduce the exposure of the products to external conditions on the way home, etc. The data to calibrate the model can be obtained from the literature (e.g. retailers' and consumers' behavioural patterns) and from statistical datasets (e.g. market shares of each retailer type).

An ABM of consumer food waste

The integrated consumer ABM-BN developed by Grainger et al. (2018d) simulates the effects of behavioural factors and social interactions on the evolution of individual opinions and actions regarding food waste, and thus on food waste generation at household level. Its structure is based on the Food Waste Model developed within the EU project H2020 REFRESH ("Resource

Efficient Food and dRink for the Entire Supply cHain") by Van Geffen et al. (2017). Also the data for calibrating the model come from a questionnaire developed within REFRESH. The questionnaire, inspired by the Motivation, Ability and Opportunity theoretical model (Thøgersen and Ølander, 1995; Rothschild, 1999), tried to measure a set of fixed features and food-related behaviours and to quantify food waste within a sample of consumer households from four pilot countries (the Netherlands, Germany, Hungary and Spain).

The features detected by the questionnaires can be grouped into six categories: (1) socio-demographics; (2) motivations (awareness of food waste consequences, attitudes toward wasting food, injunctive social norms and descriptive social norms); (3) competing goals in the food domain (health, taste, preparing time, price, having enough food and not having too much food); (4) households' food-related practices (planning, buying, overviewing stocks, cooking, storing and leftovers management); (5) opportunities (availability of products, accessibility of stores, availability of space and storage equipment, etc.); (6) abilities (difficulty with accurate planning, creative cooking and assessing food safety; and knowledge of how to prolong shelf life); (7) psychographics (awareness of parents, perceived financial control and involvement in food preparation). The data from the questionnaires were expressed probabilistically in a consumer Bayesian network.

As a first step, simulated populations are generated with a process based on data from the REFRESH consumer questionnaire. Then, the ABM evolves according to the following intra-step dynamics:

1. For each agent, one of the six competing goals related to food is selected for discussion.
2. For each agent, the agents within her individual social network whose average opinion on the six competing goals is closer than a given threshold are selected for discussion.
3. The agent changes her opinion on the competing goal selected by averaging it with the average of her neighbours, with weights represented by the relative salience of that goal.
4. The opinions of the agent on all other goals change accordingly, following empirically observed statistical correlations between opinions.
5. The agent selected changes her *awareness* of food waste consequences by averaging it with the average of her neighbours, with weights represented by her influenceability.
6. She changes her *attitude* toward food waste by averaging it with the average of her neighbours, with weights represented by her influenceability.
7. To measure injunctive social norms (what others think), the average attitude toward food waste of each agent's neighbours is calculated and assigned to the agent.
8. To measure descriptive social norms (what we think others do), the median food waste of each agent's neighbours (net of an error, due to the lack of visibility) is calculated and assigned to the agent.
9. If there are no neighbours within the threshold of point 2, thus no change has taken place, the agent's opinions on all motivations get back to past values following a "relaxation mechanism".

Once these intra-steps have been completed for all agents, the new values of the competing goals and motivations for every agent are sent to the consumer Bayesian network. The Bayesian network returns the probability that her food waste falls within each of five classes. Then, for each agent, a specific value of food waste is extracted from her individual probability distribution. Afterwards, a new time step of the ABM starts, in which this food waste level is used as a parameter.

The consumer Bayesian network was machine-learned to identify the inherent structure of the data. Then, the arcs were reversed to obtain a structure compatible with the Food

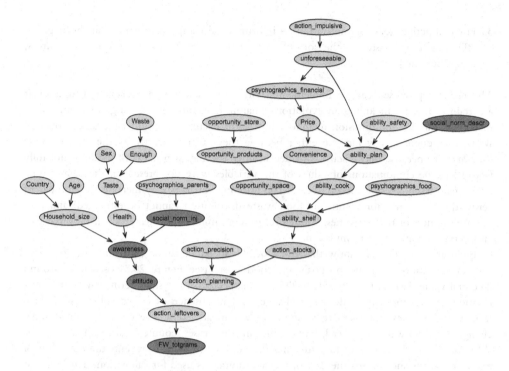

Figure 20.2 Semi-structured Bayesian network used to estimate agents' food waste levels in the integrated consumer model.

Source: Adapted from Grainger et al. (2018c, p. 15).

Waste Model (Van Geffen et al., 2017). This semi-structured Bayesian network, shown in Figure 20.2, represents a compromise between a fully structured model and a fully machine-learned one in order to reduce computational complexity. While the values of motivations and competing goals are set for each agent at each step, the other features (opportunities, abilities, psychographics and socio-demographics) are used to estimate the Bayesian network, but no hypothesis on their value is made during the single time steps.

Applications and preliminary results

To assess the potential impact on food waste of interventions insisting on a specific element of the waste-generating mechanism, changes can be applied to the baseline populations. The variables to consider can be chosen based on their impact on the food waste node in the Bayesian network. The changes can be implemented one at a time (single policy), or jointly (policy mix); then, by means of extensive simulations, the evolution of food waste can be plotted and compared to the baseline. Potential interventions on different typologies of variables include:

1. For opportunities – an incentive to purchase more efficient or more spacious freezers or fridges;
2. For abilities – the provision of training (e.g. by retailers) on the reuse of leftovers;

3. For competing goals or motivations – informational campaigns focused on the negative effects of food waste for the society (e.g. environmental damage, waste of resources, inequality, etc.).

The changes proposed can be implemented either at the onset of every simulation, or at a certain time step, including an evolution dynamic (e.g. through exchange of opinions, or through a rule for the diffusion of innovations). For example, consumers' *awareness* of food waste consequences may increase either because they are hit directly by the informational campaign, or because they discuss with peers. Since the Bayesian network model is not fully factorial (some combinations of values of the variables were not present in the dataset used to estimate it), increasing the number of conditioning variables may increase the number of zeros (the consumers for whom the food waste distribution cannot be estimated) and thus the arbitrariness of the outcomes. Therefore, only a limited set of features can be subject to an intervention in a single simulation.

Preliminary simulations show that the model is in equilibrium, with time-specific averages of motivations, competing goals and food waste (see Figure 20.3) oscillating around a central value derived from the data. This is as expected in the short term, when the composition of the populations does not change, and in absence of either policies to reduce food waste or relevant shocks (e.g., food safety scandals, etc.). The effect of motivational changes on food waste is, instead, limited and, in some cases, counterintuitive. This is probably due to social desirability bias affecting the consumers, which prevents the detection of real motivations and distorts the data of the questionnaires used for calibration. The fact that the model is essentially in equilibrium allows attention to be focused on the marginal effect of policy interventions, both cross-sectionally and dynamically.

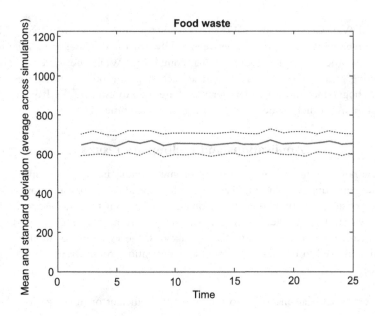

Figure 20.3 Mean and standard deviation of food waste (grams) across simulated populations at each time step.

Source: Adapted from Grainger et al. (2018c, p. 25).

Mass (energy) balance estimation

There are several examples of mass balances used to quantify food waste. The traditional mass balance approach infers food loss, waste or surplus by comparing inputs (e.g., food entering a store) and outputs (e.g., products sold to customers) alongside changes in levels of stock. In some sectors, changes to the weight of food during processing (e.g., evaporation of water during cooking) have to be considered too. This method can be applied to individual or multiple stages of the food supply chain, and has been used to estimate food waste at a national level. A broad description of this method can be found in the annex on quantification methods of the *FLW Standard* (World Resources Institute, 2016).

A unique example of mass balance is the study by Hall et al. (2009) which estimates food waste as the difference between food consumption and food supply in the United States. Unlike most traditional mass balance studies based on physical weight of food, the food waste estimate presented in Hall et al.'s paper is based on energy content of food. Details on the method are provided below. The Hall methodology further inspired others to extend and/or modify the method.

Quantifying food waste as a balance between availability, metabolism and calories consumed

Hall et al. (2009) propose that food consumption can be imputed using the mathematical model of metabolism. According to the model, consumed food provides energy to perform physical activities and support basal metabolism[1], and surplus energy from overconsumption is stored in the body as increase in body weight. The difference between food availability (US food supply data from the FAO food balance sheets) and imputed food consumption is seen as food waste. Using this method, they show that waste as share of food supply has been increasing in the US, and estimates using Hall et al.'s approach are much higher than those reported by FAO, 2011. The benefit of the approach is that while the fixed waste factors approach behind FAO implicitly assumes that consumer food waste is explained solely by food supply available to consumers, Hall et al.'s approach accounts for both the supply (food availability) and demand (consumption) side factors.[2] On the downside, the estimates of waste are highly aggregated (in calories per capita) without any information on waste associated with the underlying individual food commodities. Figure 20.4 shows their main results. While using FAO's approach yields a more or less stable percentage of available food being wasted by consumers (line connecting solid squares), the energy balance approach shows that this percentage has been steadily rising over the decades (solid line).

Some extensions of Hall et al. (2009) include Hiç et al. (2016) and Verma et al. (2016). Both adapt the Hall method to cross-section data, and show how this approach can be extended globally.

Hiç et al. apply the Hall et al. method to a larger set of countries to obtain waste estimates and quantify greenhouse gas emissions associated with food waste to have increased by 300% in the last 50 years. Their estimates of per capita per day waste stands at 516 kcal (for year 2010) in comparison to FAO's 214 kcal (Kummu et al., 2012, based on FAO, 2011) for years 2005–07. Figure 20.5 shows selected findings from Hiç et al. (2016). Globally, food production has outpaced food requirements and waste has been steadily increasing (Figure 20.5(a)). At a finer level, however, we see a lot of variation across countries

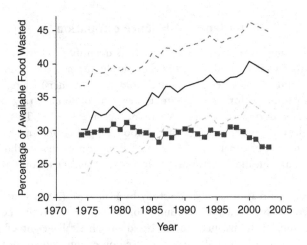

Figure 20.4 Comparison of results for US consumer food waste using FAO approach and the energy balance approach.

Source: Adapted from Hall et al. (2009).

(Figure 20.5(b)). While some countries are facing food deficit, others produce and waste more than they require.

Verma et al. start by using Hall et al.'s method to obtain consumer waste data for a set of countries where WHO body weight data is available and use a statistical relationship (based on the fact that consumers with higher incomes waste more food) to make out-of-sample predictions. Their results show food waste estimates of 526 kcal (2005) and 727 kcal (2011).[3] They also provide a monetary threshold beyond which food waste in a country becomes a real problem. They further show that standard consumption elasticities are usually overestimated on account of food waste and how to correct for those in an applied simulation model. The main limitation is that they implicitly assume that food availability and body weights in all underdeveloped countries follow the path as already observed in the developed world. Figure 20.6 shows a graphical representation of their estimates of food waste (kcal/capita/day) for individual countries (panel (a)). The darker the shading, the higher the food waste per capita. This pattern, however, reverses for panel (b), which represents responsiveness of consumer food waste to increases in a measure of consumer affluence, highlighting how waste increases as countries grow richer.

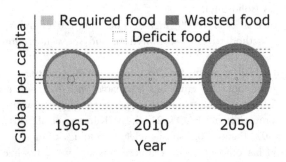

Figure 20.5a

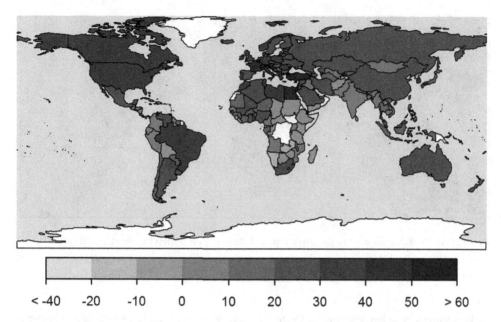

Figure 20.5b Global and country food waste estimates.
Source: Adapted from Hiç et al. (2016).

Conclusions

Discrete event simulation

The single piece of published research in this area has illustrated that application of DES to household food waste is promising. The method allows known dynamics around food waste

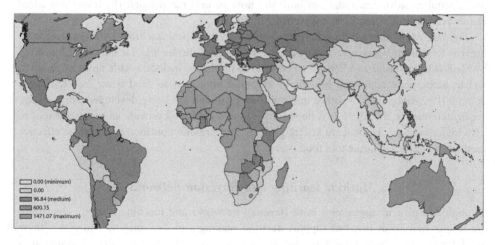

Figure 20.6a

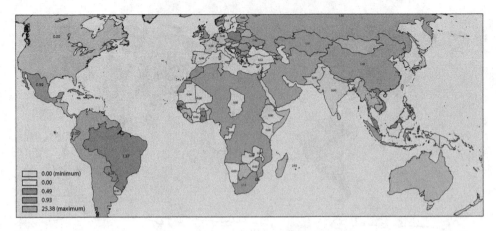

Figure 20.6b Predicted food waste (kcal/day/cap) and waste responsiveness to affluence (2011).
Source: Verma et al. (2016).

to be incorporated, has brought to life many characteristics of waste prevention and allows estimation of their importance. The modelling has also been able to estimate the effect of changes that it would be hard to test in a real-world setting. For instance, it would be difficult to measure a change in milk waste from changing any single factor, e.g. increasing the shelf life of milk, for both methodological and practical reasons.

The results demonstrate that activities with a positive impact on waste prevention (e.g. adjusting purchases according to stock levels) do not always eradicate waste: they usually reduce the quantity wasted or the likelihood of waste being produced, but do not guard against any chance of waste being produced.

Moreover, this model can act as a tool for explaining how waste generation can be conceptualised. It can engage people on the subject and therefore can be used in many contexts to facilitate conversations – most notably, it illustrates that the generation of waste in the home requires an understanding of both the flow of material through the home and social factors relating to the use of that material.

The Milk Model showed promise in helping answer practical questions by those seeking to prevent food from being wasted. For this reason, work is under way (at the time of writing) by Sheffield University and WRAP to extend the model: to include a wide range of products and to incorporate additional household dynamics important to food waste (see Kandemir et al., 2019). Alongside this, other milk simulation models are being developed (for instance, see Stankiewicz et al., 2019). It is hoped these new models will provide an important tool to help understand this particularly knotty problem and provide guidance on the most effective methods for reducing household food waste.

Machine learning and Bayesian networks

Though complex in appearance both Bayesian networks and machine learning algorithms are simply new tools that can support decision making and data analysis. However, there are limitations to both modelling approaches. It should be stressed that Bayesian networks and machine learning algorithms have allowed the identification of dependencies among variables, but not their direction and their mechanisms (i.e. causality). Understanding why age and country-level differences occur may be of paramount importance for designing better food waste policy interventions, and needs further research via multiple methods. Nevertheless, the probabilistic understanding of the drivers of food waste that have been showcased in Grainger et al. (2018a, 2018b, 2018d) allows future action and research.

Agent-based modelling

ABMs are well suited for studying a phenomenon like the generation of food waste, which results from the aggregation of individual decisions and whose drivers are complex and interrelated. In the framework of the EU Horizon 2020 REFRESH two ABMs were developed to study, respectively, the interaction between innovation adoption and food waste generation in the retail sector, and the process of food waste generation at consumer level. A relevant innovation of the consumer ABM consisted in its integration with Bayesian networks analysis techniques (Grainger et al., 2018d). These models can be used to test the impact of interventions against food waste. Practitioners need to pay particular attention to the data obtained for calibration to obtain reliable results.

Mass (energy) balance estimation

Adoption of Sustainable Development Goals (SDGs) as part of the 2030 Agenda for Sustainable Development necessitates finding a way to measure the present situation and progress. SDG 12 seeks to "ensure sustainable consumption and production patterns", including a specific target on food loss and waste. In order to measure progress toward achieving SDG 12, two indices have been proposed: a Food Waste Index and a Food Loss Index. The Food Loss Index has already been created by FAO, however the Food Waste Index is still under development. With some modifications, this method could generate a globally comparable Food Waste Index using limited available data in a transparent manner. Mass balance estimation could also be used to enhance macro modelling concerning food waste and consumption specifically due to its implications for the standard income elasticity of consumption.

Notes

1 As measured by physical activity level depending on lifestyle: vigorously active, moderately active, sedentary; and basal metabolic rate dependent on body weight.
2 There is work looking at demand side drivers, for example Britton et al. (2014) attempt to look at demand side drivers but analysis is limited to the UK or other specific countries.
3 These are the numbers based on revisions to their 2016 work and can be obtained from the authors.

Acknowledgements

Many thanks to Dr. Prajal Pradhan for providing us the modified figures from Hiç et al. (2016). The DES section of this work was co-funded by the Economic & Social Research Council Impact Accelerator (Project title: "Simulating Household Food Waste: A Research and Policy Model"), and WRAP.

References

Barr, S. (2007). Factors Influencing Environmental Attitudes and Behaviors: a U.K. Case Study of House-hold Waste Management. *Environment and Behavior*, 39(4), 435–473. doi:10.1177/0013916505283421

Britton, E., Brigdon, A., Parry, A., & LeRoux, S. (2014). Econometric Modelling and Household Food Waste (pp. 1–65). *WRAP*. Retrieved from www.wrap.org.uk/sites/files/wrap/Econometrics%20Report.pdf

Canali, M. et al. (2014) Drivers of Current Food Waste Generation, Threats of Future Increase and Oppor-tunities for Reduction. Available at: www.eu-fusions.org/index.php/download?download=111:drivers-of-current-food-waste-generation-threats-of-future-increase-and-opportunities-for-reduction

Delaney, W. and Vaccari, E. (1989). *Dynamic Models and Discrete Event Simulation*. New York, NY, USA: Marcel Dekker, Inc.

Evans, D. (2012). Beyond the Throwaway Society: Ordinary Domestic Practice and a Sociological Approach to Household Food Waste. *Sociology*, 46(1), 41–56. doi:10.1177/0038038511416150

Farmer, J. D. and Foley, D. (2009). The economy needs agent-based modelling. *Nature*, doi:10.1038/460685a

Grainger, M. J. et al. (2018a). The Use of Systems Models to Identify Food Waste Drivers. *Global Food Security*, 16, March 2018, 1-8. doi:10.1016/j.gfs.2017.12.005

Grainger, M. J. et al. (2018b). Model Selection and Averaging in the Assessment of The Drivers of Household Food Waste to Reduce The Probability of False Positives. *PLoS ONE*, 13(2), doi:10.1371/journal.pone.0192075

Grainger, M., Piras, S., Righi, S., Setti, M., Stewart, G. & Vittuari, M. (2018c). *Behavioural Economics: Linking Bayesian and Agent-Based Models to Assess Consumer Food Waste*. REFRESH Deliverable D4.4. Newcastle-Upon-Tyne, UK: Newcastle University.

Grainger, M.J., Stewart, G.B., Piras, S., Righi, S., Setti, M., and Vittuari, M. (2018d). *Model Integration. Integrated Socio-Economic Model on Food Waste*. H2020 REFRESH. Newcastle-Upon-Tyne, UK: Newcastle University.

Gustafsson, J., Cederberg, C., Sonesson, U. & Emanuelsson, A., 2013. The methodology of the FAO study: Global Food Losses and Food Waste-extent, causes and prevention, FAO, 2011.

Hall, K. D., Guo, J., Dore, M., & Chow, C. C. (2009). The Progressive Increase of Food Waste in Amer-ica and Its Environmental Impact. *PLoS ONE*, 4(11), e7940. doi:10.1371/journal.pone.0007940

Hiç, C., Pradhan, P., Rybski, D., & Kropp, J. P. (2016). Food Surplus and Its Climate Burdens. *Environ-mental Science & Technology*, 50(8), 4269–4277. doi:10.1021/acs.est.5b05088

Kandemir, C, Quested, T, Reynolds, C, Fisher, K., & Devine, R. (2019) Household food waste simula-tion model: Investigation of interventions for staple food items waste, 26th EurOMA Conference,17-19 June 2019, Helsinki, Finland.

Koivupuro, H. K. et al. (2012). Influence of Socio-Demographical, Behavioural and Attitudinal Factors on The Amount of Avoidable Food Waste Generated in Finnish Households. *International Journal of Consumer Studies*, 36(2), March 2012, 183–191.doi:10.1111/j.1470-6431.2011.01080.x

Kummu, M., de Moel, H., Porkka, M., Siebert, S., Varis, O., & Ward, P. J. (2012). Lost Food, Wasted Resources: Global Food Supply Chain Losses and Their Impacts on Freshwater, Cropland, and Fertil-iser Use. *Science of The Total Environment*, 438, 477–489. doi:10.1016/j.scitotenv.2012.08.092

Parizeau, K., von Massow, M., & Martin, R. (2015). Household-Level Dynamics of Food Waste Production and Related Beliefs, Attitudes, and Behaviours in Guelph, Ontario. *Waste Management*, Jan, 35: 207–217.doi:10.1016/j.wasman.2014.09.019

Quested, T. (2013). The Milk Model: Simulating Food Waste in the Home. Retrieved from www.wrap.org.uk/sites/files/wrap/Milk%20Model%20report.pdf

Rogers, E.M. (2010). *Diffusion of Innovations*. New York, NY, USA: Simon and Schuster.

Rothschild, M.L. (1999). Carrots, Sticks, and Promises: A Conceptual Framework for The Management of Public Health and Social Issue Behaviors. *The Journal of Marketing*, 6(4), 86–114.

Setti, M. et al. (2016). Italian Consumers' Income and Food Waste Behavior. *British Food Journal*, 118(7), 1731–1746. doi:10.1108/BFJ-11-2015-0427

Sonesson, U. et al. (2005). Home Transport and Wastage: Environmentally Relevant Household Activ-ities in The Life Cycle of Food. *Ambio*, 34(4–5), 371–375. doi:10.1579/0044-7447-34.4.371

Stancu, V., Haugaard, P., & Lähteenmäki, L. (2016). Determinants of Consumer Food Waste Behaviour: Two Routes to Food Waste. *Appetite*, Jan, 1(96), 7–17. doi:10.1016/j.appet.2015.08.025

Stankiewicz, Sebastian K., Auras, Rafael, & Selke, Susan (2019).Modeling American Household Fluid Milk Consumption and their Resulting Greenhouse Gas Emissions. *Sustainability*, 11(7), 2152.

Thøgersen, J., and Ølander, C.F. (1995). "Perceptions of waste and recycling. A qualitative analysis." In The 20th Annual Colloquium of IAREP, The International Association for Research in Economic Psychology, August 1995, Frontiers in Economic Psychology. Bergen, Norway: Norwegian School of Economics and Business Administration.

Van Geffen, L., van Herpen, E., & van Trijp, H. (2017). Quantified consumer insights on food waste: Pan-European research for quantified consumer food waste understanding, Report of the EU project REFRESH, D1.4.

Verma, M., de Vreede, L., Rutten, M., & Achterbosch, T. (2016). Modelling Food Waste Calories Wasted: Data, Estimates, and MAGNET Module. *Unpublished manuscript*.

Wenlock, R. W. and Buss, D. H. (1977). Wastage of edible food in the home: a preliminary study. *Journal of human nutrition*. Dec, 31(6), 405–411.

World Resources Institute (2016). *Food Loss and Waste Accounting and Reporting Standard*. Washington, DC, USA: WRI.

WRAP. (2007). 'We Don't Waste Food' www.wrap.org.uk/sites/files/wrap/We_don_t_waste_food_-_A_household_survey_mar_07.db6802f9.6397.pdf

WRAP (2012). *Household Food and Drink Waste in the United Kingdom*. Banbury: WRAP, 2013.

PART V

Solutions to food waste?

The question mark in the title to Part V's hints at the potential for hubris in presenting a series of neat 'solutions' to what could certainly be considered a 'wicked' problem (Batie, 2000). As earlier chapters demonstrate, the complexity of causation and interpretation of food wastage, and the multiple forms, scales, and places at which it manifests, leave the question of 'solutions' similarly complex and challenging. The chapters here delineate just some of the solutions that have been gaining visibility, resources, and sometimes critique, in different parts and places of the food chain. Authors range from the fields of food sciences to marketing to critical theory, and include practitioners from campaign organisation Feedback. Some pinpoint the decision-making processes that affect human eating behaviours, others consider the potential for technological interventions, while others examine political and structural barriers to solutions premised simply on managing 'end-of-pipe' symptoms (Corvellec, 2012). Part V's juxtaposition of diverse disciplinary approaches, and ways of understanding different solutions, highlights some of the political and practical contexts affecting how certain solutions may take hold at different times and in different places. For example, Martin Bowman, Karen Luyckx, and Christina O'Sullivan's chapter on animal feed notes how the 'backyard pig' has long been fed on food scraps, but is rooted in the specific experience of UK food policy and its industrialised pig production, which has intensified (and politicised) the challenges of how to manage cross-border flows of food and disease (Law and Mol, 2008). A key concern remains: how far might certain solutions in fact lead to more food waste, either through the shunting of causation or manifestation to different parts of food supply chains, or through distraction from underlying causes and thus creating even deeper damage?

Jane Midgley's chapter, 'Surplus food redistribution', draws on the rich literature addressing the charitable redirection of foods rendered surplus to the requirements of corporate agribusiness (see also Cloke and Giles, this volume). Midgley highlights variation between regulatory contexts and models of redistribution, but notes the dominant imaginary and narrative of redistribution as 'win-win' solution to both food waste and food insecurity (see also Lougheed and Spring, this volume). She acknowledges ethical dilemmas raised, asking 'why is it only the use of food that has been categorised as surplus that is deemed appropriate to sustain people who are food insecure?'. Her chapter raises questions of rights and responsibilities – of governments, different kinds of 'communities' and individuals. Midgley's chapter compares the diverse values, actors, practices, and policy contexts characterising surplus food redistribution spaces, narratives, and trajectories. It unpicks some of the practical and theoretical complexity underlying concepts of 'surplus' and 'waste', providing conceptual resources for understanding some of these diverse implications for redistribution as a solution to food waste. How do such practices reveal, and shape, contemporary food economies that generate prodigious quantities of wasted food, and vulnerable people?

Bowman, Luyckx, and O'Sullivan's chapter considers redistribution not to humans, but to animals. Rooted in Feedback's 'The Pig Idea' campaign to reverse the 2001 UK ban on feeding surplus food to pigs in the wake of the devastating Foot and Mouth Disease (FMD) outbreak, it notes ongoing disparities and changes in wealth and meat consumption as a key contextualising concern. The chapter offers one practical mitigation of meat production impacts: feeding surplus food to animals, which they argue could reduce overall greenhouse gas emissions from food while freeing up grain to feed hungry people (the mechanisms by which this redistribution might occur is beyond the chapter's scope). They explore legal and regulatory levers to incentivise such surplus redirection in regionally specific ways. They propose ways to overcome significant barriers to such shifts, particularly biosecurity concerns in the wake of the FMD crisis, highlighting heating and fermentation techniques currently used in Korea and Japan as well as import controls. They argue that the main problem was not the feed itself, but poorly designed regulation and enforcement. Could these suggestions overcome some of the challenges for such enforcement outlined by Law and Mol (2008), who note that in contrast to histories of the 'backyard pig', contemporary meat production's intensification and profit-led motivations, combined with global disparities in both disease prevalence and meat/feed prices, 'makes illegality appealing'. Bowman et al. provide some answers, such as surplus food treatment being separated from farms. Tensions between scientific, economic, political, and economic influences on the nexus of food waste, safety, and quality is a theme that runs through a number of chapters (see also Milne, 2012; Spring, Adams and Hardman, 2019).

As Law and Mol (2008) argue, feeding surplus food to industrially raised pigs is only possible given the excessive quantities of 'metabolic surplus' produced by consumers and restaurants in rich nations. Recalling debates about the sustainability of relying on charitable food donations to address food insecurity (Iafrati, 2016), the question is raised of what happens to these 'solutions' if a focus is placed on *prevention* rather than *management* of food excesses. Alex V. Barnard and Marie Mourad's chapter, 'From dumpster dives to disco vibes', compares social movements' analyses and diagnoses of the food waste problem and its solutions. It provides tools for better understanding the (sometimes ambiguous) motivations and goals of movements that create public spectacles and engagements with wasted food. It critiques the effects of the normative positioning of 'food waste' as the explicit and primary focus of policy and campaigns, rather than its being treated as a marker or symptom within broader analyses of waste economies, food systems, and governance or political logics. Their comparison of Food Not Bombs, 'freeganism', and Disco Soupe highlights differences within, as well as between, movements, drawing out the ambiguous implications of the success of 'food waste' as both trope and material means of campaigning. Does Disco Soupe's approach to inclusion, fun, and safety regulations, dilute its capacity to effect transformative change; indeed, what does 'transformative change' look like, and how might we recognise it?

Leaving aside the question of food waste's structural causes, the chapter by Monica C. LaBarge, Sarah Evans, Beth Vallen, and Lauren G. Block interrogates the micro-encounters mediating eating experiences and their potential for the kinds of waste generation that characterise wealthy, high-consumption societies. It explores the effects of labelling, packaging, and eating environments (the latter through the notions of 'tablescapes' and 'plates-capes') on perceptions of value, size, quality, and safety that might affect quantities eaten or discarded. The authors do not consider whether food eaten that exceeds bodily needs might be considered 'waste', which Buller (2015) calls 'metabolic waste'.[1] Nevertheless, LaBarge et al. draw on consumer research studies exploring the role of date labels, package/portion/plate size, and factors such as household incomes on waste literacy and behaviours. Date labelling, as Milne (2012) shows, arose as a response to consumer concerns around freshness and technopolitical concerns around food safety and has only more recently been publicly problematised in relation to food waste. It is important to recognise variation in date-labelling regulations, practices, and geographies, as a film by the Harvard Food Law and Policy Clinic viscerally laid bare (FLPC, 2016). LaBarge et al. confirm that safety concerns still often outweigh concerns for wastage. However, their chapter comes closer than others to sensory, embodied, and psychological aspects through which questions of pleasure, value, and 'enough-ness' are navigated. Exemplifying the increasing consideration of marketing (and marketing studies) to questions of social and environmental impacts and producer responsibilities, the chapter contrasts with studies arguing that branding, packaging, and eating environments themselves drive overconsumption, and thus waste (e.g. Cloke, this volume).

The chapter by Mohamed A. Gedi, Vincenzo di Bari, Roger Ibbett, Randa Darwish, Ogueri Nwaiwu, Zainudin Umar, Deepa Agarwal, Richard Worrall, David Gray, and Tim Foster details work under way at the University of Nottingham to explore bio-economical potentials for the 'upcycling' or re-valorisation of materials previously considered as waste. Primarily defined here as ways in which financial value can be recouped from products usually considered valueless to industry, the authors also note other valuable properties accruing from these processes: use values of nutrients for returning to food products, or structural or cleansing properties for turning into useful products. These may provide more circular and renewable resources for industry, such as plant-based rather than petroleum waxes, or orange oils for cleaning products. While many of us will have heard of entrepreneurs turning end-of-day market produce into jams, or spent grain and grounds into intriguing new concoctions, and while businesses have long attempted to recoup value from less-valuable offcuts, trimmings, or animal parts, Gedi et al. describe techniques and properties that reveal the micro-chemical affordances of supposedly 'inedible' peels and husks that a social-scientific perspective alone would miss.

Jan Mayer and Jaz Hee-jeong Choi's chapter modestly reports potentials for waste prevention within the catering industry. Giving useful insight into the methodologies and challenges of conducting participatory research in hard-to-research places (such as the busy working environment of a professional restaurant), the chapter acknowledges a range of factors at play in wastage from restaurants, which they categorise as operations and processes (e.g. menu design and procurement practices), internal factors (e.g. staff skills and experience), and external factors (e.g. weather and volatile demand). Some of these insights could indeed be applied to other domains of food wastage, such as manufacturing (Blake, 2019). While clarifying the limitations of their approach (based on prototyping and workshopping a digital app that could collate existing data on factors affecting wastage), they share important considerations for co-designing real-life applications, which must be built on close understanding of the busy, stressful nature of catering work. As such, applications must be intuitive and fit seamlessly into such working environments; how could these insights be applied to non-digital 'solutions' for food waste prevention in different places?

Part V's closing chapter by Daniel Hoornweg, Scott Lougheed, Mark Walker, Ramy Salemdeeb, Tammara Soma, and Christian Reynolds, reviews options available when 'higher' rungs of the food recovery hierarchy, including prevention and redistribution, are not possible. Detailing some of the contexts, costs, and environmental impacts of different 'downstream' options for food waste, comparing source reduction, collection, recycling, composting, incineration, and landfilling for countries of different income levels. The authors conclude by looking at these options against future decarbonisation scenarios, with a reminder that solutions must be contextually sensitive and consistently reviewed for their appropriateness and impacts.

Note

1 Indeed, this Handbook does not address the gap noted by Alexander et al. (2013, p. 479) around the bodily and technical infrastructures of food's metabolism or conversion to waste both inside and outside of bodies, or the 'centrality of bodies and shit' for food/waste studies.

References

Alexander, C., Gregson, N. and Gille, Z. (2013). *Food Waste*. in Murcott, A., Belasco, W., & Jackson, P. (Eds.). *The Handbook of Food Research*. London, New York: Bloomsbury Academic.
Batie, S. S. (2000). Wicked problems and applied economics. *American Journal of Agricultural Economics, 90*(5), 1176–1191.
Blake, M. (2019). The multiple ontologies of Surplus food. *Europe Now Journal*, 1–9.
Buller, H. (2015). *Waste provocations: Introductory symposium remarks. Royal geographical society food geographies working group*, Available at https://foodmatterssymposium.wordpress.com/2015/09/17/food-waste-symposium-introductory-remarks/
Corvellec, H. (2012). *Normalising excess: An ambivalent take on the recycling of food waste into biogas*, (Research in Service Studies No. 15). Available at https://ism.lu.se/fileadmin/files/rs/wp/WP_15_NOV_2012.pdf
Evans, D. (2014). *Food Waste: Home Consumption, Material Culture and Everyday Life*. London: Bloomsbury.
Fisher, A. (2017). *Big Hunger: The Unholy Alliance between Corporate America and Anti-Hunger Groups*. Cambridge, MA: MIT Press.
FLPC (2016). *Expired: Food waste in america. film by harvard food law and policy clinic and racing horse productions*. Available at https://vimeo.com/154439089
Heynen, N. (2010). Cooking up non-violent civil-disobedient direct action for the hungry: "Food Not Bombs" and the resurgence of radical democracy in the US. *Urban Studies, 47*(6), 1225–1240.
Iafrati, S. (2016). The sustainability of food bank provision: What happens when demand outstrips supply?, *Journal of Poverty and Social Justice 24*(3), 307–310.
Law, J., and Mol, A. (2008). Globalisation in practice: On the politics of boiling pigswill. *Geoforum, 39*(1), 133–143.
Milne, R. (2012). Arbiters of waste: Date labels, the consumer and knowing good, safe food. *The Sociological Review, 60*, 84–101.
Tomlinson, I. (2013). Doubling food production to feed the 9 billion: A critical perspective on a key discourse of food security in the UK. *Journal of Rural Studies, 29*, 81–90.

21

SURPLUS FOOD REDISTRIBUTION

Jane Midgley

Introduction

This chapter focuses on surplus food redistribution. Surplus food is food that is edible and safe for human consumption and has been generated by different failures within food industry supply chains and their practices (such as logistical errors, mislabelling, oversupply as well as order declines, among many reasons; see Midgley, 2014, 2019; Mourad, 2016; Schneider, 2013; Stuart, 2009). Once food is identified as 'surplus' by producers, manufacturers and retailers this categorisation indicates that the food is potentially available to other organisations that use alternative forms of supply and exchange ('redistribution'), and through these activities work toward achieving its safe consumption. These efforts are frequently underpinned by an environmental rationale that seeks to utilise the food to prevent the waste of food, the associated costs of its landfilling and lost resources expended in growing/raising, processing, manufacturing and distributing the foodstuff. The chapter begins by exploring different approaches to the redistribution of surplus food to contextualise the process of redistribution and the diversity of practices that this can encompass. The chapter then moves to consider the ways in which surplus food and redistribution can be conceptualised, before exploring how these may inform how surplus food redistribution is regulated in different national settings. The chapter shows that while attention and contestation are focused on the surplus food material, more critical insights are necessary to explore the redistribution process and the various re-allocations of responsibility for reducing waste and hunger as well as the various values and relations that are incorporated into this exchange and the encounters and actions that redistribution may stimulate.

A typology of surplus food redistribution

This section provides an overview of the different ways in which surplus food is moved from food industry actors to other organisations, whether they be a commercial or social distributor (the latter may include either charitable or social enterprise organisations; see WRAP, 2018). This is not, and cannot be, a complete overview, as different organisations will each have their own motivations and practices in using surplus food, in addition to operating in varying regulatory contexts (discussed later). In an effort to help guide and promote discussion the overview is organised by a broad two-fold typology, based on gener-alised characteristics, described as 'brokerage' and 'challenger' models, with illustrative examples based on information made publicly available by those organisations.

Brokerage: corporate donation for redistribution

It is well documented that the recent attention given to surplus food and its redistribution began as an emergency or temporary response to the pressures felt by households and com-munities in the United States of America (USA) following the 'rediscovery of hunger' in the 1960s (Poppendieck, 1998). The subsequent economic downturns, and allied reductions in national government spending on social and welfare budgets during the later 1970s and 1980s, saw the growth of surplus stocks being redistributed in the form of emergency food aid to those who were identified as being food insecure (without regular affordable access to safe and culturally appropriate food) and thus were at risk of hunger from poverty (Poppen-dieck, 1998). This emergency food aid response model became known as a 'food bank'. This model sees industry transfers of surplus food (at reduced cost or free donation) that would otherwise go to waste being deposited with a food bank organisation (typically a charity) and which is stored and then released to another organisation responding to hunger and food insecurity in their community. Over time, food banks have become a regularised and recognised institution in both the food and welfare landscapes for many communities throughout the world, although spatial coverage and access to these redistribu-tors remains ad-hoc (Poppendieck, 1998; Tarasuk and Eakin, 2005). The flow of food between organisations may include recipient charities paying a subscription fee to the food bank to cover its running costs, or the food bank itself may pay a fee to be a member of a larger network of food banks gaining access to additional resources (e.g. food sources and legal advice) and adhere to the network's governance arrangements, and allied procedures and practices, such as Feeding America (USA), FareShare (UK), and Die Tafel (Germany). Nor do all food banks belong to larger networks as some prefer to keep their independence. The development of this increasingly dominant model of surplus food redistribution achieved through 'brokerage' activities between food industry and the charitable and volun-tary sector has seen food bank activities in 31 countries across the global North and South, which has provided food to 7.78 million people since the first food bank opened in 1967 (Global Foodbanking Network, 2018).

Food banks operate in different ways with regard to the extent of their direct interaction with the general public/food insecure; some may offer direct low-cost resale of food to the public, and/or meal provision as opposed to 'parcels' of food supplies, in addition to their dis-tributing foods to other charitable organisations (Die Tafel, in Germany reflects this mixture of redistribution and food access provision; see Baglioni et al., 2017). Moreover, in the USA and South Korea food banks are linked in part to government policy and programme delivery, whereas in other nations such as the UK and Japan they have become a representation of gov-ernment inaction toward hunger and insecurity (Lindenbaum, 2016; Cloke et al., 2017; Kimura, 2018). At this juncture it is important to note the distinction in food bank terminology between the UK and many other nations. To the rest of the world redistribution organisations such as the UK's FareShare would be recognised as a food bank (obtaining industry-sourced donations and redistributing this to franchise members and partner organisations), however in the UK they are not described as such. In the UK 'food banks' are generally understood as organisations that collect donated food from within their community for their community (Lambie-Mumford, 2013); importantly this includes donations from the general public and this sourcing practice demarcates most of the UK food banks as not being 'surplus' food redistributors or working to prevent food waste. In the UK 'food banking' has become typified by the work of the Trussell Trust network and their self-describing their activities as food banking. The Trussell Trust is a franchise network of organisations (informed by Christian principles) who offer publicly donated food as emergency food parcels direct to the public, with access conditional on the households being in temporary crisis which is established by their referral from a range of local agencies and charitable actors (see Lambie-Mumford, 2013; Cloke et al., 2017; Lindenbaum, 2016). As such these activities may more closely resemble 'food pantries' as discussed outside the UK.

The 'win-win' equation of reducing both food waste and hunger through the solution of surplus food redistribution forms the main focus of debates that have become associated with the brokerage format and their contestation (Poppendieck, 1998). This equation is clearly illustrated when industry donors and redistributors translate the amounts (weight) of food saved into the numbers of meals created. While this equation is a crude estimation, it does illustrate what surplus food redistribution 'achieves', and signifies an intention to reduce the amounts of edible food being disposed of as waste while at the same time increasing access to food. As such there is a need to recognise the different motivations of various actors in the redistribution relationship that leads them to take responsibility for supplying and utilising surplus food, which, as discussed later in the chapter, may be voluntary or a legal requirement in different regulatory contexts (see Mourad, 2016; Swaffield et al., 2018). Amid increasing global awareness of food waste and food insecurity there has been a growth in surplus food being made available (including branded products) for redistribution by corporate actors, and recognition of the value of these actions in contributing to their corporate social responsibility, and informing perceptions and wider practices of both consumers and industry actors (see Consumer Goods Forum (2016), a partnership that represents 400 global retailers and manufacturers of consumer goods).

However, food industry actions are subject to criticism. Riches (2018) argues that corporate actors fail to exhibit social solidarity with those who are unable to access commercially retailed food by their continued generation of surplus and direction of this food category to charitable redistribution. Riches' critique notes that the solution of redistribution offered by brokerage approaches does not encourage the food industry to prevent or reduce the generation of excess food but serves as a way to manage their 'waste', which has been argued to be economically beneficial by reducing food waste disposal costs that would accrue if the food was not redistributed, especially if this food donation is encouraged by tax incentives (Lindenbaum, 2016; Lohnes and Wilson, 2018; Riches, 2018). This leads to what is the fundamental problem associated with the brokerage model in that these 'waste problems' are resolved by handing on excess food to organisations to provide food for the vulnerable and food insecure (whether free or at reduced cost). This argument also applies to social supermarkets whereby reduced cost surplus food is offered to individuals who become members of this commercial form of redistribution (as opposed to food banks and other surplus redistribution actions discussed here that would be described as social or charitable redistribution actors; see WRAP, 2018). The customers/members of social supermarkets are recognised as being in, or on the cusp of, poverty and are often provided with additional wrap-around advisory services (Schneider, 2013; Lindenbaum, 2015; Power, 2018). Thus, there is a moral dilemma closely associated with brokerage approaches as to why is it only the use of food that has been categorised as surplus that is deemed appropriate to sustain people who are food insecure? This brings with it attendant issues of stigma and potential lack of dignity in using such sources and the variable experiences of users in what has been called the 'dark-side' of food banking (van der Horst et al., 2014) which has been well documented by a range of ethnographic studies (Garthwaite, 2016; Henderson, 2004; Tarasuk and Eakin, 2005; Warshawsky, 2010; Williams et al., 2016). Moreover, the 'halo effect' associated with doing the 'right thing' or 'good work' means there has been comparatively little criticism of redistributors or providing charity organisations (Poppendieck, 1998); although this is beginning to change (see Henderson, 2004; Wakefield et al., 2013; Williams et al., 2016; Lohnes and Wilson, 2018). Many of the studies document food bank organisations working with surplus food but not all do, and so caution is needed when exploring the values and actions associated with the different foodstuffs as well as organisational ethos and practices in responding to structural inequalities that give rise to food insecurity (Wakefield et al., 2013; Cloke et al., 2017).

Authors have also stressed that surplus food redistribution efforts detract from national governments' failures to provide, respect and fulfil their citizens' 'right to food' (Riches, 2011, 2018; Lambie-Mumford, 2013). The right to food is a basic socio-economic right located in the United Nations (UN) International Covenant on Economic, Social and Cultural Rights (article 11, 1966 expanded by CESCR 1999, comment 12) that requires public institutions, typically governments, to ensure that they provide adequate means for people to afford and access adequate food. Many governments have ratified the UN treaties containing these provisions but have not subsequently incorporated this right into law and nor do they work to fulfil its aims (Riches, 2011, 2018).

As charities and other voluntary organisations work to reduce hunger and food insecurity through the brokerage model, these very issues are argued to have become depoliticised as the organisations have become reliant on surplus food donations and, in turn, become incorporated into food system practices. For example, reliance on the extensive amounts of donated foodstuffs may prevent organisations from publicly criticising donors (Warshawsky, 2010). As this form of charitable surplus redistribution has grown, so too has redistribution organisations' responsibility for managing hunger. Consequently, a key part of the social contract between a state and its citizens has become the responsibility of essentially a diverse grouping of private charitable and commercial actors; this shift and the associated role of food banks within it has seen them variously described as para-state institutions, an example of the 'shadow state' (c.f. Wolch, 1990) and neoliberal platoons (Warshawsky, 2010; Wakefield et al., 2013; Lindenbaum, 2016; Cloke et al., 2017; Riches, 2018). As local communities and charities take on responsibility for hunger they become part of local governance arrangements (however knowingly) and control access to food and the means by which this is distributed (Warshawsky, 2010; Wakefield et al., 2013). A further critique of this activity is the extent to which brokerage and other redistribution activities are underpinned by volunteer (no-wage) labour, which includes both volunteer time and also resources such as private transport to move the donated food. This relies on communities rather than industry or government to bear the considerable cost of both staffing and managing this process and surplus food resource. The extent of this volunteer contribution and practical articulation of the surplus redistribution process is suggested by the following examples of volunteer hours and numbers: in the UK during 2017 it was estimated that food banking volunteers (recognising the diversity of organisations that fall within this term) contributed 4,117,798 hours of labour which, if this had been paid at the national living wage, equated to £30,883,482 (Independent Food Aid Network, www.foodaidnetwork.org.uk/food-bank-volunteer-hours), whereas in the USA Food Rescue US collects food from 700 industry donors (bakers, farmers' markets, restaurants and canteens as well as grocers) and matches this supply to the needs of 575 receiving organisations, with this brokerage activity made possible by 3,300 rescuers who collect and deliver the food, which since 2011 has provided over 26 million meals (https://foodrescue.us).

At the same time, there is also evidence of a desire by brokerage organisations to expand their activities to reduce hunger and food waste. This is exemplified by the following quote from the Global FoodBanking Network (GFN). The GFN deploys the idea of the win-win relationship between reducing food waste and countering hunger through redistribution, but also hints at the (geo)political pressures of international charitable aid and a desire for a more locally determined form of food provision:

> 'Food banks are an **environmental asset** as they procure wholesome, surplus food that might otherwise end up as waste throughout the supply chain and redirect it away from landfills to social service organizations that feed the hungry [. And b] ecause food banks' success relies on the management of local community leaders rather than temporary foreign aid, **the concept is positioned for long-term, sustainable success**' which can in turn be locally adapted.
>
> *(GFN, 2018; original emphasis)*

Food banks and other redistributors providing food aid/hunger relief (outwith humanitarian crisis) are depicted as lacking the power to challenge either the structural inequalities (poverty) that they may be trying to respond to, although realistically this is not within their capabilities and it is unfair to expect this, or as previously noted to challenge food industry actors and their practices (Lohnes and Wilson, 2018; Poppendieck, 1998; Riches, 2018). Indeed, with the exception where there is a legal requirement to donate surplus food, the decision to make food available for redistribution, and subsequent power in the relationship is held by the donor.

Attempts to redress power inequalities and attain a greater diversity of foods within the brokerage format are seen by more direct initiatives and relations being formed (see Food Rescue US mentioned earlier and Food Zheroes in London). In these new initiatives, food industry actors offer available surplus via on-line platforms and mobile applications (the broker) directly to charity and community organisations (typically represented by community kitchens/soup kitchens, food pantries and homeless shelters). The community organisations can then decide if they want to accept the particular mix of foodstuffs being offered and contact their volunteers who collect and transport the food between sites. In turn, the efforts to match supply to demand may deflect criticism of industry actors passing on waste to charities, as well as the difficulties of working with fluctuating amounts and types of donated foods that many organisations struggle with and which can query the viability of this model (Lohnes and Wilson, 2018; Poppendieck, 1998; Riches, 2018; Tarasuk and Eakin, 2005). Moreover, these technological brokers do not require a physical (warehousing) space to log, store and redistribute food that more traditional food banking models rely on. As surplus food utilisation grows alongside such innovations we are seeing particular retailers align themselves with particular donation platforms as well as donating to particular broker/food bank networks (such as Food Cloud in Ireland or Fareshare Go and Neighbourly in the UK). It has been argued that this makes it more difficult for new actors to become involved in working with surplus food and further institutionalises the processes associated with distribution activities (Wills, 2017). Such arrangements may exemplify how this process requires trust to be built between partners to guarantee how food will be managed and its integrity protected in the redistribution process (Midgley, 2019).

Challenger models

The previous section has highlighted the growth of the brokerage model of surplus food redistribution as being a solution to both food waste and food insecurity. The brokerage format has become integrated into social welfare landscapes across the world, particularly in high- and middle-income countries, as well as a response to acute hunger and direct control over food sources in low- and middle-income countries. While this redistribution work is underpinned by a range of motivations and political actions, it contrasts with the 'challenger' model of surplus food redistribution where more radical politics, accompanied by less conditional and more plural and collective means of accessing and sharing food are practised. Global examples which readily fit within this format, albeit informed by different politics, are Food Not Bombs and Disco Soupe discussed in Chapter 23. In combination, such diverse organisations' activities 'bring a complicated assemblage of ethical values – including charity, equitable exchange, unconditionality, reduction of food waste, anti-war, anti-capitalism – to the table' (Cloke et al., 2017, p. 711).

Consequently, under the challenger formats I have included actors whose activities directly question and rework the industry donation–charitable consumption nexus represented by the brokerage model. One means by which this is illustrated are actions that typically involve the communal sharing of surplus food in some way (whether this is sharing the consumption of a meal, or the sharing of facilities on a temporary basis to prepare and host a meal) that enables redistribution actions to constitute more diverse economic performances and relations (Gibson-Graham, 2008; McLaren and Agyeman, 2015). This generates further activism in the food and waste systems, as while these redistribution actors work to obtain surplus food to prevent safe food going to waste, they typically open up the opportunity to consume this food to the wider public. These actions do not just value the surplus food but may also work to create different social and economic arrangements. One example is the Real Junk Food Project (https://therealjunkfoodproject.org) wherein a network of UK (and global) social enterprises run cafés with dishes comprised solely of surplus food, and/or operate 'Sharehouses' (stores) where surplus food can be accessed by any member of the public on a 'pay-as-you-feel' basis. 'Pay-as-you-feel' enables people to contribute any amount of money that they determine is appropriate and/or can afford in exchange for the meal/food they have just eaten, this payment is often completed anonymously, but it also enables and acknowledges payment in-kind and non-monetary means such as by volunteer time or skills. This provides the opportunity for making food available via redistribution with its consumption following expected social norms (choice of food, consumed alongside others, acknowledged by payment/exchange of some kind) without stigma, and the opportunity to interact and be with a diverse range of people from different backgrounds and circumstances (Midgley et al., 2018). This, in turn, provides an opportunity for people to question and recognise the multiple values and benefits (economic, social, environmental, and their own political and ethical stance, etc.) that the redistribution and consumption of the surplus food offers (ibid.). This is illustrated by the statement shown in Figure 21.1, displayed in a café which was part of the Real Junk Food Network.

Other examples include FoodCycle, which since 2008 has operated in the UK to serve communal meals made from surplus food that is cooked in premises where kitchens are unused at a particular time (www.foodcycle.org.uk). As well as initiatives with a growing global reach such as 'Feeding the 5000' public pop-up meal events, initiated by Feedback, a UK-based organisation that campaigns for food waste reduction as part of a more sustainable food system. At the time of writing (early 2019) there have been 50 communal meals

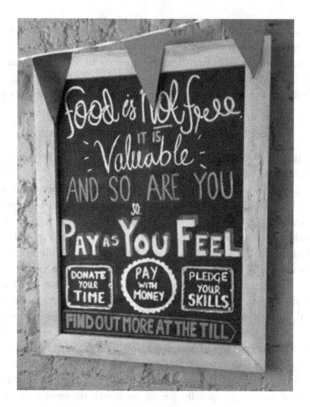

Figure 21.1 Food Is Valuable statement.
Source: Author, 2018.

in cities worldwide where 5,000 people have been served. The events aim to raise public awareness through the visibility and free participation in the meal, and in turn engage local politicians and businesses to bring together a coalition of actors to generate local and national change (https://feedbackglobal.org/campaigns/feeding-the-5000/). Through these alternative formats, surplus food redistribution and its consumption is clearly connected to food waste reduction efforts but is asserted as a clear political statement which the redistribution is portrayed as facilitating, and, in the case of communal meals, makes these issues visible (rather than the invisibility associated with food banking; see Tarasuk and Eakin (2005)). This enables a range of outcomes that are framed as being inclusive and plural in their focus (e.g. countering social isolation, building local collaborations) rather than directing efforts and activism solely on those experiencing food insecurity which is often associated with brokerage approaches.

Summary

This section has outlined a two-fold typology to help readers grasp some of the different ways in which surplus food is managed through either brokerage or challenger models. While this is not a definitive typology, the distinctions between the two formats underpin and inform current research, policy and practitioner actions and debates. This has emphasised the increasingly diverse means by which surplus food is directed toward consumers: brokerage formats have become closely associated with actions that serve specific groups (i.e. 'the hungry') and which have become institutionalised in different policy contexts to varying extents, whereas those efforts that seek to re-imagine and make visible the practices of surplus food redistribution on a more inclusive basis are more readily associated with strategies of challenger formats.

Conceptualising surplus food redistribution

Surplus is an ambiguous category and this owes much to its being positioned on a continuum between the two extremes of value and waste (Evans, 2012). In these discussions, both value and waste are primarily concerned with economic value, and so when a good fails to fulfil its expected economic value this marks the turning point wherein the good becomes categorised as surplus by its owner. Attempts to then recover its economic value see goods sold at reduced price or become de-commodified or gifted, with this categorisation emphasising a separation from the norms of market circulation and associated practices (Henderson, 2004). However, a good's categorisation as surplus does not negate a connection to its original intended use or that this use value has been lost (Henderson, 2004; Gregson et al., 2007, 2013; Evans, 2018). As such, surplus can reflect a 'stickiness' of the good's original cultural meaning(s) and value(s) and which have prevented its disposal (Douglas, [1966]). Consequently, surplus along with waste and value are cultural categorisations that reflect the arrangement and interaction of different relationships in different contexts (O'Brien, 2011). Given that the surplus good may retain the possibility of being used/consumed in the future, this has led to surplus being conceived as an interim or holding category that spatially and/or temporally pauses an item's movement to waste and allows time for its potential use (or disposal) to be identified and realised; with either outcome being dependent on the different social, economic, technological and political arrangements that structure the goods' flow (Hetherington, 2004 following Munro, 1995; Henderson, 2004; O'Brien, 2011; Gregson et al., 2013; Evans, 2018; Midgley, 2019).

Surplus food is constructed as something that has lost its economic or commodity value but still has the possibility of being able to be utilised to its full extent as edible, safe, nourishing food. Indeed, Evans (2018, p. 114) suggests that '"food" rarely crosses a line to simply and unproblematically become stuff that is "waste"' and this process can be 'understood in relation to multiple and complex movements' or placings that serve to structure and direct its movement toward either consumption or waste. Thus, while surplus food can be readily identified by industry donors, it is the combination of different aspects such as policy levers, the existence of a redistribution organisation and its capacity for (directly or remotely) managing the food that enables surplus food to be directed toward consumption rather than waste options.

A range of theoretical perspectives offer further insights into surplus food redistribution. Marxist economic theory has been used to conceptualise surplus food redistribution as an alternative circuit of capital to obtain use value while suspending its exchange value, as it is diverted from its expected path and commodity flow (Henderson, 2004). Henderson's work emphasises the often contradictory social relations that become articulated and embodied in the circulation of this 'decommodified commodity'. Lindenbaum (2015) extends this argument to suggest that surplus food redistribution is a means by which capitalism creates an Other to stabilise itself and exploit actions elsewhere in the food system. These elements include: production subsidies and incentives, trade policies that lead to surplus generation, as well as tax breaks to corporations to donate rather than waste food, in addition to the extensive amounts of volunteer/unpaid labour utilised by charitable organisations to collect, redistribute and prepare surplus food for consumption (Lindenbaum, 2015; Lohnes and Wilson, 2018).

In turn, Appadurai's (1986) economic anthropological essay on the 'social life of things' responds to Marxian understandings of commodities and explores how people attribute value to things, and how things circulate. This suggests that while commodities may move due to their agreed commercial value, other attributes (discursive meanings and values) may be attached or detached over time in different social-cultural contexts that offer differing regimes of value and which inform its trajectory (Appadurai, 1986). Importantly, it is not just how a thing moves in and out of its commodity state (and value) but also how a thing may be diverted to follow a different path. The latter diversions, Appadurai notes, are often generated by crisis or new demands, which are often politically mediated and consequently inscribed with power relations. Thus, by following a diverted trajectory rather than expected path, the social life of things can offer insights into how we might approach the various values that are attached and/or detached to food as it is identified as surplus and moves through the redistribution process. Moreover, Evans (cf. Appadurai, 1986) makes the point that 'the trajectories of things and their movement through people's homes and regimes of value relate to identity work, categorisations of other, and boundary drawing' (Evans, 2018, p. 118). This comment relates to the identification, storage and consumption of leftover (surplus) food informed by social relations and the desire to keep these actions contained within a private setting such as the household or family unit, but this helpfully refers back to the moral and cultural ordering and contextual valuation of things (cf. Douglas, [1966]). The quote prompts reflection that once a thing, such as a surplus foodstuff, enters the public realm, this opens up the process and practices of redistribution to public scrutiny which includes not just 'categorising things but also the attendant processes of categorising persons' (Evans, 2018, p. 118). I would argue that this has contributed to the tensions associated with brokerage approaches, and which are being explicitly engaged with by challenger models making the surplus food redistribution publicly visible.

Different areas of economic sociology have also been used to explore surplus food redistribution. Midgley (2014, 2019) has argued that as market arrangements are constantly evolving, marketisation theory (cf. Çalişkan and Callon, 2010) enables a focus on the devices and practices that these arrangements generate to resolve and manage various matters of concern, with surplus food and its attendant social and environmental concerns and contexts being such matters. The uncertainties associated with managing surplus food, as it overflows its original economic framing, may enable new arrangements with new actors and devices (such as challenger formats or web-based platforms facilitated by broker organisations) to order and manage the foodstuff's future consumption. Elsewhere, Swaffield and colleagues (2018) worked with convention theory (cf. Boltanski and Thevenot, 1991) and its framework for exploring normative qualities that structure exchange which are expressed through different 'orders of worth' that enable evaluation, justification and legitimate actions associated with surplus food. They identified civic ('doing the right thing'), market (financial) and opinion (brand reputation) related justifications for food retailer, redistribution actors and food waste campaigners' actions and how these created the basis for coordinating surplus food donation and redistribution, as well as how these different pressures and positions combine to structure motivations for taking action on food waste and surplus food.

Policy actions and surplus food redistribution

The various means by which a food could flow toward waste are the subject of different waste management options presented as 'hierarchies'. Waste hierarchies, now also referred to as 'use' hierarchies, offer a pre-determined set of options that aim to prevent waste arising and if this is not possible attempt to generate the least harmful environmental impact by suggesting a series of next best possible uses of a material (food) through its optimisation (surplus food consumption via redistribution), reuse, recycling, recovery (such as anaerobic digestion) and ultimately, if wasting is not preventable, final disposal, which for food wastes is typically incineration or landfill (Mourad, 2016; Papargyropoulou et al., 2014). This is promoted differently in various settings and by different institutions across the world; for example, the 'SAVE FOOD Global Food Loss and Waste' initiative, led by the Food and Agricultural Organisation of the United Nations, works to prevent safe edible food transitioning to waste in the face of food insecurity and hunger. The Environmental Protection Agency/United States Department for Agriculture suggests that one optimal use of 'extra' food is to 'feed hungry people' as part of its 'food recovery hierarchy'. In the UK, this is described as surplus food for redistribution promoted by the 'use hierarchy' of the Waste Resources Action Programme (WRAP is an organisation working with government, industry and communities to generate economic benefit through encouraging resource efficiencies). The hierarchy provides a clear direction to any food business or organisation handling food as to what could and should be done with food once they recognise that they will not be able sell/use the food as they initially expected. The hierarchy helps to identify and make available surplus foodstuffs from retailers and manufacturers' stocks by presenting it as one of the first options that should be considered (releasing it from other flows that would have directed the food toward other uses within the hierarchy, such as anaerobic digestion) and speeds up this process so that identification occurs early in industry practice (Midgley, 2014, 2019). However, the hierarchy ignores the food's edibility and relies on the potential donor to seek non-waste solutions (Bradshaw, 2018) and, in making food available for redistribution, industry actors do not follow a solely environmental rationale and justify actions by including the moral arguments associated with countering hunger (Mourad, 2016; Swaffield et al., 2018). Thus, the hierarchy works as an 'allocative tool' for wastes (Bradshaw, 2018) and where efforts are made to find alternative solutions these may build in pre-existing 'solutions' such as feeding the hungry and reproduce existing structural problems, as well as fail to engage with the economic realities of these suggested actions. For example, keeping surplus food safe within the food system in addition to its collection, repackaging, transportation and handling are argued to create a barrier to charitable redistribution, and one of the UK's leading social redistribution organisations, FareShare, continues to campaign for the UK government to create a fund to offset these costs (estimated at £15 million in 2018) to ensure that it is cheaper for the food industry to donate edible food than direct it to waste options (see #feedpeoplefirst, https://fareshare.org.uk/get-involved/feedpeoplefirst/). Mourad's (2016) study of actors in France and the United States revealed how the different solutions offered by hierarchies are often in competition due to different policy levers for different waste solutions working against each other. Consequently, while locating the potential for surplus food consumption within waste frameworks may work to help release the commercial supply of surplus food for redistribution, it creates a discursive contamination that associates surplus food as being a waste material and part of the waste stream, rather than safe edible food, and generates further tensions as to why it is this category of food that is articulated as being suitable for consumption by the vulnerable.

The ways by which different political values are translated into legislation also act to encourage, or prevent, flows of surplus food where safe and possible to do so, toward human consumption. The United States' Bill Emerson Food Donation Act (1996), otherwise known as the 'Good Samaritan' Act, is perhaps the most famous example of this. The Act works to limit the liabilities to prosecution for food industry and other actors, when donating food in good faith, should anyone consuming the food become ill, and likewise for those organisations who are distributing the food for consumption. Yet, in Australia where similar legislation exists this does not cover situations where the food is sold to consumers, even at a nominal or heavily subsidised price. This is argued to prevent more diverse redistribution responses by social enterprises such as community or social supermarkets and contributes to the dominance of food banking and pantry approaches (Wills, 2017).

In Europe, both the French and Italian governments introduced legislation during 2016 that sought to encourage the supply of surplus food from the food industry for charitable redistribution. French regulation requires that any supermarket with a footprint of 400 m^2 and above must supply safe surplus food nearing its best-before date to foodbanks for onward distribution, otherwise they risk a fine. In turn, the receiving charity must manage the food in ways that protect the food and maintain its integrity. In contrast to the French requirements and its penalty for non-compliance, Italian legislation aimed to encourage the supply of surplus food for consumption by documenting the amounts donated, for which the donor received a corresponding reduction in waste taxes, and which complemented a pre-existing limited liability/Good Samaritan law for corporate donations. These national legislative actions complement existing EU regulations on food donation (see regulations EC/178/2002; EC/852/2004) that require any food exchanged between food businesses to be safe, of good quality, and fully traceable in its supply, whether this exchange is via the market or freely donated. Thus, surplus food under EU law is regulated and subject to the same standards as any other food item and is not legally recognised or managed as waste (Midgley, 2019). Essential to all EU policy actions is the presence of an organisation that is responsible for the food under various food safety laws. However, regulation is argued to lag behind societal and technological innovations with regard to surplus food flows, such as those practised in community fridge sharing organisations (Morrow, 2019).

The protections that the different legislatures have put in place aim to counter the anxiety and concerns as to how donations are managed by receiving organisations. This contrasts with the UK where, other than EU food safety regulations in operation, equivalent efforts have typically been undertaken by some of the larger redistribution organisations who have developed their own 'assurance' guidelines for managing the food they receive, including reproducing audit and inspection, and traceability regimes in their own and receiving charities' practice as part of different ways in which 'trust in the process' of surplus food redistribution is achieved as a way to alleviate various concerns (Midgley, 2014, 2019). This reflects the continuing stance of UK governments in favouring a 'voluntary approach' that encourages the food industry to work with WRAP toward making greater amounts of surplus food available for redistribution rather than this being achieved by legislative intervention, with successive UK parliaments voting against members' bills to introduce requirements for the food industry to donate safe surplus food for redistribution (Midgley, 2014, 2019; Priestley, 2016).

Concluding discussion

This chapter has provided an overview of surplus food generated by food industry practices and the charitable and commercial organisations that, through their redistribution activities, seek to prevent safe, edible food entering the waste system and utilise this food for consumption. The two-fold typology presented above provides a framework for interrogating surplus food and characterises the different redistribution models actors are choosing to work with, discussed alongside critiques of these approaches. The main differences between the brokerage and challenger models are found in the practices that are undertaken during redistribution and the different values and relations that the redistribution process enrols and expresses. Brokerage models have a tendency to obtain and utilise surplus food to support greater food access to those who are food insecure as well as reducing food wastage, whereas challenger models share this motivation but work to embrace more radical political actions and diverse economic practices through redistribution, with redistribution becoming an act of exchange and also political and social encounter.

There is nothing inherent to surplus food as a material that prescribes its consumption as only for the hungry and food insecure, as the challenger models are emphasising. The use of surplus food as a temporary response providing emergency relief to hunger and food insecurity provided by essentially private (for profit or not-for-profit) organisations has now become a more permanent feature of social safety-nets worldwide; this re-allocates both the foodstuff and the responsibility for food security to both industry donors and redistribution actors. Contributing to this process' institutionalisation has been the application of waste/use hierarchies in promoting a ready 'solution' that works with, and hence contributes to the reproduction of, existing food system practices and structural inequalities. This is complemented by additional legal and policy interventions that provide donor protections and embed donation requirements into expected practice.

As such we need to pay attention not just to the surplus food material but also the processes of its redistribution and the diversity of practices this can enrol in different contexts. This chapter has focused on surplus food redistribution within the global North; however, as redistribution initiatives emerge in the global South more attention is needed to explore surplus food and redistribution within these settings. A key part of this will require continued critical engagement as to how diverse social, economic, cultural, technological and political relations and values are reproduced or disrupted by redistribution arrangements.

References

Appadurai, A. (1986) 'Introduction: commodities and the politics of value', in *The Social Life of Things: Commodities in Cultural Perspective*, A. Appadurai (Ed). Cambridge, UK: Cambridge University Press, 5–63.
Baglioni, S., De Pieri, B. and Tallarico, T. (2017) 'Surplus food recovery and food aid: The pivotal role of non-profit organisations, insights from Italy and Germany', *Voluntas* 28: 2032–2052.
Boltanski, L., and Thevenot, L. (1991) *On Justification: Economies of Worth*. Paris: Gallimard.
Bradshaw, C. (2018) 'Waste law and the value of food', *Journal of Environmental Law* 30: 311–331.
Çalişkan, K., and Callon, M. (2010) 'Economization, part 2: A research programme for the study of markets', *Economy and Society* 39: 1–32.
Cloke, P., May, J. and Williams, A. (2017) 'Geographies of food banks in the meantime', *Progress in Human Geography* 41: 703–726.
Committee on Economic, Social and Cultural Rights (CESCR) (1999) *Substantive Issues Arising in the Implementation Of The International Covenant On Economic, Social and Cultural Rights: General Comment 12 (Twentieth Session, 1999), The Right to Adequate Food (Art.11), E/C.12/1999/5*. United Nations Economic and Social Council.
Consumer Goods Forum, CGF (2016) *Food waste: Commitments and achievements of CGF members*. CGF available at https://consumergoodsforum.com. accessed 06 December 2018.
Douglas, M. (2002[1966]) *Purity and Danger*. London: Routledge Classics.
Evans, D. (2012) 'Binning, gifting and recovery: The conduits of disposal in household food consumption', *Environment and Planning D: Society and Space* 30: 1123–1137.

Evans, D. (2018) 'Rethinking material cultures of sustainability: Commodity consumption, cultural biographies and following the thing', *Transaction of the Institute of British Geographers* 43: 110–121.

Garthwaite, K. (2016) 'Stigma, shame and "people like us": An ethnographic study of foodbank use in the UK', *Journal of Poverty and Social Justice* 24: 277–289.

Gibson-Graham, J.K. (2008) 'Diverse economies: Performatives practices for "other worlds"', *Progress in Human Geography* 32: 613–632.

Global FoodBanking Network, GFN (2018) *The state of global food banking 2018: Nourishing the world.* GFN, available at https://foodbanking.org/food-banking-poised-to-play-a-key-role-in-achieving-zerohunger/. accessed 06/12/2018.

Gregson, N., Watkins, H., & Calestani, M. (2013) 'Politicla markets: recycling, economization and marketization', *Economy and Society* 42: 1–25.

Gregson, N., Metcalfe, A., & Crewe, L. (2007) 'Moving things along: The conduits and practices of divestment in consumption', *Transactions of the Institute of British Geographers*, New Series 32: 187–200.

Henderson, G. (2004) '"Free" food, the local production of worth, and the circuit of decommodification: A value theory of surplus', *Environment and Planning D: Society and Space* 22: 485–512.

Hetherington, K. (2004) 'Secondhandedness: consumption, disposal, and absent presence', *Environment and Planning D: Society and Space* 22: 157–173.

Kimura, A.H. (2018) 'Hungry in Japan: Food insecurity and ethical citizenship', *The Journal of Asian Studies* 77: 475–493.

Lambie-Mumford, H. (2013) '"Every town should have one": Emergency food banking in the UK', *Journal of Social Policy*, 42: 73–89.

Lindenbaum, J. (2016) 'Countermovement, neoliberal platoon or re-gifting depot? Understanding decommodification in US food banks', *Antipode* 48: 375–392.

Lohnes, J., and Wilson, B. (2018) 'Bailing out the food banks? Hunger relief, food waste, and crisis in Central Appalachia', *Environment and Planning A* 50: 350–369.

McLaren, D., and Agyeman, J. (2015) *Sharing Cities: A Case for Truly Smart and Sharing Cities.* Cambridge, MA: MIT Press.

Midgley, J. (2019) 'Anticipatory practice and the making of surplus food', *Geoforum* 99: 181–189.

Midgley, J., Jeffries, J., Aitken, D., Dravers, N., & Skinner, M. (2018). A *Recipe for Success? Identifying Social and Community Impacts in the Work of Community Cafés: The Case of Re-f-use Pay as you Feel Café.* End of award project report. Newcastle University, Newcastle upon Tyne.

Midgley, J.L. (2014) 'The logics of surplus food redistribution', *Journal of Environmental Planning and Management* 57: 1872–1892.

Morrow, O. (2019) 'Sharing food and risk in Berlin's urban food commons', *Geoforum* 99: 202–212.

Mourad, M. (2016) 'Recycling, recovering and preventing "food waste": Competing solutions for food systems sustainability in the United States and France', *Journal of Cleaner Production* 126: 461–477.

Munro, R. (1995) 'The disposal of the meal', in *Food Choice and the Consumer*, D Marshall (Ed). London: Blackie Academic and Professional, 313-326.

O'Brien, M. (2011) *A Crisis of Waste? Understanding the Rubbish Society.* London: Routledge.

Papargyropoulou, E., Lozano, R., Steinberger, J., Wright, N., & Bin Ujang, Z. (2014) 'The food waste hierarchy as a framework for the management of food surplus and waste', *Journal of Cleaner Production* 76: 106–115.

Poppendieck, J. (1998) *Sweet Charity: Emergency Food and the End of Entitlement.* London: Penguin Books.

Food Power (2018) *The role of community food retail,* Available at https://sustainweb.org/foodpower. accessed 06/12/2018.

Priestley, S. (2016) *Food waste.* House of Commons Library Briefing paper CBP07552, available at https://parliament.uk/commons-library

Riches, G. (2011) 'Thinking and acting outside the charitable food box: Hunger and the right to food in rich societies', *Development in Practice* 21: 768–775.

Riches, G. (2018) *Food Bank Nations: Poverty, Corporate Charity and the Right to Food.* London: Routledge.

Schneider, F. (2013) 'The evolution of food donation with respect to waste management', *Waste Management* 33: 755–763.

Stuart, T. (2009) *Waste: Uncovering the Global Food Scandal.* London: Penguin.

Swaffield, J., Evans, D., & Welch, D. (2018) 'Profit, reputation and 'doing the right thing': Convention theory and the problem of food waste in the UK retail sector', *Geoforum* 89: 43–59.

Tarasuk, V., and Eakin, J.M. (2005) 'Food assistance through "surplus" food: Insights from an ethnographic study of food bank work', *Agriculture and Human Values* 22: 177–186.

van der Horst, H., Pascucci, S., & Bol, W. (2014) 'The "dark side" of food banks? Exploring emotional responses of food bank receivers in the Netherlands', *British Food Journal* 116: 1506–1520.

Wakefield, S., Fleming, J., Klassen, C., & Skinner, A. (2013) '*Sweet Charity*, revisited: Organizational responses to food insecurity in Hamilton and Toronto, Canada', *Critical Social Policy* 33, 427–450.

Warshawsky, D. (2010) 'New power relations served here: The growth of food banking in Chicago', *Geoforum* 41: 763–775.

Williams, A., Cloke, P., & May, J. (2016) 'Contested space: The contradictory political dynamics of food banking in the UK', *Environment and Planning A* 48: 2291–2316.

Wills, B. (2017) 'Eating at the limits: Barriers to the emergence of social enterprise initiatives in the Australian emergency food relief sector', *Food Policy* 70: 62–70.

Wolch, J. (1990) *The Shadow State: Government and Voluntary Sector in Transition*. New York: The Foundation Centre.

WRAP, The Waste and Resources Action Programme (2018) *Surplus food redistribution in the UK; 2015 to 2017*, information sheet, available at https://wrap.org.uk/content/surplus-food-redistribution-wrap%E2%80%99s-work

22

KEEPING UNAVOIDABLE FOOD WASTE IN THE FOOD CHAIN AS ANIMAL FEED

Martin Bowman, Karen Luyckx and Christina O'Sullivan

Introduction

For thousands of years, humans have fed pigs on food waste, using up leftovers and agricultural by-products and producing pork. It is likely that pig domestication began not through humans actively capturing them, but when pigs entered human settlements to forage (Nelson and Archaeology 1998). Pigs' appetites cleared away everything from kitchen food waste to animal viscera and human excrement, preventing what would otherwise have created a breeding ground for rodents, insects and diseases – pigs converted this into manure fertiliser and meat (Sauer 1972; Nemeth 1995). Sometimes, recycling waste was the primary reason for their cultivation (Nemeth 1995). When pigs were not reared in woodlands on acorns and nuts, in more agricultural and industrial areas, they were primarily fed on leftovers and by-products from the human food chain. For most of human history, these were the primary ways of feedings pigs, with other diets being economically unviable.

A shift came in the nineteenth century when the price of cereals in the US dropped so low that it started to make economic sense to feed them to pigs, and from this point onward in the US and Europe pigs were increasingly reared on cheap grains. However, a return to using food waste feeds was made in times of scarcity such as the World Wars of the twentieth century. During the Second World War, King George VI and the UK government backed the newly created Small Pig Keeper's Council, which encouraged communities to share pigs in 'pig clubs' and collect kitchen swill to feed them as a 'national service' (Stuart 2009, p. 247). The practice has since slowly declined in modern pig farming and was completely ended in Europe with the introduction of a ban on the feeding to all livestock of meat-containing food waste following the UK Foot and Mouth Disease (FMD) outbreak in 2001. However, the backyard pig globally continues to be fed on leftovers. And in response to a lack of landfill for food waste and the soaring cost of imported feed ingredients, Japan and South Korea now have industrial treatment plants delivering food waste-based feed to commercial pig farms. In this chapter we explore how bringing the practice of feeding of food waste to livestock into the twenty-first century can help us respond to certain urgent challenges posed to the environment by our food system and consumption patterns.

Livestock farming and food waste: two challenges to tackle in creating a sustainable food system

Currently, the richest 10% of people in terms of income globally are responsible for almost half of global lifestyle consumption emissions (Oxfam 2015). This inequality extends to food – if every country in the world adopted the UK's 2011 average diet and meat consumption, 95% of global habitable land area would be needed for agriculture – up from 50% of land currently used (Ritchie and Roser 2017). Currently, 36% of calories produced by the world's harvested crops are being used as animal feed, but only 12% of those calories makes it to human consumption in the form of meat and dairy (Cassidy et al. 2013). Moreover, livestock production occupies approximately 75% of agricultural land (Foley et al. 2011) and is growing rapidly. The livestock industry is responsible for 14.5% of global emissions factoring in land use change impacts (Gerber and FAO 2013, p. 14), and if dramatic action is not taken, greenhouse gases (GHGs) from the food system are projected to constitute more than half of the total GHG emissions associated with human activities by 2050 (Bajželj 2014). As nine billion people are expected on the planet, and the three billion people set to enter the global middle classes by 2050 (WWF 2017, p. 7) are likely to increase their consumption of animal-based food, tackling the dietary question is a global priority.

Feed is responsible for a substantial proportion of meat's environmental impact, especially in the case of omnivorous non-ruminant livestock such as pigs and chickens which rely on soya, fish meal and feed grains. For example, in the UK, feed contributes 78% of the total carbon footprint of pork production (Fry and Kingston 2009, pp. 1–2). It is essential to both reduce the scale of meat production and consumption, and to reduce the environmental impact of the meat that is produced. Meanwhile, the production of food that is wasted uses up 1.4 billion hectares of land – 28% of the world's agricultural area (FAO 2013b, p. 6). This is the equivalent to the land area of China and India combined. The FAO estimate that global food waste accounts for 8% of total anthropogenic GHG emissions, nearly as much as global road transport emissions (FAO 2013a). A recent study 'Drawdown' concluded that global reduction of food waste was the third most important action that could be taken to reduce global carbon emissions (Project Drawdown 2017).

Turning food waste into animal feed falls at the intersection of two key challenges: reducing the environmental impact of meat production and reducing food waste. The UN estimates that enough grain could be freed to feed an extra three billion people if all livestock globally was fed with surplus and by-products of the food industry (UNEP 2009). McKinsey Global Institute estimate that the alleviation on land, water, fossil fuels and other resources created by resource efficiency, including food waste reduction, would lead to lower and less-volatile food prices (Dobbs et al. 2011, p. 11). Cutting food and agricultural waste by half could reduce the area of global cropland by around 14% and GHG emissions by 22–28% compared to a scenario achieving optimal yields through sustainable intensification alone. Adding healthy diets – with a significant reduction in energy-rich foods such as sugars and saturated fats, including livestock products – to a scenario of reduced waste and optimal yields, would lead to a further reduction in the area necessary for cropping by an estimated 5%, pasture by 25% and the total GHG emissions by 45% (Bajželj 2014).

Replacing even small quantities of conventional livestock feed with surplus food could lead to significant carbon savings. One study found that switching 10% of total broiler chicken feed in Europe alone to a food waste mix which includes leftover pumpkins, mushrooms and yoghurt, could lead to a total avoidance of 6.2 million Metric tonnes of CO_2 emissions to the atmosphere annually (Gillman 2018). A similar adoption of food surplus as part of livestock feed globally could lead to a 'reduction of natural land transformation by 30% and agricultural land occupation by 12%' (Gillman 2018). Certain by-products from agriculture and manufacturing, such as brewers' grains, wheat grain unsuitable for bread flour and whey, are already routinely used in animal feed. The former foodstuff processing industry in Europe transforms an estimated 5 million tonnes of leftover bread and other cereal and confectionary goods into feed ingredients (EFFPA 2018). However, as will be discussed below, there is significant additional potential for keeping food waste in the supply chain as animal feed.

Animal feed in the food use hierarchy

There has been a growing international consensus that a 'food use hierarchy' is needed to prioritise the most environmentally preferable destinations for food that is currently wasted. WRAP's hierarchy is commonly used (see Figure 22.1).

A more comprehensive list of food waste destinations is provided in the Food Loss and Waste Standard (Hanson et al. 2017, p. 37). All use of surplus food as animal feed should occur within the framework of this food use hierarchy, so only food that is not edible for humans or is difficult to prevent from occurring in the first place, should be sent to animal feed. However, compared to anaerobic digestion or composting, using surplus food as animal feed scores better on 12 out of 14 environmental (e.g. eutrophi-cation, eco-toxicity) and health (e.g. carcinogens) indicators (adapted from Salemdeeb et al. 2017; see Figure 22.2).

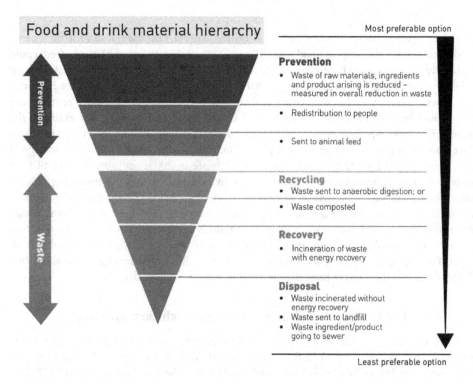

Figure 22.1 Food use hierarchy.
Source: WRAP (2014).

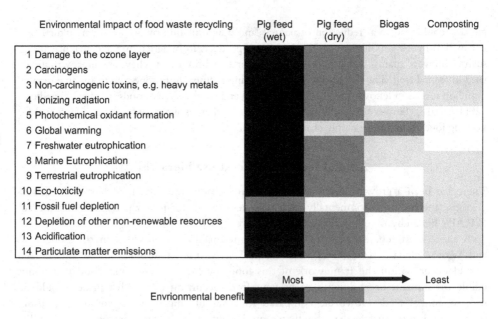

Figure 22.2 Environmental impact of food waste recycling.
Source: Salemdeeb et al. (2017).

The calculations in the study were based on the current UK energy mix for the energy needed to render the surplus food safe. If more renewable energy was used, feed could potentially beat biogas and compost on all indicators. This suggests that policy makers need to be sensitive to regional specifics (Evans 2013, p. 53), while still incentivising the hierarchy as a general guide. Governments could analyse which combination of fiscal incentives and taxes would be most effective at moving food up the food use hierarchy. For example, the charges for disposing food waste introduced by the Japanese Food Recycling Law have played an important role in encouraging the food industry to send its leftovers to animal feed. South Korea banned the landfilling of food waste in 2005, and now 45% of all food waste is treated for animal feeding, another 45% by composting, and the remaining 10% by other alternatives such as anaerobic digestion (Kim et al. 2011). However, it is important that incentives do not have perverse effects. In the case of Europe, food waste that is avoidable or suitable for redistribution to people or animals has been drawn down the food use hierarchy to anaerobic digestion (AD) due to the incentives to this sector (Wunder *et al.* 2018). For example, the latest food waste data of the UK's largest retailer Tesco show that 19,898 tonnes of food fit for human consumption went to AD in 2017/18.

The environmental impact of pig and chicken farming

In 2013, pig meat was the most consumed meat globally, at an average 16 kg per capita per year, closely followed by 15 kg for poultry meat (Ritchie and Roser 2017). The most dramatic rise comes from China, which produced nearly half of the world's pork by 2017 (TRASE 2018b). China's demand for animal feed has skyrocketed in line with this – exports of soy from Brazil to China have risen by 300% over the last decade, now making up two-thirds of Brazil's soy exports and accounting for half of the total deforestation risk associated with Brazilian soy exports (TRASE 2018b). Meanwhile, China's annual food waste is estimated to be 195 million tonnes (Mo et al. 2017, p. 638).

Pigs globally contribute an estimated 668 million tonnes CO_2eq of emissions, and chickens contributed 612 million tonnes CO_2eq (Müller and Mottet 2017). Land used to grow pigfeed globally amounts to a total of 94 million hectares, of which 45.1 million hectares is cereal grains and 39 million hectares is oil seed and oil seed cakes (Müller and Mottet 2017). Ninety-seven per cent of global soya production (Steinfeld et al. 2006), and 74% of maize (Cassidy et al. 2013, p. 4) are used as animal feed. Over the past 50 years, production of soy has increased faster than any other crop, from 27 million tonnes to 269 million tonnes, and the UN Food and Agriculture Organization predicts that global soy production may reach 515 million tonnes by 2050 (WWF 2017, p. 10).

Of meat produced in EU countries, broiler chickens have the highest soya content at 1,089 g per kg, pork contains 508 g/kg and beef contains 456 g/kg (Kroes and Kuepper 2015, p. 12). As omnivores, pigs and chickens need high-protein diets and with meat-containing food waste currently off the menu, soya is the next best source of protein. Dou et al. (2018) reviewed 23 studies for nutritional components in consumption-stage food waste and found an average protein content of 19.2% (Dou et al. 2018) which is sufficient for growing and finishing pigs (Edwards 2002). While technology in the Japanese system is making great progress in homogenising the nutritional content of food waste-based feeds, more research is necessary to deal with the inevitably variable nutritional content of food waste and for the modern pig it may be necessary to provide a mix of conventional and food waste-based feed.

Even so, the protein content of food waste-based feeds is promising in terms of reducing the demand for land to grow soya. With South America still by far the largest soy producer in the world, this in turn would reduce pressures on highly biodiverse areas such as the Gran Chaco region in Argentina, which has lost 22% of its forests between 1990 and 2015, primarily for soybean farming and cattle ranching, resulting in over 3 billion tonnes of CO_2 emissions (Mighty Earth et al. 2018, p. 5). Efforts to tackle deforestation, such as the Brazilian Soy Moratorium and 'Cerrado Manifesto', currently focus on the Amazon and Cerrado in Brazil, and provide perverse incentives for big feed companies like Bunge and Cargill to shift deforestation to frontiers such as Argentina and Paraguay (Mighty Earth et al. 2018, p. 14).

However, being in the global spotlight has not stopped deforestation in Brazil either. In May 2018, five traders and multiple soy farmers were fined a total of US $29 million by the Brazilian government for soybean cultivation and purchasing that is connected to illegal deforestation (Byrne 2018). Two of the five companies fined – Cargill and Bunge – are among the top five soy exporters from Brazil, and some of the few companies that have adopted zero deforestation commitments. The fine demonstrates the vulnerability of the companies' systems and the fact that they cannot guarantee that their sources are deforestation free (Vasconcelos and Burley 2018). The TRASE tool highlights the continued risk faced by soy traders regarding supply chain deforestation risk (TRASE 2018a). Perhaps the starkest indication that sustainable sourcing schemes are not enough is that in 2017 an area the size of Italy was deforested, the second highest area deforested since records began in 2001 – the most deforestation occurred in 2016 (Carrington et al. 2018).

Efforts have been made to reduce soy use in feeds and replace them with other sources of protein, but these are not always environmentally beneficial. For instance, rapeseed feeds are often a by-product of biodiesel made from rapeseed, which emits roughly 20% more CO_2 than diesel or petrol (Herman et al. 2016, p. 7), while encroaching on agricultural land. Using insects as animal feed has been a much-touted development, and forms part of the solution. However, according to a key Life Cycle Assessment (van Zanten et al. 2015), using larvae meal as animal feed results in decreased land use but increased global warming potential and energy use, mostly because of the additional energy needed for growing and processing the larvae. The environmental benefits of feeding food waste to insects and feeding these insects to livestock depend on what is fed to insects. If food waste is fresh and nutritious to feed to livestock directly, then this is the preferable option. Viruses that affect humans and farm animals can survive in insects (EFSA Scientific Committee 2015), so feeds for insects containing meat would need to be heat-treated as discussed below.

The EU ban

In Europe, any discussion of what can be safely fed to pigs must take into consideration the need to avoid a disease outbreak like the 2001 FMD epidemic, which cost the UK economy alone £8 billion and led to the slaughter of over six million animals (Bourn 2002). The experience was traumatic to the farming community, and images of burning animals shocked the public. The UK countryside was closed off to prevent spread of the disease, and the UK military were deployed to help with containment (Anderson 2002, p. 82). The FMD outbreak was sourced back to the illegal feeding of untreated food waste on a pig farm. While in hindsight it appears that the outbreak could have been significantly more limited if swifter livestock movement restrictions and mass vaccination had been deployed (Anderson 2002; European Commission 2001), the immediate ban on feeding food waste, treated or not, was understandable because of the need to send a strong signal to farmers and the public that an outbreak would never occur again. The EU swiftly followed the UK in banning the feeding of animal protein and kitchen leftovers to livestock, including omnivorous livestock.

However, the real problem was not feed, but the poorly designed regulatory framework and lax enforcement. Extremely unhygienic conditions had been found for years during inspections of the farm where the outbreak is thought to have started, but the inspector only offered informal warnings and did not report the problem or conduct more thorough inspections (Parliamentary and Health Service Ombudsman, 2007, pp. 35–36). The UK experience shows that to reintroduce meat-containing food surplus in feed for omnivorous livestock, we need a robustly regulated system that can be properly enforced, but the environmental and economic benefits of doing so outweigh the costs. As a result of the European bans on feeding animal protein and catering food waste to livestock, a deficiency in animal feed protein was created equivalent to 2.9 million tonnes of soymeal and EU imports of soymeal increased by 3 million tonnes between 2001 and 2003 (Steinfeld et al. 2006, p. 50). Many other countries followed suit, such as Australia (Department of Primary Industries and Regions 2018).

The backyard pig globally and the unregulated feeding of food waste

Globally, most pig farmers are very small in scale. About half of the 770 million people surviving on less than USD 1.90 per day depend directly on livestock for their livelihoods (FAO 2018b, p. 4). Backyard pig farms (farms with under 50 pigs) are mainly concentrated in Europe, China and South East Asia, with very low concentrations comparatively in India, most of Russia, the Middle East and Africa (FAO 2018a, p. 3). In China, the proportion of Chinese pig farming made up of backyard farms (1–49 pigs per farm) has declined dramatically from 74% in 2000 to 27% in 2015 (FAO 2018a, p. 7), but the numbers are still high due to the scale and growth of Chinese pork production. Chinese farmers generally treat food waste on-farm by boiling it for an hour first (Wang et al. 2015, p. 16). However, in Chinese rural areas, pigs are often raised in backyards in poor hygienic conditions, and in some mountainous regions pigs are often kept in open areas exposed to rodents and wildlife and fed on untreated waste products or animal carcasses, leading to high risks of disease transmission (Cui et al. 2006, p. 23).

India, due in part to its low meat consumption, has only 0.97% of the world's pig population (Kumar et al. 2016), and its concentration of backyard pigs is very low across the whole country (FAO 2018a, p. 3). Feed costs are approximately 70% of total production costs in India, leading to research interest in food waste feeds as a lower cost alternative (Kumar et al. 2016; Ravi 2017; Saikia and Bhar, no date). These studies all found neutral or positive effects of food waste feeds on pig growth – Saikia and Bhar in particular found a food waste diet was more nutritious, yielded greater pig growth and was lower cost than standard feed rations. However, these studies do not seem to acknowledge the need to heat-treat food waste to kill pathogens. One study fed raw kitchen waste to pigs (Gagrai et al. 2014), illustrating that this is legal in India, though the study found considerably less bacteria in cooked kitchen food waste. In 2012, Municipal Solid Waste Park in North West India kept livestock as recycling agents, with the pigs charged with eating food waste from hotels (*No Tech Magazine* 2014).

In many other countries, there is still little or no regulation of feeding food waste to pigs. In Brazil, farmers in one study were found to be collecting food waste from restaurants and fruit and vegetable stores in a local town, and feeding it to their pigs and chickens, often after boiling it (but not always), with no safety regulations from the Brazilian authorities (Fehr 2014, p. 37). In Kenya, some farmers collect food waste from garbage sites in urban centres to feed to their pigs – often separating it out, drying it, or boiling it first (Wambui 2017). Although some have spoken out about this practice as conducive to disease (Wambui 2017), it appears this practice is not illegal in Kenya. Backyard pig keeping is not just a phenomenon of the global South. In the UK for instance, there are 30,000 premises with pigs, including those with pet pigs, even though 92% of pork production comes from about 1,600 farms (AHDB Pork 2018). There are clear risks associated with small-scale livestock farming in terms of disease. For example, researchers have pointed to the role of poor small-scale pig farmers in the spread of African Swine Fever (ASF) in countries such as Mozambique, Nigeria and Russia as they practise emergency sales of their animals as soon as they suspect disease (Costard et al. 2015).

It is therefore important to consider smallholder pig farming in further research on the safe feeding of food waste to pigs. In addition to the challenges regarding disease risk as mentioned above, such research should also consider the positive aspects of small-scale livestock farming. Livestock can soak up and add value to agricultural by-products; they can avoid gluts going to waste. And omnivorous livestock such as pigs and chickens can turn kitchen leftovers into meat and eggs. Moreover, small-scale agroecological approaches are paramount when designing a sustainable food system that can feed the growing global population (Altieri 2009; Pretty et al. 2006).

While small-scale livestock farming may have its particular risks, it is important to note that highly concentrated large numbers of animals found in large-scale intensive farming are more susceptible to infection and increase the risk of emergence of more virulent disease strains (Garner et al. 2006; Mennerat et al. 2010; Jones et al. 2013). In contrast, village pig production may result in virus fitness loss and manifest as lower virulence viruses (Drew 2011). The high density and almost clonal nature of pig genetics can provide a 'monoculture' environment detrimental to natural resistance to pathogens and which may lead to explosive outbreaks of novel disease (Drew 2011, p. 101). There are also growing concerns about the erosion of genetic resources in livestock (Ajmone-Marsan 2010), because animal genetic diversity is critical for food security and rural development. Through the maintenance of rare breeds, smallholders play a crucial role in protecting global food security (RBST 2018), as this maintains genetic diversity, allowing farmers to select stock or develop new breeds in response to changing conditions, including climate change and new or resurgent disease threats (Hoffmann 2010).

In the US, a family farm can directly supplement the diet of its pigs with its own kitchen scraps, including those that contain unprocessed meat, without first undergoing the SHPA boiling procedure (US Department of Agriculture 2009; Leib et al. 2016). Given risks such as the presence of ASF in Europe, we believe that it will not be possible to have such an exemption in Europe. Risk management at the smallholder level will need to be proportionate to the scale of risk. For example, in their discussion on farm scale, disease epidemics and antibiotic resistance, (Gilchrist et al. 2007) consider 'a definable, small farm size with minimal numbers of animals' less risky in terms of disease prevention (p. 315). At the same time, countries would need to consider the proximity of farms of different sizes and the potential airborne spread of FMD and ASF.

Modern pig farming and use of food waste

Various countries around the world allow food waste to be fed to livestock following treatment to kill off pathogens. Catering and retail food surplus is fed to non-ruminants, especially pigs, in Japan and South Korea. In Japan, any by-products and former foodstuffs containing Animal Origin Protein, and all catering and kitchen waste, must undergo heat treatment to inactivate pathogens (30 minutes or more at 70 °C or for three minutes or more at 80 °C) (MAFF 2006). While Japanese legislation permits on-farm treatment, feed production from food waste is now mostly industrial in nature with 360 eco-feed producers, of which 47 process surplus from retailers and 29 specialise in the processing of meat-containing surplus food (Japan Ministry of Agriculture, Forestry and Fisheries 2018).

In the US the practice is permitted in about half of the states (Leib et al. 2016) but surplus must be heated throughout at boiling temperature (212 °F or 100 °C at sea level) for 30 minutes before being fed to swine (US Department of Agriculture 2009). New Zealand allows food waste containing meat to be fed to pigs if it has first been heated to 100 °C for one hour (New Zealand Legislation 2005). In South Africa it is legal to feed swill to pigs only if it is boiled for an hour or sterilised first (Den Hartigh 2016). In South Korea, there are currently strict regulations on treatment processes, registration and certification to ensure compliance (Dou et al. 2018).

In China, the practice of feeding raw swill to livestock including pigs was banned by the Chinese government in 2006, which outlawed feeding 'slops from restaurants or dining rooms without high-temperature processing' or raising 'livestock and poultry at dumping grounds or feed[ing] them with the substances dumped at such grounds' (People's Republic of China 2006, Article 43). Various methods are currently used to treat food waste in China, including aerobic fermentation, heat treatment and combined hydrothermic treatment and fermentation (Wang et al. 2015, p. 15), with the products sent to gas for energy, fertiliser and animal feed. The risks from feeding untreated food waste to pigs are still a problem in China, showing that regulation is inadequately enforced. One study found that the prevalence of Hepatitis E was higher in pigs fed on kitchen residue than on pigs fed on complete feed in China (Xiao et al. 2012) and incidence of swine trichinellosis in China is mainly caused by pigs fed with raw swill (Cui et al. 2006). While enforcing regulations to ensure the safe feeding of food waste by small-scale producers remains challenging, inspections of a growing urban food-to-feed processing industry is more feasible (Wang et al. 2015).

Using food waste as feed safely

Pigs face threats from numerous diseases globally, various of which can be spread through the feeding of contaminated food waste. ASF affects pigs and wild boar and can remain active for over four months in some meats and for years in frozen carcasses. The presence of ASF has been a concern in Eastern Europe for years, with wild boar eating untreated food waste as a cause of transmission. ASF has also recently appeared in wild boar in Belgium and on pig farms in China. As mentioned earlier, the illegal feeding of untreated food waste was the cause of the UK 2001 Foot and Mouth epidemic.

However, it is possible to produce safe feed from surplus food through heat treatment, potentially complemented with acidification (Luyckx 2018). While import controls are important to prevent illegal imports of contaminated meat (Hayrapetyan et al. 2017), we have to assume some illegal imports may happen and thus treatment has to be effective. For instance, heating meat to a minimum core temperature of 70 °C for at least 30 minutes inactivates the FMD virus, as does bringing the acidity below pH6 through fermentation or adding lactic acid for example (commercial yoghurt has a pH of 4.5) (OIE 2013b). ASF is inactivated if kept over 60 °C for 20 minutes (OIE 2013a). A more extensive list of diseases and how they can be inactivated can be found in Luyckx (2018).

In addition to the need for effective treatment, it is important to manage the risks from potential errors in transport, storage or manufacturing that could allow for the re-introduction of pathogens through cross-contamination between treated and untreated product (Adkin et al. 2014). Sound system design is key to prevent cross-contamination using 'biosecurity measures and proven logistical and Hazard Analysis and Critical Control Point measures for segregation in storage and transport' such as zoning, one directional process flows and dedicated sealed storage (Luyckx 2018, p. 4). Furthermore, given the challenge of monitoring on-farm biosecurity, in certain contexts it will be necessary to limit the production of feed from surplus food to licensed treatment plants that are located separately from any farm premises and can be inspected relatively easily. Additional risks such as plastics or dioxins must be managed as is done in the existing feed industry, such as the legislation on mycotoxin and dioxin testing in feedstuffs (Walker 2017). In Japan, many facilities use barcoding to track surplus food collection and input into food waste treatment plants, which could be replicated globally.

An additional animal health risk faced by livestock are transmissible spongiform encephalopathies or prion diseases. However, 'no scientific evidence exists to demonstrate the natural occurrence of Transmissible Spongiform Encephalopathy ("TSE") in farmed pigs, poultry and fish, which may create a basis for an intra-species progression of a TSE infection due to intra-species recycling' (EC Scientific Steering Committee 1999, section 3.4.A; European Food Safety Authority 2007). Scientists have done very thorough research to establish whether pigs can contract TSE but have found 'no infectivity' (Wells 2003). However, although the known risks are minimal, robust disease monitoring systems are needed to be vigilant of 'unknown unknowns' (Luyckx 2018, p. 6).

Feeding pigs catering food waste or feeds containing meat could lead to pigs eating surplus food feeds which might contain pork scraps. The Japanese and US models do not have an intra-species recycling ban for non-ruminants which means that traces of pork may be found in some of the treated feed. Processed proteins of porcine origin are also permitted in pig feed in New Zealand and Australia. Animals eating feed that contains traces of meat from their own species are at increased risk of contracting diseases that can be caught within their species – for this reason it is especially important that pathogens be inactivated through treatment and measures be in place to prevent cross-contamination. It is also essential to ensure strict segregation between ruminant and non-ruminant feed, as currently legislated in Japan (Ministry of Agriculture, Forestry and Fisheries (MAFF), Japan 2003).

Ethically, we must do all we can to prevent stress-induced forms of cannibalism such as the savaging of piglets by first litter gilts (young female pigs), which may account for up to 3% of piglet mortality (NADIS 2018; The Pig Site 2018), and tail- and ear-biting. The feeding of meat-containing surplus food could contribute to a reduction in these stress-induced behaviours (see below). Moreover, zoologist Bill Schutt has brought together evidence on the evolutionary and biological role of intra-species recycling, showing that in many cases it is perfectly natural (Schutt 2017). Similarly, pig nutritionists and animal welfare specialists consulted by Luyckx and Bowman (2018) see no concern from an animal welfare or health perspective, provided heat treatment and biosecurity measures are applied to inactivate pathogens. However, common-sense measures could be taken to reduce the proportion of pork that goes into pigfeed, for example by ensuring that the processed animal proteins from single-species rendering plants go to other species (i.e. chicken to pig and vice versa). It might be desirable to treat surplus food in plants dedicated to specific species.

In addition to the control of feed manufacturers, adequate and regular inspections of farms to ensure safety are also important. For instance a survey of 313 smallholder farms in the UK found that 24% of smallholders fed uncooked household food waste to their pigs, despite the ban (Gillespie et al. 2015). Existing farm inspections – for instance, for animal welfare standards – could be adapted to include checks that the farm is not feeding untreated unlicensed food waste to pigs, and to check risks of cross-contamination. Finally, governments and industry bodies should clearly communicate the requirement that only meat-containing surplus food that has been heat-treated can be fed to pigs and chickens.

Treatment and feeding models

An excellent example of a circular food-to-feed-to-food model is the Odakyu Food Ecology Centre. The Odakyu Group is a Japanese company operating a chain of department stores, hotels, restaurants and rail transport. They deliver unused food from their supermarkets, restaurants and train lines (including meat products), but not from households, to the Food Ecology Centre factory to be turned into pig feed, and they buy back the pork to sell as a premium-quality eco-product in their own stores. Currently, the Japan Food Ecology Centre (JFEC) take in 35 tonnes of surplus food per day, mostly from food-processing and retail, and produce 40 tonnes per day of eco-feed (JFEC 2015; Takahashi 2018). Due to the high disposal costs for surplus food introduced with the Food Recycling Law, JFEC can charge customers for disposal of their unused food. JFEC receives no capital assistance from the government, although their customers and suppliers may receive some subsidies for involvement in eco-feed.

Supermarket unused food is separated before it gets to the factory. When the bins arrive at the factory, the bins' barcodes are scanned and weighed to record the surplus food composition and ensure traceability. Some of the favourite foods for the pigs are rice, bread, noodles, cooking scraps, delicatessen, vegetables, tofu, milk, fruit and used tea leaves. The surplus food is then checked for contamination (less than 0.1% of the mix is likely to be non-food, e.g. plastic bags) and the food is broken up using a power hose. Surplus food waste is heated to 80 °C in 10 metric tonnes tanks, then cooled to 40 °C. Lactic acid fermentation is used for approximately six to eight hours, with a pH between 3.7–4.2, using formic acid and lactobacillus (a bacterium like that used to turn milk into yoghurt, and the same bacteria used in Yakult), which preserves the liquid feed and enhances its nutritional value. This process also inactivates disease pathogens of concern, including ASF and FMD.

Farmers can feed their pigs 100% eco-feed because JFEC can guarantee a protein content of 15 to 17% through computerised composition monitoring and the addition of a very small amount of soya (about 1% of total feed) as well as some synthetic lysine and calcium-vitamin premix. The resultant liquid feed is about 20% dry matter and has a shelf-life of about 10–14 days at room temperature. Finally, the feed is sold at half the cost of conventional feed, to around 15 medium-sized pig farmers (300 to 2,000 pigs each) within 150 km of the plant. Farmers can sell their pork at a premium as consumers appreciate the environmental value of the product (Kurishima et al. 2011). The pork is sold under a green label as 'Yoghurt-pig' which claims to have '10% more unsaturated fatty acids and 20% less cholesterol' and be 'tender, delicious, and juicy' (Stuart 2009, pp. 278–281).

Economic and welfare benefits

In December 2016, feed costs in 14 EU pig-producing countries made up between 50% and 67% of total production costs, and 65% of total production costs in the US (AHDB 2018). More widely in Europe, high volatility in feed prices has forced many pig farmers out of business (EUROSTAT 2017). Net margins for the UK pig industry between 2007–2017 ranged from a net £10/head loss to an £18/head profit in different years (AHDB 2017, p. 11). In Japan, however, industrial food-to-feed recycling plants deliver surplus food-based feed at half the cost of conventional feed (Takahashi et al. 2012, p. 36). The use of surplus food as animal feed has consistently grown in both Japan and South Korea; by 125% in Japan from 2003–2013, and by 35% in South Korea from 2001–2006 (Ermgassen et al. 2016, p. 39). In Japan, food wastes made up 5.8% of all concentrate animal feed in 2013 (Ermgassen et al. 2016, p. 42) and 52% of surplus from the Japanese food industry is now used as livestock feed (FAO 2017, p. 6). Japanese consumers choose to pay a premium for meat products they see as healthier and more environmentally friendly (Kurishima et al. 2011).

Reducing feed costs may help farmers avoid conditions associated with factory farming by investing in animal welfare. Factors associated with factory farming, such as high stocking density, a barren environment and absence of bedding and straw for rooting, are animal welfare risks associated with tail biting (European Food Safety Authority (EFSA) 2007). Moreover, feeding surplus food to pigs may improve animal welfare directly. Deficiencies of essential amino acids may exacerbate tail biting in fattening pigs, and deprivation of feeding behaviour, even when nutritional needs are met, may also contribute to tail biting in pigs (Manteca et al. 2008, p. 230). While tail biting is triggered by many variables, in certain situations it may be possible to contribute to a reduction in tail biting by replacing conventional feed with heat-treated leftovers that contain meat, allowing pigs to return to the type of diet they have evolved to eat as omnivores. Feeds made from surplus food could provide the additional food types required for a high welfare score in the foraging category for welfare outcome assessments in UK pig farm assurance schemes (Mullan et al. 2011).

Finally, reducing feed cost pressures may support farmers wishing to invest in reducing the levels of antibiotics required on UK pig farms, as would investment in alternatives such as probiotics. By 2050, drug-resistant infections are expected to cause 10 million deaths annually – becoming a bigger killer than cancer is today (Review on Anti-Microbial Resistance 2014, p. 5). Moreover, 'fermented liquid feed may strengthen the role of the stomach as the first line of defence against possible pathogenic infections by lowering the pH in the gastrointestinal tract' (Missotten et al. 2015) and can reduce coliform levels in the lower gut (Brooks et al. 2001).

Food businesses generating food waste may also benefit. For example, MGM Grand Buffet in Las Vegas in the US 'increased its food recovery amounts from 3,350 tons in 2007 to over 14,000 tons in 2011 while saving between $6,000 and $8,000 per month. Through partnerships with a local farm, these food scraps helped feed 3,000 pigs' (Leib et al. 2016).

The way forward

In the UK alone, 2.5 million tonnes of food surplus from UK manufacturing, retail and commercial catering currently leaving the food supply chain could potentially be fed to pigs – 20% of the UK's total estimated food waste (Luyckx and Bowman 2018). If the EU ban on feeding meat-containing food waste to omnivorous livestock were lifted, and heat-treated surplus food was recycled into animal feed at rates similar to Japan, we could see a 21.5% reduction in the current land use of large-scale EU pork production, saving an area of global agricultural land the size of Wales. There would also be an estimated reduction of up to 268,000 hectares of soybean production (Ermgassen et al. 2016, p. 37). In the most in-depth review of evidence to date, Feedback with other partners have recently produced detailed research for EU project REFRESH showing the considerable environmental benefits of feeding surplus food to pigs, and its feasibility from a nutritional, economic and safety perspective (Luyckx et al. 2019). The implications for the global food system are clearly extensive.

In the UK, where the ban began and memories of the 2001 FMD outbreak would perhaps be most vivid in Europe, there are encouraging signs of change. A recent survey of the pig farming industry 'found strong support (>75%) for the relegalisation of swill among both pig farmers and other stakeholders' (Zu Ermgassen et al. 2018, p. 1), provided disease risk was adequately managed. Feedback issued a survey of the UK public in 2018 which found that 93% of the survey respondents were in favour of relegalisation, and 94% of meat-eating respondents said they would buy pork from pigs fed on food waste, after it has been heat-treated to make it safe (Luyckx et al. 2019). The UK National Pig Association, who have thoroughly opposed any change in legislation until recently, said in 2018 that they are 'actively debating the question of whether we could begin feeding heat treated food waste to pigs again' (Driver 2018).

The time may be ripe for a revolution in how we feed livestock. The best use of unavoidable surplus food and by-products that cannot be redistributed for human consumption is livestock feed. We have the technology to significantly increase the safe use of food waste in feed, simultaneously reducing the environmental impact of both food waste and meat production.

References

Adkin, A., Harris, D. C., Reaney, S., Dewé, T., Hill, A., Crooke, H., Drew, T. and Kelly, L. (2014) *Assessment of risk management measures to reduce the exotic disease risk from the feeding of processed catering waste and certain other food waste to non-ruminants (Version 2.7)*. London: Department of Epidemiological Science, Animal & Plant Health Agency, Department for Environment, Food and Rural Affairs (DEFRA) Accessed. Available at http://randd.defra.gov.uk/Default.aspx.

AHDB (2017) *2016 Pig cost of production in selected countries*. AHDB Pork. Available at: https://pork.ahdb.org.uk/media/274535/2016-pig-cost-of-production-in-selected-countries.pdf (Accessed: 8 May 2018).

AHDB (2018) 'EU Cost of Production - Estimates of the current cost of pig meat production in various countries', *Accessed*. Available at: http://pork.ahdb.org.uk/prices-stats/costings-herd-performance/eu-cost-of-production/.

Ajmone-Marsan, P. (2010) 'A global view of livestock biodiversity and conservation'. *Animal Genetics*, 41, pp. 1–5.

Altieri, M. A. (2009) 'Agroecology, Small Farms, and Food Sovereignty'. *Monthly Review*, 61(3), p. 102, doi: 10.14452/MR-061-03-2009-07_8.

Anderson, I. (2002) *Foot and Mouth Disease 2001: Lessons to be Learned Inquiry Report for the British Prime Minister and the Secretary of State for Environment, Food and Rural Affairs*. Available at: https://webarc hive.nationalarchives.gov.uk/20100809105008/http://archive.cabinetoffice.gov.uk/fmd/fmd_re port/report/index.htm.

Bajželj, B. (2014) 'Importance of food-demand management for climate mitigation'. *Nature Climate Change*, 4, pp. 924–929.

Bourn, J. (2002) *The 2001 outbreak of foot and mouth disease: report by the Comptroller and Auditor-General*. London: National Audit Office Accessed. Available at https://nao.org.uk/wp-content/uploads/2002/06/0102939.pdf.

Brooks, P. H., Beal, J. D. and Niven, S. (2001) 'Liquid feeding of pigs: potential for reducing environmental impact and for improving productivity and food safety'. *Recent Advances in Animal Nutrition in Australia*, 13, p. 16.

Byrne, J. (2018) 'Traders, farmers fined over links to deforestation in Cerrado', *feednavigator.com*, 24 May. Available at: https://feednavigator.com/Article/2018/05/24/Traders-farmers-fined-over-links-to-deforestation-in-Cerrado (Accessed: 20 June 2018).

Carrington, D., Kommenda, N., Gutiérrez, P., Levett, C., Carrington, D., Kommenda, N., Gutiérrez, P. and Levett, C. (2018) 'One football pitch of forest lost every second in 2017, data reveals', *The Guardian*, 27 June. Available at: https://theguardian.com/environment/ng-interactive/2018/jun/27/one-foot ball-pitch-of-forest-lost-every-second-in-2017-data-reveals (Accessed: 3 September 2018).

Cassidy, E. S., West, P. C., Gerber, J. S. and Foley, J. A. (2013) 'Redefining agricultural yields: from tonnes to people nourished per hectare'. *Environmental Research Letters*, 8(3), p. 034015, doi: 10.1088/1748-9326/8/3/034015.

Costard, S., Zagmutt, F. J., Porphyre, T. and Pfeiffer, D. U. (2015) 'Small-scale pig farmers' behavior, silent release of African swine fever virus and consequences for disease spread'. *Scientific Reports*, 5, p. 17074, doi: 10.1038/srep17074.

Cui, J., Wang, Z. and Hu, D. (2006) 'The epidemiology of swine trichinellosis in China during 1999–2004'. *Helminthologia*, 43(1), p. 21–26, doi: 10.2478/s11687-006-0005-1.

Den Hartigh, W. (2016) 'EU considers swill feeding for pigs to curb food waste', *Farmer's Weekly*, 27 January. Available at: https://farmersweekly.co.za/agri-news/south-africa/eu-considers-swill-feeding-for-pigs-to-curb-food-waste/(Accessed: 3 September 2018).

Department of Primary Industries and Regions, S. A. (2018) *Swill feed*. Available at: http://pir.sa.gov.au/biosecurity/animal_health/pigs/swill_feed (Accessed: 3 September 2018).

Dobbs, R., Oppenheim, J., Thompson, F., Brinkman, M. and Zornes, M. (2011) *Resource Revolution: Meeting the world's energy, materials, food, and water needs*. New York, United States: McKinsey Global Institute. Available at: https://www.mckinsey.com/~/media/McKinsey/Business%20Functions/Sus tainability/Our%20Insights/Resource%20revolution/MGI_Resource_revolution_full_report.ashx (Accessed: 30 April 2018).

Dou, Z., Toth, J. D. and Westendorf, M. L. (2018) 'Food waste for livestock feeding: Feasibility, safety, and sustainability implications'. *Global Food Security*, 17, pp. 154–161, doi: 10.1016/j.gfs.2017.12.003.

Drew, T. W. (2011) 'The emergence and evolution of swine viral diseases: to what extend have husbandry systems and global trade contributed to their distribution and diversity?'. *Revue Scientifique et Technique de l'OIE*, 30(1), pp. 95–106, doi: 10.20506/rst.30.1.2020.

Driver, A. (2018) *NPA responds to calls for return of feeding waste to pigs*. Available at: http://npa-uk.org.uk/NPA_responds_to_calls_for_return_of_feeding_waste_to_pigs.html (Accessed: 5 September 2018).

EC Scientific Steering Committee (1999) *Intra-Species Recycling - Opinion on : the risk born by recycling animal by-products as feed with regard to propagating TSE in non-ruminant farmed animals. Adopted on 17 September 1999*. Committee, p. 8. Available at: https://ec.europa.eu/food/sites/food/files/safety/docs/sci-com_ssc_out60_en.pdf (Accessed: 5 April 2018).

Edwards, S. (2002) Feeding organic pigs. A handbook of raw materials and recommendations for feeding practice. Newcastle upon Tyne, UK: University of Newcastle.

EFFPA (2018) *European Former Foodstuff Processors Association*. Available at: https://effpa.eu/(Accessed: 16 September 2018).

EFSA Scientific Committee (2015) 'Risk profile related to production and consumption of insects as food and feed'. *EFSA Journal*, 13(10), p. 4257, doi: 10.2903/j.efsa.2015.4257.

Ermgassen, Z., KHJ, E., Phalan, B., Green, R. E. and Balmford, A. (2016) 'Reducing the land use of EU pork production: where there's swill, there's a way'. *Food policy*, 58, p. 35–48.

European Commission (2001) *Final Report of a Mission Carried Out in Uruguay from 25 to 29 June 2001 in Order to Evaluate the Situation with Regard to Outbreaks of Foot and Mouth Disease*. Food and Veterinary Office, DG(SANCO)/3342/2001 – MR Final. Available at: http://ec.europa.eu/food/fs/inspections/vi/reports/uruguay/vi_rep_urug_3342-2001_en.pdf.

European Food Safety Authority (2007) 'Certain Aspects related to the Feeding of Animal Proteins to Farm Animals - Scientific Opinion of the Panel on Biological Hazards'. *EFSA Journal*, 5(11), p. 576, doi: 10.2903/j.efsa.2007.576.

European Food Safety Authority (EFSA) (2007) 'The risks associated with tail biting in pigs and possible means to reduce the need for tail docking considering the different housing and husbandry systems - Scientific Opinion of the Panel on Animal Health and Welfare'. *EFSA Journal*, 5(12), p. 611, doi: 10.2903/j.efsa.2007.611.

EUROSTAT (2017) *Pig farming sector - Statistical portrait 2014 - Statistics Explained*. Available at: http://ec.europa.eu/eurostat/statistics-explained/index.php/Pig_farming_sector_-_statistical_portrait_2014 (Accessed: 8 May 2018).

Evans, D. (ed.) (2013) *Waste Matters*. (1 edition). Malden, MA: Wiley-Blackwell.

Gerber, P. J. FAO (eds) (2013) *Tackling climate change through livestock: a global assessment of emissions and mitigation opportunities*. Rome: Food and Agriculture Organization of the United Nations.

FAO (2013a) *Food Wastage Footprint & Climate Change*. FAO, p. 4. Available at: http://fao.org/3/a-bb144e.pdf (Accessed:30 April 2018).

FAO (2013b) *Food wastage footprint: Impacts on natural resources - Summary report*. Rome: FAO.

FAO (2017) *Livestock solutions for climate change*. Food and Agriculture Organisation of the United Nations. Available at: http://fao.org/3/a-i8098e.pdf?utm_source=twitter&utm_medium=social%20media&utm_campaign=faoclimate (Accessed: 9 May 2018).

FAO (2018a) 'African Swine Fever Threatens People's Republic of China: A rapid risk assessment of ASF introduction', p. 20.

FAO (2018b) *Shaping the future of livestock sustainably, responsibly, efficiently*. FAO. Available at: www.fao.org/3/i8384en/I8384EN.pdf (Accessed:4 September 2018).

Fehr, M. (2014) 'The management challenge for household waste in emerging economies like Brazil: Realistic source separation and activation of reverse logistics'. *Waste Management & Research*, 32 (9_suppl), pp. 32–39, doi: 10.1177/0734242X14541985.

Foley, J. A., Ramankutty, N., Brauman, K. A., Cassidy, E. S., Gerber, J. S., Johnston, M., Mueller, N. D., O'Connell, C., Ray, D. K., West, P. C., Balzer, C., Bennett, E. M., Carpenter, S. R., Hill, J., Monfreda, C., Polasky, S., Rockström, J., Sheehan, J., Siebert, S., Tilman, D. and Zaks, D. P. M. (2011) 'Solutions for a cultivated planet'. *Nature*, 478(7369), pp. 337–342, doi: 10.1038/nature10452.

Fry, J. and Kingston, C. (2009) *Life Cycle Assessment of Pork Report*. Environmental Resources Management. Available at: https://pork.ahdb.org.uk/media/2344/lifecycelassmntofporklaunchversion.pdf (Accessed: 7 May 2018).

Gagrai, L.K., Tiwary, B.K., Prasad, A. and Ganguly, S., (2014) Study on microbiology of intestines of swine fed with kitchen waste. Int. J. Curr. Microbiol. App. Sci, 3(1), pp. 577–581.

Garner, M. G., Hess, G. D. and Yang, X. (2006) 'An integrated modelling approach to assess the risk of wind-borne spread of foot-and-mouth disease virus from infected premises'. *Environmental Modeling & Assessment*, 11(3), pp. 195–207, doi: 10.1007/s10666-005-9023-5.

Gilchrist, M. J., Greko, C., Wallinga, D. B., Beran, G. W., Riley, D. G. and Thorne, P. S. (2007) 'The Potential Role of Concentrated Animal Feeding Operations in Infectious Disease Epidemics and Antibiotic Resistance'. *Environmental Health Perspectives*, 115(2), pp. 313–316, doi: 10.1289/ehp.8837.

Gillespie, A., Grove-White, D. and Williams, H. (2015) 'Should cattle veterinarians be concerned about disease risk from smallholder and pet pigs?', in *Middle European Buiatric Congress 10th ECBHM Symposium*. Maribor, Slovenia. Maribor.

Gillman, S. (2018) *Turning food waste into animal feed could take a chunk out of livestock emissions, Horizon: the EU Research & Innovation magazine*. Available at: https://horizon-magazine.eu/article/turning-food-waste-animal-feed-could-take-chunk-out-livestock-emissions_en.html (Accessed: 17 April 2018).

Hanson, C., Lipinski, B., Robertson, K., Dias, D., Gavilan, I., Gréverath, P., Ritter, S., Fonseca, J., van Otterdijk, R., Timmermans, T., Lomax, J., O'Connor, C., Dawe, A., Swannell, R., Berger, V., Reddy, M., Somogyi, D., Tran, B., Leach, B. and Quested, T. (2017) *Food Loss and Waste Accounting and Reporting Standard*. Washington, DC: World Resources Institute, p. 160.

Hayrapetyan, H., Nierop Groot, M. and Zwietering, M. (2017) *Analysis of the APHA report Assessment of risk management measures to reduce the exotic disease risk from the feeding of processed catering waste and certain other food waste to non-ruminants*. Task 6.3.3. REFRESH.

Herman, M.-O., Mayrhofer, J. and Mayrhofer, J. (2016) *Burning Land, Burning the Climate: The biofuel industry's capture of EU bioenergy policy*. Oxford: Oxfam International, p. 44.

Hoffmann, I. (2010) 'Climate Change and the characterization, breeding and conservation of animal genetic resources'. *Animal Genetics*, 41, pp. 32–46.

Japan Ministry of Agriculture, Forestry and Fisheries (2018) *EcoFeed in Japan*. Available at: http://maff.go.jp/j/chikusan/sinko/lin/l_siryo/attach/pdf/ecofeed-43.pdf (Accessed: 7 September 2018).

JFEC (2015) 'Activities of the Japan Food Ecology Center. Presentation at the Expo Milano'. Available at: http://env.go.jp/en/earth/sdgs/g7_sdgs_1st/session2_03.pdf.

Jones, B. A., Grace, D., Kock, R., Alonso, S., Rushton, J., Said, M. Y., McKeever, D., Mutua, F., Young, J., McDermott, J. and Pfeiffer, D. U. (2013) 'Zoonosis emergence linked to agricultural intensification and environmental change'. *Proceedings of the National Academy of Sciences*, 110(21), pp. 8399–8404, doi: 10.1073/pnas.1208059110.

Kim, M.-H., Song, Y.-E., Song, H.-B., Kim, J.-W. and Hwang, S.-J. (2011) 'Evaluation of food waste disposal options by LCC analysis from the perspective of global warming: Jungnang case, South Korea'. *Waste Management*, 31(9), pp. 2112–2120, doi: 10.1016/j.wasman.2011.04.019.

Kroes, H. and Kuepper, B. (2015) *Mapping the soy supply chain in Europe*, p. 27. Available at: http://assets.wnf.nl/downloads/mapping_the_soy_supply_chain_in_europe_wnf_12_may_2015_final_1.pdf (Accessed: 15 August 2018).

Kumar, A., Roy, B., Sirohi, R., Singh, Y. and Singh, D. N. (2016) 'Effect of Bread Waste Feeding on Growth Performance and Carcass Traits of Crossbred Pigs'. *Journal of Animal Research*, 6(2), p. 297, doi: 10.5958/2277-940X.2015.00178.3.

Kurishima, H., Hishinuma, T. and Genchi, Y. (2011) The Effect of CO_2 Information Labelling for the Pork Produced with Feed Made from Food Residuals. *Towards Life Cycle Sustainability Management* (pp. 349–356). Dordrecht: Springer, doi: 10.1007/978-94-007-1899-9_34.

Leib, E., Balkus, O., Rice, C., Maley, M., Taneja, R., Cheng, R., Civita, N. and Alvoid, T. (2016) *Leftovers for Livestock: A Legal Guide for Using Food Scraps as Animal Feed*. Available at: www.chlpi.org/wp-content/uploads/2013/12/Leftovers-for-Livestock_A-Legal-Guide_August-2016.pdf.

Luyckx, K. (2018) *REFRESH Task 6.3.3 Expert seminar on the risk management of using treated surplus food in pig feed*. Expert Seminar Report WP6 Task 6.3.3. Wageningen University & Research, Netherlands. Available at: http://eu-refresh.org/sites/default/files/REFRESH%20animal%20feed%20expert%20seminar%20report%20final%2012.04.18.pdf Wageningen University & Research, Netherlands (Accessed: 25 April 2018).

Luyckx, K. and Bowman, M. (2018) *Feeding Surplus Food to Pigs Safely: A win-win for farmers and the environment*. London: Feedback Available at: https://feedbackglobal.org/wp/wp-content/uploads/2018/07/Pig-Idea-UK-policy-report.pdf (Accessed: 3 September 2018).

Luyckx, K., Bowman, M., Broeze, J., Taillard, D. and Woroniecka, K. (2019) *Technical guidelines animal feed: The safety, environmental and economic aspects of feeding treated surplus food to omnivorous livestock*. *REFRESH Deliverable 6.7*. Available at: https://eu-refresh.org/results.

MAFF (2006) *Guideline for Ensuring Safety of Feeds Using Food Residues, etc.* Available at: http://famic.go. jp/ffis/feed/obj/Guideline_for_Feeds_Using_Food_Residues.pdf (Accessed: 3 April 2018).

Manteca, X., Villalba, J. J., Atwood, S. B., Dziba, L. and Provenza, F. D. (2008) 'Is dietary choice important to animal welfare?'. *Journal of Veterinary Behavior: Clinical Applications and Research*, 3(5), pp. 229–239, doi: 10.1016/j.jveb.2008.05.005.

Mennerat, A., Nilsen, F., Ebert, D. and Skorping, A. (2010) 'Intensive Farming: Evolutionary Implications for Parasites and Pathogens'. *Evolutionary Biology*, 37(2–3), pp. 59–67, doi: 10.1007/s11692-010-9089-0.

Mighty Earth, FERN and Regnskogfondet (2018) *The Avoidable Crisis - The European meat industry's environmental catastrophe.* Mighty Earth. Available at: http://mightyearth.org/wp-content/uploads/2018/04/ME_DEFORESTATION_EU_English_R8.pdf (Accessed: 19 June 2018).

Ministry of Agriculture, Forestry and Fisheries (MAFF), Japan (2003) 'New Guidelines on Prevention of Intermixing of Animal Origin Proteins in Ruminant Feeds'. 15 Shoan No. 1570. Available at: http://famic.go.jp/ffis/feed/obj/1509161570_eng.pdf (Accessed: 17 July 2018).

Missotten, J. A., Michiels, J., Degroote, J. and De Smet, S. (2015) 'Fermented liquid feed for pigs: an ancient technique for the future'. *Journal of Animal Science and Biotechnology*, 6, p. 1, doi: 10.1186/2049-1891-6-4.

Mo, W., Man, Y. and Wong, M. (2017) 'Use of food waste, fish waste and food processing waste for China's aquaculture industry: Needs and challenge'. *The Science of the total environment*, (613–614), pp. 635–643. doi: 10.1016/j.scitotenv.2017.08.321.

Mullan, S., Edwards, S. A., Butterworth, A., Whay, H. R. and Main, D. C. J. (2011) *A pilot investigation of possible positive system descriptors in finishing pigs.* Available at: https://ingentaconnect.com/content/ufaw/aw/2011/00000020/00000003/art00014 (Accessed: 9 July 2018).

Müller, M. and Mottet, A. (2017) Livestock, climate, and environment: Trends, challenges, and alternative pathways. Brussels, Belgium, p. 19.

NADIS (2018) *Pig Health - Savaging of Piglets, National Animal Disease Information Service.* Available at: http://nadis.org.uk/bulletins/savaging-of-piglets.aspx (Accessed: 8 July 2018).

Nelson, S. M. and Archaeology, U. of P. M. A. S. C. for (1998) *Ancestors for the pigs: pigs in prehistory.* Pennsylvania, US.: Museum Applied Science Center for Archaeology, University of Pennsylvania Museum of Archaeology and Anthropology.

Nemeth, D. (1995) 'On Pigs in Subsistence Agriculture'. *Current Anthropology - CURR ANTHROPOL,* 36, doi: 10.1086/204358.

New Zealand Legislation (2005) *Biosecurity (Meat and Food Waste for Pigs) Regulations 2005.* Available at: http://legislation.govt.nz/regulation/public/2005/0150/latest/DLM332617.html?search=ts_act%40bill%40regulation%40deemedreg_food+waste+for+pigs_resel_25_a&p=1 (Accessed: 3 April 2018).

No Tech Magazine (2014) 'Animals as the Answer to Recycling Food waste', *No Tech Magazine.* Available at: www.notechmagazine.com/2014/07/animals-as-the-answer-to-recycling-food-waste.html (Accessed: 31 August 2018).

OIE (2013a) 'African Swine Fever. OIE Technical Disease Cards. World Organisation for Animal Health.' Available at: http://oie.int/fileadmin/Home/eng/Animal_Health_in_the_World/docs/pdf/Disease_cards/AFRICAN_SWINE_FEVER.pdf.

OIE (2013b) 'Foot and Mouth Disease. OIE Technical Disease Cards. World Organisation for Animal Health'. Available at: http://oie.int/fileadmin/Home/eng/Animal_Health_in_the_World/docs/pdf/Disease_cards/FOOT_AND_MOUTH_DISEASE.pdf

Oxfam (2015) *Extreme Carbon Inequality.* Oxfam. Available at: https://d1tn3vj7xz9fdh.cloudfront.net/s3fs-public/file_attachments/mb-extreme-carbon-inequality-021215-en.pdf (Accessed: 4 April 2018).

Parliamentary and Health Service Ombudsman (2007) The introduction of the ban on swill feeding HC 165. 6th Report Session 2006–2007. London: The Stationery Office, p. 94. Available at: https://www.gov.uk/government/uploads/system/uploads/attachment_data/file/250386/0165.pdf (Accessed: 4 March 2018).

People's Republic of China (2006) *Animal Husbandry Law of the People's Republic of China.* Available at: https://ecolex.org/details/legislation/animal-husbandry-law-of-the-peoples-republic-of-china-lex-faoc082613/(Accessed: 3 September 2018).

The Pig Site (2018) 'Savaging of Piglets (Cannibalism)', *The Pig Site.* Available at: http://thepigsite.com/pighealth/article/260/savaging-of-piglets-cannibalism/(Accessed: 8 July 2018).

AHDB Pork (2018) *Pig Production.* Available at: https://pork.ahdb.org.uk/pig-production/(Accessed: 8 July 2018).

Pretty, J. N., Noble, A. D., Bossio, D., Dixon, J., Hine, R. E., Penning de Vries, F. W. T. and Morison, J. I. L. (2006) 'Resource-Conserving Agriculture Increases Yields in Developing Countries'. *Environmental Science & Technology*, 40(4), pp. 1114–1119, doi: 10.1021/es051670d.

Project Drawdown (2017) *Drawdown: Solutions, Drawdown*. Available at: http://drawdown.org/solutions.

Ravi, P. (2017) 'CHEMICAL COMPOSITION OF KITCHEN WASTE FOR PIG FEEDING'. *International Journal of Science, Environment and Technology*, 6, 7.

RBST (2018) 'UK's Native Livestock Breeds - Protecting and Developing a Unique Asset. Submission to EFRA Committee inquiry into Brexit'. Available at: http://data.parliament.uk/writtenevidence/committeeevidence.svc/evidencedocument/environment-food-and-rural-affairs-committee/brexit-trade-in-food/written/71607.htmlRBST.

Review on Anti-Microbial Resistance (2014) *Antimicrobial Resistance: Tackling a crisis for the health and wealth of nations*. London. Available at: https://amr-review.org/sites/default/files/AMR%20Review%20Paper%20-%20Tackling%20a%20crisis%20for%20the%20health%20and%20wealth%20of%20nations_1.pdf (Accessed: 30 April 2018).

Ritchie, H. and Roser, M. (2017) *Meat and Seafood Production & Consumption, Our World in Data*. Available at: https://ourworldindata.org/meat-and-seafood-production-consumption.

Saikia, P. and Bhar, R. (no date) 'Influence of Kitchen food waste on growth performance of grower piglets.pdf'. *Veterinary World*, 3, pp. 34–36.

Salemdeeb, R., Zu Ermgassen, E. K. H. J., Kim, M. H., Balmford, A. and Al-Tabbaa, A. (2017) 'Environmental and health impacts of using food waste as animal feed: a comparative analysis of food waste management options.'. *Journal of cleaner production*, 140, pp. 871–880.

Sauer, C. O. (1972) *Seeds, spades, hearths, and herds: the domestication of animals and foodstuffs*. Cambridge, MA: MIT Press.

Schutt, B. (2017) *Cannibalism: A Perfectly Natural History*. Chapel Hill, NC: Algonquin Books (Accessed: 8 July 2018).

Steinfeld, H., Pierre Gerber, T. D. W., Castel, V. and Haan, C. D. (2006) 'Livestock's Long Shadow: Environmental Issues and Options. Rome: Food and Agriculture Organization of the United Nations', *Accessed*. Available at: http://fao.org/docrep/010/a0701e/a0701e00.HTM.

Stuart, T. (2009) *Waste: Uncovering the Global Food Scandal*. London: Penguin.

Takahashi, K. (2018) JFEC Operational costs. Personal Communication. 4 December 2018.

Takahashi, T., Kohira, K., Horinouchi, S., Iwakiri, M. and Irie, M. (2012) 'Effects of Feeding Level of Eco-feed mainly composed of Bread from Box Lunch Factory on Pig Performance, Carcass Characteristics and Pork Quality'. *Nihon Danchi Chikusan Gakkaihou*, 55(1), pp. 33–40, doi: 10.11461/jwaras.55.33.

TRASE (2018a) 'Assessing deforestation risk in Brazilian soy exports', *Trase Yearbook 2018*, 7 June. Available at: https://yearbook2018.trase.earth/chapter5/(Accessed: 16 July 2018).

TRASE (2018b) 'Yearbook 2018 - Brazilian soy supply chains: linking buyers to landscapes', *Trase Yearbook 2018*, 8 June. Available at: https://yearbook2018.trase.earth/chapter4/(Accessed: 13 August 2018).

UNEP (2009) *The environmental food crisis: the environment's role in averting future food crises: a UNEP rapid response assessment*. Arendal, Norway: UNEP.

US Department of Agriculture (2009) *Swine Health Protection; Feeding of Processed Product to Swine, 6 C.F.R. §; 166 (2009)*. Available at: https://aphis.usda.gov/animal_health/animal_dis_spec/swine/downloads/interim_rule_pro-products.pdf (Accessed: 7 May 2018).

van Zanten, H. H. E., Mollenhorst, H., Oonincx, D. G. A. B., Bikker, P., Meerburg, B. G. and de Boer, I. J. M. (2015) 'From environmental nuisance to environmental opportunity: housefly larvae convert waste to livestock feed'. *Journal of Cleaner Production*, 102, pp. 362–369, doi: 10.1016/j.jclepro.2015.04.106.

Vasconcelos, A. and Burley, H. (2018) *Soy traders in Cerrado under fire for illegal activities, Medium*. Available at: https://medium.com/trase/soy-traders-in-cerrado-under-fire-for-illegal-activities-3138f4d4d4e1 (Accessed: 20 June 2018).

Walker, M. (2017) Food and Feed Law: Compendium of UK food and feed legislation. Department for Business, Energy and Industrial Strategy London, UK Available at: https://assets.publishing.service.gov.uk/government/uploads/system/uploads/attachment_data/file/638967/Foodfeedlaw_Apr_Jun2017.pdf (Accessed: 8 July 2018).

Wambui, C. (2017) *If you feed your pigs garbage waste, then prepare for diseases, Daily Nation*. Available at: https://nation.co.ke/business/seedsofgold/If-you-feed-your-pigs-garbage-waste-then-prepare-for-diseases/2301238-4158826-7vhs4dz/index.html (Accessed: 3 September 2018).

Wang, H., Pang, J., Ma, C. and Sui, C. (2015) *National review on food waste recycling into animal feeding in China.* Hanoi: Blue Barrels, Beijing Institute of Technology, CIRAD, INRA 21 Available at: https://umr-selmet.cirad.fr/content/download/4050/29632/version/3/file/BIT_REPORT_FW2FEED_CHINA.pdf (Accessed: 30 August 2018).

Wells, G. A. H. (2003) 'Studies of the transmissibility of the agent of bovine spongiform encephalopathy to pigs'. *Journal of General Virology,* 84(4), pp. 1021–1031, doi: 10.1099/vir.0.18788-0.

WRAP (2014) *Why take action: legal/policy case | WRAP UK.* Available at: http://wrap.org.uk/content/why-take-action-legalpolicy-case (Accessed: 17 April 2018).

Wunder, S. *et al.* (2018) *Food waste prevention and valorisation: relevant EU policy areas. Report of the REFRESH Project, D3.3 Review of EU policy areas with relevant impact on food waste prevention and valorization.*

WWF (2017) *Appetite for Destruction: Summary Report.* World Wildlife Fund. Available at: https://wwf.org.uk/sites/default/files/2017-10/WWF_AppetiteForDestruction_Summary_Report_SignOff.pdf (Accessed: 11 April 2018).

Xiao, P., Li, R., She, R., Yin, J., Li, W., Mao, J. and Sun, Q. (2012) 'Prevalence of Hepatitis E Virus in Swine Fed on Kitchen Residue'. *PLoS ONE,* 7(3), doi: 10.1371/journal.pone.0033480.

Zu Ermgassen, E., Kelly, M., Bladon, E., Salemdeeb, R. and Balmford, A. (2018) 'Support amongst UK pig farmers and agricultural stakeholders for the use of food losses in animal feed'. *PLOS ONE,* 13(4), p. e0196288, doi: 10.1371/journal.pone.0196288.

23

FROM DUMPSTER DIVES TO DISCO VIBES

The shifting shape of food waste activism

Alex V. Barnard and Marie Mourad

On a brisk November day in 2013, nearly 100 people—most of them homeless—gather in People's Park, Berkeley, for a free outdoor meal, cooked from excess food donated by local grocery stores in nearby squats and cooperatives by self-described anarchist activists. Five thousand miles away in Belleville Market, Paris, two dozen well-educated young people peel and chop vegetables that they have saved from being thrown away, preparing a warm ratatouille for passers-by drawn in by the sound of disco music. Both events are possible because, in each country, these activists are able to tap into enormous streams of surplus food that would otherwise be discarded. Yet the participants in each event understand what they are doing in dramatically different ways: in the first, they identify themselves as part of Food Not Bombs (FNB), a movement that fights for food as a "right not a privilege" as part of a wider protest against war, poverty, and capitalism. In the second, members of Disco Soupe (DS) imagine that, through "conviviality" and collective cooking in public spaces, they are pushing for public policies to reduce corporate and consumer food waste. They are "interrogating"—but not overthrowing—the existing agro-food system.

Since 2010, food waste has become an issue of public concern for policymakers, environmental non-governmental organisations, and advocates for corporate social responsibility (Mourad, 2016). Discussions over food waste have become increasingly technical, as a wide range of stakeholders debate how food waste should be measured, which actors along the food chain bear greatest responsibility, and what kind of nudges and incentives can increase donations to food waste or reduce produce left to rot in consumers' refrigerators (Chaboud and Daviron, 2017). But if food waste may appear as an enormous ecological and social challenge, the scale of the problem does not, in and of itself, explain how the issue came to be singled out for special attention. While activists like those in FNB have long denounced food waste as one of a host of problems within the modern agro-food system, food waste is now distinctive in the apparently general consensus around the need to address it (Cloteau and Mourad, 2016).

In this chapter, we point out that recent movements *against* food waste build on a long history of movements *around* food waste, often of a much more contentious flavour. We examine three social movements—Food Not Bombs, freeganism, and Disco Soupe—that all engage in a similar tactic: publicly reclaiming and redistributing recently discarded food. Although these movements speak of food waste in general, in truth they are focused on a particular kind of excess food: "ex-commodities." As one of us has argued (Barnard, 2016), ex-commodities are goods produced for sale which are still consumable but which are, nonetheless, expelled from the market into dumpsters because they cannot be profitably sold.[1] As other scholars in this volume (see Giles, Chapter 1) have shown, the contemporary confluence of increasing agricultural productivity, a highly consolidated food distribution market, and the weakening of some traditional public policies for dealing with food surpluses (such as stockpiling excess food or dumping it on developing countries) have combined to generate an expanding mass of such ex-commodities. In this chapter, we show how the differences between these movements stem in part from their divergent understandings of both the origins of and solutions to ex-commodification.

For FNB, the discovery of ex-commodified food in the 1980s was, at least at first, a boon for activists who wanted to create (and feed!) communities organised around principles of solidarity, direct democracy, and vegetarianism. Like FNB, freeganism—a movement which gained prominence in the 2000s, whose participants attempt to minimise their participation in capitalism by living off ex-commodified food, space, and household goods—treated food waste as a powerful symbol of capitalism's malfunctioning. They made it even more central to their message, however, through dumpster-diving "trash tours" in New York City. This greater media and public exposure to food waste may have contributed to growing interest in the topic by the 2010s. Over this period, participants in a new movement—Disco Soupe— looked at the same ex-commodified food and saw not a tool to overthrow the capitalist food system, but an opportunity to make it more efficient and sustainable.

All three of the movements we study have affiliates in cities around the world. However, this chapter draws on our observations of the East Bay chapter of FNB near San Francisco, the group of freegans organised around the website Freegan.info in New York, and the Paris DS group. None can claim to be representative of their respective movements as a whole. However, these three sites have been central to the development of each: San Francisco saw some of the most visible conflicts between FNB and the authorities in the 1990s, New York hosted the freegan group with by far the most media exposure in the 2000s, and the Parisian DS initially coordinated the movement's expansion in the 2010s. Jumping from the U.S. to France to some extent follows attention to food waste itself, as France has been the home to some of the most prominent public policies against food waste (Mourad, 2015).

The authors cooked and served dozens of meals with these groups between 2007 and 2016. We also attended organising meetings, trainings, and conferences put on by each. Although Mourad did the majority of research with DS and Barnard with FNB and freegan. info, each author also spent some time observing and interacting at the other's primary research site, a form of "collaborative ethnography" intended to increase the "depth, breadth, and reliability of data" (Bennett, Cordner, Klein, Savell, and Baiocchi, 2013, p. 525). We supplemented our participant observation of FNB by interviewing two key organisers. We interviewed 21 participants in freegan.info and examined materials written by freegans. Our study of DS is complemented with nine semi-structured interviews and analysis of the group's internal documents and messages. We present the three movements in roughly chronological order, highlighting the links between them. We conclude by reflecting on the broader lessons they propose about efforts to reduce food waste.

Food not bombs: free meals against capitalism

No movement is cut from whole cloth, and the redistribution of free, surplus goods has a long history in U.S. politics. In October 1966, a group calling themselves "the Diggers" (after a 17th-century English peasant movement dedicated to abolishing private property) began distributing free food to the hippies and homeless congregating in the Haight-Ashbury district of San Francisco. Propheseying oncoming ecological doom, the Diggers called for a rapid transition away from industrialism and capitalism (Belasco, 2007, p. 18). Not content only to preach, however, they sought to construct the new, post-capitalist society they saw as necessary, creating "free stores" to distribute donated, surplus, or stolen goods and offering free medical care and housing. Across the bay, the Black Panthers were creating a series of "survival programmes" to provide food, education, and health care to impoverished black communities, relying also on donations and surplus (Bloom and Martin, 2013).

Although direct lines are difficult to draw, FNB was part of this political lineage, which linked redistribution of free goods in public space to challenges to capitalism, urban exclusion, and environmental destruction (Heynen, 2010; Spataro, 2016). The group started in 1981 as an offshoot of movements that used non-violent civil disobedience to protest nuclear power (see Epstein, 1991). According to FNB's website, the movement's first act was to serve a meal outside the Federal Reserve Bank in Boston in order to "protest the exploitation of capitalism and investment in the nuclear industry."[2] By serving free, surplus food in public to anyone regardless of need or condition, the group sought to differentiate itself from churches and charities as well as demonstrate how its core principles—vegetarianism or veganism, consensus-based decision-making, and non-violence—could be used as the basis for a more just and peaceful world. Keith McHenry, one of the movement's founders, told us in an interview that recovered food was an effective vehicle for this message:

> The whole idea that food was free really blew people's minds: the message that you could have as much as you want, because it was rescued, and that we didn't anticipate or expect or even need money, and that—on top of that—it was great food which was well-presented. That had a profound impact on people, and that's why we adopted that model permanently for FNB ... It got people to think outside the box about all kinds of social and cultural issues. They started asking: 'Why is food withheld from people who need it? Why is food so expensive? And why is food a commodity when everyone needs it?'

In short, for McHenry and his friends, public meals were a way of enacting their vision for a post-capitalist food system; what allowed them to do it was ex-commodified food.

Ex-commodified food was not just useful in FNB's visible occupations of public space, then, but also in sustaining FNB activists themselves. One morning in 2012 we jointly helped prepare a meal in "Fort Awesome," a cooperative house in Oakland California replete with chicken coops, extensive organic gardens, and solar panels. We met Manuel, an El Salvadorian immigrant who was serving as the "bottom-liner," the person taking responsibility for ensuring that the meal was ready on time. Manuel told us he was currently living in a squat and spending much of his time operating a free bike workshop in a low-income neighbourhood. FNB was important to him not just as a way to express his politics to others, but also for his own survival: as he explained:

> We're all political in every part of our lives. But we also need some stability …
> and for that, you need a place to live, you need a reliable source of food. You
> have to create some kind of a structure.

Offering free food is, for the group, simultaneously a way to bring in new participants, sustain existing ones, and show solidarity with the surrounding community. FNB chapters also serve as entry points for anarchist subcultures and communities claiming to build a new society "in the shell of the old" (Edwards and Mercer, 2007; Heynen, 2010; Giles, 2013). FNB is born of a sub-culture in which food waste is one of many different types of discarded objects (appliances, bikes, or clothes, for example) that help activists lead lives that they saw as partly outside of capitalism (Clark, 2004; Carlsson, 2008). Shantz (2005, p. 12) observes the ethos of recovery in anarchist community spaces that participants in groups like FNB frequent:

> It is not uncommon for anarchist infoshops to be almost fully outfitted with goods
> found in dumpsters. Many infoshops provide free tables of useful goods that have
> been dumpstered, cleaned up and, where necessary, repaired as a means to get use-
> able items to people who would not otherwise be able to afford them.

FNB is thus part of what Carlsson (2008, p. 181)—describing a range of urban utopian projects across the U.S. such as community gardens in abandoned lots, cars running on discarded vegetable oil, or bike workshops using discarded parts—calls a "politically-informed embrace of working with waste."

The East Bay FNB chapter in which we both participated over a period of months saved hundreds of pounds of food a week from the trash. The group served seven meals a week, having missed only two (owing to extremely inclement weather) in the last 20 years. It did so with little infrastructure beyond a beat-up truck used to pick up donations. Cooking was done in a rotation of cooperative houses, meals were served on picnic benches in public parks, and who would show up on a given day was anyone's guess. As we observed, participants demonstrated an impressive ability to work with whatever produce they recovered, which they combined with purchased rice and beans. The group paid for these with money accumulated by reselling discarded furniture they discovered on the streets of Oakland and Berkeley. This kind of ingenuity was on display in New Orleans, too, where FNB managed to reach people stranded by Hurricane Katrina while large and better funded charitable organisations such as the Red Cross were scrambling (Spataro, 2016).

At the same time, the group was deliberately disconnected from other efforts around food redistribution. Group members emphatically did not see themselves as working in common cause with other organisations that provide food for some of the same homeless and precarious individuals FNB targets with its meals (see, also, Heynen, 2010). At 81 years of age, Anne had been a regular cook for East Bay FNB since her retirement. When asked about her "volunteering", she bristled:

> I don't like the word volunteer, or really charity either. I'm doing this to make
> a political statement … The reason we are in Food Not Bombs and not some church
> or charity is because we believe that food is a human right and not a commodity. We
> demonstrate that by serving meals and giving away food participating in the Food
> Not Bombs community is a meaningful and positive political act.

The group's pamphlets and its participants emphasise their "resistance to oppressive capitalist society" and commitment to "change the system," the latter understood as meaning much more than simply altering stores' wasteful practices and offering a band-aid for unequal access to food. Ultimately, for FNB, solving food waste is not the main issue. In the short term, a more efficient food system with less food waste would even make achieving the real goals of FNB—providing "solidarity" to the destitute and supporting anti-capitalist, anti-war activists—more difficult.

What's contentious about free food?

If the activists of FNB believe that sharing free food and other rescued resources is something far more contentious than simply providing charity to those in need, the authorities have consistently agreed. In the 1990s, an offshoot of FNB claimed to have opened up hundreds of squats in abandoned buildings and was housing up to 500 homeless people a night in San Francisco (Parson, 2010). The city arrested 325 members of San Francisco FNB over a three-year period, and the movement's public meals and appropriation of housing that was ex-commodified and taken off the market was problematic enough to be raised as an issue in the 1995 mayoral race. As one activist we spoke with who was involved in FNB at the time recounted, when the time came for arrested FNB participants to go to court,

> We would all go to the hall of injustice [the courthouse], and we all stood outside, and we were trying to hand out bagels, and the cops would confiscate the bagels. And we'd shout, "shame, shame, shame," and so we have a photograph of a pile of bagels with a bunch of cops in riot gear surrounding it.

FNB played a role in feeding participants in the wave of mass protests against free trade and global financial institutions across the U.S. and Western Europe in the late 1990s and early 2000s (Graeber, 2009). For some of the people we met in the East Bay, seeing FNB at these protests was their entry point into the movement. Carol explains that she came to FNB "from the inside," having spent years "eating Food Not Bombs bagels" at anti-war, anti-nuclear, and anti-incarceration demonstrations.

This anti-globalisation movement lost steam in the face of post-9/11 police suppression, but FNB has not disappeared: in fact, it claims anywhere between 500 and 1,000 loosely affiliated chapters around the world, including nine in France. In 2012, for example, we accompanied FNB activists as they brought food to "Occupy the Farm," an attempt to reclaim a small patch of farmland in Albany, California from impending development by Whole Foods (see Figure 23.1). Somewhat paradoxically, ex-commodities from the existing capitalist food system were used to support a movement that envisioned a post-capitalist food system with neither commodities nor food waste.

Yet even as food waste has become a public concern and organisations seeking to reduce it have received increasing recognition and funding, FNB's own efforts to reclaim ex-commodities have faced increasing resistance because of the political message they attach to them. A 2014 report found that 31 U.S. cities had taken actions to restrict food sharing for the homeless (Stoops, 2014); some of these group feeding laws were a direct response to FNB, leading to arrests from Southern California to Florida (Heynen, 2010). FNB provided support for the Occupy Wall Street encampments of fall 2011 (Sbicca and Perdue, 2013), which were themselves systematically shut down by the police, partly based on claims that the encampments—including their kitchens—were unhygienic (Liboiron, 2012).

Figure 23.1 "Occupy the Farm" in Albany, California, supported by FNB, in 2012.
Source: Alex Barnard (used with permission).

FNB has certainly not gone away, but it is not the most prominent voice in the food waste landscape. Instead, the last decades have seen a striking increase in the prominence of "lifestyle politics" as people turn away from public protest toward individual practices (Haenfler, Johnson, and Jones, 2012; Bennett et al., 2013). While the ideological and tactical affinities between the two are undeniable, the rise of freeganism is arguably an intermediate step in the transition to making food waste a stand-alone issue whose solutions rest less in collective protest and more in individual practices.

Freegans: diving in, opting out

In 1994, shortly after being released on bail before his trial for serving food in San Francisco without a permit, FNB co-founder Keith McHenry embarked on a "Rent Is Theft" speaking tour throughout the United States and Canada. After a presentation in Edmonton, he went with a group of local FNB "kids" who were in a punk band to a local health food store. As he tells it:

> At first, we went in, and they had samples everywhere, so we thought we could get breakfast by eating the samples. And we were all vegan, so we were just eating the vegan samples. But eventually, the workers said, "You're just eating samples, you're not even buying anything. You have to leave."

McHenry, confident that any health food store was bound to have a plethora of unsold—i.e. ex-commodified—products on hand, suggested that the group go out back:

> There were these four massive dumpsters. There were a lot of us, maybe eight or nine people, and I was in a dumpster and discovered this huge wheel of imported

cheese from France, priced at like $250. It was covered in wax, and it hadn't even been cracked, and it was so huge that I couldn't even lift it up to the rim of the dumpster.

Despite being vegan, McHenry thought the top-notch cheese was too good to pass up: "I called out to everyone, 'I can't believe I just found this cheese. To heck with being vegan, let's be "freegan"!' So that was it, where the word came from."[3]

McHenry ultimately left the wheel of cheese in the dumpster, but he carried the tale of the legendary find with him. In Gainesville Florida, he told the "wheel of cheese" story at the Civic Media Center, an alternative community space. One attendee liked the word "freegan" enough to write a short manifesto entitled *Why Freegan?*[4] While McHenry originally used "freegan" to refer only to food, the tract presents a much broader vision:

> There are two options for existence: 1) waste your life working to get money to buy things that you don't need and help destroy the environment or 2) live a full satisfying life, occasionally scavenging or working your self-sufficiency skills to get the food and stuff you need to be content, while treading lightly on the earth, eliminating waste, and boycotting everything. Go![5]

As the author went on to explain, those choosing option 2 were engaged in the "ultimate boycott" directed against "EVERYTHING—All the corporations, all the stores, all the pesticides, all the land and resources wasted, the capitalist system, the all-oppressive dollar, the wage slavery, the whole burrito!" The pamphlet enumerates an array of strategies for "withdrawing from it [capitalism] and never using money," but the most notable one is "dumpster diving" ex-commodified goods from the trash bins of commercial establishments. As the section on FNB should make clear, none of these practices was really new, but the pamphlet grouped them under a single banner.[6]

Scholars have documented self-identified freegans in cities across North America, Europe, and Australia (Edwards and Mercer, 2007; Gross, 2009; Carolsfeld and Erikson, 2013) and online freegan communities claim thousands of members. Most studies describe freegans as predominantly male, young, and coming from relatively privileged backgrounds and with high levels of post-secondary education. Although freegans vary in the extent to which they squat, hitch-hike, engage in voluntary-employment, and other strategies enumerated by *Why Freegan?* there is one common thread: nearly every self-identified freegan we talked to dumpster dives for food.

Our research focused in particular on a group in New York City organised around the website "freegan.info." The group formed in 2003 out of the ferment of direct-action environmental and anti-globalisation movements (which themselves were fed, literally and figuratively, by FNB), and a realisation among a group of activists that trying to target individual corporate bad actors seemed fruitless. As the official freegan.info story recapitulates:

> After years of trying to boycott products from unethical corporations responsible for human rights violations, environmental destruction, and animal abuse, many of us found that no matter what we bought we ended up supporting something deplorable. We came to realize that the problem isn't just a few bad corporations but the entire system itself.[7]

Like FNB, then, freegan.info started out of a concern for much more than just food waste. Indeed, freegan.info experimented over time with a wide range of self-styled anti-capitalist projects, including a free bike workshop that used salvaged bike parts, "Really Really Free Markets" where discarded goods were redistributed, and sewing "skill-shares" that taught activists to repair second-hand clothes.

Nonetheless, the group is best known for its "trash tours": publicly announced dumpster dives that recovered still edible food on the sidewalks outside grocery stores. While freegan. info, like FNB, used such ex-commodified food as a resource for sustaining an activist community, trash tours made it more central as a materialisation of the moral failings of capitalism. Moreover, aside from moments where the police cracked down on their public meals, FNB usually attracted little interest from the broader public. Over time, however, freegan.info events began to attract increasing media attention, which participants realised was primarily out of interest in the spectacle of wasted food and people willing to eat it not out of necessity, but as an act of protest.

Each freegan.info tour culminated with what they called a "Waving the Banana at Capitalism" speech, in which a freegan.info participant would use particular items to highlight different ills: discarded chicken to talk about animal exploitation, or tomatoes from Mexico to decry trade deals (Barnard, 2011; see Figure 23.2). Freegan activists recognised, as Clark (2004, p. 25) puts it, that "Through the most sophisticated branding, packaging, and advertising, American food commodities work hard to conceal the labour, spatial divides, and resources that went into making the food." Marx (1976, p. 164) classically called this process by which we are so dazzled by the useful features of capitalist products that we fail to see the exploited labour going into them the "fetishism of commodities." As Cynthia, a freegan.info and animal rights activist who got her start chasing off buffalo hunters in Yellowstone explained, freegan.info trash tours were a chance to unveil these realities:

> Seeing all the waste exposes very clearly the priorities in our society, that making a profit is more important than feeding people, than preserving the environment, than making use of resources, than honouring peoples' time, labour, love, and effort. What we see with waste is that once something cannot make money, it is discarded and of no value.

Through trash tours, freegans rediscovered what ex-commodities really were, as one put it at the end of an impassioned speech:

> We're here to reclaim all this, because we view this as wealth ... We're actually living amongst massive amounts of wealth, and until we actually reclaim it and share it with everybody around us, everything is going into the trash. Meanwhile, we have an opportunity to live in abundance. It's all actually there, we're just trained to think that it's only valuable if it came from a store.

Through trash tours, then, freegans were unveiling another form of fetishism: the "fetish of waste" (Barnard, 2016), by which the ex-commodities that are discarded in the regular operation of capitalism are nonetheless hidden from us, the useful features obscured by our conviction that anything in the garbage must be dirty and useless.

What kind of "solution" to food waste did freegan.info propose? On the one hand, freegan.info was always focused on denouncing "the system"—usually going beyond "the food system" to "the capitalist system" as a whole. For years, the group decided *not* to

Figure 23.2 A "Waving the Banana" speech during a trash tour in New York in 2008.
Source: Alex Barnard (used with permission).

engage in what they deemed "naming and shaming" particularly wasteful stores, out of a fear that doing so would imply that shopping at stores other than those they targeted was ethic-ally unproblematic. Moreover, the group was frequently torn between a desire to reduce food waste and an awareness that an abundance of edible discarded food was part of what allowed some of them to survive on the margins of capitalist society while still living in New York City. At an individual level, freegans often insisted that perfecting personal prac-tices had little to do with addressing the problems posed by waste, despite the great lengths many took to distance their daily lives from consumer capitalism. As Carol, one freegan.info activist who quit her job in the corporate world for full-time activism, put it, "The point isn't my lifestyle and how pure or impure it is. It [freeganism] is not about [taking] shorter showers. It's about making a political point and changing hearts and minds."

In actuality, though, freegans were early adopters of some of the everyday behaviours that mainstream contemporary advocates for reducing food waste now promote. Regular freegan.info meetings almost always started with the informal sharing of food that freegans had found in excess or which did not fit their specific needs. Monthly freegan "feasts"—shared meals pre-pared with only dumpster-dived food—required that freegans learn to cook with what they had, rather than run to the corner store to purchase what they thought they needed. Cynthia explained how freegans were building community through food, critiquing the way that, in cities, "people aren't treating food as social glue which sticks community together."

Freeganism, we realised, requires spending much more time gathering, storing, and preparing food than most Western consumers are accustomed to committing to. In evaluating food safety, freegans—like some contemporary food waste campaigns—encouraged their audiences to look beyond "best-" and "sell-by" dates. As David, one of freegan.info's founders, told a group of students: "We have false ideas about what constitutes fresh food. A lot of food tastes better when it looks worse. But those are not the tactile and aesthetic qualities people look for when they purchase produce." Newcomers came with a predictable range of questions about food safety, and were told by one experienced freegan, "I never look at the sell-by date, it's irrelevant to me. It's about the condition of the food: you smell it, you taste it, and if it's horrible, don't [eat it]."

Although hygiene concerns were a frequent reason for shutting down FNB's public meals, it was precisely this "ick" factor that freegans leveraged to make their activities so attention-grabbing. Douglas (1966) argues that all societies hold powerful "pollution rules" that separate the clean and dirty, sacred and profane, virtuous and wicked. In his work on dumpster-diving punks, Clark (2004, p. 28) found that

> for those ... who were raised White or middle class, dumpsters and dumped food dirty their bodies and tarnish their affiliation with a White, bourgeois power structure. In this sense, the downward descent into a dumpster is literally an act of downward mobility.

For many freegans, too, dumpster diving was a way of symbolically distancing themselves from their own privileged backgrounds and, for some, past employment in mainstream, corporate jobs.

As they insisted, freegans also engaged with these "pollution rules" strategically and instrumentally. When freegans ate "polluted" food and showed that it was still good, they simplify that the store managers, consumers, and social norms that led to ex-commodification were, in fact, dirty, profane, and wicked, while reclaiming waste was, ultimately, clean and virtuous. The perfect example came when an ABC reporter asked, "What do you say to people who say, 'There you are on the street, digging through trash, this is gross, this is disgusting'?" One media-savvy freegan replied: "Well, I'd say what's gross and disgusting is the fact that this food is being thrown out in the first place." If freegans built on the strategies for using waste piloted by FNB, this example highlights how the group further developed the idea of using food waste symbolically and instrumentally as well to call attention to a broader anti-capitalist message. This message coexisted uneasily, however, with a set of practices that, at least to some observers, seemed like an over-the-top fixation on personal carbon footprint and individual (non-)consumptive practices.

From anti-capitalism to anti-waste

By 2010, freegan.info claimed to have been the object of 600 news stories from dozens of countries. But the group also faced a series of problems. There were tensions within the New York group around those who saw freeganism as an all-encompassing anti-capitalist practice, and those who saw it simply as a common-sense way to eat cheaply while reducing waste. While the leaders of freegan.info wanted to publicise the existence of ex-commodified food as much as possible, other dumpster divers resented the new attention to what had previously been a discreet practice. They blamed freegan.info and the media it attracted for an apparent uptick in frequency with which discarded food had been deliberately destroyed through pouring bleach on it or slashing it with a knife.

These observations were not limited to New York City. Jeremy Seifert, a filmmaker who released a 2010 documentary about waste at Trader Joe's supermarkets in the United States, told the authors that a few years later:

> I've found a lot of locked dumpsters at some of the stores, for sure. I think they are quietly doing that to avoid more films and videos being put out. They refuse to adopt a corporate-wide policy, which means that they allow each individual store to determine their giving. Some stores might give some of the food, but don't want to deal with fruits and vegetables, so they're going to throw that away ... There's probably still significant waste happening, so they're locking dumpsters to avoid the scandal of it.[8]

Outside of New York, a few dumpster divers in the Netherlands, France, and the U.K. were actually arrested for recovering wasted food (Wardrop, 2011; de Vries and Abrahamsson, 2012; Goutorbe, 2015). Although there seems to be no systematic study of the criminalisation of food recovery worldwide, O'Brien (2012) suggests that practices of gleaning and dumpster diving could become more difficult as more food waste is diverted into waste-to-energy facilities or municipal composting programmes. In effect, it might be getting harder to access ex-commodities because those ex-commodities are being re-commodified.

Indeed, one of the paradoxical impacts of freeganism's rise may be that it has made its own practice more difficult through helping call attention to food waste and stimulating actions to reduce it. In early 2014, the authors attended a conference put on by GreenCook, an EU-funded collaboration between governments, businesses, and non-profits centred on reducing food waste. The keynote speaker was Tristram Stuart, a British public activist-intellectual who, by his own narrative, first became interested in food waste through "skip dipping"—recovering food from dumpsters—in London (Stuart, 2009, p. 5). He opened his remarks by asking, "Who here has ever been dumpster diving?" We raised our hands, but the other 250 people—mostly government functionaries, corporate sustainability officers, and high-level NGO employees—looked confused. Still, Stuart himself told us afterwards that:

> [b]y taking journalists round the back of supermarkets, showing them what was there, and serving them dinner based on it, and being able to very articulately talk about how this fit into a global problem generated a lot of media. It certainly sparked a lot of interest on the part of policymakers and companies ... I absolutely think freeganism was *the* original instigator of this new wave of global action on food waste.

Of course, the convergence of a global financial crisis and concerns about food supplies (see Chapter 1, this volume) set the structural stage for broader public concern over food waste. Nonetheless, since reducing food waste is not the automatic or even obvious way of addressing a growing population and rising precarity, policy entrepreneurs like Stuart and social movements like freeganism were a necessary ingredient of putting food waste onto the agenda (Evans, Campbell, and Murcott, 2012).

Yet even as it has grown in attention, the meanings attached to food waste have changed. For example, Jonathan Bloom (2010, pp. 11, 28) wrote in his frequently cited book *American Wasteland* that solving food waste is a "triple bottom line" solution that benefits consumers, businesses, and the environment, adding that "By trimming our waste and recovering the low-hanging fruit (literally and figuratively!), we can help feed hungry Americans, bolster our economy, combat global warming, and make our society that much more ethical." Stuart

(2009, p. 294), distancing himself from many dumpster divers' (including, perhaps, his own) radical critiques of the food system, declared "reducing food waste" to be "uncontroversial" and "relatively painless." Similarly, the United Nations' Think.Eat.Save project speaks of a cultural "paradigm" that enables food waste, but assures us that "with relative ease and a few simple changes to our habits, we can significantly shift this paradigm."[9]

These approaches are emblematic of a much-studied process of the transformation of seemingly radical environmental claims into initiatives that rely on voluntary corporate commitments, technological advances, and consumer choices (see, e.g., Bartley, 2003; Jaffee, 2012). Food waste programmes treat food waste as a problem, in and of itself, that can be tackled on its own terms without a structural transformation of economic or even food systems. This understanding, we show in the next section, was picked up by DS.

Disco Soupe: "Yes, we cut"

DS has more recent origins than both FNB and freeganism. Inspired by an event called "Schnippeldisko" ("Peeling Disco") in Germany[10]—organised by youth affiliated with the global slow-food movement—the group held its first event in France in March 2012. Its stated mission was raising awareness about and encouraging non-confrontational action against food waste in a collective and participative way, creating "conviviality" through music and cooking.[11] The group spread quickly, holding 60 events in 25 cities between March 2012 and May 2013 and claiming around 600 active members in 2018.[12] Although not formally affiliated with one another, the concept has been adopted by self-organised groups in, among other places, New York City ("Disco Soup"), Madrid ("Disco Sopa"), São Paulo ("Disco Xepa"), Rotterdam ("Disco Soep"), and Namyangju, Korea ("Yori Gamu").

Like freegan.info and FNB, DS acquires ex-commodified food, which would otherwise go to waste. The group mostly obtains donations directly from supermarkets or wholesalers, rather than "dumpster diving" their discards. Meals are supposed to be cooked collaboratively and served in public to anyone, regardless of need. Similarly to FNB, the group insists that these features distinguish it from more "mainstream" soup kitchens and emergency food providers. DS also claims to embody its principles by eschewing hierarchical, formal structures in favour of consensus-based decision-making and loosely affiliated chapters with no designated leaders or officers.

Some DS participants were even closely affiliated with the kind of anarchist, direction-action currents that gave birth to freeganism and FNB. At 26, Lea decided to stop her studies on urban planning to dedicate herself to DS. In 2014, she lived in an illegally occupied squat in the 20th district of Paris and explained that her action with DS was "political, in a certain way." As she elaborated in a discussion on the DS Facebook group:

> Distributing free food in the public sphere in a festive way is itself a form of claim: acting is not always acting *against* something, but it can consist in offering free activities that cannot be controlled. The idea of testing new systems of valuation not based on the market is political.

She even referred to the concept of "temporary autonomous zones" popularised by the global justice movement (Bey, 1985), joking that DS meals provide "temporary autonomous soup." For a few members of DS, then, claiming discarded food and occupying public spaces with live music, outdoors or indoors, at marketplaces, in community centres or squats, and during festivals or community events, were the key aspects of DS.

Most DS organisers, despite the exceptions noted above, tended to come from similarly privileged but less politically engaged backgrounds than those in freegan.info or FNB. The objective of DS's public meals was not to place blame on corporations or consumers but to raise general awareness among "citizens" and gain media attention. By inventing play-on-words like "we peel good!" and creating posters with smiling vegetable faces, some DS participants further emphasised their non-confrontational approach. As Pauline, a 30-year-old business school graduate working for a social enterprise, explained, the value of DS events is to talk to the "average Joe" and to attract people who would not be involved in more radical forms of activism. As she herself acknowledged, "I wouldn't do this if it were not for DS ... some radical groups are too closed or badly organised ... or less fun." Sébastien, a 27-year-old journalist organising DS events, noted that DS had benefitted from broader attention to food waste issues. But, he added, "If we just talked about food waste, there would be less interest. But there is music, too."

One of the central goals of DS is to "raise awareness against food waste" and it joined major international organisations in pointing to consumers as key to addressing the issue. For some DS participants, the way individuals related to the food itself during the meal preparation was exemplary of how consumers could change their practices. During DS meals, people exchanged tips for cooking with leftovers or parts of vegetables such as carrot tops that usually go to waste (see Figure 23.3). Participating in a DS event was, for their mostly young attendees, a chance to increase their knowledge around food by discovering rare vegetables or exotic fruits that they would not usually use and learning how to cook them. The group further encouraged "food education" with special tables for children who learn how to chop with plastic knives.

Figure 23.3 A Disco Soupe meal preparation in Paris in 2014.
Source: Yann Deva (with permission).

Some participants viewed the time spent preparing and cooking as imparting a sense of the value of food, particularly to items that would have been thrown away for cosmetic reasons. We observed one organiser voluntarily leaving some blemished parts of the fruits for participants. "The aim is to make them cut out the bad parts," she explained, "to sensitise them." Spring, Adams, and Hardman (2019) argue that such "visceral pedagogies" have the potential to allow individuals to re-imagine themselves as skilled actors in assessing and preparing food, rather than being relegated to the status of passive consumers. But if the events sought to empower their participants to address food waste, it could muddle the origins of that waste in the first place. After all, DS events intended to influence consumers relied on ex-commodities produced by retailers, who were nonetheless not the direct targets of these educational efforts.[13]

Such practices of re-valuing a-typical foods were not so far from the practices on view at a freegan feast, but they were intended to inform consumers' purchasing decisions in a way freegan.info events, needless to say, were not. One DS event organiser explained her discomfort with how an event might fail to increase awareness of the need to buy locally produced vegetables: "I always feel super weird when we cook a ratatouille [a stew made with summer vegetables] in the middle of the winter. What are we communicating to these people? They still follow the supermarket standards." Reflections like this show that, in the eyes of many DS organisers, a single awareness-raising event could spark enduring changes. One woman described the first DS event she "coordinated":

> There are the small posters ... but the very fact of doing a Disco Soupe speaks for itself. You are in the concrete aspects of waste ... They tell you "so many tons [of waste], so much stuff ..." but then you *see* the quantities, quantities and quantities [she added gestures imitating mountains of food]. You think that all of this would not have been eaten ... You spend an hour to chop: nothing can be more concrete!

She went on to explain, "Now when I chop an apple I think about this moment [saving a piece of a partly rotten apple during the DS] and I cannot throw away the entire apple!" DS thus appeared as an example of a "lifestyle-based movement" (Haenfler, Johnson, and Jones, 2012) of the kind freegans explicitly derided, even as both groups endorsed similar practices.

Is DS emblematic of a process of de-politicisation of food waste? DS members often debate whether or not they are "*politique*," but in the sense that the most common meaning of the French word relates to affiliation with political parties. This point was explicitly clarified during their first "Disco Campus" (general assembly) in 2013: "we are *politique*, not *partisan*," that is to say "political" but without party affiliation. In their eyes, public meals put positive pressure on decision-makers in government and companies. In this respect, the strength of DS was precisely that it is both well-organised enough to be taken seriously by institutions and non-confrontational enough to attract a wide array of people to its events and organising meetings. DS meals in France scrupulously follow laws and regulations regarding public events, in terms of legal structures, insurance, and permits. The same is true for how they obtain food—the group makes formal agreements with some markets and supermarkets and offers donation certificates—and food safety—"soupers" use gloves and the main organisers of DS underwent certified hygiene training.

Groups like FNB are, of course, not indifferent to food safety, and concerns about the particular health vulnerabilities of the precarious people they served commonly came up in the East Bay. Some FNB groups may even seek permits and follow hygiene requirements with the instrumental goal of avoiding the ire of the authorities. For at least some in DS, these same practices also had a tactical function, albeit one that reflected a very different overall strategy. When debates arose about the use of gloves that generate plastic waste, Jules, who quit his job as a consultant to devote himself full-time to the group, made it clear that even if the gloves do not ensure more hygiene, "they make it visible, it's not like washing your hands. That way passers-by see we are serious." DS further displays its legitimacy to outside institutions through a formalised annual report and financial statements. For a time, DS even functioned with subsidies from Paris's municipal government—a stark contrast to the decades of arrests of FNB participants by the city government in San Francisco.

Ultimately, for most Disco Soupers, solutions to food waste can be found in partnership —not conflict—with food processing and retailing companies. Pauline and Stéphanie, who both studied in prestigious business schools before participating in the founding of DS in 2012, represented DS in working groups and meetings instigated by the French Ministry for Agriculture and Food during negotiations for the "National Pact to Fight Food Waste" in 2013. Reflecting on her experience, Pauline insisted that all actors involved in those negotiations—mostly large catering and retail companies along with agro-industry representatives —had "good intentions" and that the focus should be on finding solutions. "If you offer a cheap and easy solution, they [producers and retailers] are going to be okay," she explained, "they would even pat you on the back." She proudly observed that the Pact was an opportunity for DS to launch an official partnership with a major French retail chain.

Although the meals they prepared shared similarities with those put on by FNB and the "feasts" put on by freegans, they also suggested that the politics around food waste had clearly shifted. One of our informants told us that when she attempted to start a new DS group in the south of France in 2013, she actually contacted the local FNB chapter. As she reported, however, "They even came to one of our events, but we did not really talk. They are much more radical ... we are not on the same wave-length at all." A key part of the difference, we argue, is that what was once a symptom of a malfunctioning food system had become, for DS, a problem-in-itself, that could be addressed in partnership with the very institutions previous movements denounced.

Conclusion: a new world out of/without waste

Even though they expended a great deal of effort trying to educate both consumers and policymakers, the leaders of DS often looked at the masses of people who stopped by an event for a cup of free soup and asked, "What will they remember from this Disco Soupe? They are just here for fun." One of the founders of freegan.info similarly lamented that the group's "trash tours" seemed to encounter the same quantity of waste despite years of efforts: "We've done so little with it [the media]. We've just done exposing, exposing, and exposing, and if you do that enough, people just get numb to it." While scholars have debated whether practices such as dumpster diving can, in and of themselves, have a meaningful direct ecological impact (Scheinberg and Anschütz, 2006; Brosius, Fernandez, and Cherrier, 2013), it is clear that none of the three groups reviewed in this chapter was actually directly putting a dent in the estimated 40% of food going to waste in France or the United States.[14] Moreover, the contribution of each group to shifting public policies around food waste is difficult to pin down.

Taken together, though, these movements nonetheless offer valuable lessons, including for those focused on more operational, technical, and policy-based solutions for food waste. First, critics have noted the close imbrication between the corporate food system and an increasingly bureaucratised system of food banks that provide an outlet for their excess (Fisher, 2017; Lohnes and Wilson, 2018). The movements we study, however, show the potential of decentralised and democratically governed networks in recovering and redistributing food. Second, in events such as "freegan feasts" and DS street parties, we saw how "rescuing" food—by repurposing it for new recipes or performing emergency surgery to cut out rotting parts—can actually be fun. What is often presented as an ecological duty of consumers to be more responsible can also become a source of a renewed sense of mastery and skill with respect to food. Finally, all three organisations point to how reducing food waste can also be tied to attempts to rebuild community, especially in urban spaces where food consumption is frequently hurried, atomised, and done in private.

If all three movements share some solutions to food waste, though, they saw food waste itself—particularly in the form of ex-commodities, which we defined as goods that are still useful, but which are abandoned because they cannot be profitably sold—in radically different ways. For FNB, food waste provided a resource for sustaining anarchist communities on the margins of capitalism, in the same way as abandoned buildings turned into squats or vacant lots transformed into gardens. Freeganism also tapped into food waste as a valuable resource, but, to a much greater extent than FNB, mobilised it as a potent symbol as well. Exposing that neoliberal capitalism poured natural resources, human labour, and animal exploitation into the production of commodities, only to discard them, offered a visible indictment of the system as a whole. Although some DS participants voiced similar ideas in private, they ultimately treated food waste as a problem in its own right, one that could be solved through consumer practices and public policy which contributed to incremental steps toward broader changes in the food system. FNB and freegan.info imagined constructing a new world out of waste; DS imagined keeping much the same world but taking waste out of it.

This is not to say that FNB and freegan.info did not see food waste as a problem. One critical article claimed that "[There is] a quandary inherent in the freegan movement" because "if they succeed in their overriding goal, and society ends up becoming less wasteful, the freegan lifestyle will no longer be possible" (Halpern, 2010). Most freegans and FNB participants we talked to *did* want their practices of waste reclamation to go obsolete— they were just convinced that, to do so, capitalism would become obsolete as well. The partial success of public policies against food waste in the U.K. and in France in the 2010s —with decreasing quantities of food being discarded[15]—suggests that policymakers really can address some portion of food waste without reconfiguring the food system as a whole.

This implies there was some merit to DS's consensual approach. But as certain sources of food waste dry up—whether via locking dumpsters, diverting organic matter into waste-to-energy plants, or reselling "ugly" fruits and vegetables—it is worth reflecting on what other kinds of politics and movements might be crowded out.

Notes

1 Appadurai (1986, p. 16) introduces the concept of "ex-commodity" to refer to "things retrieved, either temporarily or permanently, from the commodity state and placed in some other state," but without theorising the place of ex-commoditisation in capitalism. Our use of ex-commodity has the most affinities with Giles' (2014) notion of "abject capital" (see, also, Chapter 1 in this volume). If we take seriously Marx's notion that capital is "value in motion" (see Harvey, 1999, p. 199), then ex-commodities are the things that must be expelled from the market to keep capital moving. This mass of ex-commodities, both external to the normal circuits of capital yet in

constant relation with it, constitutes abject capital, whose future remains ambiguous. Once recovered and used to expose the waste-making processes of contemporary capitalism, "ex-commodities" thus in effect become what he calls "counter-commodities" (Giles, 2014, p. 108).

2 http://foodnotbombs.net/faq.html (Retrieved October 18, 2018).

3 The relationship between veganism and freeganism is more complex than this joke lets on. Many freegans joined the movement after a long history of animal rights activism, and chose to move to freeganism when they realised even vegan products came with their own history of ecological devastation and exploitation (see Barnard, 2016).

4 The veracity of this story was confirmed by Shteir (2012).

5 https://freegan.info/ (Retrieved October 18, 2018).

6 Many of these practices have now been associated with the label "freeganism," but few of the people we met in California identified with the term "freegan" and many long-term avid waste reclaimers had never even heard of it.

7 https://freegan.info/ (Retrieved October 18, 2018).

8 The CEO of Trader Joe's has also been celebrated as a leader in helping to develop secondary markets for otherwise-discarded food, through his Daily Table store (Alvarez and Johnson, 2011). We think this is a striking example of how more formal, mainstream attempts to reduce food waste can crowd out informal food recovery practices.

9 www.thinkeatsave.org/ (Retrieved March 21, 2019).

10 http://slowfoodyouth.de/was-wir-tun/schnippeldisko/ (Retrieved January 25, 2019).

11 www.facebook.com/DiscoSoupe/info (Retrieved October 18, 2018).

12 *Rapport d'activité, mars 2012-mai 2013 (Report of Activity, March 2012-May 2013)*, Disco Soupe, 2013. All translations from French by Mourad.

13 We are grateful to a reviewer for this point.

14 Of course, the more "mainstream" efforts to address food waste, through charitable donations or corporate social responsibility programmes, have not necessarily put a "dent" in food waste, either. This gives some life to the critique by FNB and freegan.info participants that ex-commodities are part and parcel of modern capitalist food systems.

15 *Baromètre 2018 de la valorisation des invendus en grande distribution*, Comerso, 2018. According to this study led by a food redistribution organisation, 34% of supermarkets implemented actions against food waste following the 2016 Food Waste Law. Other indicators suggest that the law had a significant impact.

References

Alvarez, J. B., & Johnson, R. C. (2011). *Doug Rauch: Solving the American Food Paradox* (SSRN Scholarly Paper No. ID 2014326). Rochester, NY: Social Science Research Network. Retrieved from: http://papers.ssrn.com/abstract=2014326

Appadurai, A.. (ed.) (1986). Introduction: Commodities and the Politics of Value. In *The Social Life of Things: Commodities in Cultural Perspective* (pp. 3–63). Cambridge, UK: Cambridge University Press.

Barnard, A. V. (2011). "Waving the Banana" at Capitalism: Political Theater and Social Movement Strategy Among New York's 'Freegan' Dumpster Divers. *Ethnography*, *12*(4), 419–444.

Barnard, A. V. (2016). *Freegans: Diving into the Wealth of Food Waste in America* Minneapolis, MN: University of Minnesota Press.

Bartley, T. (2003). Certifying Forests and Factories: States, Social Movements, and the Rise of Private Regulation in the Apparel and Forest Products Fields. *Politics & Society*, *31*(3), 433–464.

Belasco, W. J. (2007). *Appetite for Change: How the Counterculture Took On the Food Industry* (2nd ed.). Ithaca, NY: Cornell University Press.

Bennett, E., Cordner, A., Klein, P. T., Savell, S., & Baiocchi, G. (2013). Disavowing Politics: Civic Engagement in an Era of Political Skepticism. *American Journal of Sociology*, *119*(2), 518–548.

Bey, H. (1985) *T.A.Z.: The Temporary Autonomous Zone, Ontological Anarchy, Poetic Terrorism*. The Anarchist Library. Retrieved from https://theanarchistlibrary.org/library/hakim-bey-t-a-z-the-temporary-autonomous-zone-ontological-anarchy-poetic-terrorism

Bloom, Jonathan (2010). *American Wasteland: How America Throws Away Nearly Half of Its Food*. Cambridge, MA: Da Capo Lifelong Books.

Bloom, Joshua, & Martin, W. E. (2013). *Black Against Empire: The History and Politics of the Black Panther Party*. Berkeley, CA: University of California Press.

Brosius, N., Fernandez, K. V., & Cherrier, H. (2013). Reacquiring Consumer Waste: Treasure in Our Trash?. *Journal of Public Policy & Marketing, 32*(2), 286–301.

Carlsson, C. (2008). *Nowtopia: How Pirate Programmer, Outlaw Bicyclists, and Vacant-Lot Gardeners Are Inventing the Future Today!* Oakland, CA: AK Press.

Carolsfeld, A. L., & Erikson, S. L. (2013). Beyond Desperation: Motivations for Dumpster™ Diving for Food in Vancouver. *Food and Foodways, 21*(4), 245–266.

Chaboud, G., & Daviron, B. (2017). Food losses and waste: Navigating the inconsistencies. *Global Food Security, 12*, 1–7. doi: 10.1016/j.gfs.2016.11.004

Clark, D. (2004). The Raw and the Rotten: Punk Cuisine. *Ethnology, 43*(1), 19–31. Doi: 10.2307/3773853

Cloteau, A., & Mourad, M. (2016). Action publique et fabrique du consensus, Public policy and consensus-making. *Gouvernement et action publique, 1*, 63–90. Doi: 10.3917/gap.161.0063

de Vries, K., & Abrahamsson, S. (2012, March 27). Dumpsters, Muffins, Waste, and Law. Retrieved April 1, 2012, from http://discardstudies.wordpress.com/2012/03/27/dumpsters-muffins-waste-and-law/

Douglas, M. (1966). *Purity and Danger: An Analysis of the Concepts of Pollution and Taboo*. London, UK: Routledge.

Edwards, F., & Mercer, D. (2007). Gleaning from Gluttony: An Australian Youth Subculture Confronts the Ethics of Waste. *Australian Geographer, 38*(3), 279–296.

Epstein, B. (1991). *Political Protest and Cultural Revolution: Nonviolent Direct Action in the 1970s and 1980s*. Berkeley, CA: University of California Press.

Evans, D., Campbell, H., & Murcott, A. (2012). A Brief Pre-History of Food Waste and the Social Sciences. *The Sociological Review, 60*, 5–26.

Fisher, A. (2017). *Big Hunger: The Unholy Alliance between Corporate America and Anti-Hunger Groups*. Cambridge, MA: MIT Press.

Giles, D. B. (2013). *"A Mass Conspiracy To Feed People": Globalizing Cities, World-Class Waste, and the Biopolitics of Food Not Bombs*. PhD Thesis: University of Washington.

Giles, D. B. (2014). The Anatomy of a Dumpster: Abject Capital and the Looking Glass of Value. *Social Text, 32*(1118), 93–113.

Goutorbe, C. (2015, February 4). Hérault : des glaneurs de poubelles au tribunal. *La Depeche*. Retrieved from www.ladepeche.fr/article/2015/02/04/2043246-herault-des-glaneurs-de-poubelles-au-tribunal.html

Graeber, D. (2009). *Direct Action: An Ethnography*. Oakland, CA: AK Press.

Gross, J. (2009). Capitalism and Its Discontents: Back-to-the-Lander and Freegan Foodways in Rural Oregon. *Food and Foodways, 17*(2), 57–79.

Haenfler, R., Johnson, B., & Jones, E. (2012). Lifestyle Movements: Exploring the Intersection of Lifestyle and Social Movements. *Social Movement Studies, 11*(1), 1–20.

Halpern, J. (2010 June 4). The Freegan Establishment. *The New York Times*, MM58.

Harvey, D. (1999). *The Limits to Capital*. New York: Verso.

Heynen, N. (2010). Cooking Up Non-Violent Civil-Disobedient Direct Action for the Hungry: 'Food Not Bombs' and the Resurgence of Radical Democracy in the U.S. *Urban Studies, 47*(6), 1225–1240.

Jaffee, D. (2012). Weak Coffee: Certification and Co-Optation in the Fair Trade Movement. *Social Problems, 59*(1), 94–116.

Liboiron, M. (2012). Tactics of Waste, Dirt and Discard in the Occupy Movement. *Social Movement Studies, 11*(3–4), 393–401.

Lohnes, J., & Wilson, B. (2018). Bailing Out the Food Banks? Hunger Relief, Food Waste, and Crisis in Central Appalachia. *Environment and Planning A: Economy and Space, 50*(2), 350–369. Doi: 10.1177/0308518X17742154

Marx, K. (1976). *Capital: Volume 1*. (B. Fowkes, Trans.). London, UK: Penguin.

Mourad, M. (2015). *France Moves Towards a National Policy Against Food Waste* (No. R-15-08-B). Washington, DC: National Resources Defense Council. Retrieved from http://switchboard.nrdc.org/blogs/jberkenkamp/food_waste_inspiration_the_fre.html

Mourad, M. (2016). Recycling, recovering and preventing "food waste": competing solutions for food systems sustainability in the United States and France. *Journal of Cleaner Production, 126*, 461–477. Doi: 10.1016/j.jclepro.2016.03.084

O'Brien, M. (2012). A 'Lasting Transformation' of Capitalist Surplus: From Food Stocks to Feedstocks. *The Sociological Review, 60*, 192–211.

Parson, S. M. (2010). *An Ungovernable Force: Homeless Activism and Politics in San Francisco, 1988–1995.* (Dissertation). University of Oregon, Eugene, OR.

Sbicca, J., & Perdue, R. (2013). Protest Through Presence: Spatial Citizenship and Identity Formation in Contestations of Neoliberal Crises. *Social Movement Studies, 13*(3), 309–327.

Scheinberg, A., & Anschütz, J. (2006). Slim Pickin's: Supporting Waste Pickers in the Ecological Modernization of Urban Waste Management Systems. *International Journal of Technology Management & Sustainable Development, 5*(3), 257–270.

Shantz, J. (2005). One Person's Garbage, Another Person's Treasure. *Verb, 3*(1), 9–19.

Shteir, R. (2012). *The Steal: A Cultural History of Shoplifting.* New York: Penguin.

Spataro, D. (2016). Against a De-Politicized DIY Urbanism: Food Not Bombs and the Struggle Over Public space. *Journal of Urbanism: International Research on Placemaking and Urban Sustainability, 9*(2), 185–201. Doi: 10.1080/17549175.2015.1056208

Spring, C., Adams, M., & Hardman, M. (2019). Sites of Learning: Exploring Political Ecologies and Visceral Pedagogies of Surplus Food Redistribution In the UK. *Policy Futures in Education,* 1478210318819249. Doi: 10.1177/1478210318819249

Stoops, M. (2014). *Food-Sharing Report: The Criminalization of Efforts to Feed People in Need.* Washington, DC: National Coalition for the Homeless.

Stuart, T. (2009). *Waste: Uncovering the Global Food Scandal.* New York: W. W. Norton & Company.

Wardrop, M. (2011, June 1). Woman in Court for Taking "Waste" Food from Tesco Bins. *Telegraph.* Retrieved from www.telegraph.co.uk/news/uknews/crime/8548653/Woman-in-court-for-taking-waste-food-from-Tesco-bins.html

24

THE EFFECTS OF LABELLING, PACKAGING AND THE EATING ENVIRONMENT ON CONSUMER-GENERATED FOOD WASTE

Monica C. LaBarge, Sarah Evans, Beth Vallen
and Lauren G. Block

Food waste generated by consumers represents a substantial proportion of food loss—estimates range from 40% (CEC, 2017) to over 50% (Lipinski et al., 2013). A typical four-person American household discards roughly $1,500 worth of usable food every year (Smith, 2014), and the largest share of food loss and waste in North America—67 million tons per year—occurs at the individual or household level, with the remaining share accounted for by producers and retailers (CEC, 2017). One of the potential ways to impact this significant source of food waste is to examine factors that can contribute to food waste that occurs at the consumer level, such as the impact of food labelling and packaging, as well as the eating environment that surrounds food consumption (Block et al., 2016).

The manner in which information about food, and food itself, are presented to people has been reliably demonstrated to influence the quantity of food that people decide to purchase, take, and eventually consume. Most studies on decision making have explored the impact of variables related to food presentation and information up to the point of the consumption decision; in this chapter, we consider work that examines how and why waste may be generated as a consequence of individuals consuming less or more of a food depending on the format or other aspects of the food's conveyance, such as labelling, packaging and the eating environment (e.g., the tablescape or serveware). Decisions about how food is delivered or presented to people are frequently controllable by producers, retailers or others in the food supply production process, and so developing a more complete picture of the potential impact of these factors on food waste is an important step toward reducing consumer-originated waste (Schneider and Lebersorger, 2009). Additionally, as individuals, marketers and policy makers grow increasingly concerned with the social impact of consumption, research exploring when, how, and in what quantities people dispose of products, including food, is increasing in relevance.

In this chapter, we identify and review existing research in the domains of consumer psychology, food marketing, environmental science, agricultural economics and other relevant areas to explore what empirical work exists to document the effects the properties of food labelling, packaging and the eating environment have on consumer-originated food waste, and highlight potential directions for future research aimed at understanding and mitigating these effects.

Labelling

Food labelling can encompass a range of information about a particular food, including: the name, contents, origin and appearance of a product; nutritional data (e.g. calories, grams of fat, sodium or sugar, serving size, etc.); or safety or freshness-related information. It is that last type of label that has been most clearly linked to food waste and which is discussed here.

There are four label types that are frequently used by producers and retailers to indicate some date-related information about the quality or safety of the food in question: (1) best by (or best before), (2) sell by, (3) fresh by, and (4) use by (FSA, 2018). However, research shows substantial consumer confusion related to these terms. The "best by" label is intended to be a guideline for the point at which a food is at its highest quality, but people frequently misinterpret it to mean the date when the food is no longer safe to eat. In contrast, the "use by" date is an indication of food safety, although people frequently misinterpret it by believing the food is still safe to consume a few days after the date (Abeliotis et al., 2014). Still other products are labelled "sell by," which is a date meant for retailers but whose inclusion is also confusing for people when they are purchasing or consuming the product. There are also labels like "fresh by" that are understood to indicate product quality by consumers; however, they are not officially recognized by any regulatory standards (Wilson et al., 2017).

Individuals reported expecting to waste the least of food products that are labelled with the "use by" label, followed by the less-frequently used "fresh by," whereas they expected to waste the most of foods with "best by" and "sell by" labels (Wilson et al., 2017). Given the variation in labelling practices and confusion about what each term means, as well as the fact that people report being unwilling to take any risk with foods that are close to the expiration date (Cox and Downing, 2007), it is unsurprising that roughly 20% of food waste is thought to stem from confusion around date labels (Brook Lyndhurst, 2011). Being "past the date on the label" has been indicated by people as a driver for 30% of disposal choices (Brook Lyndhurst, 2011), in most cases leading them to throw out food that is still safe to eat (Abeliotis et al., 2014). A large national survey in the US found that 70% of individuals believe food that is past the package date has a higher chance of making people sick (Qi and Roe, 2016), and 90% of respondents in a large UK study reported paying very close or moderate attention to date labels (Brook Lyndhurst, 2011).

References to and reliance on date labels do not appear to be uniform across different types of foods. People are most likely to rely on or require external information such as labels when they are not confident in their own ability to judge the quality of the food; for example, evaluations of meat and dairy products as edible or waste were most likely to be based primarily upon the date on the label, whereas people were more confident about using their own judgement to assess the safety and quality of fresh fruit and vegetables (Brook Lyndhurst, 2011). One study focusing solely on dairy products found that individuals were more willing to consume yogurt when it had a "best before" label in comparison to a "use by" label, but that was not found to be the case for milk or cheese (Thompson et al., 2018), suggesting that not all foods are perceived equally with respect to date labelling. These findings suggest that there may be some inherent aspects of different food types such that they are judged as being differentially risky to consume closer to the date past which they could be unsafe to eat (Tsiros and Heilman, 2005). Additional research is necessary to determine what is driving those perceptions, be it a compositional element of the food itself, an assessment of the degree of transformation the food has undergone before reaching the end consumer, or some other psychological bias.

The literature shows that food labels influence individuals' food waste behaviours at different times across the acquisition and consumption process. This influence starts at the point-of-sale, such that people begin to use date labels in store to estimate how likely they are to waste food: some researchers have found that individuals anticipated being more likely to waste foods that are close to the expiration date while shopping (Aschemann-Witzel et al., 2017), while others have found that people expect to waste less of a product the further in the future the date on the label (Wilson et al., 2017). Wilson and colleagues (2017) term this expected amount of food that will eventually be discarded "premeditated food waste," and found that it interacts with willingness-to-pay, a measure of perceived product value. They suggest that increasing perceptions of value of the food, perhaps by reminding people of the value they themselves placed on the food at the time at which it was purchased, may help to reduce premeditated and realized food waste.

One of the tactics used by grocery retailers to sell food that is close to its expiry date is to offer it at a discount. It has been suggested that such price offers may increase the potential for food waste (Porpino et al., 2016), but empirical studies have shown that people explicitly take into account the possibility of waste due to the proximity of the food to its expiry date when considering whether or not to buy it (Aschemann-Witzel et al., 2017). As such, evaluations of the monetary value (as a combination of the price discount and its ultimate price) are traded off against assessments of how likely the food is to be wasted versus eaten or preserved (e.g., via freezing). Other studies have also demonstrated that price reductions do not change individuals' willingness to consume products that are close to their expiry dates (Thompson et al., 2018), suggesting that price discounts offered based on date labels do not generally affect individuals' perceptions of quality or safety. Additionally, Theotokis et al. (2012) have shown that this practice of providing discounts based on the expiration dates of food can actually have positive impacts on brand evaluation: when consumers are familiar with the practice, expiration date pricing does not affect perceptions of brand quality, and such perceptions can actually be significantly increased when the practice is framed as a cause-related marketing strategy.

Sen and Block (2008) have demonstrated an "ownership" bias, or endowment effect, such that individuals' willingness to consume a perishable food product past its "fresh by" date was greater when they already owned the product than when they did not, and this ownership-basis also decreased people's estimates that they would get sick from the product when it was past its freshness date. One large-scale study found that foods that have been removed from their packaging and no longer have a date label on them are less likely to be wasted than those that retain their original packaging and label (Brook Lyndhurst, 2011), while another study found that, for foods like leftovers without dates, people conceptualize their own standards or "eat-by" dates (Mavrakis, 2014). Taken together, this diminished sensitivity to a date label depending on ownership status, storage choices, or degree of transformation suggests that although date labels act as anchors by which people base judgements of desirability, quality and/or safety, they can also be malleable. In the case of safety-related labelling this could pose a problem, but in the case of small differences in quality, this represents a possible opportunity to encourage people to be more flexible about labelling practices such as "best by" dates, potentially reducing food waste.

The extent to which the packaging, which acts as a delivery mechanism not only for food but also for the labels just described, can affect food waste is reviewed next.

Packaging

Studies have demonstrated that roughly 20–25% of household food waste can be attributed to packaging issues, primarily because people find the quantity of food in the package exceeds consumers' actual needs and is too much to fully use before the best before date or before the food spoils (Williams, 2012). People are well aware that package size is a driver of their food waste, and yet they continue to buy large packages, often because of their own lay theories about "large = better value" (Haws and Winterich, 2013). These and other psychological biases and misestimations about packaging, as well as a range of demographic and lifestyle factors, can all have significant effects on food waste.

Larger is better bias

The bias people have toward larger packages as a proxy for better value frequently leads to over-buying (Ganglbauer et al., 2013) or "supersizing" (Dobson and Gerstner, 2010). People have been shown to perceive foods as being significantly cheaper (per unit weight) when contained in larger packaging compared to smaller, even in such extreme cases as when the packaging of the smaller container was half the size of the larger one but the contents themselves remained the same (Wansink, 1996). This effect is heightened when comparing standard packaging (in terms of shapes and sizes), which is perceived as smaller in quantity compared to uniquely shaped packaging (e.g., a bottle of apple juice shaped like an apple, a bottle of lemonade with ripples and curves, a glass instead of a plastic bottle; Folkes and Matta, 2004). This misestimation can have significant effects on food waste, particularly if the food contained in the larger package is less shelf-stable and likely to spoil quickly.

Demographic and lifestyle factors

A range of lifestyle and socio-economic status variables impact levels of food waste, both generally, as well as in the context of food packaging; here we will present general findings about food waste first, followed by package-specific research. Income, for instance, has been shown to have an effect on food waste, although its impact has varied across studies: some studies show higher income households produced more food waste overall (Schneider and Obersteiner, 2007), and still others do not observe any correlation between income and food waste (Williams et al., 2012). Interestingly, research has also found that lower income households, as well as those who were price conscious and those who took advantage of promotions (i.e., BOGOF offers and discounted products) produced less food waste than other households (Silvennoinen et al., 2014). This last finding suggests the possibility of a set of knowledge or skills that helps minimize waste, whether due to environmental or economic concerns. The potential for a type of "waste literacy," perhaps as a subset of food literacy, may provide an interesting avenue for future research. In the context of the relationship between income, food waste and packaging waste, one study found that higher income households produced more packaging waste compared to food waste, whereas lower income households produced more food waste compared to packaging waste (Bolaane and Ali, 2004), suggesting there is an ideal balance between the amount of food and the amount of packaging it requires.

Household composition and lifestyle factors can also influence food waste. For example, single-person households have been shown to produce the most average per person food waste (Mallinson et al., 2016), while individuals who rely on pre-packaged foods tend to produce less organic waste but more packaging waste than households who prepare more food from scratch (Parizeau et al., 2015). Taken together, this suggests a relationship between waste, packaging size and price, such that smaller packages of food—which may be more appropriate for smaller households as well as being more efficient in terms of reducing food waste—may also be less affordable (or at least are perceived to be so). Mallinson et al. (2016) draw the conclusion that many pre-packaged foods are both over-priced and provide too much food for small households, which leads to both food waste and higher food costs. The question remains, however, as to whether the extent of waste savings from pre-packaged foods represents a reduction in *actual* waste (e.g., via better controlled portion sizes) versus simply shifting waste backwards in the supply chain (i.e., the trim and other waste created through food preparation is no longer consumer-originated but occurs during mass-processing and packaging stages) (Parizeau et al., 2015).

It has also been demonstrated that people are more likely to throw away poorer quality fresh produce if it is pre-packaged or chosen for them (e.g., in online grocery shopping) versus when they choose it themselves; in the former case, they feel less responsible for it (Ilyuk, 2018). This suggests a "shift of blame" effect that might also be found in the context of leftovers that people did not prepare for themselves, such as those from a large restaurant meal. This again suggests that ownership status (see Sen and Block, 2008) has complex effects on food waste, ranging from who currently owns the food to who originally picked it or prepared it. Future research might explore conditions that accentuate or attenuate this ownership bias.

Evaluations of packaging versus of food

The condition of the packaging is also an important contributor to food waste. For instance, people see external imperfections on packaging (i.e., a dent in a soup can) as an indication of contamination or perceive there to be a health and safety risk, which increases the likelihood they will throw it away (White et al., 2016). Another series of studies demonstrated that individuals are more likely to recycle larger, more whole pieces of "garbage" (in this case, paper), but put smaller, damaged recyclable items into the garbage (Trudel and Argo, 2013). These suggest that judgements of how "intact" or "whole" a food is may affect the likelihood of it being discarded. In the context of food waste, it might be worth examining to what extent that completeness or degree of transformation the food has undergone (i.e., raw carrots versus cooked, cut-up carrots) influences an individual's willingness to dispose of it.

One of the biggest issues related to packaging and food waste is termed the "food waste-packaging paradox," which refers to the trade-off between making smaller portions to cut down on food waste at the expense of increasing packaging waste (Porpino et al., 2015; Verghese et al., 2015). A majority of people believe that packaging waste is a bigger concern than food waste (Cox and Downing, 2007; Williams, 2011; Principato et al., 2015), likely because food is biodegradable whereas most (plastic) packaging is not (Cox and Downing, 2007). Some analyses have tried to examine the environmental trade-offs between the environmental impact of producing and transporting food versus the impact of packaging, and generally have concluded that slightly increasing packaging waste for the sake of reducing food waste is warranted for some foods that alone have a high environmental impact (e.g., meat and dairy) (Williams, 2011). Recommendations to address this problem include greater availability of smaller portions that are priced so as to limit the appeal of "bulk-buying", which increases the likelihood of food waste due to errors in forecasting. Packaging designs such as resealable, subdivided or generally smaller packages, and storage advice on the label may also aid people in preserving uneaten food portions (Verghese et al., 2015).

Portion size

Oversized portions, whether in the foodservice sector or at home, have been identified as drivers of a significant portion of food loss and waste (Gunders, 2012). Approximately 30% of food is estimated to be consumed directly out of commercial food packages (Wansink, 1996). Because package size influences consumption, in that people have been shown to eat more from larger packages (Wansink, 1996), to the extent that some of the increased amount of food taken from larger packages remains uneaten, it has the potential to contribute to food waste.

The way that food is packaged and labelled has also been shown to influence perceptions of portion size and, thus, consumption and waste. For example, using real sales data on yogurt and cookies, researchers found that people tended to buy more of a food product when the recommended serving size presented on the packaging was smaller, because they perceived it as healthier (i.e., smaller serving size equals fewer calories; Elshiewy et al., 2016). Even the pictures of food on the package, rather than the size or shape of the packaging itself, can have an impact on perceptions of the quantity of food contained therein (Young, 2005); packages showing a larger quantity of food (e.g., seven versus four cookies, four versus one cracker) were perceived as containing a larger quantity and larger serving size inside (Madzharov and Block, 2010). A possible implication of these findings is that people may misestimate how much is contained in a given package depending on serving size specifications or visual depictions; these biases could either increase or decrease food waste, depending on the direction of misestimation.

In an intervention designed to make portion sizes more salient, researchers inserted a red chip every five or seven potato chips within a serving tube (similar to the packaging of Pringles) and found that doing so both reduced consumption of chips by over 50% as well as improved estimates of the number of potato chips consumed (Geier et al., 2012). They suggest that such interventions may work by making monitoring of eating easier and more salient for individuals; they may introduce a normative element in terms of portion size; and/or may introduce a pause within an automatic eating sequence that could otherwise continue uninterrupted (Geier et al., 2012). Given that researchers have found that the smaller the amount of leftovers, the more likely they are to be thrown away (Mavrakis, 2014), it is possible that altering the packaging of bulk foods (e.g., chips, crackers, cookies, etc.) in such a way as to cue distinct portions could result in less food waste, since it would be easily apparent how many portions were left in a package and people could make more informed value assessments.

Although a significant proportion of food is eaten directly from a package, an even larger amount is served out of or onto other types of serveware and consumed at a table. These environmental elements surrounding food have also been shown to directly affect food waste, as discussed next.

The eating environment

Food consumption behaviour is also heavily influenced by the environment that surrounds food; in particular, the platescape (the serveware—e.g., bowls, plates, glasses and utensils used) and the tablescape (the furniture or table on which food is presented) can influence the amount of food taken and consumed, and ultimately wasted. The surface area of the average dinner plate increased by 36% from 1960 to 2007 (Wansink and Van Ittersum, 2007), and since the size of a plate or bowl has been demonstrated to significantly affect how much food is served, the size of those portions affects both the amount of food actually consumed (Sobal and Wansink, 2007) as well as how much is wasted.

Serveware

The research around the effects of different types of serveware on consumption is well established. A recent meta-analysis (Holden et al., 2016) confirmed previous findings that people have been shown to serve themselves significantly more when their plates, bowls or other containers were larger or wider (Wansink and Van Ittersum, 2006; Wansink et al., 2006; Sobal and Wansink, 2007). The shape of serveware can also have an impact on the amount of food or liquid taken; the shape of glasses and cups influences the amount of liquid perceived to be in them (Raghubir and Krishna, 1999), and people serve themselves more when filling "3-D" shaped containers (like bowls with spherical shapes that fill in three dimensions) compared to "1-D" shaped containers (such as a plain cylinder, that only appears to fill upwards; Chandon and Ordabayeva, 2009). Other studies have found that serveware can also have a direct effect on waste; for example, one study found that hotels with smaller breakfast buffet plates (21 cm) had 19% less food waste than hotels with larger (24 cm) plates (Kallbekken and Sælen, 2013). In all these cases, only about 90% of the food taken is consumed (Robinson et al., 2015), so increased serving size due to larger serveware has implications for both over-consumption and food waste.

Beyond size, other serveware differences have also been shown to affect consumption and waste. Williamson and colleagues (2016) demonstrated that people who were served food on permanent (i.e., hard plastic) plates both ate more and wasted less those who were served on disposable (i.e., paper) plates. They also discovered, using an implicit association test, that participants were significantly faster at categorizing foods on paper plates into the "stop eating" category and those on permanent plates into the "keep eating" category (Williamson et al., 2016). Although in this study the food was not perceived as being of different quality depending on which type of plate was used, other studies have demonstrated a perceptual difference in food quality depending on the type of container. For example, liquids served in styrofoam cups were rated as lower quality than the same liquid served in a glass cup, potentially due to the role of haptic feedback in assessments of quality and satisfaction (Krishna and Morrin, 2007). Finally, utensil type can also influence the amount of food taken (and wasted). Foods eaten with a spoon have been shown to be perceived as less calorie dense and smaller in size, whereas serving or eating with a fork increases perceptions of calorie density and quantity, thus reducing the overall amount served or eaten (Szocs and Biswas, 2016). Even nutrition experts are subject to these biases related to utensils; when given larger spoons (3 ounces versus 2 ounces), they served themselves 14.5% more food (Wansink et al., 2006). In cases where food is served using spoons, especially large ones, but eaten using forks, more food may be served than consumed, which could potentially increase food waste.

Tablescape

Characteristics of the tablescape can also affect the amount of food taken, consumed and wasted. Portion sizes are perceived as smaller when food is served on a smaller table, whereas larger tables lead to perceptions of larger portions, which leads to taking less food (Davis et al., 2016). In the case of smaller tables, people compensate for this by serving themselves more. If individuals overcompensate by taking more than they actually can or want to eat, there is an increased potential for food waste. Studies have also demonstrated that the variety and abundance of food served in a buffet setting increases the amount of food that people take (Sobal and Wansink, 2007), and that when a given quantity of food is separated into more, separate bowls, people served themselves more (Kahn and Wansink, 2004). In a study explicitly examining food waste in a buffet setting, people who chose the larger plates wasted 135% more food than did those who chose smaller plates (who wasted about 14% of their food). When self-serving a second time, people who had larger plates and who had overserved themselves the first time also had a tendency to repeat that behaviour, even if the second serving was onto a smaller plate (Wansink and Van Ittersum, 2013).

Finally, the organization and aesthetic elements of the tablescape also affect consumption, and potentially waste. When food was clearly organized into recognizable patterns on a table, people took less food than when food was presented in a less organized way (Kahn and Wansink, 2004). Moreover, contrasting tablecloth colours with plate colours (i.e., white and red) accentuate the plates' diameter, consistent with the optical illusion of relative size perceptions of circles (called the Delboeuf Illusion). This visual effect makes people more likely to over serve themselves (Van Ittersum and Wansink, 2011), with attendant potential effects on food waste.

Identity-related issues

Finally, there is also a range of identity-related issues that affect how and how much food is served. Caregivers, in a desire to fulfil the role of "good mother," often over-prepare food in order to have a table that is replete with varied and plentiful portions (Evans, 2011; Graham-Rowe et al., 2014), particularly for family gatherings (Porpino, 2016). This not only influences the amount of food prepared, served and eaten—which all affect food waste as identified previously—but also the amount of food purchased to stock cabinets, as part of the motivation to provide abundance and comfort, consistent with avoiding "not having enough" (Food Waste Avoidance Benchmark Study, 2009) and being seen as a "good provider" (Porpino, 2016). Given problems of misestimation discussed previously, this desire for abundance over scarcity has the potential to increase food waste at several steps within the consumption process. Finally, the amount of effort expended in producing food to be served at a significant occasion, such as a family holiday dinner, can also influence food waste; a study based on the food journey of American Thanksgiving Day found that people are much less willing to throw away leftovers from a meal that took a long time to prepare (Wallendorf and Arnould, 1991).

Having reviewed the research related to food waste in each of the areas of labelling, packaging and the eating environment, we turn next to areas of potential future research.

Future research

In summary, confusion about date labelling causes a significant amount of food waste, though there is some variance in use of date labels depending on such factors as the type of food in question, the "ownership" status of the food, and when storage of the food has been separated from its date label. Research also suggests that larger packages increase the amount of food that individuals purchase, how much they serve themselves, and likely how much food they waste, although this last would benefit from additional empirical support beyond the research presented here. Despite somewhat inconsistent findings about household income and food waste, it is clear that smaller households often either pay more per unit for smaller packages of food, or have a more challenging time controlling food waste, or both. Additionally, smaller packages have the paradoxical effect of decreasing food waste but increasing packaging waste, often placing people in an environmental dilemma. Packaging also affects portion size, with attendant effects not only on health but also increasing the potential for food waste. Finally, various aspects of the eating environment, such as the tablescape, the platescape, or the person preparing or serving the food, can all have a significant effect on the amount of food served and eaten. However, most research has focused on the effects of the eating environment on food consumption rather than directly on food waste, which suggests this is an area in need of further empirical investigation.

When reviewing the research presented here, three primary gaps emerge. First, a substantial amount of research on food waste is descriptive in nature, focusing on attitudes and behaviours related to food waste, as well as measuring actual quantities wasted. In order to be able to design interventions that will truly tackle not only the behaviour in question, the underlying motivations or psychological processes that drive the behaviour are important to acknowledge and understand. Second, of the existing research that does delve into these psychological processes, much of it stops short of making the explicit (and empirical) connection to what smaller or larger amounts of food, as affected by factors such as labelling, packaging and the eating environment, ultimately mean for quantities of food waste. Finally, few papers make any recommendations about interventions or practical steps that marketers, producers or individuals themselves could take with respect to how controllable factors related to food conveyance could be modified or altered to reduce food waste.

In order to attempt to fill some of these gaps, we present some potential research questions that address the practical and theoretical gaps identified throughout this chapter (see Table 24.1). While not all-encompassing, they may provide a roadmap for research that seeks to close these gaps and influence food waste through changes in labelling, packaging, and the eating environment. Existing research in these areas has demonstrated that such an impact is possible, though much remains to be confirmed and acted upon to truly capture the myriad ways in which such aspects of food presentation affect food waste.

Table 24.1 Sample research questions

Theoretical questions	Practical questions
What properties of food lead them to be judged as differentially safe to consume after the best by date, or affect willingness to waste? Degree of transformation (i.e., how close the food is to its raw state)? Other processes such as fermentation, pasteurization, cutting into smaller pieces, or cooking? Importance or centrality to a dish (e.g., milk in cereal vs small amount of cream in a sauce)?	To what extent does the standardization of date labels (e.g., Leib et al., 2013; FSA, 2018) include a concerted education campaign for consumers around "best by" labels in particular, to clarify after what period of time, for different types of foods, food is still safe to eat?
What is the relationship between estimations of value of a food (and thus likelihood of being	Given that people appear to take into account the likelihood of food becoming waste when evaluating

(Continued)

Table 24.1 (Cont).

Theoretical questions	Practical questions
wasted) at different points in the consumption process? Wilson et al. (2017) suggest that some proportion of food is estimated to be "predetermined" food waste as early as at the point-of-purchase, and individuals assign a value to it at that point. Given findings about ownership bias, do those estimations and perceptions of value change once the product has been brought home?	food that is offered at a discount to try to reduce waste at the producer or retailer level, what tactics could be employed to provide people with tools to reduce their own waste if they do buy such reduced foods (i.e., quick and easy recipes, freezer bags, etc.)?
What presentation format or intervention has the greatest potential to take advantage of the demonstrated "adjustment" element of people applying the anchoring and adjustment process demonstrated to be at work in the context of date labelling? Are there boundary conditions under which date labels truly serve as anchors and cannot be adjusted?	What practical tools can be created that decouple date labels from foods (via storage, etc.), without negative effects on health or food safety but that also encourage people to use their own judgement as to when a food could be eaten versus should be discarded?
Given findings of time- or goal-inconsistent behaviours related to food consumption and waste, what labelling, packaging or eating environment cues might reduce such inconsistencies?	Could more obvious (i.e., front-of-package) labelling of serving or portion size help mitigate the larger is better bias? Or implementing price labels that include per-portion cost, rather than per-weight or volume pricing, as is currently the more common case?
Is there a set of skills that could constitute a type of "waste literacy", perhaps as a subset of food literacy? What might those skills or knowledge look like? How could it be generated or improved?	Are there ways to produce smaller portions of food at comparable prices to larger packages, thus allowing smaller households to better manage their food waste?
How do choice, "blame" (Ilyuk, 2018) and "ownership" (Sen and Block, 2008) in the context of food waste interact with preparation and serving of food? That is, are people more or less likely to discard food that has been prepared and served to them by someone else, compared to if they did either of those themselves?	What types of packaging could help mitigate the packaging-waste paradox, while still allowing for the portion size and reduced food waste benefits that come from smaller package sizes?
What other psychological cues (e.g., priming, alternative goal activation) could be presented to reduce the influence of the "good provider" identity on overpreparation of food, and thus increased amounts of food waste?	What packaging options (e.g., inserting markers indicating serving size—Geier et al., 2012) could exist to cue people as to serving size, and what impact could such packaging cues have on consumption and waste?
How does research balance issues of health against goals of reducing food waste? Given concerns about obesity and over-consumption of food, to what extent can food waste be decreased without encouraging people to "clear their plates"?	Can serveware that is less likely to encourage people to serve themselves more food (e.g., smaller or hard plastic versus paper plates, "unidimensional" containers, forks versus spoons) be marketed as such? Is that a characteristic that (some) people would value?

References

Abeliotis, K., Lasaridi, K., & Chroni, C. (2014). Attitudes and behaviour of Greek households regarding food waste prevention. *Waste Management & Research*, 32(3), 237–240.

Aschemann-Witzel, J., Jensen, J. H., Jensen, M. H., & Kulikovskaja, V. (2017). Consumer behaviour towards price-reduced suboptimal foods in the supermarket and the relation to food waste in households. *Appetite*, 116, 246–258.

Block, Lauren G., Keller, P.A., Vallen, B., Williamson, S., Birau, M.M., Grinstein, A., Haws, K.L., LaBarge, M.C., Lamberton, C., Moore, E.S., Moscato, E.M., Reczek, R.W., & Tangari, A.H. (2016). Food waste at the intersection of marketing and consumers: an analysis of food loss and food squander. *Journal of Public Policy & Marketing*, 35(2 – Fall), 292–304.

Bolaane, B., & Ali, M. (2004). Sampling household waste at source: lessons learnt in Gaborone. *Waste Management & Research*, 22(3), 142–148.

CEC. (2017). *Characterization and Management of Food Loss and Waste in North America*. Montreal and Canada: Commission for Environmental Cooperation. p. 48.

Chandon, P., & Ordabayeva, N. (2009). Supersize in one dimension, downsize in three dimensions: Effects of spatial dimensionality on size perceptions and preferences. *Journal of Marketing Research*, 46(6), 739–753.

Cox, J., & Downing, P. (2007). *Food Behaviour Consumer Research: Quantitative Phase*. Banbury, UK: WRAP.

Davis, B., Payne, C. R., & Bui, M. (2016). Making small food units seem regular: how larger table size reduces calories to be consumed. *Journal of the Association for Consumer Research*, 1(1), 115–124.

Dobson, P. W., & Gerstner, E. (2010). For a few cents more: Why supersize unhealthy food?. *Marketing Science*, 29(4), 770–778.

Elshiewy, O., Jahn, S., & Boztug, Y. (2016). Seduced by the label: How the recommended serving size on nutrition labels affects food sales. *Journal of the Association for Consumer Research*, 1(1), 104–114.

Environment Protection Authority (2012). *Food Waste Avoidance Benchmark Study 2009*. Sydney, Australia. Retrieved from http://www.frankston.vic.gov.au/files/34d7963e-24ab-455b-a1f5a22300d89be2/Love_food_hate_waste.pdf

Evans, D. (2011). Blaming the consumer – once again: The social and material contexts of everyday food waste practices in some English households. *Critical Public Health*, 21(4), 429–440.

Folkes, V., & Matta, S. (2004). The effect of package shape on consumers' judgments of product volume: attention as a mental contaminant. *Journal of Consumer Research*, 31(2), 390–401.

FSA (2018, January 8). Best Before and Use-By Dates: Understanding 'Best Before' and 'Use-By' Dates on Food Labels and How You Must Treat them Differently. Retrieved September, 2018, from www.food.gov.uk/safety-hygiene/best-before-and-use-by-dates.

Ganglbauer, E., Fitzpatrick, G., & Comber, R. (2013). Negotiating food waste: Using a practice lens to inform design. *ACM Transactions on Computer-Human Interaction (TOCHI)*, 20(2), 11.

Geier, A., Wansink, B., & Rozin, P. (2012). Red potato chips: Segmentation cues can substantially decrease food intake. *Health Psychology*, 31(3), 398.

Graham-Rowe, E., Jessop, D., & Sparks, P. (2014). Identifying motivations and barriers to minimizing household food waste. *Resources, Conservation and Recycling*, 84, 15–23.

Gunders, D. (2012, August). "Wasted : How America Is Losing Up to 40 Percent of Its Food from Farm to Fork to Landfill." *NRDC Issue Paper*. Retrieved March, 2016, from www.nrdc.org/food/files/wasted-food-ip.pdf.

Haws, K. L., & Winterich, K. P. (2013). When value trumps health in a supersized world. *Journal of Marketing*, 77(3), 48–64.

Holden, S. S., Zlatevska, N., & Dubelaar, C. (2016). Whether smaller plates reduce consumption depends on who's serving and who's looking: a meta-analysis. *Journal of the Association for Consumer Research*, 1(1), 134–146.

Ilyuk, V. (2018). Like throwing a piece of me away: How online and in-store grocery purchase channels affect consumers' food waste. *Journal of Retailing and Consumer Services*, 41, 20–30.

Kahn, B. E., & Wansink, B. (2004). The influence of assortment structure on perceived variety and consumption quantities. *Journal of Consumer Research*, 30(4), 519–533.

Kallbekken, S., & Sælen, H. (2013). 'Nudging' hotel guests to reduce food waste as a win–win environmental measure. *Economics Letters*, 119(3), 325–327.

Krishna, A., & Morrin, M. (2007). Does touch affect taste? The perceptual transfer of product container haptic cues. *Journal of Consumer Research*, 34(6), 807–818.

Leib, E. B., Gunders, D., Ferro, J., Nielsen, A., Nosek, G., & Qu, J. (2013). *The Dating Game: How Confusing Food Date Labels Lead to Food Waste in America*. New York: Harvard Food Law Clinic and National Resources Defense Council.

Lipinski, B., Hanson, C., Lomax, J., Kitinoja, L., Waite, R., & Searchinger, T. (2013, June). "Reducing Food Loss and Waste." *World Resource Institute*, 1–40. Retrieved from: http://unep.org/wed/docs/ WRI-UNEP-Reducing-Food-Loss-and-Waste.pdf.

Lyndhurst, Brook (2011). *Consumer Insight: Date Labels and Storage Guidance*. Banbury, UK: WRAP.

Madzharov, A. V., & Block, L. G. (2010). Effects of product unit image on consumption of snack foods. *Journal of Consumer Psychology*, 20(4), 398–409.

Mallinson, L. J., Russell, J. M., & Barker, M. E. (2016). Attitudes and behaviour towards convenience food and food waste in the United Kingdom. *Appetite*, 103, 17–28.

Mavrakis, B. A. (2014). The generative mechanisms of 'food waste'in South Australian household settings (Doctoral dissertation, Flinders University).

Parizeau, K., von Massow, M., & Martin, R. (2015). Household-level dynamics of food waste production and related beliefs, attitudes, and behaviours in Guelph, Ontario. *Waste Management*, 35, 207–217.

Porpino, G. (2016). Household food waste behavior: avenues for future research. *Journal of the Association for Consumer Research*, 1(1), 41–51.

Porpino, G., Parente, J., & Wansink, B. (2015). Food waste paradox: antecedents of food disposal in low income households. *International Journal of Consumer Studies*, 39(6), 619–629.

Porpino, G., Wansink, B., & Parente, J. (2016). Wasted positive intentions: the role of affection and abundance on household food waste. *Journal of Food Products Marketing*, 22(7), 733–751.

Principato, L., Secondi, L., & Pratesi, C. A. (2015). Reducing food waste: an investigation on the behaviour of Italian youths. *British Food Journal*, 117(2), 731–748.

Qi, D., & Roe, B. E. (2016). Household food waste: multivariate regression and principal components analyses of awareness and attitudes among US consumers. *PloS one*, 11(7), e0159250.

Raghubir, P., & Krishna, A. (1999). Vital dimensions in volume perception: Can the eye fool the stomach?. *Journal of Marketing Research*, 36(3), 313–326.

Robinson, E., Nolan, S., Tudur-Smith, C., Boyland, E. J., Harrold, J. A., and Halford, J. C. G. (2015). The not so clean plate club: Food self-served won't always result in food eaten. *International Journal of Obesity*, 39(January), 376.

Schneider, F. & Lebersorger, S. (2009). Households attitudes and behavior towards wasting food – a case study. In: Cossu, D. and Stegmann (eds), *Proceedings of 12th Sardinia 2009 Symposium*, Cagliari: CISA Environmental.

Schneider, F. & Obersteiner, G. (2007). Food waste in residual waste of households – regional and socio-economic differences. In: Proceedings of the Eleventh International Waste Management and Landfill Symposium, Sardinia, Italy, pp. 469–470.

Sen, S., & Block, L. G. (2008). "Why my mother never threw anything out": The effect of product freshness on consumption. *Journal of Consumer Research*, 36(1), 47–55.

Seo, J. Y. and Yoon, S. (2013). Feel Sorry For the Cake in Trash? The Effect of Food Types on Consumers' Food Waste Perceptions. In: Botti, S. and Labroo, A. (eds), *NA-Advances in Consumer Research*, Volume 41. Duluth, MN: Association for Consumer Research.

Silvennoinen, K., Katajajuuri, J. M., Hartikainen, H., Heikkilä, L., & Reinikainen, A. (2014). Food waste volume and composition in Finnish households. *British Food Journal*, 116(6), 1058–1068.

Smith, E. (2014, June). Spoiler Alert. *The Atlantic*. Retrieved March, 2016, from www.theatlantic.com/ magazine/archive/2014/06/spoiler-alert/361626/.

Sobal, J., & Wansink, B. (2007). Kitchenscapes, tablescapes, platescapes, and foodscapes: Influences of microscale built environments on food intake. *Environment and Behavior*, 39(1), 124–142.

Szocs, C., & Biswas, D. (2016). Forks over Spoons: The impact of cutlery on calorie estimates. *Journal of the Association for Consumer Research*, 1(1), 161–174.

Theotokis, A., Pramatari, K., & Tsiros, M. (2012). Effects of expiration date-based pricing on brand image perceptions. *Journal of Retailing*, 88(1), 72–87.

Thompson, B., Toma, L., Barnes, A. P., & Revoredo-Giha, C. (2018). The effect of date labels on willingness to consume dairy products: Implications for food waste reduction. *Waste Management*, 78, 124–134.

Trudel, R., & Argo, J. J. (2013). The effect of product size and form distortion on consumer recycling behavior. *Journal of Consumer Research*, 40(4), 632–643.

Tsiros, M., & Heilman, C. M. (2005). The effect of expiration dates and perceived risk on purchasing behavior in grocery store perishable categories. *Journal of Marketing*, 69(2), 114–129.

Van Ittersum, K., & Wansink, B. (2011). Plate size and color suggestibility: the Delboeuf Illusion's bias on serving and eating behavior. *Journal of Consumer Research*, 39(2), 215–228.

Verghese, K., Lewis, H., Lockrey, S., & Williams, H. (2015). Packaging's role in minimizing food loss and waste across the supply chain. *Packaging Technology and Science*, 28(7), 603–620.

Wallendorf, M., & Arnould, E. J. (1991). "We gather together": consumption rituals of Thanksgiving Day. *Journal of Consumer Research*, 18(1), 13–31.

Wansink, B. (1996). Can package size accelerate usage volume? *The Journal of Marketing*, 60(3), 1–14.

Wansink, B., & Van Ittersum, K. (2006). The visual illusions of food: Why plates, bowls, and spoons can bias consumption volume. *The FASEB Journal*, 20(4 - March), 618.

Wansink, B., & Van Ittersum, K. (2007). Portion size me: downsizing our consumption norms. *Journal of the American Dietetic Association*, 107(7), 1103–1106.

Wansink, B., & Van Ittersum, K. (2013). Portion size me: Plate-size induced consumption norms and win-win solutions for reducing food intake and waste. *Journal of Experimental Psychology: Applied*, 19(4), 320.

Wansink, B., Van Ittersum, K., & Painter, J. E. (2006). Ice cream illusions: bowls, spoons, and self-served portion sizes. *American Journal of Preventive Medicine*, 31(3), 240–243.

White, K., Lin, L., Dahl, D. W., & Ritchie, R. J. (2016). When do consumers avoid imperfections? Superficial packaging damage as a contamination cue. *Journal of Marketing Research*, 53(1), 110–123.

Williams, H. (2011). Food packaging for sustainable development (Doctoral dissertation, Karlstad University).

Williams, H., Wikström, F., Otterbring, T., Löfgren, M., Gustafsson, A. (2012). Reasons for household food waste with special attention to packaging. *Journal of Cleaner Production*, 24(March), 141–148.

Williamson, S., Block, L. G., & Keller, P. A. (2016). Of waste and waists: The effect of plate material on food consumption and waste. *Journal of the Association for Consumer Research*, 1(1), 147–160.

Wilson, N. L., Rickard, B. J., Saputo, R., & Ho, S. T. (2017). Food waste: The role of date labels, package size, and product category. *Food Quality and Preference*, 55, 35–44.

Young, L. R. (May 23, 2005). *The Portion Teller: Smartsize Your Way to Permanent Weight Loss*. New York: Publishers Weekly, p. 75.

25

UPCYCLING AND VALORISATION OF FOOD WASTE

Mohamed A. Gedi, Vincenzo di Bari, Roger Ibbett,
Randa Darwish, Ogueri Nwaiwu, Zainudin Umar,
Deepa Agarwal, Richard Worrall, David Gray and Tim Foster

Introduction

By 2050 the ever-growing global population is expected to reach over 9 billion people, with India's population predicted to exceed that of China (Chandrasekaran, 2012). Consequently, demand for natural resources to feed the world has also increased, creating scarcity of such resources. It has been noted that food waste is estimated to be one-third of global food production (Gustafsson et al., 2013) and could be up to 1.3 billion metric tonnes lost per year (Pleissner and Lin, 2013). In Europe the food waste figure is estimated to be about 88 million tonnes corresponding to around 173 kg per capita (Tonini et al., 2018) whereas in the United States 3.84×10^7 tonnes of food were lost in 2014 (RedCorn et al., 2018). In Asia very large amounts of food waste are being generated by means of agricultural production practices, food transportation and storage, and human food consumption activities (Ong et al., 2018). Though specific data is scarce in Africa, the problem is equally huge since storage facilities are in short supply.

Disposal of vast amounts of organic waste causes loss of resources and huge environmental impact due to the multiple processes involved in its life cycle, most of which ends up as landfill. However, if 'waste' can be used to generate income, then it should be considered as a resource (Salihoglu et al., 2018). Traditional methods of waste disposal, including incineration and use of landfill (see Chapter 27), may lead to uncontrolled release of greenhouse gases (Matsakas et al., 2017), hence, food waste valorisation is regarded as a better option (Burange et al., 2011) because it can be converted to other beneficial uses. A broad definition of valorisation or upcycling might include other waste treatment methods such as composting, anaerobic digestion or animal feed (see Chapters 22 and 37). However, in the context of this chapter we take a narrower definition. Specifically, where technology and innovation are applied to create new efficient methods for utilising available resources (i.e. wasted food) in more sustainable fashion: to create new food, new by-products for food and feed formulations, new high value-added food and feed components or other novel products from wasted food. This final option involves creating products for other sectors of the economy, where valorised materials could be utilised. Products might include packaging materials, commodity chemicals for other industries, biofuel or bioenergy sources and as composting materials (soil fertilisers). Following the waste hierarchy, when valorisation and other waste management approaches are not possible and all waste minimisation has been attempted, then landfill is the final option.

Many recent food valorisation studies have focused on plant-based by-products of widely used crops. These include brewers' spent grains (Ikram et al., 2017; Cappa and Alamprese, 2017; Cooray and Chen, 2018; Tišma et al., 2018), spent coffee beans (Páscoa et al., 2013; Brazinha et al., 2015; Kovalcik et al., 2018) and okara of soy bean (Fu et al., 2017; Quintana et al., 2018; Santos et al., 2018), by-products from fruits such as, the pomace of apple (Perussello et al., 2017; Singha and Muthukumarappan, 2018), grape (Peixoto et al., 2018; Quiles et al., 2018; Saurabh et al., 2018; Šporin et al., 2018) and olive (Aliakbarian et al., 2011; Bonetti et al., 2016; Borroni et al., 2017; Galanakis et al., 2018; Peixoto et al., 2018; Quiles et al., 2018; Saurabh et al., 2018; Šporin et al., 2018), as well as citrus peels (Lota et al., 2000; Scordino et al., 2005; Masmoudi et al., 2008; Chedea et al., 2010), and by-products from vegetables, such as pomace of tomato (Li et al., 2018; Mehta et al., 2018), carrot (Kaisangsri et al., 2016; Majzoobi et al., 2017; Psimouli and Oreopoulou, 2017; Yu et al., 2018) and potato peel (Othman et al., 2017; Mushtaq et al., 2017; Jeddou et al., 2017). These are selected examples representing cereals, pulses, oil crops, fruits, vegetables and tubers. For further examples and target ingredients of each by-product see Table 25.1. Other by-products of animal origin from meat, dairy, poultry and fish and seafood have also been valorised in recent years (Asghar et al., 2011; Jayathilakan et al., 2012).

This chapter highlights examples of developments in the valorisation of fractions from agri-residue feed-stocks, micro nutrients from green field biomass, and waxes from bran and concludes with a recent business case study.

Some similar information to that in Table 25.1 relating to fruits and vegetables was also reported by Galanakis (2015).

Valorisation of fractions from agri-residue feed-stocks for protein and fibre

Protein products from brewers' spent grains (BSG)

Spent grain is a major by-product from the brewing industry, which consists of the wet solid material remaining after the mashing process, after the majority of starch and soluble sugars have been extracted from the malt prior to fermentation of the wort liquor. Several hundreds of thousands of tonnes of BSG are produced by breweries in the UK annually, which are sold primarily as a low-value ruminant feed (Aliyu and Bala, 2011). The nutritional content for feed applications is acceptable, where typically BSG contains around 25% protein and around 60% polysaccharides on a dry mass basis (Mussatto et al., 2006). However, as-made wet BSG consists of only 25–30% solids after pressing, which not only lowers deliverable nutritional value but also leads to microbial instability resulting in a low storage life of maybe 2–3 days.

The high protein content of BSG, mainly insoluble hordeins, raises the possibility of further processing to separate a protein-enriched product, which would have higher economic value for both feed and also for human nutrition or wellbeing supplements or as cosmetic ingredients. Most investigations have centred on the prospect of digesting the protein

Table 25.1 Agri-food by-products and their valuable target compounds

Plant origin	By-product	Target ingredient	Reference
Apple	Pomace	Dietary fibre (pectin), phytochemicals (phenolic compounds)	Perussello et al., 2017
Grape	Pomace	Dietary fibre	Peixoto et al., 2018; Saurabh et al., 2018; Šporin et al., 2018; Quiles et al., 2018
Mango	Peel, seed and kernels	Vitamins, polyphenols, enzymes and dietary fibre and phenolic compounds	Torres-León et al., 2016; Shabeer et al., 2016
Tomato	Skin, peel and seeds	Carotenoids (lycopene, lutein and β-carotene, vitamin A), dietary fibre, new food ingredient	Mehta et al., 2018; Li et al., 2018
Citrus (e.g. mandarin orange and lemon)	Peel, by-product	Essential oil (limonene), carotenoids, hesperidin, essential pectin	Scordino et al., 2005; Chedea et al., 2010; Lota et al., 2000; Masmoudi et al., 2008
Kiwi	Pomace	Dietary fibre	Martin-Cabrejas et al., 1995
Pear	Pomace, peel	Dietary fibre	Martin-Cabrejas et al., 1995; Koubaa et al., 2016
Carrot	Pomace,	Carotenoids (some being vitamin A), fibre	Majzoobi et al., 2017; Psimouli and Oreopoulou, 2017; Kaisangsri et al., 2016; Yu et al., 2018
Blackcurrant	Seeds residue after oil extraction	Phenols	Bakowska-Barczak et al., 2009
Apricot	Kernel	Protein	Dhen et al., 2018
Cauliflower	Floret and curd	Pectin	
Olive	Wastewater pomace, wasteoil	Polyphynols, carotenoids and hydroxytyrosol	Galanakis et al., 2018; Borroni et al., 2017; Bonetti et al., 2016; Aliakbarian et al., 2011
Potato	Peel	Amylase, polyphenols, fibre	Mushtaq et al., 2017; Sepelev and Galoburda, 2015
Barley/starchy crops	Breweries' spent grains	Fibre-enriched foods, laccase and polyphenols, prebiotic oligosaccharide, lignin and cellulose	Sajib et al., 2018; Cappa and Alamprese, 2017; Ohra-aho et al., 2016; Pierre et al., 2011)
Soybean	Okara	Isoflavones, encapsulation of Lactobacillus plantrarum and dietary fibre	Santos et al., 2018; Quintana et al., 2018; Fu et al., 2017
Sugar cane/ beet	Bagasse	Cellulose and lignin	Gabov et al., 2017

component using protease enzymes, of which a wide range are commercially available for food applications (Celus et al., 2007). Extraction yields in excess of 70% are quoted, where extracts will consist of lower molecular weight fragments and peptides, resulting from the hydrolysis reactions required to reduce chain length to increase solubility. Although the process is simple, operating at 50–60 °C, considerable further process effort is required to recover the protein concentrate as a solid, with also the requirement to adjust the pH by acid addition to neutralise the additional amino acid end groups resulting from hydrolysis. The final product may, therefore, have a relatively high mineral content.

Other fractionation methods are based around wholly physical processing, where it has been found that wet milling will preferentially break up the protein-bearing aleurone tissue of the spent grain, leaving particles of a much finer texture than the other polysaccharide components which constitute the sheaf of the grain (Kirsty, 2006). Yields of 40–50% of the total protein have been achieved by simple wet sieving, although the protein in the concentrate is insoluble in its native tertiary form so will have limited techno-functional properties. Also there are significant costs attributed to the watering and drying operations that are required to obtain a stable dry product. This means that to valorise this wasted food involves considerable capital expenditure and, hence, high commercial risk.

Protein concentrates from potato by-products

Potatoes are grown commercially on a large scale, either for direct use as a vegetable dish, or for further processing to manufacture products such as fries, mash and snacks. Additionally, the crop is utilised as a feedstock for production of starch, as used as a food ingredient or for industrial applications. The potato tuber consists of flesh comprised of cells containing multiple starch granules, which are surrounded by the cell cytoplasm, bounded by a thin cell wall comprised of polysaccharides including structural cellulose.

During starch production the flesh is macerated and the starch and cytoplasm or juice are separated physically, for example by sieving or centrifugation, leaving a fibrous cell wall residue. Historically the juice was considered a waste product but in more recent times it is appreciated that it contains a significant amount of soluble protein, mainly patatins but also various protease inhibitors (Ralet and Guéguen, 2000). Hence protein recovery is now standard as a process step in starch production, usually achieved by heating and/or acidification to denature and insolubilise the protein as a solid (Karup Kartoffelmelfabrik). However, denaturation destroys the techno-functional attributes of the protein and therefore alternative separation techniques based on ultrafiltration (Wojnowska et al., 1982) or expanded bed adsorption chromatography (Strætkvern et al., 1998) have been developed. These technically elegant solutions retain the protein in the native state, allowing it to be spray-dried and hence delivering properties such as foam formation, stabilisation and emulsification when rehydrated as a food ingredient.

The development of new techniques for protein recovery has prompted investigations to consider whether waste or low-grade potatoes from crop harvesting and sorting might also be processed to separate out a protein concentrate as an added value by-product. While endeavours are made to reduce spoilage and to maximise the proportion of grade 1 crop, inevitably a significant proportion of the crop is down-graded and is either sold as animal feed as stock potatoes or is sent for anaerobic digestion. Processes may be considered where the sub-grade feedstock is macerated as in starch production, and where a simpler centrifugation step allows separation of juice from the remaining starch-containing flesh, which would still have value for anaerobic digestion. The protein-containing juice can then be further processed using ultrafiltration or adsorption chromatography to extract a protein concentrate. However, from a commercial perspective the decision to invest in expensive additional capital equipment will depend on certainty regarding the value and market size of a potato protein isolate, especially as this is likely to be a new commercial direction of a traditional potato sorting and packaging business.

Functional fibre and other products from citrus waste

Citrus juice is produced on a large scale for the drinks industry. Consequently, large quantities of pith and peel are generated as by-products, which must be further processed to convert into other useful products, rather than simply treated as waste. Their utilisation offers broad applications in a wide range of food products due to the number of unique functionalities such as adding viscosity, freeze/thaw stability, moisture retention and nutritional value by fat replacement, among others (Dhingra et al., 2012; Zhu et al., 2018). Technologies have been developed to score or rasp the outer skin layer, the flavedo, to rupture pockets containing essential oils such as limonene. This oily layer can be physically separated from the wash water by centrifugation, giving rise to a valuable flavour and aroma product, useful in foods and also in household products such as surface cleaners, and in cosmetics (Ciriminna et al., 2014). The remaining pith is typically dewatered by pressing and dried as pellets for animal feed, or alternatively it can be further processed, possibly within a different business, for extraction of valuable pectin. Pectin has many uses, depending on the fruit or vegetable source, as a gelling or thickening agent or stabiliser in the food and drinks industry.

Pectin extraction is usually carried out by a hot water treatment, with adjustment of pH to solubilise the pectin component, which is then precipitated usually by addition of isopropanol non-solvent and then dried as a powder (Yeoh et al., 2008). However, yields are typically quite low, maybe only 5% of total pectin content, so the remainder is retained in the pulp fibre residue. While development effort goes into improving extraction yields, the residual pectin content of the fibre residue may lead to the possibility of producing a fibre product with good techno-functional and nutritional properties (Figuerola et al., 2005).

A number of citrus fibre products are currently marketed, where the manufacturing technology has been carefully optimised to avoid collapsing the porous fibre microstructure, allowing a high level of reswelling on rehydration (Rondeau-Mouro et al., 2003; Lundberg, 2005). The variety of components retained in the fibre enable a range of applications, including controlled flavour release and fat replacers (in foods) as well as controlled drug release in biopharmaceuticals (Abbas et al., 2010; Abdelhameed et al., 2016). Citrus fibres are also used as egg replacers, thickeners, emulsifiers and ingredients for controlling taste perception (Fernández-Ginés et al., 2003; Arltoft et al., 2008; de Moraes Crizel et al., 2013; Song et al., 2016; Agarwal et al., 2018). The ability of the cellulose fibres to bind water is a key functionality required for reducing fat in meat products (Song et al., 2016). Consumption of citrus fibres has also been linked to health benefits, with positive effects established for blood glucose and cholesterol (Fuller et al., 2016; Jiang et al., 2018). The same technologies used in the citrus juice industry could potentially also be used to process sub-standard or damaged citrus fruit rejected during the sorting and packing operations in a fruit supply business. Additional challenges would exist, in that damaged fruit may not be as easy to handle through the rasping operation for separation of limonene, or through other handling and physical operations. Microbial damage may also lead to contamination of the various desired products, so an additional level of sorting of sub-standard fruit may be required to ensure efficient use of food material. Issues are again concerned with the risk of capital investment, where the addition of equipment for extraction and drying has to be compared against disposal costs, or alternatively the cost of installation of anaerobic digestion.

Fibre materials from pea haulm

Peas are grown widely as a commercial crop in the UK and in other countries, where the varieties of vining peas have been bred to assist large-scale mechanised agricultural practices. The crop can be harvested using sophisticated mechanical harvesters, something like a combine, which collect up the entire plant and then split the pods and separate the peas by a combination of mechanical and centrifugal action in the harvester body (*Farmers Weekly*, 2016). This efficient method allows the peas to be taken away at intervals by accompanying trailer and, in some businesses, they are then shipped directly to freezing plants to ensure maximum freshness.

The crushed green material from the empty pods and the rest of the plant is dropped from the rear of the harvester back onto the field, to be ploughed in for the next crop. While some retention of green biomass generated is required for soil quality, it is likely that at least a proportion of this residue would be available for separate collection and processing for other feed and food applications. One possibility is to juice this whole material, for example using an industrial screw press, to separate out a green juice fraction, leaving a comminuted pulp material as a further residue. The green juice has considerable potential as a nutritional ingredient, with a high concentration of protein and essential vitamins, oils and minerals, which could be spray- or freeze-dried to give a stable powder product (Torcello-Gómez et al., 2019). The residual pulp has a fibrous texture, consisting of stem, leaf and pod structural tissues of the plant, also containing some protein and useful micronutrients, which has potential as a dietary fibre product. However, in its as-produced state the residual pulp is likely to have poor sensory texture, and further processing would be required to reduce particle size to a level where any sensation of grittiness or stringiness is lost. Milling could be carried out in the wet state, for example using a colloid type mill, although efficiencies may not be high, especially if water is added to improve flow, which would then need to be removed by centrifuge or pressing. Alternatively, the as-produced material could be dried prior to a dry milling operation, for example ball milling or hammer milling (Larrauri, 1999). However, with either approach there would inevitably be significant mechanical and thermal energy demands which would affect overall process economics. This would need to be balanced against the likely value of the product for food or feed applications.

Valorisation of fractions from agri-residue feed-stocks for micro nutrients

While the previous section focused on the fibre from pea harvest field residues, this section highlights the micronutrients of pea harvest field residues, which refers to the green leaves, vine, stems/haulm and crops left behind the harvesters. Millions of tonnes of green haulm/residuals are generated from agricultural production every year in the United Kingdom (Torcello-Gómez et al., 2019). The green residuals from various plants have been reported to contain a wide range of valuable macro- and micronutrients. Much of these are concentrated in an abundant organelle called the chloroplast found in plant cells. Chloroplasts are lens-shaped bodies with a diameter of approximately 5–10 µm and it is here that the major part of a plant's vital nutrients are made via photosynthesis (Gross, 2012).The recovery of chloroplasts from green food waste leads to increased nutritional content per unit mass as compared to the fresh leaf (Gedi et al., 2017). The derivation of the nutrient-rich particulate fraction from green biomass is simple and has real potential to provide functional ingredients to food and feed. Pea vine straw/haulm is a good example of green field residue left after harvesting peas that is rich in chloroplasts. Generally, green leafy biomasses consist of water (80–90%) and fibre with chloroplasts which makes up around 10–20% of the total biomass.

From a biochemical perspective, osmotic solutions, such as sugar, are used to isolate chloroplasts. Innovative procedures for chloroplast isolation have been developed (Gedi et al., 2017; Torcello-Gómez et al., 2019) to enable their use as functional food/feed ingredients. The method is simple and environmentally friendly and is based on juice extraction by physical fractionation from green plant materials and recovery of the chloroplast-rich fraction (CRF) by centrifugation. Major and minor nutrients (total lipids, proteins, ash and carbohydrates; and omega-3, β-carotene, lutein, α-tocopherol and ascorbic acid, respectively) of the biomass from pea vine straw/haulm have been concentrated using this physical method (Torcello-Gómez et al., 2019). Results show that the CRF recovered from fresh pea vine straw/haulm consisted of a number of essential micronutrients such us α-linolenic acid (C18:3n-3), β-carotene, lutein and α-tocopherol.

Another recent study also explored the nutritional composition of CRF extracted from various green biomasses (Gedi et al., 2017). Vitamin E (α-tocopherol), pro-vitamin A (β-carotene), and lutein were all greater in CRF preparations as compared to their original leaf materials. Of the minerals, iron was most notably concentrated in CRF. The study concluded that CRF consisted of higher concentrations of essential micronutrients, such as α-tocopherol, β-carotene, lutein, α-linolenic acid (C18:3n-3) and trace minerals (Fe and Mn) compared with their original leaf materials on dry weight basis. Therefore, CRF could be used as a concentrated source of nutrients in food/feed formulations.

Recovering nutritionally rich fractions of chloroplasts from field green residuals/green waste biomasses could create new sustainable and functional food ingredients, enriched with essential micronutrients, which is in theory more bioaccessible than nutrients in chloroplasts enclosed by a cell wall. This approach may provide a way to ensure that poorer societies have access to food rich in valuable micronutrients. However, the current cost of deployment at scale mean that this goal would be a long-term ambition. Furthermore, it would require cultural, social, technological and economic change to be deployed at scale. In addition, there could be a range of commercial opportunities to use isolated chloroplasts in food and feed formulations.

Valorisation of fractions from agri-residue feed-stocks for waxes

The limited availability of fossil resources together with increasing demand for sustainable and environmentally friendly alternatives has driven a growth in the interest of renewable feed-stocks to produce biofuels, high-value chemicals, and materials for food, pharma and cosmetic applications. Among those are lipids, which due to their poor solubility in aqueous media and affinity for hydrophobic systems require a different recovery approach. The bran removed from cereal kernels (rice, wheat, and oat), seeds left from juice production, date palm (Al Bulushi et al., 2018), and maize germ (Nikiforidis and Kiosseoglou, 2009) are only a few examples of by-products where lipids represent a relevant fraction. These lipid compounds currently are, or could be exploited to satisfy different market demands, including: nutraceutical supplements (omega-3 oil and lipophilic vitamin supplements), nutritional (edible oils from rice bran and maize germ), coatings (waxes), animal feed formula ingredients. Lipids are an important and large family of biomolecules with various functional activities (structural, nutritional and antioxidant) and structures. Among the lipids of industrial interest, plant waxes represent a relatively small fraction (by weight) of the waste biomass but with great potential to be re-integrated into the supply chain as high-added value chemicals and materials. This is primarily because plant waxes offer a suitable alternative to petroleum-based waxes. This technological functionality, together with consumers' preference for sustainable and natural plant products in healthcare and cosmetic applications, has determined a growth in the commercial demand of natural plant waxes over the last few years (Attard et al., 2018b). From a chemical perspective, waxes are a mixture of several hydrophobic compounds: wax esters (compounds resulting from the ester-ification of a fatty acid with a fatty alcohol), fatty acids and fatty alcohols, ketones, *n*-alkenes and other minor compounds. In plants, waxes are usually deposited on the outer surface of the leaves or straw to reduce water loss and are therefore often referred to as 'cuticle waxes'. There-fore, this biological localisation allows the design of processes targeting the biomass surface as a first step in the valorisation process. As part of their work on the development of an integrated holistic biorefinery,[1] Attard and co-workers (Attard et al., 2018b) have reported in a series of publications the composition of waxes recovered from various feed-stocks and compared the effect of extraction conditions, *n*-hexane versus supercritical CO_2 ($scCO_2$) extraction, on the chemical profile of the final wax extract (Attard et al., 2016, 2018a, 2018b). The authors clearly demonstrated two key advantages associated with the use of the $scCO_2$ approach: (1) selective fractionation of wax compounds, which can be achieved by fine-tuning the extraction condi-tions *via* pressure and temperature adjustments. The wax fractions characterised by different chemical profiles and physical properties may find application in a number of products ranging from lubricants, to personal care and cosmetics; (2) increased downstream processing yields of the biomass for the production of second-generation biofuels and/or of surfactants.

A parallel stream of research with great potential for wax exploitation is oleogelation. This has emerged in the last decade and aims at using waxes in food applications. The word oleogelation refers to the use of non-triglyceride molecules to create lipid gels, referred to as oleogels. Oleogels are gels where the continuous phase is an edible oil (olive, soy bean, sun-flower, etc.) as opposed to hydrogels where the continuous phase is aqueous. It has been shown that various plant waxes are effective oleogelators since they are required in small amounts (from as low as 1%, by weight) to produce self-standing gels (Blake et al., 2014). From a colloidal point of view, wax molecules form a continuous network of interconnected crystals immobilis-ing the oil, thus providing it with a solid-like consistency. The morphology of the crystals, their ability to immobilise the oil, and the overall consistency of the gels depends on the type of wax and on the process adopted to form the oleogels (Blake et al., 2014). Unpublished work carried out in our laboratories has demonstrated that the cooling rate affects the size of the crystals in rice bran wax (RBW) based oleogels. RBW is a by-product of rice bran oil production (an oil produced from rice bran) and is an approved additive in foods (E908). RBW is known to form crystals that appear as bright needle-like particles when visualised using polarised light micros-copy (Dassanayake et al., 2009). Micrographs in Figure 25.1 show the microstructure of two oleogels containing 2% RBW in rapeseed oil and formed applying different cooling profiles. It can be clearly noticed that the cooling rate significantly affects the size of the crystals: when formed under rapid cooling (Figure 25.1a) crystals are significantly smaller than those formed under slow cooling (Figure 25.1b). Wax based oleogels have also been successfully applied in baked products, demonstrating they are a valuable alternative to saturated and *trans*-fats but more research is needed in this area (Yılmaz and Öğütcü, 2015).

Waxes are ubiquitous plant materials given their physiological functional role. When util-ised as functional sustainable biomaterials, waxes' physical properties and composition as well as the specific chemical features of individual molecules (i.e. fatty acid and alcohol chain length, presence of minor compounds, and the relative abundance of molecules), depend on a wide number of factors including plant species, part of the plant used for extraction, grow-ing conditions and stage of growth, and recovery method. Furthermore, processing and

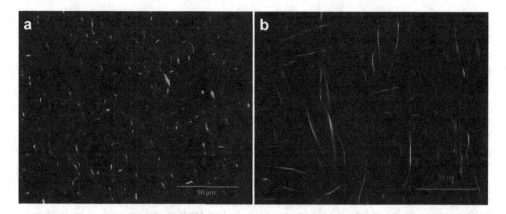

Figure 25.1 Microstructure visualisation of 2% RBW oleogel in rapeseed oil. Crystals appear as needle-like particles. (a) Rapid cool, (b) slow cool.

formulation approaches can be tailored to create structures and products with the desired functionality. Therefore, there is a virtually infinite number of combinations that could be engineered to offer new sustainable solutions to deliver innovation using waxes obtained from agri-food by-products. These biomaterials could be used to replace saturated and *trans*-fats in foods as well as petroleum-based waxes in healthcare and cosmetics.

Business case study: turning food by-products into functionalised food ingredients

Parfitt, Barthel and Macnaughton (2010) commented that the Food and Agriculture Organization of the United Nations (FAO), established in 1945, had reduction of food losses within its mandate especially reduction of post-harvest losses to address world hunger. The report highlighted attempts made to quantify global food waste over several decades. However, the assessments are reliant on limited datasets and the data suggested that strategies such as life cycle costing for processing and value-added reuse of food waste products may reduce the environmental burden (De Menna et al., 2018). With a view to reduce these losses, valorisation studies were globally executed in the last few decades. The most common conclusions from the current literature are that (1) more studies need to be carried out to apply new findings into industrial-scale applications or need to be scaled up and (2) are currently applicable only in animal feed. This trend has been going on since the late 1970s and was boosted during the past decade by the growing concern of the socio-economic impact of wastes from agri-food activities (Domínguez-Perles et al., 2018). It was noted that wastes have limited uses such as landfilling or composting. Advanced valorisation alternatives should be developed to maximise the value derived (Lin et al., 2014) from food waste sources.

Here we present a business case study titled 'NewTrition', financed by the Newton/Bhabha Fund and sponsored by United Kingdom and Indian governments. The aims of the project are to identify, quantify and evaluate by-products in the UK, Europe and India; turn by-products into functionalised ingredients suitable for use in human food applications; and develop new positive nutrition snack products by manufacturing by-products. The collaborators for the project are: University of Nottingham, Indian Institute of Food Processing Technology, Siddharth Starch and PepsiCo. The partners for the consortium were selected based on their potential to create value in new product development (Emden et al., 2006). By-products of food products A, B and C (not mentioned due to intellectual property protection) from PepsiCo were selected for the project. With over $63 billion in net revenue in 2015 and more than 250,000 employees, PepsiCo is among the largest food and beverage companies. In addition, PepsiCo's products are sold in over 200 countries and territories worldwide and at least 22 brands in its portfolio generate more than US$1 billion each in retail sales every year. As stated on the sustainability section of PepsiCo's website, their vision is to deliver top-tier financial performance over the long term by integrating sustainability into their business strategy. This is hoped to substantially increase products sales, 'reduce our environmental impact' and 'advance respect for workers' fundamental human rights'.[2] To achieve this, the company aims to transform their portfolio and offer healthier options by reducing added sugars, saturated fat and salt content. According to the website, positive nutrition by adding whole grains, fruits and vegetables and proteins is encouraged. Furthermore, the website states that access to healthier options will be provided to underserved communities. A four directional approach is expected to drive PepsiCo's vision which includes working to achieve positive water impact, reduce greenhouse gases by up to 20% before 2025, enable material source sustainability and, in particular, reduce and eliminate waste. To reduce waste, recycling is encouraged and no waste from direct operations shall be sent to landfill in future. Importantly, the website states that it is a company ambition that wastes from food shall be halved.

The project is on track and is currently in the second year out of the planned 2.5 years. Though detailed information cannot be published at this time, the by-products of products A, B and C are currently used for animal feed and selected with the objective of producing new ingredients with enhanced positive nutrition profile and final products with increased dietary fibre content. To date, the by-products have been successfully upgraded from low-value animal feed material to higher value-added human food. Safe ingredients and final products with higher dietary fibre content made using new ingredients have been obtained. Products developed were well accepted in initial sensory tests. Pilot-scale production is in progress and new product launches may be achieved after completion of the project. Upon product launch, it is expected that waste reduction and lower carbon emissions across the supply chain will be achieved.

Conclusions

This chapter has introduced the concepts of upcycling and valorisation of food waste by highlighting some work carried out at the University of Nottingham. We have also provided a case study where food by-products are transformed into functionalised food ingredients that are safe to consume; the overall process results in reduced carbon emissions across the supply chain. Some of these products have elevated dietary fibre content and were well accepted in initial sensory tests. We hope that we have shown that though very technical, valorisation and the bio-economy offer new untapped methods to transform food waste in the future.

Notes

1 A holistic biorefinery is an operation that can valorise different types of waste/resources into biomass, biofuel, biomaterials and bioenergy at one single site. This has emerged from circular economy concepts. In practical terms this type of operation would mean that maximum value/resources could be extracted from any type of waste stream at one site and fed back into the economy.
2 www.pepsico.com/sustainability/performance-with-purpose/planet

References

Abbas, KA, SM Abdulkarim, AM Saleh, and M Ebrahimian 2010. Suitability of viscosity measurement methods for liquid food variety and applicability in food industry-A review, *Journal of Food, Agriculture, & Environment*, 8: 100–107.

Abdelhameed, Ali Saber, Gary G Adams, Gordon A Morris, Fahad M Almutairi, Pierre Duvivier, Karel Conrath, and Stephen E Harding 2016. A glycoconjugate of Haemophilus influenzae Type b capsular polysaccharide with tetanus toxoid protein: hydrodynamic properties mainly influenced by the carbohydrate, *Scientific Reports*, 6: 22208.

Agarwal, Deepa, Louise Hewson, and Tim J Foster 2018. A comparison of the sensory and rheological properties of different cellulosic fibres for food, *Food & Function*, 9: 1144–1151.

Aliakbarian, Bahar, Alessandro A Casazza, and Patrizia Perego 2011. Valorization of olive oil solid waste using high pressure–high temperature reactor, *Food Chemistry*, 128: 704–710.

Aliyu, Salihu, and Muntari Bala 2011. Brewer's spent grain: a review of its potentials and applications, *African Journal of Biotechnology*, 10: 324–331.

Arltoft, D, F Madsen, and R Ipsen 2008. Relating the microstructure of pectin and carrageenan in dairy desserts to rheological and sensory characteristics, *Food Hydrocolloids*, 22: 660–673.

Asghar, Ali, Faqir Muhammad Anjum, and Jonathan C Allen 2011. Utilization of dairy byproduct proteins, surfactants, and enzymes in frozen dough, *Critical Reviews in Food Science and Nutrition*, 51: 374–382.

Attard, Thomas M, Camille Bainier, Marine Reinaud, Alexandra Lanot, Simon J McQueen-Mason, and Andrew J Hunt 2018a. Utilisation of supercritical fluids for the effective extraction of waxes and Cannabidiol (CBD) from hemp wastes, *Industrial Crops and Products*, 112: 38–46.

Attard, Thomas M, Natalia Bukhanko, Daniel Eriksson, Mehrdad Arshadi, Paul Geladi, Urban Bergsten, Vitaliy L Budarin, James H Clark, and Andrew J Hunt 2018b. Supercritical extraction of waxes and lipids from biomass: a valuable first step towards an integrated biorefinery, *Journal of Cleaner Production*, 177: 684–698.

Attard, Thomas M, C Rob McElroy, Richard J Gammons, John M Slattery, Nontipa Supanchaiyamat, Claire Lessa Alvim Kamei, Oene Dolstra, Luisa M Trindade, Neil C Bruce, and Simon J McQueen-Mason 2016. Supercritical CO2 extraction as an effective pretreatment step for wax extraction in a Miscanthus biorefinery, *ACS Sustainable Chemistry & Engineering*, 4: 5979–5988.

Bakowska-Barczak, Anna M, Andreas Schieber, and Paul Kolodziejczyk 2009. Characterization of Canadian black currant (Ribes nigrum L.) seed oils and residues, *Journal of Agricultural and Food Chemistry*, 57: 11528–11536.

Blake, Alexia I, Edmund D Co, and Alejandro G Marangoni 2014. Structure and physical properties of plant wax crystal networks and their relationship to oil binding capacity, *Journal of the American Oil Chemists' Society*, 91: 885–903.

Bonetti, A, S Venturini, A Ena, and C Faraloni 2016. Innovative method for recovery and valorization of hydroxytyrosol from olive mill wastewaters, *Water Science and Technology*, 74: 73–86.

Borroni, Virginia, Maria Teresa González, and Amalia Antonia Carelli 2017. Bioproduction of carotenoid compounds using two-phase olive mill waste as the substrate, *Process Biochemistry*, 54: 128–134.

Brazinha, C, M Cadima, and JG Crespo 2015. Valorisation of spent coffee through membrane processing, *Journal of Food Engineering*, 149: 123–130.

Al Bulushi, Karima, Thomas M Attard, Michael North, and Andrew J Hunt 2018. Optimisation and economic evaluation of the supercritical carbon dioxide extraction of waxes from waste date palm (Phoenix dactylifera) leaves, *Journal of Cleaner Production*, 186: 988–996.

Burange, Anand, James H Clark, and Rafael Luque 2011. Trends in food and agricultural waste valorization,*Encyclopedia of Inorganic and Bioinorganic Chemistry*: 1–10. https://onlinelibrary.wiley.com/doi/abs/10.1002/9781119951438.eibc2425

Cappa, Carola, and Cristina Alamprese 2017. Brewer's spent grain valorization in fiber-enriched fresh egg pasta production: modelling and optimization study, *LWT-Food Science and Technology*, 82: 464–470.

Celus, Inge, Kristof Brijs, and Jan A Delcour 2007. Enzymatic hydrolysis of brewers' spent grain proteins and technofunctional properties of the resulting hydrolysates, *Journal of Agricultural and Food Chemistry*, 55: 8703–8710.

Chandrasekaran, Margam. 2012. *Valorization of food processing by-products* (CRC Press).

Chedea, Veronica S, Panagiotis Kefalas, and Carmen Socaciu 2010. Patterns of carotenoid pigments extracted from two orange peel wastes (Valencia and Navel var.), *Journal of Food Biochemistry*, 34: 101–110.

Ciriminna, Rosaria, Monica Lomeli-Rodriguez, Piera Demma Cara, Jose A Lopez-Sanchez, and Mario Pagliaro. 2014. Limonene: a versatile chemical of the bioeconomy, *Chemical Communications*, 50: 15288–15296.

Cooray, Sachindra T, and Wei Ning Chen 2018. Valorization of brewer's spent grain using fungi solid-state fermentation to enhance nutritional value, *Journal of Functional Foods*, 42: 85–94.

Dassanayake, Lakmali Samuditha K, Dharma R Kodali, S Ueno, and K Sato 2009. Physical properties of rice bran wax in bulk and organogels, *Journal of the American Oil Chemists' Society*, 86: 1163.

De Menna, Fabio, Jana Dietershagen, Marion Loubiere, and Matteo Vittuari 2018. Life cycle costing of food waste: a review of methodological approaches, *Waste Management*, 73.

de Moraes Crizel, Tainara, André Jablonski, Alessandro de Oliveira Rios, Rosane Rech, and Simone Hickmann Flôres 2013. Dietary fiber from orange byproducts as a potential fat replacer, *LWT-Food Science and Technology*, 53: 9–14.

Dhen, Nahla, Ines Ben Rejeb, Hager Boukhris, Chokri Damergi, and Mohamed Gargouri 2018. Physico-chemical and sensory properties of wheat-Apricot kernels composite bread, *LWT*, 95: 262–267.

Dhingra, Devinder, Mona Michael, Hradesh Rajput, and RT Patil 2012. Dietary fibre in foods: a review, *Journal of Food Science and Technology*, 49: 255–266.

Domínguez-Perles, Raúl, Diego A Moreno, and Cristina García-Viguera 2018. Waking up from four decades' long dream of valorizing agro-food byproducts: toward practical applications of the gained knowledge, *Journal of Agricultural and Food Chemistry*, 66: 3069–3073.

Emden, Zeynep, Roger J Calantone and Cornelia Droge 2006. Collaborating for new product development: selecting the partner with maximum potential to create value, *Journal of Product Innovation Management*, 23: 330–341.

Farmers Weekly. 2016. Exotic and unusual harvesters – peas, beans and spinach, *Farmers Weekly*. https://www.fwi.co.uk/arable/exotic-unusual-harvesters-peas-beans-spinach.

Fernández-Ginés, JM, J Fernández-López, E Sayas-Barberá, E Sendra, and JA Pérez-Alvarez 2003. Effect of storage conditions on quality characteristics of bologna sausages made with citrus fiber, *Journal of Food Sience*, 68: 710–714.

Figuerola, Fernando, María Luz Hurtado, Ana María Estévez, Italo Chiffelle, and Fernando Asenjo. 2005. Fibre concentrates from apple pomace and citrus peel as potential fibre sources for food enrichment, *Food Chemistry*, 91: 395–401.

Fu, Zong-qiang, Min Wu, Xiao-yu Han, and Lei Xu. 2017. Effect of okara dietary fiber on the properties of starch-based films, *Starch-Stärke*, 69: 1700053.

Fuller, Stacey, Eleanor Beck, Hayfa Salman, and Linda Tapsell 2016. New horizons for the study of dietary fiber and health: a review, *Plant Foods for Human Nutrition*, 71: 1–12.

Gabov, Konstantin, Jarl Hemming, and Pedro Fardim 2017. Sugarcane bagasse valorization by fractionation using a water-based hydrotropic process, *Industrial Crops and Products*, 108: 495–504.

Galanakis, Charis M, Philippos Tsatalas, Zenovia Charalambous, and Ioannis M Galanakis 2018. Polyphenols recovered from olive mill wastewater as natural preservatives in extra virgin olive oils and refined olive kernel oils, *Environmental Technology & Innovation*, 10: 62–70.

Galanakis, Charis Michel. 2015. *Food waste recovery: processing technologies and industrial techniques* (Academic Press).

Gedi, Mohamed A., Rhianna Briars, Felius Yuseli, Noorazwani Zainol, Randa Darwish, Andrew M. Salter, and David A. Gray 2017. Component analysis of nutritionally rich chloroplasts: recovery from conventional and unconventional green plant species, *Journal of Food Science and Technology*, 54: 2746–2757.

Gross, Jeana. 2012. *Pigments in vegetables: chlorophylls and carotenoids* (Springer Science & Business Media).

Gustafsson, J, Christel Cederberg, Ulf Sonesson, and Andreas Emanuelsson. 2013. The methodology of the FAO study: global food losses and food waste-extent, causes and prevention"-FAO, 2011 (SIK institutet för livsmedel och bioteknik).

Ikram, Sana, LianYan Huang, Huijuan Zhang, Jing Wang, and Meng Yin 2017. Composition and nutrient value proposition of brewers spent grain, *Journal of Food Science*, 82: 2232–2242.

Jayathilakan, K, Khudsia Sultana, K Radhakrishna, and AS Bawa 2012. Utilization of byproducts and waste materials from meat, poultry and fish processing industries: a review, *Journal of Food Science and Technology*, 49: 278–293.

Jeddou, Khawla Ben, Fatma Bouaziz, Soumaya Zouari-Ellouzi, Fatma Chaari, Semia Ellouz-Chaabouni, Raoudha Ellouz-Ghorbel, and Oumèma Nouri-Ellouz. 2017. Improvement of texture and sensory properties of cakes by addition of potato peel powder with high level of dietary fiber and protein, *Food Chemistry*, 217: 668–677.

Jiang, Yang, Jinhua Du, Liguo Zhang, and Wenqian Li. 2018. Properties of pectin extracted from fermented and steeped hawthorn wine pomace: a comparison, *Carbohydrate Polymers*, 197: 174–182.

Kaisangsri, Nattapon, Ryan J Kowalski, Isuru Wijesekara, Orapin Kerdchoechuen, Natta Laohakunjit, and Girish M Ganjyal 2016. Carrot pomace enhances the expansion and nutritional quality of corn starch extrudates, *LWT-Food Science and Technology*, 68: 391–399.

Kirsty, Schwencke V. 2006. Sustainable, cost-effective, and feasible solutions for the treatment of brewers' spent grain, *Master Brewers Association of the Americas*, 43: 199–202.

Koubaa, Mohamed, Francisco J Barba, Nabil Grimi, Houcine Mhemdi, Wael Koubaa, Nadia Boussetta, and Eugène Vorobiev 2016. Recovery of colorants from red prickly pear peels and pulps enhanced by pulsed electric field and ultrasound, *Innovative Food Science & Emerging Technologies*, 37: 336–344.

Kovalcik, Adriana, Stanislav Obruca, and Ivana Marova 2018. Valorization of spent coffee grounds: a review, *Food and Bioproducts Processing*, 110.

Larrauri, JA. 1999. New approaches in the preparation of high dietary fibre powders from fruit by-products, *Trends in Food Science & Technology*, 10: 3–8.

Li, Na, Ziqian Feng, Yuge Niu, and Liangli Yu. 2018. Structural, rheological and functional properties of modified soluble dietary fiber from tomato peels, *Food Hydrocolloids*, 77: 557–565.

Lin, Carol Sze Ki, Apostolis A Koutinas, Katerina Stamatelatou, Egid B Mubofu, Avtar S Matharu, Nikolaos Kopsahelis, Lucie A Pfaltzgraff, James H Clark, Seraphim Papanikolaou, and Tsz Him Kwan 2014. Current and future trends in food waste valorization for the production of chemicals, materials and fuels: a global perspective, *Biofuels, Bioproducts and Biorefining*, 8: 686–715.

Lota, Marie-Laure, Dominique de Rocca Serra, Félix Tomi, and Joseph Casanova. 2000. Chemical variability of peel and leaf essential oils of mandarins from citrus reticulata blanco, *Biochemical Systematics and Ecology*, 28: 61–78.

Lundberg, B. 2005. Using highly expanded citrus fiber to improve the quality and nutritional properties of foods, *Cereal Foods World*, 50: 248.

Majzoobi, Mahsa, Zahra Vosooghi Poor, Gholamreza Mesbahi, Jalal Jamalian, and Asgar Farahnaky 2017. Effects of carrot pomace powder and a mixture of pectin and xanthan on the quality of gluten-free batter and cakes, *Journal of Texture Studies*, 48: 616–623.

Martin-Cabrejas, MA, RM Esteban, FJ Lopez-Andreu, K Waldron, and RR Selvendran 1995. Dietary fiber content of pear and kiwi pomaces, *Journal of Agricultural and Food Chemistry*, 43: 662–666.

Masmoudi, Manel, Souhail Besbes, Moncef Chaabouni, Christelle Robert, Michel Paquot, Christophe Blecker, and Hamadi Attia 2008. Optimization of pectin extraction from lemon by-product with acidified date juice using response surface methodology, *Carbohydrate Polymers*, 74: 185–192.

Matsakas, Leonidas, Qiuju Gao, Stina Jansson, Ulrika Rova, and Paul Christakopoulos 2017. Green conversion of municipal solid wastes into fuels and chemicals, *Electronic Journal of Biotechnology*, 26: 69–83.

Mehta, Deepak, Priyanka Prasad, Rajender S Sangwan, and Sudesh Kumar Yadav 2018. Tomato processing byproduct valorization in bread and muffin: improvement in physicochemical properties and shelf life stability, *Journal of food science and technology*, 55: 2560–2568.

Mushtaq, Qudsia, Muhammad Irfan, Fouzia Tabssum, and Javed Iqbal Qazi 2017. Potato peels: a potential food waste for amylase production, *Journal of Food Process Engineering*, 40: e12512.

Mussatto, Solange I, Giuliano Dragone, and Inês Conceicao Roberto 2006. Brewers' spent grain: generation, characteristics and potential applications, *Journal of Cereal Science*, 43: 1–14.

Nikiforidis, Constantinos V, and Vassilios Kiosseoglou 2009. Aqueous extraction of oil bodies from maize germ (Zea mays) and characterization of the resulting natural oil-in-water emulsion, *Journal of Agricultural and Food Chemistry*, 57: 5591–5596.

Ohra-aho, Taina, Piritta Niemi, Anna-Marja Aura, Marco Orlandi, Kaisa Poutanen, Johanna Buchert, and Tarja Tamminen 2016. Structure of brewer's spent grain lignin and its interactions with gut microbiota in vitro, *Journal of Agricultural and Food Chemistry*, 64: 812–820.

Ong, Khai Lun, Guneet Kaur, Nattha Pensupa, Kristiadi Uisan, and Carol Sze Ki Lin. 2018. Trends in food waste valorization for the production of chemicals, materials and fuels: Case study South and Southeast Asia, *Bioresource Technology*, 248(Part A): 100–112.

Othman, Siti Hajar, Siti Amirah Mohammad Edwal, Nazratul Putri Risyon, Roseliza Kadir Basha, and Rosnita A Talib. 2017. Water sorption and water permeability properties of edible film made from potato peel waste, *Food Science and Technology*, 37: 63–70.

Parfitt, Julian, Mark Barthel, and Sarah Macnaughton 2010. 'Food waste within food supply chains: quantification and potential for change to 2050', *Philosophical Transactions of the Royal Society of London B: Biological Sciences*, 365: 3065–3081.

Páscoa, Ricardo NMJ, Luís M Magalhães, and João A Lopes 2013. FT-NIR spectroscopy as a tool for valorization of spent coffee grounds: application to assessment of antioxidant properties, *Food Research International*, 51: 579–586.

Peixoto, Carla M, Maria Inês Dias, Maria José Alves, Ricardo C Calhelha, Lillian Barros, Simão P Pinho, and Isabel CFR Ferreira 2018. Grape pomace as a source of phenolic compounds and diverse bioactive properties, *Food Chemistry*, 253: 132–138.

Perussello, Camila A, Zhihang Zhang, Antonio Marzocchella, and Brijesh K Tiwari 2017. Valorization of apple pomace by extraction of valuable compounds, *Comprehensive Reviews in Food Science and Food Safety*, 16: 776–796.

Pierre, Guillaume, Frédéric Sannier, Romain Goude, Armelle Nouviaire, Zoulikha Maache-Rezzoug, Sid-Ahmed Rezzoug, and Thierry Maugard 2011. Evaluation of thermomechanical pretreatment for enzymatic hydrolysis of pure microcrystalline cellulose and cellulose from Brewers' spent grain, *Journal of Cereal Science*, 54: 305–310.

Pleissner, Daniel, and Carol Sze Ki Lin 2013. Valorisation of food waste in biotechnological processes, *Sustainable Chemical Processes*, 1: 21.

Psimouli, V, and V Oreopoulou 2017. Carrot fibre enrichment of fat reduced cake, *Quality Assurance and Safety of Crops & Foods*, 9: 265–274.

Quiles, Amparo, Grant M Campbell, Susanne Struck, Harald Rohm, and Isabel Hernando 2018. Fiber from fruit pomace: a review of applications in cereal-based products, *Food Reviews International*, 34: 162–181.

Quintana, G, E Gerbino, and A Gómez-Zavaglia 2018. Valorization of okara oil for the encapsulation of Lactobacillus plantarum, *Food Research International*, 106: 81–89.

Ralet, Marie-Christine, and Jacques Guéguen 2000. Fractionation of potato proteins: solubility, thermal coagulation and emulsifying properties, *LWT-Food Science and Technology*, 33: 380–387.

RedCorn, Raymond, Samira Fatemi, and Abigail S Engelberth 2018. Comparing end-use potential for industrial food-waste sources, *Engineering*, 4(3), June 2018: 371–380.

Rondeau-Mouro, C, B Bouchet, B Pontoire, P Robert, J Mazoyer, and A Buléon 2003. Structural features and potential texturising properties of lemon and maize cellulose microfibrils, *Carbohydrate Polymers*, 53: 241–252.

Sajib, Mursalin, Peter Falck, Roya RR Sardari, Sindhu Mathew, Carl Grey, Eva Nordberg Karlsson, and Patrick Adlercreutz 2018. Valorization of Brewer's spent grain to prebiotic oligosaccharide: Production, xylanase catalyzed hydrolysis, in-vitro evaluation with probiotic strains and in a batch human fecal fermentation model, *Journal of Biotechnology*, 268: 61–70.

Salihoglu, Guray, Nezih Kamil Salihoglu, Selnur Ucaroglu, and Mufide Banar 2018. Food loss and waste management in Turkey, *Bioresource Technology*, 248(Part A), January 2018: 88–99.

Santos, Vidiany A Queiroz, Camila G Nascimento, Carla AP Schimidt, Daniel Mantovani, Robert FH Dekker, and Mário Antônio A Da Cunha 2018. Solid-state fermentation of soybean okara: Isoflavones biotransformation, antioxidant activity and enhancement of nutritional quality, *LWT*, 92: 509–515.

Saurabh, Chaturbhuj K, Sumit Gupta, and Prasad S Variyar 2018. Development of guar gum based active packaging films using grape pomace, *Journal of Food Science and Technology*, 55: 1982–1992.

Scordino, Monica, Alfio Di Mauro, Amedeo Passerini, and Emanuele Maccarone 2005. Selective recovery of anthocyanins and hydroxycinnamates from a byproduct of citrus processing, *Journal of Agricultural and Food Chemistry*, 53: 651–658.

Sepelev, Igor, and Ruta Galoburda 2015. Industrial potato peel waste application in food production: a review, *Res Rural Dev*, 1: 130–136.

Shabeer, Munazza, M Tauseef Sultan, Muhammad Abrar, M Suffyan Saddique, Muhammad Imran, Muhammad Saad Hashmi, and Muhammad Sibt-e-Abbas. 2016. Utilization of Defatted Mango Kernel in Wheat-Based Cereals Products: Nutritional and Functional Properties, *International Journal of Fruit Science*, 16: 444–460.

Singha, Poonam, and Kasiviswanathan Muthukumarappan 2018. Single screw extrusion of apple pomace-enriched blends: extrudate characteristics and determination of optimum processing conditions, *Food Science and Technology International*, 24(5): 447–462. 1082013218766981.

Song, Junhong, Teng Pan, Jianping Wu, and Fazheng Ren 2016. The improvement effect and mechanism of citrus fiber on the water-binding ability of low-fat frankfurters, *Journal of Food Science and Technology*, 53: 4197–4204.

Šporin, Monika, Martina Avbelj, Boris Kovač, and Sonja Smole Možina 2018. Quality characteristics of wheat flour dough and bread containing grape pomace flour, *Food Science and Technology International*, 24: 251–263.

Strætkvern, Knut O, Jurgen G Schwarz, Dennis P Wiesenborn, Elias Zafirakos, and Allan Lihme 1998. Expanded bed adsorption for recovery of patatin from crude potato juice, *Bioseparation*, 7: 333–345.

Tišma, Marina, Anita Jurić, Ana Bucić-Kojić, Mario Panjičko, and Mirela Planinić. 2018. Biovalorization of brewers' spent grain for the production of laccase and polyphenols, *Journal of the Institute of Brewing*, 124: 182–186.

Tonini, Davide, Paola Federica Albizzati, and Thomas Fruergaard Astrup 2018. Environmental impacts of food waste: learnings and challenges from a case study on UK, *Waste Management*, 76: 744–766.

Torcello-Gómez, Amelia, Mohamed A Gedi, Roger Ibbett, Khatija Nawaz Husain, Rhianna Briars, and David Gray 2019. Chloroplast-rich material from the physical fractionation of pea vine (Pisum sativum) postharvest field residue (Haulm), *Food chemistry*, 272: 18–25.

Torres-León, Cristian, Romeo Rojas, Juan C Contreras-Esquivel, Liliana Serna-Cock, Ruth E Belmares-Cerda, and Cristóbal N Aguilar 2016. Mango seed: functional and nutritional properties, *Trends in Food Science & Technology*, 55: 109–117.

Wojnowska, Irena, Stefan Poznanski, and Włodzimierz Bednarski 1982. Processing of potato protein concentrates and their properties, *Journal of Food Science*, 47: 167–172.

Yeoh, S, J TAG Shi, and TAG Langrish 2008. Comparisons between different techniques for water-based extraction of pectin from orange peels, *Desalination*, 218: 229–237.

Yılmaz, Emin, and Mustafa Öğütcü 2015. The texture, sensory properties and stability of cookies prepared with wax oleogels, *Food & Function*, 6: 1194–1204.

Yu, Guoyong, Jia Bei, Jing Zhao, Quanhong Li, and Chen Cheng 2018. Modification of carrot (Daucus carota Linn. var. Sativa Hoffm.) pomace insoluble dietary fiber with complex enzyme method, ultrafine comminution, and high hydrostatic pressure, *Food Chemistry*, 257: 333–340.

Zhu, Xindi, Brock Lundberg, Yanling Cheng, Lei Shan, Junjie Xing, Peng Peng, Paul Chen, Xiangzhong Huang, Dong Li, and Roger Ruan 2018. Effect of high-pressure homogenization on the flow properties of citrus peel fibers, *Journal of Food Process Engineering*, 41: e12659.

26

EXPLORING THE POTENTIAL OF DIGITAL FOOD WASTE PREVENTION IN THE RESTAURANT INDUSTRY

Jan Mayer and Jaz Hee-jeong Choi

Introduction

In 2017, the Australian restaurant industry entered its fifth consecutive year of constant growth (IBIS World, 2018). Culinary tourism and changing social trends (e.g. consumers turn to restaurants because of busier lifestyles) are fuelling the industry's revenue, which is expected to grow by 3.5% over the next five years (IBIS World, 2018). Because of consumers' increasing demand for quality food and dining experiences, Australian cuisine is moving beyond the tropes and limitations of its colonial and Indigenous heritage, with influences from the Asia-Pacific region and Europe. In alignment with a growing sustainable food movement, modern Australian cuisine is centred around locally sourced ingredients, reinterpretation of traditional foods, and sustainable use of resources.

Despite the increasing awareness of food sustainability from both the consumers and industry, the restaurant industry remains one of the largest producers of food waste in Australia and other parts of the world, especially in more economically developed countries (Gustafsson et al., 2006). In Australia, the food and beverage industry creates an estimated 858,305 tonnes of food waste every year, of which only 8% is recovered or recycled (Alsco, 2015). Influential chefs around the world are starting to address this issue as part of what is often referred to as the sustainable cuisine movement, exploring ways of achieving holistic sustainability. Efforts to revive the traditional cooking methods, which maximize the use of each ingredient to reduce waste, are on the rise. More direct waste reduction endeavours are also evident. For example, Jost Bakker – a Dutch chef and environmentalist – opened Melbourne's first "zero waste" restaurant Brothl, where he reuses byproducts from fine dining restaurants in the same city, such as Attica and Rockpool. To promote sustainability, Bakker also created Greenhouse, a pop-up restaurant built with recycled material, designed to produce zero waste and to be relatively self-sufficient; hundreds of potted strawberry plants are incorporated into the restaurant's façade, fruits from which are then used in the kitchen. For the 2015 Milan Expo, Massimo Bottura – a world renowned Italian chef – launched the project Refettorios, where soup kitchens collect and cook with surplus products from local supermarkets, restaurants, and catering firms. During the 2014 Olympics in Rio de Janeiro, a Refettorio soup kitchen repurposed surplus food from the Olympic village.

While such strategies help to prevent food waste and promote sustainability, they remain small in number, with limited replicability and applicability, in particular for small, independent restaurants. Larger corporations are starting to recognize the economic and environmental consequences of food waste, applying modern technology to prevent food waste and reduce costs. In the retail sector, a large supermarket chain started using machine learning in combination with traditional supply chain solutions to improve fresh food replenishment (Glatzel et al., 2016).

In between the attempts of renowned chefs and large food services to prevent food waste, there are numerous small, independent restaurants that comprise the majority of the Australian food service sector (The Intermedia Group, 2017). Such small-to-medium restaurants (SMRs) are often resource-tight with little financial and organizational flexibility and thus require cost-effective food waste prevention strategies that address the specific challenges in SMRs. However, tools that focus on food waste prevention in SMRs remain limited (Christ and Burritt, 2016). Our study aimed to address the lack of practical tools by exploring the potential of digital technologies to support food waste prevention in SMRs.

Current literature

Food waste in the restaurant industry

Governments and policymakers around the world proposed ambitious plans to reduce global food waste in the coming decades. The European Union introduced its Sustainable Development Goals as part of the Circular Economy Package in September 2015, with the aim to halve food waste at consumer and retail levels by 2030. In November 2017, the Australian government introduced its National Food Waste Strategy in order to halve Australia's food waste by 2030 (Commonwealth of Australia, 2017).

Brotherton (2012) describes the food service industry to be inclusive of hotels, restaurants, and contract food services (e.g. workplace canteens, university or hospital dining). The volume of food waste within the complex network of food service industry has also been investigated. Kranert et al. (2012) evaluated the volume of food waste along the food supply chain in Germany, classifying the food service industry as the second largest producer of food waste, accounting for 17% of total losses. The Swiss food service industry is the third largest producer of food waste (18%) after households and food production (Betz et al., 2015). Okazaki et al. (2008) surveyed the food waste volume and recycling habits across 8,253 licensed food establishments in Hawaii as well as food producers and retailers, and found that food establishments generated approximately 336,510 tonnes of food waste per year. After retailers, restaurants were identified as the second largest source of food waste, generating an annual 103,617 tonnes. Contract food services (i.e. schools and daycare, correctional and medical facilities) accounted for approximately 35,978 tonnes of food waste.

Recent studies on food waste have focused mainly on hotels, contract food services, and chain restaurants. Betz et al. (2015) introduced four waste categories to categorize food waste generation: storage loss, preparation loss, serving loss, and plate waste. The waste categories were used to quantify the amount of food waste in two contract food services in Switzerland. Silvennoinen et al. (2015) determined the volume and sources of food waste in the Finnish food service sector by weighing originally edible food waste in 40 contract food service outlets over a period of 200 days. Food waste was separated into kitchen waste, serving loss, and plate waste. A majority of Finnish contract food services use self-service buffets resulting in high amounts of serving loss, when more food is produced than consumed. Other food services such as restaurants, diners, and cafés were included, but participated over a shorter, one-day research period. Based on these findings, Heikkilä et al. (2016) developed an illustrative framework categorizing sources of food waste in the Finnish food service sector. A qualitative research approach with employees of three contract food services identified eight elements affecting food waste, such as product development and procurement, business model, and customers. This study is of particular interest as we used the illustrative framework as a baseline for the analysis of interview data, as will be shown in the subsequent sections of this chapter.

In most countries, the food service industry consists largely of small-to-medium-sized enterprises such as restaurants, cafés, and pubs with varying business models, operation sizes, and financial constraints. Australians "love to eat out", especially in these places, which make up 57.9% of the restaurant industry (The Intermedia Group, 2017). In this chapter, we refer to these as SMRs. Currently, research focusing on SMRs is limited, which may be the result of higher entry barriers (harder to engage with mostly already resource-tight SMRs) and means to map, measure, and experiment within SMRs' management structures, which tend to be less systematic and more diverse, compared to their larger counterparts. Therefore, it remains unclear how findings from previous studies about different food service industries may apply to SMRs as they can differ significantly from how corporate and contract food services are structured, operate, and manage food waste (Assaf et al., 2011; Lee et al., 2016). Our study aims to contribute to addressing this gap, building on the existing research to explore the challenges and opportunities for reducing food waste that are unique to SMRs.

Use of digital technologies in the food service industry

Interests in the intersection between food and digital technologies have been growing rapidly (Choi et al., 2014; Choi and Graham, 2014). Digital technologies are widely used in the restaurant industry today, particularly the point of sales (PoS) systems. Modern PoS systems provide a platform that can enhance the customer experience and streamline restaurant operations beyond payment. For example, Oracle offers a PoS solution that, among other things, provides reporting and analytics, inventory management, and labour management, making it one of the most important technologies for all involved in the restaurant's daily operations. Reducing food waste is an inherently participatory process (Strotmann et al., 2017). Thus PoS systems can play an important role in facilitating it, yet they are currently rarely used for that purpose.

Other, though less widely used, systems offer additional functions to tackle food waste, showing promising early results but with some limitations. For example, LeanPath provides a food waste prevention strategy combining weighing stations with real-time analysis and reports. Ikea, a Swedish-founded multi-national furniture company, recently announced that it would integrate LeanPath's digital scales and analytics software in its restaurants and cafés, with an aim to halve their food waste. Results from an early phase of the project indicate that some Ikea restaurants were able to halve their food waste by using the system;

importantly, restaurants were able to maintain lower food waste rates throughout the project's duration. Similarly, Winnow, a system using AI to classify and document food waste, reports a reduction of food waste by 50% and food cost between 3–8%. While the collection and documentation of food waste data may support waste reduction by, for example, preventing the overproduction of food, independent SMRs are likely to find it financially challenging to acquire access to – often costly – proprietary hardware or software. For this reason, many consider that practical tools supporting food waste prevention in the restaurant industry are underdeveloped (Baldwin et al., 2011; Pirani and Arafat, 2014), signally an opportunity to exploring the potential of accessible digitally supported food waste prevention in the specific context of SMRs.

Potential perils of digital platforms

Digital platforms can bridge the gap between stakeholders through real-time communication, fostering close relationships, and reducing the time for administration, but often come with substantial financial, social, and environmental costs to others in related networks if not the users of the technologies themselves. For example, Airbnb, a platform for short-term renting, is often criticized for worsening housing affordability in major cities (Lee, 2016). Digital platforms in food-related domains also face similar issues. For example, delivery services such as Foodora often require uses and purchases of mobile phones and vehicles (e.g. bikes, scooters, and cars), which can negatively contribute to environmental sustainability; they can also impose financial burdens on individual delivery workers who often bear the costs for repairs and maintenance themselves while having no access to social security and a regulated legal framework that traditional employment provides (Scholz, 2017).

In recognition of these potential perils, our study aimed to go beyond simply transferring the responsibility to elsewhere in the chain or networks of which the user forms a part. We also tried to remain aware of apparent and less visible consequences of our design decisions during the development of a digital platform. Our focus thus remained firmly on designing an accessible digital platform that would, to the best of our abilities, assist SMRs in reducing food waste, while not creating further economic, technical, and social challenges.

Research problem and aims

As mentioned earlier in this chapter, Heikkilä et al. (2016) introduced an illustrative framework for food waste prevention. Based on participatory workshops with employees from three different communal food services, they identified eight key elements affecting food waste, including product development and procurement, business concept, management, professional skills, communication, diners, competitors, and society. While generally useful, effective food waste prevention strategies for SMRs need to be designed specifically for SMRs, taking into account their unique challenges and constraints. Our study directly addressed this with the following research questions:

1 Where and how do SMRs waste food?
2 How might digital technologies support food waste prevention in SMRs?

To answer these questions, we applied a design-inclusive research (DIR) approach, involving interviews and focus groups, development of a prototype, and its evaluation and further discussions with its different potential user groups.

Materials and methods

We undertook qualitative research to gain nuanced insights into the rich contexts in which chefs and kitchen staff work among different SMRs. These contexts can differ significantly and are subject to various factors such as an SMR's management or business model (Heikkilä et al., 2016). Applying a DIR approach, we conducted semi-structured interviews, on-site observations, and focus groups, and inductively analysed the data to reveal characteristics, using a grounded theory approach.

Despite our initial aspirations to engage with participatory design approaches, we were unable to do so for two main reasons: first, the imposed limit in the time and scope of the project, which made it challenging for the main researcher (a Master's student in Engineering) to learn and make use of a wide range of design approaches, and relatedly; second, because of the challenges with ensuring meaningful participation from people working in SMRs in the research process. This chapter, for us, thus serves to be both a recognition of our specific methodological decision and reflection on how similar endeavours could better occur in the future, not only for learners in design but also for commercial endeavours, which may take advantage of shorter, simpler, and often compromised – user-centric – methods of engagement.

Design-inclusive research

As a DIR project (Horváth, 2007), our study involved three phases: (1) an exploratory research phase, (2) a creative design phase, and (3) a confirmatory research phase. The exploratory phase, also called pre-study, comprises the actions oriented to exploration, induction, and deduction (Horváth, 2007). The aim of the pre-study is, among other things, the aggregation and construction of knowledge related to the research problem, the critical analysis of current and existing approaches, and defining research questions and aims of the design activities.

In our study, the exploratory research phase included an extensive literature review on current research activities related to food waste followed by semi-structured interviews with eight SMRs. Suitable restaurants were selected according to the three key criteria: that they have (1) fewer than 50 employees, (2) no more than five branches, and (3) no affiliation to franchises or chains. Interview participants included head chefs, managers, and kitchen staff with exposure to a wide range of restaurant processes – for example, procurement and recipe development. The interviews were semi-structured and conducted on-site, allowing participants to "show and tell" the challenges and their experiences with food waste in the restaurant.

We applied the concept of data saturation, bringing new participants to the study until the point of diminishing return – that is, further interviews do not provide new knowledge (Bowen, 2008; Miles and Hubermann, 1994). Nvivo, a qualitative data analysis software, was used to support our data analysis. A total of eight participants working at eight different restaurants in Brisbane and Melbourne were recruited. While keeping the question open and flexible, some of the key questions addressed the eight dimensions of the food waste framework by Heikkilä et al. (2016). We paid close attention to carefully analyse the interview data, following the approach introduced by Silverman (2017) to achieve two goals: (1) to reflect on, and where appropriate, revise the framework suitable for SMRs, and (2) to help shape the design and development of a digital prototype, supporting food waste prevention in SMRs. By carefully transcribing each interview, the basic features of "interviewer-interviewee talk" (Silverman, 2017) were preserved, with fillers and half-finished sentences included in the transcription. As they often convey meaning, omitting these features can alter how certain sentences or even paragraphs are interpreted.

Questioning multiple dimensions of food waste with diverse stakeholders provided comparative insights into related interactions, processes, and internal/external factors in SMRs, which allowed for reflexively revising Heikkilä's framework in the SMR context. We also designed and developed a digital prototype, with its key functions, as well as user interface and experience, being informed by the findings of the exploratory research phase.

In the confirmative research phase, we evaluated the prototype's potential to support food waste prevention in SMRs by conducting separate workshops with seven restaurant experts and six lay users. By involving lay users, we were able to examine not only the related usability and user experience but also whether the prototype can make complex restaurant processes more approachable for untrained employees or emerging entrepreneurs.

Participants interacted with the prototype, playing through example scenarios such as ordering supplies for the next day. During the interaction, they engaged in the "think aloud" method of evaluation (Jaspers et al., 2004) by speaking aloud their current thoughts and feelings associated with their actions – for example, by describing what they are doing, thinking, and where needed, indicating where they get stuck or feel confused by the interface. Subsequent to the example scenarios, participants were asked to reflect on their experience interacting with the prototype. After the interaction, we provided "idea cards", i.e. index cards that contain ideas on how the prototype and software in general can support other restaurant processes. Participants were asked to discuss and rank the "idea cards" according to potential impact and applicability. All workshop activities were audio-recorded and transcribed for further analysis using Nvivo.

Results and discussion

In this section, we present the results of our study stemming from the three – exploratory, creative, and confirmatory (Horváth, 2007) – research phases.

Food waste in SMRs

During the exploratory research phase we focused on the sources and drivers of food waste in SMRs. Initial analysis of interview data and field notes revealed the ubiquitous nature of food waste. Combining our findings and existing food waste frameworks (Betz et al., 2015; Heikkilä et al., 2016; Pirani and Arafat, 2016), we devised an illustrative framework focused on SMRs, describing food waste as the interaction of three domains: restaurant operations and processes, internal factors, and external factors.

Restaurant operations and processes

In participating SMRs, food waste occurred in every process throughout the restaurant operations. As participants acknowledged, it is the "little things" that add up and eventually become a significant amount of food waste. These "little things" can range from choosing appropriate portion sizes when developing new recipes to how staff peel an onion during preparation, often carried out by different individuals. Therefore, understanding each restaurant process and how they coalesce to form the overall operations is critical in under-standing where and how food waste is generated in SMRs.

The restaurant operations consist of two basic circular phases: planning and operations. The planning phase is comprised of the processes such as product development (recipe and menu creation) and supplier selection (finding and selecting suitable suppliers). How often the planning phase is run depends on the type of SMR, its business model, and manage-ment. Some SMRs create new recipes and menus every day based on what they find on the market, others change the menu seasonally, looking for suppliers who can provide the required ingredients. The operations phase represents a restaurant's day-to-day operations including procurement, preparation, and service. Procurement generally involves ordering ingredients from various suppliers. These and other ingredients are then prepared for service. During service dishes are cooked, assembled and served to customers. Among participating SMRs, the operations phase is repeated once a day with service once or twice a day.

The processes that comprise the restaurant operations are the primary sources of food waste in SMRs. Participants particularly emphasized that recipe and menu creation can be significant sources of food waste when the portion sizes are not appropriately considered. One participant stated: "There are a lot of places that give you a lot of food, 80% of people can't finish it and then it goes to the bin. And that is a massive amount of waste."

Besides product development, participants considered procurement especially a complex and error-prone process that is generally the responsibility of an experienced chef. In the food service industry, demand is highly volatile and subject to numerous factors often out-side of an SMR's control – for example, the weather, local events, and public holidays (Gunders, 2012). Hence, procurement typically involves uncertainty and guesswork. One participant referred to working out order amounts as a "juggling act". To cope with this uncertainty, participants tended to order more ingredients than necessary for a given period of time, to avoid running out of food during service. This practice can generate significant amounts of waste and a substantial financial loss if excessive ingredients are not used for other purposes.

Overall, restaurant processes can be seen as the primary sources of food waste. The level of skills and experience involved in effective and creative product development and procurement have direct and significant implications for the amount of food waste generated. Continued skills development across various processes is necessary but can be overly time-consuming for already resource-tight SMRs despite their awareness.

Internal factors

While restaurant operations and processes are primary sources, they are not solely responsible for food waste in SMRs. Internal factors such as management and business model can affect food waste by shaping restaurant processes. This can affect where and how food waste is generated. For example, an SMR with the business model of serving very large portions to increase their competitive edge will subsequently generate more plate waste, because cus-tomers will have difficulty finishing their food. Most participating SMRs did not have a dedicated management but distributed managerial responsibilities across multiple roles. For example, the head chef oversees the "back of the house" processes while the general man-ager organizes the service and customer relations. Thus, having clear, consistent core values understood, if not embodied, by staff was perceived to be crucial. For example, one partici-pant, who operates a plant-based restaurant in Brisbane, promoted sustainability as a core value, managing all restaurant processes accordingly:

In every way we try to think of ways on how we can reduce our impact and our footprint on our industry and community. So, a lot of the wood used [for interiors] are scrapped chips. We try to minimize the amount of plastics and non-reusable containers that come into our business from suppliers.

This sustainable mindset is also reflected in the restaurant's dishes, where ingredients are sourced locally, portion sizes are carefully monitored, and if necessary, adjusted, and every edible part of an ingredient is used. On the contrary, SMRs without a clearly identified unique and/or sustainability-related value indicated that "it is almost easier to ignore [food waste] than to enforce [documenting it]".

The key internal factors identified in our study include business model, management, professional skills, and communication. While this is not a complete list, it demonstrates how internal factors influence restaurant processes, affecting the volume of food waste that is generated within an SMR, as well as clear inter-relations with operations and processes as identified in the previous section.

External factors

External factors are generally outside of an SMR's control. Nonetheless, they can significantly influence the restaurant's operations and processes and thus affect where and how food waste is generated. While SMRs have limited control over external factors, they can observe their effect on processes in order to minimize food waste. Based on the findings of Heikkilä et al. (2016) we identified four key external factors, including demand (e.g. local events, the weather, competitors), suppliers, customers, and society. Volatile demands complicate the procurement process, which often leads to over ordering and increased food waste from spoilage. Diners are a significant source of food waste, as our interviews and previous research confirmed. Yet, diner-related food waste can be difficult to prevent. For example, a participant from Melbourne observed plate waste and adjusted the portion sizes. While this reduced the overall plate waste, customers continue to leave food on their plates because of arbitrary reasons – for example, a dislike of pizza crusts leading to them not being consumed and so wasted.

Revisiting the food waste framework

The three elements restaurant processes, internal factors, and external factors form the building blocks of our food waste framework (Figure 26.1). It must be noted that the sources and drivers of food waste can change significantly between enterprises. Therefore, our framework should be viewed as a broader scaffolding of diverse, inter-related, and at times conflicting elements across restaurant processes, internal factors, and external factors in the order of the most to least controllable.

- *Processes*: processes are primary sources of food waste, i.e. they directly generate food waste. While processes are primary sources, they are also the easiest to control and adjust.
- *Internal factors*: internal factors are secondary sources of food waste, i.e. they do not generate food waste directly but affect the amount of food waste generated by processes. Internal factors can be controlled but it is generally more resource-intensive than adjusting processes.
- *External factors*: external factors are secondary sources of food waste, affecting the volume of food waste that is generated by SMR processes. External factors can be observed but not controlled.

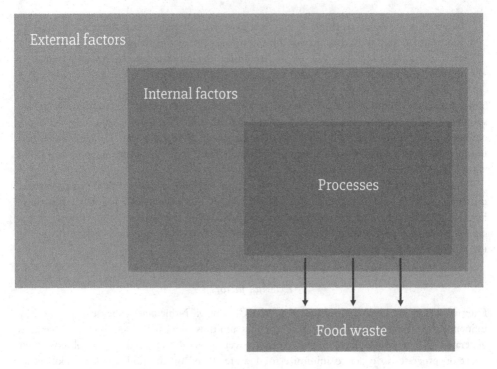

Figure 26.1 An illustrative framework describing food waste at the intersection of restaurant processes, internal, and external factors.

Prototype development

We focused on the procurement process for prototyping, particularly the demand management and ordering of supplies, because of the following reasons:

- The majority of participants called procurement an especially complex, time-consuming, and error-prone process, involving repetitive tasks and uncertainty.
- As such, procurement is generally the responsibility of an experienced chef (e.g. head or sous chef), it can create bottlenecks and put additional pressure on the senior chefs.
- Procurement errors often lead to substantial food waste and financial loss.

Considering the prevalence of digital, networked technologies within restaurant environments – for example, using phones or tablet devices for PoS processes – a lightweight digital application can be integrated without significant disruptions. Some of the key advantages of integrating digital applications include that they can automate repetitive tasks, freeing up employees' time for creative tasks; through data analysis, they can provide key information such as expected demand and inventory data during procurement, reducing uncertainty and guesswork; by streamlining and guiding users through the procurement process, they can reduce complexity, making ordering more approachable for less experienced employees, and; a scaffolded procurement process can reduce human error, preventing food waste and financial loss. During the exploratory research phase, we noticed significant differences between SMRs that were managed by experienced chefs and entrepreneurial SMRs with less experienced management. To make the prototype accessible for a majority of employees regardless of their level of experience and skills, we designed "restaurant personas" that highlighted the differences between more established and entrepreneurial businesses. Furthermore, using additional standard human-centred design methods, we created a streamlined procurement process, and journey maps for key processes, such as ordering supplies for the next day, to identify current "pain points" and "make or break" moments (see Figure 26.2).

We used the restaurant's menu as a baseline for ordering supplies, in recognition of its significant role in generating food waste. The menu used in the prototype consists of a relatively small number of dishes: three entrées, four mains, and three desserts. Each dish has attached to it a recipe, containing a list of ingredients with quantities. These quantities are used to calculate the required order amounts to assist with procurement processes. The user enters the expected demand for each dish on the menu, which is displayed next to each dish and calculated based on sales figures, reservations, local events, and weather data (see Figure 26.3). Providing key

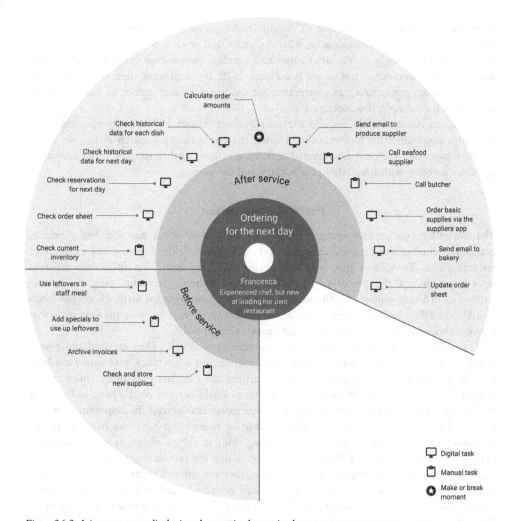

Figure 26.2 A journey map displaying the required steps in the procurement process.

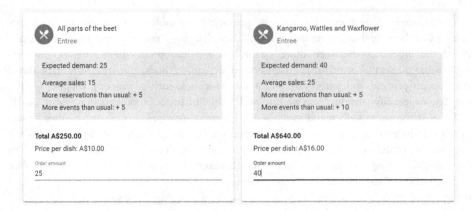

Figure 26.3 The software prototype provides the expected demand during the procurement process.

information can reduce stress related to decision-making under uncertainty. Subsequently, the software calculates the order amounts, splits the order, and sends it to the respective suppliers designated by the user (e.g., the meat order to a butcher, the produce order to a farmer, the dairy order to a wholesaler, and so on) (see Figure 26.2). By automating these repetitive, time-consuming tasks, participants can concentrate on creative tasks that cannot be carried out by machines – for example, developing recipes.

While we chose to only include the procurement process in the prototype, there are numerous possibilities for interventions. During the confirmatory research phase, we tested the prototype and explored how digital technologies may further support other restaurant processes together with hospitality professionals and lay users.

Prototype evaluation

The aim of the confirmative research phase is to bring in outside knowledge and expertise, evaluating whether the design artefact supports concepts developed during the exploratory research phase. To achieve this, hospitality experts and lay users were invited to different workshops, to test the prototype, playing through example scenarios such as creating a menu or ordering supplies for the next day. This user test provided feedback on the functionality, usability, and user experience of the prototype, as well as other possible ways that digital technologies may support food waste prevention in SMRs.

The participants provided positive and constructive feedback. They enjoyed the prototype's simplicity, which helped to complete procurement in a quick and understandable way. In particular, they saw potential in automating the calculating of order amounts, yet stated that the accuracy of calculated order amounts would need to be adequate to be useful in the real kitchen environment. In general, participants emphasized the importance of certainty and trust; a chef who uses the system has to be assured that her order has been placed successfully. Furthermore, participants saw strong value in the provision of key information (e.g. reservations, sales data, and inventory levels) during the procurement process.

At the same time, participants also raised questions and offered additional points for consideration. For example, work in the kitchen can be stressful and requires constant multitasking. Food waste prevention strategies in general, and new digital technologies in particular, will need to integrate seamlessly into existing processes. If introducing a new process complicates day-to-day operations, it can be difficult to gain the acceptance of staff. Further-more, the interaction must be intuitive with a low cognitive load, as workers in SMRs often work long shifts at irregular hours.

We acknowledge that the study relied only on participants' evaluation of the prototype, which might differ substantially from evaluating the real-world deployment and use of a fully developed version in a restaurant. In its current state the prototype cannot be used in an actual restaurant environment. Various features were only visually, not functionally, presented to allow for more focused and meaningful evaluation within the given time constraints. Furthermore, our software prototype focused on tasks related to the procurement at the expense of other restaurant processes such as recipe and menu creation. Nonetheless, the study confirmed the potential of supporting food waste prevention through the use of accessible digital technology.

Possible digital strategies for SMRs

Following the prototype evaluation, participants used the idea cards to identify key oppor-tunities for digitally supported food waste prevention in SMRs, and to probe additional pos-sibilities beyond what our study could cover. Opportunities were identified surrounding three key areas, including "Recipe creation", "Inventory", and "Suppliers". Participants offered some possible scenarios – for example, emphasizing the importance of inventory control, to avoid ordering excess ingredients, participants suggested the technology may pro-vide real-time monitoring of the ingredients in stock and their expected shelf life, alerting when an ingredient drops below a certain threshold.

Further, participants demonstrated their understanding about the importance of considering the broader food ecosystem. While a comprehensive system might significantly reduce food waste in SMRs, isolated interventions will not automatically result in an overall change along the food supply chain (Göbel et al., 2015). Isolated prevention strategies in SMRs, without effective communication and collaboration with other constituents of the broader food service ecology, merely move food waste to other stakeholders – for example, the suppliers and produ-cers. Thus the technology must be open, inclusive, and encourage collaboration.

By reviewing and synthesizing the overall findings, we derived a set of key criteria for digital food waste prevention strategies in SMRs:

- *Simplicity*: they must be easy to use, set up, and maintain regardless of the user's experi-ence, professional skills, and occupation.
- *Integration*: they must integrate seamlessly into existing restaurant processes.
- *Versatility*: they must adapt to different restaurant types, sizes, business models, and phil-osophies, as SMRs exist in diverse forms, including casual and fine dining, cafés, pubs, and bars.
- *Setup/initial cost*: they must be affordable and cost-effective. In an industry with notori-ously low profit margins, SMRs often cannot justify substantial investment in digital technologies.
- *Connectivity*: they must recognize their impact on other stakeholders (e.g. suppliers and producers) and minimize the risk of a bullwhip effect within the broader food service ecology (i.e. food waste is merely moved along the supply chain).

The derived criteria for digital food waste prevention strategies can help assess and guide related digital developments, as well as other future design endeavours around food waste prevention in SMRs.

Conclusions

In this chapter, we presented a study that aimed to address the challenges SMRs face in their endeavour to reduce food waste by better understanding their practices, processes, needs, and wants, and exploring opportunities for digital technologies to aid their endeavours in effective and accessible ways. To achieve this, we applied a DIR approach. We first conducted semi-structured interviews with participants from eight SMRs in Brisbane and Melbourne in Australia. Based on the findings of the exploratory phase, we developed (1) an illustrative framework describing food waste as the interaction of restaurant processes, internal factors, and external factors, and (2) a digital prototype supporting the procurement process, a significant source of food waste within SMRs. Then we invited experts currently working in SMRs and lay users to participate in focus groups where they evaluated the prototype and discussed additional possibilities for related future digital technologies.

Based on participants' feedback, we derived five criteria for (digital) food waste prevention strategies: simplicity, integration, versatility, setup and initial cost, and connectivity. These broad categories can be flexibly used to assess the existing, and guide future developments of digital strategies for food waste prevention within the SMR context. We are certainly not claiming that these are definitive. Rather, it is our hope that these will be further interrogated and revised by others in the future.

Similarly, we acknowledge some of the key limitations of our study. Its relatively small scale focusing on a selected restaurant process made it possible to design a prototype based on the knowledge and experience of the participants. While it was our intention to have flexible and minimal engagement with the participants out of understanding and respect for their limited time and resources, having more diverse representations from and of SMRs throughout the process could have not only produced findings for the researchers but also led to increasing understanding among the staff and their work and overall capacity building, resulting in direct benefit to the participants.

Further, having both more participation and participants might have led to more fine-grained identification of internal and external factors, possibly revealing feasible opportunities to address what might now be considered "out of control". It would likely have led to identifying and creating different ways for SMRs to communicate, share resources, and care for one another beyond formalized associations. Any design attempting to create change that could benefit a particular group (in this case, SMRs) is an inherently political act, which may, for various reasons, be seen as a threat to the (non-)participants with different "objectives, logics, and values" (Schwittay, 2014).

The food service industry is a dynamic and open ecosystem, engendering diverse, often competing agendas. Even within a defined sector such as SMRs, a wide range of practices, processes, values, and voices exist. Thus meaningful and inclusive co-creation is necessary to ascertain more impactful outcome, including acceptance and collaboration across the food sector toward reducing food waste. Our study is a small but active call for such careful design toward sustainable food futures.

References

Alsco. 2015. "The Food Waste Problem and Tips to Reduce It — Alsco Australia." Availalabe at www.alsco.com.au/2015/07/food-waste-reality-check-tips-reduce-food-waste-hospitality-sector/?lipi=urn%3Ali%3Apage%3Ad_flagship3_pulse_read%3Bs%2F4xr4f1R5Skf7gbPFnNwQ%3D%3D. Retrieved 2018-09-14.

Assaf, A George, Margaret Deery, and Leo Jago 2011. "Evaluating the performance and scale characteristics of the australian restaurant industry." *Journal of Hospitality & Tourism Research* 35 (4): 419–436.

Baldwin, Cheryl, Nana Wilberforce, and Amit Kapur 2011. "Restaurant and food service life cycle assessment and development of a sustainability standard." *The International Journal of Life Cycle Assessment* 16 (1): 40–49.

Betz, Alexandra, Jürg Buchli, Christine Göbel, and Claudia Müller. 2015."Food waste in the Swiss food service industry - Magnitude and potential for reduction." *Waste Management* 35: 218–226.

Bowen, Glenn A. 2008. "Naturalistic inquiry and the saturation concept: a research note." *Qualitative Research* 8 (1): 137–152.

Brotherton, Bob. 2012. *International Hospitality Industry*. Oxford: Elsevier.

Choi, Jaz Hee-jeong, Foth, Marcus, & Hearn, Gregory N. (Eds.) (2014) Eat Cook Grow: Mixing Human-Computer Interactions with Human-Food Interactions. MIT Press: Cambridge, MA.

Choi, Jaz Hee-jeong & Mark Graham 2014. "Urban food futures: ICTs and opportunities." *Futures: The Journal of Policy, Planning and Futures Studies* 62 (Part B): 151–154.

Christ, Katherine Leanne, and Roger Burritt 2016. "Material flow cost accounting for food waste in the restaurant industry." *British Food Journal* 119 (3): 600–612.

Commonwealth of Australia. 2017. *National Food Waste Strategy: Halving Australia's Food Waste by 2030*. Technical Report. Canberra. www.environment.gov.au/system/files/resources/4683826b-5d9f-4e65-9344-a900060915b1/files/national-food-waste-strategy.pdf.

Glatzel, Christoph, Matt Hopkins, Tim Lange, and Uwe Weiss. 2016. "The Secret to Smarter Fresh-Food Replenishment? Machine learning." Available at www.mckinsey.com/industries/retail/our-insights/the-secret-to-smarter-fresh-food-replenishment-machine-learning?cid=other-eml-alt-mip-mck-oth-1611. Retrieved 2018-09-14.

Göbel, Christine, Nina Langen, Antonia Blumenthal, Petra Teitscheid, and Guido Ritter 2015. "Cutting food waste through cooperation along the food supply chain." *Sustainability* 7 (2): 1429–1445.

Gunders, Dana. 2012. "Wasted: How America is losing up to 40% of its food from farm to fork to landfill." NRDC Issue Paper 1–26.

Gustafsson, Inga-Britt, Åsa Öström, Jesper Johansson, and Lena Mossberg 2006. "the five aspects meal model: A tool for developing meal services in restaurants." *Journal of Food-Service* 17 (2): 84–93.

Heikkilä, Lotta, Anu Reinikainen, Juha Matti Katajajuuri, Kirsi Silvennoinen, and Hanna Hartikainen. 2016."Elements affecting food waste in the food service sector." *Waste Management* 56: 446–453.

Horváth, Imre. 2007. "Comparison of Three Methodological Approaches of Design Research." In *Guidelines for a Decision Support Method Adapted to NPD Processes*.

IBIS World. 2018. *Restaurants - Australia Market Research Report*. Melbourne: Technical Report.

The Intermedia Group. 2017. *Eating out in Australia: 2016 in Review*. Glebe, NSW: Technical Report, The Intermedia Group. www.the-drop.com.au/wp-content/uploads/2016/11/EatingOutinAustralia_2017_Respondent-Summary.compressed.pdf.

Jaspers, Monique WM, et al. 2004. "The think aloud method: a guide to user interface design." *International Journal of Medical Informatics* 73 (11–12): 781–795.

Kranert, M., G. Hafner, J. Barabosz, H. Schuller, D. Leverenz, A. Kölbig, F. Schneider, S Lebersorger, and S. Scherhaufer 2012. *Ermittlung der weggeworfenen Lebensmittelmengen und Vorschläge zur Verminderung der Wegwerfrate bei Lebensmitteln in Deutschland*. Stuttgart: Technical Report. www.bmel.de/SharedDocs/Downloads/Ernaehrung/WvL/Studie_Lebensmittelabfaelle_Langfassung.pdf?__blob=publicationFile.

Lee, Craig, Rob Hallak, and Shruti R. Sardeshmukh. 2016."Drivers of success in independent restaurants: A study of the Australian restaurant sector." *Journal of Hospitality and Tourism Management* 29: 99–111.

Lee, Dayne. 2016. "How airbnb short-term rentals exacerbate los angeles's affordable housing crisis: Analysis and policy recommendations." *Harvard Law & Policy Review* 10.

Miles, Mathew B, and Michael A Hubermann 1994. *Qualitative Data Analysis: An Expanded Sourcebook*. 2nd ed. Thousand Oaks, CA: Sage Publications.

Okazaki, W K, S Q Turn, and P G Flachsbart 2008. "Characterization of food waste generators: A Hawaii case study." *Waste Management* 28 (12): 2483–2494.

Pirani, Sanaa I, and Hassan A Arafat. 2014."Solid waste management in the hospitality industry: A review." *Journal of Environmental Management* 146: 320–336.

Pirani, Sanaa I, and Hassan A Arafat. 2016."Reduction of food waste generation in the hospitality industry." *Journal of Cleaner Production* 132: 129–145.

Scholz, Trebor. 2017. *Uberworked and Underpaid: How Workers Are Disrupting the Digital Economy.* Cambridge, UK: Polity Press.

Schwittay, Anke. 2014. "Designing development: Humanitarian design in the financial inclusion assemblage." *PoLAR: Political and Legal Anthropology Review* 37 (1): 29–47.

Silvennoinen, Kirsi, Lotta Heikkilä, Juha Matti Katajajuuri, and Anu Reinikainen. 2015."Food waste volume and origin: Case studies in the Finnish food service sector." *Waste Management* 46: 140–145.

Silverman, David. 2017. "How was it for you? The Interview Society and the irresistible rise of the (poorly analyzed) interview." *Qualitative Research* 17 (2): 144–158.

Strotmann, Christina, Christine Göbel, Silke Friedrich, Judith Kreyenschmidt, Guido Ritter, and Petra Teitscheid 2017. "A participatory approach to minimizing food waste in the food industry—A manual for managers." *Sustainability* 9 (1): 66–87.

27

FOOD WASTE MANAGEMENT, TREATMENT AND DISPOSAL OPTIONS

A review and future considerations

Daniel Hoornweg, Scott Lougheed, Mark Walker, Ramy Salemdeeb, Tammara Soma and Christian Reynolds

Introduction

There is clear direction on the prevention, management and treatment of wasted food through the use of a "food waste hierarchy" (Metcalfe et al., 2017). Many levels of government from national or federal, through to municipal bodies recognise the use of a hierarchy in the selection of how to prevent and manage food waste (see Figure 27.1).

The food waste hierarchy, depicted in Figure 27.1, stipulates that governments should prioritise efforts (presented in order of most to least preferable in terms of its environmental impact) to (1) reduce food waste, (2) redistribute the surplus and fit-for-consumption food to humans or use it as animal feed, (3) recycle food waste by composting it in an enclosed environment or sending it for anaerobic digestion where both energy and digestate could be produced, and finally, (4) dispose it via incineration or in a landfill (WRAP, 2016a). These options are grouped into two categories: food waste upstream options where food waste arising is either prevented or diverted from being disposed of or recycled using existing food waste processing options, and food waste downstream treatment options where food waste is disposed of using one of the existing food waste treatment options mentioned above (i.e., composting, anaerobic digestion, incineration or landfill).

Other chapters in this Handbook examine the "higher" parts of the hierarchy such as donation/redistribution (see Chapter 21: Midgley) or animal feed (see Chapter 22: Bowman, Luyckx and O'Sullivan). However, for completeness, this brief chapter outlines the "lower" downstream recycling, recovery and disposal aspects of the food waste hierarchy. Drawing upon previous reviews of the subject (Hoornweg et al., 1999; Hoornweg and Bhada-Tata, 2012; Laurent et al., 2014a, 2014b; Salemdeeb and Al-Tabbaa, 2015a, 2015b; Salemdeeb et al., 2017, 2018; Zheng et al., 2017), this chapter describes the disposal route, and provides a summary of their current and future environmental consequences under different decarbonisation scenarios.

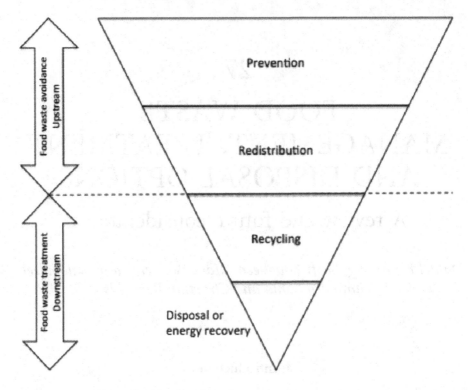

Figure 27.1 The food waste hierarchy.
Source: Adapted from WRAP (2016b).

Food waste composition

Food waste can be regarded as an organic waste material with a high moisture content (up to 80–95%) and a high salt content. When processed as a mixed food waste rather than a single type of food waste suitable for high value valorisation (see Chapter 25: Gedi et al.), it contains differing levels of protein, starch, fat and other organic matter, and is rich in nitrogen, phosphorus, potassium, calcium and other trace elements. Due to the variety of storage and disposal routes, mixed food waste may include harmful chemicals, pathogenic microorganisms, flies, cockroaches and rats. These potentially harmful or dangerous factors require that household food waste be disposed almost every day in some (high temperature) countries or cities. To negate the dangers to public health, waste management infrastructure has developed to specifically treat and manage food waste (Reynolds et al., 2011).

The task (and expense) of food waste management (collection, processing and disposal) traditionally falls to local or municipal authorities. In order to reduce the costs to councils, household food waste has traditionally been mixed with other municipal solid waste (MSW) prior to landfill disposal. However, this method of collecting waste has had a detrimental impact on our environment.

Hoornweg and Bhada-Tata (2012) found typical waste collection methods to be one of the following:

1. *House-to-house*: waste collectors visit each individual house to collect garbage. The user generally pays a fee for this service.
2. *Community bins*: users bring their garbage to community bins that are placed at fixed points in a neighbourhood or locality. MSW is picked up by the municipality, or its designate, according to a set schedule.
3. *Kerbside pick-up*: users leave their garbage directly outside their homes according to a garbage pick-up schedule set with the local authorities (secondary house-to-house collectors not typical).
4. *Self delivered*: waste generators deliver the waste directly to disposal sites or transfer stations, or hire third-party operators (or the municipality).
5. *Contracted or delegated service*: businesses hire firms (or municipality with municipal facilities) who arrange collection schedules and charges with customers. Municipalities often license private operators and may designate collection areas to encourage collection efficiencies.

Separate food waste collection has been in operation in some municipalities now for over a decade (Bernstad and la Cour Jansen, 2011), and municipal governments have begun to adopt new food waste treatment methods and practices. It should be noted, however, that existing disposal methods may be entrenched, having been shaped by long-standing government policy and finances, politics, planning and geographical considerations; for instance, many municipalities are locked into five- or ten-year waste disposal contracts, and can then only put out to tender for change. Other considerations that impact food waste management option selection include land availability, size and population density and the degree of urbanisation, as well as broader community factors such as water resources (for sewer disposal), income and lifestyle factors, cultural and eating habits, education levels and community environmental awareness.

The two generalised methods of treating food waste can be classified as either centralised treatment or on-site/decentralised/informal treatment. Moving "down" the waste hierarchy split these then further into four categories: biological technologies, mechanical biological treatment, thermal technologies and landfill technologies (WSN Environmental Solutions, 2005). These treatment methods are summarised in Table 27.1 by country income level. Centralised treatment is the primary method of food waste treatment and includes collection, separation and treatment of food waste. It is traditionally run by local government and/or private contractors.

In centralised treatment, household food waste is stored in home either "wet" – directly in a house bin prior to collection – or "dry" – in a bench top container (such as a "kitchen caddy") to dry off the liquid, then seal the waste into a biodegradable or paper bag. In the summer time, in the hot countries (such as Australia), many councils suggest that food waste can be stored in the fridge or freezer until organics collection day in order to reduce odour (Zero Waste SA, 2010). During home storage of food waste, biological changes can occur to the food waste including a loss of carbon and nutrients (Bernstad and la Cour Jansen, 2012). This food waste is then collected for treatment by the municipality. The various treatment methods will be further outlined below.

Decentralised, on-site or informal food waste treatment is where the food waste is treated by the household itself without being transferred to the council's garbage collection system. For developed countries, Reynolds et al. (2014) classified the following informal methods: home composting, animal disposal (to worms, chickens, dogs or other), to sewer or macerator/garburator (a food waste processor under kitchen sink), to charity, or via illegal disposal.

Table 27.1 Comparison of solid waste management practices by income level

Activity	Low income	Middle income	High income
Source reduction	No organised programmes, but reuse and low per capita waste generation rates are common.	Some discussion of source reduction, but rarely incorporated into an organised programme.	Organised education programmes emphasise the three "R's" – reduce, reuse, and recycle. More producer responsibility and focus on product design.
Collection	Sporadic and inefficient. Service is limited to high visibility areas, the wealthy, and businesses willing to pay. High fraction of inerts and compostable impact collection – overall collection below 50%.	Improved service and increased collection from residential areas. Larger vehicle fleet and more mechanisation. Collection rate varies between 50 to 80%. Transfer stations are slowly incorporated into the solid waste management system.	Collection rate greater than 90%. Compactor trucks and highly mechanised vehicles and transfer stations are common. Waste volume a key consideration. Aging collection workers often a consideration in system design.
Recycling	Although most recycling is through the informal sector and waste picking, recycling rates tend to be high both for local markets and for international markets and imports of materials for recycling, including hazardous goods such as e-waste and ship-breaking. Recycling markets are unregulated and include a number of "middlemen". Large price fluctuations.	Informal sector still involved; some high technology sorting and processing facilities. Recycling rates are still relatively high. Materials are often imported for recycling. Recycling markets are somewhat more regulated. Material prices fluctuate considerably.	Recyclable material collection services and high technology sorting and processing facilities are common and regulated. Increasing attention toward long-term markets. Overall recycling rates higher than low and middle income. Informal recycling still exists (e.g. aluminium can collection). Extended product responsibility common.
Composting	Rarely undertaken formally even though the waste stream has a high percentage of organic material. Markets for, and awareness of, compost lacking.	Large composting plants are often unsuccessful due to contamination and operating costs (little waste separation); some small-scale composting projects at the community/ neighbourhood level are more sustainable. Increasing use of anaerobic digestion.	Becoming more popular at both backyard and large-scale facilities. Waste stream has a smaller portion of compostable than low- and middle-income countries. More source segregation makes composting easier. Anaerobic digestion increasing in popularity. Odour control critical.

(Continued)

Table 27.1 (Cont).

Activity	Low income	Middle income	High income
Incineration	Not common, and generally not successful because of high capital, technical, and operation costs, high moisture content in the waste, and high percentage of inerts.	Some incinerators are used, but experiencing financial and operational difficulties. Air pollution control equipment is not advanced and often by-passed. Little or no stack emissions monitoring. Governments include incineration as a possible waste disposal option but costs prohibitive. Facilities often driven by subsidies from OECD countries on behalf of equipment suppliers.	Prevalent in areas with high land costs and low availability of land (e.g., islands). Most incinerators have some form of environmental controls and some type of energy recovery system. Governments regulate and monitor emissions. About three (or more) times the cost of landfilling per tonne.
Landfilling/ dumping	Low-technology sites usually open dumping of wastes. High polluting to nearby aquifers, water bodies, settlements. Often receive medical waste. Waste regularly burned. Significant health impacts on local residents and workers.	Some controlled and sanitary landfills with some environmental controls. Open dumping is still common. CDM projects for landfill gas are more common.	Sanitary landfills with a combination of liners, leak detection, leachate collection systems, and gas collection and treatment systems. Often problematic to open new landfills due to concerns of neighbouring residents. Post-closure use of sites increasingly important, e.g. golf courses and parks.
Costs (see Annex E of Hoornweg and Bhada-Tata (2012))	Collection costs represent 80 to 90% of the MSW management budget. Waste fees are regulated by some local governments, but the fee collection system is inefficient. Only a small proportion of budget is allocated toward disposal.	Collection costs represent 50% to 80% of the MSW management budget. Waste fees are regulated by some local and national governments. More innovation in fee collection, e.g. included in electricity or water bills. Expenditures on more mechanised collection fleets and disposal are higher than in low-income countries.	Collection costs can represent less than 10% of the budget. Large budget allocations to intermediate waste treatment facilities. Up front community participation reduces costs and increases options available to waste planners (e.g., recycling and composting).

Source: Adapted from Hoornweg and Bhada-Tata (2012)

Recycling via biological treatment

Biological treatment recycles the nutritive value of the food waste back into material that can be used to grow new food. The two most common biological treatment methods for food waste are anaerobic digestion (AD) and composting.

AD is a process that involves the biological breakdown of food waste in the absence of oxygen in a closed and controlled environment (Smith et al., 2001). It includes the stages of hydrolysis, acidogenesis, acetogenesis and methanogenesis. It is a well-established technology in the UK, where there are 254 operational AD sites (Defra 2016; Defra, 2019). Food waste is an ideal substrate for AD as it contains 80–97% of volatile solid (VS)/total solid (TS), 70–90% water per total weight, and a carbon to nitrogen ratio (C:N) range from 14.7–36.4 (Zhang et al., 2007, 2014). For the main stage of AD, the pH, temperature, nutrient level, C:N ratio are important for the efficient operation of the process (Tampio et al., 2014; Zhang et al., 2014). Thus, if the type of food waste changes in the AD, the reaction speed and output of the AD reactor will change. The scale of an AD plant can vary from industrial through to "small-scale" AD reactor units that are suitable to rural areas. The scale also can alter the speed of the AD reaction. Due to this variability, the development of small-scale anaerobic digesters is still facing great challenges due to long reaction times and low methane gas production (Zhang et al., 2016). Material outputs from AD include a biogas with a high methane content that is suitable for the generation of heat and power; and a nutrient-rich solid or liquid output (digestate) that can be used as a soil improver and substitute synthetic fertiliser.

Composting is a process that includes the biological breakdown of food waste aerobically in an enclosed environment (via microorganisms such as bacteria and fungi), with accurate temperature control and monitoring. It is a well-established technology in the UK for the treatment of both food and garden waste mixtures. There are a number of different industrial composting systems which include aerated static pile composting, high fibre composting, in-vessel composting, tunnel composting, windrow composting, vermicomposting, and microbial composting. Also, there are other small-scale composting processes such as community-based composting (Tramhel, 2012), and the composting bin which have been used for residential and community decentralisation waste treatment. The time needed to compost effectively can vary with the exact process, but can be over six weeks (Recycled Organics Unit, 2007; Tweib et al., 2011). Outputs from composting include a soil conditioner rich in nutrients that could be used as a substitute to synthetic fertiliser.

Recovery via thermal treatment

Energy can be recovered from food waste via thermal treatment. This energy recovery is typically carried out through incinerating (a mass-burn) a mixed waste stream of food waste and other municipal wastes. This incineration of mixed waste can result in a 90% reduction of the original volume and 70–80% of the mass (Lombardi et al., 2015; Kumar and Samadder, 2017). Waste to Energy (WtE) (or Energy from Waste (EfW)) plants are now commonly employed to use the heat produced from the thermal plant heat for electricity production. In some countries which have less land available, incineration has become one of the most important treatment methods alongside other thermal conversion technologies such as gasification and pyrolysis (Astrup et al., 2009). Incineration was previously recommended as a low-carbon and low-cost fuel option in the UK Energy White Paper (Department of Trade and Industry, 2007). At the end of 2014, 8.6 million tonnes of waste were processed in 74 incinerators and there were an additional 134 sites permitted for building (Defra 2016; Defra, 2019). The high moisture content of up to 80% in food waste has led to the need to pre-treat and co-combust with coal or other mixed wastes (such as plastics) in order to ensure that the incineration is operating efficiently (Lombardi et al., 2015). However, even under optimum conditions, the energy efficiency is only 18–34% depending on the scale and the specific technology used. Outputs from incineration include energy recovery in the form of electricity, heat or both; bottom ash is the main residual from the incineration of food waste. Representing around 20–30% of the original waste feed by weight, it is usually recycled into aggregates for use in the construction industry; and fly ash, which is hazardous material that is composed of fine particulate matter and gas-cleaning reagents (mainly lime, activated carbon, dioxins and furans). These two types of ashes are typically sent to landfill.

Other advanced thermal treatment options are *gasification* and *pyrolysis*. These are both complex processes that involve physical and chemical interactions. They are more complex and costly to operate and maintain than incineration (Lombardi et al., 2015). Gasification generally takes place at temperatures in excess of 600 °C in the presence of oxygen-enriched air or pure oxygen. The net electricity production efficiency is approximately 23–31%, depending on plant size (Viganò et al., 2010). Pyrolysis takes place at 400–800 °C in a rotary kiln, which is indirectly heated by a portion of the flue gases (approximately 20%) from syngas combustion. This process produces steam which drives a steam turbine generator for power generation. The gross electric conversion efficiency is about 16%. However, this treatment method is limited to specific food waste flows such as cooking oil (Lombardi et al., 2015).

Compared to conventional combustion, pyrolysis is less well-established as a technology, with experimental facilities in countries such as Canada failing to demonstrate economic feasibility at scale (Pearson, 2015; Sandor, 2015).

Disposal

Disposal of food waste without the extraction of any value is the lowest level of the food waste hierarchy. In most cases this can mean the disposal of the food waste down the sewer (without further AD) or disposal to a landfill.

Sewer disposal is another method to dispose of food waste. There are currently two types of sewage disposal mechanism. As described by Zheng et al. (2017), the first type uses an electrically driven mixer to macerate food waste in combination with water to flush the homogenate into the sewer system. The second type is an advance on the first in that it dehydrates the macerated food waste to produce either a compost material for potting mix or for transferal into an MSW bin (Lundie and Peters, 2005; Battistoni et al., 2007; Iacovidou et al., 2012). In the USA and in most industrialised countries, sewer disposal options have been available for several decades. These have proved to be a very convenient way for residents to dispose of and treat food waste, especially for those who are living in apartments and small units within urban areas. However, a problem with sewer disposal is the impact on the sewage and waste water infrastructure (Marashlian and El-Fadel, 2005; Evans et al., 2010), with "fatbergs" and blockages created due to the sewer systems not having been designed to take food waste. Assessment of the capacity of any waste water or sewerage system must be undertaken before it is used as a primary food waste disposal and treatment route.

Traditional landfill sites have caused serious public health issues in the past and have had detrimental environment impacts, including air pollution, methane emissions, water pollution, leachate and litter problems. For instance, each tonne of organic/food waste sent to landfill will produce between 300–1,000 kg of CO_2 due to anaerobic methanogenesis occurring within the sealed landfill (Manfredi et al., 2009; Zaman and Reynolds, 2015). Therefore, countries – such as Scotland – have already introduced new measures to reduce the biodegradable waste landfilled (Scottish Government, 2012). Currently there are six common technologies that are used for landfill treatment: open dump, conventional with flares, conventional with energy recovery, standard bioreactor, flushing bioreactor and semi-aerobic landfills (Manfredi and Christensen, 2009). See Table 27.2 for further discussion of landfill types. Open dumps have now been

Table 27.2 Further classification of landfills

	Operation and engineering measures	Leachate management	Landfill gas management
Semi-controlled dumps	Few controls; some directed placement of waste; informal waste picking; no engineering measures	Unrestricted contaminant release	None
Controlled dump	Registration and placement/compaction of waste; surface water monitoring; no engineering measures	Unrestricted contaminant release	None
Engineered landfill/controlled landfill	Registration and placement/compaction of waste; uses daily cover material; surface and ground water monitoring; infrastructure and liner in place	Containment and some level of leachate treatment; reduced leachate volume through waste cover	Passive ventilation or flaring
Sanitary landfill	Registration and placement/compaction of waste; uses daily cover; measures for final top cover and closure; proper siting, infrastructure; liner and leachate treatment in place and post-closure plan	Containment and leachate treatment (often biological and physico-chemical treatment)	Flaring with or without energy recovery

Source: Adapted from Hoornweg and Bhada-Tata (2012)

banned in many countries due to the impact on the environment and toxicity concerns, while some of the other technologies are still in use worldwide.

Even after a 100-year timeframe, landfills may continue to release gas and leachate that might still impact humans and eco-systems. Up to 50% of carbon and 99% of heavy metals from waste may remain in the landfill at the end of the 100-year time horizon; landfill gas and leachate collection systems may have a reduction in efficiency over time (Manfredi and Christensen, 2009).

Environmental impacts comparison of recovery and recycling methods now and in a decarbonising economy

Greenhouse gas (GHG) emissions from food waste have emerged as a major concern. The FAO have estimated that if the emissions associated with global food loss and waste were a country, they would be the third largest emitting country in the world (FAO, 2013, 2016), this is equal to 4.4 $GtCO_2$ eq, or about 8% of total anthropogenic GHG emissions annually. The organic nature of food waste, the collection vehicles, and waste disposal methods all contribute to the environmental impacts of food waste. Along with the prevention and reduction of avoidable food waste, changing the collection method and the treatment methods can be effective methods of further reducing the environmental impact of unavoidable food waste.

Multiple studies have compared food waste downstream management options for recovery and recycling (incineration, composting and AD) (Laurent et al., 2014a, 2014b;

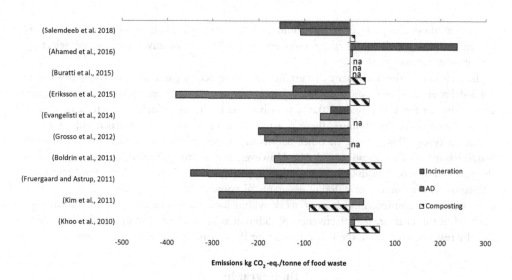

Figure 27.2 Results of ten life cycle analysis studies reporting GHG emissions per tonne of food waste treated by incineration, AD, or composting. "na" are provided where a study has not included a technology in their analysis. Where a study reported several scenarios for the same option, the mean value for all scenarios is shown.

Salemdeeb and Al-Tabbaa, 2015a, 2015b; Salemdeeb et al., 2017, 2018; Zheng et al., 2017). The assessment of environmental impacts is complex as uncertainties in the LCA data make it difficult to determine the best treatment option.

Figure 27.2 indicates ten life cycle analysis studies that compare (at least two of the) treatment methods of incineration, composting and AD (Khoo et al., 2010; Boldrin et al., 2011; Fruergaard and Astrup, 2011; Kim et al., 2011; Grosso et al., 2012; Evangelisti et al., 2014; Buratti et al., 2015; Eriksson et al., 2015; Ahamed et al., 2016; Salemdeeb et al., 2018). Figure 27.2 compares each result as kg of CO_2 equivalent per tonne of food wasted. Multiple studies show that any of these treatment options can have positive or negative impacts. This difference is due to differences in the system boundaries of the assessment, the quantity of food waste treated, and the lifespan of the facilities.

The previous studies reported a large variation in the global warming potential (i.e. volumes of GHG emissions), and some broad patterns emerge. Four out of six studies conclude that incineration with energy recovery has the greatest environmental benefits, while only two studies conclude in favour of AD. This could be explained due to the high energy input required to operate an AD facility (compared to incineration) and the additional diesel consumption required to set up a separate food waste collection system (Burnley et al., 2011). In addition, variations in the biogas yield and the type of substituted energy adopted in reviewed studies contribute significantly to these discrepancies. For example, Eriksson et al. (2015) reports AD results that are four times larger than those reported in Salemdeeb et al. (2018). This substantial difference could be attributed to the assumption made by Eriksson and his colleagues that the entire theoretical yield of biogas was produced, while other studies such as Salemdeeb et al. (2018) are based on actual AD plant figures; Eriksson et al.'s study also assumes that biogas replaces diesel as a fuel for city buses.

Due to these complexities in environmental impacts (and when no other information is present), following the food waste recovery hierarchy is a positive step toward selecting a treatment method.

In addition to the assessment of current environmental impacts of food waste treatment, Salemdeeb et al. (2018) also calculated future environmental impacts, based on the future energy mix of the UK economy (i.e. a decarbonised economy). Their results indicate that as UK electricity mix decarbonises, there is a reduction in overall environmental impact across treatment types. This increase in other decarbonised energy generation slightly decreases the positive impacts of incineration and AD. However, the positive effects of composting remain the same. It is worth noting the issue of appropriate scale and the need to allow room for adaptation in the context of differing geographical context. Specifically, adoption of particular food waste management models must work within local circumstances. Due to the findings outlined in this chapter, the effectiveness of different waste management options must be continually reassessed to ensure the best outcome for the environment, and the economy.

Bibliography

Ahamed, A., Yin, K., Ng, B.J.H., Ren, F., Chang, V.W.C., Wang, J.Y., 2016. Life cycle assessment of the present and proposed food waste management technologies from environmental and economic impact perspectives. *J. Clean. Prod.*, 131, 607–614. doi:10.1016/j.jclepro.2016.04.127

Astrup, T., Fruergaard, T., Christensen, T.H., 2009. Recycling of plastic: Accounting of greenhouse gases and global warming contributions. *Waste Manag. Res.*, 27, 763–772. doi:10.1177/0734242X09345868

Battistoni, P., Fatone, F., Passacantando, D., Bolzonella, D., 2007. Application of food waste disposers and alternate cycles process in small-decentralized towns: A case study. *Water Res.*, 41, 893–903. doi:10.1016/j.watres.2006.11.023

Bernstad, A., la Cour Jansen, J., 2011. A life cycle approach to the management of household food waste - A Swedish full-scale case study. *Waste Manag.*, 31, 1879–1896. doi:10.1016/j.wasman.2011.02.026

Bernstad, A., la Cour Jansen, J., 2012. Review of comparative LCAs of food waste management systems – Current status and potential improvements. *Waste Manag*, 32(12), December, 2439–2455.

Boldrin, A., Andersen, J.K., Christensen, T.H., 2011. Environmental assessment of garden waste management in the Municipality of Aarhus, Denmark. *Waste Manag.*, 31, 1560–1569. doi:10.1016/j.wasman.2011.01.010

Buratti, C., Barbanera, M., Testarmata, F., Fantozzi, F., 2015. Life Cycle Assessment of organic waste management strategies: An Italian case study. *J. Clean. Prod.*, 89, 125–136. doi:10.1016/j.jclepro.2014.11.012

Burnley, S., Phillips, R., Coleman, T., Rampling, T., 2011. Energy implications of the thermal recovery of biodegradable municipal waste materials in the United Kingdom. *Waste Manag.*, 31, 1949–1959. doi:10.1016/j.wasman.2011.04.015

Defra, 2019. *UK Statistics on Waste.* Waste Statistics Team, Defra, London.

DEFRA, 2016. *Digest of Waste and Resource Statistics – 2015 Edition.* Department for Environment, Food and Rural Affairs, London.

Department of Trade and Industry, 2007. *Meeting The Energy Challenge: A White Paper On Energy: A White Paper On Energy (cm.).* 7124th ed. Tso (the Stationery Office), London.

Eriksson, M., Strid, I., Hansson, P.-A., 2015. Carbon footprint of food waste management options in the waste hierarchy – a Swedish case study. *J. Clean. Prod.*, 93, 115–125. doi:10.1016/j.jclepro.2015.01.026

Evangelisti, S., Lettieri, P., Borello, D., Clift, R., 2014. Life cycle assessment of energy from waste via anaerobic digestion: A UK case study. *Waste Manag.*, 34, 226–237. doi:10.1016/j.wasman.2013.09.013

Evans, T.D., Andersson, P., Wievegg, Å., Carlsson, I., 2010. Surahammar: A case study of the impacts of installing food waste disposers in 50% of households. *Water Environ. J.*, 24, 309–319. doi:10.1111/j.1747-6593.2010.00238.x

Fao, 2013. Food wastage footprint. Impacts on natural resources. Summary Report. Food wastage footprint Impacts on natural resources 63.

FAO, 2016. *Food Wastage Footprint & Climate Change.* Rome.

Fruergaard, T., Astrup, T., 2011. Optimal utilization of waste-to-energy in an LCA perspective. *Waste Manag.*, 31, 572–582. doi:10.1016/j.wasman.2010.09.009

Grosso, M., Nava, C., Testori, R., Rigamonti, L., Viganò, F., 2012. The implementation of anaerobic digestion of food waste in a highly populated urban area: An LCA evaluation. *Waste Manag. Res.*, 30, 78–87. doi:10.1177/0734242X12453611

Hoornweg, D., Bhada-Tata, P., 2012. *What a Waste: A Global Review of Solid Waste Management.* World Bank, Washington, DC.

Hoornweg, D., Thomas, L., Otten, L., 1999. Composting and its applicability in developing countries. World Bank working paper series 8, 1–46.

Iacovidou, E., Ohandja, D.-G., Gronow, J., Voulvoulis, N., 2012. The household use of food waste disposal units as a waste management option: A review. *Crit. Rev. Environ. Sci. Technol.*, 42, 1485–1508. doi:10.1080/10643389.2011.556897

Khoo, H.H., Lim, T.Z., Tan, R.B.H., 2010. Food waste conversion options in Singapore: Environmental impacts based on an LCA perspective. *Sci. Total Environ.*, 408, 1367–1373. doi:10.1016/j.scitotenv.2009.10.072

Kim, M.-H., Song, Y.-E., Song, H.-B., Kim, J.-W., Hwang, S.-J., 2011. Evaluation of food waste disposal options by LCC analysis from the perspective of global warming: Jungnang case, South Korea. *Waste Manag.*, 31, 2112–2120. doi:10.1016/j.wasman.2011.04.019

Kumar, A., Samadder, S.R., 2017. A review on technological options of waste to energy for effective management of municipal solid waste. *Waste Manag.*, 69, 407–422. doi:10.1016/j.wasman.2017.08.046

Laurent, A., Bakas, I., Clavreul, J., Bernstad, A., Niero, M., Gentil, E., Hauschild, M.Z., Christensen, T.H., 2014a. Review of LCA studies of solid waste management systems–part I: Lessons learned and perspectives. *Waste Manag*, 34(3), March, 573–588.

Laurent, A., Clavreul, J., Bernstad, A., Bakas, I., Niero, M., Gentil, E., Christensen, T.H., Hauschild, M.Z., 2014b. Review of LCA studies of solid waste management systems–part II: Methodological guidance for a better practice. *Waste Manag.*, 34, 589–606. doi:10.1016/j.wasman.2013.12.004

Lombardi, L., Carnevale, E., Corti, A., 2015. A review of technologies and performances of thermal treatment systems for energy recovery from waste. *Waste Manag.*, 37, 26–44. doi:10.1016/j.wasman.2014.11.010

Lundie, S., Peters, G.M., 2005. Life cycle assessment of food waste management options. *J. Clean. Prod.*, 13(3), February, 275–286.

Manfredi, S., Christensen, T.H., 2009. Environmental assessment of solid waste landfilling technologies by means of LCA-modeling. *Waste Manag.*, 29, 32–43. doi:10.1016/j.wasman.2008.02.021

Manfredi, S., Tonini, D., Christensen, T.H., Scharff, H., 2009. Landfilling of waste: Accounting of greenhouse gases and global warming contributions. *Waste Manag. Res.*, 27, 825–836. doi:10.1177/0734242X09348529

Marashlian, N., El-Fadel, M., 2005. The effect of food waste disposers on municipal waste and wastewater management. *Waste Manag. Res.*, 23, 20–31. doi:10.1177/0734242X05050078

Metcalfe, P., Moates, G., Waldron, K., 2017. Detailed hierarchy of approaches categorised within waste pyramid. Refresh.

Pearson, M., 2015. After Plasco: City looks to increase diversion, find new technology | Ottawa Citizen [WWW Document]. URL https://ottawacitizen.com/news/local-news/after-plasco-city-looks-to-increase-diversion-find-new-technology (accessed 7.9.19).

Recycled Organics Unit, 2007. *Recycled Organics Dictionary and Thesaurus: Standard Terminology for the New South Wales Recycled Organics Industry, 3rd edn Recycled Organics Unit.* University of New South Wales, Sydney, Australia.

Reynolds, C.J., Mavrakis, V., Davison, S., Høj, S.B., Vlaholias, E., Sharp, A., Thompson, K., Ward, P., Coveney, J., Piantadosi, J., Boland, J., Dawson, D., 2014. Estimating informal household food waste in developed countries: The case of Australia. *Waste Manag. Res.*, 32, 1254–1258. doi:10.1177/0734242X14549797

Reynolds, C.J., Thompson, K., Boland, J., Dawson, D., 2011. Climate change on the menu? A retrospective look at the development of South Australian municipal food waste policy. *Int. J. Clim. Change Impacts Respon.*, 3 (3), 101–112.

Salemdeeb, R., Al-Tabbaa, A., 2015a. A hybrid life cycle assessment of food waste management options: A UK case study, in *The ISWA 2015 World Congress.* International Solid Waste Association, Antwerp, pp. 334–339. doi: 10.13140/RG.2.1.2264.7925.

Salemdeeb, R., Al-Tabbaa, A., 2015b. An ecological assessment of food waste composting using a hybrid life-cycle assessment, in Clift, R. (ed.), *The 8th Conference of the International Society for Industrial Ecology.* International Society for Industrial Ecology, Surrey. https://www.researchgate.net/publication/

280683030_AN_ECOLOGICAL_ASSESSMENT_OF_FOOD_WASTE_COMPOSTING_ USING_A_HYBRID_LIFE_CYCLE_ASSESSMENT.

Salemdeeb, R., Bin Daina, M., Reynolds, C., Al-Tabbaa, A., 2018. An environmental evaluation of food waste downstream management options: A hybrid LCA approach. *Int. J. Recycling Org. Waste Agric.*, 7, 1–13. doi:10.1007/s40093-018-0208-8

Salemdeeb, R., Font Vivanco, D., Al-Tabbaa, A., Zu Ermgassen, E.K.H.J., 2017. A holistic approach to the environmental evaluation of food waste prevention. *Waste Manag.*, 59, 442–450. doi:10.1016/j.wasman.2016.09.042

Sandor, A., 2015. City Looks to New Waste Solution Following Plasco Failure. [WWW Document]. URL www.cfra.com/news/2015/02/11/city-looks-to-new-waste-solution-following-plasco-failure (accessed 8. 27.18).

Scottish Government, 2012. The Waste (Scotland) Regulations 2012 (No. Issue 2014, Number 148.). The Scottish Government.

Smith, A., Brown, K., Ogilvie, S., Rushton, K., Bates, J., 2001. Waste management options and climate change: Final report to the European Commission. Waste management options and climate change: Final report to the European Commission.

Tampio, E., Ervasti, S., Paavola, T., Heaven, S., Banks, C., Rintala, J., 2014. Anaerobic digestion of autoclaved and untreated food waste. *Waste Manag.*, 34, 370–377. doi:10.1016/j.wasman.2013.10.024

Tramhel, J., 2012. Using participatory urban design to integrateorganic solid waste management into urban agriculture: A case study from Cayagan de Oro City in the Phillipines, in Robertss, M. (ed.), *Sustainable Cities: Local Solutions in theGlobal South*. International Development Research Centre, Ottawa, ON, pp. 147–159.

Tweib, S.A., Rahman, R.A., Kalil, M.S., 2011. A literature review on the Composting. *International Conference on Environment and Industrial Innovation IPCBEE 12*.

Viganò, F., Consonni, S., Grosso, M., Rigamonti, L., 2010. Material and energy recovery from Automotive Shredded Residues (ASR) via sequential gasification and combustion. *Waste Manag.*, 30, 145–153. doi:10.1016/j.wasman.2009.06.009

WRAP, 2016a. Why take action: Legal/policy case | WRAP UK [WWW Document]. URL www. wrap.org.uk/content/why-take-action-legalpolicy-case (accessed 7.8.19).

WRAP, 2016b. *Quantification of Food Surplus, Waste and Related Materials in the Grocery Supply Chain*. WRAP, Banbury, UK.

WSN Environmental Solutions, 2005. *Your Easy Guide to Waste Technologies*, WSN Environmental Solutions, New South Wales.

Zaman, A., Reynolds, C., 2015. The economic and bio-energy production potential of South Australian food waste using Anaerobic digestion, in: *Unmaking Waste 2015 Conference Proceedings. Zero Waste SA Research Centre for Sustainable Design and Behaviour*, Adelaide, SA, pp. 336–347. URL https://www.unmakingwaste.org/conference-proceedings/

Zero Waste SA, 2010. Valuing our food waste South Australia's Household Food Waste Recycling Pilot Summary Report - 2010.

Zhang, C., Su, H., Baeyens, J., Tan, T., 2014. Reviewing the anaerobic digestion of food waste for biogas production. *Renew. Sust. Energ. Rev.*, 38, 383–392. doi:10.1016/j.rser.2014.05.038

Zhang, Q., Hu, J., Lee, D.-J., 2016. Biogas from anaerobic digestion processes: Research updates. *Renew. Energ.*, 98, 108–119. doi:10.1016/j.renene.2016.02.029

Zhang, R., El-Mashad, H.M., Hartman, K., Wang, F., Liu, G., Choate, C., Gamble, P., 2007. Characterization of food waste as feedstock for anaerobic digestion. *Bioresour. Technol.*, 98, 929–935. doi:10.1016/j.biortech.2006.02.039

Zheng, M., Orbell, J.D., Fairclough, R.J., 2017. *Household Food Waste Treatment Technologies - A Systematic Review*. Victoria University, Melbourne.

PART VI

Debates in food waste studies and looking ahead

The final part of the Handbook brings together chapters that do not necessarily offer solutions to food waste, or as other parts of this book have done, analyse national regulations and policies, or focus on a particular food sector per se. Rather, these concluding chapters advance more questions, identify tensions and debates in the field of food waste studies, and re-frame or re-conceptualise well-received terminologies in food waste. In essence, the chapters elucidate some of the complex, tangled and 'wicked' nature of the food waste 'problem' as seen through differing economies, geographies, technological interventions, academic disciplines, and power relations. What can be surmised throughout the chapters in Part VI is that there are conflicting imaginaries and interpretations of appropriate approaches, frameworks, and futures of addressing food waste.

Scott Lougheed and Charlotte Spring's chapter, 'Conduits that bite back: challenging the "win-win" solutions of food recalls and redistribution' posits that there are 'conflicting visions' with regard to the merits of various solutions for wasted food. The chapter reconceptualises these practices as *divestment*, implying that which aims to maintain a desired order of things through various *conduits* (Gregson et al. 2007). To divest means to sever existing relations, yet it also entails creating new relations and also spaces. Drawing on their respective fieldwork, Lougheed and Spring compare and contrast spaces of food recall and redistribution, identifying how certain routes of divestment aim to ensure that wasted food materials are removed, or 'taken care of', yet can in some cases 'bite back' in potentially harmful and unexpected ways (such as was the case with the foot and mouth disease outbreak, caused by untreated food waste fed to ruminants). As such, debating food waste solutions requires attention in navigating contradictory interests of trying to 'close loops' and achieve environmental or societal benefits, yet to regulate materials flows in the interest of biosecurity. This is particularly important when considering how supposedly 'win-win' solutions might backfire when conduits 'bite back'.

In 'Are you buying food waste? The roles technologies can play in (re)designing the food retail experience', Geremy Farr-Wharton, Timur Osadchiy, and Peter Lyle explore the role of new technologies such as artificial intelligence, wearables, drones, blockchain, and virtual reality. The authors ask how these may be mobilised to redesign food purchasing practices and to improve the sustainability of retail practices. While the chapter showcases diverse future scenarios envisaging how new technologies may disrupt the status quo of food waste practices, the disruptive role of said technologies may also create collateral damage. Grounded in Science and Technology Studies literature, they articulate scenarios that, albeit speculatively, ask questions such as what happens when new technologies become 'too smart' or 'too automated' for our own good. They provide an example of a 'smart' fridge which automatically ordered and procured more milk once a bottle was emptied, despite the consumer not necessarily wanting or needing to purchase extra milk. The chapter highlights how technologies will increasingly become more embedded in the future of food waste solutions, debates, and in some cases, yield unexpected problems.

In Chapter 30, 'A brief overview of current food waste research: the what, why, how and future directions', Jessica Aschemann-Witzel, Ezra Ho, and Tammara Soma give an overview of the 'what, why and how' of food waste studies by reviewing core literature that often identity *types* of food waste (*the what*), *causes* of food waste (*the why*), and potential *solutions* to food waste (*the how*). However, beyond these three core categories (acknowledging that these categories can also be fluid), the authors note a massive gap in the field of food waste studies, which has contributed to a lack of food waste data and research into what was formerly considered the 'Big Four' (BRIC) advancing economies, namely Brazil, Russia, India and China (it has recently added South Africa, making 'BRICS'). The authors argue that as these countries expand economically and continue on a trajectory of development that heralds distinctive patterns of food production, consumption, and distribution, it is critical to consider how these economies may impact the reconfiguration of not only regional agriculture and agribusinesses, but also overall global food consumption and wasting trends. The chapter calls upon food waste scholars, policymakers, and practitioners to consider the strong potential for cross-cultural learning in reducing food waste. Studying trajectories of BRICS economies is important from a food system perspective, but there is also much to learn from multicultural perspectives as to how food can – and should – be revalued, cooked, and enjoyed. As such, the authors of this chapter (a Dane, a Singaporean, and a Canadian-Indonesian) conclude that the future of food waste studies and food waste solutions should be a diverse one.

Martin Bowman's chapter, 'Challenging hegemonic conceptions of food waste: critical reflections from a food waste activist', is rooted in years of campaigning against food waste for the organisation formerly known as 'Feeding the 5000', now Feedback. Taking up an argument familiar to other political economy analyses in this Handbook (e.g. Cloke's and Giles' chapters), Bowman critiques 'hegemonic conceptions' that allow food's wastage to be cast as an unfortunate by-product of food systems that can be tweaked without the radical overhaul that Feedback advocates. Importantly, such overhaul requires situating food waste within broader systems of production, profit, distribution, labour, and histories of dispossession and vast, uneven, power concentrations. Mobilising around these struggles as root causes of food wastage, Bowman argues that solving the issue of food waste requires allying with political movements beyond those focusing on 'food waste' alone. It is not, he argues, sufficient to reform current practices through tweaks. In light of ongoing imperialist and post-colonial legacies, 'transformist' solutions that interrogate wealth and resource redistribution are vital. Bowman calls upon fellow activists to develop counter-hegemonic narratives that question the inherently unequal and unjust foundations of a dominant economic focus on seemingly endless economic growth.

28

CONDUITS THAT BITE BACK

Challenging the 'win-win' solutions of food recalls and redistribution

Scott Lougheed and Charlotte Spring

Introduction

Every year developed countries recall[1] tens-of-thousands of tonnes of food. The United States alone recalls annually enough food to feed over 20,000 humans for a year, or the mass of 100 blue whales (Johnson 2015). A single US charity also redistributes billions of meal-equivalents of donated food (Feeding America n.d), while charitable redistribution of unwanted, unsold or unsaleable (but not recalled) food has been increasing globally (see Midgley, this volume). The UK's largest surplus food redistributor grew from redistributing 5,500 tonnes in 2013/4 to 16,992 tonnes in 2017/8 (FareShare 2018), while rising demand for 'emergency' food aid continues to stir debate (Osborne and Hopkins 2018). The numerous and diverse efforts to manage the flows of contaminated, unsold, or rejected food are often pitched as win-win solutions that resolve the environmental consequences of food waste while bringing about social (and economic) benefits (Mirosa et al. 2016). However, as we demonstrate, the claimed environmental/social 'win-win' is not guaranteed. Rather, these solutions may 'bite back' (Tenner 1996), by which we mean that they possess the capacity to create new and unintended problems or exacerbate the very problems these interventions attempted to remediate. Recalled, unsold, or otherwise unwanted products (hereafter 'divested food') pose a logistical challenge for manufacturers, importers, or processors, as these flows of surplus organic material and packaging raise myriad public health, environmental, ethical, and business concerns. As such we argue that there is a need to attend to the vitality of divested food (Bennett 2009, O'Brien 2012)—its capacity to affect and be affected—as it moves through the *conduits* by which it is *divested*. This shift in the language of waste—to that of divestment and conduits—offers critical analytical purchase that reveals the subtler issues associated with downstream or 'end of pipe' solutions for food waste (Gille 2007).

Conceptualising food's reverse flows

We bring together seemingly disparate examples of food wasting—rejecting, recalling, or redistributing unsold foods—under the unified language of *divestment* and the *conduits* along which the material is subsequently moved. Thinking in terms of divestment and conduits encourages an accounting of the new sets of relations that processes of divestment create and avoids the conceptual externalising of materials considered waste (Hetherington 2004, Gregson et al. 2007, Lepawsky and Mather 2011, Hird 2012). By better accounting for these relations of divestment, a richer picture of the costs and consequences of divestment emerges (insofar as they can be understood and accounted for), allowing for a more nuanced assessment of the costs of downstream 'management'—no matter how creatively that management takes place—and the merits of upstream prevention.

While often the outcome of different antecedents, we conceptualise divested food (and 'waste' generally) as enrolling new actors, entering complex (re)circulations, creating challenges and opportunities for redistribution and reuse. We examine how regulatory regimes, food safety, and ascendant moral concerns around hunger, shape material flows of food into and out of moments and spaces where waste/value, use/non-use are performed. Divesting food raises contradictory biopolitical concerns around public safety, on one hand, and unequal food access on the other, raising questions of the knowability of food risk and the constellations of knowledge constituting 'edibility'. We show that there are conflicting visions among participants about the relative merit of the various available conduits for divested food, while power relations and physical infrastructures tend to reproduce path-dependencies for 'disposing' of 'waste' through linear conduits, in spite of diverse available options and critical discourses promoting prevention rather than production reliant on excess (see also Chapters 1, 4, and 23, this volume).

Drawing on field work conducted in the domains of surplus food redistribution (Spring) and recalled food (Lougheed), we put forward a view of food redistribution and disposal as comprised of assemblages of human and more-than-human actants. These assemblages possess the capacity to 'bite back', presenting socio-political and environmental challenges to the past, present, and future of 'solutions' to food waste. By adopting a relational ontology and a new vocabulary of food wastage, we demonstrate how solutions to food waste contain generative potential for disruption and biting back in unanticipated (and unanticipatable) ways. We provide broader analytical insights that complicate notions of 'waste' and 'wasting' as a category and a practice, respectively. Most critically, despite the imminent risk and contradiction, many food waste solutions ultimately fail to address the reason food became waste in the first place and serve to discursively reinforce the normativity of wastage.

Conceptualising divestment

Gille (2010: 1050) argues that any definition of waste needs 'to leave open the opportunity to demonstrate the material and social consequences of one type of waste material metamorphosing into another as it traverses the circuits of production, distribution, consumption, reclamation, and "annihilation"'. To move beyond the conceptual limits of conventional understandings of the noun and verb 'waste', Gregson et al. (2007: 187) refer to *divestment*: a practice enacted to maintain the desired order of things, such as the elimination of broken objects, excess material, dirt, or contamination from a given space (e.g., a home, the curb, a retail shelf, or a packing plant). Unlike a Douglassian claim that order is (re)produced by externalising dirt from a given society (Douglas 2002), divestment acknowledges that practices of re-placing 'dirt' involve both severing existing and *creating new* relations, and spaces. These geneses are always provisional and always carry the possibility of 'biting back' (Gille 2007: 2013).

The concept of *conduits* refers to the various pathways or routings by which divestment takes place and along which divested material flows. Conduits may include landfills, food charities, freegan cafés, anaerobic digesters (AD), household and industrial composters, mouths, and the intermediate steps and processes in between (Munro 1995). A given object may be divested through any number of conduits (Hetherington 2004), and the availability or lack of conduits shapes choices around consumption (Munro 1995). In our context of corporations divesting food, the choice (and availability) of conduits, and conduits' various capacity to imply surplus or excess, can impact corporate social responsibility portfolios, legal liability, regulatory compliance, and financial bottom lines.

Divestment excises some relations while generating others as material moves through and between conduits. For example, a grocer's donation of near-expiry food to food charities severs the relationship between the grocer and the product while establishing new relations between the food charity, the donated food, and the charity's clients. Conduits act on the divested material, such as by destroying it, repurposing it, or decomposing it. Conduits can also act on the divestor, such as by providing tax credits and enhancements to corporate social responsibility portfolios for grocers who donate to food charities. Divestment (re)produces particular processes of social ordering (Gregson et al. 2007), such as the reliance of companies using donations to reduce divestment costs, government relying on food charity to provide social welfare rather than state institutions, or the use of bins rather than AD to divest recalled food.

In sum, divestment (or, conventionally, wasting) is a 'disruption of, and termination of particular associations and arrangements of material in the world, to bring about new associations, arrangements, and conjunctures' constituted as conduits of material flows (Gregson and Crang 2010: 1068). The recent and growing emphasis on the environmental impacts of food waste and the social injustice of food insecurity mean that there is growing interest in closing the loop on these divested materials. To borrow terminology from Gregson et al. (2007), the imperative is to move from conduits in which 'excess' is disposed of, to conduits in which 'surplus' is recovered and capitalised.

Methods

This chapter is based on two research projects conducted by the authors. Data are derived from interviews with key informants; participant and non-participant observation; and documentary analysis of Canadian Food Inspection Agency documents[2] pertaining to the 2012 XL Foods recall obtained through Access to Information and Privacy requests. Lougheed's food recall study included semi-structured interviews with 23 participants, with observation in three facilities devoted to depackaging and secure product destruction. Spring's study of food charity and redistribution included interviews with 36 participants. A total of 15 observation sites were visited by Spring, including food banks, pay-as-you-feel-cafés, and commercial redistribution outlets. The combined 59 participants spanned food production, distribution, and sale; government regulation; corporate and academic consulting and law; waste disposal and reclamation; food redistribution, charity, and activism.

The afterlife of recalled food

It is an October morning in southern Ontario, Canada and I (Lougheed) am standing inside a large industrial building, which was formerly a slaughterhouse. The smell that pervades my nostrils is not blood or flesh. Instead, it is a milky sweet smell of rejected meal replacements. To my left, a pair of workers are removing six-packs of the meal replacements from cardboard boxes. The six-packs move along a conveyor and are shredded. The shards of plastic are caught on a second conveyor belt and deposited into a second recycling bin. The contents spill down into a vat and are pumped into a large tank. Yelling over the din of the shredding machine, Ken, who runs this depackaging operation, has just finished explaining that they have two liquid tanks due to 'a valuable lesson that we learned here, and I knew as a kid: that you don't mix acids with dairy … so we keep juice over here, and dairy over here'. It is a lot of work to empty these tanks if the contents coagulate and turn into a thick mass.

The contents of these tanks will eventually be transported to ADs where bacteria will break it down, producing a nutrient-rich sludge used for fertiliser, and methane that will be burned to generate electricity. Not all companies have the means or the will to hire Ken to divert their divested food from landfill, some companies sell their food too cheaply to be able to justify his services.

To my right are pallets of various food products: children's snacks, condiments, and pantry staples, among others. Ken leads me to a section of the warehouse with rails and chains in a grid across the ceiling. Pig carcasses hung from this ceiling during the building's past life. Like much of the food that passes through it, this building has been recycled, saved from indefinite vacancy and dilapidation. Visible just beyond this room are the large table-saws used to break down pig carcasses, decommissioned and in the dark. Large metal doors with chains and locks bracket off this section of the warehouse. They were useful for keeping rooms cold in the slaughterhouse days, but they serve a different purpose today:

> If product does happen to come in as in the case of XL Foods beef, that's why you see all the chains and the locks on all the doors. Because everything came in with the CFIA [Canadian Food Inspection Agency] inspectors. We would lock all of these doors, they would tag them, and they would allow only certain doors to be open at certain times. Everything was secured, so they [CFIA] would come in in the morning, make sure the seals weren't broken and away we'd go. And that was just to protect you, and protect me, and protect everybody else.
>
> *(Ken, Depackager 2015-10-07)*

Ken is referring to XL Foods, Canada's largest beef processor, who was implicated in Canada's largest food recall, which involved 5,000 tonnes of beef contaminated with the deadly *E. coli* O157:H7 pathogen in 2012. Some of the recalled product came to him to be depackaged and sent to industrial rendering where it would become meat and bone meal for pet and livestock feed. Like the slaughterhouse, the food that now passes through this building is being given a second life, and Ken goes to great lengths—security cameras, log books, card-lock doors, and well-paid staff—to ensure that second life is not spent in the landfill where most recalled food goes, surreptitiously at an employee's home, or on the grey or black markets, as has been documented in the past (*New York Times* 1992).

This scene contrasts with images of boxes of XL Foods-produced beef being bulldozed into landfill cells that appeared on national media outlets across the country, stirring public outcry (see Figure 28.1; Boesveld 2012, The Huffington Post 2012). What a waste of perfectly good food while millions of Canadians are food insecure. Why not cook it and sell it to the poor (The Huffington Post 2012) or render it into animal feed (indeed some was)? Why recall it at all, since with proper cooking it would, in theory, be safe (Boesveld 2012)? The sheer size of the recall and the highly public use of landfill as one of several conduits for the beef brought into public consciousness the nexus between the safety of (industrial) food production, food waste, and hunger. This media attention was nevertheless a too-simplistic glance at the complexities of the afterlife of rejected food, which we will now unpack.

Figure 28.1 XL Foods beef being bulldozed into landfill cell.
Source: Photo courtesy of Ray Juska.

Despite being the de facto conduit for recalled food, study participants were ambivalent about landfill's merits. Some saw landfill as easy, inexpensive, and secure. Others claimed landfill was expensive, environmentally harmful, and lacked long-term security offered by other conduits. Among proponents, landfilling was an unproblematic default conduit for their recalled food and food waste generally. It was a path of least resistance. One food producer, discussing divesting of cheese recalled in their first and only recall in their over-100-year history:

> One of the inspectors from the CFIA ... and I wound up going to the dump, and she witnessed me ... pitching it into the dump ... I don't think we even explored other options. The product needed to be rendered completely inedible, so we had to stab all the boxes with a pitchfork and make sure it was exposed to air [so] it spoiled, and that people wouldn't steal it out of the garbage I guess. They [CFIA] were going as far as saying I needed to get coloured bleach to dump on all of it, but I didn't know where to get that, so they just let it go.

> There really wasn't any other discussion about like ... a grinder or something like that. We just needed to prove to them that it needed to be disposed of and it was not going to be available to us to resell it somehow. I don't even know why we'd wanna do something like that.

> (Paul, Cheese Producer 2017-01-31)

As this quote suggests, Paul had not considered options other than landfill for disposing of their recently recalled cheese; the landfill had always been where they sent any off-batches of cheese that did not meet specification (but were not recalled). This was a sentiment reflected by a regional retailer. Their protocol for stores was to place any wastes, including recalled food, into their compactors for destruction. When asked if they had considered alternatives such as reclamation or AD, the director of food safety said:

> We just haven't. There's no reason against it, or for it. Our process at this point has worked so we've kept it status quo. If the organisation grows is that something we might want to explore? It could be, absolutely, it just hasn't crossed our path yet.
>
> *(Director of Food Safety, regional retailer, 2015-12-10)*

Other retailers were aware of alternatives to landfill offered by third-party logistic firms and recall services companies, but the most common response was that 'it just doesn't work for us' (Director Food Safety, national retailer A 2015-09-03). In many cases the combination of inexpensiveness, convenience, nation-wide applicability, and security of landfilling aligned more closely with participants' priorities. In this respect, the practice of landfilling is a product of a linear conceptualisation of the supply chain—a logical alternative to originally intended consumption—since materials disposed of in this manner, in theory, do not re-enter the food or feed systems. For many study participants, and as demonstrated in waste studies more generally, landfilling is perceived as a largely infallible conduit, placing material securely out of sight and out of mind, reproducing the notion that waste can unproblemat-ically be externalised to society's benefit (Hird 2015).[3]

Conduits, however, are permeable. There is the possibility of divested food 'seemingly disappearing only to return again unexpectedly and perhaps in a different place or in a different form' (Hetherington 2004: 162). The mobilities of divested material are complex, and divested products can re-emerge, sometimes in innocuous ways such as on the tables of freegans who gleaned the food from bins, and sometimes in unexpected and harmful ways. Two cases demonstrating the more dramatic consequences of these mobilities are Bovine Spongiform Encephalopathy (BSE) and Foot and Mouth Disease (FMD). Outbreaks of these diseases have been linked to practices of looping surplus organic material back into the food supply for economic (and environmental) benefit that may otherwise have been externalised as excess. BSE is associated with cows eating feed comprised of other ruminant animals (e.g., sheep and other cows). FMD in the UK was traced back to the practice of feeding improperly heat-treated food waste (i.e., swill) to pigs (Law 2006, Law and Mol 2008).

Feeding pigs swill could decrease the environmental impact of pork production in Europe by over 20% and also reduce the environmental harms of landfilling the divested food (Zu Ermgassen et al. 2016). However, the safety of this practice for curtailing the spread of diseases like FMD requires the careful regulation of the contents and heat treat-ment of swill. It was precisely a failure to regulate these practices that led to the FMD out-break in the UK in 2001, resulting in the culling of over 10 million animals, whose carcasses were buried or burned (Uhlig 2002).

The vitality of conduits and divested food exceed human control and prediction, the activities over the long term not easily human-readable, and the risks 'epistemologically distant' (Carolan 2006: 234). Care must be taken navigating the at-times mutually exclusive imperatives of closing loops for the benefit of the environment and corporate bottom lines, and the impera-tive to regulate and curtail material flows in the interest of biosecurity. These circulations can be fragile; as Law (2006) demonstrates, the failure of a single farmer or renderer to comply with regulations is all that is needed for an outbreak and international agricultural disaster to occur (Law and Mol 2008, Zu Ermgassen et al. 2016). Biosecurity crises such as FMD and BSE put a strain on the biopolitical imperative to maintain a separation of healthy and diseased life and serve as a cautionary tale concerning the potential implications of closing certain material loops.

While the priority for handling recalled products is to ensure that they are completely corrected or irreversibly destroyed, things do not always go these ways. Reflecting Hetherington's (2004) observation that disposal is never final, divested products can potentially re-emerge in unexpected and sometimes dangerous ways. In 1985, a Canadian tuna cannery was closed by the federal food safety authorities for unsanitary conditions. The remaining inventory of 25–50 million cans of tuna deemed unfit for human consumption was sold to a US company and relabelled as cat food under four different brand labels (*New York Times* 1992, 1995). In 1992, approximately 40,000 of those relabelled cans were once again labelled as Ocean King brand tuna. After several illnesses and discovery of a cat food label under the Ocean King label, the FDA requested a recall and laid criminal charges against Ocean King.

Some conduits, while working in the interest of security and public health, are at odds with grassroots environmental movements such as freeganism.

> I mean the whole notion of dumpster [bin] divers is alive and well and what you don't want is throwing whole cases of product into the back of a dumpster and somebody coming along and saying, 'look at all that stuff, it's perfectly edible' and they try it and oh, this is good, and off it goes into the grey market.
>
> *(David Acheson, Food Industry Consultant)*

The growing use by retailers of compactors that crush material in hard-to-access metal containers rather than open bins and covering recalled products in denaturing agents such as bleach has drawn criticism from freegans and food waste advocates for preventing recovery of 'good food' (DeMar 2005, Stuart 2009). These denaturing practices are justified by critics of bin-diving as playing an important role in preventing the consumption or redistribution of harmful products. This is because while humans can often detect spoilage (which while unpleasant, is typically harmless) with sight, smell, or taste, the hazards that lead to product recalls are not so easily detected by these human senses.

Confounding things further is that within bins (destined for landfill or elsewhere), safe and unsafe material are intermixed in unpredictable ways, resulting in edible food being rendered potentially harmful along the course of the conduit (Mancini and Vellani 2016). That which is divested does not stay within the intended conduits and maybe act in unexpected ways that defy the knowledge or intention of the original divestor, to 'act back' (Gregson et al. 2007: 198). Denaturing and compacting have thus emerged as security practices in response to the permeability of conduits such as bins of divested food destined for landfill.

Conduits for recalled food have the effect of rendering food *in*edible (with varying success) in the interest of securing brands from reputational harm and securing the public from foodborne hazards (for more on the biopolitics of recalled food, see Lougheed and Hird 2017). Inversely, one can point to efforts to render or retain food surpluses as *edible* in the interests of another key dimension of biosecurity, that of preventing hunger. The following examples highlight divestment practices and conduits adopted for the redistribution of food surpluses to manage 'first world hunger' (Riches 1997).

Concurrent to the knowledge politics and microbiological techniques by which publics and regulators have come to 'see' and problematise food safety (Milne 2012), recent decades have seen growing problematisation of hunger in wealthy countries, especially following welfare reform and retrenchment (Riches 1997, Tarasuk and Eakin 2005, Loopstra et al.

2018). Publicly visible contradictions between abundant food supplies going to waste and the spectre of public hunger have galvanised efforts to secure that food for 'bellies, not bins'. This section shifts from practices of recalling and securing *in*edibility to practices of divestment in conduits for redistributing surplus food and securing its *edibility* in the UK. These practices are considered in two contexts. The first relates to the affective labour by (often unpaid) charity workers and activists enacting care to ensure food is not only safe and edible but also appropriate and desirable. The second context is ensuring compliance with donors, usually the very supply-chain actors requiring integration conduits for food recovery that can afford them economic and reputational benefits. While affording a supposed eco-social 'win-win', the following account nevertheless highlights the 'acting-back' of such practices.

Securing edibility in the afterlife

It is October 2016 and I (Spring) am spending a day at a warehouse, termed the 'anti-supermarket', on the outskirts of a north England city where a surplus food redistribution activism network was founded in 2013. A section of the warehouse is open to the general public. With shutters instead of automatic doors and hand-painted signs instead of corporate brands, it resembles a discount food store comprising shelves, fridges, boxes, and pallet-loads of food that 'shoppers' can take in exchange for a donation, from fresh and frozen produce to myriad 'nonperishables'. A separate section is for receiving and sorting newly intercepted food. Here, I sit on an upturned supermarket delivery tray, helping a volunteer rinse packeted food items. These had been jumbled together in a refuse bag, causing yoghurt to spill over other items. The volunteer insists that these may nevertheless be perfectly good, if only we can rinse off the yoghurt to determine what they are. The supermarket that donated this jumbled array, he tells me, is notoriously poor at arranging food for donation in such a way as might prevent such breaches.

Despite faint abjection in my reaction to rootling through the yoghurt-strewn bag, I marvel at the care the volunteer takes to wash each item, categorising them according to type and storage requirements. Additional labour is required of both volunteer and retail employees who must change their divestment practices if donation to needy people is to displace the incumbent conduits of compactors and waste bins more typically used in maintaining the shelf turnover essential to the generation of profit for retailers and other forward supply-chain participants (Giles 2016).

This additional labour includes sorting practices to rescue and maintain not only edibility but appropriateness and desirability of foodstuffs, exemplified by the yoghurt rinsing (Figure 28.2). Re-configuring donated products to a state suitable for the anti-supermarket shelves involves considerable affective labour, including washing off matter-out-of-place (yoghurt splatters) produced by ingrained labour practices typical of a retail employee accustomed to the speed and convenience of the bin. While on the surface this labour is an attempt to avoid harming food recipients' dignity by providing inferior-quality food, this care for food also constitutes an attempt to re-normalise food devalued by capitalist logics—to convert 'excess' to 'surplus' (Gregson et al. 2007)—as the following section shows.

Scholars have critiqued the reliance on unpaid labour in charitable food redistribution as the enrolling of volunteers to serve corporate needs to divest unsold food rather than relying on the paid labour of landfill or compost (e.g. Tarasuk and Eakin 2005), while providing a 'moral safety valve' for the discomfort citizens feel about hunger in wealthy nations (Poppendieck 1998). The 'anti-supermarket' volunteer described his work as motivated by detestation of unnecessary food waste, satisfaction in retaining its use value, receipt of free

Figure 28.2 Affective labour: sorting through divested wholesaler produce for potential redistribution to people.

Source: Spring.

food, and avoiding being a 'wage slave'. He thus expressed a different moral gauging of divested food from critiques of voluntary food aid work. The warehouse's founder rejected its identification as a food bank, vociferously critiquing the latter's potential stigmatisation of those categorised as poor enough to access 'food aid'. Many network actors' praxis was rooted in freegan discourse (Barnard 2016), arguing that food is divested due not to its inedibility, but its non-profitability. Echoing the concerns of the public about food waste in the wake of the XL Foods beef recall, the implication is that food's use-values do not necessarily correspond to its relegation as excess and can be rescued through the appropriate conduits. Refusing to redistribute food to 'needy' people alone, and endeavouring to raise public awareness about the economic and environmental injustice of profit-motivated wastage, the activist network treated the 'anti-supermarket' as a hub for multiple conduits: food divested in bins and recovered through 'interception', or directly donated, was subsequently passed along through deliveries to 'pay-as-you-feel' cafés around the city, schools, catered events, and 'pop-up' stalls.

The network attempted to shift the perception of 'rescued food' away from something solely suitable to feed those in poverty, and instead instil diverse purposes and values to devalued commodities: to stimulate new eating spaces, educate children, and tighten loops in urban food procurement. The warehouse was thus part of multiple conduits, requiring significant investment in infrastructural arrangements as well as labour. Distinct conduits, depending on their nature (e.g. the desire among schools for 'healthy' food) can place add-itional demands on those tasked with handling, sorting, and allocating hard-to-predict food flows. As the network's scale and popularity has grown, its founders have maintained a goal of 'putting itself out of business'—a goal that has, at times, conflicted with daily imperatives to rescue food and supply it to a growing range and number of conduits.

Contrasting with biopolitical efforts to secure potentially hazardous food through recalls, then, is the biopolitical imperative of securing a population's access to food. Nally (2011: 46) cites the adoption of the language of food *insecurity* rather than hunger to argue that 'the politics of food is now firmly embedded in a neoliberal apparatus of security'. The impera-tives of safety and access can come into direct conflict. While seeking to oppose itself to a supermarket or food bank, the redistribution network's warehouse nevertheless found itself embroiled in a controversy that highlights its imbrication in broader processes of regulating food flows in the interests of public safety. The event highlighted contradictory divestment imperatives of redistribution activists and food safety authorities. The case highlights the ambiguous status of new spaces and organisations claiming a repurposed role for 'ex-commodities' (Barnard 2016), as well as tensions between socio-environmental imperatives to mitigate food waste impacts and biosecurity imperatives that mirror tensions inherent in food recall.

The redistribution network was attempting to prevent future food wastage through edu-cating visitors about determining food's edibility through sensory engagement rather than reliance on expiry dates. As noted, food hazards are not necessarily detectable by human senses alone; Milne (2012) has shown how microbiological techniques have 'revealed' food risks in new ways (Lougheed and Hird 2017). The resulting array of regulatory legislation in the form of date stamps follow such knowledge-making but also decades of campaigns to secure governmental intervention in relationships between manufacturers and consumers. The nascent spaces, actors, and practices that assemble around redistribution conduits, how-ever, invite new uncertainties around the interpretation of expiry dates.

Some months following my visit to the warehouse, it was reported in local and national media that Trading Standards inspectors had summoned the redistribution network's founder to a hearing following an inspection. The summons letter was shared on the network's Facebook page, quoting that inspectors had 'discovered 444 items which were 6,345 days past the use-by date'. Food aid charities redistributing surplus food have generally observed the compliance requirements of donor supermarkets not to distribute food past the use-by date (intended to indicate a cut-off for safety of higher-risk foods, unlike the best-before date which indicates peak quality). The network had allowed certain such items to be dis-tributed through the 'anti-supermarket' or served in the cafés, with some members arguing that volunteers and eaters (often one and the same) should use 'common-sense' judgement in assessing the edibility of presumed over-cautious date margins. The case prompted certain suppliers to cut off donations, highlighting donors' concerns around the reputational and safety implications of conduits receiving their divested products, and divestors' power to stymie flows toward conduits that 'bite back'.

Midgley (2013) analyses how redistribution organisations must manage values attached to divested foods, including liabilities such as expiry dates. The inspector's summons of the food redistribution network highlights how the latent regulatory power of such technologies can shift from governmentality of consumer conduct (i.e. self-management in the interests of public wellbeing) toward a heavier-handed imposition of power, where evidence of non-compliance threatens the viability of the 'feeding people' conduit. Retaining food as edible contrasts with other forms of distribution favoured by major donors (AD has been a fast-growing conduit that arguably competes with redistribution; Mourad 2015). The conduit of making rejected foods available through the 'anti-supermarket' acted back, not only on donors, but on those activist and charitable organisations investing considerable labour and developing spatial infrastructures to secure divested food as edible.

Discussion and conclusion

The present cultural moment in many western countries is characterised by simultaneous and interrelated preoccupations with hunger, food safety, and waste. In responding to these concerns, government, the food and waste industries, non-profit organisations, activists, and individual consumers find themselves at the nexus of multiple environmental and (bio)political concerns that may, at times, be at odds with each other. In lieu of upstream interventions in waste generation comes the exploitation of an increasingly diverse range of conduits for divestment. Some of these conduits provide apparent environmental and social benefits, but these arrangements are fragile as they butt up against the vitality of conduits, divested food, and limits of human control.

Conduits may bite back, contributing to a range of negative outcomes. These include the dismantling of alternative food (re)distribution pathways and economically damaging, epidemiologically risky, and immensely wasteful food scares. The ongoing reliance, for example, of the slaughter/feed/food industrial complex on industrial rendering, and renewed calls from environmental campaigners for the return of 'pig buckets' in protest at what is seen as overly-cautious and wasteful legislation to prevent closed-loop animal feed from surplus (Bowman's chapter, this volume) must contend with the history such conduits share with devastating disease outbreaks of BSE and FMD. In the case of rendering, the divested fat and protein are transported, processed using energy-intensive methods into raw material for use as animal feed, transported to feed mills, eventually being fed to animals to be converted into fats and proteins for human consumption (and hopefully not subsequently recalled). Similarly, redistribution to humans requires vans, fridges, warehouses, and cooking facilities whose environmental impacts are rarely considered.

We have shown how specific divestment practices undergirding specific conduits require significant inputs of logistical, spatial, and affective labour for the management of food products whose status as surplus, and thus bearing the potential for reputational or biophysical harm, requires the coordination of multiple interests: producers, inspectors, volunteers, and eaters. Divestment is argued to be the 'counterpart to appropriation' (Gregson et al. 2007) yet ethnographic analysis demonstrates how conduits for divested food are generative of new ties and relationships, evident in the image of redistribution as 'creating social value' (Mirosa et al. 2016) and recall as protecting various publics. Additionally, divested food remains tied to its commodity form through, as shown, the printing of expiry date labels, meaning that those handling surplus food must manage such traces (Midgley 2013), their meaning/interpretation, and the material 'acting-back' of food that operates an inevitable teleology of decay (Evans 2014). Food's capacity to disgust and make ill, as well as nourish and delight, makes recall and redistribution spaces places for the management of trust.

Particularly in the case of redistribution, care must be taken in the positioning of eventual recipients' 'common-sense' in determining edibility; the history of food regulation challenges perceptions of regulation as arbitrary and servile to profiteering: rather, it has grown from consumer-led campaigns for protection against 'wily manufacturers' and the tendency for intensifying food systems to exacerbate food risks (Juska et al. 2003, DeLind and Howard 2008). Our comparison of the spaces, labour, and legislative histories surrounding redistribution and recall has revealed a central biopolitical tension between the imperative to secure food's inedibility in the interests of public safety (in the case of recall), and the at-times competing imperative to retain surplus food's edibility in the interests of food justice and anti-waste public sentiment.

Which brings us to our concluding argument. The potential value extracted from closing organic material loops is not only contingent on 'the inventiveness, skill, facilities, networks, and distribution channels' (Reinert 2012: 71), but also on uncertain limits on the extent to which organic material can be cycled through processes of capitalism before biting back. The capacity for recall and redistribution conduits to 'bite back' in often unanticipated ways leads us to consider how both recall and redistribution reflect fundamental inequities endemic to contemporary food production and distribution systems. If 'divestment is foundational to contemporary levels of consumerism' (Gregson et al. 2007: 187), it is also foundational to overproduction, as others have theorised (Barnard 2016, Giles 2016).

Reading food waste through concepts of conduits and divestment expatiates the complexity and often spatially and temporally distributed implications of, in this case, two contrasting instantiations of biopolitics. Thinking in terms of conduits as socio-material flows broadens the analytical landscape, working against certain foreclosures such as the 'exteriority' of 'waste' and the marginalisation of poverty, volunteer and affective labour, and food insecurity. We suggest that this analytical lens be used in future scholarship as it facilitates a critical engagement with the complexities and contradictions of the productive processes of assembling waste and waste management.

We have thus broadened the conceptual apparatus of divestment and conduits from a focus on households to institutional and market actors. The dominant system is predicated on competitive abundance, fuelled by the availability of cheap calories. Unsold or recalled materials are costly and carry real or perceived risks, limiting or prohibiting production capacity, and as such are 'moved along' in ways that prioritise a return to production. While large food businesses' prime purpose is to generate profit for shareholders, access to food is predicated on one's capacity to pay. 'Moral economies' for addressing hunger have been replaced by market mechanisms (Nally 2011) such that a common public refrain for solving hunger is: to produce ever-cheaper food; provide state-sponsored subsidies (e.g., food stamps) offering a minimal level of support and reproduce a reliance on inexpensive food; or to instantiate charitable redistribution in such a way that ex-commodities can be re-enrolled into the management of poverty without threatening prices, a solution that fails to address socioeconomic inequities underlying uneven food access. Producing ever-cheaper food, implies the further intensification of food production systems whose globalisation and centralisation already exacerbates the kinds of contamination risks that underlie food recalls (Juska et al. 2003, DeLind and Howard 2008).

The problems outlined are multi-dimensional and manifold. What is required, and what our proposed conceptualisations facilitate, is addressing questions of how the scale and intensification of the food system in the service of cheap food and profit margins intersect with (failures to remediate) poverty, food safety, and sustainability. One critical move to mitigate these problems would be to reduce income inequality while simultaneously shifting toward a food system that more adequately accounts for the true costs of production. While a less intensive, more ecologically sustainable food system would result in increased food prices, the answer to not alienating those on low incomes is to boost incomes to levels that enable not only survival, but shared participation in more socially and environmentally just food economies (Fabian Society 2015). This pair of simultaneous interventions would counteract the forces that push people to rely on secondary food redistribution and address supply-chain tendencies that externalise costs to the detriment of human and environmental health.

Notes

1 The removal from the market of a product that violates relevant laws (e.g., food safety laws) or private standards.
2 Specifically: a copy of their Issue Management System summarising CFIA staff activities and correspondence with other agencies and companies concerning a specific food safety event.
3 Though as Gay Hawkins (2001) notes, and as reflected by the anxieties felt by some in this study, being out of sight in the landfill does not necessarily mean out of mind.

References

Barnard A. (2016) *Freegans: Diving into the Wealth of Food Waste in America*. Minneapolis, MN: University of Minnesota Press.
Bennett J. (2009) *Vibrant Matter: A Political Ecology of Things*. Durham: Duke University Press.
Boesveld S. (2012) 'XL foods trashes tonnes of recalled beef even though food experts say it's safe to eat'. *National Post*. http://nationalpost.com/news/canada/xl-foods-trashes-tonnes-of-recalled-beef-even-though-food-experts-say-its-safe/wcm/559610cc-3b5b-47ff-994e-6f3942c6edf7
Carolan M. S. (2006) 'Risk, trust and "the beyond" of the environment: A brief look at the recent case of mad cow disease in the United States'. *Environmental Values* 15(2): 233–252.
DeLind L. B., and Howard P. H. (2008) 'Safe at any scale? Food scares, food regulation, and scaled alternatives'. *Agriculture and Human Values* 25: 301–317. DOI: 10.1007/s10460-007-9112-y
DeMar G. (2005) 'Making dumpster diving possible'. *American Vision*. https://americanvision.org/1472/making-dumpster-diving-possible/
Douglas M. (2002) *Purity and Danger: An Analysis of Concepts of Pollution and Taboo*. New York: Taylor.
Evans D. (2014) *Food Waste: Home Consumption, Material Culture and Everyday Life*. London: Bloomsbury.
Fabian Society. (2015). Hungry for change: The final report of the Fabian commission of food and poverty. www.fabians.org.uk/wp-content/uploads/2015/10/Hungry-for-Change-web-27.10.pdf
FareShare. (2018). UK still way behind France in putting surplus food to good use. *FareShare*. https://fareshare.org.uk/uk-france-surplus-food-good-use/
Feeding America. (n.d.). Our network. *Feeding America*. www.feedingamerica.org/our-work/food-bank-network.html
Giles D. B. (2016) 'The work of waste-making: Biopolitical labour and the myth of the global city'. In: J. P. Marshall and L. Connor (eds.), *Environmental Change and the World's Futures: Ecologies, Ontologies and Mythologies*. London: Routledge, pp. 81–95.
Gille Z. (2007) *From the Cult of Waste to the Trash Heap of History: The Politics of Waste in Socialist and Postsocialist Hungary*. Bloomington, IN: Indiana University Press.
Gille Z. (2010) 'Actor networks, modes of production, and waste regimes: Reassembling the macro-social'. *Environment and Planning A* 42: 1049–1064. DOI: 10.1068/a42122
Gregson N., and Crang M. (2010) 'Materiality and waste: Inorganic vitality in a networked world'. *Environment and Planning A* 42: 1026–1032. DOI: 10.1068/a43176
Gregson N., Metcalfe A., and Crewe L. (2007) 'Moving things along: The conduits and practices of divestment in consumption'. *Transactions of the Institute of British Geographers* 32: 187–200.
Hawkins G. (2001) 'Plastic bags: Living with rubbish'. *International Journal of Cultural Studies* 4: 5–23. DOI: 10.1177/136787790100400101
Hetherington K. (2004) 'Secondhandedness: Consumption, disposal, and absent presence'. *Environment and Planning D* 22(1): 157–173.
Hird M. J. (2012) 'Knowing waste: Towards an inhuman epistemology'. *Social Epistemology* 26: 453–469. DOI: 10.1080/02691728.2012.727195
Hird M. J. (2015) 'Waste, environmental politics and dis/engaged publics'. *Theory, Culture & Society* 34: 187–209. DOI: 10.1177/0263276414565717

The Huffington Post. (2012) 'Tainted tweet continues to fuel uproar'. *Huffington Post*, www.huffington post.ca/2012/10/23/danielle-smith-tainted-tweet-reaction_n_2006329.html

Johnson N. (2015) 'We recall 100 blue whales' worth of meat a year'. *Grist*, http://grist.org/food/we-recall-100-blue-whales-worth-of-meat-a-year/

Juska A., Gouveia L., Gabriel J., et al. (2003) 'Manufacturing bacteriological contamination outbreaks in industrialized meat production systems: The case of E. coli O157: H7'. *Agriculture and Human Values* 20: 3–19.

Law J. (2006) 'Disaster in agriculture: Or foot and mouth mobilities'. *Environment and Planning A* 38: 227–239.

Law J., and Mol A. (2008) 'Globalisation in practice: On the politics of boiling pigswill'. *Geoforum* 39: 133–143. DOI: 10.1016/j.geoforum.2006.08.010

Lepawsky J., and Mather C. (2011) 'From beginnings and endings to boundaries and edges: Rethinking circulation and exchange through electronic waste: From beginnings and endings to boundaries and edges'. *Area* 43(3): 242–249. DOI: 10.1111/j.1475-4762.2011.01018.x

Loopstra R., Fledderjohann J., Reeves A., and Stuckler D. (2018) 'Impact of welfare benefit sanctioning on food insecurity: A dynamic cross-area study of food bank usage in the UK'. *Journal of Social Policy* 47: 437–457.

Lougheed S. C., and Hird M. J. (2017) 'Food security and secure food in the anthropocene'. *Crime, Law and Social Change* 68: 499–514. DOI: 10.1007/s10611-017-9699-x

Mancini M., and Vellani N. (2016) 'Heres how much food Walmart throws away over 12 days'. *CBC*. www.cbc.ca/news/business/marketplace-walmart-food-waste-1.3814719

Midgley J. (2013) 'The logics of surplus food redistribution'. *Journal of Environmental Planning and Management* 57(12): 1872–1892.

Milne R. (2012) 'Arbiters of waste: Date labels, the consumer and knowing good, safe food'. *The Sociological Review* 60: 84–101.

Mirosa M., Mainvil L., Horne H. et al. (2016) 'The social value of rescuing food, nourishing communities'. *British Food Journal* 118(12): 3044–3058. DOI: 10.1108/BFJ-04-2016-0149

Mourad M. (2015) 'Recycling, recovering and preventing "food waste": Competing solutions for food systems sustainability in the United States and France'. *Journal of Cleaner Production* 126: 461–477.

Munro R. (1995) 'The disposal of the meal'. In D. Marshall (ed.) *Food Choice and the Consumer*. New York: Blackie Academic and Professional, pp. 313–325.

Nally D. (2011) 'The biopolitics of food provisioning'. *Transactions of the Institute of British Geographers* 36 (1): 37–53.

New York Times. (1992) 'Cat food relabeled as tuna for people'. *New York Times*. www.nytimes.com/1992/03/24/nyregion/cat-food-relabeled-as-tuna-for-people.html

New York Times. (1995) 'Man charged in sale of cat food as tuna'. *New York Times*. www.nytimes.com/1995/02/12/nyregion/man-charged-in-sale-of-cat-food-as-tuna.html

O'Brien M. (2012) 'A "lasting transformation" of capitalist surplus: From food stocks to feedstocks'. *The Sociological Review* 60(2): 192–211. DOI: 10.1111/1467-954X.12045

Osborne H., and Hopkins N. (2018, August 28). Revealed: Ministers' plan to research effect of policies on food bank use. *The Guardian*, www.theguardian.com/society/2018/aug/01/revealed-ministers-plan-to-research-effect-of-policies-on-food-bank-use

Poppendieck J. (1998) *Sweet Charity? Emergency Food and the End of Entitlement*. New York: Viking.

Reinert H. (2012) 'The disposable surplus: Notes on waste, reindeer, and biopolitics'. *Laboratorium. Russian Review of Social Research* 4(3): 67–83.

Riches G. (1997) *First World Hunger: Food Security and Welfare Politics*. London: Macmillan/New York: St Martins.

Stuart T. (2009) *Waste: Uncovering the Global Food Scandal*. New York: WW Norton & Company.

Tarasuk V., and Eakin J. (2005) 'Food assistance through "surplus" food: Insights from an ethnographic study of food bank work'. *Agriculture and Human Values* 22(2): 177–186.

Tenner E. (1996) *Why Things Bite Back: Technology and the Revenge of Unintended Consequences*. New York: Knopf.

Uhlig R. (2002) '10 million animals were slaughtered in foot and mouth cull'. *Telegraph*. www.telegraph.co.uk/news/uknews/1382356/10-million-animals-were-slaughtered-in-foot-and-mouth-cull.html

Zu Ermgassen E. K. H. J., Phalan B., Green R. E., et al. (2016) 'Reducing the land use of EU pork production: Where there's swill, there's a way'. *Food Policy* 58: 35–48.

29

ARE YOU BUYING FOOD WASTE?

The roles technologies can play in (re)designing the food retail experience

Geremy Farr-Wharton, Timur Osadchiy and Peter Lyle

The epidemic of food waste

Food waste is a growing pandemic facing the world (Light et al., 2017). This waste is comprised of organic materials that have entered the waste stream and were originally intended for consumption (Schneider & Obersteiner, 2007). Food waste has preceding and subsequent social, economic and environmental impacts associated first with the processes from farm-to-plate, and second, with the waste management process (Farr-Wharton, 2015; Heller & Keoleian, 2000). A number of industries, such as the food retail industry (e.g. food retailers and businesses, restaurants, food chains) have implemented numerous strategies targeting the reduction of food waste at various stages along their supply chains, resulting in approximately 3–5% of once consumable foods entering the waste stream (Garcia-Garcia et al., 2017; Parfitt et al., 2010). However, strategies targeting the domestic market are struggling to gain traction or are ineffective, as the household sector continues to contribute approximately 20–40% of food purchases to landfill as a result of spoilage or discarded food (Caswell, 2008; Schneider, 2008).

Consumers and food retailers are in misalignment when it comes to reducing food waste. Retailers aim to reduce food 'shrinkage' (including food waste occurring as a result of unsold products) and increase food purchases, as much as possible, regardless of whether the food is consumed prior to spoilage. However, retailers are under social pressures to reduce waste across their supply chain, which encompasses domestic settings (Gunders, 2012; Parfitt et al., 2010). For example, the 'ugly food' movement (Mortimer, 2015) aimed at improving the consumption of imperfect food. Consumer decision-making practices are significantly influenced by marketing ploys designed to encourage consumers to purchase as much food as possible, regardless of whether the product will be consumed or not (Tsiros & Heilman, 2005). This encourages poorly informed and impulsive decision-making about purchasing food, which consequently serves as a significant driver for the creation of food waste in domestic settings, resulting in oversupplies of food in storage (e.g. refrigerator, freezer or pantry) and poor food nutrition and wasted money (Farr-Wharton et al., 2014; Vidgen & Gallegos, 2010).

Over-production, over-supply and over-buying – all encouraged by our current economic configuration – are among major sources of food waste (Girotto et al., 2015; Papargyropoulou et al., 2014; Smil, 2004). There are a number of issues contributing to the surplus of food in the supply chains of the restaurant and food retail industry. In many cases that is the effect of poor communication, inaccurate sales forecasting and lack of logistical planning (Mena et al., 2011). Ganglbauer et al. (2012), as part of their research, looked into the reasons behind why consumers buy foods in larger quantities than are needed or could be consumed in a reasonable amount of time. As with the industry, on the household level the surplus constitutes a lack of prior planning (i.e. not creating shopping lists), change in plans (e.g. purchase of foods for a specific recipe that was then not cooked) or buying larger quantities for a lower price (bulk purchases). Such behaviour results in more than half of food ending up in waste, because it was not consumed in time (Williams et al., 2012). The lack of environmental education is another big contributor to the problem. In seeking causes of waste in the food manufacturing, wholesaling and retailing industries in the UK and Spain, Mena et al. (2011) have found that management did not even consider waste as an important problem. In a study by Neff et al. (2015), 42% of respondents demonstrated some level of awareness about food waste and only 16% sought information about reducing it. A survey of 147 participants in New Zealand conducted by Tucker and Farrelly (2016) have shown that binning food is a normal practice for three-quarters of households, instead of composting, for example. As one of the action points in the study was minimising food waste, Tucker and Farrelly (2016) proposed providing clear and accessible information and education, for example, as part of educational programmes in schools. Indeed, despite efforts by charities, scientific communities and governments to promote environmental sustainability, this knowledge is mainly available on demand when consumers actively seek the information. The ubiquity of technology could bridge this gap and provide this information right at the time when a behaviour causing the food waste occurs. For example, when a consumer buys more items than they need or when a particular food in their fridge approaches its best-before date. These possible solutions are of course limited by their focus on the individual as the source of changing a systemic problem.

From a systems perspective (e.g. a comprehensive view of all components of the system), consumers and retailers are both in alignment for reducing food waste in general, yet remain at odds regarding how best to achieve this. Further, because the percentage of food waste entering the waste stream is significantly higher in domestic settings, interventions targeting domestic food waste have tended to focus solely on the domestic dwelling. This has been at the expense of interventions targeting earlier stages of consumer decision-making regarding food, such as the food purchasing stage (e.g. consumer grocery shopping). We could find only a handful of studies exploring interventions during consumer food procurement, which among other similarly implemented strategies, attempted to supplement or support more informed consumer decision-making (Clear et al., 2016; Farr-Wharton et al., 2013; Hirsch et al., 2016; Ng et al., 2015; Park et al., 2017; Shipp et al., 2013; Stevens et al., 2017). Many of these interventions targeted nutritional advice and very few aimed to reduce wastages. This may suggest that there are unique challenges for implementing consumer purchasing support interventions within food retail outlets or that such interventions are particularly challenging to embed within retailers, because they may run counter to the economic incentive to sell more food, such as the reduction in bulk purchases, which is a key marketing tactic. Instead, alternative interventions, which are sensitive to both the consumer and food retailer's needs, are required.

The food and technology landscape in the food retail sector

Enabling and emerging technology adoption for the food retail sector is not a new phenomenon. There continue to be numerous opportunities for the sector to leverage these technologies to support, for example, process and procedural efficiencies (Piotrowicz & Cuthbertson, 2014), reduced waste associated with smart packaging (Ghaani et al., 2016), and tracking food supply chains to improve logistical proficiencies, food providence and food safety (Tian, 2017). The sector is also leveraging membership programmes to understand more about what their consumers are purchasing, when, and how much, through big data and business intelligence to improve the way they market their products to their consumers (Carolan, 2018). Through these membership programmes, food retailers can promote the sale of particular products to encourage purchasing, which can also be used to reduce shrinkage of products. Other enabling and emerging technologies have also been implemented to improve the accessibility for their customers as they traverse through stores. Key examples of these technologies, include: (1) digital screens for product price updates, rather than printed price tags, (2) self-service kiosk for straight through processing of transactions, and (3) automatic scanners, such as the Regi-Rob (Corporation, 2017), which scan products as they are entered into a basket or trolley, among others. As new technologies emerge, they will continue to play a role in shaping the way the food retail sector interacts with its customers.

Understanding the current food retail experience is critical

Currently, existing technologies mainly focus on addressing the food waste on either consumer or restaurant and food retail side. On either side of the issue, these solutions are generally developed around the distribution of foods approaching the best-before date or tracking and analysing the food waste behaviour to prevent it in the future. It is important for future interventions to explore opportunities to support both the food retailer in their business and consumers in purchasing food that is best suited to their needs and desires, while aiming to avoid wasting food. This is a significant deficiency in current works targeting consumer food waste reduction in a food retail experience context.

There are many models of distribution of low-demand or foods in excess developed for the business. For example, a Denmark-based company Too Good To Go (TooGoodToGo, 2018) developed a mobile application of the same name that provides a communication channel for restaurants to inform their clients about big discounts on foods they did not sell during a day. Similar to that, the application NoFoodWasted (NoFoodWasted, 2018) produced in the Netherlands allows local supermarkets to advertise discounts on foods with an ending shelf life. A food delivery service, Gebni (Gebni, 2017), based in New York, provides a mobile application that adjusts restaurant menu prices according to real-time demand. An organisation FoodCloud (FoodCloud, 2016) from Ireland provides supermarkets with a cloud-based solution that helps to distribute unsold foods to charities and community groups. Despite being creative solutions addressing food waste at the business level, these solutions transfer responsibility to a consumer who may still end up disposing products soon after the purchase. Thus, there is still a demand for a technology that allows early prevention of the food waste. The company Winnow Solutions (Winnow, 2018) developed a system for restaurant kitchens that covers that need. The system offers tools for tracking and analysing disposing behaviour in the food production pipeline. The tracking element consists of digital scales for a kitchen bin and a touchscreen user interface. When staff dispose of food into the bin, it is automatically weighed. On the touchscreen, the staff need to map the name of the food from the restaurant menu and the stage of production at which the food is being disposed. A cloud software combines that information with prices of the disposed foods to estimate losses for the business and pinpoint sources of food waste in the production line. These reports help restaurants to avoid the food waste, save money and time of the staff, for example, by rapidly identifying and removing the least popular foods among clients from their menu.

Similar to the restaurant and retail food retail industry, there is a technology that helps to redistribute excessive foods available to households. A social enterprise OLIO (OLIO, 2018) founded in the UK, with more than half a million users, aims to connect neighbours with each other and local shops to facilitate sharing of soon to expire foods. In contrast to avoiding food waste through redistribution of soon to expire foods, another promising direction for a digital food waste solution is preventing over-purchasing behaviour in the first place. One such example is a mobile application for food management called No Waste (NOWASTE, 2017). The application offers a smart shopping list that tracks purchased products and alerts a user if some of the products approach their best-before date. It also helps to better organise storage of foods according to recommendations from manufacturers and increase the lifespan of foods. In a study by Aydin et al. (2017) that conceptualises a similar mobile application, authors added elements of behaviour change and persuasive design theories to encourage better food management. Nipping the food waste in the bud, for example by preventing over-purchasing behaviour, is the basis of a successful solution. However, a more effective technology should at least offer comprehensive coverage of the problem from these two sides, consumer and retail. Such technology could be applied at the touchpoint of these two parties, which is online shopping.

A food waste prevention tool for online shopping experience could inform consumers of their over-buying behaviour and the associated consequences. A key to such experiences could be personalisation. People normally buy products to be consumed in a several day period. Estimating intake needs for long periods of time (e.g. a week) can be a challenging task, especially for a big family. Even with prior planning, the challenges of estimating intake needs can lead to rushed purchasing of foods that were not needed and eventually expire. Thus, a personalised shopping experience could assist that planning and make it more accurate by predicting consumption needs and alerting their clients when they exceed those needs. For example, before purchasing any products a user could specify physical characteristics of all members of their family. In this way the system can estimate their energy needs for a single day, for example, from their basal metabolic rate (McNab, 1997). When the client adds groceries to a basket the system can predict how long it would take to consume those products. It can then alert the user, if there are any items that are likely to expire within that period and should be consumed quicker. The system can even assist dietary targets of its users, for example, by alerting them if they clearly exceed their calorie needs.

Personalised online shopping experiences will give retailers and manufacturers an insight into the post-shelf life of their products. This information would serve as a fuel for an accurate forecast of product demand and purchasing behaviour of their clients that would help to avoid over-production and over-supply. Moreover, online food retailers could borrow some of the aforementioned methods of attracting more customers to soon to expire products by advertising lower prices on them. For example, discounted and relevant products could be recommended along with other products already selected by a customer. Such recommendation-based systems are already a long-time practice of the online shopping experience and produce suggestions mainly based on customers' purchasing history and reviews (Linden et al., 2003; Osadchiy et al., 2019). The longevity of a product's shelf life and the level of demand could be used as another parameter for these recommender systems to facilitate the sales.

(Re)Designing consumer engagement with a digitally transformed food retail sector

Understanding how enabling technologies will be adopted, adapted and altered in the future is fundamental to exploring the ways in which these technologies will be used to digitally transform the food retail experience. Such technologies can play a significant or subtle role in shaping that experience in vastly different ways. We explore three scenarios, which we feel have a high possibility of redesigning the food retail experience. We articulate the current state, explore the potential future state, and investigate the likely positive and negative implications they may have on both the retailers and consumers, and, indeed, on the food ecosystem.

Scenario 1: robotics, autonomous vehicles, dark stores and the full-circle online shopping experience

In this scenario, we explore how robotics are, and will continue to transform how food retailers manage their engagement with their customers, as well as improve their business practices and logistics. As part of articulating the current state of this scenario, we refer to food retailers as those who have larger chain stores, who implement relatively uniform procedures and practices depending on the size and rating of the store.

The current state

Modern brick and mortar grocers are designed to maximise customer experience and to encourage product purchases through leveraging marketing ploys and catering to the needs and interests of end consumers. To capitalise on every available opportunity, food retailers must provide the infrastructure to encourage as many people as possible to enter their stores. Involved in this process are relatively simple logistical, albeit expensive, complexities, such as providing parking spaces and increasing accessibility for their consumers. There is also a need to provide enough space throughout their store for their customers to traverse aisles and dedicated space for payment facilities. There is significant investment required for this infrastructure, which smaller food retailers may struggle to absorb, leading to smaller stores and a potential reduced market share. Restocking foods onto the shelves, monitoring food expiration, managing the store, and ensuring payment facilities are staffed appropriately requires labour commitments by food retailers, for which there are also associated costs. Emerging and enabling technologies have the capability to reduce the costs associated with infrastructure by removing the need for such infrastructure. However, this would have significant implications for reshaping the way consumers interact with food retailers as well as spatial implications related to land use.

The future state

As a result of the challenges and considerations, and as a potential means of overcoming them, the concept of a food retail 'dark store' has surfaced in recent years (Jones & Livingstone, 2015). Food retail dark stores, as the name suggests, are designed for low human engagement and intervention, where customers are catered for through online purchases only and the process of consumer food procurement is automated as much as possible. Some designs of food retail dark stores demonstrate a drive through-like interaction, where food products are pre-ordered online and picked up in a single instance. This removes the need for key infrastructure, such as parking lots and space dedicated for consumers to traverse aisles. As payment is completed online, no infrastructure or staffing requirements associated with payments are necessary. For this reason, economically, food retail dark stores provide a useful mechanism to reduce costs, while catering to consumers' food needs and interests. They also present opportunities to significantly lower food waste, as intended food purchases of customers are known prior to picking them up. As a result, the food procured by the food retailer can be more precise and targeted. In order to store food efficiently, robotics can be used to move food around the store. Robots have already been extensively tested in such settings (Marques et al., 2017; Santana, 2018) and are already in established use within sectors such as logistics and manufacturing.

Dark stores also present opportunities for autonomous vehicles to be involved in delivering food purchases to consumers (Mileham, 2016). For example, Amazon.com, Inc. has invested extensive resources into exploring the opportunities for drones to play a role in parcel delivery, tailoring the experience for consumers who purchase products online. While there are challenges associated with this technology currently (Ramadan et al., 2017), this enabling technology complements a dark store strategy effectively and may improve engagement with consumers, while simplifying operations for food retailers. Driverless cars present yet another opportunity for dark stores to prosper in the future. These cars, while currently legislated that they must be operated with a human present, may reach a stage where this is not required. In such a setting, food orders can be purchased online by the end consumer and a driverless vehicle could go pick it up at the retail outlet as an automated process. This removes the logistical consideration for the consumer, providing a more convenient scenario for them to procure their food, and again, supporting the food retailer in reducing their costs. However, automated experiences regarding food have been explored previously with mixed results. The infamous example of when a smart fridge (Rothensee, 2007) procured milk automatically once a present bottle was empty demonstrated that consumers do not necessarily desire automation regarding food (Wei et al., 2011; Lueg, 2002). However, as these enabling and emerging technologies become more popular, and they are integrated into the food retail environment, we are likely to witness a significant redesign of the food retail experience. This redesign may also come with unintended consequences; as Gille (2012) noted, food waste solutions limited to a single country or to one part of the chain may create collateral damage in other parts of the food supply chain.

Scenario 2: the gut microbiome, digital reality and the digitally shaped in-store experience

In this scenario, we explore the emergence of the gut microbiome and how technology, such as digital reality technology (e.g. augmented reality), delivered through smartphones can aid food retailers in digitally transforming the shopping experience for consumers, to improve their consumption of healthier foods, and tailored purchases toward an individual's needs, in order to reduce shrinkage.

The current state

During food shopping, it can be challenging for consumers to navigate the food products that are most beneficial to their own personalised health, given the complexities with: nutritional information (e.g. font size and level of assumed knowledge of nutritional intake), choice and variety of options, brands, food allergies and intolerances, and lists of ingredients. Further, as a result of a flurry of information relating to diets and health, an extensive array of diet programmes, and targeted product marketing, the process of food selection is more complex than ever, with marketers leveraging the Paradox of Choice (Schwartz, 2004) – when faced with many choices and little time, no choice is optimal, meaning individuals continue to purchase the same food items again and again to minimise complex decision-making. This can make it fundamentally challenging to alter and maintain diets for improved health and wellbeing.

Our diets fundamentally shape our health (World Health Organization, 2003). The prevalence of obesity and diabetes in First World countries is demonstrating the poor quality of diets, largely comprising of energy-dense and highly processed foods, which is damaging our health and increasing risks of disease (Prentice & Jebb, 2003). As the prevalence in food intolerances (allergies) also rises (Hadley, 2006), it is critical to support the diverse food needs of consumers. Technology can play a significant role in supporting better food choices for consumers by removing, or at the very least, reducing the complexity of choices and individualising the advice provided.

The future state

Within the literature and in more widely distributed media, there has been a recent surge in interest regarding the gut microbiome of humans (Schmidt, 2015). The gut microbiome consists of trillions of microbes, also known as bacteria, which serve a number of purposes, including playing a role in maintaining the health of an individual. Diet and exercise are the two most influential factors that have a significant impact on the gut microbiome, with approximately equal weighting. Poor diets are known to create imbalances or reduce diversity of microbes in the microbiome, which can impact health (Bull & Plummer, 2014). As obesity and food intolerances continue to rise, it is important that decision support regarding food be provided to individuals at the point of choice, rather than point of purchase. Many interventions have targeted food decision-making practices in reflection, post-purchase, and this is too late. These interventions will often only provide reflections of the food purchased and not necessarily alternatives for the next time they need decision-making support regarding food choices. This information is simply too late or requires individuals to remember key details during the next time they are making decisions about food choices.

Technology can play a role in providing decision support at point of choice. Point of choice is when the consumer is deciding which product to remove from the shelf, among a variety of brands and similar products. Therefore, for a technology to be useful in this context, it needs to provide the necessary information to the individual to aid them in making the decision about which product to choose. Smartphones are one of the most pervasive technologies available today and many individuals have a smartphone on them wherever they go. Given the prevalence of these devices, they are an obvious choice to engage users at the point of choice regarding food. Some people are already using apps to aid them in checking shopping lists or understanding which products are low in, for example, sugar or salt. However, pulling out a smartphone to check every product may be time intensive or cumbersome. Embedding technologies, such as augmented reality into a smartphone may also have its associated challenges, such as having to hold a phone in front of you, as you search for the products you are after (Ahn et al., 2015; Olsson et al., 2013). However, this approach would enable consumers to quickly identify the foods that are best suited to them as they traverse the aisles of the stores. If consumers are able to feed into the device what dietary requirements were best suited to their health, this would enable food retailers to market particular foods to consumers more effectively. It may also provide greater transparency about the foods a consumer is likely to purchase during a shop, prior to them even entering a store. This scenario has been one of the greatest challenges for the food retail sector to achieve and goes beyond simple food retail membership programmes designed to improve transparency of purchases. Understanding what the consumer will likely purchase in a shop means that food retailers can leverage more focused food procurement, reducing the potential for shrinkage.

In the future, other technologies, such as smart glasses, can be used to replace smartphones in providing the desired information at point of choice. Smart glasses would still leverage augmented reality to provide key information about products, perhaps even providing a virtual pathway for the consumer to traverse in order to quickly locate the products they are after. However, unlike smartphones, smart glasses have the potential to naturalise the interaction between the consumer and the products they seek, in that they would not need to hold their phone in front of them as they traverse the aisles of the store. Smart glasses are not a mainstream technology that has been widely adopted. This is as a result of limitations with the technology (e.g. battery life), rather than the utility of these devices. As a result, with rapid improvements to emerging technology occurring, this technology will likely play a key role in the future for consumers and food retailers.

Scenario 3: food providence and safety, blockchain, and improved outcomes for consumers and food retailers

In this scenario, we explore how blockchain can be leveraged to support better outcomes for both consumers and food retailers. We investigate the influence blockchain may have on food provisioning and safety, and how consumers and food retailers will benefit from this technology. This scenario can be used to improve 'trust' in food, thereby improving more informed decision-making regarding food and increasing purchases of currently less desirable and imperfect food, such as those targeted in the 'ugly food' movement (Mortimer, 2015). This process will ultimately reduce shrinkage for retailers and wastes across the supply chain.

The current state

Food waste occurs at all stages of the food supply chain from harvest through to food retailers' shelves and end consumers. Before appearing on a table, food sometimes travels from one continent to another, risking expiration during transportation or spoilage in a poorly managed warehouse (Parfitt et al., 2010). Maintaining recommended storage conditions at every stage of the supply chain to preserve the quality of food is a significant challenge. According to the Food and Agriculture Organisation, one contributing factor to the issue is the lack of communication and coordination between parties across food supply chains (FAO, 2011). Thus, an effective and sustainable solution to minimising food waste must involve collaboration between all stakeholders at the global level. Real-time traceability of products and monitoring environmental conditions (e.g. temperature, humidity) at every stage of distribution can make that collaboration transparent (Aung & Chang, 2014). In addition to other benefits, such as improved food safety, a transparent system can help in revealing sources of food waste in the supply chain.

The future state

A commonly proposed solution for tracing each individual product through the supply chain is attaching unique identifiers (e.g. Radio Frequency Identification (RFID) tags or bar codes) to them (Aung & Chang, 2014; Tian, 2016). At every stage of distribution, stakeholders involved in the process can make relevant records (e.g. storage conditions, packaging and processing) into a centralised system and access product history when required. However, a centralised solution potentially becomes a corrupted monopoly involving tampered-with and falsified information (Tian, 2016). Blockchain offers a promising decentralised alternative to this problem. Instead of an editable profile stored in a database, all information is sealed into a blockchain certificate that follows a product throughout its lifecycle. Events added into the certificate are validated by all members of the process and no individual is able to amend the certificate. A spoiled food can be instantly and reliably traced back to a place and point in time where, for example, recommended storage conditions were incorrectly implemented. There are still challenges in implementing the food traceability with the blockchain, such as high costs, that will be overcome with the development and wider adoption of the technology (Tian, 2016). A related challenge is the accessibility for all parties in the supply chain, and the trust that the verifiable information added to the chain is indeed trustworthy. Nevertheless, transparency and accountability enabled by the blockchain are expected to disrupt the food supply chain (Kshetri, 2018).

Apart from the reduction of food waste in the distribution process, the usage of blockchain can significantly reduce the number of food fraud incidents and increase food safety (Galvin, 2017). The source of contamination or infection in food can be traced and identified in seconds, instead of weeks, helping to confine cases of food poisoning and saving billions in costs for the global healthcare market. From the consumer perspective the blockchain technology will enable more informed and safer food choices based on improved trust in the food they purchase. For retailers, they can use the improved consumer trust in the food they sell to include currently less desirable foods, such as those with blemishes and imperfections (Farr-Wharton et al., 2014), which will reduce shrinkage and waste across the supply chain. Indeed, these data would be most useful to food retailers and health authorities. Having access to the full history of a product stored in a blockchain would provide instant access to information about the farm the food originated from and whether that food is actually organic or free range as stated on the packaging, providing them with a significantly different food retail experience to the present.

Conclusion

Targeting a zero waste culture concerning food is essential to improve food security and reduce the ecological, social and spatial impact of food waste. This will require systemic change, and the responsibility of reducing food waste is shared across every stage of the food supply chain, with consumers and food retailers able to play a key role. Technology is already disrupting and transforming markets and the food retail sector is not shielded from this process. We explore three high-level scenarios of how technologies can be leveraged by consumers and the food retail sector, to improve the experience of end consumers and improve outcomes for food retailers, while reducing food waste systemically. While these scenarios are speculative in nature, they are grounded in current research and aim to provide guidance for future research, policy design and industry to improve the interaction between consumers and food retailers in a way that results in the reduction of food waste.

References

Ahn, J., Williamson, J., Gartrell, M., Han, R., Lv, Q., & Mishra, S. (2015). Supporting healthy grocery shopping via mobile augmented reality. *ACM Transactions on Multimedia Computing, Communications, and Applications (TOMM), 12*(1s), 16.

Aung, M. M., & Chang, Y. S. (2014). Traceability in a food supply chain: safety and quality perspectives. *Food Control, 39,* 172–184.

Aydin, A., Micallef, A., Lovelace, S., Li, X., Cheung, V., & Girouard, A. (2017). *Save the Kiwi: encouraging better food management through behaviour change and persuasive design theories in a mobile app.* Paper presented at the proceedings of the 2017 CHI conference extended abstracts on human factors in computing systems.

Bull, M. J., & Plummer, N. T. (2014). Part 1: the human gut microbiome in health and disease. *Integrative Medicine: A Clinician's Journal, 13*(6), 17.

Carolan, M. (2018). Big data and food retail: nudging out citizens by creating dependent consumers. *Geoforum, 90,* 142–150.

Caswell, H. (2008). Britain's battle against food waste. *Nutrition Bulletin, 33*(4), 331–335.

Clear, A. K., O'neill, K., Friday, A., & Hazas, M. (2016). Bearing an open "Pandora's box": HCI for reconciling everyday food and sustainability. *ACM Transactions on Computer-Human Interaction (ToCHI), 23*(5), 28.

Corporation, P. (2017). The Industry-first experimental demonstration of "Regi-Robo(TM)", an entirely automated robotic checkout system and RFIDs (electronic tags) at Lawson Panasonic-Mae store. Retrieved from https://news.panasonic.com/global/topics/2017/46190.html

FAO, G. (2011). Global food losses and food waste–Extent, causes and prevention. *SAVE FOOD: An Initiative on Food Loss and Waste Reduction.*

Farr-Wharton, G. (2015). *Mobile interaction design approaches for reducing domestic food waste.* (Doctor of Philosophy Doctorate), Queensland University of Technology.

Farr-Wharton, G., Foth, M., & Choi, J. H. J. (2013). *EatChaFood: challenging technology design to slice food waste production.* Paper presented at the proceedings of the 2013 ACM conference on pervasive and ubiquitous computing adjunct publication.

Farr-Wharton, G., Foth, M., & Choi, J. H. J. (2014). Identifying factors that promote consumer behaviours causing expired domestic food waste. *Journal of Consumer Behaviour, 13*(6), 393–402.

FoodCloud. (2016). FoodCloud. Retrieved from https://food.cloud/

Galvin, D. (2017). *IBM and Walmart: Blockchain for food safety.* PowerPoint presentation.

Ganglbauer, E., Fitzpatrick, G., & Molzer, G. (2012). *Creating visibility: understanding the design space for food waste.* Paper presented at the proceedings of the 11th international conference on mobile and ubiquitous multimedia.

Garcia-Garcia, G., Woolley, E., & Rahimifard, S. (2017). Optimising industrial food waste management. *Procedia Manufacturing, 8,* 432–439.

Gebni. (2017). Gebni. Retrieved from https://gebni.com/

Ghaani, M., Cozzolino, C. A., Castelli, G., & Farris, S. (2016). An overview of the intelligent packaging technologies in the food sector. *Trends in Food Science & Technology, 51,* 1–11.

Gille, Z. (2012). From risk to waste: global food waste regimes. *The Sociological Review, 60,* 27–46.

Girotto, F., Alibardi, L., & Cossu, R. (2015). Food waste generation and industrial uses: a review. *Waste Management, 45,* 32–41.

Gunders, D. (2012). Wasted: how America is losing up to 40 percent of its food from farm to fork to landfill. *Natural Resources Defense Council, 26,* 1–26.

Hadley, C. (2006). Food allergies on the rise?: determining the prevalence of food allergies, and how quickly it is increasing, is the first step in tackling the problem. *EMBO reports, 7*(11), 1080–1083.

Halupka, V. A. (2012). *Food Media.* Keio University.

Heller, M., & Keoleian, G. (2000). *Life Cycle-Based Sustainability Indicators for Assessment of the US Food System.* Ann Arbor, MI: Center for Sustainable Systems, University of Michigan, 42.

Hirsch, T., Lim, C., & Otten, J. J. (2016). *What's for lunch?: a socio-ecological approach to childcare nutrition.* Paper presented at the proceedings of the 2016 ACM conference on designing interactive systems.

Jones, C., & Livingstone, N. (2015). Emerging implications of online retailing for real estate: Twenty-first century clicks and bricks. *Journal of Corporate Real Estate, 17*(3), 226–239.

Kshetri, N. (2018). 1 Blockchain's roles in meeting key supply chain management objectives. *International Journal of Information Management, 39,* 80–89.

Light, A., Powell, A., & Shklovski, I. (2017). *Design for existential crisis in the anthropocene age.* Troyes, France: Paper presented at the proceedings of the 8th international conference on communities and technologies.

Linden, G., Smith, B., & York, J. (2003). Amazon. com recommendations: item-to-item collaborative filtering. *IEEE Internet computing, 1,* 76–80.

Lueg, C. (2002). On the gap between vision and feasibility. In *Lecture Notes in Computer Science (including subseries Lecture Notes in Artificial Intelligence and Lecture Notes in Bioinformatics), 2414,* 45–57. Springer Verlag. https://doi.org/10.1007/3-540-45866-2_5

Marques, F., Gonçalves, D., Barata, J., & Santana, P. (2017). *Human-Aware Navigation for Autonomous Mobile Robots for Intra-factory Logistics.* Paper presented at the international workshop on symbiotic interaction.

McNab, B. K. (1997). On the utility of uniformity in the definition of basal rate of metabolism. *Physiological Zoology, 70*(6), 718–720.

Mena, C., Adenso-Diaz, B., & Yurt, O. (2011). The causes of food waste in the supplier–retailer interface: evidences from the UK and Spain. *Resources, Conservation and Recycling, 55*(6), 648–658.

Mileham, R. (2016). Prime movers [transport drones]. *Engineering & Technology, 11*(4), 70–72.

Mortimer, G. (2015). Taste over waste: ugly food movement winning friends. *The Conversation.* Retrieved from https://theconversation.com/taste-over-waste-ugly-food-movement-winning-friends-38987

Neff, R. A., Spiker, M. L., & Truant, P. L. (2015). Wasted food: US consumers' reported awareness, attitudes, and behaviors. *PLoS One, 10*(6), e0127881.

Ng, K. H., Shipp, V., Mortier, R., Benford, S., Flintham, M., & Rodden, T. (2015). Understanding food consumption lifecycles using wearable cameras. *Personal and Ubiquitous Computing, 19*(7), 1183–1195.

NoFoodWasted. (2018). NoFoodWasted. Retrieved from www.nofoodwasted.com/

NOWASTE. (2017). No waste. Retrieved from www.nowasteapp.com/

OLIO. (2018). OLIO. Retrieved from https://olioex.com/

Olsson, T., Lagerstam, E., Kärkkäinen, T., & Väänänen-Vainio-Mattila, K. (2013). Expected user experience of mobile augmented reality services: a user study in the context of shopping centres. *Personal and Ubiquitous Computing, 17*(2), 287–304.

Osadchiy, T., Poliakov, I., Olivier, P., Rowland, M., & Foster, E. (2019). Recommender system based on pairwise association rules. *Expert Systems with Applications, 115,* 535–542.

Papargyropoulou, E., Lozano, R., Steinberger, J. K., Wright, N., & Bin Ujang, Z. (2014). The food waste hierarchy as a framework for the management of food surplus and food waste. *Journal of Cleaner Production, 76,* 106–115.

Parfitt, J., Barthel, M., & Macnaughton, S. (2010). Food waste within food supply chains: quantification and potential for change to 2050. *Philosophical Transactions of the Royal Society B: Biological Sciences, 365* (1554), 3065.

Park, S. Y., Kim, S., & Leifer, L. (2017). *"Human chef" to "computer chef": culinary interactions framework for understanding HCI in the food industry.* Paper presented at the international conference on human-computer interaction.

Piotrowicz, W., & Cuthbertson, R. (2014). Introduction to the special issue information technology in retail: toward omnichannel retailing. *International Journal of Electronic Commerce, 18*(4), 5–16.

Prentice, A. M., & Jebb, S. A. (2003). Fast foods, energy density and obesity: a possible mechanistic link. *Obesity reviews, 4*(4), 187–194.

Ramadan, Z. B., Farah, M. F., & Mrad, M. (2017). An adapted TPB approach to consumers' acceptance of service-delivery drones. *Technology Analysis & Strategic Management, 29*(7), 817–828.

Rothensee, M. (2007). A high-fidelity simulation of the smart fridge enabling product-based services.

Santana, P. (2018). *Human-aware navigation for autonomous mobile robots for intra-factory logistics.* Paper presented at the symbiotic interaction: 6th international workshop, symbiotic 2017, Eindhoven, The Netherlands, December 18–19, 2017, Revised Selected Papers.

Schmidt, C. (2015). Mental health: thinking from the gut. *Nature, 518*(7540), S12-S15.

Schneider, F. (2008). *Wasting food – an insistent behaviour.* Paper presented at the proceedings of waste - the social context, international conference, Edmonton, Alberta; Canada.

Schneider, F., & Obersteiner, G. (2007). *Food waste in residual waste of households–regional and socio-economic differences.* Cagliari, Italy: Paper presented at the proceedings sardinia, eleventh international waste management and landfill symposium.

Schwartz, Barry. 2004. *The paradox of choice: Why more is less.* New York: Ecco.

Shipp, V., Flintham, M., Mortier, R., Graf, B. A., Maqbool, M., & Parhizkar, B. (2013). *Understanding underutilisation: methods for studying fruit and vegetable buying behaviours.* Paper presented at the proceedings of the 2013 ACM conference on pervasive and ubiquitous computing adjunct publication.

Smil, V. (2004). Improving efficiency and reducing waste in our food system. *Environmental Sciences, 1*(1), 17–26.

Stevens, G., Bossauer, P., Neifer, T., & Hanschke, S. (2017). *Using shopping data to design sustainable consumer apps.* Paper presented at the 2017 Sustainable Internet and ICT for sustainability (SustainIT).

Tian, F. (2016). *An agri-food supply chain traceability system for China based on RFID & blockchain technology.* Paper presented at the Service Systems and Service Management (ICSSSM), 2016 13th International Conference on.

Tian, F. (2017). *A supply chain traceability system for food safety based on HACCP, blockchain & Internet of things.* Paper presented at the service systems and service management (ICSSSM), 2017 international conference on.

TooGoodToGo. (2018). Save delicious food and fight food waste. Retrieved from https://toogoodtogo.co.uk/en-gb/

Tsiros, M., & Heilman, C. M. (2005). The effect of expiration dates and perceived risk on purchasing behavior in grocery store perishable categories. *Journal of marketing, 69*(2), 114–129. https://doi.org/10.1509/jmkg.69.2.114.60762

Tucker, C. A., & Farrelly, T. (2016). Household food waste: the implications of consumer choice in food from purchase to disposal. *Local Environment, 21*(6), 682–706.

Vidgen, H. A., & Gallegos, D. (2010). Food literacy: time for a new term or just another buzzword? *Journal of the Home Economics Institute of Australia, 17*(2), 2–8.

Wei, Jun, Roshan Lalintha Peiris, Jeffrey Tzu Kwan Valino Koh, Xuan Wang, Yongsoon Choi, Xavier Roman Martinez, Remi Tache, Veronica Halupka, and Adrian David Cheok. "Food Media: exploring interactive entertainment over telepresent dinner." In *Proceedings of the 8th International Conference on Advances in Computer Entertainment Technology*, p. 26. ACM, 2011.

Williams, H., Wikström, F., Otterbring, T., Löfgren, M., & Gustafsson, A. (2012). Reasons for household food waste with special attention to packaging. *Journal of Cleaner Production, 24*, 141–148.

Winnow. (2018). Winnow solutions. Retrieved from www.winnowsolutions.com/

World Health Organization. 2003. *Diet, Nutrition, and the Prevention of Chronic Diseases: Report of a Joint WHO/FAO Expert Consultation* (Vol. 916). World Health Organization – Technical Report Series.

30

A BRIEF OVERVIEW OF CURRENT FOOD WASTE RESEARCH

The what, why, how and future directions

Jessica Aschemann-Witzel, Ezra Ho and Tammara Soma

Introduction

Over the past decade, food waste has risen in prominence within environmental research and policy circles. Although food waste is hardly an iconic environmental issue, it is deeply implicated and is connected with major environmental problems. Of the nine planetary boundaries – systems that sustain human and natural life on Earth – four have already exceeded natural limits (Steffen et al., 2015). And these four – biological diversity, biochemical flows, climate change, and land-use change – are all closely related to the contemporary food production system. Because food production is tightly coupled to energy and water consumption, not to mention associated with fertiliser inputs and carbon emissions, planetary sustainability can only be achieved through balancing the food-energy-water nexus (Kibler et al., 2018). A keyword search for 'food waste' in academic databases as well as the growing number of comprehensive reviews published on the matter in recent years reflect a rapidly growing interest in food waste research (Aschemann-Witzel et al., 2015; Block et al., 2016; de Steur et al., 2016; Schanes et al., 2018; Soma, 2018).

Indeed, the seminal 'Global Food Losses and Food Waste' report published by the Food and Agriculture Organization, and the much-cited fact of '1/3 of all food is wasted', have been common references in the literature (FAO, 2013). In 2015, through its Target 12.3, the United Nations explicitly mentioned the aim of halving food waste levels by 2030 as part of the Sustainable Development Goals (UN, 2015). This target has played an important role especially for policy makers and environmental organisations in underlining the strategic role of food waste research for achieving sustainability goals. In short, addressing food waste is increasingly recognised to be a key component of sustainable development.

In this chapter, we aim to provide a brief overview of food waste research, and discuss future directions in the field of food waste studies, with a focus on a call for more research in emerging economies (Soma & Lee, 2016). For new scholars entering this field, it is useful

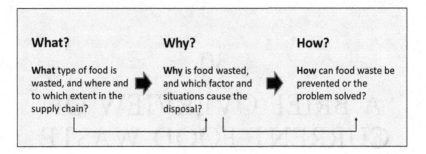

Figure 30.1 The what, why and how of current food waste research.

to recognise that while research on food waste is diverse, the research questions in food waste studies can be roughly categorised into studies questioning the '*what*', the '*why*', and the '*how*' (see Figure 30.1). We recognise that these categories tend to overlap across studies, and we use them for analytical and organisational purposes. Studies exploring the 'what' focus on how much and which food is wasted. Likewise, studies that examine the reasons and drivers of food waste address the 'why'. Last, studies addressing the 'how' present intervention studies that attempt to reduce food waste in experimental settings. In the following sections, we will further explore each stream of research.

First stream: the what?

This first stream of the literature aims to define and identify the problem of food waste, namely measuring the type of food that is wasted and where. Quantifying food waste is challenging not only because there are many different categories of food types – for which there are different loss figures due to the nature of particular food groups – but also because food waste can occur throughout the supply chain due to various reasons (Edjabou et al., 2016; Schmidt & Matthies, 2018). Moreover, studies also distinguish between food 'loss' and food 'waste', where the former is defined by the FAO (2014) to refer to any 'decrease in quantity or quality of food', and the latter is defined as food that is 'left to spoil or expire as a result of negligence by the actor (predominantly, but not exclusively, the final consumer)'. Although food waste quantification studies have grown exponentially, there is still no standardisation of methods. As a result, it is difficult to distinguish between food loss and food waste, leading to most studies aggregating such figures (See Bellemare et al., 2017; Xue et al., 2017 for thorough discussions).

It is important to note that the question of where food waste occurs is highly dependent on the operating context, which in turn affects the reason food is wasted or lost. It is generally accepted that in high-income, industrialised countries, upwards of 50% of food waste occurs at the household level (i.e. at the consumption and disposal stages) (Hall et al., 2009). In contrast, low-income countries tend to experience much of their food waste at the agricultural, post-harvest, processing, and transportation stages. Due to this difference, food waste studies in high-income countries tend to focus on the household or out-of-house locations such as restaurants or grocery stores (Betz et al., 2015; Cicatiello et al., 2017; Parizeau et al., 2015), while studies in low-income countries tend to examine the food waste at particular stages of the pre-consumption supply chain (Gangwar et al., 2014; Mwangi et al., 2017). However, several studies are starting to focus on consumer food waste in low-income countries, noting that the rise in middle-class population and supermarket revolution are changing food consumption patterns (Aschemann-Witzel et al., 2018, 2019; Lee & Soma, 2016; Soma, 2018).

In summary, we have a rough idea of where food waste occurs in different contexts. However, this understanding is obscured by a lack of standardised methodologies and poor data quality (Xue et al., 2017). Moreover, global coverage of food waste quantification is highly uneven, reflecting the inequalities in knowledge production (e.g. Abiad et al., 2018). Accordingly, the bulk of studies conducted in households are situated in the industrialised North, dominated by the US, UK, Australia, and Northern and Western European countries.

Second stream: the why?

The second stream of literature explores the causes of and reasons for the occurrence of food waste, namely, why food is wasted, and the factors and situations that cause disposal. Beyond identifying the extent and structure of the problem, this research stream generally focuses on the drivers of food loss and waste, and how actions at one point in the supply chain affect another stage, thus emphasising the interdependencies and interconnectivity of the food supply chain.

As noted in the first stream, the drivers of food waste are highly context dependent. Factors such as a country's level of economic development, regulations, state of food infrastructure, transportation, access to food storage and processing technologies, societal and cultural norms matter in how food is wasted (or not) (e.g. Chalak et al., 2016). In low-income countries, it is generally accepted that food waste mostly occurs in pre-consumption stages because of the lack of appropriate and effective technologies (Bahadur et al., 2016). For instance, a lack of agricultural technologies results in an inefficient processing of grains. Improper handling and defective packaging may lead to significant amounts of food being damaged. Furthermore, poor transportation and communications networks may impede farmers and distributors from transporting food to where there is demand, resulting in substantial food spoilage. For example, in a recent and preliminary estimation of food waste in Brazil, Dal'Magro and Talamini (2019) suggest that up to 43.7% of the national annual food supply was wasted or lost, much of it due to inappropriate handling, defective packaging or poor transportation conditions. On the consumer side, issues around culture, class and income can also be a driver in the power differential, which allows one group to determine what is food and what is waste (Soma, 2017).

In contrast, in high-income countries, the drivers of food waste are quite different given the bulk of studies focus on consumer and household dynamics. Moreover, depending on the assumptions underpinning a study (i.e. what can and should be studied), studies of household food waste can arrive at different rationales and drivers of food waste (Reynolds et al., 2019; Stancu et al., 2016). On one hand, studies informed by a psychological approach are based on the individual as the unit of analysis. These studies aim to quantify the influence of personal, cognitive, or socio-demographic factors on behaviour (Abdelradi, 2018; Graham-Rowe et al., 2014; Visschers et al., 2016). These studies are typically conducted within disciplines which share a positivist epistemology, such as psychology, economics and quantitative sociology. While quantifying behaviour factors around food waste may predict intention from factors such as income or commitment to environmental values, it does not necessarily predict the actual behaviour (Schanes et al., 2018). Nonetheless, such studies have informed us about how different segments of the population, whether by age, gender, class, or education, are likely to waste food (or not) (Delley & Brunner, 2017; Gaiani et al., 2018; Mallinson et al., 2016).

On the other hand, as opposed to the psychological approach which places the individual as the central unit of analysis and focuses interventions on improving consumer food literacy (see lovefoodhatewaste.ca; van der Werf et al., 2018; WRAP, 2008), a social practice approach widens the scope of analysis to consider the social context around how people consume and dispose of food. In such studies, the central unit of analysis becomes food-related practices, which refer to the everyday actions of purchasing, storing, cooking and disposing of food (Evans, 2011, 2014). In contrast to psychological approaches which establish contributing factors a priori, practice-based studies tend to adopt an open-ended research orientation and are typically conducted through the more interpretive subdisciplines of sociology, geography and anthropology (Cetina et al., 2005). Accordingly, a practice-based approach aims to identify the socially shared contexts, experiences and knowledge that influences particular actions leading to food waste outcomes. For instance, the proliferation of freezers in modern homes has allowed households to store a greater amount of food. However, due to the rapid pace of urban lifestyles, household routines tend to be guided more by improvisation rather than planning, leading to a mismatch between food acquisition and consumption (Hebrok & Heidenstrøm, 2019; Romani et al., 2018). As a result, households, for example, tend to accumulate food until it turns bad or people decide it is unsafe to eat (van Boxstael et al., 2014; Watson & Meah, 2012). Similarly, a focus on marketing *practice* shows how certain business decisions such as offering bulk discounts or maintaining high aesthetics standards for produce can lead to unnecessary food waste (de Hooge et al., 2018; Eriksson et al., 2017; Gruber et al., 2016). In summary, the drivers of food waste are multifaceted, and vary by context and according to disciplinary inquiry.

Third stream: the how?

Finally, the third stream of research focuses on interventions and on evaluating the effectiveness of initiatives to reduce food waste generation.

Given that food waste in global South countries occur in post-harvest stages of the supply chain, interventions have focused on addressing food loss and waste in and around the farm. On one level, the solution to food waste in global South countries can seem straightforward through the right application of technological fixes. Investments in appropriate agricultural technologies, and in transportation and telecommunications infrastructures would likely result in the efficiencies needed to avoid post-harvest food loss and wastage (Institute of Mechanical Engineers, 2013). For example, investments in low-tech measures such as bio-fuelled fruit dehydrators could reduce post-harvest loss due to decomposition (Hodges et al., 2011). Yet on another level, as Bahadur et al. (2016) caution, shoring up post-harvest technological deficiencies might not necessarily result in a reduction in overall food wastage, as low-income countries' food waste problems come to resemble food waste patterns in the global North. Moreover, it is also important to place efforts to combat food waste in the context of other policy priorities in low-income countries, such as enhancing food security, economic (re)structuring, or social welfare. In an environment characterised by competing priorities and poor governance, food waste interventions need to synergise well with other socio-economic objectives. For instance, to improve economic opportunities while reducing food waste, scholars and policy makers might want to explore opportunities for better investment in low-cost and low-tech processing infrastructure. This can take the form of value – food waste into inputs for food additives and products to alleviate food poverty (Torres-Leon et al., 2018), or the (re)organisation of municipal waste management systems to provide employment opportunities for the informal sector (Hettiarachchi et al., 2018).

In the case of high-income countries, efforts have largely focused on influencing consumer behaviour to reduce food waste. Despite the philosophical differences between psychological and practice-based approaches to understanding food waste, interventions tend to appear more similar than different from each other, and this might be due to the practical-ities of organising the funding, the logistics of organising such interventions, and the import-ance of holistic approaches in combating food waste. Shifting consumer behaviour by providing more information is still the mainstay of interventions, with campaigns seeking to inform people about the social, economic and environmental costs of wasting food (Bernstad et al., 2013). Other campaigns seek to provide consumers with the knowledge to employ more appropriate storage or food planning practices, in effect tackling confusion over best-before dates and perceptions of health risks that feature prominently in practice-based studies (Hebrok & Heidenstrøm, 2019; Schmidt & Matthies, 2018). Likewise, both psychological and practice-based approaches acknowledge the role of contextual factors, and attempt to modify them. What practice-based approaches identify as socially shared ideas and infrastruc-tures around food-related practices (provisioning, storage, cooking and consumption), psy-chological approaches refer to as 'choice architectures', for instance in the retail environment, that are amenable to interventions through 'nudging' (Jaeger et al., 2018; Kall-bekken & Sælen, 2013).

However, although much ink has been spilled investigating and understanding consumer food waste behaviour, surprisingly little work has been done on conducting intervention studies and evaluating them. In Reynold et al.'s (2019) review on consumption-stage inter-ventions between 2006–2017, of the 304 food waste studies identified, only 17 featured interventions of some sort. Of these, the most successful ones involved initiatives that relied on technical/technological interventions such as a reduction in portion or plate size, policy changes such as modifying dietary guidelines, and information provision campaigns. Even then, they argue that most intervention studies suffer from poor design, small sample sizes, and lack of theoretical rigour, concluding that 'there is a lack of research surrounding inter-ventions designed to reduce the amount of food waste generated, and a lack of evidence of the ease with which it is possible to scale up previous smaller interventions' (23). For instance, most interventions are short-term and tend to rely heavily on self-reported methods. This makes it hard to ascertain a strong causality between the intervention and any reported reductions in food waste.

In summary, interventions to reduce food waste occur throughout the supply chain. While such measures tend to rely on technological innovation, it is important to bear in mind that there is no one-size-fits-all approach, and that interventions need to be tailored to the operating context. In fact, as noted by Gille (2012, 27), 'food waste solutions that are limited to innovation in a few sites or countries will likely exacerbate existing inequalities'. In many cases, although food waste is the focus, researchers should recognise the inevitabil-ity of working in an environment of multiple, competing priorities, and attempt to create win-win solutions that enhance systematic sustainability. Compared to the evidence base of understanding where and why food is wasted, our knowledge of how to effectively reduce food waste is still limited. There need to be more concrete and measured efforts to establish what works to reduce food waste.

The future of food waste research

In the preceding sections, we have attempted to provide the reader with a brief overview of food waste research to highlight the breadth, complexity and interdisciplinary nature of the field. Although by no means exhaustive, this exercise in outlining the contours of current food waste research helps us to identify pathways from which to chart innovative directions for the field.

Perhaps the single, biggest weakness across the literature reviewed is the knowledge inequalities between global North and global South countries. As several other commentators have noted, food waste research reflects the dominance of global North societies not only in knowledge production, but also in the framing of the problem, the methodologies and in developing the solutions. Studies throughout the supply chain tend to focus on high-income countries (Reynolds et al., 2019; Xue et al., 2017). This imbalance may be because high-income countries are often easier and more convenient for researchers to work in, and because this is where many academics who have funding for research as well as training for and access to academic publishing, live and work. More importantly, this imbalance highlights potential issues within low-income countries to critically assess and evaluate their own food systems, especially taking into consideration their own cultural framework and context.

While there is a need to equalise food waste research between the global North and South, the rise of emerging economies – in particular the so-called BRICS grouping consisting of Brazil, Russia, India, China and South Africa – poses new and challenging questions for food waste research. Not only are these societies rapidly expanding in economic and political terms, but their development heralds distinctive patterns of food production, distribution and consumption that will have lasting implications for global food sustainability. As the special issue by McKay et al. (2016) notes, the rise of the BRICS economies, coupled with their growing engagement with middle-income countries has resulted in the reconfiguration of national and regional agrarian and agribusiness dynamics. Even as these new actors assert themselves on the regional and global stage, jostling with Northern centres of capital and expertise, it is unlikely they represent an entirely new paradigm of organising food systems. Large-scale production of commodities by corporate agribusinesses, vertically and horizontally integrated supply chains, consumer-facing supermarket chains, and convenience food suggest more continuities than disruptions to the global food system. In particular, the large-scale establishments of supermarkets as well as the introduction of more fast and convenience food in these emerging societies will have a significant impact on the socio-technical infrastructures underpinning the kinds of foods people have access to, and also influence how they store, consume, and waste it.

While it is tempting to assume the reproduction of the current system, we should be wary of such extrapolations. Even if affluence generally imposes a high resource cost, preliminary examinations of households in emerging societies are quite diverse and context matters. In a study of South African households from two different Johannesburg municipalities, Oelofse et al. (2018) found no statistically significant correlation between household incomes and food disposal levels. Moreover, these households were found to generate very low levels of food waste, averaging 5% of total household waste. Similarly, for the case of Indian households in Bhopal, while Pandey et al. (2018) show differences in practices of reuse and recycling according to income levels, they also show that households across income levels share similarity in how they divert food waste in productive ways, whereby kitchen waste is almost never thrown away, and is typically fed to animals. However, there are other studies posing the opposite. For example, Ramukhwatho et al. (2016) in a survey of 210 households in South Africa found that high-income households waste more food, especially staples such as porridge. In Indonesia, access to a particular type retail (for example, modern supermarkets) is income-related, and a study in Bogor, found that the correlation between higher income and a larger amount of food waste generation is statistically significant (Soma, 2019).

Although far from conclusive, such findings suggest that households in emerging societies possess a repertoire of knowledge, skills and material resources that enable them to manage their food resources and waste in sustainable ways or through patterns of consumption that promote 'buy today eat today' (Soma, 2018). While possibly counterintuitive, such findings highlight how inequalities in knowledge production can prejudice our interpretations. As Henrich et al. (2010) argue, the greater share of the current studies on human psychology and behaviour reflect an extremely small segment of the world. Such studies typically draw samples from populations in Western, Educated, Industrialised, Rich, and Democratic (WEIRD) countries, and when compared to non-WEIRD populations, show high variability in cognitive traits such as perception, motivation, categorisation and reasoning styles. In short, what we commonly understand to be fundamental assumptions around behaviour *should not* be assumed to be the default. In the context of understanding food waste in emerging contexts, we need to be cautious of importing very basic assumptions around how things work, and what will work. What remains to be seen is how these food practices will evolve as the socio-technical fabrics of these societies modernise, transforming everyday life. Given the rapid development of these emerging countries, food waste researchers need not only to develop a robust evidence base, but also to engage with policy and development networks to pre-empt being locked into unsustainable trajectories for food systems.

Conclusion

Finally, we hope to suggest a novel direction for food waste studies. While our brief overview of food waste literature has highlighted the multidisciplinary nature of food waste research, we feel that even more cross-disciplinary and cross-cultural engagements are needed to address future challenges. In studies of Western households, one constant theme in the realm of policy interventions has been the focus on individual consumers as a unit analysis. Therefore, with regard to reducing food waste, recommendations have revolved around improving food literacy and raising awareness on how to better purchase, cook, manage and store food. Examples include improving culinary knowledge that would enable individuals to make more productive use of leftovers. Culinary knowledge and practices are also implicated in the need for temporal flexibility as households navigate the tensions between procuring and consuming foodstuffs they can use on short notice. Given that knowledge of and around food preparation is profoundly social and cultural, it is surprising that there has been little exploration of its relevance in food waste interventions (with the exception of Soma, 2017). On a basic level, cultivating a versatile repertoire of culinary practices would leverage and enhance households' existing abilities to maximise productive use of food. On a deeper level, engagement with culinary practice could piggyback on the growing popularity of 'slow' and 'mindful' living found in contemporary Western cultures, and hopefully contribute as another counterbalance against the rapid societal rhythms that have an impact on environmental degradation and resource exploitation (for a spiritual perspective on tackling food waste see Chapter 3 by Yoreh and Scharper). Moreover, any cross-cultural introduction or comparison of culinary practices would be relatively acceptable given that exposure to multicultural cuisines have become part of everyday life in Western metropoles. To conclude, what this conversation means for the what, the why and the how of food waste research is that food waste studies scholars will increasingly rely on multidisciplinarity and incorporate multicultural perspectives to address this global and systemic issue. Doing so will expand the repertoire of possible solutions and the framing of the problem.

References

Abdelradi, F. (2018). Food waste behaviour at the household level: A conceptual framework. *Waste Management*, 71, 485–493.

Abiad, M. G., & Meho, L. I. (2018). Food loss and food waste research in the Arab world: A systematic review. *Food Security*, 10(2), 311–322.

Aschemann-Witzel, J., De Hooge, I., Amani, P., Bech-Larsen, T., & Oostindjer, M. (2015). Consumer-related food waste: Causes and potential for action. *Sustainability*, 7(6), 6457–6477.

Aschemann-Witzel, J., Giménez, A., & Ares, G. (2018). Convenience or price orientation? Consumer characteristics influencing food waste behaviour in the context of an emerging country and the impact on future sustainability of the global food sector. *Global Environmental Change*, 49, 85–94.

Aschemann-Witzel, J., Giménez, A., Ares, G. (2019). Household food waste and the reasons why: Consumer's own accounts and how it differs for target groups. *Resources, Conservation and Recycling*, 145, 332–338.

Bahadur, K C. K., Haque, I., Legwegoh, A., & Fraser, E. (2016). Strategies to reduce food loss in the global South. *Sustainability*, 8(7), 595.

Bellemare, M. F., Çakir, M., Peterson, H. H., Novak, L., & Rudi, J. (2017). On the measurement of food waste. *American Journal of Agricultural Economics*, 99(5), 1148–1158.

Bernstad, A., la Cour Jansen, J., & Aspegren, A. (2013). Door-stepping as a strategy for improved food waste recycling behaviour–Evaluation of a full-scale experiment. *Resources, Conservation and Recycling*, 73, 94–103.

Betz, A., Buchli, J., Göbel, C., & Müller, C. (2015). Food waste in the Swiss food service industry–Magnitude and potential for reduction. *Waste Management*, 35, 218–226.

Block, L. G., Keller, P. A., Vallen, B., Williamson, S., Birau, M. M., Grinstein, A., Haws, K. L., LaBarge, M. C., Lamberton, C., Moore, E. S., & Moscato, E. M. (2016). The squander sequence: Understanding food waste at each stage of the consumer decision-making process. *Journal of Public Policy & Marketing*, 35(2), 292–304.

Cetina, K. K., Schatzki, T. R., & von Savigny, E. (eds.). (2005). *The Practice Turn in Contemporary Theory*. London and New York: Routledge.

Chalak, A., Abou-Daher, C., Chaaban, J., & Abiad, M. G. (2016). The global economic and regulatory determinants of household food waste generation: A cross-country analysis. *Waste Management*, 48, 418–422.

Cicatiello, C., Franco, S., Pancino, B., Blasi, E., & Falasconi, L. (2017). The dark side of retail food waste: Evidences from in-store data. *Resources, Conservation and Recycling*, 125, 273–281.

Dal'Magro, G. P., & Talamini, E. (2019). Estimating the magnitude of the food loss and waste generated in Brazil. *Waste Management & Research*, 37 (7), 706-716, 0734242X19836710.

de Hooge, I. E., van Dulm, E., & van Trijp, H. C. (2018). Cosmetic specifications in the food waste issue: Supply chain considerations and practices concerning suboptimal food products. *Journal of Cleaner Production*, 183, 698–709.

de Steur, H., Wesana, J., Dora, M. K., Pearce, D., & Gellynck, X. (2016). Applying value stream mapping to reduce food losses and wastes in supply chains: A systematic review. *Waste Management*, 58, 359–368.

Delley, M., & Brunner, T. A. (2017). Foodwaste within Swiss households: A segmentation of the population and suggestions for preventive measures. *Resources, Conservation and Recycling*, 122, 172–184.

Edjabou, M. E., Petersen, C., Scheutz, C., & Astrup, T. F. (2016). Food waste from Danish households: Generation and composition. *Waste Management*, 52, 256–268.

Eriksson, M., Ghosh, R., Mattsson, L., & Ismatov, A. (2017). Take-back agreements in the perspective of food waste generation at the supplier-retailer interface. *Resources, Conservation and Recycling*, 122, 83–93.

Evans, D. (2011). Blaming the consumer–once again: The social and material contexts of everyday food waste practices in some English households. *Critical Public Health*, 21(4), 429–440.

Evans, D. (2014). *Food Waste: Home Consumption, Material Culture and Everyday Life*. London and New York: Bloomsbury Publishing.

FAO. (2013). *Food Wastage Footprint: Impacts on Natural Resources - Summary Report*. Rome, Italy: Food and Agricultural Organisation. FAO.

FAO. (2014). *Definitional framework of food loss*. Rome, Italy: Food and Agricultural Organisation. FAO.

Gaiani, S., Caldeira, S., Adorno, V., Segrè, A., & Vittuari, M. (2018). Food wasters: Profiling consumers' attitude to waste food in Italy. *Waste Management*, 72, 17–24.

Gangwar, R. K., Tyagi, S., Kumar, V., Singh, K., & Singh, G. (2014). Food production and post harvest losses of food grains in India. *Food Science and Quality Management*, 31, 48–52.

Gille, Z. (2012). From risk to waste: global food waste regimes. *The Sociological Review*, 60, 27–46.

Graham-Rowe, E., Jessop, D. C., & Sparks, P. (2014). Identifying motivations and barriers to minimising household food waste. *Resources, Conservation and Recycling*, 84, 15–23.

Gruber, V., Holweg, C., & Teller, C. (2016). What a waste! Exploring the human reality of food waste from the store manager's perspective. *Journal of Public Policy & Marketing*, 35(1), 3–25.

Hall, K. D., Guo, J., Dore, M., & Chow, C. C. (2009). The progressive increase of food waste in America and its environmental impact. *PloS One*, 4(11), e7940.

Hebrok, M., & Heidenstrøm, N. (2019). Contextualising food waste prevention-Decisive moments within everyday practices. *Journal of Cleaner Production*, 210, 1435–1448.

Henrich, J., Heine, S. J., & Norenzayan, A. (2010). The weirdest people in the world? *Behavioral and Brain Sciences*, 33(2–3), 61–83.

Hettiarachchi, H., Meegoda, J., & Ryu, S. (2018). Organic waste buyback as a viable method to enhance sustainable municipal solid waste management in developing countries. *International Journal of Environmental Research and Public Health*, 15(11), 2483.

Hodges, R. J., Buzby, J. C., & Bennett, B. (2011). Postharvest losses and waste in developed and less developed countries: opportunities to improve resource use. *The Journal of Agricultural Science*, 149 (S1), 37–45.

Institute of Mechanical Engineers. (2013). Global food: Waste not, want not. London: Institute of Mechanical Engineers. Retrieved from: www.imeche.org/docs/default-source/reports/Global_Food_Report.pdf?sfvrsn=0.

Jaeger, S. R., Machín, L., Aschemann-Witzel, J., Antúnez, L., Harker, F. R., & Ares, G. (2018). Buy, eat or discard? A case study with apples to explore fruit quality perception and food waste. *Food Quality and Preference*, 69, 10–20.

Kallbekken, S., & Sælen, H. (2013). 'Nudging' hotel guests to reduce food waste as a win–win environmental measure. *Economics Letters*, 119(3), 325–327.

Kibler, K. M., Reinhart, D., Hawkins, C., Motlagh, A. M., & Wright, J. (2018). Food waste and the food-energy-water nexus: A review of food waste management alternatives. *Waste Management*, 74, 52–62.

Lee, K. and Soma, T. (2016) From 'farm to table' to 'farm to dump': emerging research on household food waste in the global south, in Anderson, C., Brady, J. and Levkoe, C. (eds.) *Conversation in Food Studies*, 243–266. Winnipeg: University of Manitoba Press.

Mallinson, L. J., Russell, J. M., & Barker, M. E. (2016). Attitudes and behaviour towards convenience food and food waste in the United Kingdom. *Appetite*, 103, 17–28.

McKay, B. M., Hall, R., & Liu, J. (2016). The rise of BRICS: Implications for global agrarian transformation. *Third World Thematics: A TWQ Journal*, 1(5), 581–591.

Mwangi, J. K., Mutungi, C. M., Midingoyi, S. K. G., Faraj, A. K., & Affognon, H. D. (2017). An assessment of the magnitudes and factors associated with postharvest losses in off-farm grain stores in Kenya. *Journal of Stored Products Research*, 73, 7–20.

Oelofse, S., Muswema, A., & Ramukhwatho, F. (2018). Household food waste disposal in South Africa: A case study of Johannesburg and Ekurhuleni. *South African Journal of Science*, 114(5–6), 1–6.

Pandey, R. U., Surjan, A., & Kapshe, M. (2018). Exploring linkages between sustainable consumption and prevailing green practices in reuse and recycling of household waste: Case of Bhopal city in India. *Journal of Cleaner Production*, 173, 49–59.

Parizeau, K., von Massow, M., & Martin, R. (2015). Household-level dynamics of food waste production and related beliefs, attitudes, and behaviours in Guelph, Ontario. *Waste Management*, 35, 207–217.

Ramukhwatho, F. R., Du Plessis, R., & Oelofse, S. H. (2016). Household food wastage by income level: A case study of five areas in the city of Tshwane Metropolitan Municipality, Gauteng Province, South Africa. *Proceedings of the 23rd WasteCon Conference* 17-21 October 2016, Johannesburg, South Africa.

Reynolds, C., Goucher, L., Quested, T., Bromley, S., Gillick, S., Wells, V. K., Evans, E., Koh, L., Kanyama, A. C., Katzeff, C., Svenfelt, Å., & Jackson, P. (2019). Consumption-stage food waste reduction interventions-What works and how to design better interventions. *Food Policy*, 83, 7–27.

Romani, S., Grappi, S., Bagozzi, R. P., & Barone, A. M. (2018). Domestic food practices: A study of food management behaviors and the role of food preparation planning in reducing waste. *Appetite*, 121, 215–227.

Schanes, K., Dobernig, K., & Gözet, B. (2018). Food waste matters- A systematic review of household food waste practices and their policy implications. *Journal of Cleaner Production*, 182, 978–991.

Schmidt, K., & Matthies, E. (2018). Where to start fighting the food waste problem? Identifying most promising entry points for intervention programs to reduce household food waste and overconsumption of food. *Resources, Conservation and Recycling*, 139, 1–14.

Soma, T. (2017). Gifting, ridding and the "everyday mundane": The role of class and privilege in food waste generation in Indonesia. *Local Environment*, 22(12), 1444–1460.

Soma, T. (2018). (Re) framing the food waste narrative: Infrastructures of urban food consumption and waste in Indonesia. *Indonesia*, April (105), 173–190.

Soma, T. (2019). Space to waste: The influence of income and retail choice on household food consumption and food waste in Indonesia. *International Planning Studies*. 10.1080/13563475.2019.1626222.

Stancu, V., Haugaard, P., & Lähteenmäki, L. (2016). Determinants of consumer food waste behaviour: Two routes to food waste. *Appetite*, 96, 7–17.

Steffen, W., Richardson, K., Rockström, J., Cornell, S. E., Fetzer, I., Bennett, E. M., Biggs, R., Carpenter, S. R., De Vries, W., De Wit, C. A., & Folke, C.(2015). Planetary boundaries: Guiding human development on a changing planet. *Science*, 347(6223), 1259855.

Torres-Leon, C., Ramirez, N., Londoño, L., Martinez, G., Diaz, R., Navarro-Macias, V., Alvarez-Pérez, O. B., Picazo, B., Villarreal-Vázquez, M., Ascacio-Valdes, J., & Aguilar, C. N. (2018). Food waste and byproducts: An opportunity to minimize malnutrition and hunger in developing countries. *Frontiers in Sustainable Food Systems*, 2, 1–17.

UN. (2015). Sustainable developments goals: Goal 12: Ensure sustainable consumption and production patterns. United Nations.

van Boxstael, S., Devlieghere, F., Berkvens, D., Vermeulen, A., & Uyttendaele, M. (2014). Understanding and attitude regarding the shelf life labels and dates on pre-packed food products by Belgian consumers. *Food Control*, 37, 85–92.

van der Werf, P., Seabrook, J. A., & Gilliland, J. A. (2018). Food for naught: Using the theory of planned behaviour to better understand household food wasting behaviour. *The Canadian Geographer/Le Géographe canadien,* 63(3), 478–493.

Visschers, V. H., Wickli, N., & Siegrist, M. (2016). Sorting out food waste behaviour: A survey on the motivators and barriers of self-reported amounts of food waste in households. *Journal of Environmental Psychology*, 45, 66–78.

Watson, M., & Meah, A. (2012). Food, waste and safety: Negotiating conflicting social anxieties into the practices of domestic provisioning. *The Sociological Review*, 60, 102–120.

WRAP. (2008). The food we waste. Banbury, UK: Waste and Resources Action Programme (WRAP).

Xue, L., Liu, G., Parfitt, J., Liu, X., Van Herpen, E., Stenmarck, Å., O'Connor, C., Östergren, K. & Cheng, S. (2017). Missing food, missing data? A critical review of global food losses and food waste data. *Environmental Science & Technology*, 51(12), 6618–6633.

31

CHALLENGING HEGEMONIC CONCEPTIONS OF FOOD WASTE

Critical reflections from a food waste activist

Martin Bowman

Food waste is a rare example of an environmental issue that apparently unites people across the political spectrum. In order to build public consciousness and influence those in power, it has made strategic sense for the food waste movement to cultivate a relatively depoliticised image. It is a tribute to its success that food waste as an issue has now been taken up by organisations ranging from the United Nations and the World Bank to Tesco. Widespread public awareness and networks of food waste organisations have also been built.

However, as powerful actors become involved, they are creating and entrenching certain ideological framings of the food waste problem and its solutions. We are at a critical juncture where rules are beginning to be fought over and laid down, which will lock in approaches to dealing with food waste long into the future – such as reduction targets, regulation, subsidies and voluntary frameworks. While public engagement in the issue is high, it is vital that food waste campaigners harness this energy to push for progressive policies. To do this, they must: (1) develop a clear critique of why dominant conceptions of food waste and its solutions are sometimes ineffective or regressive, (2) articulate clear progressive alternatives and solutions, and (3) have a clear strategy for influencing high-level political decisions to achieve these alternative pathways. This chapter provides a sketch of how to achieve this, first exploring how hegemonic conceptions of food waste conceal deeper causes of food waste rooted in capitalism, neoliberalism and colonialism, and positing counter-hegemonic narratives that can be used to open up new transformist visions for a more just society, within ecological limits.

Core to this chapter is the notion of hegemony – which, in the tradition of Gramsci (1992), I use to mean the political power exercised by one group over others, closely associated with the dominance of certain ideas which powerful groups promote as 'common sense' to perpetuate the consent of general society to the neoliberal capitalist systems that sustain those power relations. I critique both capitalism and its neoliberal form, which promotes free-market competition, minimal state control or regulation beyond facilitation of markets, and prioritising the market as the primary, efficient allocator of resources.[1]

This chapter is rooted in my experience of working for environmental organisations Feedback and This Is Rubbish on various food waste campaigns. The campaigning styles of these organisations has ranged from research, to lobbying governments, to petitions, to meeting with businesses, to generating media scandals and more. These approaches offer many lessons for strategic engagement with power to leverage enduring policy changes. However, this chapter also aims to map out how future food waste activism could develop beyond what previous approaches have attempted, through grappling with the hegemonic conceptions underpinning certain 'solutions'. The urgency of the crises of climate change and global inequality demand that we raise our ambition – this chapter is intended as a rallying call to food waste activists (myself included) to rise to that challenge. First, I explore how the binary conception of food 'loss vs. waste' eclipses power relations that activists must challenge.

'Food loss' vs. 'food waste': eclipsing power relations

The FAO distinguishes between 'food losses' which occur at the 'production, postharvest and processing stages in the food supply chain', and 'food waste' which occurs at retailer and consumer level (FAO, 2011). Sustainable Development Goal (SDG) 12.3 reporting is separated into the FAO's Food Loss Index[2] and UN Environment's Food Waste Index (FAO, 2019). The EU's frameworks, such as the Platform on Food Losses and Food Waste, and the wording of the revised Waste Framework Directive repeat the loss/waste distinction (EU, 2018). Numerous reports repeat the narrative of food loss vs. waste even if they do not use the terms – for instance, Project Drawdown states that in low-income countries wastage is 'generally unintentional' at earlier stages of the supply chain, whereas in rich countries, 'wilful food waste' occurs mainly at retailer and consumer level (Project Drawdown, 2017, np).

In this narrative, developing countries experience primarily food loss as a result of poor technical infrastructure (Venkat, 2011), and developed countries primarily experience food waste because of wasteful consumer habits. This is highly misleading. Retail food waste is usually small in rich nations compared to food waste in other businesses – for instance, only 0.26 million tonnes of UK food waste occurs at retail compared to 1.85 million tonnes in manufacturing (WRAP, 2018) and an estimated 2.5 million tonnes at primary production (Quinn, 2017b). Also, food waste occurring prior to retail is often roughly equivalent or larger than consumer food waste in rich countries – between 30% (FUSIONS, 2016) and 54% (STOA, 2013) of the EU's food waste occurs before retail. I thus use the term food waste throughout this chapter to refer to all food that is used below its environmental and social potential, wherever it occurs in the supply chain.

Disastrously, the distinction has become increasingly embedded in international efforts to tackle food waste – often through SDG 12.3: 'By 2030, halve per capita global food waste at the retail and consumer levels and reduce food losses along production and supply chains, including post-harvest losses' (UN, 2016). This sets a specific target for halving food waste but only vague reduction for food loss. Champions 12.3, a group of global leaders set up to drive progress toward SDG 12.3, recommends that countries should apply the 'halve per capita' target to food losses too – and this should cover 'from the point that crops and livestock are ready for harvest or slaughter' (Hanson, 2017). This recommendation should be actively championed by activists, as otherwise it may be overlooked by governments. The distinction also implies that supply chain 'losses' are not caused by human socio-economic arrangements, such as power imbalances in the supply chain, which would require not just technical solutions but institutional and systemic changes (Gille, 2013). Drivers of food waste such as poor refrigeration and storage are replaced by other problems in rich countries, causing comparable levels of pre-retail food waste (FAO, 2011).

These problems are mainly driven by power relations across supply chains – as studies by environmental charity Feedback have found. A Feedback survey of UK farmers (Bowman, 2018) found that respondents often reported overproducing because there was pressure to always meet buyer orders, or risk losing contracts. This often leads to greater price volatility – gluts of produce lead to price crashes, and farmers plough produce back in as it becomes uneconomical to harvest. Many respondents experienced cosmetic outgrading – one producer interviewed was wasting 25% of their carrots, 21 million portions of produce per year, mainly on cosmetic grounds. Many believed that retailers had influenced consumers to be fussy over appearance, and that supermarket dominance of UK retail had led to fewer outlets for lower grade produce. The survey also found that retailers and middlemen often use cosmetic rejections as a way to cancel orders, raising standards in times of glut or lower demand to regulate supply. Respondents experienced other Unfair Trading Practices (UTPs) including order cancellations from retailers unpredictably switching suppliers in search of the cheapest offer. The Groceries Code Adjudicator, the UK's regulator of UTPs, found evidence that UTPs cause widespread food waste (Quinn, 2017a). Gille (2013) also argues that costs and risks are externalised onto farmers by their buyers, citing Clapp (1994) who similarly found quality standards were tightened by contracting companies during overproduction. Through these methods supermarkets ensure a reliable stream of produce of the highest grade possible, relatively insulated from price fluctuations. Successful campaigning from European NGOs including Feedback helped lead to the EU agreeing new UTP legislation in 2018 (Wills, 2019), which will go some way to protecting producers (including those exporting to the EU), but more needs to be done.

Feedback's investigations into farmers in the global South exporting to Europe found similar power dynamics, including last-minute order cancellations and flexing cosmetic standards (Colbert, 2017). For instance, Peruvian citrus fruit producers reported that often they experienced a 50% exportability rate for tangelo oranges, mostly for cosmetic reasons. Fruits rejected from export were then often dumped domestically, depressing prices and often forcing farmers to bury 10–40% of total production. This represents a huge loss of money, time and resources. Small-scale producers tend to be excluded from supplying supermarkets because they lack the 'infrastructure, technology, financing and institutional support needed' to comply with their 'increasingly stringent quality-control and certification standards' (UNI Global Union, 2012, p. 14). Complying with these standards often demands upscaling to industrial agricultural practices reliant on inputs such as industrial fertilisers, which prioritise short-term productivity over long-term sustainability (Gascón, 2018).

The food 'loss' versus 'waste' binary is a hegemonic narrative that eclipses these power relations and transformative solutions to them, deflecting focus onto consumer behaviour change in the global North and enabling companies to expand into lucrative markets in the global South (as purported saviours of technical food loss issues). Large and rapidly growing consumer markets such as India and China are major targets of expansion for supermarkets and global agribusiness – food waste reduction is a valuable tool to leverage entry. For instance, when the Indian parliament was discussing whether to lift restrictions on Foreign Direct Investment in retail in 2010–11, Carrefour submitted recommendations, claiming they would modernise Indian supply chains to reduce food waste (Antony and Macaskill,

2011). Appeals to increase efficiency and reduce wastefulness have historically been used to draw land into industrial agriculture and commodify food systems. For instance, Locke's theory of 'wastelands', which argued that unenclosed commons constitute waste because they are unproductive compared to cultivated land, was pivotal in justifying primitive accumulation – violent colonial expropriation of land in the colonies to convert it into privately owned cultivated land (Gidwani and Reddy, 2011).

Some food waste *does* occur in the global South due to lack of storage and infrastructure – but the role of wealthy nations' exploitation of poorer countries in creating (and perpetuating) this situation is often overlooked. Economic growth and the political dominance of Europe and the US depended on colonialism. Involving millions of hours of slave labour exploited, land used to produce food and resources in the colonies freed up labour power domestically for industrial pursuits (Pomeranz, 2001). Colonies were devastated – for instance, India experienced no increase in per capita income under colonial rule between 1757–1947, and from 1872–1921 the average life expectancy of Indians fell by 20% (Davis, 2002). Post-colonial exploitation is ongoing. In 2012, developing countries received just over $2 trillion, including aid, investment and income from abroad, but $5 trillion flowed out of the developing world to rich countries – a net $3 trillion outflow, 24 times the size of the global annual aid budget (Hickel, 2017). This is a combination of debt repayments, repatriated profits, intellectual property rights payments and capital flight.[3]

Money draining from the global South has eroded nations' capacity to invest in vital infrastructure to prevent food wastage – and this situation will only be reversed once structural problems are fixed. This will require the global food waste movement to ally with broader struggles – such as to cancel poor country debts, clamp down on capital flight and close tax havens, end loans conditional on damaging neoliberal reforms, stop arms sales to oppressive regimes and end unequal exchange.[4] Liberalising markets to allow greater access to multinational corporations has historically often entrenched uneven development and capital flight. Growing export-oriented crops rather than prioritising local nutritional needs is partially a legacy of colonialism, and partially perpetuated more recently by Structural Adjustment Programmes and free trade agreements which bind the global South into pursuing their 'comparative advantage' and producing raw materials such as export-oriented cash crops (Klein, 2008), locking them into declining terms of trade and highly unequal power relationships that generate risks of waste.

These forms of exploitation and colonialism have long been underpinned by capitalist crises of overproduction and underconsumption, as explained by Marx (1965) and Harvey (1985, 2018).[5] Capitalist crises partially manifest in the overproduction of food, leading to the destruction of food surpluses alongside underconsumption, i.e. 'food poverty' (O'Brien, 2013). When farmers plough food back into the soil because it is uneconomical to harvest, this is in part because demand has been depressed by low wages which render poorer workers (and the unemployed) unable to afford food at an economical price. Such food insecurity is often hegemonically understood as individuals' personal failings and/or laziness, rather than structurally driven. Simultaneously, capitalists escape squeezes on profits by exerting downward pressure on the wages of food industry workers – the cost to US taxpayers of Walmart workers relying on public assistance programmes due to low wages is estimated at $6.2 billion (Americans for Tax Fairness, 2014). Supermarkets can pass some of the pressures of tight profit margins onto their suppliers through the mechanisms described previously, with many farms relying on cheap migrant labour and subsidies to survive.

When the rate of profit in the productive economy declines, excess money floods into speculative trading and real estate instead in search of higher returns, or demand is artificially boosted through encouraging debt – as happened in the 2008 financial crash. Speculation is risky short-term trading based on predicted market price fluctuations (Soederberg, 2004). Due to weakened regulation of commodities markets, during the early 2000s speculators came to hold the majority of long contracts for commodities like wheat and soy, causing prices to trade at substantially higher prices than if based on supply and demand alone (Jones, 2010). This led to significant price volatility and speculative bubbles – manifesting in widespread hunger and food riots in 2008. Despite this, the EU's recent regulations to restrict food derivatives trading have been weakened (Chow, 2017).

A fertile area of research would be to study the effect such commodity speculation has on food waste; how during price bubbles, artificially expensive food might fail to reach people who need it and be destroyed, and price crashes could mean food is not economically viable to harvest. Clapp and Isakson (2018) analyse the negative role financialisation and speculative trading has played with food. Meanwhile, countries or regional alliances may sometimes collude to escape crises of overaccumulation by transferring negative effects to other countries via economic policies, a key driver of colonialism and defined by Harvey (1985) as 'spatial fixes'. For instance, subsidies to farmers in the global North keep food prices lower, mitigating domestic hunger and political unrest, and keeping more farmers in business. This shifts the problem to the global South, where loans conditional on neoliberal reforms have left farmers with minimal protection against cheap imports, causing millions of small-scale farmers to be displaced into slums (Weis, 2007). This section has explored the historical roots of how capitalist drives for profit and growth have driven colonialism and exploitation that continue to the present. The next section links these drivers of food waste to the pressing challenges of today's environmental crises.

Food waste and the urgency of climate crisis

Urgent action is needed to fight climate change. The COP21 summit in 2015 agreed to limit climate change to 1.5 °C of warming. However, this goal depends on 'Nationally Determined Contributions' – and the total of these voluntary pledges currently puts us on course for about 3–3.2 °C *if* the pledges are met (UNEP, 2019). Climate change resulting in a 4 °C rise would be extremely dangerous: some regions could be 15 °C warmer (Martinez, 2017), and yields could collapse for many crops, causing widespread hunger (World Bank, 2012). High temperatures are likely to increase food spoilage and more unpredictable weather will likely increase waste from volatility and hedging against it.[6]

The Jevons Paradox and notion of rebound effects shed some light on why emissions reductions are so challenging. First advanced by English economist William Stanley Jevons in the nineteenth century, the Jevons Paradox states that 'in a capitalist system, growth of efficiency normally leads to an increase in scale of the economy … more than negating any ecological gains made' (Foster et al., 2010, p. 105). For instance, Jevons observed that improved efficiencies in the use of coal led its price to drop, attracted more investment and increased demand (Jevons, 1866). Thus, paradoxically, greater efficiency in resource use often leads to *increased* consumption of resources.

The 'rebound effect' is a less extreme version of this effect, where the negative impacts on overall resource consumption growth arising from efficiency only partially offset efficiency savings. Any reductions in food waste are likely to save someone money, which can either be saved – and must find profitable investment in further production or depreciate in value – or spent on consumption. For instance, a family may save money by wasting less food, and spend it on a holiday flight, or save it in a pension fund that invests in fossil fuels.

Or a food business reducing food waste might invest the saved money in expanding production or diversifying into livestock. Salemdeeb et al. (2017) found that this rebound effect may reduce greenhouse gas (GHG) savings per tonne of household food waste saved by up to 60%. WRAP (2009) found that the rebound effect could reduce potential emissions savings from food waste reduction by up to half. Overall GDP growth provides a structural driver for rebound effects, offsetting sectoral emissions savings. Hickel and Kallis (2019) demonstrate that the strong link between GDP growth and emissions growth has never historically been decoupled at the speed needed to achieve the emissions reductions necessary to keep us even below 1.5 °C warming – which needs to be roughly 12% per year for rich countries. Despite driving environmental crises, GDP growth is currently not successfully alleviating global poverty. Just 5% of all new income generated since 1990 went to the poorest 60% of humanity – at this rate, to ensure every person earns above $5/day would take over 200 years, and the global economy would have to grow to 175 times its present size (Woodward, 2015), impossible within environmental limits.

Marx argued that nature and labour are the parents of 'use value' (intrinsic usefulness) and in the attempt to convert them into exchange value (monetary worth), capitalism often exploits them, undermining its own basis (Marx, 1938). Growing exchange value therefore drives the commodification of natural resources, creating 'metabolic rifts'- disruptions in complex ecological processes like the nitrogen cycle- by extracting natural resources to funnel them into linear supply chains, ejecting by-products as waste (Foster et al., 2010).

There is a growing movement for de-growth or 'steady state' economics as an alternative to endless growth. Hickel (2017) argues that efficiency improvements and clean energy technologies can contribute to reducing emissions by, at most, 4% per year, but to reach 10% overall reductions rich countries will have to downscale production and consumption by about 6% per year. But shrinking of GDP is compatible with increases in happiness, equality and positive economic activity, such as renewable energy infrastructure (Jackson, 2016). GDP is the ultimate measure of exchange value – but arguably use value is more important. GDP does not factor in how equitably money is distributed, or whether monetary value has negative societal impacts (e.g. crime or war), and disregards non-monetised labour such as volunteering or care, or non-monetised environmental benefits such as a safe climate. Alternatives to GDP such as the Genuine Progress Indicator could be used by governments to measure economic activity of genuine positive value to society (Kubiszewski et al., 2013).[7]

A world of abundance and inequality

De-growth, dismantling post-colonial exploitation, and critiques of neoliberal capitalism need to become mainstreamed for the necessary changes to gain traction, but may be frightening, unchartered territory for many. Nine billion people are expected on the planet, with 3 billion set to enter the global middle classes, by 2050 (WWF, 2017). This makes feeding the world a daunting prospect, and de-growth conjures images of recession and hardship. Food waste provides an excellent entry point to explain that there are abundant resources to meet everyone's needs if they were distributed more equally – even when GDP is shrinking. Dominant narratives have fixated on the solution to global food poverty being increased food production (Tomlinson, 2011) – but Stuart (2009) estimates that if a third of the world's food is wasted, this would be enough to provide for the entire nutritional needs of an extra 3 billion people. If 25% of the world's food is unnecessarily wasted, this represents a loss of approximately 675 trillion litres of water, enough for the household needs of nine billion people using 200 litres a day (Stuart, 2009). One study concluded that reducing food waste was the third most important measure globally that could be taken to avert climate change (Project Drawdown, 2017). The production of food that is wasted uses 28% of the world's agricultural land (FAO, 2013), equivalent to the area of China and India combined. Stuart (2009) roughly estimates that 50–100% of man-made GHG emissions could be offset by reforesting land currently used to grow wasted food. These may be over-estimates (better food waste data is needed to tell), but the scale of resources wasted is not in doubt. Research commissioned by the Committee on Climate Change estimates that halving UK food waste would save 941,000 hectares of UK land, though this ignores food waste on farms and land savings overseas (CEH and Rothamsted Research, 2019).[8]

This message of abundance alongside hunger creates a powerful sense of intuitive injustice and could be used as a bridge to systemic critique – that the root of these material resource inequalities is the allocation of commodified resources according to the market, and thus inequalities in wealth. In 2017, the eight richest people in the world owned as much wealth as the poorest 50% of humanity (Oxfam, 2017). In most European countries, the poorest half of the population owns less than 5% of the wealth (Piketty, 2014). This inequality translates into environmental impact. The richest 10% of people in terms of income globally are responsible for 49% of global lifestyle consumption emissions, and the poorest 50% are responsible for only 10% (Oxfam, 2015). If every country in the world were to adopt the US's 2011 average diet, 140% of global habitable land area would be needed for agriculture (Ritchie and Roser, 2017). Londoners use 6.63 hectares globally each, 41% of which is for food production (Weis, 2007). In production, emissions are even more unequally weighted. Since 1988, 100 corporate and state producing entities account for 71% of global industrial GHG emissions (Griffin, 2017). Wealthier people are also more likely to have capital invested in production associated with emissions – currently, the wealthiest 10% own roughly 80–90% of global private capital (Piketty, 2014).

In the context of such inequality, asking individuals to 'vote with their wallets' to fix the food system, by buying 'wonky' vegetables or organic food, is not enough (Alkon and Guthman, 2017). Such tactics may yield some change but are limited by the assumption that the market subserviently reacts to consumer demands, and in an equitable way. If the market reacts to a 'one dollar, one vote' system, then the vast inequalities between consumers means resources will be allocated on the basis of the needs of wealthier consumers, such as the disproportionate land dedicated to rich consumer meat consumption. Marx argued that world trade is mainly driven by the needs of production (Marx, 1963). The even greater inequalities in who owns capital and production shows clearly how these powers could override the needs of consumers or smaller businesses. The 'one dollar, one vote' market system is itself the source of the unequal distribution of power and resources – so the central task must be to fix this system. Reducing food waste in rich countries – especially through individual behaviour change – will not automatically mean that the poorest will be able to access adequate food, until the structures distributing food, land and wealth are reorganised (although reduced waste can free up resources for these new systems). A radical food waste vision could include redistribution of resources and wealth through the state, ensuring the right food is grown in the right places according to need, food sovereignty approaches, and challenging social structures that unjustly distribute and concentrate wealth[9] (Riches and Silvasti, 2014). Currently, however, preferred policy approaches tend to favour voluntary action from business; the following section asks whether this is enough.

Food industry actors often argue that competition and efficiency will naturally drive businesses to reduce waste to minimise costs – thus, voluntary initiatives rather than stronger regulation are seen as the most appropriate approach (STOA, 2013, p. 92). Champions 12.3

found high financial returns for food waste reduction (Hanson and Mitchell, 2017). However, the types of food waste prevalent in global North countries are often the result of externalities, so incentives to reduce food waste are not internal to the business and require regulation or mediation to resolve – such as the Groceries Code Adjudicator regulating UTPs in the UK, or WRAP mediating between supermarkets and their suppliers to solve cross-supply chain issues leading to food waste (see Porter's chapter, this volume).

When the RSPB conducted an analysis of the effectiveness of over 150 voluntary schemes, it found that most set unambitious targets, many failed to achieve these targets or were undermined by low rates of private sector participation, and concluded that voluntary approaches cannot be an effective alternative to regulation (RSPB, 2015). WRAP's Courtauld 2025, where UK businesses voluntarily sign up to measure and target the reduction of their food waste, targeted 20% reduction by 2025 (inadequate to meet SDG 12.3), and has suffered problems of low participation (Quinn, 2017c). Nevertheless, voluntary agreements are rapidly becoming the dominant framework used to tackle industry food waste, forming part of a reformist strategy in line with neoliberal notions that businesses will act efficiently and environmentally if left unregulated. Instead of leaving the task to voluntary agreements, food waste activists could build pressure for the following: binding statutory targets to halve food waste from farm to fork by 2030; penalties and incentives to move food waste up the food waste hierarchy; compulsory food waste reporting for all large food businesses; regulation of UTPs; and adequate public funding for food waste prevention research and programmes. To refocus efforts on businesses, a helpful reframing is that food waste is more concentrated in large businesses than throughout millions of separate consumer households, so interventions here may be more effective and yield quicker environmental gains, such as preventing the 21 million portions of carrots wasted on one UK farm mentioned previously.

A majority of food waste-concerned civil society groups currently prioritise setting up social enterprises or charitable food redistribution projects, which can serve to bring communities together around the sharing of food. However, problematic aspects of voluntary food redistribution as a solution to hunger identified by researchers and campaigners include their being under-resourced, socially stigmatising, patchy in coverage, and vulnerable to fluctuating food stocks according to the availability of food surpluses. Most importantly, food redistribution charities do not have the power to guarantee universal access to affordable nutritious food, and by plugging gaps in welfare and employment systems, arguably ease pressure on governments to guarantee safety nets. Poppendieck (2014) outlines how food redistribution in the US developed as a political response to public outrage over the destruction of huge agricultural surpluses in the 1930s to keep up prices alongside the mass poverty of the Great Depression. In the 1960s, US anti-poverty campaigners decided to pursue reform and expansion of food provision programmes, rather than entitlements of cash assistance, allying with politicians in Congress 'who feared the poor would spend cash unwisely' (Poppendieck, 2014, p. 182). This arguably undermined campaigns for structural, preventative approaches to poverty.[10]

Food redistribution charities need to vocally challenge government policies that lead to food poverty, such as cuts to social safety nets, lax labour laws and regressive taxation. Food waste movements could promote the Human Right to Food, as enshrined in the *International Covenant on Economic, Social and Cultural Rights* (Riches and Silvasti, 2014). Focus should be on designing food waste and food poverty out of the system in the first place. I believe that many people do want structural change, but some disciplining factors prevent focus on this. Many workers for redistribution charities rely on corporate donations of food meaning that, to a certain extent, they need to serve CSR objectives or risk partners removing support. Being too radical risks groups losing 'insider' status with policymakers or businesses. Charities also frequently rely on grant funding, the political scope of which is almost always significantly shaped by the political leanings of the extremely rich (McGoey, 2015). Food redistribution and events organisation are also very volunteer, time and resource intensive – diverting capacity from system-targeted campaigning. Portions of the media edit out complexity in favour of simple solutions like 'give surplus food to the poor', rather than framing food waste and food poverty as separate problems requiring systemic solutions (Arcuri, 2019). Food waste activists must find ways to bypass these restrictions, such as grassroots fundraising, efforts to get unrestricted funding, pushing at the boundaries within the constraints of restricted funding, or diverting unpaid volunteering energy from redistribution projects to campaigning.[11] The following section returns to the question of how the food waste movement can challenge the kinds of historically rooted global inequalities described earlier, and notes the potential role for resource transfers and agroecology.

The richest 10% of the human population currently causes 49% of global consumption-linked emissions, and to stay within safe emissions levels, we need to restrict agricultural land expansion to virtually nil (Government Office for Science, 2011). Therefore, to avoid overstepping planetary boundaries (Rockström et al., 2009), developing countries replicating the growth and consumption patterns of wealthier countries would be ecologically disastrous. This is immediately pressing, with BRIC countries like China and India experiencing vast, growing populations and rapid economic growth. Rich countries, therefore, need to make sharp emissions cuts proportional to their disproportionate historical emissions responsibility, transferring money as compensation to help poorer countries develop toward carbon-free economies (Climate Equity Reference Project, 2019; Jackson, 2019) – possibly partially administered through a 'global feed-in tariff' (Klein, 2015). A similar model could be applied to food waste reduction, funding large-scale technology and knowledge transfer (including storage and cool-chain technology) and food waste prevention programmes targeting the greatest environmental impacts. However, technological solutions are not enough – more importantly, poorer countries can work to develop more economically and politically just systems than neoliberal capitalism.

In 2010, the UN Special Rapporteur on the Right to Food published a report recommending agroecology as a means of delivering greater food sovereignty and the right to food (De Schutter, 2010). Agroecology seeks to enhance agriculture by mimicking nature; its benefits include ecological impacts, yield per acre, farmer incomes and empowerment, and food poverty reduction (IAASTD, 2009). It promotes regional small-scale food systems, publicly funded farmer-to-farmer collaboration, greater investment in public goods such as research and infrastructure, and regulatory protections. The food waste movement could ally with agroecology movements like La Via Campesina by forming coalitions and strategically working together for political change. Food waste aims could be integrated into an agroecology framework through advocacy for massive public investment in storage and cool-chain infrastructure for small-scale farmers, localising food production to reduce spoilage from long-distance transit, and publicly funding information sharing on food loss reduction via farmer-to-farmer networks. It could advocate for protections for small-scale farmers, including against food surplus dumping by rich countries, and for the cultivation of land primarily for regional consumption to reduce food poverty. Where farmers do export produce, it could empower farmers through cooperatives and unions so that they are less at the mercy of retailers and middlemen, and regulate UTPs (Wills, 2019). To conclude this chapter, the final section compares campaign tactics for achieving some of these aims.

Beyond reformism: transformist strategies for the food waste movement

To build effective strategies it is helpful to distinguish between different campaigning approaches. Scholte (2002, p. 284) distinguishes between reformists, who seek to correct perceived 'flaws in existing regimes while leaving underlying social structures intact', and transformists who 'aim for a comprehensive change of the social order'. Reformists tend to adopt 'insider' strategies, e.g. trying to build consultative relationships with government and/or businesses, whereas transformists tend to be less able or willing to form such relationships (see also Barnard and Mourad's chapter, this volume). Stavrianakis (2010, p. 62) reflects that 'the outsider position is widely seen as a useful foil for the insiders, in that it creates political pressure that allows insiders to make progress on incremental reforms' but less often considered is that insiders 'co-opt the available room for manoeuvre, thus further diminishing the possibility of more fundamental change'. For example, Klein (2015, p. 203) documents how, through the 1970s, environmentalists had a wave of successes, graduating from outsiders at protests to being at the centre of law-making, becoming the 'ultimate insiders, able to wheel and deal across the political spectrum'. However, during the 1980s, many large environmental groups realised that unless they embraced the new free-market ideology of Reagan or Thatcher, they would be relegated back to outsider status – so they made a strategic decision to try to act within those frameworks.

To tackle the urgent existential threats of climate change and social inequality, environmentalists can no longer afford a neutral, apolitical stance to maintain their insider status with neoliberal politicians or businesses. The radical changes necessary to save our planet pose a threat to neoliberal thinking and business interests, and will be fiercely opposed. As crises of capitalism set in, the neoliberal 'centre' has been destabilised and the dark spectre of fascism is rising, allied closely with climate change denialism which shuts out environmentalists completely, and scapegoating migrants (who will become more numerous if ecological disasters drive them to migrate). For instance, far-right parties are consistently growing in popularity across Europe (Tartar, 2017) and already-elected far-right leaders like Trump and Bolsonaro have quickly acted to expel environmentalists from government and replace them with extractivist industry champions (Dillon and Sellers, 2018). However, there is hope – because progressive movements have risen also. Critical left-wing movements, including the nascent mainstreaming of socialist values to electoral politics in the UK and US, show that transformist movements can be radical, broad-based and inclusive, and have a clear strategy to win power and implement progressive policies.

I argue that there is a need for the food waste movement to encourage these progressive movements to adopt policies implementing the radical change needed to avoid climate breakdown, including the transformist solutions to food waste reduction mentioned in this chapter. These progressive movements display receptiveness to new and radical ideas, but also include a spectrum of political forces, from centre-left politicians still supportive of neoliberalism, to more progressive leftists; hence this will be a struggle. Alexandria Ocasio-Cortez's proposals for a Green New Deal in the US and calls emerging for a Green New Deal within the UK's Labour Party offer inspiring policy examples (LabourGND, 2019) – integrating de-growth thinking would be a welcome addition to these proposals. Then, the priority is to get those political parties into office quickly, to enact the changes needed. These processes will require engaging with groups with different world views and values. I propose that activists employ narratives like those of 'abundance alongside hunger' named above, to open conversations around global inequalities and structural injustices, before presenting positive systemic changes as the solution. Food can be used as a way to create communities, initiate meaningful conversations, and draw people into political movements. Nevertheless, the priority must be strategic engagement with hegemony to win radical changes. Nothing less than transformist solutions are demanded by the severity of the environmental and social crises we face.

Notes

1 Klein (2008) provides an accessible history.
2 This excludes food left unharvested in the field from compulsory reporting, though countries can choose to optionally report this.
3 Hickel's (2017) book *The Divide* explores how global inequality has arisen and been perpetuated.
4 Campaigns tackling systemic causes of global poverty, mainly focused on the global South, include Tax Justice Network (www.taxjustice.net), Jubilee Debt Campaign (jubileedebt.org.uk), Bretton Woods Project (www.brettonwoodsproject.org), Third World Network (twn.my), Global Justice Now (www.globaljustice.org.uk), and Campaign Against the Arms Trade (www.caat.org.uk).
5 See also Giles' and Barnard & Mourad's chapters, this volume.
6 The Tyndall Centre (www.tyndall.ac.uk) and Food Climate Research Network have excellent resources for exploring links between food and climate.
7 For further reading, and to find academic networks supporting degrowth economics, see www.degrowth.org.
8 See Chapter 22 in this volume for more on how shifts to plant-based diets and livestock fed on surplus food could liberate even more land for carbon sequestration through mass eco-system restoration.
9 Examples of some innovative democratic alternatives to distribution of food, incorporating right to food and agroecology approaches, can be found in the People's Food Policy (www.peoplesfoodpolicy.org).
10 A struggle continuing through the work of organisations including Why Hunger and the 'Closing the Hunger Gap' conferences.
11 Barnard and Mourad's chapter compares the political work of different food redistribution organisations. For an alternative media framing, see Garthwaite, Spring and Fisher (2019).

References

Alkon, A. and Guthman, J. (eds) (2017) *The New Food Activism*. California: University of California Press.
Americans for Tax Fairness. (2014) *Walmart on Tax Day*. Washington: Americans for Tax Fairness. Available at: https://americansfortaxfairness.org/files/Walmart-on-Tax-Day-Americans-for-Tax-Fairness-1.pdf.
Anderson, K. (2012) 'Climate change going beyond dangerous – Brutal numbers and tenuous hope', *Development Dialogue*, 61, pp. 16–40.
Antony, A. and Macaskill, A. (2011) 'Indian panel said to pave way for Wal-Mart, Tesco to open stores', *Bloomberg*, 22 July. Available at: www.bloomberg.com/news/articles/2011-07-22/india-panel-said-to-pave-way-for-wal-mart-tesco-with-investment-approval.
Arcuri, S. (2019) 'Food poverty, food waste and the consensus frame on charitable food redistribution in Italy', *Agriculture and Human Values*. doi:10.1007/s10460-019-09918-1.
Bowman, M. (2018) *Farmers talk food waste*. Feedback. Available at: https://feedbackglobal.org/wp/wp-content/uploads/2018/02/Farm_waste_report_.pdf.
CEH and Rothamsted Research. (2019) *Quantifying the impact of future land use scenarios to 2050 and beyond - Final Report*. Committee on Climate Change. Available at: www.theccc.org.uk/wp-content/uploads/2018/11/Quantifying-the-impact-of-future-land-use-scenarios-to-2050-and-beyond-Full-Report.pdf (Accessed: 13 May 2019).
Chow, H. (2017) *The long, hard fight against food speculation, global justice now*. Available at: www.globaljustice.org.uk/blog/2017/feb/23/long-hard-fight-against-food-speculation.
Clapp, J. and Isakson, S. R. (2018) *Speculative Harvests*. Nova Scotia, Canada: Fernwood Publishing.
Clapp, R. (1994) 'The moral economy of the contract', in Little, P. (ed), *Living Under Contract: Contract Farming and Agrarian Transformation in Sub-Saharan Africa*. Madison, Wisconsin, United States: University of Wisconsin Press, pp 78-97.

Martin Bowman

Climate Equity Reference Project (2019), *Climate Equity Reference Project*, Available at: https://climateequityreference.org/.

ClimateFairshare. (no date). Available at: www.climatefairshares.org/.

Colbert, E. (2017) *Causes of food waste in international supply chains*. Feedback. Available at: https://feedbackglobal.org/wp-content/uploads/2017/05/Causes-of-food-waste-in-international-supply-chains_Feedback.pdf.

Davis, M. (2002) *Late Victorian Holocausts*. London: Verso Books.

De Schutter, O. (2010) *Agroecology and the right to food*. United Nations Office of the Special Rapporteur on the Right to Food. Available at: www.srfood.org/images/stories/pdf/officialreports/20110308_a-hrc-16-49_agroecology_en.pdf.

Dillon, L. and Sellers, C. (2018) 'The environmental protection agency in the early trump administration: Prelude to regulatory capture', *American Journal of Public Health*, 108(2), pp. S89–S94. doi:10.2105/AJPH.2018.304360.

EU. (2018) *Directive (EU) 2018/of the European Parliament and of the Council of 30 May 2018 amending Directive 2008/98/EC on waste*. Available at: https://eur-lex.europa.eu/legal-content/EN/TXT/PDF/?uri=CELEX:32018L0851&from=EN (Accessed: 1 August 2018).

FAO. (2011) *Global Food Losses and Food Waste: Extent, Causes and Prevention*. Rome: FAO. Available at: www.fao.org/3/a-i2697e.pdf.

FAO. (2013) *Food wastage footprint: Impacts on natural resources - Summary report*. Rome: FAO.

FAO (2019) *SDG indicator 12.3.1 - global food losses, food and agriculture organization of the United Nations*. Available at: www.fao.org/sustainable-development-goals/indicators/1231/en/ (Accessed: 29 June 2019).

Foster, J. B., Clark, B. and York, R. (2010) *The Ecological Rift: Capitalism's War on the Earth*. New York: NYU Press.

FUSIONS. (2016) *Estimates of European Food Waste Levels*. Stockholm: European Commission Available at: www.eu-fusions.org/phocadownload/Publications/Estimates%20of%20European%20food%20waste%20levels.pdf.

Garthwaite, K., Spring, C., & Fisher, A. (2019, March 25). It's not the hungry who gain most from food banks – it's big business. *The Guardian*. https://www.theguardian.com/commentisfree/2019/mar/25/big-business-food-banks-subsidise-reputation

Gascón, J. (2018) 'Food waste: A political ecology approach', *Journal of Political Ecology*, 25(1), pp. 587–601. doi:10.2458/v25i1.23119.

Gidwani, V. and Reddy, R. N. (2011) 'The Afterlives of "Waste"', *Antipode*, 43(5), pp. 1625–1658.

Gille, Z. (2013) 'From risk to waste: global food waste regimes', in Evans, D. (ed), *Waste Matters*. 1st edition. Malden: Wiley-Blackwell, pp. 27–46.

Government Office for Science. (2011) *The Future of Food and Farming: Final Project Report*. London: Foresight. Available at https://assets.publishing.service.gov.uk/government/uploads/system/uploads/attachment_data/file/288329/11-546-future-of-food-and-farming-report.pdf.

Gramsci, A. (1992) *Prison Notebooks*. New York: Columbia University Press.

Griffin, P. (2017) *The carbon majors database: CDP carbon majors report 2017*. CDP. Available at: www.cdp.net/en/reports/downloads/2327.

Hanson, C. (2017) *Guidance on interpreting sustainable development goal target 12.3*. Champions 12.3. Available at: https://champs123blog.files.wordpress.com/2017/10/champions-12-3-guidance-on-interpreting-sdg-target-12-3.pdf.

Hanson, C. and Mitchell, P. (2017) *The business case for reducing food loss and waste*. Champions 12.3. Available at: www.wrap.org.uk/sites/files/wrap/Report_The%20Business%20Case%20for%20Reducing%20Food%20Loss%20and%20Waste.pdf.

Harvey, D. (1985) 'The geopolitics of capitalism', in *Social Relations and Spatial Structures*.ed. Derek Gregory and John Urry. London: Macmillan, pp. 128–163. doi:10.1007/978-1-349-27935-7_7.

Harvey, David (2018), *The Limits to Capital*. London: Verso.

Hickel, J. (2017) *The Divide*. London: William Heinemann.

Hickel, J. and Kallis, G. (2019) 'Is green growth possible?', *New Political Economy*, pp. 1–18. doi:10.1080/13563467.2019.1598964.

IAASTD (2009) *Global report*. B. D. McIntyre and International Assessment of Agricultural Knowledge, Science and Technology for Development. Washington, DC: Island Press.

International Organisation for Migration. (2015) *A complex nexus, international organization for migration*. Available at: www.iom.int/complex-nexus.

504

Ivanova, D., Vita, G. and Steen-Olsen, K. (2017) 'Mapping the carbon footprint of EU regions', *Environmental Research Letters*, 12(5). doi:10.1088/1748-9326/aa6da9.

Jackson, T. (2016) *Prosperity without Growth*. 2nd edition. London: Routledge.

Jackson, T. (2019), *Zero Carbon Sooner — The case for an early zero carbon target for the UK*, CUSP, Available at: https://www.cusp.ac.uk/themes/aetw/zero-carbon-sooner/.

Jevons, W. S. (1866) *The Coal Question*. London: Macmillan.

Jones, T. (2010) *The Great Hunger Lottery*. London: Global Justice Now. Available at: www.globaljustice.org.uk/sites/default/files/files/resources/hunger_lottery_report_6.10.pdf.

Klein, N. (2008) *The Shock Doctrine*. London: Penguin.

Klein, N. (2015) *This Changes Everything*. London: Penguin.

Kubiszewski, I., Costanza, R., Franco, C., Lawn, P., Talberth, J., Jackson, T. and Aylmer, C. (2013) 'Beyond GDP: Measuring and achieving global genuine progress', *Ecological Economics*, 93, pp. 57–68. doi:10.1016/j.ecolecon.2013.04.019.

LabourGND. (2019) *Labour for a green new deal, labour for a green new deal*. Available at: www.labourgnd.uk/.

Lauderdale, J. M. E. (1804) *An Inquiry Into the Nature and Origin of Public Wealth*. Edinburgh: Arch. Constable & Company.

Lenin, V. I. (1939) *Imperialism, The Highest Stage of Capitalism*. Moscow: Foreign Languages Publishing House.

Martinez, R. (2017) *Creating Freedom*. New York: Pantheon Books.

Marx, K. (1938) *Critique of the Gotha Program*. New York: International Publishers.

Marx, K. (1963) *The Poverty of Philosophy*. New York: International Publishers.

Marx, Karl (1965), *Das Kapital: A critique of political economy*. ed. H. Regnery. New York: International Publishers.

McGoey, L. (2015) *No Such Thing as a Free Gift*. London: Verso Books.

Mol, A. P. (2003) *Globalization and Environmental Reform*. Cambridge, MA: MIT Press.

O'Brien, M. (2013) 'A "lasting transformation" of capitalist surplus: From food stocks to feedstocks', in Evans, D. (ed), *Waste Matters*. 1st ed. Malden, MA: Wiley-Blackwell, pp. 192-211.

Oxfam. (2015) *Extreme Carbon Inequality*. Oxfam. Available at: https://d1tn3vj7xz9fdh.cloudfront.net/s3fs-public/file_attachments/mb-extreme-carbon-inequality-021215-en.pdf.

Oxfam. (2017) *An Economy for the 99%*. Oxfam. Available at: www-cdn.oxfam.org/s3fs-public/file_attachments/bp-economy-for-99-percent-160117-en.pdf.

Peters, G. P., Minx, J. C., Weber, C. L. and Edenhofer, O. (2011) 'Growth in emission transfers via international trade from 1990 to 2008', *Proceedings of the National Academy of Sciences*, 108(21), pp. 8903–8908. doi:10.1073/pnas.1006388108.

Piketty, T. (2014) *Capital in the Twenty-First Century*. Cambridge, MA: Harvard University Press.

Pomeranz, K. (2001) *The Great Divergence: China, Europe, and the Making of the Modern World Economy*. Princeton, New Jersey, United States: Princeton University Press.

Poppendieck, J. (2014) 'Food assistance, hunger and the end of welfare in the USA', in Riches, G. and Silvasti, T. (eds), *First World Hunger Revisited*. London: Palgrave Macmillan, pp 176–190

Project Drawdown. (2017) *Drawdown: Solutions, drawdown*. Available at: www.drawdown.org/solutions.

Quinn, I. (2017a) 'Forecast and promo failures driving waste warns Tacon', *The Grocer*, 24 November. Available at: www.thegrocer.co.uk/home/topics/waste-not-want-not/forecast-and-promo-failures-driving-waste-warns-tacon/560504.article.

Quinn, I. (2017b) 'From farm to food waste: The pre-farmgate fight', *The Grocer*, 19 October. Available at: www.thegrocer.co.uk/home/topics/waste-not-want-not/from-farm-to-food-waste-the-pre-farmgate-fight/559044.article.

Quinn, I. (2017c) *Major suppliers pulled over failure to back Courtauld 2025*, *The Grocer*. Available at: www.thegrocer.co.uk/waste-not-want-not/major-suppliers-pulled-over-failure-to-back-courtauld-2025/559073.article.

Riches, G. and Silvasti, T. (eds) (2014) *First World Hunger Revisited*. London: Palgrave Macmillan.

Ritchie, H. and Roser, M. (2017) *Meat and seafood production & consumption, our world in data*. Available at: https://ourworldindata.org/meat-and-seafood-production-consumption.

Rockström, J., Steffen, W., Noone, K., Persson, Å., Chapin, F. S. I., Lambin, E., Lenton, T. M., Scheffer, M., Folke, C., Schellnhuber, H. J., Nykvist, B., de Wit, C. A., Hughes, T., van der Leeuw, S., Rodhe, H., Sörlin, S., Snyder, P. K., Costanza, R., Svedin, U., Falkenmark, M., Karlberg, L., Corell, R. W., Fabry, V. J., Hansen, J., Walker, B., Liverman, D., Richardson, K., Crutzen, P. and

Foley, J. (2009) 'Planetary boundaries: Exploring the safe operating space for humanity', *Ecology and Society*, 14(2). doi:10.5751/ES-03180-140232.

RSPB. (2015) *Using regulation as a last resort? Assessing the performance of voluntary approaches.* RSPB. Available at: http://ww2.rspb.org.uk/Images/usingregulation_tcm9-408677.pdf.

Salemdeeb, R., Vivanco, D., Al-Tabbaa, A. and Zu Ermgassen, E. (2017) 'A holistic approach to the environmental evaluation of food waste prevention', *Waste Management*, 59, pp. 442–450. doi:10.1016/j.wasman.2016.09.042.

Scholte, J. A. (2002) 'Civil society and democracy in global governance', *Global Governance*, 8(3), pp. 281–304.

Schröder, E. and Storm, S. (2018) *Economic growth and carbon emissions: The road to 'hothouse earth' is paved with good intentions.* 84. Institute for New Economic Thinking. Available at: www.ineteconomics.org/uploads/papers/WP_84.pdf.

Smucker, J. (2017) *Hegemony How-to: A Roadmap for Radicals.* Chico, California, United States: AK Press.

Soederberg, S. (2004) *The Politics of the New International Financial Architecture: Reimposing Neoliberal Domination in the Global South.* New York: Zed Books.

Stavrianakis, A. (2010) *Taking Aim at the Arms Trade.* London: Zed Books.

Stern, N. (2006) *Stern review: The economics of climate change.* Available at: http://unionsforenergydemocracy.org/wp-content/uploads/2015/08/sternreview_report_complete.pdf.

STOA. (2013) *Technology options for feeding 10 billion people - options for cutting food waste.* Science and Technology Options Assessment for the European Parliament, p. 159. Available at: www.europarl.europa.eu/RegData/etudes/etudes/join/2013/513515/IPOL-JOIN_ET%282013%29513515_EN.pdf.

Stuart, T. (2009) *Waste: Uncovering the Global Food Scandal.* London: Penguin.

Tartar, A. (2017) 'How the populist right is redrawing the map of Europe', *Bloomberg*, 11 December. Available at: www.bloomberg.com/graphics/2017-europe-populist-right/.

Tomlinson, I. (2013) 'Doubling food production to feed the 9 billion: A critical perspective on a key discourse of food security in the UK', *Journal of Rural Studies*. (Food Security), 29, pp. 81–90. doi:10.1016/j.jrurstud.2011.09.001.

UN. (2016) *Goal 12, sustainable development goals knowledge platform.* Available at: https://sustainabledevelopment.un.org/sdg12.

UNEP. (2019) *Emissions Gap Report 2018.* United Nations Environment Programme, Nairobi: UNEP.

UNI Global Union. (2012) *Walmart's global track record and the implications for fdi in multi-brand retail in India.* Available at: www.uniglobalunion.org/sites/default/files/attachments/pdf/FDI_Report.pdf.

Venkat, K. (2011) 'The climate change and economic impacts of food waste in the United States', *International Journal on Food System Dynamics*, 2(4), pp. 431–446. doi:10.18461/ijfsd.v2i4.247.

Weis, T. (2007) *The Global Food Economy: The Battle for the Future of Farming.* London and New York: Zed Books.

Wiedmann, T. and Schandl, H. (2015) 'The material footprint of nations', *Proceedings of the National Academy of Sciences*, 112(20), pp. 6271–6276. doi:10.1073/pnas.1220362110.

Wills, T. (2019) *What is the EU's new unfair trading practices directive? Traidcraft exchange.* Available at: www.traidcraft.org.uk/traidcraft-in-depth/2019/2/19/what-is-the-eus-new-unfair-trading-practices-directive.

Woodward, D. (2015) 'Incrementum ad absurdum: Global growth, inequality and poverty eradication in a carbon-constrained world', *World Economic Review*, 4, pp. 43–62.

World Bank. (2012) *Turn down the heat: Why a 4C warmer world must be avoided.* World Bank. Available at: http://documents.worldbank.org/curated/en/865571468149107611/pdf/NonAsciiFileName0.pdf.

World Resources Institute. (2016) 'The Roads to Decoupling', 5 April. Available at: www.wri.org/blog/2016/04/roads-decoupling-21-countries-are-reducing-carbon-emissions-while-growing-gdp.

WRAP. (2009) *Meeting the UK Climate Change Challenge: The Contribution of Resource Efficiency.* London: WRAP.

WRAP. (2018) *WRAP restates UK food waste figures to support united global action.* Available at: www.wrap.org.uk/content/wrap-restates-uk-food-waste-figures-support-united-global-action.

WWF. (2017) *Appetite for destruction.* World Wildlife Fund. Available at: www.wwf.org.uk/sites/default/files/2017-10/WWF_AppetiteForDestruction_Summary_Report_SignOff.pdf.

INDEX

RFPM *see* Remote Food Photography Method
rice 44, 199–200, 213, 322–323, 372–373
rice bran wax (RBW) 420, 421
Riches, G. 8, 43, 351
Richter, B. 135, 279
Ridoutt, B. G. 227
Righi, Simone 254, 326–343
right to food 352, 500
robotics 475–476
Roe, B. 263, 265
Roman Catholic Church 59, 62, 76n14
Roodhuyzen, D. M. A. 137
Russell, S. V. 134, 264
Russia 2, 44, 368, 456, 488
Rustemeyer, Jenny 15n2

Sælen, H. 145
safety *see* food safety
Sage, C. 68
Sahakian, Marlyne 158, 187–206
Saikia, P. 369
Sainsbury's 32, 70, 71
Salemdeeb, Ramy 158, 207–224, 348, 443–454, 498
Saloma, Czarina 158, 187–206
sampling 260–261
Saudi Arabia 158, 217–221
SAVE FOOD Global Food Loss and Waste initiative 161, 358
scenario technique 238, 240–249, 438
Schachter-Shalomi, Zalman 57
Schanes, K. 132
Scharper, Stephen Bede 22, 55–64
Schatzki, T. R. 274
Schneider, Felicitas 79, 84, 93, 114–128
Scholte, J. A. 502
schools 145, 148, 267n1
Schutt, Bill 372
Schwittay, Anke 440
Scotland 58, 164, 169n29; agricultural production losses 85; Zero Waste Scotland 257, 261, 262
Scott, S. 277
SDGs *see* Sustainable Development Goals
Seattle 25, 27–28, 29–31, 34
secondary retail markets 32–33
Seifert, Jeremy 47, 391
self-efficacy 298, 303, 306
self-interest 293–294, 306
sell-by dates 39, 46, 71, 119, 133–134, 390, 401; *see also* best-before dates; use-by dates
Sen, S. 402
Senegal 45
Seng, Bunrith 190, 193
Serres, Michel 15n6
serveware 405–406, 409
service sector 80, 144–156, 201, 429–430; Australia 226; digital technologies 430–440;

New Zealand 230–231; South Africa 216; *see also* restaurants
serving waste 145–146, 147–148, 150, 429–430
Setti, Marco 254, 326–343
sewage 131, 157, 226, 445, 449
Shackleton, C. M. 214
"shadow economies" 24, 29–31, 32
Sharp, Anne 254, 293–310
shelf-life 119–120, 296, 328, 474
Shenoy, Megha 158, 187–206
Shilling, C. 4
shopping 133, 271, 279, 296, 326, 474; *see also* over-purchasing; purchasing; retailers
Shove, E. 272
shrinkage 100, 103, 110n5; new technologies 471, 473, 478, 479; retail food waste 115
Silvennoinen, Kirsi 80, 144–156, 430
Silverman, David 432–433
Simons, D. W. 95
simulation 327–328, 331, 336
Singapore 188
Sky Woman 320–321
Smaje, C. 120
small-to-medium restaurants (SMRs) 429, 430, 431–440
smart technology 456, 476
smartphones 4, 476, 477; *see also* apps
Smith, Andrew F. 4, 22, 37–54
Smithers, R. 46
Sobal, J. 257
social innovation 254, 311–325
social justice 5, 62, 200, 311
social movements 5, 6, 47–48, 346, 381–399
social norms 272, 294, 334, 354, 390
social practice approach 137, 485–486
social supermarkets 351
socio-demographic factors 131–132
socioeconomic status 12, 214, 403
sociology 272, 311, 357, 485, 486
sociotechnical relationships 69–70, 72, 76n18
Soma, Tammara 1–19, 158; Asia 187–206; food waste management 348, 443–454; food waste studies 456, 483–492; household food waste 136, 189; Islamic values 60; social innovation 254, 311–325
Somalia 44
sorting waste materials 261
source reduction 446
South Africa 158, 207–217, 247; animal feed 370; cost of food waste 249; food waste studies 456, 488; household food waste 131; retail food waste 115, 121
South Korea: animal feed 363, 366, 370, 373; data 188, 189; food banks 350; marketing 135; over-purchasing 119; spending on food 38; surveys 263; waste disposal 42–43
Southerton, D. 273, 279

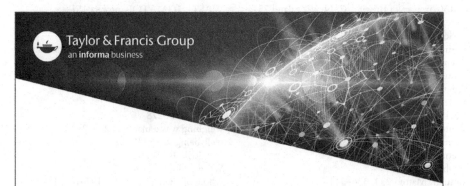

Printed in the United States
by Baker & Taylor Publisher Services